Social Inequality

The eleventh edition of *Social Inequality: Forms, Causes, and Consequences* is an introduction to the study of social inequality. Fully updated statistics and examples convey the pervasiveness and extent of social inequality in the United States. The authors use an intersectional perspective to show how inequality occurs, how it affects all of us, and what is being done about it.

With more resources and supplementary examples, exercises, and applications embedded throughout to aid students' learning and visualization of important concepts, the book provides a rich theoretical treatment to address the current state of inequality. In line with current affairs, the authors have expanded the content to include:

- An intersectional approach throughout the chapters;
- A stronger emphasis on the connections between poverty, wealth, and income inequality;
- New case studies on the opioid epidemic, COVID-19, the lead poisoning crisis, and climate change;
- A new focus on the rise of right-wing movements.

With additional content and classroom extensions available online for instructors, *Social Inequality* remains an ideal and invaluable overview of the subject and provides undergraduate students with a robust understanding of social inequality from a sociological perspective.

Heather M. Fitz Gibbon is a Professor of Sociology at the College of Wooster. Her research focuses on poverty in micropolitan regions, motherhood within the welfare system, and childcare systems. She has been a community-based researcher, evaluating anti-poverty and family literacy community programs.

Anne M. Nurse is a Professor of Sociology at the College of Wooster. Her published work is on juvenile corrections and child sexual abuse prevention. She most recently published *Confronting Child Sexual Abuse*.

Charles E. Hurst is an emeritus Professor of Sociology at the College of Wooster. His work focuses on issues of social status, comparative poverty and inequality, and the uses of theories in understanding contemporary problems. Recently, these interests also include studies of status in Amish communities in Ohio.

Social Inequality

Forms, Causes, and Consequences

Eleventh Edition

Heather M. Fitz Gibbon, Anne M. Nurse,
and Charles E. Hurst

Routledge
Taylor & Francis Group

NEW YORK AND LONDON

Cover image: © iStock/monstArrr_

Eleventh edition published 2023
by Routledge
605 Third Avenue, New York, NY 10158

and by Routledge
4 Park Square, Milton Park, Abingdon, Oxon, OX14 4RN

Routledge is an imprint of the Taylor & Francis Group, an informa business

© 2023 Taylor & Francis

The right of Heather M. Fitz Gibbon, Anne M. Nurse, and Charles E. Hurst to be
identified as authors of this work has been asserted in accordance with sections 77
and 78 of the Copyright, Designs and Patents Act 1988.

First edition published by C.V. Mosby 1979
Tenth edition published by Routledge 2019

Library of Congress Cataloging-in-Publication Data
Names: Fitz Gibbon, Heather M., author. | Nurse, Anne, 1968- author. |
Hurst, Charles E., author.
Title: Social inequality : forms, causes, and consequences / Heather M. Fitz Gibbon,
Anne M. Nurse and Charles E Hurst.
Description: Eleventh edition. | New York, NY : Routledge Books, 2023. |
Includes bibliographical references and index.
Identifiers: LCCN 2022005572 (print) | LCCN 2022005573 (ebook) |
ISBN 9781032027395 (hardback) | ISBN 9781032027371 (paperback) |
ISBN 9781003184966 (ebook)
Subjects: LCSH: Equality--United States. | United States--Social conditions.
Classification: LCC HN90.S6 H87 2023 (print) | LCC HN90.S6 (ebook) |
DDC 305.0973--dc23/eng/20220302
LC record available at https://lccn.loc.gov/2022005572
LC ebook record available at https://lccn.loc.gov/2022005573

ISBN: 9781032027395 (hbk)
ISBN: 9781032027371 (pbk)
ISBN: 9781003184966 (ebk)

DOI: 10.4324/9781003184966

Typeset in Goudy
by KnowledgeWorks Global Ltd.

Access Support Material: www.routledge.com/9781032027371

Contents

List of Figures

List of Tables

List of Boxes

Preface

Like past editions, this eleventh edition of *Social Inequality: Forms, Causes, and Consequences* is an introduction to the study of social inequality from a sociological perspective aimed at undergraduate students and the general public. This book conveys the pervasiveness and extent of social inequality in the United States using an intersectional perspective to show how inequality occurs, how it affects all of us, and what is being done about it. We provide a rich theoretical treatment that addresses the current state of inequality through the use of up-to-date statistics and current examples. The book additionally provides useful exercises for students, and suggestions for in-classroom discussion.

This edition benefits from a variety of changes that have significantly strengthened the text.

- We thread a more intersectional approach throughout the chapters and, where applicable, address the impact of COVID-19.
- We have reorganized the poverty and wealth chapter to provide a stronger emphasis on the connections between poverty, wealth, and income inequality.
- The class chapter now focuses on definitions of class and policies that affect the class structure in the United States.
- The gender chapter has been reworked to provide a more cohesive theoretical framework.
- The health chapter includes new case studies on the opioid epidemic, COVID-19, the lead poisoning crisis, and climate change.
- In the chapter on social movements, we have added information about the rise of right-wing movements.
- The concluding chapter addresses possible new policy suggestions in light of the volatile political climate in which we are living.

The eleventh edition is divided into five major parts. *Part 1* examines the scope of inequality, with a focus on issues such as income, wealth, status, and power. *Part 2* outlines general explanations of inequality. The classical arguments included are those of Marx, Weber, Durkheim, and Du Bois, while the contemporary theories discuss how inequalities become durable and persistent. Specifically, we look at functionalist and labor market theories and outline how material and symbolic resources are hoarded. Finally, we address the importance of micro-level processes, such as identities and interactions. The chapters in *Part 3* ask who benefits and who loses by inequality: Chapters 8–11 discuss gender, sexuality, and race and include a chapter combining immigration, religion, and place. *Part 4* includes two chapters of intersectional case studies on inequality: the first focuses on health and the environment, and the second on crime and the criminal justice system. Finally, *Part 5* addresses processes of change and stability in the structure of social inequality through discussions of social movements and potential policy alternatives. The book concludes with a glossary of many of the basic terms used in the text.

Acknowledgments

Although any shortcomings in the book are our own responsibility, any improvements in this edition are due in large part to others. We would like to thank our outstanding research assistant, Lauren Ganson. Thanks also to the editorial staff at Taylor and Francis for guiding us kindly and wisely through the publication process.

We would like readers to know that this book was originally written by Charles Hurst, and he was the sole author for the first eight editions. Two new authors were added in the ninth edition, but they can only be credited with building off the incredibly strong foundation Chuck created. We value not only Chuck's sociological wisdom but also his friendship and sense of social justice.

We are all indebted to our families for their support during this project. From the Fitz Gibbon family, we thank Stewart, Andrew, and Thomas, and from the Nurse/Thompson family, we are grateful to John, Alexander, Jacob, and Gabriel.

An Introduction to the Study of Social Inequality

Fernando was brought into the United States illegally by his mother when he was five years old. He is now 29 and works as a lab technician in the San Francisco Bay Area. A recipient of DACA (Delayed Action for Childhood Arrivals, a program that allows people like Fernando to stay in the country and work legally), he is consumed with anxiety because of past attempts by the federal government to end the DACA program. If he loses his DACA status, he would have to return to Mexico, a country he barely remembers. He told a reporter, "I have no clue what they would do .... Would they come knocking on my door, putting me in detainment facilities, put me on a plane and have someone else take care of my stuff? Would they round everyone up? I would be afraid of losing everything, losing my friends, having to start over again in a place I barely know. I can still speak Spanish, but as far as living a life there, it wouldn't be mine." (Sanchez, 2018)

April had worked for 16 years at her firm and was finally promoted to supply chain director. But then March of 2020 arrived, and the pandemic forced her son's school to close. Like so many mothers, she found herself in the impossible situation of trying to juggle a full-time job and childcare. Ultimately she was laid off from what she described as her dream job. (Miller, 2021)

Landon, an Iraqi War vet from Idaho, was one of the people who stormed the Capitol on January 6, 2021. In an interview, he said, "I don't regret being there, the idea was to confront our lawmakers. The idea was to try and have a voice and try and, you know, speak for people and just be like, you know, we're not getting what we want from our lawmakers." Landon's comments reflect a sense of voicelessness. But research on the riot also shows that the majority of participants, like Landon, were from states where the population of racial minorities is growing, suggesting another possible motive involves concerns about the distribution of power. (Feuer, 2021; Husler et al., 2021; MacFarlane et al., 2021)

The stories above are real and are drawn from recent news reports. Fernando, April, and Landon are all worried about the impact of inequality in their own lives and in society more generally, but the particular focus of their concerns differs, depending on their individual identities, experiences, and backgrounds. What issues of inequality worry you? You might be thinking about the student loans you have taken out to pay for your education. Or perhaps you are concerned that American society has gone too far in granting rights to particular minority groups. The goal of this book is to give you tools to enable you to think about these kinds of issues in a larger context. What is inequality? Why do we have it? Is it good or bad? This chapter begins with an introduction to the topic of inequality and is followed by some key questions involving how we perceive inequality, the level of inequality in the United States compared to other countries, and whether inequality is desirable and/or inevitable. We conclude with the terms and concepts you will need throughout the text.

DOI: 10.4324/9781003184966-1

Thinking about Social Inequality

You need not look far to find articles in the popular press decrying the rise of inequality in the United States and around the world. Many have likened this era to the famous gilded age of the late nineteenth century. Justin Fox in *Bloomberg* described the gilded age as an era of "exploding economic inequality, stagnant living standards, growing concern about monopolies, devastating financial crises ... brazen political corruption, frequent pronouncements that the American republic was doomed, and seemingly unending turmoil over race and national identity" (Fox, 2018). For many of us, this characterization sounds disturbingly familiar. The share of income that the top 1 percent controls is now as high as it was in the gilded age (see Figure 1.1), and inequality is present and affects us at all stages of our lives.

Think of your own experiences. Even when young, we hear of people as being from a "bad neighborhood," as not being "our kind," as being "above" or "below" us. We hear epithets aimed at persons because of their race, ethnicity, gender, or sexual orientation. As youths, we notice that because of the way they dress, where they live, and who their parents are, some children are treated differently and have more or fewer opportunities than others. We are also smart enough to see that there are class differences associated with different schools and even churches. These economic differences show no sign of disappearing, and in fact, they are at a record high.

Economically, the gap between the top and the bottom has increased, and class mobility has stagnated in the last few decades. The middle class has been particularly hard hit. In 1970, they received 62 percent of the nation's income. By 2019, that number had dropped to 43 percent. Similarly, the percent of people in the middle class dropped from 61 percent to 51 percent over the same period (Horowitz et al., 2020). This apparent decline of the middle class has

Figure 1.1 Share of Income in the United States for the Top 1 percent and Bottom 50 percent, 1913–2021.
Source: Created from World Inequality Database (2021).

significant ramifications for democracy. Scholars as far back as Aristotle have stressed the importance of a large and prosperous middle class for the stability, cohesiveness, and productivity of a society (Pressman, 2007). Yet throughout the United States, the number of middle-class neighborhoods has declined, while both poor and rich neighborhoods have grown. Additionally, the middle class has declined most precipitously in cities because skilled jobs for non-college graduates that were concentrated in urban areas have been automated or outsourced. This has forced formerly middle-class people to take low-income jobs that require little specialization (Autor, 2019). Leicht and Fitzgerald put the matter bluntly: "*Middle-class prosperity in the late twentieth and early twenty-first centuries is an illusion*" (2006, p. 4, italics in original).

As we see in Figure 1.1, the share of income controlled by the richest members of our society dropped from the early part of the century to the 1950s, then stayed relatively flat until the 1970s. Since that time, the overall trend has been one of rapid growth. This phenomenon of increasing income inequality is not unique to the United States. Nicholas Bloom, a professor at Stanford, who was quoted in the *New York Times*, said, "This is a truly global phenomenon, and I don't know any serious economist who would deny inequality has gone up. The debate is over the magnitude, not the direction" (Schwartz, 2016).

Poverty increased in 2020, but it had been on a slight downward trajectory for the six years prior. Nonetheless, over the whole period, the percentage of families and children in poverty has remained over 10 percent and is higher than it was in 2000 (US Census Bureau, 2021j). At the same time, the 2020 compensation of chief executive officers (CEOs) in the top 500 US corporations was 351 times that of the average worker (Mishel & Kandra, 2021). Figure 1.2 demonstrates that while the income of the average worker has remained reasonably flat, the income of CEOs has increased dramatically.

As we can see in Figure 1.3, wealth—the value of what a family owns—is even more highly polarized than income in the United States, with a small percentage controlling most of the resources. Economic inequality thrives in the United States.

Among those especially affected by inequality are blue-collar workers whose manufacturing plants have moved or shut down. In 2018, for example, General Motors announced that several North American plants would be idled, with 3,300 immediate layoffs and the threat of as many as 14,000 in the long run. This happened, at least in part, because of imports of cheap Chinese steel. GM employee Nanette Senters stated:

> To just say, "You're done," is wrong. Yes, a company is supposed to make money. But they did get all kinds of money from those tax cuts, and they are still doing this. I am so disappointed. They always take things out on workers. (Campbell, 2018)

Economists are increasingly recognizing the impact of technology on the decline of the middle class, with some citing that at least half of the wage gap over the past 40 years is due to the automation of tasks that used to be done by people (Lohr, 2022).

The injurious impact of inequality is not confined to the working class and the poor. In recent years, as companies downsize to meet competition and maintain profits, the effects of social and economic forces pushing people into different economic circumstances have been increasingly felt by those in the white-collar ranks. Many of the jobs lost at General Motors were white-collar jobs (Boudette, 2018).

Is one of your personal concerns the cost of college? A recent study finds that rising income inequality in the United States can explain over half of tuition increases since 1990. Colleges are ranked by their quality, which is measured by the abilities of their students. To enroll as many high-ability students as they can, colleges have to admit many who cannot afford the tuition, thus requiring significant grants or discounts. To cover those grants, colleges are forced to charge

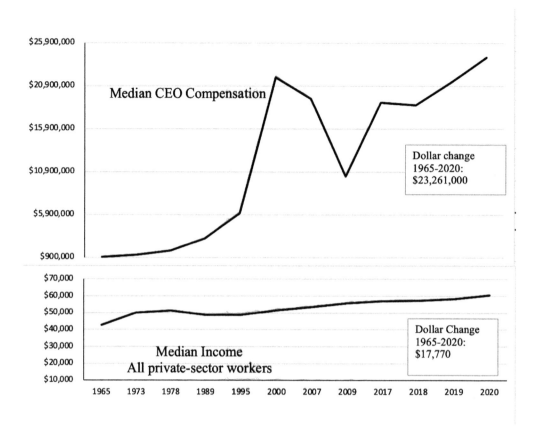

Figure 1.2 Median CEO Compensation and Median Income of Workers, 1965–2020.
Source: Created with data from the Economic Policy Institute (Mishel & Kandra, 2021).

the richest students more. Thus, the more inequality that exists, the higher the sticker price of college (Cai & Heathcote, 2022).

While many people are experiencing downward mobility, advances in computer and information technologies as well as federal policies such as tax reforms and deregulation have created opportunities for others to become phenomenally rich. In 2018, Wall Street's yearly bonus pool came to $27.5 billion. This amount "is more than three times the combined incomes of the 600,000 Americans employed fulltime at minimum wage" (Reich, 2021, p. 46). In 2021, J.P. Morgan and Goldman Sachs raised their bonus pool by 40 percent for investment bankers (Foley, 2021).

The statistics and stories above demonstrate the persistence of inequalities, but they also show their complexity. Let's look back at the three stories presented at the beginning of this chapter. All three of these individuals express insecurity and fear in our current environment of rampant inequality. But their fears are different, depending on their identities and backgrounds. For Fernando, his ethnic background and citizenship status are central to his concerns. April expresses the concerns of working women, and Landon feels he lacks power. These stories tell us that inequalities are located in a complex matrix of identities—race, class, gender, nationality, and sexuality (among others) are all statuses that individually and in combination intersect to bring about different experiences of inequality. This idea, called intersectionality (defined briefly below and more extensively in Chapter 7), is a central and guiding concept for this text.

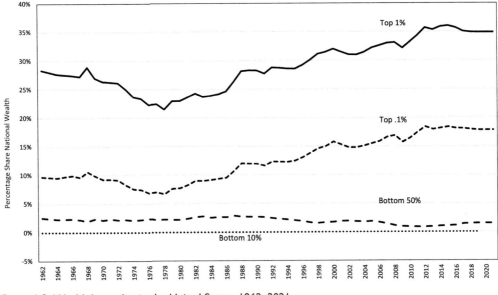

Figure 1.3 Wealth Inequality in the United States, 1962–2021.
Source: Amended from data from World Inequality Database (2021).

BOX 1.1 A PLAGUE ON INEQUALITY?

In the fourteenth century, the Black Plague led to soaring wages and a decrease in inequality, as the deaths of over 75 million caused labor shortages and thus greater bargaining power for workers (Jedwab et al., 2020; Steverman, 2020). Similarly, the Great Depression of the 1930s was followed by decreasing levels of both income and wealth inequality. Are these two events representative? Do massive events such as pandemics or severe economic downturns always decrease economic inequality? While the Black Plague led to an albeit brief decline in inequality, a look historically at other pandemics demonstrates that the evidence is mixed. With some pandemics, such as the various cholera outbreaks, inequality declined simply because so many poor people died. In others, such as the Spanish Flu of 1918, the economic disruptions outweighed deaths, leading to an increase in the number of poor (Alfani, 2020).

It is too early to know what effect the COVID-19 pandemic will have on rates of inequality—as with the historic record, the evidence thus far is mixed. In the short run, we know that many have gotten much richer during the pandemic (Oxfam International, 2021). Surprisingly, US households have thus far increased their wealth during the pandemic by $13.5 trillion, compared to an $8 trillion reduction following the mild 2001–2002 recession and an $8 trillion reduction in wealth following the 2008 recession. Unprecedented government investment in the economy seems to have greatly buffered the effects of the pandemic, temporarily increasing the wealth of many, including those in the middle to lower ranks of the income ladder (though for those at the bottom, the increase was due to stimulus checks and is likely to be temporary). Still, over 70 percent of this increase in household wealth went to the top 20 percent of income earners, driven in great part by increases in the stock market and a boom in housing prices. This rapid increase in housing prices (a 23 percent increase between 2020 and 2021) is making homeownership impossible for many. High-paying jobs (those paying more than $60,000) rose by 2 percent in 2020, but low-income jobs decreased by 24 percent. "The Americans who gained the most during 2020 were the ones who had the most to begin with" (McCaffrey & Shifflett, 2021).

Yet, at the time of writing, current labor shortages suggest that this might be a moment where workers are gaining a modicum of bargaining power. Support for unions has reached a contemporary high, and workers are quitting their jobs at record rates. In fact, in September of 2021, a record 4.1 million workers quit (Hess, 2021; Picchi, 2021). Many of those quitters were in low-paid, high turnover jobs. To quote one pet store worker, "My life is not worth a dead-end job" (Bhattarai, 2021). We don't know yet if this is just a temporary blip. But all of this begs the question: Do economic disruptions such as recessions or pandemics make inequality worse or make it better?

Inequality in the United States in Global Context

As we will explore further in Chapter 2, the United States has notably high levels of inequality. In Table 1.1, you can see how we rank against other large industrial countries. The Gini Index is a measure of inequality with "0" representing a situation of complete equality and 1 a situation of complete inequality. Our number is 0.39. Looking more broadly around the world, generally, countries lower in living standards by United Nations measures have inequality levels that exceed those in industrial nations. In terms of regions of the world, Europe is the least unequal and the Middle East the most unequal (Alvaredo et al., 2018).

Table 1.1 Income and Inequality among Households within Selected Rich Industrial Countries: 2017–2019

Country	Gini Coefficient	Country	Gini Coefficient
Australia	0.33	Greece	0.31
Austria	0.28	Ireland	0.3
Belgium	0.26	Italy	0.33
Canada	0.3	Netherlands	0.29
Denmark	0.26	Norway	0.26
Finland	0.27	Sweden	0.28
France	0.3	Switzerland	0.3
Germany	0.29	United States	0.39

Source: OECD (2022), https://data.oecd.org/inequality/income-inequality.htm. Depending on the country, data gathered was from 2017 to 2019.

Note: In Chapter 3, you will notice that we give a different Gini Coefficient for the United States. This is because the OECD calculates Gini using post-tax and transfer income, whereas many other organizations use pre-tax and transfer.

American Perceptions of Inequality

Now we have a little bit of information about the level of inequality in the United States. Were you surprised? It turns out that most Americans have significant misperceptions about inequality, income, and wealth. In fact, in a recent survey, respondents from 40 countries were asked about the distribution of wealth and income in their society. They were given five diagrams from which to choose. One diagram, for example, was shaped like a diamond (with a large middle class and small upper and lower classes). Another diagram was a pyramid with a wide base (indicating lots of poor people) and a few people at the top. Only 29 percent of Americans were able to accurately identify the model that represents the United States. Looking at the scores from the other countries, the US ranked about the middle in terms of our knowledge of inequality

(Gimpelson & Treisman, 2018). Interestingly, later analyses with the same survey data revealed that perceptions of inequality are linked to one's own class. Richer people tend to believe that there is less inequality in their societies than do poorer people. It is likely that this is because of **homophily**—the tendency for people to spend time with others who are like them. The people in our lives provide us a **reference group** with which we compare ourselves and understand our world. If everyone you know, for example, is rich, it is easy to overestimate the percentage of rich people in the country (Knell & Stix, 2020).

Conventional wisdom, and some research, suggest that Americans tend to underestimate the true level of inequality in the country (Hauser & Norton, 2017). Where do our perceptions of inequality come from? One factor is media coverage: people are more likely to express concerns about the economy and its fairness if the media has been heavily covering inequality issues. Where people live matter too (Diermeier et al., 2017). One study looked at perceptions of inequality among New Yorkers. They found that people who lived in more economically diverse areas tended to perceive higher levels of inequality than those who lived in homogeneous areas (Minkoff & Lyons, 2019). Americans also appear to use state-level economic indicators (including the percent of poverty and unemployment as well as changes in the income share of the top socioeconomic tier) to assess the level of inequality. Interestingly, the political ideology of the state in which people live also matters with residents of more liberal states adjusting their perceptions of inequality more strongly in response to poverty and unemployment (Franko, 2017). A study with adolescents found that African Americans and those whose parents had low levels of education tend to give higher estimates of inequality (Flanagan & Kornbluh, 2019).

Is Inequality Desirable or Undesirable?

Some scholars think of inequality as a source of integration in society. Some argue, for example, that inequality in rewards is a way of making sure that critical occupations are filled with the most qualified persons. That is, since rewards provide motivation to do certain tasks, the structure of inequality is really an incentive system that helps the whole society survive. Other analysts contend that economic and other kinds of inequality create divisiveness between the haves and the have-nots, men and women, minorities and majorities. This is in large part because these groups are not equally likely to believe that the system of inequality is fair. Nor do they agree that inequality works to the benefit of the entire society rather than only a few select groups. Because of this, inequality is more likely to instigate conflict than it is to strengthen cohesion between groups and in society in general.

In some ways, Americans are attracted to equality; in other ways, they view inequality as justified. Part of the problem here is that people think about different things when they think about inequality, and people feel differently about the various kinds of equality/inequality; thus, the meaning of equality/inequality is not self-evident. For example, Bryan Turner (1986) identified four basic kinds of equality: (1) equality of human beings—that is, the notion that basically, we are all the same and equally worthy as persons; (2) equality of opportunity—the idea that access to valued ends is open to all; (3) equality of condition—that is, that people all start from the same position; and (4) equality of results or outcome, or equality of income. The latter is the most radical of the four and the one most likely to incite controversy.

Americans feel quite differently about equality of opportunity than they do about equality of income, and groups feel differently about the fairness of the system. A national poll conducted by the Pew Research Center, 2012, found that 70 percent of Americans feel that the government should adopt policies to enhance equality of opportunity, but less than half support policies that directly redistribute income. This shows that they feel any fair distribution of goods should be based more on equality of *opportunity* rather than equality of *result*. More recent research appears to support these conclusions. When asked, "In the future, should it be a priority for the president and Congress to reduce income differences between people with high incomes and those with low incomes?" a minority of Americans said that it should be a "very important priority." This included 27 percent of the top 1 percent, 34 percent of those with high and middle incomes, and 42 percent of low-income respondents (NPR, Robert Wood Johnson Foundation, and the Harvard T.H. Chan School of Public Health, 2020).

Perceptions of economic inequality are generally viewed differently and separately from views of racial and gender inequality. With racial and gender inequality, inequalities of *outcome* are seen as evidence of inequalities of *opportunity*. That is, if we find that there are differences in outcome by race, it is a fair assumption that there are unfair obstacles in the way of some, and thus the inequality is seen as unjust. With economic inequality, however, inequality of outcome coexists with inequality of opportunity—and inequality of outcome may be due to differences in efforts or skills rather than to opportunity. Thus, as McCall suggests, an intersectional model of income inequality should ask:

> How are perceptions of rising class inequality affected: by perceptions of trends in racial and gender inequality? by racial and gender differences in education, wealth, poverty, employment, and residential segregation? by racial and gender identities? and by intersections of these with social class identities and social movements? (2014, p. 30)

Regardless of whether Americans support the general idea of inequality, most agree that we have too much of it today. About two-thirds think that the current amount of income inequality is too large, and 61 percent believe wealth and income should be more equally distributed (Siripurapu, 2020). Most Americans—as well as residents of other countries—believe there should be a limit on the amount of inequality. An international survey of sixty countries, including the United States, showed that citizens are concerned about the levels of inequality and that most believe that the key explanation for inequality is selfishness among the rich. This belief in selfishness is more likely in countries experiencing high levels of corruption and is a contributor globally to beliefs that inequality is unfair and something that governments need to address (Almås et al., 2022).

In sum, a majority of Americans appear to support the *principle* of income inequality as being fair, but they do not see the present system as necessarily equitable. They also underestimate the extent of economic inequality in the country, and they are decidedly split on whether the government should do something about income inequality. It is clear that Americans' attitudes about inequality are complex and often contradictory.

Is Inequality Inevitable?

Perhaps the most basic issue relates to the inevitability of inequality. It is important to clarify that reference is being made here to *institutionalized* rather than *individual* inequality (i.e., structured inequality between categories of individuals that are systematically created, reproduced, legitimated by sets of ideas, and relatively stable). We would not be studying this phenomenon if it were not a prominent feature of contemporary society with significant consequences. To ask whether it is inevitable is to address the origins of inequality (i.e., whether it is caused by natural or artificial factors). If social inequality is directly linked to conditions inherent in the nature of groups of individuals or in society, then little might be expected to eliminate it. On the other hand, if such inequality arises because of the conscious, intentional, and freely willed actions of individuals or the structures they create in society, then perhaps it can be altered.

One side argues that inequality is always going to be present because of personal differences among individuals either in the form of basic differences in their own makeups or differences in the amount of effort they expend. A large majority of Americans would appear to agree. A recent poll, for example, found that 43 percent of Americans think that the rich got that way because they worked harder than other people (42 percent said it was due to advantages they had been given) (Dunn, 2018). If there is an open society and if people vary in their talents and motivations, then this would suggest that inequality is inevitable, a simple fact of society. "Some inequalities come about as a result of unavoidable biological inequalities of physical skill, mental capacity, and traits of personality," argued Cauthen (1987, p. 8) in his treatise on equality. Some early philosophers also argued that there are "natural" differences between individuals; in fact, some people still maintain that differences of this type separate the sexes, resulting in the inevitability of inequality. Aristotle took the position that "the male is by nature superior, the female, inferior; and the one rules, and the other is ruled" (Kriesberg, 1979, p. 12). These and other explanations of inequality will be discussed in detail later.

Other theorists have argued that inequality is inevitable because as long as certain kinds of tasks are more necessary for the survival of the society than others, and as long as those who are able to perform those tasks are rare, social inequality of rewards among individuals is needed to motivate the best people to perform the most difficult tasks. Under these conditions, the argument goes, inequality cannot be eradicated without endangering society.

On the other side of the fence are those who argue that economic inequality is not inevitable and is largely the by-product of a system's structure and not the result of major differences in individual or group talents, characteristics, and motivations. Rousseau, for example, linked the origins of inequality to the creation of private property (Dahrendorf, 1970, p. 10). It is the characteristics of the political economy and the firms and labor markets within it that are primary determinants of differences in income and wealth. Where a person works and in what industry have major effects on income. Certainly, the job changes resulting from downsizing would suggest this. Essentially, then, this argument states that it is not human nature and individual differences but rather structural conditions that determine where an individual winds up on the ladder of economic inequality. Discrimination is another of those conditions. If the conditions that generate social inequality are artificial creations of human actions, then they can be changed, and economic inequality is not inevitable, nor is it necessarily beneficial for the society and all its members. We will examine this controversy more thoroughly in later chapters.

Key Terms and Usages

Social Inequality and Stratification

As we use it in this text, "inequality" refers to situations where people have different amounts of something valuable. That could be a material thing such as food or income, or it could be invisible like **prestige** or education. Inequality is not necessarily problematic if most people agree that it is fair. For example, in surveys conducted all over the world (including the United States), about three-quarters of respondents say performance and effort are legitimate determinants of pay differences (Evans et al., 2010). In other situations, however, we do not think inequality is fair—for example, if we started distributing income based on people's height, we might hear some protest. But we will explore this question further in later chapters.

Social stratification is related to inequality, but it refers to a "rare form of disparity that clusters social units by layers, or *strata*, which are homogenous with respect to a wide range of goods (both autonomous and relative) and which occupy a single, well-defined rank order" (Tilly, 1998, p. 27). In simpler terms, social stratification refers to a situation where people have unequal access to various resources based on the group they belong to, including material goods, power, symbolic goods, and social status. If the inequality is due to a person's membership in a particular group rather than individual characteristics, this is stratification, not simply inequality (McLeod & Nonnemaker, 1999, p. 321). In this text, we are using "social inequality" and "stratification" interchangeably.

Globalization

Another term that is central to understanding inequality is globalization. **Globalization** has been defined in two basic ways, one which is narrowly economic and another which incorporates a variety of dimensions and is sometimes referred to as the "grand" theory of globalization. In this latter view,

> Globalization refers to a multidimensional set of social processes that create, multiply, stretch, and intensify worldwide social interdependencies and exchanges while at the same time fostering in people a growing awareness of deepening connections between the local and the distant. (Myers, 2014, p. 45)

This definition includes not only increasing economic ties between countries but also closer cultural and social ties. A narrower conceptualization of globalization views it as a strictly economic phenomenon involving the increase in direct investment, flow of workers, and free trade between countries. It is primarily this latter definition that we will use in our assessment of globalization's impact on inequality among nations and within the United States.

Intersectionality

First coined by Kimberlé Crenshaw (1989), the term **intersectionality** refers to the idea that people experience inequality differently, depending on their particular status. Thus, while gender inequalities are certainly consequential, Black women face very different discrimination than do White women. Inequalities represent a "matrix of domination" (Collins & Bilge, 2016), whereby intersecting statuses and identities combine to create a system of exploitation and domination. To fully understand the lived experiences of inequality, we need to understand how the combination and intersection of statuses affect our lives.

Representing Race and Ethnicity

As have many, we struggle with how we should speak about groups that are raced. When referring to individuals or groups that have a race associated with them, such as Black Americans, do we capitalize the "B" in Black? And what about the "W" in White? Arguably the preferred style, particularly since the recent racial justice protests, has been to capitalize "B" but not "W" (Tharps, 2014). Early sociologist W.E.B. Du Bois was perhaps the first to capitalize the reference to race, asking that the "N" in negro be capitalized, in the words of the Associated Press, "conveying an essential and shared sense of history, identity and community among people who identify as Black, including those in the African diaspora and within Africa" (Associated Press, 2020). Capitalizing "B" (and the first letter in Asian Americans, Hispanics, and Native Americans) conveys respect for groups that have been historically marginalized.

Why then capitalize the "W" in White? We have been persuaded by recent statements by the National Association of Black Journalists (2020) and the prominent historian of race, Nell Painter, that "whenever a color is used to appropriately describe race then it should be capitalized, including White and Brown." We are not so much concerned by the lack of parallelism by capitalizing one and not the other—clearly, the life experiences of groups have not been parallel, and it is absolutely reasonable for language to reflect those differences. But more convincing is that idea that by capitalizing one and not the other, we are implying that race is only salient for people of color. White then becomes the invisible, unraced default: "In terms of racial identity, White Americans have had the choice of being something vague, something unraced and separate from race. A capitalized 'White' challenges that freedom, by unmasking 'Whiteness' as an American racial identity as historically important as 'Blackness'—which it certainly is" (Painter, 2020).

We have generally chosen to use the term "Hispanic" to refer to people with ancestry in the Spanish-speaking world. We discuss the origin of this term in detail in Chapter 10. We also occasionally use the term "Latino." Polls indicate that both these terms are acceptable to people who identify as being in the category but that there is a slight preference for "Hispanic." While the term "Latinx" appears to be growing in popularity, the majority of Hispanics have not heard of it, and there is considerable controversy over its use (Noe-Bustamante et al., 2020). For this reason, we do not use it. If larger numbers of Hispanic people choose to self-identify as Latinx, we will make the change in future editions of this book.

Gender-Neutral Language Choices

In Chapter 8 of this text, we cover the links between gender and inequality. We will learn that increasing numbers of Americans—particularly young Americans—are identifying as trans, nonbinary, or genderqueer. While most of this group continue to use the terms "she" and "he," about a quarter prefer other pronouns. We firmly believe that people should be able to choose the names they are called, as well as their pronouns. For this reason, throughout the text, we use she/him when that is a person's preference. Where we are unsure, or where a person has stated a desire for nonbinary pronouns, we use the term "they." There are other non-gendered pronouns (ze, for example), but polls indicate that "they" is by far the most popular (The Trevor Project, 2020).

Organization of the Book

The text is divided into four major parts. Part 1 addresses the extent of inequality in its various forms. Chapters 2–5 focus on specific forms of inequality that concern resource *outcomes* (i.e., income/wealth, poverty, social status, and power) which are distributed unequally among individuals and groups in the United States. Part 2 presents the primary general explanations for social inequality, with Chapter 6 including information about how the classical theorists, Marx, Weber, Durkheim, and Du Bois, understand inequality. Chapter 7 analyzes more contemporary explanations, ranging from functionalist theories to social reproduction and constructionist theories to intersectional theories. In Part 3, we look at significant categories according to which we distribute resources. These include gender, sexual orientation, race/ethnicity, immigration status, place, and religion. All of these categories (discussed in Chapters 8–11) affect the distribution of wealth, status, and power in our society.

Having discussed the extent and explanations of inequality in the first three parts of the book, we then turn to the pervasive *consequences* of inequality for individuals and society. Chapter 12 looks at how health and the environment have a profound impact on the outcomes of individual people and communities. In Chapter 13, we examine crime and the criminal justice system. We ask how categories including socioeconomic position, race, and gender affect the steps in the criminal justice process from the chances of being arrested to the likelihood of being given a long sentence. Street crimes, white-collar crimes, and hate crimes are each discussed. We also show how inequality plays a role in determining who commits a crime in the first place.

Part 5 of the book explores the possibility for change. In Chapter 14, we examine how social movements—both current and historical—have changed inequality. These movements include the labor, civil rights, and women's movements as well as #metoo and #BlackLives Matter. All of these movements can be viewed as reactions to inequalities that were perceived as unjust. Chapter 15 is a chance to think about alternatives to our current system and ways that you might be able to become involved in changing how goods are distributed in society.

Each chapter ends with a short set of questions and film suggestions, addressing some critical issues raised by the chapter. They are aimed at forcing you to come to grips with central problems in inequality, often by looking at inequality in your own life. The *Web Connections* sections suggest various websites where you can get more information and which you can use as bases for course exercises. These should broaden and deepen your understanding of inequality. Many chapters also contain brief boxes addressing specific issues to be analyzed or questions for discussion. Each issue is introduced to serve as a point of departure for classroom discussion. Finally, a *Glossary of Basic Terms* used in the text follows the last chapter (terms appearing in the glossary are represented in bold in the body of the chapters).

The lines separating the social sciences are often vague, the result being that discussions in the book often will draw on the work of economists, anthropologists, as well as sociologists, and others. In addition, there is material from other countries. These inclusions, hopefully, result in a more thorough and well-rounded perspective on the structure and process of social inequality in the United States.

Summary

Social inequality has been a popular topic in recent years, with increasing attention from the media and from policy makers. But many discussions of social inequality lack an in-depth understanding of how inequality operates at the intersections of the various statuses we occupy in society. This book addresses the complexities of social inequality, outlining its nature and extent, who is most affected, and possible solutions for remedying it.

So far, we have learned that inequality has increased greatly over the years, both in the United States and globally. Generally, economic inequality is greater in poorer countries, although there are major variations among industrial nations. When compared to its industrial counterparts, the United States ranks at the top in terms of its income and wealth inequality. Research tells us that Americans hold significant misperceptions about the level of inequality in society but that, in general, they would prefer to see a more equitable distribution of wealth and income.

Critical Thinking

1. Try to think of a personal relationship you have with someone who is unequal to you in some way, and yet the inequality appears to have few negative effects on you or your relationship. What characteristics lessen the impact of inequality in this relationship? Discuss some lessons from this relationship that might be used to diminish the negative effects of inequality in society as a whole.

2. Is social inequality a problem that demands the full attention of society, or is it merely a personal problem of those living below the middle class? Explain your answer.

3. Is it possible for *equality* in political power to exist alongside economic *inequality*?

4. Gazing into your crystal ball, do you think the long-run impact of increasing relationships among peoples around the world will lead to a leveling of inequalities among them, or will it solidify or increase existing inequalities?

Web Connections

Several of the following chapters use information obtained from national polls, many of which are published on the Internet. The National Council on Public Polls suggests that among the questions you should consider before accepting poll results are the following: (1) Who sponsored and who conducted the poll? (2) Is the sample large enough and representative of the whole population? (3) Were any important groups excluded from the poll? (4) Was the technique used in the interview likely to affect the answers received? (5) Was the wording of the questions neutral or biased in some way? (6) Are the survey results still valid or are they out-of-date? (Carr, 2005).

PART I

Extent and Forms of Social Inequality

2 Poverty, Wealth, and Inequality

In the next several chapters, we consider different forms of inequality: economic, status, gender, sexuality, racial, and political. We start here with economic inequality since it is what people most associate with inequality and because income/wealth differences are strongly related to all other forms of inequality. Why are we discussing poverty, wealth, and income all together? The focus of this book is *social* inequality, which, as we identified in the last chapter, is a system whereby resources are distributed unequally based on group membership. More importantly, for our purposes, this system involves intersecting and interlocking forms of inequality. While we will demonstrate the extent of economic inequality, our main goal is to unpack the *nexus* between poverty, wealth, and income inequality. That is, we look at how the massive increase in wealth and income at the top is connected to the impoverishment of those at the bottom. And we examine how both processes are closely related to other forms of inequality including race, gender, citizenship, disability, and sexuality.

Income and Wealth Inequality in the United States

John Mitchell, a restaurant server living in Philadelphia, was thrilled when he received rental assistance at the start of the pandemic. The restaurant he worked at had closed, and he was unable to pay his rent. The federal assistance kept him in his home, but with the pandemic surging again in January, he was facing eviction once again, but there were now few supports available: "This has just been hell," he told reporters (Kasakove & Thrush, 2022). As he himself faced illness, he was uncertain how he would support himself and his ailing mother.

This is a familiar story repeated across the country: in the middle of the pandemic, one in eight families with children were having difficulty feeding their families, and one in seven renters nationwide were behind in rent. The effects were felt most among Black and Latinx families (CBPP, 2021b), with 62 percent of Hispanic Americans and 54 percent of Black Americans reporting the loss of income during the pandemic, compared with 45 percent of White Americans (Morrison et al., 2021). Globally, decades of progress in reducing poverty were severely reduced (Beaumont, 2021)—estimates are that the number of those living in extreme poverty might have increased from 200 million people to half a billion during the pandemic (Berkhout et al., 2021).

Temporary pandemic relief packages, such as the eviction supports described above, helped to reduce these poverty levels: in the summer of 2021, relief programs helped to cut poverty nearly in half compared with pre-pandemic levels (DeParle, 2021). But as these supports are ending, many worry that the poverty levels will rise quickly again without further changes to how we support those in financial need.

At the same time, the wealthiest individuals have gotten much richer during the pandemic. The total wealth of billionaires in the United States is up 35 percent since the beginning of the pandemic, with $3.4 trillion added to the wealth of billionaires. And more than half of that

DOI: 10.4324/9781003184966-3

wealth increase was accountable by only the top 20 billionaires—for example, Elon Musk's net worth "skyrocketed an incredible 540 percent, from 27 billion in early January 2020 to more than $170 billion today" (Peterson-Withorn, 2021).

Some of these outcomes are specific to the conditions of the pandemic, but they both illustrate and exacerbate central dynamics involved with poverty, wealth, and income distribution. The precarity experienced by John Mitchell and the power and wealth of Elon Musk are not isolated and separate events—it is no accident that as the economy suffers a crisis, the rich get richer and the poor get poorer. We commonly heard during the pandemic that we were all in this together—we were all in the same boat. But that is not exactly true. We experienced the same storm, but we were most certainly not in the same boat. Some, like Jeff Bezos, were in a $500 million yacht, so large it needs its own yacht with a helipad to ferry passengers back and forth (Morrow, 2021), and others were hanging on for life on debris left from the storm.

In the last chapter, we outlined some broad trends in income and wealth inequality in the United States and globally. Here we look deeper into the scope and complexity of these current and historical inequalities, wherever possible providing an intersectional perspective.

Income and Wealth Defined

The meaning of the terms *income* and *wealth* may seem obvious, but they are often confused in everyday speech. *Money income*, as defined by the Census Bureau, includes money from virtually all sources, including wages or salaries, social security, welfare, pensions, and others. There are some advantages to using money income when assessing the extent of economic inequality. In the first place, it is certainly more immediately quantifiable than many other measures, such as real estate. Second, income is highly valued in US society and serves as a basis on which people are evaluated by others. Third, income inequalities saturate and are reflected in a number of other economically related areas. Unemployment, inflation, farm and food prices, rent control, gender discrimination, racism, and welfare are all areas that involve income-differential issues. Think about your own income and the myriad ways it is related to other areas of your life.

It turns out that while money income is important, it only tells us one piece of the story about economic inequality. This is because it does not include the value of stocks, real estate, or other noncash economic assets. Income is also just a snapshot in time, failing to capture the trajectory an individual may be on if, for example, they are just beginning in a lucrative career. On a larger scale, national data on income may be unrepresentative because it is usually obtained from tax returns. The Internal Revenue Service finds that income is underreported and not all persons who are required to file income tax returns do so. The majority of underreported income is from businesses or self-employment because these are sources that are hard for the IRS to track (IRS, 2020). Related to this, high-income earners are more likely to underreport income than low-income earners (Guyton et al., 2021).

Measuring wealth as well as income gives us a more complete measure of a family's economic power since it consists of the value of all the family's assets minus its debts. Thus, wealth includes the value of homes, automobiles, businesses, savings, and investments. Even this measure, however, does not reflect the access of the wealthy to financial tools that serve to enhance their economic opportunities and market situation. For example, ownership of a great deal of stock in a corporation that is **interlocked** or directly connected with other corporations may give an individual indirect influence over the economic behavior of the latter organizations. This shows how wealth has economic implications beyond the actual size of a person's holdings. Economic opportunities are at least in part a function of the economic tools one has at their disposal.

There is little consensus on how to measure the distribution of wealth. There are several reasons for this. First, information about wealth is difficult to obtain. Virtually all data about it come from various field surveys and administrative records (such as tax records). Often, individuals are hesitant to be interviewed, and this is especially true of the wealthy, who, for several reasons, may be sensitive about their wealth. Sherman (2017) conducted in-depth interviews with New Yorkers in their thirties and forties who had a household income of over $250,000. She commented:

> In the interviews, most people described themselves as reluctant to talk about money in any detail with anyone except their partners and sometimes other close family members. They described money as deeply private—'more private than sex,' in the words of one psychotherapist I interviewed. (p. 18)

Sherman found that her interviewees were very concerned about anonymity, and they felt deeply ambivalent about their wealth, making them unwilling to be honest about the true extent of their holdings or spending. As a result, it is likely that what wealthy people report on surveys may not be accurate.

Income and Wealth in US History

If ever there was a time when equality was present, it surely must have been when the United States was first being established. Many of the early colonists left their European homelands to escape oppression of one kind or another. The goal was to live in the "land of the free," where the streets were thought to be paved with gold. In the Declaration of Independence, the Founding Fathers used "the voice of justice" to enumerate the offenses committed against the then new American people and to demand freedom and equality for all.

While some, such as Alexander Hamilton and Thomas Jefferson, argued about whether the government should or should not take a strictly egalitarian form, many believed the period was one where "the hierarchies of social rank and inherited status gave way to a social order grounded in radical principles of social equality" (Dahl, 2018, p. 47). The Founders espoused the belief that "all men are created equal" and later devised a constitution that had among its objectives to "establish justice." In his famous visit to the United States, Alexis de Tocqueville (1966) was surprised by the "equality of conditions" that seemed to prevail in the youthful country. And although he believed wealth was certainly present, no one group held a monopoly on it. Indeed, de Tocqueville believed that wealth moved about quite a bit in the country.

But from the beginning, this supposed equality was possible only because others were not free: "in the heart of the nation that had laughed about prejudices and that had set itself the goal of erecting a state with the least conceivable class differences, there existed from the very beginning the worst of all caste differences that, unheeded, grew to a threatening girth, namely a slavery based on race and color" (Du Bois, 1906, p. 243). These **caste** differences were established from the start of the nation and built the framework on which later income and wealth differences would proceed (Wilkerson, 2020). Thus, "in a conceptual sense, American colonists developed their notions of freedom not despite but because of slavery by contrasting their own status a freeman with that of their slaves. In a material sense, individual freedom rested on the economic independence afforded by the profits from slave labor" (Dahl, 2018, p. 5).

Though levels of inequality were lower during the very early history of the United States, social historians, poring over probate records, tax forms, and old census documents, have found a decidedly different America than one might have expected. Studies of wealth distribution in the early United States consistently point to the fact that wealth inequality was a clear and constant condition during this period. Income inequality existed in the Colonies, but it was less pronounced than it was in England and in other north-western European countries at the time. Notably, it was also far lower than in the present-day United States (Lindert & Williamson, 2016).

The relatively higher levels of equality in income and wealth among White people during the early years of the nation were partially based on rapid economic growth. Also important was the provision of large tracts of land to free White men for no or very low cost. This was a model of **settler colonialism**, or "a distinct form of colonialism aimed at the expropriation of native land rather than the exploitation of native labor" (Dahl, 2018, pp. 1–2). Under settler colonialism, there was wide distribution of cheap land through the violent dispossessions of the lands of indigenous peoples.

After 1774, there was an increasing trend toward inequality in the United States. Lindert and Williamson (2016) looked at income data and found evidence that income inequality increased dramatically during the period between 1774 and 1860. In fact, the rate of increase was the highest in American history until it was surpassed in the 1970s. Levels of inequality rose across the nation, but there was also evidence of an increasing divide between the North and the South and between urban and rural people. After Emancipation in 1863, income concentration began to increase substantially in the North at the same time that it decreased in the South. These two effects largely canceled each other out so that, on average, income inequality rose only moderately over the period (Lindert & Williamson, 2016).

The concentration of wealth in the nineteenth century appears to have peaked during the period from 1850 to 1870. In 1870, estimates are that the 1 percent of all adult individuals controlled 39.8 percent of the nation's wealth, a bit higher than today's rate of 34.8 percent (Sutch, 2017, p. 600). A small percentage had great wealth, but large numbers had little if any. Wealth concentration was more pronounced in the South due to the reality that "the (B)lack population had little opportunity and insufficient time to accumulate a level of wealth appropriate to their age and recently endowed income" (p. 600). Real estate discrimination also meant that Black people were generally unable to own land. The main conclusion to be drawn is that at least from the mid-eighteenth to the mid-nineteenth centuries, there was high and increasing concentration of wealth in the United States.

As American moved into the World War I, estimates suggest that the richest 1 percent held between 35 percent and 40 percent of all wealth, and then, at the outset of the Great Depression in 1928, their wealth began to decline, reaching just under 23 percent by 1950 (Piketty, 2014). There were moderate increases during the 1950s, but the wealth share of the top 1 percent stayed mostly stable or declined up until the 1980s (Keister & Moller, 2000). Income inequality also decreased until the 1970s, resulting in levels of equality not seen in the country since 1774 (Lindert & Williamson, 2016). These decreases in wealth and income inequality involved factors such as the destruction of financial property due to the wars, increasing financial regulation after the depression, and increasing trade barriers.

Income Inequality: Trends from 1980 to Today

Income data from 1980 to 2020 reveal high and increasing inequality. Table 2.1 summarizes information on how US households were distributed among different income categories in 1980, 1990, 2000, 2010, and 2020. Presenting the data in these increments is useful because it can illustrate broad trends. At the same time, it hides variability within each period.

Looking at the top line in the income distribution in Table 2.1, we see that the percentage of families with incomes below $15,000 has declined over the period (from 12.2 percent in 1980 to 9.4 percent in 2020). At the same time, the percentage of those with incomes of at least $100,000 rose far more dramatically (doubling from 17 percent to 33.6 percent). The percentages of those in the $25,000–$74,999 categories have generally declined. While shifts in the top and bottom categories in Table 2.1 may suggest that economic conditions have improved since 1980, we need to reserve judgment until we have additional information.

Table 2.1 Percentage Distribution of Households by Income Level: 1980–2020

Income	1980	1990	2000	2010	2020
Under $15,000*	12.2	11.1	9.3	11.2	9.4
$15,000–$24,999	10.7	10.1	9.3	10.7	8.7
$25,000–$34,999	10.3	9.5	9.3	9.4	8.1
$35,000–$49,999	14.6	13.9	13.1	13.3	11.6
$50,000–$74,999	21.2	19.5	17.7	16.8	16.5
$75,000–$99,999	14	13.7	13.2	12.4	12.2
$100,000–$149,999	12	13.8	15.4	14.1	15.3
$150,000–$199,999	3.2	4.8	6.8	6.3	8
$200,000 and above	1.8	3.7	6.2	5.9	10.3
Median Income	$52,461	$56,966	$62,512	$57,904	$62,773

*   Median income measured in 2020 adjusted dollars using CPI-U-R5, Table C-1.

Source: US Census (2021i). Tables A-2 and C-1, https://www.census.gov/library/publications/2021/demo/p60-273.html

First, it is important to note that, while wages have risen over time, they have not risen at the rate they have in the past. One way to see this is to compare wages to the growth in productivity. In theory, as companies produce more goods, wages should rise at about the same rate. This was the reality during the 30 years after World War II. But in the period between 1979 and 2019, the two rates diverged, with productivity increasing 72.2 percent but wages rising only 17.2 percent (Economic Policy Institute, 2021). Part of the explanation lies in the fact that an increasing proportion of the national income has gone to profits and capital and less to wages and salaries. At the same time, some wage earners have benefited with the top 1 percent seeing their wages rise by 160 percent over the period (Mishel & Kandra, 2020b). CEOs were particularly advantaged. In Chapter 1, we described how, in 2019, the average CEO made about 320 times the compensation of the average worker. This compares to a ratio of 21 to 1 in 1965 and 61 to 1 in 1989 (Mishel & Kandra, 2020a).

It can be difficult to visualize income inequality and how it changes over time. Figure 2.1 provides a graphical view of the percentage of income obtained by different quintiles of the population starting in 1980. A quintile is simply a fifth (20 percent) of the population. The top quintile of income earners, for example, are the 20 percent of people who earn the most (80 percent of the population earns less than they do). The "middle quintile" would be the people who earn more than 40 percent of people in the population but less than the top 40 percent of income earners.

The data show that the percentage of all income going to the bottom and middle quintiles of the population has declined since 1980, while that going to the top 20 percent has increased from 44.1 percent to 52.2 percent in 2020. The top 5 percent alone received over 23 percent of all income in 2020.

Trends in the Gini Ratio also indicate the increasing concentration of income in the United States. In 1980, the Gini Index (pre-tax and transfer money income) for US households stood at 0.40; by 2018, it had risen to 0.49, the highest of any highly developed country in the world (US Census Bureau, 2021i).

The middle and lower classes are well aware of the recent declines in their economic fortunes. About 48 percent of Americans said that their income has fallen behind the cost of living (Parker et al., 2016). On average, about two-thirds of a family's income comes from employment earnings (not including business, farm, and self-employment), but the proportion is much greater for those

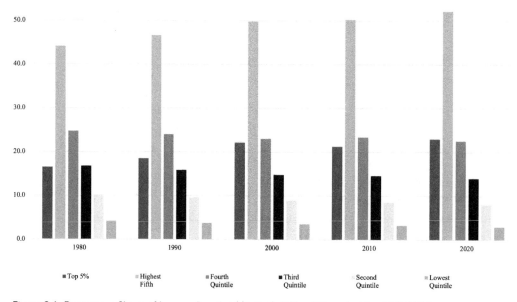

Figure 2.1 Percentage Share of Income Received by Each Fifth of Households, 1980–2020.

Source: US Census Bureau (2021j), Table H-2, https://www.census.gov/data/tables/time-series/demo/income-poverty/historical-income-households.html

in the middle class (Bhutta et al., 2020). It should not be surprising, then, that the acceleration in income inequality since 1980 is due heavily to the increase in earnings inequality, especially between those in the top 10 percent and the rest of the working population. Those earnings differences partly reflect a polarizing increase in both high- and low-paying jobs alongside a decrease in middle-wage positions (Gould, 2020).

It might be reasonable to think that unemployment plays a role in today's high level of income inequality. It turns out, however, that while unemployment is clearly important in determining individuals' income, it cannot explain societal increases in inequality. In 2021, the unemployment rate was 5.8 percent, up slightly due to the pandemic from a historic low of less than 4 percent in 2020 (US Bureau of Labor Statistics, 2021b). These low rates are clearly not driving inequality. Instead, researchers find that shifts in the **occupational structure** (including the rise of **contingent work**), declines in the power of unions and the rise of right-to-work laws, a lagging minimum wage, and globalization account for most of these changes (Keller & Olney, 2017; Solow, 2015).

Another driver of inequality and a source of stress for the lower and middle class involves increasing costs. Housing is a good example. In 1984, the average family paid 30 percent of their income for housing; by 2020, that number was 34.9 percent. Notably, those families in the lowest quintile today spend 42.9 percent of their income on housing (US Bureau of Labor Statistics, 2021h). Higher education costs have also risen dramatically, causing real hardship for the middle class (see Box 2.1) (Seltzer, 2017).

Not surprisingly, income inequalities are not distributed evenly across racial and ethnic groups. Table 2.2 outlines the trends in income distribution across several groups from 1980 to 2020. The percentage of those earning below $25,000 has declined for all groups, but the percentage of those earning over $150,000 has greatly increased, and those in the middle have seen their incomes decline. The racial group to experience the greatest increase in income is non-Hispanic White households, with Black households reporting the smallest increase.

Photo 2.1 Evictions are a common problem for the poor in the United States.
Source: Shutterstock/TLF Images.

BOX 2.1 STUDENT LOAN DEBT

Student loans are a significant problem in the United States. Currently, the debt on these loans totals more than 1.7 trillion dollars, with the average debt for a bachelor's degree at over $36,000 (Siripurapu & Speier, 2021). Many economists worry about the effect of student loans at both the individual and societal levels. High levels of student debt are linked to the jobs people take after college. For example, research shows that people with high loans face more health issues, psychological stress, and lower life satisfaction (Kim & Chatterjee, 2019). People with high loans are also more likely to take higher-paying private sector jobs, rather than jobs that more directly serve the public interest (like work in non-profits) (Rothstein & Rouse, 2011). Loan debt affects the economy when it prevents people from buying houses, slowing the housing market. There are even concerns that student loans have become an economic "bubble" that may burst and lead to another recession. While economists disagree about the likelihood of this happening, some believe that if there were to be massive default on loans, it could have ripple effects throughout the economy.

Education is much more expensive in the United States than in other countries and costs have increased quickly—rising 500 percent since 1985. This is because many other countries invest more heavily in their education systems, making it less expensive for students. In Denmark, for example, higher education is not only free, but students receive a monthly stipend to help them pay living expenses. This policy is predicated on the idea that abilities and interests should drive students going to college, not socioeconomic standing (Noack, 2015). Additionally, a more educated workforce helps the economy by increasing labor productivity. In the United States, states with highly educated workforces tend to have higher average wages. This is partly because a more educated workforce attracts high-tech and other high-paying industries. States benefit when wages are high because tax revenues increase (Berger & Fisher, 2013).

Table 2.2 Percentage of Households by Income Level, by Race and Hispanic Origin: 1980–2020 Incomes in 2020 Dollars

	1980	1990	2000	2010	2020
Household Incomes Below $25,000					
Non-Hispanic Whites	19.9	17.6	16.1	18.5	15.6
Black	40.8	38.3	29.1	35.4	29.7
Hispanic	29.6	29.6	22.9	27.2	20.4
Asian	–	15.5	13.4	17.2	13.7
Household Incomes between $25,000 and $74,999					
Non-Hispanic White	45.6	42.6	37.9	38.2	34.5
Black	43.6	41.1	43.4	41.2	40.7
Hispanic	49.6	47.3	46.7	45.8	43.4
Asian	–	34.8	31.6	31.9	26.8
Household Incomes between $75,000 and $149,0000					
Non-Hispanic White	28.5	30	30.9	28.8	29.3
Black	14.2	17.4	21.2	18.3	20.6
Hispanic	20.8	19.3	24.2	20.7	25.6
Asian	–	34.7	32.6	29.5	27.4
Household Incomes $150,000 and Higher					
Non-Hispanic White	5.9	9.8	15.2	14.3	20.7
Black	1.3	3.1	6.1	5	8.9
Hispanic	2.3	3.8	6.2	6.3	10.6
Asian	–	15	22.4	21.3	32.1

Source: US Census Bureau (2021j), Table H-17, www.census.gov/data/tables/time-series/demo/income-poverty/historical-income-households.html

Some care should be taken in interpreting income data for Asian people because the category masks significant differences by ethnicity. For example, in 2016, people of Indian descent had an average household income of about $110,000, while Burmese people earned just under $39,000. Bangladeshis and Hmong people also have low average incomes and high rates of poverty (Wilson & Mokhiber, 2017). These within-group differences among Asians are so significant that they have the greatest level of income inequality of any racial/ethnic group, with Asians at the 90th percentile of income having 10.7 times the income of Asians at the 10th percentile. The equivalent figures are 9.8 for Black people, 7.8 for White people, and 7.8 for Hispanics (Kochhar & Cilluffo, 2018). The Hispanic category, like the Asian category, also contains a huge amount of diversity. Importantly, it includes both native and foreign-born people, masking important differences in inequality between them. We discuss these disparities at greater length in the immigration section in Chapter 11.

Table 2.2 illustrates the percentage of households from each racial/ethnic group in income brackets. We see a similar story when we look at the *share* of income received by each quintile across racial groups. Table 2.3 illustrates that between 1980 and 2020, Non-Hispanic White households in the top 20 percent income category increased their share of income from 43.4 percent to 51.2 percent, while those in the bottom quintile decreased their share from 4.4 percent to 3.2 percent. This pattern holds for all groups. Similarly, the Gini coefficient for all groups increases, with the greatest increase among non-Hispanic White individuals and the lowest among Hispanic households.

Table 2.3 Share of Aggregate Income Received by Bottom 20 percent, Middle 60 percent, and Top 20 percent within White, Black, Asian, and Hispanic Households: 1980–2020

	1980	1990	2000	2010	2020
Non-Hispanic Whites					
Bottom 20%	4.4	4.2	3.7	3.6	3.2
Middle 60%	52.2	50	47	47.1	45.4
Top 20%	43.4	45.8	49.3	49.4	51.3
Gini Index	*0.392*	*0.416*	*0.455*	*0.458*	*0.478*
Blacks					
Bottom 20%	3.7	3.1	3.2	2.7	2.4
Middle 60%	49.2	48	47.8	46	43.5
Top 20%	47.1	49	49	51.3	54.1
Gini Index	*0.439*	*0.464*	*0.458*	*0.487*	*0.514*
Hispanics					
Bottom 20%	4.3	4	4	3.5	3.5
Middle 60%	51.1	49.7	47.4	47.1	46.8
Top 20%	44.5	46.3	48.5	49.4	49.7
Gini Index	*0.405*	*0.425*	*0.444*	*0.458*	*0.46*
Asians					
Bottom 20%	–	–	–	2.9	2.9
Middle 60%	–	–	–	48.8	46.8
Top 20%	–	–	–	48.3	50.3
Gini Index				*0.456*	*0.476*

Source: US Census Bureau (2021c), Tables H-2/H-4, https://www.census.gov/data/tables/time-series/demo/income-poverty/historical-income-households.html

Note: Data for Asians prior to 2010 are not available.

You might have noted the absence of American Indians in Table 2.3. This is because the Census has not yet provided equivalent updated data for this group. Using slightly older data, we know that the economic status of American Indians lags behind that of other groups. In 2016, the median household income for American Indians and Alaskan Natives was $39,719, which was 69 percent of the national average. About 26 percent of American Indians/Alaskan Natives had incomes that put them below the poverty line, double the national average (Wilson & Mokhiber, 2017).

Racial/ethnic differences in income intersect with inequalities by gender. Figure 2.2 demonstrates notable trends in income among full-time workers since 1990. While men of all ethnic and racial groups represented here earn more than women, Asian men and women report the greatest increases in income, while Black and Hispanic men report the lowest increases over the years. White and Asian men held the highest incomes, with the income of Asian men on average twice that of Hispanic women. Black and Hispanic women reported the lowest income.

We will explore possible explanations for these differences in inequality by race and gender further in later chapters. To understand fully the complexity of the inequalities, however, we need to look also at differences in wealth.

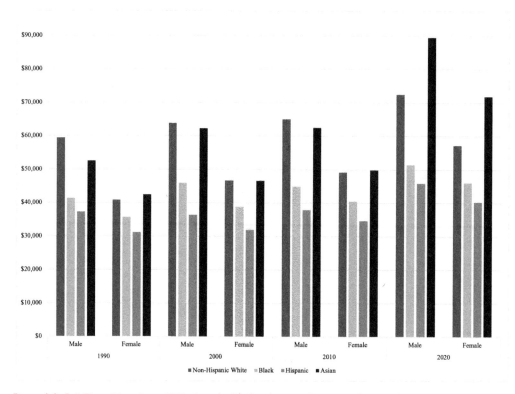

Figure 2.2 Full-Time, Year-Round Workers by Median Income, Race, and Sex, 1990–2020.

Source: US Census Bureau (2021l), Table P-36, https://www.census.gov/data/tables/time-series/demo/income-poverty/historical-income-people.html

Wealth Inequality: Current Trends

In 2019, the median wealth or **net worth** of households, that is, the value of all their assets minus their debts, was just over $121,760. Figure 2.3 shows net worth by quintile. You might notice that the bottom quintile does not appear in this chart. This is because their net worth is negative, indicating that they owe more than they own. The wealthiest 20 percent owned almost 90 percent of all net worth in 2019.

Not surprisingly, income and wealth are highly correlated: In 2021, people who were in the top 1 percent in income had almost 10 times the wealth of the bottom 20 percent. This is the widest wealth gap in the 35 years since the Federal Reserve began keeping records. The upper class (the top 10 percent of income) had an average of $1.6 million in wealth in 2019, while the lower class (the bottom 20 percent) possessed only $9,800 in wealth (Bhutta et al., 2020). But note that the correlation isn't perfect: look back to Figures 1.1 and 1.3 in Chapter 1 for an illustration. While the top 1percent in income controlled 19.1 percent of income in the United States in 2019, the top 1percent in *wealth* controlled 34.87 percent of the wealth (World Inequality Database, 2021).

Financial or *non-home* wealth, that is, wealth involving only stocks, mutual funds, and other investments, was even more concentrated than overall net worth in 2019. The top 10 percent possessed over 90 percent of all stocks, mutual funds, and other investments. Stock ownership has become increasingly concentrated over time with 93.6 percent of stocks held by the top 10 percent—as with overall net worth, this is the highest level of inequality in the last 35 years (Wolff, 2021). In 2019, only 35 percent of Americans owned stocks, bonds, or mutual funds (this

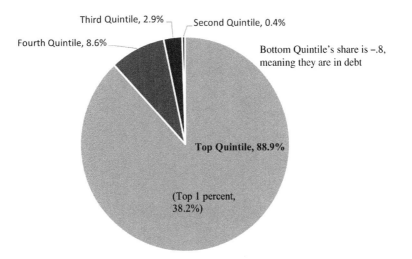

Figure 2.3 Percentage Share of Wealth by Quintile, 2019.
Source: Based on Wolff (2021). *Household Wealth Trends in the United States 1962 to 2019.*

did not include retirement accounts) with upper income Americans five times more likely to be owners of this type of financial wealth (Igirlnik, 2020). In sum, all the evidence indicates a highly unequal distribution of wealth in the United States.

The reasons for the increasing concentration of wealth in recent years are related to the differences in the types of wealth held by various income groups. That is, their assets are distributed differently. Figure 2.4 shows that in 2019, the vast majority of the wealth of the richest 1 percent was in stock, mutual funds, financial securities, or business investments; less than 9 percent of their wealth was in their principal home. In contrast, those with much less wealth are likely to have their wealth in savings accounts and home ownership. Over 60 percent of the wealth of the bottom 60 percent of households was in their homes. Under 4 percent was in stock, mutual funds, or financial securities.

Most of the households in the middle and at the bottom of the wealth distribution rely almost completely on wages and salaries to pay their bills. Many are heavily in debt. In 1963, those in the bottom 10 percent had no wealth, but in 2016 the equivalent families were $1,000 in debt (The Urban Institute, 2017). Given these debts, most people in the lower quintiles have little money to invest in the stock market; nor can they save for the long term. Needless to say, mounting debt and the inability to save make wealth accumulation extremely difficult and directly affect the transmission of wealth to the next generation.

The constraints placed on poorer families mean that they are less able to provide inheritances to their children, leaving the latter with little or no wealth on which to build. This is another reason why wealth inequality is so important—its accumulation has direct implications for economic inequality among the children of today's families. As a basis for future economic status, wealth (or its absence) helps to stabilize, reproduce, and even exacerbate economic inequality in future generations (Oliver & Shapiro, 2006). Inheritances contribute to the maintenance of wealth inequality over generations because

> [these] head-start assets … often include paying for college, substantial down-payment assistance in buying a first home, and other continuing parental financial assistance … This inherited wealth allows its recipients to live economically and socially beyond where their own achievements, jobs, and earnings would place them. (Shapiro, 2004, pp. 2–3)

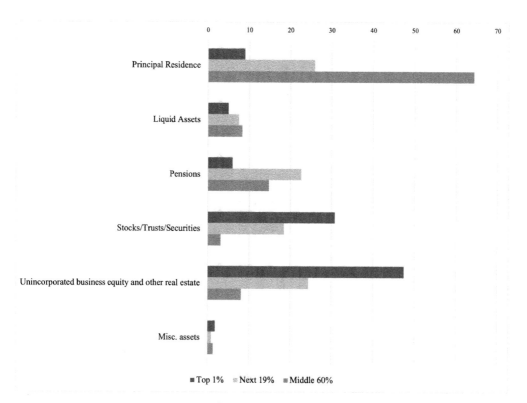

Figure 2.4 Percentage Distribution of Asset Types by Household Wealth Rank, 2019.
Source: Based on Wolff (2021). *Household Wealth Trends in the United States, 1962 to 2019.*

Between 1989 and 2007, 38 percent of the top bracket of income earners (and 45 percent of the top bracket of wealth holders) received an inheritance. The equivalent percentages for the lowest brackets were 15 and 9. The size of the inheritances of the top bracket was 27 times those of the lowest bracket (Wolff & Gittleman, 2014). The likelihood of inheriting wealth is strongly related to race, with 29.9 percent of White individuals receiving an inheritance, compared to 10.1 percent of Black people and 7.2 percent of Hispanic people (Bhutta et al., 2020).

The large amount of wealth owned by a very small percentage of the population raises questions about its origin. Historically, family and inheritance have been major sources of wealth among the corporate rich in the United States. Only a minority obtained their initial wealth through entrepreneurship or personal saving. Gift and estate laws have done little to stem the flow of inherited wealth to subsequent generations. Wealth is kept in the family, and this is one reason why the extended family is such an important institution among the rich. The social, cultural, and economic capital passed on to children helps them maintain and even increase their wealth.

Today, however, technological innovation is becoming a more prevalent source of wealth. About 60 percent of the individuals on *Forbes* 2020 list of the 400 richest Americans obtained their wealth in the technology, service, food and beverage, manufacturing, media, or investment industries. To be included on the 2020 *Forbes* richest list, one's wealth had to have been at least $2 billion. Together, the net worth of these 400 individuals totaled $3.2 trillion, up $240 billion from 2019 (Forbes, 2021). Many of the people on the list started their own businesses or are self-employed—few achieved their vast wealth because of inheritance. But these 400 people do not represent most wealthy Americans. For most, inheritance still plays an important role in laying a foundation for wealth accumulation.

What characteristics are related to the amount of wealth one has? Certainly, race, ethnicity, and gender are factors that are involved. We explore these differences in depth in Chapters 8 and 10, but it is important to note here that, on average, Black and Hispanic people, as well as Native Americans have significantly less wealth than White and Asian people. In 2019, the median net worth of non-Hispanic Black people was $9,000, for Hispanics, it was $14,000 and for non-Hispanic Whites, it was $160,200 (Wolff, 2021). On average, Asian households hold more wealth than do White households, but—as we mentioned above—the number for Asians masks high levels of inequality within the group. Wealth data have not been collected for Native Americans for many years, making comparisons difficult, but high levels of poverty suggest that wealth levels are low (Asante-Muhammad et al., 2017).

How wealth is concentrated matters since it affects how well a family can survive economic shocks. For example, because the wealth of Black and Hispanic households is more likely to be concentrated in their primary residences, they are more likely to be harmed in financial downturns (see Table 2.4). This was evident in the 2008 recession—while the net worth for White households dropped 6.58 percent following the recission, it fell by 9.76 percent for Black households and 10.62 percent for Hispanic households.

Wealth differences are difficult to calculate by gender because most statistics are measured at the household level rather than being disaggregated to the individual level, and home ownership is assumed (sometimes wrongly) to be shared by couples (Shiffer-Sebba & Behrman, 2021). But there are some clear indications that there is a gender gap in wealth. Of the 400 on the *Forbes* list, only 56 are women. And of these 56 women, only 11 are self-made, meaning that most received their wealth through inheritance—three of the richest women are from the Walton family (Walmart), and three are from the Mars family (Mars candy). Women are estimated to own only 32 cents to every dollar owned by men, and women of color own far less—while the median wealth for single White men is estimated at $28,900, for single Black women it is $200, and for single Black mothers it is $0 (McCulloch, 2017).

Family type is another important factor that determines the level of wealth, with married-couple households possessing about three to four times the wealth of single-headed households. Among age groups, those in the 65–74 age bracket had the most net worth, and those under 35 the least. Finally, the wealth of those with college degrees far exceeds that of less educated individuals (Eggleston et al., 2020).

Table 2.4 Distribution of Assets by Race: 2019

	All	Non-Hispanic Whites	Blacks	Hispanics
Principal Residence	26.9	24.6	46.8	51.4
Liquid Assets	6.8	6.7	10	6
Pension Accounts	15.5	15.7	19.7	13.4
Stocks, Mutual Funds, Trusts	20	21.2	4.6	7.3
Uninc. Business Equity or Real Estate	29.4	30.2	17.9	21.5
Miscellaneous Assets	1.4	1.5	1	0.4

Source: Based on Edward Wolff (2021). *Household Wealth Trends in the United States, 1962–2019: Median Wealth Rebounds … But Not Enough.*

Understanding Poverty in the United States

The distribution of income and wealth discussed above provides a portrait of economic inequality, but that portrait is incomplete without an understanding of both why poverty happens and how extensive it is in the United States. We begin with an outline of the theoretical perspectives on poverty, followed by a description of the nature and depth of poverty in the United States.

Theoretical Explanations for Poverty

Why are some people rich and some people poor? As we'll see in Chapter 4, Americans have many theories explaining why some people fare well and others poorly. But what does sociological research tell us? Not surprisingly, there are many theories, but they can be categorized into four major groups: individualistic, structural, political, and relational frameworks (Brady, 2019; Desmond & Western, 2018).

Individualistic theories argue that people are either rich or poor because of the qualities they possess, because of their behavior, or because of their culture. Qualities might include things such as human capital, including investment in education or skills training, or attributes such as intelligence or perseverance. Individualist theories that focus on behavior point to things like becoming a single mother or not participating in the labor market (Brady, 2019, p. 157).

A common individualist sentiment is one expressed by Sawhill of the Brookings Institute that poverty would be greatly reduced if people were truly ready for parenthood, meaning "completing their education, securing a steady job, and having a committed partner with whom to share the tasks of both earning a living and raising children. The ideal would be education, work, marriage, children—in that order" (Sawhill, 2014, p. 14). For example, family composition, including declining marriage rates and an increase in female-headed households might explain higher levels of poverty (Aber et al., 2015, p. 20; Brown, 2010).

In the 1960s, Oscar Lewis famously argued that poverty in and of itself constitutes a separate culture that perpetuates itself and contributes to continued poverty (Lewis, 1966). This "culture of poverty" argument maintains that the values that people in poverty hold serve to keep them poor and that this culture is passed on to future generations creating an ongoing cycle. Lewis included values such "fatalism, helplessness, dependence, and inferiority" (p. 23), arguing that communities with a prevalence of these attitudes maintained a greater level of inter-generational poverty. Few sociologists subscribe to a robust cultural of poverty argument today, in part because many see it as "blaming the victim," but arguments that culture does play some role in the reproduction of poverty are gaining traction (Small et al., 2010). Examples of cultural frameworks that may exacerbate poverty include attitudes toward parenting, willingness to work hard in school, or attitudes toward sexual behavior (Akerlof & Kranton, 2010; Carter, 2005; Lareau, 2011). These more contemporary theories argue that culture provides "schemas and repertoires that guide poor's behavior" (Brady, 2019, p. 158).

Structural theories maintain that poverty arises in particular "demographic or economic contexts" (Brady, 2019, p. 161) and that this macro context establishes the "rules of the game" that determine who is rich and who is poor (Calnitsky, 2018). Structural explanations include macro-level changes such as deindustrialization (the shift away from manufacturing), large-scale economic growth, severe economic dislocations such as recessions, or large-scale policy reforms such as welfare reform or civil rights reforms (Desmond & Western, 2018). Demographic factors include phenomena such as **"neighborhood effects"** (Sampson, 2008; Sharkey, 2013) or the idea that the type of neighborhood you grow up in affects your life chances (see Chapter 11 for a discussion of neighborhood effects).

Structure is related to behavior because it provides the context in which it occurs. For example, women may choose to forgo marriage because there are no labor market opportunities for men (Edin & Kefalas, 2011; W. J. Wilson, 2012)—this is a behavior, but it arises within the context of joblessness. Sometimes structural contributors are more directly related to poverty, as in the case of a major shift in the kinds of skills employers are seeking or a spatial mismatch between where jobs are and where people seeking jobs live (Easley, 2018).

Structural theorists argue that simply looking at individual decisions or behavior does not adequately explain poverty. While it might be true that individuals can improve their level of education and thus be less likely to be in poverty, it doesn't hold that if everyone were better educated, there would be no poverty if the structure of the job market remained unchanged (Calnitsky, 2018). Think of it, Rank (2004) argues, as a game of musical chairs, where one chair is always left out. The system is structured such that some people are going to lose. A society might penalize bad decisions with poor economic outcomes (women who have children and don't get married are more likely to be poor), but it turns out that higher penalties don't decrease the prevalence of bad behavior (countries with the highest penalties for being a single mother don't have the lowest prevalence of lone parenting) (Brady et al., 2017).

Political theories focus on power relations within a society—who has the power to make policy and establish the rules of the game (Brady, 2019). As we will talk about in Chapter 5, political theorists argue that those with more power are able to control the institutions that determine who wins and who loses. The powerful control the resources people need to survive and determine whether or not to expand the welfare state and redistribute resources (Nelson, 2012). Researchers find a lower level of poverty in democracies "where Left parties have controlled government, unionization is higher, and women are a greater share of parliaments" (Brady, 2019, p. 164). In his recent analysis of how our political structure has "rigged the system," Robert Reich stresses that it is important for us to ask "whom the market has been organized to serve" (Reich, 2021). To understand inequality, we must focus on "systemic changes that have caused the wealth and power of a few to dramatically increase during the last forty years at the expense of the many" (p. 24). Policies such as the deregulation of the finance sector, or changes in the tax structure, Reich argues, were put in place by those in power to reward themselves and their friends.

Relational theories, the fourth approach to income and wealth inequality, focus on the relationships between people. Similar to power theorists, relational theorists argue that poverty or wealth are "not simply the by-product of one's attributes or historical outcomes but [are] also actively produced through unequal relationships between the financially secure and insecure" (Desmond & Western, 2018, p. 310). Poverty or wealth can be seen as the outcome of the relationships between groups of people, such as "landlords and tenants (Desmond, 2016), city developers and slum dwellers (Sassen, 2014), and police and citizens (Stuart, 2016)" (Desmond & Western, 2018, p. 310).

We will expand on relational theories more fully with a discussion of Marx and Tilly in Chapters 6 and 7, but central to the approach is a recognition that poverty and wealth do not occur independently. Rather, they arise through a "power relationship whereby the rich take advantage of the poor and profit from their vulnerability" (Desmond & Western, 2018, p. 311). Compared with a political approach, relational theorists move beyond an argument that suggests that those individuals in power hoard resources to maintain their power to a recognition that the key to wealth and income imbalance is the relationships between actors, in particular relationships of exploitation (Avent-Holt & Tomaskovic-Devey, 2014; Sakamoto & Kim, 2010). Those at the top remain so because they exploit the work of others by paying them less than they are worth.

Which of these theories is correct? We all know or have heard of individuals who are in poverty because of bad choices they have made or because of bad luck. As you will see, however, research consistently indicates that it is incorrect to explain all—or even most—poverty using individualistic explanations. For that reason, and because we are interested in understanding the social processes that lead to poverty, we focus on structural, political, and relational theories throughout the rest of the text.

Who Are the Poor?

This is not an easy question to answer because of continuing disagreements about how "poverty" should be measured. The federal poverty measure (usually referred to as the **poverty line**) considers pre-tax income from all sources to determine one's income level. Consequently, it does not include the value of noncash benefits or the effect of taxes and tax credits on income. The poverty line varies by one's age, family size, and composition. For example, in 2021, individuals were defined as poor if their total income fell below $12,880, and a family of four with two parents and two children under 18 years of age had to have a gross income of under $26,500 to be classified as poor.

The federal poverty line is problematic because it is based on a household spending formula that is outdated. Since its inception in the mid-1960s, the poverty line has been calculated by estimating the cost of a minimally nutritious diet. At that time, food represented one-third of an average family's budget—the poverty line has therefore been calculated by multiplying the cost of food by three. Today, this formula is no longer representative of family expenses because the average family spends less than one-third of their income on food and more than they did in the 1960s on housing and other expenses. Alternative poverty measures that address these issues, such as the Supplemental Poverty Measure developed by the National Academy of Sciences, indicate that poverty levels are higher than those obtained using the official measure. For example, in 2019, the poverty rate as estimated by this measure was 11.7 percent, or 1.2 percental points above the official measure (US Census Bureau, 2020b). However, because longitudinal governmental data on poverty are based on it, the official poverty measure will be used in the present discussion.

In contrast to the long-term movement toward greater income and wealth inequality, trends in official poverty rates have been more erratic since 1980, going up in the early 1980s before declining and then rising again in 1989 (see Figure 2.5). They began to decline again in 1993 and did so for the remainder of the decade before increasing again in 2001, and then more dramatically during the Great Recession of 2008–2010. In 2020, the poverty rate stood at 11.4 percent, representing 37.2 million individuals, down from 11.8 percent (38.1 million) in 2018. As you can see, the last six years have seen a slow decrease in the poverty rate (US Census Bureau, 2021e).

As we will discuss further in Chapter 4, the racial and ethnic composition of the poor is not what stereotypes suggest. White individuals make up the largest group, but as Figure 2.6 shows, the share of those in poverty has increased for Hispanics and Native Americans over the past four decades. In 1990, Hispanic people composed only 17.9 percent of the poor, and by 2020 they represented 27.9 percent. Another rapid increase in the share of poverty has been among Native Americans, representing 1.3 percent of poor in 1990 and 2.1 percent in 2020 (US Census Bureau, 2021e).

While White people represent the largest group of those in poverty, Black people have the highest *rate* of poverty at 19.5 percent, over twice that of Whites, with Hispanic individuals close behind (Table 2.5). The rate of poverty among Asians is nearly equal to that of Whites.

Table 2.5 indicates that the poverty rate for families with female householders is about five times that of married-couple families, and the poverty rate for children is noticeably higher than that for any other age group. In 2020, 16.1 percent of children under 18 were in poverty, compared with the national poverty rate of 11.4 percent. In all the years represented, women have a higher poverty rate than men, though the differences have narrowed a bit over the years. In 2020, 12.6 percent of all women were in poverty, compared with 10.2 percent of men.

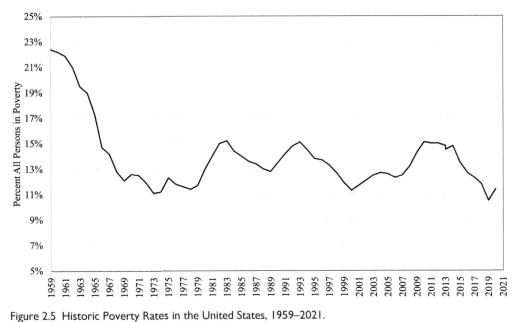

Figure 2.5 Historic Poverty Rates in the United States, 1959–2021.

Source: US Census Bureau (2021e), Table 2, https://www.census.gov/data/tables/time-series/demo/income-poverty/historical-poverty-people.html

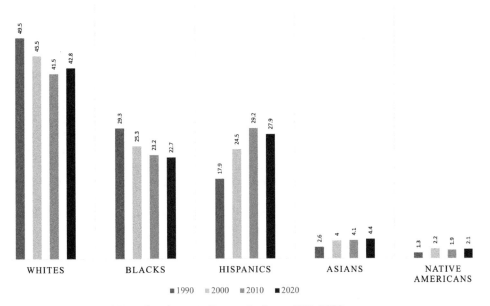

Figure 2.6 Percentage of Total Population in Poverty by Race, 1990–2020.

Source: US Census Bureau (2021e), Table 2, https://www.census.gov/data/tables/time-series/demo/income-poverty/historical-poverty-people.html

Table 2.5 Poverty Rates by Race, Sex, Age, and Family Status: 1990–2020

	Poverty Rate (% in Poverty)				
	1990	2000	2010	2015	2020
All Persons	13.5	11.3	15.1	13.5	11.4
Under 18 Years Old	20.6	16.2	22	19.7	16.1
18 to 64 Years Old	10.7	9.6	13.8	12.4	10.4
65 and Older	12.2	9.9	8.9	8.8	9
Whites, Non-Hispanics	8.8	7.4	9.9	9.1	8.2
Blacks	31.9	22.5	27.5	24.1	19.5
Hispanics	28.1	21.5	26.5	21.4	17
Asians	12.2	9.9	12.2	11.4	8.1
Native American	28.5	23.2	28.8	23.3	19.8
Married-Couple Families	5.7	4.7	6.2	5.4	4.7
Female-Headed Families	33.4	25.4	31.6	28.2	23.4
Male-Headed Families	12	11.3	15.8	14.9	11.4

Source: US Census Bureau (2021e), Tables 2, 3, 4, 7 and 24, https://www.census.gov/data/tables/time-series/demo/income-poverty/historical-poverty-people.html

While a popular stereotype is that most poor people live inside principal cities, data indicate that the majority actually live in rural areas. Rural poverty is high partly because of increasing unemployment due to large-scale trends such as mechanization and globalization (US Census Bureau, 2021a). Poverty is higher in the South and West than in the Northeast or Midwest. Mississippi, Alabama, Arkansas, Kentucky, and Louisiana were among the states with 2020 poverty rates that were well above the national average. Mississippi had the highest poverty rate with 19.6 percent. In contrast, the rates in Alaska, Connecticut, Hawaii, Maryland, and New Hampshire were significantly lower than the national average (US Census Bureau, 2020c).

Within the population of people in poverty, some are poorer than others. For example, some have incomes that are very near the poverty threshold, whereas the incomes of others fall well below. Two measures are used to indicate how far an individual's or family's income falls below their poverty threshold. One of these is a *ratio* that compares their actual income with their poverty threshold. A ratio of 1.00 indicates that their income is exactly the same as the threshold. A ratio below 1.00 is a measure of how far *below* poverty the person's or family's income falls; conversely, a ratio above 1.00 indicates how far their income is *above* the poverty threshold. In 2020, about 55 percent of the population, or almost 18 million individuals, had incomes that were *less than half* of the amount that the government uses to classify them as poor. Over five and a half million children lived in families with this level of income (US Census Bureau, 2021j).

The second measure used to show the depth of poverty is the **income deficit**, which is the difference between a family's income and its poverty threshold. In 2020, the average poor family's income deficit was $11,318, which means that their income was actually $11,318 below the poverty threshold. Thus, they were not only poor but *very* poor (US Census Bureau, 2021i).

Dimensions of Poverty

Amartya Sen (US Census Bureau, 2021b) famously argued that poverty is more than the deprivation of income:

It can involve not only the lack of necessities of material well-being, but also the denial of opportunities of living a tolerable life. The lives could be prematurely shortened, made hard, painful, or hazardous, deprived of understanding and communication, and robbed of dignity, confidence and self-respect. It is ultimately in the poverty of the lives that people can lead that poverty manifests itself. (pp. 4–5)

Poverty is multidimensional, representing several aspects of deprivation, including, among others, health, education or literacy, social isolation, housing, sanitation, and hunger. For example, the Global Multidimensional Poverty Index, developed by the United Nations (United Nationals Development Programme, 2020), uses ten indicators of poverty to rank global poverty and understand the lived experiences of those at the bottom of the income and wealth hierarchy in each country.

Beyond these particular indicators, there are several broader dimensions of poverty that capture a more nuanced understanding of those at the bottom. These include (1) the lived experience of poverty and how that fits with who we define as poor; (2) the duration of poverty—that is, whether it is chronic and ongoing or episodic; and (3) the depth of poverty.

Poverty is clearly not just an abstract concept. It is a lived reality experienced daily by millions of Americans. But what does it mean to feel poor? When we use absolute measures of poverty, like the official poverty line, we establish a clear border demarcating the poor from the not poor. The advantage of an absolute measure is that it is comparable over time and cross-nationally, and it provides a clear indicator for determining policy solutions. But weaknesses are that an absolute measure cannot "capture relative economic deprivation at the country level or the need for higher outlays for economic well-being in richer countries" (Ravallion, 2020, p. 168). For a quick domestic example, think about whether those living at the poverty line earning $12,760 per year living in New York City have the same life chances as do those living in rural Alabama. The people living in New York City clearly experience poverty in a different way than in the low cost of living in rural Alabama.

To better capture the nuances of experiencing poverty, researchers have begun using relative measures of poverty. Under these, poverty can be defined simply as "having too few resources or capabilities to participate fully in a society" (Smeeding, 2016, p. 21). Relative measures ask what the needs are in a particular place and time and allow for a more complex understanding of the lived experience of poverty (Brady & Parolin, 2020, p. 2344). Here is an odd example: most of us would argue that objectively having a flush toilet means that you are better off than not having one. But in the 1920s, when flush toilets became the standard in housing, many low-income housing units without toilets were deemed inhabitable and were condemned. Families were left with no housing and thus were worse off than they were before. The cost of participating in society at that time suddenly included having flush toilets, so those without them were relatively poor. This reality would not have been captured with an absolute measure of poverty.

A second key variable in understanding the causes, nature, and remediation of poverty is its *duration* for individuals and households. Researchers make the distinction between chronic poverty, or the situations where people experience poverty for most of their lives, or even across generations, and episodic or situational poverty, or the phenomenon where one traumatic event such as losing a job leads to a temporary state of poverty. For most people, poverty is not chronic (only a little over 6 percent experience chronic poverty), though rates of chronic poverty for non-Hispanic White individuals are over twice that for Black and Hispanic individuals (Mohanty, 2019). Chronic poverty is more likely to be multidimensional, meaning that those experiencing poverty for longer periods of time are more likely to also experience other forms of deprivation, such as a low quality of housing or social isolation. Chronic poverty is more likely to lead to poverty "traps," or a particular component of poverty that limits someone's ability to leave poverty (Alkire et al., 2017).

An example of a poverty trap is related to welfare—it is known as the **benefits cliff**, or the situation where a small increase in wages makes someone ineligible for benefits such as food stamps or childcare allowances. In Ohio, for example, a woman making $11.50 per hour qualifies for food assistance, Medicaid, and child support. A simple $3 increase in her hourly pay means that she loses the food assistance and Medicaid and has to pay significantly more for childcare. She ends up losing money if she accepts a promotion or pay increase (Coccia, 2021). The result is likely to be the perpetuation of chronic poverty.

Finally, the depth of poverty is important for understanding lived experience and for comparing levels of poverty cross-nationally. Sociologists use the terms "deep" and "extreme" poverty to describe the most severe levels of poverty. These levels can be measured absolutely, as do some who define it as living on less than $2 per day in the United States (Edin & Shaefer, 2015). By this measure, in 2019, about 2.6 percent of population reported living in deep poverty (Prahalad, 2019). Similarly, the World Bank defines extreme poverty globally as those who live below $1.90, representing over nine percent of the world's population, and rising during the pandemic to 150 million in 2020 (The World Bank, 2020). As we saw above in the discussion of absolute and relative poverty, however, these measures are potentially problematic because they do not represent objective standards of need, which vary by location and time (Brady & Parolin, 2020; Smeeding, 2016).

Extreme and deep poverty can be defined using more relative measures. "To say that individuals are in 'deep' or 'extreme' poverty simply means that the gap between resources and needs is deeper or more extreme" (Brady & Parolin, 2020, p. 2344). An example of a relative measure would be tagging the measurement of the poverty line to the median income. Thus, Brady and Parolin (2020) measure deep poverty as representing those falling below twenty percent of the median income and extreme poverty as falling below ten percent of the median income. By these measures, 2.23 percent of the US population, or 7.2 million people were in deep poverty in 2016, and 1.15 percent (3.7 million) were in extreme poverty. This level is a clear increase in both rates since the 1990s—from 1995 to 2016, deep poverty increased by 48 percent.

Extreme poverty is often most visibly seen among those who lack consistent or adequate housing. Determining how many people are unhoused, however, is a difficult matter. Because

Photo 2.2 It is common to associate poverty with the inner city, and indeed central cities have the highest poverty rates of any residential area. But rural poverty is also significantly higher than the national average. The poverty rate for those living outside.

Source: William Griffith/Shutterstock.

of methodological differences, national surveys yield wildly different appraisals on the extent of homelessness in the United States, with estimates ranging from several hundred thousand to several million. Estimates based on single counts at a given time ("point-in-time counts") tend to be lower than estimates based on counts of those who are unhoused sometime during a period of time ("period prevalence counts"). One point-in-time study estimated that there were 580,000 unhoused individuals during the month of January 2021, an increase of 2 percent compared with 2019 (US Department of Housing and Urban Development, 2021).

Point-in-time estimates suggest that homelessness has decreased since 2007 by about 10 percent, despite a slight increase over the past two years. Homeless rates differ greatly by state, however, with several states experiencing large increases since 2007. For example, homelessness increased by 45.8 percent in New York and 19.9 percent in Washington, DC. The states with the largest decreases include Florida, Texas, Georgia, and New Jersey (US Department of Housing and Urban Development, 2021). Of the unhoused people counted in one night in January 2020, nearly 20 percent were children. Of the adults, 6 in 10 were male and minorities were disproportionately represented. Just over one-half of 1 percent were transgender or non-gender-conforming people. Not surprisingly, a higher degree of homelessness is found in urban than in rural areas. The composition of the unhoused population in a given area generally reflects the composition of the local population (Lee et al., 2010).

Several factors have been linked to homelessness, primarily low wages and the lack of affordable housing. The higher cost of housing is due in large part to declines in the building of affordable private homes and public housing. In addition, stagnation in wages and the decline in the value of the minimum wage have made decent housing difficult to obtain for low-wage workers. This has left a larger poor population competing for smaller numbers of affordable residences. The increased demand has pushed rents up. The destruction or conversion of housing units for other

Photo 2.3 Over the last decade and a half, the proportion of people who are hungry has increased, and many of these individuals are also unhoused. While single men are still the modal group, children, women, and minorities are composing a higher percentage of the homeless. Violent crimes against the unhoused have also been on the increase.

Source: "Homeless sleeping" by Franco Folini is licensed under CC BY-SA 2.0.

purposes, along with gentrification, has worsened the problem. When asked, most people without homes also list unemployment, evictions, and poverty as major causes of their homelessness (Aurand et al., 2018).

Health difficulties and the associated lack of services available to unhoused people have helped maintain homelessness. The declining value of public assistance benefits, a lack of low-cost treatment options for mental illness and drug addiction, and high numbers of people re-entering society from prison contribute as well. During the Great Recession, homelessness among families increased as the number of foreclosures rose. Thus, many of the elements that affect the extent of homelessness are "macroprocesses" related to the government and market economy (National Alliance to End Homelessness, 2018). And it is the poor who are especially vulnerable to shifts in these processes.

US Poverty and Welfare in Comparative Perspective

When we look across the world, we find that some populations not only have much higher rates of poverty but also have degrees of poverty that are significantly more abject than those found in the United States. The greatest numbers living in extreme poverty, less than $1.90 per day, are in South Asia, Central and Sub-Saharan Africa, and East Asia, respectively. India alone is estimated to have 21.2 percent of its population living in severe poverty. In some countries, such as Madagascar and Malawi, over three-quarters of the population is in extreme poverty. Overall, in 2019 over 740 million people, or 9.6 percent of the world population was living in extreme poverty. This is expected to dramatically increase with COVID-19 (Hughes et al., 2021).

The United States does not compare well to other rich industrial nations on relative poverty rates. As we see in Table 2.6, the United States has the second-highest poverty rate in this group. The lowest poverty rates are found in Scandinavian nations, as well as other major European nations. Similarly, Denmark and Finland had child poverty rates that were over five times lower than the US rate—among 38 OECD nations, the United States has the fifth-highest relative child poverty rate (OECD, 2021c). Combining life expectancy, expected years of schooling, mean years of schooling, and gross national income per capita into an index of quality of life called the Human Development Index (HDI), the United Nations ranked the United States 17th (United Nations Development Programme, 2021). Clearly, the United States does not rate well in these comparisons of poverty levels.

When we compare the poverty rates to income inequality, we see that while there are some patterns, it is not always the case that the countries with the highest inequality also have the highest poverty rates. Italy, for example, ranks reasonably high on poverty rates but quite low on income inequality.

Why might the United States have higher levels of poverty and inequality than most other rich democracies? Several factors are at play, including cultural values that discourage extensive government involvement in the lives of individuals, a market economy that emphasizes free exchange and competition and drives the society toward greater income inequality, and welfare policies that do not have a large impact on reducing poverty.

Societies with free, largely unregulated market economies tend to have higher degrees of economic inequality than other nations where governments are more actively involved in economic matters (Birchfield, 2012). In the former, given an assumption of equal opportunity for all, the operation of an open market determines the outcome and distribution of goods and resources among the people. Let the chips fall where they may, so to speak.

In the abstract, Americans tend to subscribe to conservative values of small government, a free economy, and individual responsibility. "The United States differs from most nations that achieve lower poverty rates because of its emphasis on work and self-reliance for working-age adults, regardless of the wages workers must accept or the family situations of those workers" (Smeeding, 2018).

Table 2.6 Poverty Rates in OECD Countries and Percent Share Income of 1 percent, 2019 or Latest Available

Country	Percent in Poverty	Percent Share Income 1%	Country	Percent in Poverty	Percent Share Income 1%
Costa Rica	20.5	21.6	Luxembourg	11.4	9.2
United States	17.8	18.8	New Zealand	10.9	11.9
Latvia	17.5	9.1	Portugal	10.4	11.7
Romania	17.4	13.1	Germany	10.4	13
Turkey	17.2	18.4	Poland	9.8	11.7
Israel	16.9	14.4	Austria	9.4	9.5
Bulgaria	16.7	18.6	Switzerland	9.2	11.1
South Korea	16.7	13.2	Ireland	9	11.9
Mexico	16.6	28.7	Sweden	8.9	9.1
Chile	16.5	28.1	France	8.5	10
Estonia	16.3	14.2	Norway	8.4	10.7
Japan	15.7	11.6	Netherlands	8.3	7.1
Lithuania	15.5	12.3	Belgium	8.2	8.5
Spain	14.2	12.4	Hungary	8	12.4
Italy	13.9	8.8	Slovakia	7.7	10.8
Russia	12.7	21.5	Slovenia	7.5	8.4
Australia	12.4	12.9	Finland	6.5	10.2
Greece	12.1	12.9	Czech Republic	6.1	10.4
Canada	11.8	14.8	Denmark	6.1	11.4
United Kingdom	11.7	12.9	Iceland	4.9	8.3

Source: The Organization for Economic Co-operation and Development (OECD, 2021c), https://data.oecd.org/inequality/poverty-rate.htm; World Inequality Database, https://wid.world/data/

Note: The poverty rate is the ratio of the number of people whose income falls below the poverty line compared to the total population; the poverty line is here taken as half the median household income. Consult the website to determine the latest year of the statistic.

But at the same time, evidence indicates they realize that problems may arise during the actual operation of society that demand government intervention on behalf of those who are victimized or trapped. While Americans are resistant to helping those whom they believe can help themselves (i.e., are undeserving), they tend to be generous toward those they believe are poor for reasons beyond their control (i.e., are deserving). Their feelings toward groups that are usually the focus of government assistance, such as the poor and elderly, are much warmer than those felt about the rich and big business, for example (Bartels, 2008). National surveys indicate that most people support government assistance to the poor for their basic necessities (Page, 2009). The researchers refer to this seemingly contradictory mixture of beliefs as "conservative egalitarianism." One consequence of this ambivalent stance is that while the United States has some welfare programs, they tend not to be overly generous and thus, do not drive down the poverty rate very much.

Some societies choose to devote more resources than others toward reducing poverty. As Timothy Smeeding put it: "We have more inequality and poverty than other nations because we choose to have more" (Smeeding, 2005, p. 980). More inequality means that the richest groups in our society have moved further away from the middle class and poor. Their material interests are different, and they see little need for a generous welfare program.

Summary

Poverty and wealth are inextricably bound together. As the wealthy in this country have accrued more, others are able to accrue less—this is particularly true of the middle class. In this chapter, we have looked at the historical and current extent of economic inequality in terms of both income and wealth. There have been ups and downs in economic inequality in the nation's history, but it has increased at record rates since the 1980s. Economic inequalities are not equally distributed throughout the population; people of color and women are disproportionately disadvantaged. In later chapters, we will look at the situation for gender and sexual minorities.

The second half of the chapter looked more deeply at poverty. There have been many explanations for poverty proposed. They can be grouped into individualistic, cultural, structural, and relational theories. We also learned that poverty is multidimensional and it is important to understand its lived experience, duration, and depth. People's experience of poverty is dependent on where they live and their frame of reference. Poverty in America is usually episodic rather than chronic, and there is a substantial percentage of the poor who live in extreme poverty.

Critical Thinking

1. Were you surprised by the extent of income and wealth inequality in the United States? Why or why not?
2. In your opinion, what should be the determining factors in setting a poverty threshold? Why?
3. What do you think are some ways Americans experience increasing inequality in their daily lives?
4. Provide examples of each of the four explanations of poverty that you have seen in your own lifetime.
5. Why do you think the United States fares poorly on measures of poverty and economic inequality when compared to other industrial nations?

Web Connections

The Economic Policy Institute is a non-profit research and analysis think tank that is dedicated to making the needs of low- and middle-income Americans heard in economic policy conversations. They specialize in many areas of research, including inequality and poverty. Visit their website at www.epi.org/research/inequality-and-poverty/.

Film Suggestions

Saving Capitalism (2017). Features Robert Reich looking at inequality and its impact on people's lives.

Growing up Poor in America, Episode 3 (2020). This Frontline documentary follows three poor children and their families in Ohio as they confront the COVID pandemic.

Tent City, USA (2012). This documentary shows Nashville's tent city that was created during the economic recession of 2008. The city could barely support one in five of the homeless population, so the homeless created their own city that they self-governed.

America Street (2019). A look at an African American neighborhood in Charlestown that is undergoing gentrification. It illustrates some of the processes driving income inequality.

3 Class, Governmental Policy, and Mobility

In the last chapter, we looked at wealth and poverty and how the two are linked together in a system of inequality. In this chapter, we tackle the issue of social class. What is it? How do government policies and programs attempt to redistribute income and wealth to shift the class system? And finally, we look at mobility. How easy or difficult is it to move up the social class system in the United States? As we will see in later chapters, social class has a significant impact on the prestige, power, and life chances that individuals possess. Consequently, a discussion of social class and economic inequality is critical for a full understanding of other forms of inequality.

The Everyday Reality of Class

Historically, Americans have been much less willing to talk about social **class** than citizens of other nations (Cobb, 2016). There are many reasons for this, including the image of the United States as an egalitarian society where, regardless of background, anyone can succeed, but Americans' reluctance to discuss class does not mean that they do not think about it. Social class is deeply rooted in our everyday experiences and relationships. Awareness of class differences begins early; even preschool children categorize individuals as rich or poor and make judgments about them on that basis (Horwitz et al., 2014). By elementary school, children can reliably identify social class location, and they have definite ideas about behavioral and social differences between groups (Mistry et al., 2015).

The class structure is also a subjective reality for adults. When asked to identify how many "rungs" there are on the class ladder, the majority of Americans (88 percent) identify five or more (Davidai & Gilovich, 2015). They are most likely to identify themselves ("**subjective class**"), however, as "middle class." In 2016, a survey by the Gallup Organization indicated that 58 percent of the adults interviewed considered themselves to be "middle" or "upper-middle" class, while 30 percent classified themselves as "working" class. Only 3 percent thought they were "upper class," and 8 percent labeled themselves "lower" class.

BOX 3.1 SUBJECTIVE CLASS

If someone were to ask you about your social class, what would you say? What factors would you consider? Would you include college loans in your calculations? Your future earning potential? If you are a traditional-aged college student, would you consider your parents' income? The Pew Research Center has a calculator that will show your class position based on income, region, and household size. Check it out at https://www.pewresearch.org/fact-tank/2020/07/23/are-you-in-the-american-middle-class/

Were you surprised by the result? If you could talk to the creators of the calculator, what changes might you suggest to make it more accurate?

DOI: 10.4324/9781003184966-4

How do people determine their own and others' class position? Over the last 40 years, research shows that income has come to play an increasingly large role and is now the primary indicator (Cohen et al., 2017). Interestingly, however, income is not determinative. For example, less than 10 percent of Americans who have a yearly income between $30,000 and $40,000 report that they are "lower class" even though their income is well below the nation's median. At the other end of the spectrum, only a third of people who make over $250,000 identify as "upper class" (Bird & Newport, 2017).

Education is an important factor that determines subjective class with more education leading to higher class identification. Similarly, the social class of one's family of origin helps guide people to a particular subjective class position (Hout, 2008; Speer, 2016). Research also shows that, as people age, they tend to identify with higher classes. Living in a rural area or being from Northeast United States predicts lower rankings (Bird & Newport, 2017; Speer, 2016). Occupation too factors into many people's calculation of their class; those that have a lot of freedom and autonomy and those that have lower levels of intensity (meaning that workers have enough time to complete their jobs) are generally classified as higher class (Horowitz, 2016).

A final factor influencing subjective class is race. In the past, White people ranked themselves higher in social class than did equally situated Black people—suggesting that they recognized that being White confers class privilege. In recent years, however, White people have decreased their own subjective ratings such that race does not predict overall class ranking. This may mean that they are less likely to view their race as an advantage. There remain, however, differences in how people from different races and ethnicities determine their subjective social class. Black people weigh the impact of income, education, and occupation less heavily than do White, Hispanic, or Asian people. It is possible that this is because Black people consider their status to be that of a caste—regardless of how well educated or rich they become, they are consigned to the lower ranks of the class ladder by virtue of their race (Cohen et al., 2017). What all these findings suggest is that while social class is clearly a salient concept for Americans, how people decide on their own class is complicated and based at least in part in group identity.

Two Views of the US Class Structure

We have just discussed how Americans perceive class, but what is the actual reality of the class structure? Here we will look at two common descriptions of class in America, a "socioeconomic" and a "Marxist" definition. Neither of these approaches is inherently better than the other, and each focuses on criteria that have been found to have effects on individuals' life conditions. Both approaches attempt to identify meaningful breaks in the class system, and, as such, each is useful in characterizing different aspects of economic inequality. We end the section with a hybrid model that contains characteristics of both.

Socioeconomic Definition of Class

Socioeconomic definitions of class incorporate several criteria, usually occupational status, education, and/or income. Individuals or families that fall in the same category on these dimensions are then said to be in the same social class. Generally, people receive a score based on their placement on these variables; in essence, social class is determined by a statistical score. Since these scores are continuous, with small differences in scores between individuals in adjacent positions, the class hierarchy is frequently viewed as a continuum where the boundaries between classes are not always clear and distinct. Classes may merge imperceptibly into one another, and, as a result, boundary determination becomes an important problem.

Another characteristic of this approach is that the dimensions used to measure social class are not all purely economic in nature. Occupational status is essentially a measure of the *prestige* of an occupation—that is, it reflects the subjective judgment of individuals about an occupation (for more discussion of this concept, see Chapter 4). Education is also a noneconomic phenomenon. The result is that this measure of social class is multidimensional in that it mixes economic with social dimensions of inequality. Consequently, it is often referred to as **socioeconomic status (SES)**. SES measures do not assume any kind of necessary relationship between the classes. There is no assumption, for example, that the upper and working classes are in conflict with each other. Classes are merely the result of scores on a series of socioeconomic dimensions.

An example of this approach is the Gilbert-Kahl model (2018). A condensed version of this model is presented here. The percentage of households estimated to be in each class is enclosed in parentheses.

1. *Capitalist Class (1 percent)*: Graduates of high-ranking universities who are in top-level executive positions or are heirs who have an income average of $1.5 million mainly from assets.
2. *Upper Middle Class (14 percent)*: Individuals with at least a college degree who are in higher professional or managerial positions or owners of medium-sized businesses who have incomes of about $200,000. At the top of the upper middle class, are very highly paid professionals (such as doctors or corporate lawyers) who earn hundreds of thousands of dollars but rely on their income rather than assets. This subgroup is called the "working rich."
3. *Middle Class (30 percent)*: Individuals who have high school degrees and maybe some college education who are in lower managerial or white-collar, or high-skilled, high-pay, blue-collar occupations who make about $85,000 a year.
4. *Working Class (25 percent)*: Persons with high school degrees who are in lower-level white-collar (e.g., clerical, sales workers) or blue-collar positions (e.g., operatives) whose incomes are about $40,000 per year.
5. *Working Poor (15 percent)*: Those with some high school who are service workers or are in the lowest-paid blue-collar and clerical positions who have average incomes of $25,000.
6. *Underclass (15 percent)*: Individuals with at most some high school education who work part-time, are unemployed, or are on welfare, and who have incomes under $15,000.

In surveying models of US class structure that use different kinds of socioeconomic criteria, there are some remarkable *similarities* as well as differences among them. These models, like that of Gilbert-Kahl, usually see the structure as being composed of five to seven classes rather than as a dichotomy or trichotomy. Also, the proportion of the population said to be in each class in each model is very similar. Generally, the working and middle classes, in which the majority of the population is placed, are considered to be about equal in size, and the upper class is generally said to be around 1 percent. Then, depending on whether employed as well as unemployed people are included in the lower class, its percentage can range from 10 percent to 25 percent.

Some of the most significant *differences* in traditional socioeconomic models center on the criteria used to place individuals in various classes. One notable difference lies in the distinctions made about the lower class. Some researchers simply include all those who are poor, while others draw a line between those who are poor but work and those who are chronically unemployed and poor for long periods of time. The term **underclass** came into popular use in the 1980s and 1990s to refer to the latter group. A number of critics have argued, however, that the term has come to have a pejorative and racialized meaning (Gans, 1996; Wacquant, 2007). In other words, the term is used to refer symbolically to poor urban Black people, and it implies that poverty is solely the result of deviant behavior rather than emphasizing structural roots. For this reason, we have chosen to use the term "severely disadvantaged" throughout this text except when we are discussing a model, such as Gilbert and Kahl, that uses the underclass term.

Another difference among the models of class structure concerns the way they treat white-collar and blue-collar occupations. Traditionally, blue-collar work was considered manual in nature, with white-collar work defined as nonmanual. Manual work was generally viewed as requiring physical and routine tasks rather than mental and intricate skills/tasks. Recently, however, the lines distinguishing the nature of blue-collar and white-collar jobs have become blurred. The routine nature of much low-level white-collar work has encouraged some analysts to place individuals who do this kind of work into the working class and to place those who do complex, high-skilled, well-paying blue-collar work into the middle class. As technological change occurs, and some physical labor by humans is replaced by machines, the character of the working-class changes correspondingly.

Marxist View of the Class Structure

In contrast to the continuum approach, Marxist sociologists generally object to the mixing of economic, status, and other socioeconomic variables because they believe it dilutes what Marx considered to be the core economic meaning of social class. Marx believed class was basically an economic phenomenon defined by an individual's position in the social relations of production and by control over the physical (property) and social (labor power) means of production. In other words, class is not defined by income or occupation but rather by owner-ship/control in the system of production. In this view, introducing other socioeconomic vari-ables, such as prestige or occupational status, only distorts the meaning of social class. Thus, in the Marxist definition, class is much less multidimensional in nature. Moreover, the class system is not a continuous hierarchy in which the lines between classes blur and classes merge into each other. Rather, the boundaries between the classes are discrete and clear. Classes in this view are defined by the exploitation that exists between them and by the interconnec-tion between the functions of each class. Different classes perform distinct but interrelated functions in capitalist society.

Marx believed that under capitalism, there were two major classes:

> by bourgeoisie is meant the class of modern capitalists, owners of the means of social production and employers of wage-labour. By proletariat, the class of modern wage-labourers who, having no means of production of their own, are reduced to selling labour-power in order to live. (Marx & Engels, 1969, p. 108)

Although Marx believed that the bourgeoisie and the proletariat were the primary classes, his use of such terms as "strata," "gradation," "middle classes," and "dominated classes" makes it clear that he was aware of the complexity that can characterize a concrete system of inequality. What is also apparent is that mere occupation or source of income is not the criterion used by Marx to define a class. Each class has within it a hierarchy of strata. Thus, within the proletariat, for example, individuals vary according to their specific occupations and incomes.

While some Marxists define class strictly in terms of structural position, others incorporate a social-psychological dimension into their conception, arguing that class consciousness or a shared sense of belonging and organized opposition must also be present. That is, to be in the same class, individuals must identify with each other and understand their real relationship to other classes and act on that knowledge. Kraus et al. (2011), for example, argue that the concept of class has both subjective and objective dimensions with the subjective element being a sense of unity that develops as a class emerges:

Social class reflects more than the material conditions of people's lives. Objective resources (e.g., income) shape cultural practices and behaviors that signal social class. These signals create cultural identities among upper- and lower-class individuals—identities that are rooted in subjective perceptions of social-class rank vis-a-vis others. (p. 246)

In this approach, people become a real *social* class when they acquire a common culture and political awareness. In addition to occupying the same location or position in relation to the **means of production**, then, people in the same social class "share the distinctive traditions common to their social position" (Szymanski, 1978, p. 26). This common identity, especially when it involves awareness of common exploitation and engagement in class struggle, Marx suggested, is what welds an aggregate of people into a social class, or a "class-for-itself" (Carrier & Kalb, 2015).

Perhaps the most sophisticated attempt to analyze the class structure of the United States in Marxist terms comes from Erik Wright. Wright's characterization of US class structure uses exploitation as the defining element (Western & Wright, 1994; Wright & Cho, 1992). Classes and class locations are distinguished by an individual's ability to exploit or be exploited on the basis of (1) property; (2) organizational authority; and (3) expertise or skill.

Combining these three criteria, Wright (2000) identified several class "locations" within this structure of class relationships. The specific categories in his model are shown graphically in Figure 3.1, but, in broad strokes, the most elemental distinction in Wright's model—as in Marx's—is between those who have property and those who do not (owners versus nonowners). But among *owners*, Wright separated groups based on how many people they employed. Application of the other two criteria of class location, authority and expertise, results in distinctions among nonowners. For example, supervisors and managers are distinguished by the fact that they have more authority than other workers. Positions also differ in the level of skills and expertise required, with some positions requiring advanced credentials ("experts"), others requiring less training ("skilled"), and a final category that requires no advance training ("non-skilled"). In this scheme, the owners might be considered the capitalist class, and the nonskilled workers compose the working class. The remaining groups among employees (managers, supervisors, experts, and skilled workers) might be viewed as the middle class because they have characteristics of both those above and below them. In a real sense, as Wright has put it, these employees occupy "contradictory" locations because not only are they exploited as workers, but they also exploit others because of their authority and/or expertise assets.

Wright's model gives a rather static, broad view of the class structure and how people might be located within it. But he has pointed out that class position also depends on the relationship a person has with others in their family—relationships that may link the individual to different classes. In other words, a person's own position is "mediated" by the position of others.

Owners	Employees			Relation to Authority
Capitalists	Expert Managers	Skilled Managers	Nonskilled managers	Managers
Small Employers	Expert Supervisors	Skilled Supervisors	Nonskilled Supervisors	Supervisors
Petty Bourgeoisie	Experts	Skilled Workers	Nonskilled Workers	No Authority
	Expert	Skilled	Nonskilled	

Relation to Scare Skills

Figure 3.1 Erik Olin Wright's Model of Class.
Source: Adapted from Wright (2000).

For example, a woman might be a lawyer (an "expert") while her husband is a supervisor in a factory ("nonskilled supervisor"). Wright asks how having these two different class positions in the same family affects each person's own class position. He points out that families of origin matter too—causing a college professor whose parents worked as janitors ("nonskilled workers") to experience their own class position differently from a professor whose parents were also academics ("experts"). These varying sets of relationships connect each of these workers to the class structure in different ways.

Further complicating matters, Wright points out that two individuals may be in the same class at a given time, but one is located on a clear and recognized career path that will take them to a higher position and the other is not. For example, two people might be working together at the same fast-food restaurant, but one is a college student who will end up with a high-paying job after graduation and the other is an older person without a college degree who does not have the same potential to leave fast food work for something more lucrative. This "temporal" aspect of class position means that to define class location fully, one must take into account the span of the broader career trajectory in which the current position is embedded.

A Hybrid Model

Wysong et al. (2014) propose a model that is a hybrid between a continuum and a Marxist model of class. Like Marxist models, it posits two major antagonistic classes with little movement between them. Like continuum models, however, this model sees class as embodied in people, not in occupational positions. In other words, individual people have different kinds of capital (including skills, investments, and social networks) resulting in different class positions.

In their analysis of the US economy, Wysong, Perrucci, and Wright find that class is arrayed in a double diamond shape (see Figure 3.2). The privileged class includes owners, employers, managers, and professionals, while the new working class (which makes up 80 percent of the population) includes everyone else (from professionals in non-elite firms to the self-employed to the working poor and unemployed). At the same time, the authors believe that there is a gradient of class

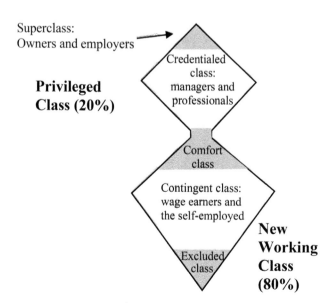

Figure 3.2 Double-Diamond Model of Class Structure and Class Segments.
Source: Adapted from Wysong et al. (2014).

within each diamond. This allows for some mobility within either the upper or lower diamonds, meaning that it is possible to move from being unemployed to being part of the working poor or to move from being a professional to an owner.

Transfer Payments and Class

What forces shape the class structure in the United States? One important determinant involves government policies. In a later section of this chapter, we look at the impact of taxation and minimum wage policy, but we start here with government payments to individuals through social programs. These are known as transfer payments and include what we commonly think of welfare as well as a range of other programs. Most transfer payments are intended to alleviate poverty.

From early in our history, the government has played a major role in addressing poverty. There has not been, however, agreement on how extensive the US government's programs should be. Over time, the public has shifted in its level of support for three different perspectives. The most stringent view—the **residual**, or conservative, view—holds that social welfare aid should only be given to the poor when their families and jobs have not been able to lift them out of poverty. In this sense, welfare is to serve a "residual" function, coming in only after other more traditional, nongovernmental sources of help have been exhausted. As this function implies, social welfare expenditures and programs are expected to be kept to a minimum, and only those who demonstrate indisputably that they are in need are considered eligible for welfare help. Even then, benefits will be low and short term so as not to discourage work. Poverty is viewed as being caused primarily by the kinds of individual explanations we discussed in the last chapter rather than by wider social or cultural conditions. Under these circumstances, there is a social stigma for those seeking welfare. Up until the New Deal, this approach to welfare dominated the US welfare system (Bell, 1987), and it still maintains a strong grip.

The second view of social welfare—the **institutional**, or liberal, perspective—has basically the opposite characteristics from the residual approach. Specifically, it assumes that social welfare programs are an integral part of the institutional structure of modern society and that, like other institutions, they play a vital role in dealing with many of the problems generated by society's social structure and events, such as business cycles and aging, which are largely inevitable. The institutional approach is consistent with the structural and relational theories of poverty. Since poverty is largely beyond people's control, they should be able to expect help without a stigma being attached to such aid. Beginning with the New Deal in the 1930s, an institutional element was formally introduced on a broad scale into the general income-maintenance system of the United States. The result is that the present system is largely a mixture of both approaches.

A third view of social welfare programs interprets them differently than either conservatives or liberals. Instead of being considered either an unnecessary burden on government or as an integral and humane part of it, this *pacifying* perspective interprets social welfare programs as a means of controlling the working class and the poor. Social welfare programs expand when there is rising unrest among these groups and contract when these groups are calm (Piven & Cloward, 2012). This placating function of welfare is closely related to the uneven operation of the capitalist economy. Oversupplies of labor lead to increases in government-sponsored programs. At the same time, however, the work requirements and benefit levels of welfare programs are stringent enough to ensure the availability of a cheap labor force to employers.

Current US income-maintenance programs can be divided into two general categories: social insurance and public assistance. Both include cash and **in-kind benefits** (goods or services). **Social insurance** is aimed at replacing income lost because of death, unemployment, disability, or retirement. Most of the social insurance programs were developed under the Social Security Act of 1935; they include old-age insurance, survivors' insurance, disability insurance, unemployment insurance, and, in many cases, workers' compensation. Medicare is also a social insurance program. These programs are financed by the insured through payroll taxes, by employers, and by the government. Eligibility for participation depends on the extent of a person's prior work history. As long as individuals satisfy certain basic requirements, they are automatically eligible for these programs. There is little stigma attached to participation because individuals are thought of as deserving of such benefits. These programs are most illustrative of the "institutional" perspective on welfare.

Public assistance programs, which have been more "residual" in terms of the assumptions built into them, are "**means-tested**" programs that aim at temporarily assisting poor individuals and families. Means-tested programs require recipients to prove that their income and assets are below a certain level. These make up what most people think of as "welfare." The major programs included in the public assistance category are Temporary Aid to Needy Families (TANF), Supplemental Security Income (SSI), Supplemental Nutrition Assistance Program (SNAP), and Medicaid. SNAP was formally known as the Food Stamp Program. In addition to these programs, local general assistance and housing also are included in this category.

Social Insurance Programs

Of all the social insurance programs, Social Security is the largest. It provides monthly benefits to eligible retired and disabled workers, as well as to their spouses, children, and survivors. Retirement benefits make up most of these expenses. In 2021, the average monthly retirement benefit was $1,554 with a maximum of $3,113 for those who retire at 66 years old (people who retire sooner get less, and those who retire later get more) (Social Security Administration, 2021). Individuals also receive different monthly payments based on an indexed average of their earnings for the 35 years in which they made the most. Each year the government sets a maximum amount of earnings that are subject to taxation and to benefits calculation (it was $142,800 in 2021). Social Security is primarily funded by a 6.2 percent tax on employers and an equivalent tax on employees. Self-employed workers pay the entire 12.4 percent themselves.

Although most of the benefits from the Social Security retirement program go to nonpoor recipients, it prevents millions from falling into poverty. In fact, estimates suggest that the program prevented 26.5 million people from being in poverty in 2019 (Fox, 2020). Despite this, Social Security has become a source of contention between younger and older generations. As its costs have gone up due to an aging population and a comparatively smaller base of workers to support it, some younger workers resent the program's immediate cost to them and worry whether it will be able to support them when they retire.

In addition to the retirement program, survivors' and disability insurance are also a part of Social Security. Under the first type, a worker's surviving dependents receive cash benefits. Disability insurance provides protection against the loss of family income resulting from a "breadwinner" being disabled. In 2021, about 11 percent of the total social security benefits was paid to disabled workers (Social Security Administration, 2021).

In 1965, Medicare was added to the Social Security package. Its purpose is to provide hospital and medical insurance for people aged 65 or older and for adults of any age who are disabled and covered by Social Security. Payment under Medicare is made directly to the care provider. At the present time, Medicare does not pay for all medical services. For example, it does not cover custodial care (help with daily activities that can be provided by a non-licensed worker) or dental care, nor does it pay for long-term nursing home care. The latter has been an issue of increasing concern, especially as the number of elderly people increases. Medicare benefits totaled $776 billion in 2020 for its 61 million enrollees, compared with over $425 billion in 2007 (Cubanski & Neuman, 2018; KFF, 2020). Medicare is funded through a 1.45 percent tax on both employers and employees (up to a cap).

The final social insurance program we discuss here is unemployment insurance. This program replaces part of a worker's wages when they are fired or laid off from a job. It is funded through a state tax on employers, as well as a federal tax (which is largely offset if employers pay their taxes on time). States run their own unemployment systems and have a great deal of latitude to set benefits, limits, and requirements. Most replace about 50 percent of a person's salary, but because it is capped, high-income workers tend to receive a lower percent than do low-income workers. Pre-pandemic, most states had a 26-week eligibility period. In March 2020, the federal government passed the CARES Act, which extended the time period of eligibility, loosened requirements, and increased payments by $600 per week (later reduced to $300) (Kovalski & Shelner, 2020). The time extension and the enhanced benefits programs have since expired. The extended benefits during the pandemic were consistent with a long history of the federal government increasing aid during economic downturns; for example, they increased unemployment benefits during the recession of 2008.

Workers who leave their jobs voluntarily or who are looking for a job for the first time are not eligible for unemployment insurance. To receive unemployment in most states, a person must be actively seeking work. There are restrictions on how long a person must have worked (or how much they must have earned). The rules about duration disqualify many low-wage workers who do seasonal or occasional work. Additionally, gig workers and students do not qualify (although these rules were loosened under the CARES Act). Different state rules have resulted in wide disparities between states in the percentage of the unemployed who actually get the benefit—from 9 percent in Mississippi to 55 percent in Massachusetts. (Kovalski & Shelner, 2020). This explains why unemployment benefits were only estimated to have pulled about 415,000 people out of poverty each year pre-pandemic (Wolfe & Blair, 2019).

Public Assistance Programs

Unlike social insurance programs, public assistance programs tend to be controversial because many of the recipients are seen as undeserving. It is with these programs that questions about fraud, laziness, and deservedness arise most often. Groups that have been the most vulnerable to poverty historically are most likely to receive public assistance. These include women, children, minorities, and the elderly.

Under the public-assistance umbrella are the TANF, SNAP, Medicaid, and SSI programs. All these programs are means-tested and most involve both federal and state funds, although the federal government has given states wide latitude in determining eligibility criteria. The benefits from the TANF and SSI programs come in the form of cash assistance, while those from SNAP and Medicaid come as in-kind benefits. Let us look briefly at each of these major programs.

TANF provides cash assistance for poor families with children. Participants are required to seek employment unless they are caring for a child under the age of six or a disabled family member. They can also avoid the work requirement if they are in a treatment program or are enrolled in school. If individuals are not able to find jobs themselves, they are given subsidized or community employment, or are required to enter a work-training program. The aim is to remove individuals from the welfare rolls as soon as possible and encourage self-sufficiency. After two years of continuous receipt, they are automatically dropped from the program and can only participate for a total of five years over their lifetimes. While TANF's overall design was created by the federal government, the program's specific eligibility rules and administration are carried out by each state which allows them to choose more stringent requirements.

On average, a qualified parent with two children received $473 from TANF per month in 2019 but just as requirements for receipt vary by state, so too do benefit amounts. Mississippi had the lowest benefit level at $151 per month and New Hampshire the highest at $777 (HHS, 2020).

It should be noted that TANF benefit levels are less than 60 percent of the poverty line in all 50 states and do not even cover the cost of an average two-bedroom apartment (Safawi & Floyd, 2020). One of the most significant failings of the TANF program is that it reaches only a minority (23 percent) of families in poverty. This is down from a high of 82 in 1979 and a level of 68 just prior to 1996, when welfare was significantly altered under President Clinton (CBPP, 2021a). Again, we see wide disparity by state, with California's TANF program reaching 70 percent of the poor, but the equivalent number in Louisiana is four. States with large proportions of Black residents tend to have lower benefit levels, so Black children are less likely to receive help (Meyer & Floyd, 2020).

Because benefit levels are low and so few poor families receive help, TANF does not have a big impact on the nation's poverty rate. Estimates suggest that only 438,000 families were pulled out of poverty by the program in 2018. That is a very small number compared to other programs like school lunch programs, which pulled over 1.2 million families out of poverty that same year (Wolfe & Blair, 2019). In 2020, federal costs for TANF were $16.8 billion. This included everything from administration to childcare, but it does not reflect the fact that states are also required to provide funding for TANF. In 2019 states contributed about 15 billion dollars to the program (CBPP, 2021a). Less than a quarter of the money was spent on basic cash assistance (down from 71 percent in 1997) (Safawi & Schott, 2021).

One of the reasons that TANF has not been effective in reducing poverty is that it is not a true entitlement program where everyone who is eligible receives funds regardless of the total cost (such as Social Security, Medicare and TANF's predecessor, Aid to Families with Dependent Children). Instead, TANF is a capped block grant program. That means that the annual expenditure is capped at $16.8 billion, as it has been for over two decades, with no adjustment for inflation, population growth, or increase in economic need.

During the pandemic, the need for assistance rose dramatically—particularly because women were forced out of the workforce in record numbers. As a result, applications for TANF went up across the nation and many states waived some of their requirements (for example, time limits, job-seeking, and in-person orientations). Most states saw much larger caseloads as a result. Some states gave out one-time lump sums to augment TANF payments. As of this writing, however, states have begun to roll back these exceptions, and it is unclear what will happen to caseloads (Meyer & Floyd, 2020; Safawi & Floyd, 2020).

BOX 3.2 ASSET LIMITS

Melissa was a low-income worker who filed for TANF to help her pay rent in the wake of a divorce from an abusive husband. Because she owned an eight-year-old car, however, she was ineligible since the car was worth more than the allowable asset limit for the program. She sold her car, but this made it much more difficult for her to become self-sufficient (Vallas & Valenti, 2014). While this case is somewhat dated, states continue to impose asset limits on many of their public assistance programs. Supporters of asset limits argue that dropping or modifying them would lead to abuse of the program. Others argue that the limits discourage saving money, something that is necessary for long-term stability. Researchers were able to assess the real-world effect when seven states dropped their asset limits and their TANF caseloads did not increase (Pew Research Center, 2016a). In 2020 Congress began considering legislation that would eliminate asset limits on TANF, SNAP, and the Low-Income Home Energy Assistance Program. It would raise the limits for the SSI program as well. All programs would retain their current work requirements and income limitations. What do you think? What are the advantages and disadvantages of asset limits?

Table 3.1 presents some of the basic characteristics of TANF participants. Contrary to the stereotype, the average TANF family tends to be fairly small, averaging fewer than two children. Most adult recipients are women, and the racial/ethnic distribution is about evenly split between White, Black, and Hispanic people with each group composing about 30 percent of the total. About 36 percent have less than high school education, and only 9 percent have more than a high school degree. Approximately 22 percent are employed. About 36 percent of the children in these families are under 6 years of age, and only 9 percent are older than 15.

SSI is another cash-benefit program aimed at people who are in financial need and who are either 65 years of age or older, blind, or disabled. Implemented in 1974, it replaced federally reimbursed programs being run by the states to help the elderly, blind, and disabled. In 2021,

Table 3.1 Characteristics of TANF Households and Recipients: 2020

Average Number of Persons in Household	3
Average Number of Children per Family	1.8
Adult Recipients	(%)
Sex	
Male	14.7
Female	85.3
Race/Ethnicity	
Hispanic	30.5
Non-Hispanic White	29.7
Black	30.8
Asian	2.4
American Indian/Alaskan Native	1.5
Multi-Racial or Other	3.3
Education (Number of Years Attained)	
No Formal Education	10
Less Than 10 Years	5
10–11 Years	20.3
12 Years	55.3
More Than High School	9.4
Citizenship Status	
US Citizen	92.9
Qualified Immigrant	6.8
Employment Status	
Employed	21.6
Child Recipients	
Less Than 6 Years Old	35.7
6–11 Years Old	34
12–15 Years Old	20.8
16–18 Years Old	9.4

Source: HHS (2021). *Characteristics and financial circumstances of TANF recipients.* https://www.acf.hhs.gov/sites/default/files/documents/ofa/fy2020_characteristics_data_final.pdf

about 7.8 million persons received federally administered SSI payments. Monthly payments for individuals averaged $585 (Social Security Administration, 2021).

SNAP is one of the major in-kind public assistance programs offered by the federal government. Benefits are deposited directly into an account that recipients can access through a plastic card (such as a debit card). The card can only be used to purchase limited types of food in authorized stores. Some states, however, are currently piloting programs that allow recipients to buy food from approved online realtors as well. To receive SNAP, a household must be under 130 percent of the poverty line and not have assets greater than $2,250 (not including assets like houses that can't be used to purchase food). The asset limit is higher if there is an elderly or disabled person living in the household. Almost half (48.9 percent) of households receiving SNAP contain at least one child under the age of 18, a full 60 percent contain at least one person over the age of 60, and about 46 percent contain a person with a disability. In over 85 percent of SNAP households, there is at least one worker (Loveless, 2020).

In 2020, the average SNAP recipient received $121 per month (about $1.40 per meal). Benefit levels were increased partway through the year due to the pandemic. Extra benefits were also issued to cover children who, due to shutdowns, were no longer receiving free or reduced price food at school. Between April and September of 2020, SNAP payments accounted for one in nine dollars spent in the US on groceries (USDA, 2021b). Most of these pandemic-related benefit enhancements have expired, but Congress authorized a permanent increase in benefits of about 21 percent in October of 2021. This increase was based on research showing that SNAP payments were too meager to cover the cost of a healthy diet (CBPP, 2021c).

SNAP benefits are based on household size as well as on the earnings of individuals. As people's earnings increase, they receive less in SNAP benefits. To encourage work, however, there is a 20 percent earnings deduction and, during non-pandemic times, 18–50 year olds can only receive SNAP three months out every 3 years unless they are working or in training at least 20 hours a week (CBPP, 2021c). There was a significant jump in 2020 and in the early months of 2021 in the number of people receiving SNAP, likely due to hardship caused by the pandemic and relaxed eligibility rules. In 2020, about 74 billion dollars were spent on SNAP, and there were about 40 million recipients (USDA, 2021a). Estimates suggest that the program kept 2.5 million people from poverty in 2019 (Fox, 2020). At the same time, only 82 percent of eligible people received benefits (USDA, 2021c).

Medicaid is another in-kind program aimed at providing financial assistance to states to pay for the medical care of low-income adults and children who earn less than 138 percent of the federal poverty level (in 2021, this was $17,774). Medicaid is different from Medicare in at least two key ways. First, it is a means-tested program, whereas Medicare provides basic benefits to a particular age group, regardless of their income. Second, Medicaid is a federal- and state-administered program, whereas Medicare is federally administered.

The Affordable Care Act, enacted in 2010, greatly expanded access and coverage of Medicaid. The federal government agreed to reimburse states 100 percent of the costs until the end of 2016 before dropping its rate to 90 percent. A Supreme Court ruling in 2012, however, allowed states to opt out of the expansion. As of 2021, twelve states have taken this option, resulting in 4 million uninsured adults who would have had coverage under the expansion (Kaiser Family Foundation, 2021). In June of 2021, Medicaid was providing coverage for over 76 million people (Centers for Medicare and Medicaid Services, 2021).

There is widespread agreement that programs such as Medicare and Medicaid have made it possible for more people to get needed medical care. Based on a comparison of states that expanded Medicaid and those that did not, it appears that the program is associated with higher rates of preventative care, lower rates of depression, less medical debt, and thousands of lives saved (CBPP, 2020). Despite these beneficial trends, however, problems still remain. For example, variations between states in their coverage rules and the services available create inequalities among individuals who are equally in need of medical care.

Taxation Policy and Class

Taxation is obviously important because it provides funding for crucial services (like roads and the military). It is also a way that the government can redistribute wealth and thus alter the class structure. But how redistributive is our taxation policy? First, it is important to note that there are several kinds of tax. Sales tax is what we pay when we buy things, and it is set at a flat rate by location. Most states (45 plus the District of Columbia) charge sales tax, but localities can add more on top of the state rate (Cammenga, 2021). That is why the sales tax rate often varies within states. Because everyone pays the same rate in the same place, however, sales tax is known as **regressive**. In other words, because the tax constitutes a larger percentage of poor people's income, it hits them harder than it does rich people.

Property tax, which is administered by localities (like cities or townships or parishes), is based on the value of land or real estate. Property tax can be very confusing because different localities assess property values in very different ways and some do not charge tax on the whole assessed value, only on some percentage. Further, in most places, elderly or disabled homeowners are allowed to either reduce or eliminate their property tax burden. Property taxes have both regressive and progressive elements. While everyone pays the same percentage, people who own more expensive homes pay more overall. Multiple reports (including from Chicago and Philadelphia), however, show that homes owned by poor and minority people have been systematically overvalued, causing the homeowners to pay too much in tax, while rich people's homes are systematically undervalued, reducing their tax burdens (Wiltz, 2020).

Income tax is imposed by the federal government, as well as by most states (41 plus the District of Columbia) (Waggoner, 2021). Income taxes are progressive. As you earn more, you pay a higher percentage of your income to the government. It should be noted, however, that as a person moves up through the tax brackets, they only pay each successively higher rate on the money over the income cut-off. In other words, if the tax rate is 10 percent for people with incomes under $10,000 but 12 percent for those between $10,001 and $20,000, a person who earns $13,000 would only pay 10 percent on the first $10,000 and 12 percent on the remaining $3,000. About 33 percent of Americans do not pay income taxes at all because their incomes are too low (Bellafiore & Mauro, 2019). The wealthy provide most of the individual tax payments received by the Internal Revenue Service. In 2018, the top 1 percent were responsible for 40.1 percent of federal tax revenue, paying at an effective rate of about 25 percent (York, 2021).

It may appear that income tax takes much more from the rich than the poor. Four points should be kept in mind, however. *First*, a large number of non-taxpayers are unemployed elderly people, and of those who are not, a significant percentage contribute payroll taxes. Payroll taxes are taken directly out of people's paychecks and provide funding for social insurance programs (Plumer, 2012). *Second*, rates are considerably lower for the rich than they have been at other points in time (Tax Policy Center, 2020). The top tax rate is 37 percent, down from the 70 percent charged between the 1950s and 1970s. *Third*, since most of the wealth of the wealthiest is in the form of stocks, a much higher percentage of the incomes of the wealthy derives from **capital gains**, which are taxed at a lower rate than earnings from employment. Work earnings are the principal source of income for those in the middle and working classes. This results in a situation where the wealthy sometimes end up with a lower tax rate than poorer people. This suggests the *fourth* point, namely, that the higher *amount* paid by the wealthy is a testament to the large size of their incomes. Conversely, the much smaller amounts of taxes contributed by those on the bottom give evidence to the meagerness of their incomes.

In truth, many of the rich pay little to no taxes at all. A recent report by Pro Publica found that Jeff Bezos did not pay income tax in 2007 and 2011, even though his wealth increased by billions of dollars. Similarly, Elon Musk paid no tax in 2018. If you look at the richest 25 Americans and calculate how much their wealth grew, they only paid an effective tax rate of 3.4 percent. How do they do this? There are many loopholes and deductions in the tax code. Additionally, increases in the value of stocks and properties are not taxed (Eisinger et al., 2021).

An important tax program with a substantial redistributive effect is the **Earned Income Tax Credit** (EITC). This program was set up to encourage employment by allowing low-earning workers, especially those with children, to receive a tax credit. It applies to people whose earnings fall below a certain level (for example, $42,158 in 2021 for a single parent with one child). The credit is scaled depending on income and family size, with a phase-out starting at a certain income level. When a person receives a tax credit, it is first applied against their tax bill (for example, if they owe $1,000 in taxes and get a $1,500 EITC, they do not owe any taxes). In addition, any money left over after taxes is refunded to the worker (in the case just mentioned, the worker would receive a check for $500). The EITC has an extremely significant impact on poverty in our country. In 2018, it pulled 5.6 million people, 3 million of whom were children, out of poverty. In other words, there would have been a full twenty-five percent more poor children without the program (CBPP, 2019). Some fear that the EITC discourages work, but research suggests that it has practically no impact on the number of hours married men work, small negative effects on married women, and positive effects on single women. In other words, single women are more likely to enter the labor market in the presence of the EITC (Hoynes, 2014).

Estate/inheritance tax is a tax charged when a person dies and passes on their wealth. An **estate tax** gets taken out of the estate before it is transferred, while an inheritance tax comes in the form of a bill to the person who inherits. The federal government imposes an estate tax as do 12 states. An additional six states have inheritance taxes. Few Americans pay the federal estate tax, however, because it is not applied unless the estate is very valuable (11.7 million dollars in 2021). It should be noted that the estate is only charged on the amount over the limit, not its whole value. Only a tiny percent (0.2) of estates qualify to pay any taxes at all. This is because, most of the time, spouses are exempt from paying and there are many discounts and deductions allowed. It is also possible for people to set up a trust to decrease the tax burden after their death. While the top federal tax rate is 40 percent, the average effective tax rate is 17 percent. US estate taxes are lower than those in the 26 of 34 other OECD countries that levy them (Huang & Cho, 2017).

There are a number of controversial aspects of estate/inheritance taxes. First, some people argue that rates should be much higher because people do not earn an inheritance, it is effectively a gift. Second, the fact that so few people pay it, and only at a low rate, means it has little impact on inequality and effectively encourages the **sedimentation** of wealth. On the other hand, some people argue that the estate tax is not fair because people are charged for unrealized capital gains. This means that if someone bought a house many years ago and it increased in value by the time of their death, the inheritor must pay taxes on the current value. In theory, the inheritor might have to sell the house (or farm) to pay the tax—and this does happen in a small number of cases each year. Because so few estates pay tax and those who inherit those estates often already have great personal wealth, however, this problem does not impact a significant number of people.

One final tax policy that has important ramifications on inequality is called the mortgage deduction. People who own homes are able to deduct some of the interest they pay on their mortgages. This policy was instituted to encourage home buying, but its primary effect has been to save well-off people a lot of money over generations. Today, however, interest rates are lower than they were in the past, and many people do not choose to itemize, so it is less important than it used to be. Also, stricter limits were put in place during the Trump administration—allowing people to only deduct interest payments up to $750,000 rather than a million dollars. It should be noted that there is no strong evidence to suggest that mortgage deductions increase home-buying, but they may encourage people to buy bigger homes (Hanson et al., 2014).

The Impact of Taxes and Transfers on Inequality

As described, the American tax system is supposed to be "progressive"—that is, to lessen income differences between income strata by taxing higher-income groups at higher rates. Social insurance and public assistance programs are intended to redistribute income to the lowest earners. To what extent do they accomplish these goals? In 2017, taxes dropped the Gini Index from 0.521 to 0.477 (Tax Policy Center, 2020). This measure, however, does not count the indirect effects of taxes. In other words, taxes are used to fund government transfer programs, which also have an impact on inequality.

Turning now to the impact of transfer programs, the Congressional Budget Office estimates that, in 2017, government transfers reduced the Gini Index from 0.52 to 0.48 (CBO, 2020). It is important to note that transfer programs may reduce inequality, but they are not a good driver of mobility. Although they help people stay on their feet during hard times, they are not large enough to significantly impact people's class standing. And as mentioned, most public assistance programs are designed so that once a person starts to achieve mobility (by getting a new job or increasing hours, for example), they become ineligible for assistance.

Looking internationally, the United States reduces inequality through transfers better than some countries but considerably worse than others. The data in Table 3.2 gives a comparative look at selected countries in 2013. Keep in mind that the Gini Index is calculated slightly differently by different organizations, so the data in Table 3.2 are not the same as those provided by the Congressional Budget Office (shown above), but they do accurately reflect international differences.

Table 3.2 shows that Canada and the United Kingdom spend more (proportionally) on transfer programs and achieve greater effects at reducing inequality. It should be noted, however, that the table only reflects transfers, not taxes. In the United States, taxes and transfers together have a stronger impact with a reduction in the Gini Index (in 2017) from 0.52 to 0.43 (CBO, 2020).

Table 3.2 Selected Countries Average Income, Percent of Income in Transfers, and Pre- and Post-Transfers Gini Index: 2013

Country	India	Russia	UK	Canada	US
Pre-Tax Income in US Dollars	3,781	24,661	32,074	42,382	46,962
Transfers as Percent of Income	2.02	5.16	8.75	5.15	2.42
Gini Index without Transfers	0.52	0.38	0.45	0.40	0.45
Gini Index with Transfers	0.51	0.36	0.37	0.37	0.43

Source: Kakwani et al. (2020). Assessing the Social Welfare Effects of Government Transfer Programs: Some International Comparisons.

Minimum Wage Policy and Class

The minimum wage is a governmental policy with a strong potential impact on inequality. The first federal minimum wage law was set at 25 cents an hour in 1938. The original bill called for 40 cents, but that figure was reduced to appease senators from the southern states (Kiger, 2021).

The bill that was passed also excluded many industries like restaurants and agriculture. These industries were, not coincidentally, those in which a third of Black workers were employed. In 1966, Congress expanded the minimum wage mandate to many of these industries, resulting in a 20 percent reduction in the level of racial income equality by the mid-1970s (Derenoncourt & Montialoux, 2020).

The minimum wage has been increased 12 times since 1938. At the time of this writing, it is set where it was in 2009, at $7.25 an hour. The minimum wage hit its highest purchasing power in 1968 when it was over eleven dollars an hour (in 2019 dollars). Today, it is at its lowest purchasing power. Many states and localities have enacted their own minimum wage laws, however, and employers in those areas are required to pay the amount that is highest (Kiger, 2021). Even today, not everyone is covered by minimum wage laws; for example, some employees at small family farms are exempt. By federal law, workers in jobs where tips are received can be paid a minimum of $2.13 an hour so long as their tips bring them up to the minimum wage. Additionally, people under the age of 20 can be paid $4.25 an hour for ninety consecutive days after they start work.

Business owners sometimes speak out against raising the minimum wage, arguing that it will not only lessen their profits but will force them to cut jobs and raise prices for consumers. But is this true? Although it seems obvious that raising wages would decrease the number of jobs, economists have found very little evidence to support the idea—not only in the United States but in a variety of other countries around the world (Manning, 2021). This may be because minimum wage increases are generally fairly low and are phased in over time. Seattle raised its minimum wage by $1.50 an hour in 2014, and there was little impact on the employment of low-wage workers. But when the city raised the minimum wage again in 2015, this time by $2.00, employers did appear to reduce work hours (Jardim et al., 2017). Similarly, San José raised its minimum wage by 25 percent. This resulted in about a one percent increase in restaurant prices (Allegretto & Reich, 2018). Research suggests that the effect of minimum wage increases on employment is quite variable and depends on the region of the country as well as the initial minimum wage (Wang et al., 2019).

It is difficult to calculate exactly how an increase in the minimum wage might impact the economy. This is because there are both direct and indirect effects. An example of an indirect effect is that because low-wage workers are more likely than high-wage workers to spend the extra money they receive from a raise, a minimum wage increase will likely have a positive impact on the economy and business owners will sell more (Hall & Cooper, 2012). Increasing the minimum wage is also likely to reduce income inequality. Research shows that, over the last thirty years, a lagging minimum wage has been a factor contributing to worsening wage inequality in the United States, particularly for women (Autor et al., 2016). Interestingly, higher minimum wages appear to be associated with lower rates of suicide (Kaufman et al., 2020) and lower rates of child maltreatment reports (Raissian & Bullinger, 2017).

Trade Policy and Class

A final government policy we discuss in terms of its impact on the class structure involves trade policy. Trade policy is obviously related to globalization as the economies of different countries become increasingly intertwined. Trade agreements and tariffs can dramatically impact the number of jobs and wages in the United States. It is extremely hard to assess whether their impact is negative or positive because they can have disparate effects on different groups of people. For example, in 2016, President Trump placed tariffs (taxes) on imported steel with the goal of increasing the number of steel worker jobs in the United States. It appears that the tariffs did meet this goal, but there were unintended consequences. Because steel was more expensive and harder to get, some companies that used it in their products had to raise prices and lay off workers.

Photo 3.1 Abandoned factories are an indicator of the decline of US manufacturing jobs.
Source: © Christian Mueller/Shutterstock.

Foreign countries started increasing their imports of products made of steel, which meant increased competition for US companies. Estimates suggest that for each job created in the steel industry, American consumers paid about $900,000 in increased prices on consumer goods (Gertz, 2020).

Free trade agreements generally lift tariffs and allow for unfettered movement of goods across borders. An example in the United States was the North American Free Trade Agreement, signed in 1994 by President George Bush, the prime minister of Canada, and the president of Mexico. While there were groups who benefited from this agreement (like farmworkers), the overall effect was to increase inequality in the United States. In fact, there is solid evidence that blue-collar workers across many industries suffered wage declines (Hakobyan & McLaren, 2016). This is likely because NAFTA reduced employment in traditionally high-paying manufacturing jobs, lessened investment in the manufacturing base, and reduced the price of many goods, thereby indirectly causing a decline in average wages. The threat of competition from foreign workers may have also caused US employees to reluctantly accept wage reductions (Mishel et al., 2007).

In 2020 Donald Trump signed the US-Mexico-Canada Agreement to replace NAFTA. While it is very similar, it contains more protections for US labor. For example, it mandates that 75 percent of a new car's parts (up from 62.5 percent under NAFTA) must be produced in North America or a tariff will be imposed. It also mandates that 40 percent of car parts must come from places where workers are paid at least $16 an hour and it requires Mexico to legalize the formation of unions (Wiseman, 2021). These restrictions are intended to reduce the incentives for American companies to move production to Mexico. Time will tell if this new agreement has an impact on wages and inequality in the United States.

Mobility

So far in this chapter, we have looked at the class structure and at how taxes, transfers, and government policies affect it. We now step back and look at class mobility. How likely is it that people move up or down? The United States as a storied land of opportunity and freedom is chronicled in many myths and fables about how the individual, no matter how humble and lowly, can succeed.

Children in US society often are told that if they work hard enough and want something badly enough, they will obtain it. They are taught that opportunities are there to be grasped if a person just has the aspirations and perseverance required to take advantage of them.

At first glance, the meaning of the term "mobility" may seem obvious—it is simply a measure of movement up or down the class ladder. Social scientists, however, use the term in a variety of ways. Here we list some of these distinctions.

- **Intergenerational vs. Intragenerational Mobility:** Most mobility studies look at mobility between generations (intergenerational). Specifically, they compare parental class standing with their children. In general, are people's children better or worse off than their parents? Intragenerational mobility looks at the possibility for class or occupational change across the life course. For example, if a person starts out as a fast-food worker, what are the chances that they can switch occupations to something more lucrative?
- **Absolute vs. Relative Mobility:** An absolute measure of mobility compares a child's adjusted income to that of their parents at the same point in their lives. It asks whether, in absolute terms, people are doing better or worse than their parents. A relative measure, in contrast, compares locations in the income structure. For example, if we divide up the income distribution into quintiles, we might ask if a child ends up in the same quintile as their parent. This is a relative measure because quintiles compare where you are to where others are.
- **Structural vs. Circulation Mobility:** Structural mobility is movement between social classes due to changes in the occupations available in society at any given time. For example, when many factories left the United States, the kinds of jobs in the economy changed, forcing people to find new kinds of work. Circulation mobility, in contrast, is movement between social classes because individual people change. The class structure stays the same, but people move up or down within it. For example, a person might obtain more education than their parents and thus have a higher position in the class structure. Many consider circulation mobility to be a better measure of the openness of a system than structural mobility because it is a more direct measure of the impact of family background on an individual's mobility. Greater openness suggests a weaker tie between background and mobility.

Americans tend to have a rosy view of the opportunities and prospects attainable in their country. A 2017 Pew survey found that about 61 percent of Americans think that people can get ahead if they just work hard (Doherty et al., 2017). Another innovative study of attitudes found that Americans overestimate US mobility compared to other countries (Davidai and Gilovich, 2015). Respondents were given a randomly ordered list of 15 different countries and asked to rank them in terms of mobility. The researchers specifically chose countries so that the correct ranking would put the United States exactly in the middle (8th of 15). Over 90 percent of respondents, however, overestimated our ranking. On average, they thought that the United States is the third most mobile society. The survey also showed that most Americans believe it is the attributes of the person rather than outside forces that are most important for advancement. But how easy is it really to advance up our class structure? Do people's children generally tend to do better than they have done?

Mobility from 1850s to 1990s

Research suggests that **intergenerational mobility** was fairly high in the United States from 1850 until the end of the century. There was considerable mobility between occupations connected to people moving to new parts of the country for better jobs. After 1900, however, intergenerational mobility strongly decreased (Long & Ferrie, 2013). The trend turned around again after World

War II, likely because veterans received occupational training while in the military and then were able to take advantage of the educational opportunities afforded by the GI Bill. This allowed them to strengthen their human capital and later attain higher wages and more prestigious occupations than their fathers (Teachman & Tedrow, 2004).

Research suggests that circulation mobility increased between 1957 and 1962 and that a son's occupation became less dependent on that of his father. In other words, the system of inequality appears to have been more open in 1962 than in the earlier years (Blau & Duncan, 1967; Featherman & Hauser, 1978). Most of the mobility, however, took place in the middle of the occupational hierarchy, for example, in upper blue-collar positions, while the top and bottom were fairly closed, suggesting "barriers to movement across class boundaries" (Featherman & Hauser, 1978, p. 180). This has been substantiated for the period from 1972 to 1985 as well. The decline in the association between an individual's social background and where they end up occupationally appears to have been linked to the rise in the proportion of workers who had higher education. This was the case for both men and women (Hout, 1988).

When Featherman and Hauser (1978) discovered that mobility increased during the late 1950s and early 1960s, they projected that it was part of a long-term trend of increasing openness and decreasing inheritance of class. It soon became clear, however, that their projection was wrong. Instead, evidence suggests that intergenerational mobility slowed and even began to decline during the 1980s (Aaronson & Mazumder, 2008). During the 1990s, intergenerational mobility at the top and bottom of the economic hierarchy remained restricted. In other words, there was a distinct tendency for individuals born into a high- or low-status family to remain in that position (Hertz, 2005; Mazumder, 2005). For example, it was estimated that a son born into the top 10 percent of the income hierarchy had at least a 1 in 5 chance of attaining the same position, but that one born into the bottom 10 percent had only a 1 in 100 chance of moving up into the top income decile. The chances were much greater that the latter would remain at the bottom (Bowles & Gintis, 2002). Nam's (2004) study of sons from low-income and high-income backgrounds confirmed this conclusion, finding that intergenerational transmission for those in the high-income group increased over time but that the chances of low-income persons moving up from their poorer position did not change significantly.

Current US Mobility Patterns

Some scholars predicted that there would be drops in social mobility in the United States as our levels of income inequality increased. The link between income inequality and social mobility has been well established. For example, looking at the country level, we see that high-income inequality is strongly associated with low social mobility (Corak, 2013). This effect is called the Great Gatsby Curve after the upwardly mobile character Jay Gatsby in the novel by F. Scott Fitzgerald.

While some studies have found the Gatsby Curve to be accurate, others have found less evidence for the link. At least part of the reason for the conflicting findings is that some researchers look at relative mobility while others look at absolute mobility. Chetty et al. (2014), for example, analyzed tax returns from all US citizens born between 1980 and 1993 and found that relative mobility has changed very little from the 1970s. In a later study, however, Chetty et al. (2017) used tax returns to look at absolute mobility and found strong decreases linked to inequality. For example, while 90 percent of children born in 1940 ended up earning more than their parents, only 50 percent of children born in 1984 did so. This decline was particularly marked for the middle class. Another study similarly found that relative mobility spiked upward during the 1970s but then returned to about where it was in the 1950s and 1960s. In contrast, absolute mobility decreased in tandem with increases in inequality (Aaronson & Mazumder, 2008).

It is not entirely clear why the impact of inequality on absolute and relative mobility is so different, but one reason may be widespread income stagnation across the income spectrum. When wages do not grow, it obviously makes it difficult for people to earn more than their parents. Additionally, as described above, inequality keeps much of the income tied up in the hands of the rich so that even when there are income increases, only a minority of Americans benefit. The level of relative mobility has stayed more or less the same because much of the change in income has been in the upper end of the income distribution (the top 1 percent increasing its share of income) and has not had a lot of impact on the relative mobility of the middle class (Chetty et al., 2014; Chetty et al., 2017).

When we talk about mobility, it is important to point out that there are significant variations between racial/ethnic groups. In their landmark study of US men in the early 1960s, Blau and Duncan (1967) argued that Black people generally start out from a lower position, but instead of moving up in a manner commensurate with their education and other human capital, they are hindered at each step along the way in the attainment process. That is, their disadvantages are *cumulative*. Due to discrimination, they have a hard time getting a higher education, and when they do, the occupational returns for that education are less than those received by White people. For example, Black people with a bachelor's degree earn about 8.4 percent less than Whites with the same degree; it appears there is a similar trend for Hispanic people; those with a bachelor's degree earn only 89 percent of the income of White people with the same degree (de Brey et al., 2019).

Although not all racial and ethnic groups gain an equal mobility boost from education, a college degree significantly increases income for all groups. Smaller percentages of Black and Hispanic people compared to White and Asian people graduate from high school and obtain bachelor's degrees. At the same time, their rate of increase in college enrollment has been much higher. This is particularly notable among Hispanics, with enrollment jumping 14 percent since 2000. The enrollment of Black students also increased a significant 6 percent during the same time period. The equivalent percentage for Whites and Asians was 3 (Hussar et al., 2020). Because more Black and Hispanic students are enrolling in college, they receive more bachelor's degrees than in the past. At the same time, the graduation rate has not risen at the same pace as the enrollment rate. Only about 46 percent of Black students and 55 percent of Hispanic students enter college graduate. This compares to about 66 percent of White and Asian students (Shapiro et al., 2017). Increasing enrollment is not directly translating to an equivalent level of graduation largely because Black and Hispanic students are more likely to drop out due to financial and other concerns and a higher percentage attend schools that do not award bachelor's degrees (Krogstad & Fry, 2014).

An important study on mobility and race was released in 2018. Analysis of data from 20 million children and their parents showed that Black people and American Indians are less likely to be upwardly mobile than Whites, Hispanics, and Asians. A Black child born into the bottom quintile of income has only a 2.5 percent chance of ending up in the top quintile. This compares to 10.6 percent for Whites. Black children born into the top quintile of income have an equal chance of ending up in either the bottom or top quintile. This indicates high levels of downward mobility. What is so important about this dataset is that it is so large, the researchers were able to compare Black and White children who came from similar family structures, social classes, and even neighborhoods. They find that little of the mobility gap has to do with family structure, education, wealth, or ability. They also find that Black males are more disadvantaged in mobility than Black females. On a more positive note, Black children who move to more advantaged neighborhoods early in life tend to have higher mobility, suggesting that we could help address the mobility gap by improving neighborhood conditions (Chetty et al., 2018).

As described earlier, Americans tend to be optimistic about their chances of becoming rich even though rags-to-riches mobility is very unusual in the United States (DiPrete, 2007; Kotkin, 2010). The chances of becoming wealthy by being a **Horatio Alger**-type entrepreneur are much less for those from poor backgrounds than they are for individuals who come from middle- or upper-class families. It is paradoxical that, on the one hand, most citizens believe in the openness of US society, while on the other hand, the family one is born into has a significant effect on one's **status attainment**. Mobility matters greatly to people and has an impact on a wide range of outcomes. For example, Cherlin found that people who were downwardly mobile felt less trust in social institutions (like Congress, the educational system, and banks) and more animosity toward immigrants (Cherlin, 2016).

Summary

We asked three related questions in this chapter. First, what is the nature of the class system in the United States? It turns out that there is a lack of agreement on the exact definition and measurement of social class. There are two primary schools of thought: those who favor a Marxian definition and those who prefer a socioeconomic model. But, further complicating matters, there is disagreement even among Marxists. Marx never gave an explicit, clear-cut definition of class. He suggested various definitions and different numbers and types of social classes at different points in his writing. Nevertheless, his approach and that of contemporary Marxist analysts are clearly different from socioeconomic models. Where Marxists generally view classes as (1) discrete rather than continuous, (2) real rather than statistical creations, (3) economic in nature, and (4) conflict-ridden, socioeconomic models define classes as existing along a continuous hierarchy, largely statistically created, and being multidimensional and relatively harmonious in their relationships.

The second question this chapter addressed involved the impact of redistributive programs and policies, including transfer programs, taxes, minimum wage policy, and trade agreements on the American class structure. Problems of inequity, inadequacy, and goal conflict have permeated public assistance programs for the poor. In addition, concerns about how they affect work incentive, family composition, and effectiveness have also generated heated debate. At the same time, transfer programs do decrease the number of people in poverty, but they have only a moderate impact on inequality and do not serve as a driver of mobility. Tax policy, similarly, decreases inequality, although the impact is not strong. The EITC, however, is associated with a notable decrease in inequality. Raising the minimum wage also has the potential to decrease inequality.

Finally, we learned about the extent of mobility in the American class system. Mobility was relatively high between 1850 and 1900 but then decreased until after World War II, when it began increasing again. The 1990s saw a decrease in mobility, a trend that continues to the present moment.

Critical Thinking

1. How many classes do you think there are in America? Do you agree more with a Marxist model of class or a continuum model? Why?
2. Consider the jobs you have held. Which factors do you think led to your being employed and affected the earnings you received?
3. What do you think economic and technological conditions will be like ten years from now? How will these affect your chances of moving up or down in wealth?
4. How do you define welfare? How does that match with your classmates?

Web Connections

The US Census Bureau regularly collects data on income and poverty in the United States. Go to their website at www.census.gov and click on "topics" and then "income and poverty." United for a Fair Economy is an independent, nonprofit organization interested in greater equality that also gathers information on wealth, earnings, and income distribution and their relationship to race and democracy. They also write reports on this information. Visit www.faireconomy.org. Do you think inequality undermines democracy?

Film Suggestions

American Factory (2019). A documentary about a Chinese firm that—with great fanfare—opens a factory in a closed General Motors plant near Detroit. The film documents the tensions that emerge between the leadership and the workers.

American Winter (2013). A documentary about what happened to struggling families in the aftermath of the Great Recession of 2008–2010. Filmed over one winter, it follows a number of families in Portland, Oregon.

Masters of Deception: Social Class in American Pop Culture (2014). Examines how popular culture shapes our notions of social class in relation to a wide range of topics, including consumerism, beauty, and romantic love.

Growing Up Poor in America (2020). A documentary that follows four poor children in Ohio as the COVID-19 pandemic hits.

The American Ruling Class (2005). A "dramatic documentary musical," this film explores the lives of two students, one rich and one not rich. The story is interwoven with interviews with prominent scholars on class.

4 Status Inequality

Differences in *economic* resources are not the only basis of inequality. We also use social factors to rank people in society. Think, for example, about how students at your school are evaluated by their peers. In addition to gender and race/ethnicity, other factors such as fraternity/sorority membership, academic major, athletic participation, the regions of the country they are from, and even the residence halls in which they live serve as criteria for ranking people. Sociologists refer to this social form of inequality as **status**.

Status is defined as "a social ranking of individuals, groups, or objects as superior or inferior according to a shared standard of social value" (Ridgeway & Nakagawa, 2014, p. 3). This definition is inherently relational. Because you can't see or count your status (as you can with money), it only becomes meaningful in terms of where you stand relative to others. We know if someone has a high or low status through the amount of esteem and deference given to them by others. More often than not, we notice these social distinctions in our contacts with others; that is, they become most salient when we interact with individuals whose characteristics and lifestyles differ from our own.

Status can be afforded on the basis of education, religion, possession of "culture," type of occupation, and even speech patterns and clothing styles. It is often related to economic class, but it is not just the *amount* of wealth but the *kind* and *source* of wealth as well as how it is *used* that are ranked. It is not just the amount of education, but the kind and place of education. It is not just the earnings of the occupation but the kind of occupation it is. It is not just whether one is poor, but whether one is on welfare. If economic inequality is primarily about *quantities*, status inequality is about *qualities*.

Theories of Social Status

Max Weber is the classical theorist most associated with theories of status. As will be described in more detail in Chapter 6, he stressed the importance of distinguishing between economic class and social status, even while pointing out that they can be empirically related to each other, as when one's social status is dependent on *class* position. Weber viewed a person's *status situation* as "every typical component of the life fate of men that is determined by a specific, positive or negative social estimation of honor. This honor may be connected with any quality shared by a plurality" (Gerth & Mills, 1962, p. 187 italics in original). This means that status is ultimately a subjective assessment rendered by a community or another group. "Status is the sum of the evaluations that are 'located' in the minds of other people with whom one interacts" (Milner, 2016, p. 39). In other words, individuals are given homage and respect based on the sum of qualities, called "status characteristics," that the community considers honorable or dishonorable. There are many status characteristics, and they vary across cultures. As described, just a few of the characteristics in the United States include wealth, poverty, education, occupation, race, gender, disability, and physical attractiveness.

DOI: 10.4324/9781003184966-5

One of the ways that status characteristics lead to honor is through the stereotypes associated with them. Generally, low-status groups are portrayed with negative stereotypes, providing a rationale for showing them dishonor. The opposite is true for high-status groups. Interestingly, however, research suggests that mixed or ambivalent stereotypes about low-status groups might be more effective at maintaining their position in the hierarchy. This is because members of the low-status group are less motivated to fight against status inequality if there are positive as well as negative stereotypes attached to them (Durante et al., 2013).

One of the most powerful stereotypes that come to be affixed to status groups involves competence. While high-status people are usually assumed to be more competent than those of low status, it depends somewhat on the status characteristics they possess. A **specific status** causes people to assume competence, but only in a particular context. Athletic ability is an example. People do not assume that a great gymnast will also be a superior computer programmer. A **diffuse status**, however, transcends specific situations. Gender and disability are diffuse statuses. This means that people assume that being a woman or a person with a disability affects competence across a wide range of contexts (Ridgeway & Nakagawa, 2014).

While status is always at play in our assessments of others, it can take on more significance at some times than others. For example, Weber argued that when social and economic conditions in a community are stable, stratification by status (rather than by class or power) becomes dominant. In the United States, these conditions are frequently found in small towns where the same kin groups have lived for generations, where relationships are based on the family name, and where social connections are important. Social status also becomes more significant when access to other forms of power is weak (Milner, 2016). When people have little else to use as leverage in social situations, they use their own status conventions and goods as a means of controlling others or enhancing their social positions.

Status Groups

When people share a status characteristic, they can be considered a status group. Status groups are ranked in a certain place on a community's social hierarchy and are characterized by (1) a set of conventions and traditions, or lifestyle; (2) a tendency to marry within their own ranks; (3) an emphasis on interacting intimately—for example, eating only with others in the same group; (4) frequent monopolization of economic opportunities; and (5) emphasis on ownership of certain types of possessions rather than others (Weber, 1947). These features all reflect the tendency in status groups to establish and maintain the integrity of the boundaries that separate them from other groups. Wearing team jackets or particular types of clothes, associating with only particular kinds of people, and participating in an initiation process when becoming a member of a group are all signals that social status is operating.

As the list above indicates, to be an accepted member of a status group, a person is expected to follow the normative lifestyle of the group and to have "restrictions on 'social' intercourse" (Weber, 1947, p. 187). This means that the person is expected to associate intimately with only similar kinds of people. Consider what might happen when people in a distinct status group step out of line by violating the expected customs of the group. They might be confronted, ostracized, shunned, or punished in some other more physical way and told in no uncertain terms what they need to do to get back in the good graces of their community or group. Because status groups are separated by social and cultural boundaries, the above efforts are made to maintain them. Continuous "boundary work" is needed to reinforce status distinctions between groups.

Members of a status group try particularly hard to separate themselves from those whom they believe might contaminate the purity of the group. An extreme instance of this process exists when status group members agree to marry only among themselves (i.e., to practice

endogamy) and to chastise or shun anyone who marries outside the group. In the past, high-status families in the United States exerted a great deal of pressure on children to marry people of their own social standing. This pressure has decreased somewhat, but research suggests that when a lower-status person "marries up," they never feel entirely comfortable in their new position (Streib, 2015).

The key to status honor is "distance and exclusiveness." In her study of country clubs, for example, Jessica Holden Sherwood (2013) notes how carefully potential new members are screened and the elaborate application process that is involved before a new person is accepted. Applicants must be rich enough to afford membership but also must demonstrate the proper status markers (including dress and manners, for example). The extent and intensity of the application process are a direct indicator of the strength of the social boundary of a status group. The maintenance of a status group's cultural and social integrity requires continual vigilance of its boundaries with the outside. This is called **social closure**, a process whereby outsiders to a group are called out as not being worthy of belonging to the group and are kept from joining or participating (Massey, 2007, p. 17; Tilly, 1998, p. 13). In other words, not just anyone can be accepted. Voluntary residential segregation in a secure gated community on the part of a group is an example of how a high-status social group (rich people) separates themselves from people of lower status.

It should not be surprising that to be accepted as a member of a particular status group requires possessing certain credentials. Many see credentialism as a major tool in the practice of exclusion (Brown, 2001). Having the proper credentials might mean, for example, having a given license or educational degree before being accepted into a group. When an occupation requires a credential, it limits the number of people who qualify, thereby enhancing the earnings of the whole group (Weeden, 2002). Molly George (2013) has shown how the new occupation of "life coaches" has used credentials, professional experiences, and careful labeling to create a social status as a profession.

"Exclusion" is another mechanism by which those in powerful status groups keep others from gaining power (Massey, 2007). For example, men may attempt to keep their corporate positions exclusive by preventing women from moving to the top of the ladder. Even high-status six year olds exclude lower-status children from their play (Fanger et al., 2012). Since high status is coveted and in short supply, those at the top may change or complicate the norms to maintain their position, making it more difficult for those below them to move up and displace them. One's own status is always at the expense of someone else's social position.

Sometimes groups that are dishonored or low in status do not accept their assigned place. In these cases, they may attempt to usurp prestige by creating their own ranking system. This enhances their own social status, often to the denigration of other groups. One example is provided by Lamont (2001), who found that working-class men use their own criteria to distinguish themselves as an honorable and distinct status group from those above and below them. Rather than wealth or political power, which would relegate them to a lower status, these men use moral criteria (such as being hard-working and responsible or having integrity) to separate themselves from others. More recently, Arlie Hochschild (2018) conducted five years of fieldwork in a poor rural area of Louisiana. She found that people defined themselves and found status through a fierce sense of pride about being both hard-working and independent. These criteria allowed them to define social and cultural boundaries while providing them with a higher social status in their own eyes.

Deference and Demeanor

When ranking occurs among status groups, *deference* is expected to be shown toward those in more prestigious or honored groups. An example of deferential behavior involves greetings and titles (Goffman, 1959, 1967). For example, students are often concerned with how they should address faculty members: Should it be "Professor," "Doctor," "Mr./Ms.," or simply a first name? Some clearly feel uneasy using the latter form of address because they think it suggests a lack of respect or deference.

While those in lower statuses may show deference for those at the top, the latter can use their resources to present themselves in ways that elicit and justify such respect. They typically have the resources and motivation to appear impressive and so are able to manage situations to obtain the responses they desire. Through their demeanor, individuals of higher status can suggest that they are worthy of such deference. Demeanor is "that element of the individual's ceremonial behavior typically conveyed through deportment, dress, and bearing, which serves to express to those in his immediate presence that he is a person of certain desirable or undesirable qualities" (Goffman, 1967, p. 77). A great deal of research shows that, in situations where a group is trying to complete a task together, people assume high-status others will contribute more and better ideas. In response, the high-status actors adjust their demeanor by talking more and contributing more ideas. The group ends up taking their ideas more seriously, even if they are not as useful as suggestions made by lower-status others. This becomes cyclical with expectations leading to demeanor and then the demeanor reinforcing the original expectations (for a review of the literature, see Ridgeway & Nakagawa, 2014).

Assessment of Social Status

As described, assessing status can be difficult because it is relative and invisible. It is also complicated because it is multidimensional. Ridgeway and Nakagawa (2014) use the example of a Black female doctor interacting with a White male patient. A doctor is a member of a prestigious occupation that grants a lot of status. At the same time, this particular doctor—on the basis of her race and gender—is a member of a lower status group than her patient. So how does the patient decide how much deference to give her? In situations where a task needs to be accomplished, in this case, a medical procedure, research suggests that people aggregate all the different statuses someone has (they add and subtract them in their minds), but they put more weight on those that are relevant to the task at hand. This is an excellent example of intersectionality—when multiple statuses interact to shape interactions. In this case, the fact that the patient needs a medical procedure means he will consider the doctor's profession more heavily than either her gender or race. At the same time, he will still take gender and race into account and will accord the doctor less respect than if she were White or male.

All of us, like the patient in the example above, are constantly calculating other people's status. At the same time, we also evaluate our own; this assessment is called subjective social status. Nielsen et al. (2015) used data from a large sample of young adults to assess Americans' subjective social status. They found that, while family background (parental education and income) does have an impact, more immediate factors are weighted more heavily. These include the respondent's education, earnings, job satisfaction, job repetitiveness, household income and assets, and high school grade point average (GPA). Occupational prestige matters as well, but not as much as the other factors. Importantly, there are group differences in the assessment of subjective social status. For example, Black people give less weight to education and employment than do White people. This may be because Black people are more likely to compare themselves to others of the same race, rather than to the larger population, and to recognize the impact of discrimination in shaping educational and employment outcomes. It also appears that women count employment in their subjective social status less than do men, perhaps reflecting traditional gender notions about the importance of being the breadwinner for men (Shaked et al., 2016).

Some Key Status Characteristics in the United States

As described earlier, numerous status characteristics combine to determine the esteem in which a person is held. In this chapter, we focus on the characteristics of occupation, education, lifestyle, wealth, physical appearance, and disability. In Chapters 8–11, we will expand our discussion to include race, place, nationality, gender identity, and sexual orientation. As you read, you will notice how spheres of status are intertwined. In other words, having a lot of status in one area often translates into high status in another.

Occupation

Occupations are a basis for deference and honor, not only because of their association with valued goals (income, power, and so forth), but also because there are different levels and kinds of education and training that members undergo, as well as different types of behavior that characterize them. In other words, there are lifestyles associated with particular roles that receive different degrees of honor. Plumbers and professors are accorded different levels of honor partly because of what people associate with each of these occupations.

Over the years, there have been several attempts to rank occupations according to prestige or status. The first prestige rankings obtained were based on a 1947 survey of 2,920 individuals who were asked to classify the *general standing* of each of 90 occupations. No mention was made of prestige. The most frequently cited reasons for awarding a given occupation an excellent standing, in order of decreasing frequency, were that it paid well (18 percent), served humanity (16 percent), required a lot of previous training and investment (14 percent), and had a high level of prestige associated with it (14 percent) (Hodge et al., 1964). This list has changed over time, however. The most recent polling data gives high prestige rankings to a variety of blue-collar, white-collar, and service occupations in different institutional areas (Harris Polls, 2014). Clearly, an association with high earnings is not enough to give an occupation a high ranking; for example, real estate agents and stockbrokers are at the bottom of the list and a number of the occupations chosen as the most prestigious are those that serve humanity (fire fighter, scientist, doctor, nurse).

One somewhat surprising determinant of occupational prestige involves the level of gender segregation, with more segregated occupations receiving higher scores. In other words, both male- and female-dominated professions are judged to be more prestigious than mixed-gender occupations. Racial segregation also has an impact, but in this case, only White-dominated occupations get the prestige bump. Finally, it appears that people's positionality affects how they rank occupations (Valentino, 2019). For example, racial/ethnic minorities place a particularly high value on jobs that involve "service, care for others, and social advancements" (Pérez Huber et al., 2018, p. 14).

There is some evidence that COVID-19 has changed our ideas about occupational status. The pandemic revealed that several low-wage, historically low-prestige occupations including grocery store workers, health care workers, and garbage collectors are an absolutely essential part of the economy. This realization led to efforts to laud these workers. For example, New Yorkers clapped for healthcare workers every night at 7 pm. It is not clear, however, if there will be long-term changes in the level of prestige given their occupations, nor is it clear that their wages will be increased. In response to the appreciation they were given, some health care workers commented that "you can't eat applause"(De Camargo & Whiley, 2020).

Education

Like occupation, education is considered an important and valuable dimension of one's life. The level of education is assumed to be related to the level of knowledge and skill one has in a particular field. In addition, education prepares one for a particular status group. The type of education, as well as the place where it is received, are bases for prestige. A degree from an Ivy League school such as Yale or Harvard, or a small private school such as Amherst or Smith is quite prestigious compared to a degree from a local community college. The elitism and degree of selectivity associated with a school are linked to the level of prestige accorded to it.

Elite private secondary schools, such as Phillips Andover Academy, appeared in the 1770s. Analysis of the history of these schools supports the conclusion that they were developed as a tool for the established upper class to isolate itself and achieve social closure. Initially, the founders hoped that these schools would help separate their cultural group from the new wealth developing in industry and from the increasing numbers of lower-class immigrants. But the expense of running these schools pressured administrators to take in some of the sons of individuals who had become recently wealthy from industrial, manufacturing, or other enterprises in the latter part of the nineteenth century (Levine, 1980). These *nouveaux riches* (new rich) consequently infiltrated the boarding schools even though the established patrician families winced because the former were often seen as lacking in manners and polish.

Today, elite preparatory high schools continue to be a powerful tool used by the rich to cement class advantage and ensure solidarity. A large part of the education for students in these schools involves learning how to be proper members of their class. In his ethnography of an elite boarding school, Gaztambide-Fernandez (2009) points out that the school must teach "the symbolic materials and subjective dispositions that are required to demonstrate membership in particular status groups" (p. 11). As part of this, students must learn to believe that their privilege is legitimate. This is done both by "having individuals work hard enough so that they feel they can deserve what they have and keeping them separate from the rest of the world that doesn't share their assumptions about the highly unequal distribution of rewards" (Cookson & Persell, 2010, p. 26). In contrast, most public schools in working-class areas do the exact opposite—they discourage class consciousness and emphasize individuality and individual effort (Finn, 2012). It is rare that the two worlds meet, as boarding school students are together 24 hours a day. The hothouse, intense, closed setting of the prep school helps to foster "brick wall syndrome," a belief that exclusivity should be the norm and that there is nothing wrong with the separation of this group of students from those in the outside society (Kendall, 2002).

In recent years, pressure has been mounting on elite schools to increase both income and racial diversity. And, in fact, their student bodies have become more diverse over time although the students who attend are still disproportionately well-off (Murnane et al., 2018). While scholarships and financial aid are available, the high cost of the prestigious secondary schools makes them out of reach for most Americans. For example, the full cost for students who board at Andover for the 2021–2022 school year is $61,950. In addition to being well-off, students at private schools are also disproportionately White. About 12 percent of White children attend private elementary and secondary schools, the comparable number for Black children is 6 percent, 4 percent for Hispanics, 11 percent for Asians, and 5 percent for Native Americans (Hussar et al., 2020).

Higher education, like primary and secondary education, is segregated by class and race. For example, about 37 percent of the students in the highest income quintile attend highly selective four-year colleges. The equivalent percentage for the lowest quintile is 7 percent (Fain, 2019). Black and Hispanic students are underrepresented in college enrollment, and this is especially true at selective colleges (Carnevale et al., 2018; Hussar et al., 2020). It might be tempting to think that differences in admittance to selective colleges is a result of academic preparation. But a recent study of college admissions comparing students with the same ACT and SAT scores shows that it is income, not ability, that explains why the rich are disproportionately in colleges (Chetty et al., 2020). A second study finds that Black and Latino students with above average standardized test scores are underrepresented in selective public colleges (Carnevale et al., 2018).

One of the reasons for the overrepresentation of well-off White students in elite colleges is that, as described, they disproportionately attend top preparatory schools. A recent survey found that a full 10 percent of students who attend these private schools end up at an Ivy League college, while only 1 percent of their public school counterparts do (Gallup and NAIS, 2017). Elite private schools put forth a huge amount of effort and expense to ensure that their students go on to the most prestigious colleges in the country. Additionally, the parents of many of the children of the wealthy attended prestigious colleges themselves, making their kids eligible for legacy preferences given to the sons and daughters of alumni. This **legacy** policy illustrates not only the passing on of social status between generations but also high-status schools' tendencies toward exclusivity and boundary maintenance (Kahlenberg, 2010).

Of course, like elite secondary schools, prestigious colleges do not just admit children of the upper class. They have also become more diverse over time. The transition to these colleges can be difficult for working class and minority students, however. A study with lower-income Black and Latino students enrolled at an elite college found that many felt out of place and had difficulty adapting to the culture. Interestingly, this was much less true of the students who had attended a selective private high school. They had already learned how to navigate environments dominated by White well-off students (Jack, 2019).

The discomfort poor and minority students can feel at elite colleges is a strong indicator of how the schools reflect the lifestyles, behavior, and values of the upper class. Jose, a student interviewed in the study mentioned above commented,

> Being in this toxic environment without resources changes us. When I got here, I was invincible. Over time, I started breaking down. If I went to another school where I was comfortable, I would be more of a leader. Since coming (here), I've become quiet, more conscious, especially in the classroom. In a social setting, I'll talk to you. In class, I shut up. In a class with more people of color, people that I can relate to, I feel comfortable. The thing is (here) [Being in a class with students of color] doesn't really happen.

Jose's comment shows how the disconnect between his experiences and the culture of the elite college made it difficult for him to fully participate in the life of the institution.

Attending an elite school confers status, but as described at the beginning of this section, there are even social hierarchies within those same schools. For example, elites understand that getting into the right fraternity or sorority can provide opportunities for social networking and class cultivation. Among the values and skills learned in these organizations are the importance of screening potential members, allegiance to your "own kind" of people, and the development of social networks that will be helpful in later years (Kendall, 2002; Robbins, 2004). It is no accident that, since 1910, a full 84 percent of Supreme Court judges were fraternity members. If you exclude the four women justices, this number increases to 91 percent. The situation is similar for the presidency, with 68 percent of presidents since 1877 having pledged fraternities (Konnikova, 2014, numbers post-2014 calculated by author).

Racial and ethnic minorities were not allowed to join all-White Greek organizations until the late 1960s, and then were largely kept out by selection processes at the local level. There are no national data on the demographic composition of Greek organizations, but research done at Princeton found that about three quarters of members were White, compared to just 47 percent of the student population. It should be noted that there are a variety of multicultural fraternities and sororities today, but majority White Greek organizations still command the largest and most powerful alumni networks. People from the working and lower classes tend to be locked out of these prestigious fraternities and sororities. At Princeton, 95 percent of members were from the richest quarter of Americans. This is partly because the dues to be a Greek member are extremely high, making it unaffordable for many students, but it is also reflective of preferences given to

Photo 4.1 Even the classical architecture and spacious, finely manicured grounds of prestigious prep schools conspire to create a feeling of tradition and specialness among their students.
Source: Photo by Charles E. Hurst.

legacies (Chang, 2014). Issues of racism and elitism in the Greek system have recently sparked an "Abolish Greek Life" movement among members of fraternities and sororities at schools including Vanderbilt, Duke, and Emory (Marcus, 2020).

Fraternities and sororities are fairly obvious examples of status groups with the potential to impact later occupational success, but it turns out that even the choice of sports team can make a difference. Lauren Rivera (2015) studied the hiring processes for entry-level positions at the nation's top-tier investment banks, law firms, and management consulting firms. Clear preference was given to students from elite schools with extra points awarded to those who had engaged in activities associated with the upper class (such as lacrosse, tennis, and crew rather than football or wrestling).

Wealth

One of the reasons having a particular amount and type of *wealth* and/or income is important in determining status is because economic resources serve as a control on the kind of lifestyle one can afford. The right kind and level of consumption may gain one entrance into the upper class. The use of inherited wealth, family lineage, club membership, quality of education, and general lifestyle as criteria for membership into the established upper class helps maintain the exclusivity of that class. We have already seen how boarding schools function in this regard. Practicing endogamy also helps determine who can get into "Society."

As described in Chapter 3, some believe that the United States contains a national urban upper class with its own tradition that is tightly knit and class conscious. This upper class has been buttressed historically by institutions that serve its members, such as boarding schools, select eastern universities and colleges, and the Episcopal Church (see, for example, Domhoff, 1971; Ostrander, 1983). The upper class as a status group practices a particular kind of lifestyle with distinct rules associated with it. Specifically, children are expected to be well-bred, with manners and a sense of their importance in society. Boarding schools are a principal source of this train-ing, but family ties are also central. Keeping the family line intact and marrying the right kind of person are important. Marriages are not made as independently as might be the case in other social classes. But some restricted social activities, such as debutante balls and fox hunts, which once were prominent elements in the lifestyle of the upper class, have declined in recent years. Acceptable occupations include financier, lawyer, business executive, physician, art collector, museum director, and even architect. Living in an exclusive residence separate from middle- and lower-class neighborhoods and maintaining a second summer home are also the means by which separation from outsiders is preserved.

Upper-class families tend to have a traditional structure with a husband who is in the paid labor force and a wife who is not. Recent data show that families in which men earn over $250,000 a year have the highest rate of mothers who opt out of paid work (VerBruggen & Wang, 2019). Frequently, wealthy women are expected to be involved in charitable activities and other social events.

Evidence suggests that members of this upper-status group are concerned with maintaining their separation from others, even in death. Their burial customs and sites tend to be different from those of people from the lower classes (Cassell et al., 2005). A historical analysis of cemeteries in the United States noted the long-term attempts by the middle and upper classes to segregate themselves physically in burial sites from those of a lowlier status, and to freely use monuments and mausoleums to proclaim their status. Mausoleums and monuments have experienced a resur-gence in popularity recently. Well-off people can purchase "million dollar mausoleums" that will remind viewers of how much success was attained during one's lifetime (Chen, 2013). As these characteristics indicate, "members of the upper class not only have *more*, they have *different*" (Domhoff, 1971, p. 91).

Weber thought that status groups are ranked according to their patterns of consumption as manifested in their lifestyles (as cited in Gerth & Mills, 1962, p. 193). Many possessions have a level of prestige that differs drastically from their actual monetary value. For example, consider the relative prestige of a new Chevy pickup and an older BMW, both of which may cost the same amount. It is not so much the economic value *per se* of the consumed goods that is important, but rather the fact that these goods, especially if owned by a higher-ranking status group, serve as symbols of worth and ability. It becomes a matter of self-respect and honor to conspicuously display such goods, not merely to "keep up with the Joneses" but to surpass them if possible (Veblen, 1953).

The linkage of class position to status is most clearly seen in the arguments of Thorstein Veblen. His discussion of status applies most directly to the period up to the early part of the twentieth century. Veblen contended that manual labor had become defined as dishonorable, undignified, and not befitting one who wished to be considered of high social status. On the other hand, he argued that nonproductive labor, such as that of being a business executive, increased the probability of owning great amounts of property, which in turn increased one's status. Owning property had become, in Veblen's view, the equivalent of possessing honor. In order to show this to others, one has to engage in ostentatious displays of wealth, namely various forms of what he called "conspicuous consumption." This display serves as a symbol of one's worth and ability and covers a wide range of possessions, even such things as better-groomed lawns, ownership of prize horses, and expensive dress. Everyone battles in this competition, according to Veblen, but the upper class has the ability to be the most successful.

Especially in open and democratic societies, the salience and ranking of status symbols wax and wane over time. In one year, having a particular characteristic or possession may result in great prestige, but a few years later, that same possession may be of little social impor-tance, while another has ascended to a high position. Interestingly, it appears that the level of income inequality has an effect on the importance of status goods. An analysis of Google search terms (Walasek & Brown, 2015) suggests that people are more interested in status symbols (such as designer clothing) in states with higher levels of income inequality than in those with lower levels.

Part of Veblen's argument about conspicuous consumption was that people admired the upper class and wanted to appear to be a part of it. More recent research, however, shows a somewhat more nuanced portrait. Widespread images of all the classes can be found in the media, revealing Americans' subjective views about each group. For example, Kendall's (2011) study of newspaper and television characterizations of classes uncovered a variety of both positive and negative presentations of each class. The upper class is portrayed as just regular people who are generous, materialistic, and worthy of emulation, but also sometimes unhappy, unfulfilled, and deviant. Some media coverage portrays them as greedy and criminal. National polling data shows similar contradictory attitudes with 60 percent of Americans saying that they believe that most rich people earned their wealth, but 38 percent saying that the rich made money by "taking advantage of other people" (Ekins, 2019).

Similarly, a study by Hahl and Zuckerman (2014) found that people are suspicious of high-status actors and are more likely to see them as cold, calculating, and less authentic than low-status actors. Interestingly, people of all statuses harbor these same beliefs. This may be because people recognize that there are incentives to cheat and trample on other people to gain status. These possibilities throw into question high-status people's actions. To allay these suspicions, the researchers found that high-status people sometimes try to find ways to prove their sincerity, or they appropriate symbols of lower-status culture to signal their authenticity.

BOX 4.1 THE STRESSES OF TOO MUCH VERSUS TOO LITTLE

Throughout the text, there are numerous discussions of the negative effects of being on the bottom of the socioeconomic ladder. The poor are worse off when it comes to basic life chances such as health, hunger, and homelessness. They also have less social status and political power than others. Does this mean that the very wealthy are without significant problems? After all, they can afford the homes, vacations, and lifestyles they want. Money can provide the physical comforts and much of the security that everyone desires.

But what are the stresses, if any, associated with being wealthy? Many religious groups consider too much wealth to be dangerous because it can potentially weaken a sense of community and increase egoism. One of the authors of this text found this to be the case among the Amish (Hurst & McConnell, 2010). Wealth is seductive, but it holds hidden dangers: "It's just like eating," one Amish businessman said, "we have to eat but if we don't discipline ourselves, we become gluttons."

In their interviews with 130 millionaires, some of whom had inherited their wealth while others were self-made, Schervish et al. (1994) found that most felt that a lot of money does not guarantee happiness or that one will be taken seriously. One millionaire entrepreneur, for example, admitted that while she has been very successful, she also believes that she is often not taken seriously because she is a woman. In effect, her wealth does not save her from being a victim of prejudice. Some of the interviewed wealthy wish they had spent more time with their children. Guilt about having inherited wealth is also a recurrent theme in the self-told stories of many of these millionaires. This feeling makes many want to prove their worth by their own achievements and contributions. Wealth also draws the jealousy and envy of others, and the sense that one was just lucky or more ruthless than others.

Recent research suggests that the wealthy may differ from those in the lower class in other ways as well. For example, it appears that wealthy people score lower on tests of empathy, generosity, helpfulness, and compassion (Kraus et al., 2010; Piff et al., 2010; Stellar et al., 2012). One hypothesis that explains this finding is that poorer people are forced to rely more on personal connections for survival and, thus, they need to be very aware of the emotions of others. A related hypothesis is that poor people are more aware of their environments because they have less control and more often have to respond to threats (such as foreclosure or crime). When a person thinks they might have to respond quickly to a threat, it pays to be very aware of their surroundings and the feelings of the people around them.

   The lesson here is that while wealth may allow one to have more possessions, better health care, and a fancier lifestyle, it has its own attendant pressures and stresses. A question for you to consider is how much wealth is enough to live a happy, meaningful life. What do you think?

Poverty and Welfare

As with the upper class, there are strong images and stereotypes of poor people, and these deeply affect their status in society. Importantly, these stereotypes are linked to how we explain poverty. Throughout most of US history, Americans have focused in one way or another on alleged weaknesses among the poor themselves, rather than on structural factors, as the cause of their plight. This was heavily influenced by the English approach, codified in the Elizabethan Poor Law of 1601. This law distinguished between the deserving and undeserving poor. The undeserving were those who were seen as able to work and thus, as not worthy of any help. The stereotypes attached to this group tended to be uniformly bad. The deserving category included pregnant women, disabled people, and children (Katz, 1996). Here there were more ambivalent stereotypes, often portraying the deserving group as incompetent but warm (Durante et al., 2013).

   The willingness to accept the idea that at least some categories of poor people are responsible for their own condition makes sense, given the American value of individualism/autonomy. The quintessential image of the pioneer as someone who, when confronted by the rigors of frontier life, worked hard and took responsibility for their own fate, has been ingrained in the American psyche as what true Americans should be like. Despite the fact that most early Americans traveled and lived in groups, the idea of the rugged individual has held great appeal (Hirschfield, 2015). While perceptions of the poor as lazy and undeserving have lessened during economic downturns, even in times of extreme economic stress such as the Great Depression, the poor were by and large characterized as immoral, and relief was seen as morally suspect (Katz, 2013). Negative stereotypes and misperceptions of the poor persist today and are often reinforced by the media focusing on the personal characteristics or failings of the poor, rather than on structural or societal issues (Santiago, 2015). These distortions and stereotypes matter because research demonstrates that how we represent the plight of the poor has important consequences for public policy (Rose and Baumgartner, 2013; Santiago, 2015). We discuss some of the most prevalent and powerful myths that shape policy below:

1. *Poor people have more children than non-poor people*
   In truth, while poor families do have somewhat more children than other families, the difference is small. For example, in 2020, the average size of all US families was 3.13 people, while that of poor families was 3.42. Looking just at married couple households, the average household size was 3.16 compared to 3.57 for families in poverty (US Census Bureau, 2021b). The Bureau of Labor Statistics found that there was no difference in family size between those receiving public assistance and those not (Foster and Rojas, 2018). Thus, the differences in household composition between those on welfare and others are not nearly as great as stereotypes would suggest.

2. *Welfare encourages childbearing and discourages marriage*

In the 1990s, a group of policymakers developed a rule called the "family cap." This rule was based on the myth that women on welfare have additional children to increase their benefits. Adopted in 24 states, it capped benefits for families, meaning that if they had more children while on the TANF program, they would not receive more money. This policy change provided researchers with a real-life experiment. They were able to compare childbearing among TANF recipients in states with the family cap to those in states without it. They discovered that there was no difference, suggesting that childbearing decisions have little to do with benefit levels. In other words, people simply do not have children to get additional money (CRRJ, 2016).

Similar to concerns about childbearing, a great deal of controversy exists over whether public assistance fosters the disintegration of marriages and encourages non-marital childbirth. Most studies, however, have found no relationship between benefit levels; family dissolution, and non-marital childbirth (e.g., Kearney and Levine, 2012; W. J. Wilson, 2012). Changes in family composition are more closely tied to shifts in attitudes about families and divorce as well as to broader events in the economy. Family dissolution and reluctance to marry are related, for example, to the availability of employment opportunities for women and to concerns about the amount men (particularly Black men who face notably strong discrimination in employment) are able to contribute to the family (Edin & Kefalas, 2011).

3. *The poor waste their money on frivolous purchases*

Evidence from the 2020 Consumer Expenditure Survey conducted by the US Department of Labor suggests that poor people spend the majority of their incomes on basic needs. Table 4.1 compares the percentages and amounts of income spent on different items by households in the poorest income quintile with the percentages spent by those in the richest income quintile. Total expenditures for those in the lowest quintile are almost exactly one-fourth of those of the top quintile ($28,724 vs. $114,840). In terms of how income is spent, about two-thirds of the total is spent on housing, food, and utilities by the lowest-level households. An additional 9.7 percent is spent on health care. Significant for future quality of life, only 2.1 percent of the expenditures is put aside for insurance and pensions. In contrast, while they spend more in absolute terms in each category, smaller *percentages* are spent by the richest quintile on housing, food, and health care. But these households

Table 4.1 Average Annual Expenditures and Percentages Spent in Major Categories for Lowest and Highest Income Quintiles: 2020

Major Spending Category	Lowest Income Quintile		Highest Income Quintile	
	Amount	Percentage	Amount	Percentage
Housing	$12,317	40.9	$36,645	31.9
Food	$4,099	14.3	$12,245	10.7
Utilities	$2,757	9.6	$5,848	5.1
Health Care	$2,775	9.7	$7,931	6.9
Entertainment	$1,192	4.2	$5,940	5.2
Insurance and Pensions	$610	2.1	$19,952	17.4
Average Annual Expenditures	$28,724	100	$114,840	100

Source: BLS (2021b), *Consumer Expenditures in 2020*, Table 1101. https://www.bls.gov/cex/tables/calendar-year/mean-item-share-average-standard-error/cu-income-quintiles-before-taxes-2020.pdf

spend over eight times as much money as the lowest income group on insurance and pensions, providing them with a better foundation for a stable future.

4. *Most poor people are unemployed*

Perhaps the most consequential perception of the poor involves their attachment to work and the work ethic. As mentioned earlier, the value of work is deeply ingrained in US culture, as is the belief that most people can succeed if they try hard enough. The truth, however, is that many poor people work. Census data reveal that, in 2020, 57 percent of all poor people aged 18 to 64 held full-time jobs. An additional 21 percent worked part-time (Shrider et al., 2021 Table B-1). This resulted in a situation where a full four percent of workers who were in the labor force for at least 27 weeks were in poverty (US Bureau of Labor Statistics, 2021f). This is not surprising since working 40 hours per week for 50 weeks at the minimum wage of $7.25 would provide a household income of $14,500, just over half of the amount needed to raise a family of four (two parents, two children) above the poverty level. It should also be noted that many of the poor who do not work are either elderly or disabled.

5. *Poor people don't want to work*

The data cited above indicate that many poor individuals work, but despite their efforts, they remain poor. But do they want to work? This question has been at the forefront of public discussion during the pandemic because unemployment benefits were increased. When companies began hiring again, they were hard pressed to find workers. Many governors believed that the problem was that people simply preferred unemployment to work. Two major studies of this question found somewhat conflicting results. In one, enhanced unemployment benefits had no impact on people's willingness to return to work (Altonji et al., 2020). On the other, a 10 percent increase in benefits was correlated with a 3.6 percent decline in applications (Marinescu et al., 2021). This indicates that, if there is an effect of unemployment benefits on willingness to apply to jobs, it is fairly minimal. It is likely that other factors like a lack of childcare are more significant than the expanded unemployment benefits. Older research backs up the idea that government assistance does not reduce work. One study, for example, found that the same percentage of people work in areas with high levels of SNAP benefits as those in low benefit areas (Moffitt, 2015). The fact is that most Americans want to work. When asked if they would continue to work even if they won the lottery, 70 percent of American adults said that they would (Sawhill & Pulliam, 2018). This includes people with disabilities, nearly 70 percent of whom report a desire to work (Kessler Foundation, 2015). Interviews with poor single mothers confirm these general findings. Work "gives me a feeling of accomplishment"; it shows my children "a good example." "When I don't work, I feel useless like I'm wasting my life." "I don't want to live on welfare" (Hennessy, 2009, pp. 566–567). These findings should not be surprising given that work is a hub around which many Americans' most cherished values revolve. Work is a major source of self-esteem and identity.

6. *The vast majority of welfare recipients are people of color*

As we saw in Chapter 3, while people of color are overrepresented among TANF recipients, the actual number of White, Black, and Hispanic recipients from each group is about equal. The myth that people of color—particularly Black people—receive the lion's share of welfare, payments however, is pervasive. One reason for this belief is that Black people are disproportionately portrayed in images of the poor and welfare recipients, whereas Hispanic and White people are underrepresented (van Doorn, 2015). The stereotype about race and welfare receipt is somewhat ironic, given that policies have historically precluded many people of color from receiving welfare at all. For example, Black soldiers returning from World War II were not allowed to take advantage of the interest-free mortgage program that enabled thousands of White veterans to purchase homes. Agricultural and domestic workers, who were disproportionately people of color, were initially excluded from the Social Security Program. In the early years of TANF (then under the name ADC), states were given enough leeway that they found ways to deny most Black children support. In the 1940s and 1950s, some instituted morals-based policies, denying children aid if the mother was suspected of having sex out of wedlock. When Louisiana instituted this policy, 95 percent of the mothers who were cut off were Black—a signal of disproportionate suspicion and surveillance of those mothers (Floyd et al., 2021). Starting in the 1960s and 1970s, federal oversight ensured that more Black people could qualify for welfare (Floyd et al., 2021). This led to a significant backlash, however, and decreasing levels of public support for the programs (Ward, 2020). President Reagan deepened the stereotypes with his rhetoric about "welfare queens," women who supposedly bilked the welfare system for thousands of undeserved dollars. Today, popular stereotypes about race continue to be a major reason for the negative view of welfare and its beneficiaries (Masters et al., 2014).

7. *Many welfare recipients commit fraud*

While there are certainly welfare recipients who commit fraud, research suggests that it is only a small percentage, and that, in almost all cases, only a minor amount of money is involved (Aussenberg, 2018). Fraud is a particular problem in the Medicaid Program, but the primary beneficiaries are doctors and other health care providers. In 2017, the federal government arrested hundreds of health care workers for fraudulently charging Medicaid for prescriptions that they never purchased, for tests that were never performed, and for selling prescriptions to patients for cash (while also billing Medicaid). The fraud totaled $1.3 billion (Ruiz, 2017). At the same time, there was a surge in fraud when the CARES Act made more money available to more unemployed people during the pandemic. Because so many people needed the money right away, there were fewer safeguards to protect against fraud. These safeguards were put in place in later rounds of assistance (Iacurci, 2021).

In sum, negative, and incorrect, stereotypes of the poor and welfare recipients lead to low status and to a lack of support for welfare programs to help them. As we discuss in Chapter 14, the negative connotations about poverty have also made it difficult for poor people to band together to press for more rights. But interestingly, recent research has shown that COVID-19 caused the public's attributions of poverty to shift more toward situational factors and away from moral ones (Wiwad et al., 2021). A January 2020 Pew survey even found that about 71 percent of Americans agree that people are poor because "they have faced more obstacles in life than most other people." About 26 percent said that the people are poor because they don't work as hard as others (Pew Research Center, 2020a). It is not clear if this is a long-term trend, or if it will shift back as the impact of the pandemic fades. The answer to that question may determine the direction of public policy toward poverty and inequality going forward.

Physical Appearance and Status

While we may not often think of it in these terms, physical appearance is an important basis for social status. "In twentieth-century American society, physical beauty emerged as a resource, like wealth or talent" (Rubenstein, 2001, p. 212). Beauty, of course, is in the eyes of the beholder, but what the beholder sees and how it is interpreted are shaped by culture's values. Beauty is a social construction. The definitions of beauty and other status symbols vary among societies and even among different groups in the same society. For example, research has revealed somewhat different views of beauty in the United States by race and ethnicity (Webb et al., 2013). Beauty standards also change over time. The beauty of the human figure portrayed in a Rubens painting is not the same ideal of beauty seen today in the clothing ads of Victoria's Secret or Dior.

The term "**lookism**" refers to discrimination based on how well people conform to beauty standards. Its prevalence in society reinforces how physical attractiveness is linked to status. The impact of lookism is evident even very early in life with young children recognizing and preferring attractive people (Principe & Langlois, 2013). But beauty—like other status characteristics—is not simply valuable for its own sake, but rather because it is associated with other positive qualities. As a diffuse status, it affects perceptions of competence across domains. For example, physically attractive people are seen as more trustworthy (Zhao et al., 2015). They are also more likely to obtain jobs, although interestingly, they may be less likely to be offered jobs that are considered undesirable because employers assume that good-looking people have a sense of entitlement that will make them unhappy in those jobs (Lee et al., 2018). Once hired, attractive employees earn more than less attractive workers and are promoted more rapidly (Hamermesh, 2011; Rhode, 2010). People who are rated as physically attractive also tend to have better psychological health and lower rates of depression (Datta Gupta et al., 2016). A recent study shows that people who are rated as better-looking have a more positive outlook on life. This is probably related to the fact that they do, in fact, experience greater upward mobility than others (Urbatsch, 2018).

We see the impact of beauty in both politics and law. The authors of one study conducted an experiment in which likely voters were sent information about candidates that either included photos or did not. The respondents were then asked for whom they planned to vote. Those respondents who received photos were more likely to choose the attractive candidate over the less attractive ones (Ahler et al., 2017). In criminal cases, female defendants who are more physically attractive tend to be arrested and convicted less often (Beaver et al., 2019). While these kinds of lookism have occurred for a very long time, there is some evidence that the era of selfies has increased people's willingness to accept it (Chae, 2019).

The studies we just discussed show that being beautiful bestows many benefits, but we know that there can also be disadvantages. For example, because people expect more from highly attractive people, they can be easily disappointed when their expectations fail to match reality. One study found that beautiful people are assumed to be more cooperative than others, but if they turn out not to be so, they are harshly judged (Andreoni & Petrie, 2008). Similarly, attractive college instructors receive higher teaching evaluations and students are more likely to attend their classes but when they fall short of students' expectations, they are punished more heavily than less attractive instructors, particularly if they are men (Wolbring & Riordan, 2016). Another kind of "beauty penalty" was observed in a study of an online business lending market. Across the board, women were less likely to be offered a loan than men. Looking only at women applicants, however, the researchers found those who were physically attractive were less successful. It is possible that attractiveness is associated with femininity, which is seen as disadvantageous in the male-dominated world of business (Kuwabara & Thébaud, 2017).

Beauty is linked to inequality between individuals, but it also has an impact at the group level because it reinforces gender inequality. Many popular folktales (e.g., Cinderella, Snow White) are those that stress the value of female rather than male beauty. This consistent encouragement to be beautiful may discourage women from pursuing roles, activities, or positions that will make them appear less attractive. It also takes a great deal of time and money to achieve a culturally determined standard of beauty. This is time and money that could instead be used to fully develop women's mental, political, and economic potential (Wolf, 2002). Some argue that, as women have faced fewer external constraints on their activities, the ideal of beauty becomes an even more important way to limit their activities and reduce the chance they will try and compete in male-dominated occupations (Baker-Sperry & Grauerholz, 2003).

The widespread use by women of elective plastic surgery, liposuction, and cosmetics that promise to make them look younger suggests the importance of appearance in their lives. In 2020, over 15 million cosmetic procedures were performed in the United States. Most of these

Photo 4.2 In the United States, physical beauty is a currency that can be cashed in for improved social status. The subjective importance placed on beauty is indicated by the more than 17 million cosmetic procedures performed in the United States in 2016, according to the American Society of Plastic Surgeons. Over 90 percent of these surgeries were on women.

Source: © People Images/Getty Images.

were minimally invasive, like Botox, but 2.3 million involved surgery (American Society of Plastic Surgeons, 2021). This is fairly remarkable given that many people chose to forgo elective procedures during the pandemic.

It is well established that one of the most often-used status symbols concerns fashions in clothing. Veblen (1953) observed that clothing was particularly well suited to being a status symbol since "our apparel is always in evidence and affords an indication of our pecuniary standing to all observers at the first glance" (p. 119). Undoubtedly, how we dress affects the attitudes and behavior of others toward us.

Clothing takes on multiple meanings depending on the wearer and the location in which they are being worn. For example, in the 1970s, hoodies were associated with skaters, punk rock, and the nascent hip-hop movement (D. Wilson, 2012). After Trayvon Martin, a 17-year-old unarmed Black youth was killed while wearing a hoodie, they became a symbol of protest. In 2015, a legislator in Oklahoma proposed a law that would prohibit wearing them in public. While the legislator claimed that hoodies obscure people's face, making it easier for them to commit crimes, critics charged that the bill was racially motivated since hoodies have become associated with Black youth (Stern, 2015). Hoodies are also worn as a statement of casual cool by celebrities such as Mark Zuckerberg, the founder of Facebook. Another way that clothing is related to status is through the assumption that a person's dress indicates something about their personality or morals. This is a particular issue facing women who are encouraged to dress sexy, but not too sexy, or their moral character will be thrown into question (Griffin et al., 2013).

Research suggests that clothing frequently evokes status-related reactions. Lurie (1987) argued that brands of clothes are marked in such a way that others can distinguish the high-status piece of clothing from an imitation. Interestingly, however, more recent research suggests that companies make brand markings on some items (such as sunglasses and handbags) more subtle on their most expensive items. The researchers believe that this is because high-status "insiders" want to make it harder for lower-status others to copy their style. They also found that because other high-status people can recognize more subtle symbols, they are an effective way to communicate with insiders and achieve social closure (Berger & Ward, 2010).

One particularly important aspect of American beauty standards involves body size. Like other status characteristics, the low-status category (obesity) has negative stereotypes attached to it. A review of the literature found that these stereotypes included being sloppy, careless, and lazy (Gordon et al., 2018). This suggests that obesity is a diffuse status. As a result, stigma against overweight people is significant. For example, weight has an impact on whether people are hired and whether they are judged as competent in their jobs (Caliendo & Lee, 2013; King et al., 2016). Overweight people tend to have lower life expectancies than non-overweight people. This appears, in large part, to be due to stress caused by discrimination rather than by complications from weight (Sutin et al., 2015). Similarly, research suggests that children who are obese are less likely than others to end up attending college (Ryabov, 2018).

People are well aware that obesity is linked to negative evaluations. This leads them to both worry about their weight and to try and lose weight. For example, between 2013 and 2016, over 36 percent of adolescents tried to lose weight (45.2 percent of girls and 30.1 percent of boys) (McDow et al., 2019). While both Black and White young women are conscious of their bodies, White women are particularly likely to have negative feelings about their body shape and weight (Greenwood & Dal Cin, 2012).

Some denigrated status groups find support by spending time with other people who belong to the same status. For example, gay and lesbian people have long formed groups for activism and support. Overweight people, however, are different because they hold many of the same negative stereotypes of the group as do non-overweight people. In a survey conducted with people in a weight loss program, respondents described obese people in more negative terms than they used for those people who were not obese (Carels et al., 2009). At the same time, there are numerous examples of activism to decrease stigma. The National Association to Advance Fat Acceptance (NAAFA) was founded over fifty years ago. This civil rights group works to fight discrimination and increase acceptance.

Disability and Status

There are many reasons to consider people with disabilities as a status group. First, being able-bodied is viewed as "normal," and any deviation from that state is seen as inferior (McRuer, 2006). This becomes clear when people with disabilities are asked to explain themselves or their condition. They also face stigma and stereotyping—from images of them as sexual predators, to asexual, to violent, to being like children. They are aware of the stigma and their categorization as "other" (Jahoda et al., 2010). In other words, many people with disabilities recognize themselves as a group with common interests. As described above, disability can be considered a diffuse status because it affects assessments of competence in a wide range of areas. For example, people in wheelchairs are sometimes talked to loudly or slowly as though they are also cognitively impaired.

Even though over one in five Americans reports having a disability and disability is clearly linked with status, the topic is rarely found in inequality texts (Courtney-Long et al., 2015). This is partly because the definition of disability is complex and can cover a huge range of conditions—some permanent and others temporary, some invisible and others not. Disabilities may or may not have a severe impact on a person's ability to live independently, just as some disabilities can incur huge medical costs while others do not. People whom society sees as disabled may or may not identify that way (Grue, 2016). A person who cannot see, for example, might consider herself to be blind but not disabled. A discussion of how disability relates to inequality is difficult for all these reasons but also because the lived experience of having a disability varies widely across categories of social class, sexuality, race, age, and gender (Bérubé, 2006).

Prior to the 1960s, people tended to think of disabilities in medical terms—as an impairment rooted in an individual's body. People with disabilities were urged to cope as best they could in private. They faced many forms of discrimination, including prohibitions from some jobs and educational opportunities. Many disabled people were institutionalized in oppressive facilities that—at best—only took care of their basic needs. Schools were not required to provide any sort of accommodations, and disabled children were sometimes not allowed to enroll at all. Some cities even had ordinances prohibiting physically disabled people from appearing in public so as to not offend the sensibilities of others. The **eugenics movement**, popular in the 1920s and 1930s, argued that disabled people should be prevented from procreating. As a result, laws and policies existed that allowed for disabled women's forced sterilization. Some of these policies were in existence until the 1970s (Ko, 2016). Laws also excluded disabled people from immigrating to the United States (Longmore & Goldberger, 2000). At the same time, there were charitable efforts—such as the March of Dimes—that were intended to help people with disabilities. Most of their attention and money, however, went to trying to find a cure rather than helping improve the lives of the people who were already living with a disability (Fleischer & Zames, 2001).

At the same time that people with disabilities were isolated and discriminated against, some still found ways to support each other and fight for rights and access. In the 1930s, six young adults came together to protest a government policy that classified disabled workers as "unemployable" regardless of their actual skills. The six were all well-educated and suited for many types of work but discrimination in the private sector meant that they were unable to find employment. When the government disqualified them from employment under the New Deal's programs (such as the Work Progress Administration), it was the last straw. For nine days, they staged a sit-in at the Emergency Relief Bureau in New York City. Their action prompted over a month of large protests and media coverage. It also resulted in the formation of the League of the Physically Handicapped, which went on to fight against other instances of discrimination in hiring, as well as demanding an expansion of relief (Longmore & Goldberger, 2000). Other organized groups came into existence in the 1940s, including former residents of state mental hospitals who began meeting on the steps of the New York Public Library. Calling themselves "We Are Not Alone," they provided support for each other (Cook & Jonikas, 2002).

What we today call the Disability Rights Movement (DRM) began in the 1960s. It was much more extensive than prior activism as it sought large-scale social change. Modeled on the civil rights movement, the DRM argued that the primary reason people with disabilities fail to thrive is not their impairment, but rather discrimination and lack of opportunity. Advocacy groups that had been set up around particular impairments (wheelchair users or blind people, for example) came together on a number of different initiatives.

One of the first important federal actions to address the needs of people with disabilities was the 1973 Rehabilitation Act. This law had many provisions that affected federal jobs (and employers who received federal funds), some of which barred discrimination on the basis of disability and required measures be taken to ensure access. The law was notable because it—like the DRM—recognized that many of the problems disabled people had were a result of discrimination, not impairments. It was also notable because it was the first time disabled people were defined as a group, rather than being categorized by their particular impairments (Mayerson, 1992). While the passage of the act was seen as a victory, regulations had to be put in place before it could actually be enforced. Disability rights activists from a wide range of groups fought for years for these regulations and staged several lengthy and well-publicized sit-ins. The regulations were finally passed in 1977.

The Rehabilitation Act was an important step forward in ensuring rights for people with disabilities, but it only covered jobs that involved federal funds. Because most jobs are in the private sector, activists began to seek broader protections. Disabilities were not included in the Civil Rights Act of 1964 (which did cover race, color, religion, national origin, and sex), so many activists began the fight to enact broad legislation that could protect disability rights. The Americans with Disabilities Act of 1990 was one result of these efforts. It defined disabilities in the same way as the Rehabilitation Act as, "a physical or mental impairment that substantially limits a major life activity, such as walking, seeing, hearing, learning, breathing, caring for one-self, or working." This definition was broadened in 2009 to more clearly encompass people with diseases such as cancer or diabetes. The law does not just protect those currently disabled but also those who have had a disability in the past or who are perceived to have a disability (whether or not they actually do) (EEOC, 2009; Fleischer & Zames, 2001). People who are alcoholics are included but current illegal drug users are not (but once they stop using drugs, they are considered disabled due to addiction). The law specifies that "reasonable accommodations" that do not cause "undue hardship" be made for people with disabilities (EEOC, 2002). There are some exceptions for small businesses that employ fewer than 15 people.

The ADA's coverage of mental disabilities, particularly mental illness, was controversial. This is probably because mental illness is highly stigmatized in our society. While mental illness was ultimately included, continuing stigma puts its sufferers in a difficult position: employees (and potential employees) may not want to disclose their illness to their workplace, but if they do not disclose, they are not covered by the ADA. One study of employers found high levels of negative beliefs about people with mental illnesses. It also revealed that companies that failed to comply with the ADA were more likely to espouse these negative beliefs (Scheid, 2005).

Another area of controversy that emerged in the debate about the ADA involved the inclusion of HIV/AIDS as a disability. While most members of Congress favored it, notable conservative members resisted because they associated HIV with gay men. The minority report from the Committee on Energy and Commerce, for example, said HIV's inclusion made the ADA a

Photo 4.3 A woman in a wheelchair looks at a building that has not been made compliant with the Americans with Disabilities Act.

Source: © fstop123/Getty Images.

"homosexual rights bill" (Colker, 2004). The ADA explicitly states that homosexuality is not a disability (which is consistent with the American Psychiatric Association's *Diagnostic and Statistical Manual*, see Chapter 8) but it also excludes "gender identity disorders not caused by a physical impairment." The latter category—at the time the ADA was passed—was considered to be a psychiatric condition (for information on the current view, see Chapter 8) (Barry et al., 2016).

The ADA has broad goals. It mandates accessibility to all public programs, full access to public transportation, access to any businesses that serve the public, and an end to wage and employment discrimination. Has it accomplished its goals? It appears that the employment rate of people with disabilities actually dropped somewhat after the passage of the ADA. It is not entirely clear why this is the case. It is possible that employers were wary of having to pay for accommodations when they hired people with disabilities (DeLeire, 2000). It is also possible that more people became classified as disabled, affecting the employment rate (Hotchkiss, 2004). The ADA has resulted in increased access to businesses and workplaces, although problems remain. For example, businesses do not need to make renovations if they are not "readily achievable." This means that expensive renovations (such as adding an elevator in an old building) are not mandated (Riley, 2016). Additionally, when the ADA was written, the internet was not publicly available, so nobody thought about what website accessibility would mean. Initially, government records and forms were required to be accessible, but this did not extend to any other domain (Lauffer, 2002). In 2019, a man named Guillermo Robles, who is blind, sued Domino's because it was impossible for him to order pizza on the website, even with a screen reader. While he lost the first case, he won on appeal and the US Supreme Court declined to hear Domino's appeal, leaving the lower court ruling intact. This decision means that all businesses must make their websites accessible to people with disabilities because they are essential "places of public accommodation."

Today, thanks in large part to the DRM, many people have moved away from a strictly medical definition of disability. This new social definition acknowledges how context and discrimination shape both the experience of disability as well as what we perceive it to include. Having dyslexia, for example, would not be considered a disability in our agricultural past (Ben-Moshe & Magaña, 2014). Other popular definitions of disability downplay limitations and emphasize how disability is an essential component of human variation. They argue that for a society to be its most successful, there must be a diversity of abilities and talents from which to draw. What may appear to be a disability today could very well be an adaptation that is valuable as our society changes (Koffmar, 2015).

Looking at the population today, mobility and cognition impairments are the most common types of disability. Women report higher levels of disability than men, and Black and White people report higher levels than do Hispanic and Asian people (US Bureau of Labor Statistics, 2021d). On average, working-age people with disabilities are more likely to be poor than their non-disabled peers (Brucker et al., 2015). This is in spite of the Supplemental Security Income (SSI) program that is available to elderly poor people and to people of all ages who have a disability. This means-tested program, which we discussed in Chapter 3, provides a monthly payment to those who qualify. On average, however, the amount of SSI payments only brings the income of recipients to less than three-quarters of the poverty line (Konish, 2021). This is one of the reasons that there is a much higher poverty rate (25 percent) among people aged 18–64 with disabilities than among the non-disabled in the same age group (9.3 percent) (Shrider et al., 2021).

In 2020, the disabled population had a much higher rate of unemployment than the non-disabled (12.6 percent compared to 7.9). Remember that unemployment is defined to include only people who are actively seeking work but cannot find it. If a person is too disabled to work, they are not counted in the rate. Unemployment varied by race with Black and Hispanic people with disabilities having higher levels of unemployment than Whites and Asians. Many

---

BOX 4.2 HIGH SCHOOL STATUS GROUPS

Think about your high school experience. What was the basis for status? What social groups existed and how were they arranged in a hierarchy? These questions have held great interest for moviemakers for years. Grease, for example, portrayed the T-Birds and Pink Ladies while the *Breakfast Club* showed characters from different social strata meeting in detention. The basis for status in high school changes over time and place, however, so it is unlikely your high school resembled Rydell High. One recent study finds three kinds of status groups in high schools: conventional (which includes students who have characteristics valued in the mainstream culture like money, good looks, or sports ability), countercultural groups (based around non-mainstream activities like doing drugs or dressing goth), and racial/ethnic groups (based on racial or ethnic identification). These groups are awarded different levels of status (Crabbe et al., 2019). What do you think about how status works in high school?

---

people with disabilities (80 percent) are simply out of the workforce—some because they are elderly and do not want to work, but others because they cannot get a job (US Bureau of Labor Statistics, 2021d).

Summary

This chapter has addressed the topic of social status, a form of inequality that is analytically separate from economic inequality, even though it is frequently based on an individual's economic resources. Status also can be based on occupation, education, lifestyle, physical appearance, and disability. The type of occupation one has, the kind of education one receives, the lifestyle one pursues, and the way one appears in public are each a badge of status. Each affects how others perceive us and how they treat us. Each also forms a basis for the groups with which we identify. Status groups, particularly those with high status, find ways to exclude others and legitimize their own position.

We learned that people with disabilities face particularly pernicious forms of discrimination but, through activism, have had some success in changing stereotypes and laws. Lookism results in less favorable outcomes for people who do not conform to beauty expectations. Poor people are another low-status group, although American attitudes about them are frequently ambivalent—unlike views of welfare recipients, which are more uniformly negative. Traditional values of individualism, independence, hard work, and material success encourage a negative attitude toward those who are not economically independent. At the same time, humanitarian and community values encourage people to take care of those who are less fortunate than themselves. These divergent beliefs have resulted in a somewhat bifurcated approach to poverty programs for the needy.

Critical Thinking

1. Discuss the new forms or bases of status developing in the United States. What are they, and how important are they? Will they replace status based on older grounds? Explain your answer.
2. How can individuals present themselves to others to indicate their membership in particular status groups?
3. On an everyday basis, how do students in junior high school and high school behave to maintain or enhance their social status among their peers? That is, how do they "do" status?
4. Does the formation of tightly knit status groups encourage fragmentation in the United States, or does it simply enrich and strengthen our diversity?

Web Connections

The US Census collects information about disability in the United States. You can check out their data at www.census.gov/topics/health/disability/data.html. If you are interested in the National Association to Advance Fat Acceptance, go to their website at www.naafaonline.com/dev2/about/index.html. They have information and resources there.

Film Suggestions

Crip Camp (2020). A documentary about a camp for children with disabilities and the impact it had on the disability rights movement.

Fattitude (2017). Looks at fat shaming in the United States and the prevalence of anti-fat bias with a hope to inspire change.

Born Rich (2003). Interviews with children born into wealthy families about what it is like to be born rich.

CinemAbility (2013). Examines media representations of disabled people and analyzes the effects such representations have on their inclusion.

Good Girls (Las Niñas Bien) (2018). A rich Mexican socialite deals with the crisis of the 1982 economic meltdown and the impact on her social status.

Killing Us Softly 4 (2010). Explores media advertising and images of women.

5 Power

The exercise of power and the experience of powerlessness are implicit in all the forms of inequality. The relationships between individuals who are wealthy and nonwealthy, men and women, gay and straight, and Black and White are frequently mediated by the relative economic, social, and cultural power of the groups to which they belong, and by the intersections of power between those groups. Power has a narrow political meaning as well, relating to the varied involvement and impact of individuals and groups in the government. In this chapter, we examine this political arena of power, beginning with the images of the political power structure in the United States and whether the evidence supports those images.

Portraits of National Power Structure

The founding architects of the US national government did not agree on how large or how strong it should be, nor did they consistently agree on whether everyone should have an equal influence on government. Washington and Adams, for example, believed in the need for a strong, centralized government, while Jefferson and Madison worried that such a government would move the country toward a European-style monarchy rather than a democracy.

Arguments over how widespread such power is continue to this day. Basically, the debate boils down to one over the extent of inequality in political power. Most of these views can be listed under one of the following types: (1) pluralist, (2) power elite, or (3) ruling class. The principal issue on which these approaches differ is the degree to which they see power as being concentrated in the United States.

The Pluralist View

In 1961, Robert Dahl famously asked, "in a political system where nearly every adult may vote but where knowledge, wealth, social position, access to officials, and other resources are unequally distributed, who actually governs?" (Dahl, 1961, p. 1). His answer was that, since the founding of the country, the United States has moved from governance by an oligarchy, where a few elites are in control, to a system of pluralism. This widely debated position envisions several competing groups and organizations that hold much of the power in the country but with none holding power all of the time. There is no central or **inner circle** that dominates or coordinates the connections between these groups because each is relatively autonomous and self-interested. Each group pursues issues that are of narrow interest to its organization; in those areas, it can have influence, but in others, it has little or no power. Generally, people have similar power resources, and not one source dominates.

With **pluralism,** one is given the impression of a society that is fundamentally based on a broad system of values about which there is a widespread consensus, even though the society is

DOI: 10.4324/9781003184966-6

composed of a variety of groups with specific interests that may be different. In this society, each individual is rational and free, and their interests are taken into account in one way or another by powerful organizations such as government or corporations. Power and powerlessness do not appear to be problems. The sharing of power actually helps the society to function.

Since its introduction in the post-World War II era, pluralism has been roundly criticized (Mills, 1956). The central criticisms, based on an analysis of current events, reflect skepticism about the actual extent of democracy in society. Critics argue that the notion of pluralism was developed in a post-war environment in which economic polarization was at a historic low, thus producing a more optimistic view of democratic engagement. They point out that the issues of concern to many people are frequently not dealt with by the government. In large part, this occurs either because these individuals are not in positions to make their interests known or because their interests are of less concern than those of people who hold positions of economic and social power and whose values are represented and reflected in the government (Connolly, 1969). Second, voluntary associations such as civic groups are no longer effective representatives of the average citizen, as they have themselves become oligarchic in nature. Finally, individuals in positions of organizational power do not represent the average member. Most members of voluntary associations do not have access to power (Kariel, in Connolly, 1969, p. 16).

Because of these critiques, some theorists propose a variant of pluralism called "neopluralism" (McFarland, 2007). This approach argues that "the outcomes of various political processes stem from the interaction of a range of specific, powerful individual and collective (group) actors below, outside, surrounding, cutting across and populating states and societies" (Cerny, 2017, p. 34). Thus, neopluralists acknowledge that, while there are multiple groups vying for power in the political arena, some of these groups do have more power than others. Neopluralist models have been particularly useful in explaining global political processes whereby international non-governmental organizations (NGOs), multinational corporations, and state and local governments interact across borders, creating a fragmented, cross-cutting political process. For example, in the context of environmental activism in China, Matsuzawa (2019) argues that rather than seeing political actions as being determined by hegemonic or imperialistic processes (either in terms of the state or international organizations), global environmental projects arise and are modified through interactions between NGOs, activists, researchers, and local government officials. These are the sorts of processes the neopluralists might address.

The Power-Elite View

One of the central critiques of pluralism discussed above stemmed from C. Wright Mills and his concept of the **power elite** (Mills, 1956). Though an old theory, Mills's portrayal of the power elite has drawn an inordinate amount of attention in the years since it was written, and it represents a prime example of a theory in opposition to the pluralist position. His essential argument is that power is centralized in a power elite that was brought into being by certain historical changes. As society has grown, institutions have become more complex, and national functions have become centralized in specific institutions—namely, the economy, military, and politics.

Mills contended that the tasks in top positions in each of the three key institutions have become so similar that it is now possible for the people who occupy them to interchange positions. In other words, a top military commander can easily become the CEO of a corporation. This means that, in addition to centralization in institutions, there has been an increasing coalescence, so much so that *three* separate political, military, and corporate elites are now *one* power elite made up of individuals in the highest positions in an interconnected set of institutions, which he called the "military industrial complex." "By the power elite, we refer to those political, economic, and military circles which as an intricate set of overlapping cliques share decisions having at least national consequences" (p. 18).

The nucleus of the power elite consists of those who hold high positions in more than one of the three major institutions, as well as those, such as prestigious lawyers and financiers, who serve to knit the three institutions together. The persons within this structure have their power because of their positions, although they do tend to come from the same kinds of economic, social, and educational backgrounds and do informally intermingle. Ultimately, however, it is their position that makes them powerful in national decision-making.

Some may feel that Congress is part of the power elite, but Mills did not agree. Rather, he referred to Congress as a "semi-organized stalemate" made up of people who, since they have their eyes on re-election, are concerned largely with the fluctuating local issues of their constituencies back home. In other words, such groups as the farm bloc, labor unions, white-collar workers, and Congress really have little to do with decisions of national consequence. These groups, specifically Congress, make up a middle level of power in the United States. If the competition of groups envisioned by pluralism operates at all, it is at this level, as congressional members exchange favors and make compromises, essentially balancing each other out.

Mills (1956) further believed that the wealthy and political officers who are entrenched in local interests will not become nationally important. As he stated, "to remain merely local is to fail" (p. 39). Local society has, by and large, been swallowed up by the national system of power and prestige. This is partly due to increasing urbanization, increasing satellite status of smaller towns, improved transportation networks, and the Internet. Again, there have been changes in the structure of the society that have resulted in the appearance of a particular kind of power structure.

At the bottom of this pyramidal power structure are the large majority of people who are quickly developing into a **mass society**. Masses are characterized by the fact that they are always on the receiving end of opinions, cannot or do not effectively respond to opinions expressed in the mass media, and really have no outlet for effective action in society. Mass media, largely controlled by those on the top of the power structure, have only served to weaken communications between the top and the bottom of the structure. The media tell people what their experiences are or should be and stereotype them. Education only serves to help people "adjust" to a society that is extremely hierarchical in terms of power. Voluntary associations, although they may be viewed theoretically as a link between the individual and the people at the top, do not perform this function because as they have grown, the individuals in them feel less powerful. Power is distant and inaccessible to average members.

Mills's power-elite theory has been criticized on several grounds, including the arguments that his terminology is vague and his selection of issues to test his theory is biased. Also, he has been faulted for choosing data that support his theory and ignoring contrary evidence. Third, some critics have attacked his conception of power as being too narrow in that it omits the role that moral and other kinds of authority may play in offsetting the power of an elite. His argument that power is based on position rather than actual decision-making has also been contested, as has his contention that power only flows from the top down. After Mills's death, the power of civil rights and the women's movement to influence policy confirmed the ability of those on the bottom to organize and have an impact. Finally, some have argued that Mills attributed too much independent power to the military and too little to Congress (Domhoff, 2006; Weston, 2010).

Despite these criticisms, Mills's analysis improved the quality of the debate about power differences and initiated a stream of research on national power structure. Moreover, recent headlines have substantiated his contention about the great power that military, corporate, and political institutions have over average citizens (Bacevich, 2017).

The Ruling-Class View

As we have seen, Mills's description of the power structure is one in which a group of individuals in high positions in core institutions dominate, while those at the bottom comprise an unorganized, ineffectual mass. The bottom has little power and offers little active resistance. Rather, these individuals are manipulated and educated in a manner that makes them almost willing subordinates in the society. The **ruling-class** view similarly proposes that a small group has inordinate political power in the society and that there are important interconnections between economic and political institutions. However, aside from these similarities, the ruling-class model differs from the power-elite model in three ways:

1. Rather than stressing several types of institutions as being involved in the elite, the ruling-class view emphasizes the dominance of the economic institution and position within it.
2. The ruling-class model often views the bottom of the power structure as being more active and effectual than the working class. It can organize and bring about change in the society. In the case of the power-elite model, the mass is largely passive in response to its position, whereas in the ruling-class model, the working class can be class-conscious and organized. Thus, the relationship between those on the top and those at the bottom is characterized more fully by conflict (Bottomore, 2006).
3. The relationship between the upper class or bourgeoisie and political power is portrayed as being much tighter than is the case in Mills's power-elite theory, in which the upper class and celebrities are more tangential to the political process. In Mills's view, it is strictly *institutional position*, not *personal wealth*, that leads to political power.

G. William Domhoff's argument that rich corporate owners constitute a "dominant class" that largely controls the political process is perhaps the best representation of a ruling-class theory of US politics. Briefly, Domhoff (1998, 2009) contends that a cohesive power elite dominates federal governmental affairs, and it is composed of those members of the upper class whose wealth is heavily concentrated in corporate holdings and who actively become involved in corporate affairs and political policy-making. Consequently, their power is based in both class position and corporate attachment. In addition, these individuals have similar backgrounds, often know each other, and have general political and economic interests in common. Because of the cohesiveness founded on these similarities, the upper class "is a *capitalist* class as well as a *social* class" (Domhoff, 1998, p. 116, emphasis added). Although there may be internal disagreements over specific policies, there is broad agreement over the general direction that policy should take. The corporate-based elite dominates the political arena through its heavy influence on public opinion, participation in lobbying through its powerful interest groups, and involvement in policy formation through foundations, boardroom discussions, and various research groups.

In contrast to Mills's view of the power elite, Domhoff does not suggest there is a mass society without voice and in which no group but the elite can have any real power. Rather, he notes that unions and different liberal groups frequently conflict with the corporate rich but that, generally, it is the latter group that sets the parameters within which conflict occurs. Domhoff is quick to point out that, given the size, internal disagreements, and bases of the dominant class, his is not a conspiracy theory. Rather his argument focuses on providing evidence that there is "an upper class that is tightly interconnected with the corporate community … [and] that the social cohesion that develops among members of the upper class is another basis for the creation of policy agreements" (1998, p. 71). In sum, while Domhoff does recognize that there are other bases of power, they pale in comparison to the inordinate power exercised by those with massive economic resources. Clearly, the pouring of huge amounts of private money into the electoral process would seem to support his emphasis on economic power. In fact, a recent study of the empirical basis for theories of political inequality, including pluralism and elite theory, found evidence that economic elites have "far more independent impact upon policy change than the preferences of average citizens do" and that the average citizens' influence on policy-making is "near zero" (Gilens & Page, 2014, p. 576).

Distribution of Political Power

Each of the positions just discussed makes a different argument about political inequality on the national level in the United States. But what does the evidence suggest? One way to answer Dahl's question of who actually governs, or who has the power, is to look at the distribution of power in the political process. The degree of political power and political participation can be measured in a variety of ways, and each of these measures provides clues concerning the actual distribution of power.

Although some people feel they have little influence, perhaps they are wrong. One means by which to assess the potential political impact of a group is through its history of participation in the political process. A group obviously has to make its desires known if it is to have the possibility of gaining political power under the present system.

> Party politicians are inclined to respond positively not to group *needs* but to group *demands*, and in political life as in economic life, *needs* do not become *marketable demands* until they are backed by "buying power" or "exchange power" because only then is it in the "producer's" interest to respond. (Parenti, 1970, p. 528; emphasis in original)

Individuals and groups can make their demands known by participating in the political process through (1) voting, (2) holding political office, and/or (3) putting pressure in the form of lobbying and monetary support.

Voting

Voting is a frequently used measure of political participation. Voting turnouts for national elections in this country are well below the 80 percent turnouts found in other industrial democratic nations. Only a little over 67 percent of voting-age citizens voted in the 2020 presidential election. This lower voting rate is somewhat surprising, given that evidence suggests Americans tend to be more politically aware than adults in other similar countries. A sense that the benefits of voting are not readily apparent, recent voter registration laws, and party polarization have recently weakened participation in the US political process (Highton, 2017).

As Table 5.1 indicates, minorities and members of lower socioeconomic groups are less likely to vote than White people or those with higher educations or incomes. It is important to note, however, that when factors such as education and income are statistically controlled, Black people have a higher political participation rate than White, Hispanic, or Asian people (Darrah-Okike et al., 2021). The overrepresentation of lower socioeconomic individuals among nonvoters is exacerbated by the fact that organized efforts to get individuals to the polls focus on those who are most likely to vote anyway, that is, the affluent and more highly educated segments (Campbell, 2007). Moreover, to the extent that individuals with higher incomes and education vote for candidates and legislation that favor their positions, lower-ranking groups may suffer

Table 5.1 Voting Rates among Citizens 18 and Older in the 2012, 2016, and 2020 Presidential Elections, by Selected Characteristics

Year	2012	2016	2020
Sex			
Men	60	59	65
Women	64	63	68.4
Race and Hispanic Origin			
White, Non-Hispanic	64	65	70.9
Black	66	59	62.6
Asian	47	49	59.7
Hispanic (Any Race)	48	48	53.7
Age			
18–24	41.2	43	51.4
25–44	57.3	56.5	62.6
45–64	67.9	66.6	71
65–74	73.5	72.6	76
75+	70	68.4	72.3
Educational Attainment			
Less than High School Graduate	38	34	40.4
High School Graduate or GED	53	51	55.5
Some College/Associate Degree	64	63	69.6
Bachelor's Degree	75	74	77.9
Advanced Degree	81	80	83
Annual Family Income*			
**Less than $20,000	48	46	41.1
$20,000–$29,999	56	52	56.1
$30,000–$39,999	58	59	63.1
$40,000–$49,999	63	62	68.6
$50,000–$74,999	68	68	72
***$75,000 and over	77	76	81.2
Employment Status			
Unemployed in Labor Force	52	50	57.8
Employed in Labor Force	67	64	68.9

*   All percentages rounded to nearest whole.
** Average of three income categories (under $10,000; $10,000–$14,999; $15,0-00–$19,999).
*** Average of three income categories ($75,000–$99,999; $100,000–$149,999; $150,000 and over).

Source: US Census Bureau (2021d), *Voting and Registration in the Elections of November 2012–2020, Detailed Tables.* (https://www.census.gov/topics/public-sector/voting.html)

from the resulting political policies. Finally, poor and minority people are more likely to have felony records that, in some states, preclude them from voting. In 2020, 5.2 million Americans were prevented from voting through these laws. This represents 1 in every 16 Black persons of voting age (Uggen et al., 2020).

The effect of race on voting is complex and has changed in recent years. A key concept in the literature on voting is that of **linked fate**, or the idea that those candidates closest matching your identity are more likely to represent your interests. This is particularly interesting given the rise in diversity among candidates and given the concept of intersecting identities. In recent elections, there has been support for this concept, in varying degrees. Findings in one recent study show that women are more likely to subscribe to a belief in linked fate than are men, most particularly Black women (Bejarano et al., 2021). Black men are less likely to vote based on linked fate. In the 2018 midterm elections, race was salient for those White voters who reported a high level of White racial consciousness (Knuckey & Kim, 2020), and racial resentment was an important factor in the 2016 and 2020 elections (Buyuker et al., 2021).

Although Black voters are more likely to vote for Black candidates, the political party does matter. A study of 2010 elections showed that the presence of Black Democratic candidates increased Black voter turnout; the same was not true for Black Republican candidates (Fairdosi & Rogowski, 2015). There is some concern, additionally, that younger Black voters view the political process differently from those who are older and may be less likely to vote or support the traditional agenda of the older generation (Bositis, 2007).

The data for Hispanics in Table 5.1 have to be interpreted carefully since they only include citizens and therefore not all Hispanic adults. In 2020, 28 percent of Hispanics in the population were not citizens. The political impact of this ethnic group will no doubt increase as more become citizens. In fact, Hispanics have been increasingly courted by national candidates, in large part because they are expected to compose one-fourth of the US population by 2050 and they are the fastest-growing demographic group. Immigrant Hispanic citizens, or those not born in the United States, are more likely to vote than any other racial group, though they are also the group most negatively affected by voter suppression efforts (Darrah-Okike et al., 2021). In addition, the Hispanic population is concentrated in just eight states, states that contain 80 percent of the electoral votes needed to win the presidency (Phillips, 2018). Finally, religious and moral issues of the kind that have become prominent (e.g., abortion, same-sex marriage) complicate voting patterns for Hispanics, since they tend to vote Democratic, but many come from strong religious traditions emphasizing traditional family structures. In combination, these factors make Hispanic voters an increasingly important but complex political constituency.

As voting data suggest, some groups are, at best, only minimally involved in the political process. Those who are totally inactive are disproportionately from low-income and low-education backgrounds, whereas "complete activists" have an overrepresentation of high-status individuals in their ranks (Brady et al., 2015). The complete activists are individuals who participate in a variety of ways (voting, attending meetings, making campaign contributions, contacting officials, and so forth). They are more often wealthier and better-educated citizens (Bartels, 2008, p. 252). Business and professional groups continue to be politically involved but tend to promote the interests of the affluent and educated (Skocpol, 2007). There is also evidence to suggest that this inequality in political participation is perpetuated over generations through educational differences. Parents who are highly educated tend to be politically involved, provide a variety of politically relevant experiences to their children, and perhaps most significantly, maximize the chances of their children becoming highly educated themselves:

> In turn, well-educated offspring are likely to … have challenging and financially rewarding jobs, to develop civic skills and to receive requests for participation in non-political institutions, to be politically informed and interested, and so on. … Most of the proximate causes of political participation have their roots, at least in part, in social class background. (Verba et al., 2003, p. 58)

These differences in preparation and participation mean that "ordinary Americans speak in a whisper while the most advantaged roar" (quoted in Dionne, 2004, p. B2).

Historically, the less advantaged have also been less organized and less powerful when attempting to influence the political system. Some organizations and movements advocating their interests have sprung up in recent years—certainly, the populism across the globe that we have seen arise is a response to increasing inequality (Pastor & Veronesi, 2018)—but other influential political groups, such as unions, have declined in membership. Union members have higher rates of voting than nonmembers in similar occupations (Kerrissey, 2015), but the percentage of private-sector workers that is unionized is much smaller than that found among public-sector workers. When these conditions are combined with the fact that private-sector union members tend to have less education and lower wages than those in the public sector, the result is that the political power of the working class as expressed through voting is weakened, making political inequality between the classes greater (Rosenfeld, 2010).

In addition to lower voting rates and less participation in political activities, weakness in the political power of the working and lower classes is further indicated by the lack of government responsiveness to the arguments of these classes. An analysis of actions by congressional legislative staff members shows that staff members misrepresent the perspectives of their constituents, particularly those staff members who rely more heavily on business interests (Hertel-Fernandez et al., 2018). People who choose not to vote because they believe that the government is not responsive to their needs may not be wrong, particularly if they are not wealthy.

While class position affects political participation, some have argued that, as a basis for political advocacy, class has been supplanted by "cultural" factors. Prominent issues such as abortion, transgender individuals and athletic participation, the teaching of so-called "critical race theory," marijuana legalization, and immigration incite groups that are not organized around *class* but around religious and other *cultural* dimensions. **Status-based politics** has moved into the foreground while class-based politics has receded. Michael Hechter (2004) observes, "[t]hat status politics may be gaining in recent times is suggested by the increasing political salience of ethnicity, religion, nationalism, gender, and sexual orientation" (p. 404). But while status-based issues may be increasing in prominence, especially within the upper class, economic issues still predominate in the minds of voters. For example, the economy, health care, and economic inequality were more important to voters in 2020 than was abortion (Pew Research Center, 2020c).

Photo 5.1 Although working-class families have been among the most openly patriotic and have generally contributed their members disproportionately to serving their country militarily, they are less likely to vote or occupy political positions than are those in higher classes.

Source: William Griffith/Shutterstock.

Importantly, political participation cannot solely be explained by interest in politics or willingness to vote. Inequalities in power also predict differentials in the access to voting, via processes such as **gerrymandering** and voter suppression. Despite the passage of the Voter's Rights Act of 1965, which prohibited barriers targeting African Americans, voter dilution and suppression continued.

Named after Elbridge Gerry, the fifth vice-president of the United States and the governor of Massachusetts, gerrymandering refers to the redrawing of voting districts to benefit one party over another. Every ten years following the release of the decennial census and potential changes to the number of allotted Congressional representatives, state legislatures often redraw voting districts. For example, a party might choose to draw districts in such a way that all voters of one category, such as one race, might be clustered in one district, thus diluting the power of their vote. Gerrymandering has existed since Gerry's efforts in 1812, but technological advances such as mapping and greater access to big data have accelerated its use and increased its impact, most evidently following the 2010 census and again following the 2020 census. Indeed, "redistricting is the great game of modern politics, and the arms race for the next decade's maps promises to be the most extensive—and most expensive—of all time" (Newkirk, 2017). Redistricting efforts were a keystone priority of the Republican Party during the past two decades, as was evident in the statement from the party's REDMAP website that the "party controlling that effort controls the drawing of the maps—shaping the political landscape for the next 10 years" (cited in Newkirk, 2017). More recently, Democrats have been actively engaging in gerrymandering in states such as New York and Illinois.

How much does gerrymandering affect the outcome of elections? Certainly, the process is unpopular, with voters in the 2018 election passing anti-gerrymandering legislation in Colorado, Michigan, Missouri, and Utah (and earlier in Ohio). However, the evidence assessing the effects of gerrymandering is mixed, partly due to the presence of other confounding variables and due to disagreements about how to measure such effects. For example, based on an analysis of the 2012 elections, Goedert (2014) argues that while gerrymandering did net Republicans a few seats in Congress, most of the increased polarization of the electoral districts stems from increased urbanization rather than gerrymandering. That is, increasingly, the dense urban areas are more diverse and more Democratic, with rural areas remaining (for the most part), Republican and White. This explains in great part the disparity between the popular vote and the electoral vote—though the density of Democratic voters has increased, this population density is isolated in urban districts. Similarly, despite journalistic accounts that gerrymandering increases polarization, research suggests that demographic factors such as urbanization may be more to blame (Carson et al., 2007).

Nonetheless, there is some evidence that gerrymandering has at least modest effects on elections (Chen & Cottrell, 2016), and combined with the demographic trends noted above, these effects might be increasing. A recent report by Princeton's Gerrymandering Project (Adler & Thompson, 2018) argues that in some states, such as Ohio, gerrymandering had a substantial effect in the midterm elections. Though Democrats won 48 percent of the popular vote, representing an increase of over 5 percent, they did not add any congressional seats. And an AP study of the election in Pennsylvania suggests that the court-ordered redrawing of the highly gerrymandered maps cut the Republican statistical edge in half (Lieb, 2018). The area in dark gray in Figure 5.1 represents Pennsylvania's former 7th district, no so fondly nicknamed "Goofy Kicking Donald Duck." This district became the icon of the need to redraw Congressional districts.

As with gerrymandering, political efforts to dilute and suppress the power of voters are evident with recent voter identification laws. Strict voter identification laws are relatively new—in 2006, no states required voters to produce photo identification, today 35 do (NCSL, 2021). How is this

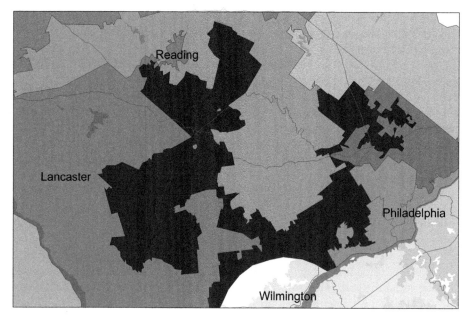

Figure 5.1 Pennsylvania's Former 7th District.
Source: Adapted from ESRI (2020).

tied to inequality? Studies demonstrate that voter identification laws have discriminatory effects due primarily to the fact that minorities and those who are less educated and lower-income are less likely to have access to photo identification (Darrah-Okike et al., 2021). Despite the recency of these laws and limited data (Highton, 2017), some current studies suggest that these laws do negatively impact the turnout of minority voters (Hajnal et al., 2017).

Holding Political Office

.Holding political office is another and more substantial means for weilding political power. Despite recent progress, White heterosexual males still dominate political positions at the federal level. Although the 117th Congress is more racially/ethnically diverse than ever before in history, 77 percent of the voting members are White, compared to just 60 percent of the US population. Democrats represent 83 percent of that diversity. There are 11 openly LGBT members in Congress (Avery, 2020; Schaeffer, 2020).

Women in general remain underrepresented in elected political positions. A record 120 (27 percent) of the 439 members of the 2020 House of Representatives were women; 24 (24 percent) of the members of the Senate are women (Blazina & Desilver, 2021). Although the first woman was elected to the House of Representatives in 1916, the influx of women into Congress is a relatively recent phenomenon, with regular increases in the number of women beginning in the 1970s. The midterm elections of 2018 resulted in the first-ever Native American women to be elected to Congress (one of these, Deb Haaland would subsequently rise to the position of the Secretary of the Interior), and a record number of women of color.

Despite the increased movement of women into elected federal positions, gender stereotypes still create obstacles. Men have more often held leadership positions and have, consequently, been thought to have stronger leadership qualities. Whereas men are viewed as being more forceful, sure of themselves, and knowledgeable, women are generally seen as being more compassionate, relational, and open to compromise. Stereotypes are also one of the reasons women are less likely than men to consider running for office (Bos et al., 2021; Carli & Eagly, 2007; Dolan, 2005; Palmer & Simon, 2010). Counteracting these pressures has been the international women's movement, which has fostered an increase in participation by women in the political process (Paxton et al., 2006). Internationally, however, women still lag behind men in holding legislative positions. Worldwide in 2021, only 10 women served as heads of state and 13 served as heads of government, and only 21 percent of cabinet members were women. Moreover, in only a small number of countries do women compose more than 30 percent of members of parliament (UN Women, 2021).

In addition to gender and race, socioeconomic status has also been tied to holding political office. Historically, most members of Congress not only have been White men, but also members of the middle or upper class, and a majority have been lawyers, bankers, or other businessmen. The Congress of 2021 was similarly composed; the vast majority were in business or law with only a handful in blue-collar labor (Congressional Research Service, 2021). The overrepresentation of individuals from higher-status backgrounds is clearly continuing in Congress.

For over two decades, Dye (2002) documented the characteristics, backgrounds, and interconnections of the institutional elite in the United States. He included in his definition of elites all those who occupy positions of high authority in the governmental, media, educational, civic/cultural, military, financial, industrial, and legal institutions in the United States. Considering only the governmental elite—that is, those who occupy the top positions in the executive, legislative, and judicial branches—almost 75 percent have law or other advanced degrees. More than 40 percent are graduates of highly prestigious private universities or colleges. Women and African Americans, as might be expected, are grossly underrepresented.

What is the meaning of these studies in terms of the perspectives on power presented earlier? If the essence of pluralism is the presence of a rough balance of power between constituencies with different interests, then these data clearly do not support the pluralist position. Some groups—most notably women, racial minorities, and working- or lower-class individuals—are seldom found in national-level offices of political power. To the extent that these offices are a principal means by which to gain and exercise political power, and that incumbents reflect and work for their own

Photo 5.2 Women and minorities are underrepresented on Capitol Hill in Washington, DC. In 2020, only 27 percent of the House of Representatives and 24 percent of Senate members were women. Racial and ethnic minorities composed 23 percent of Congress.

Source: Wikicommons/Noclip.

interests, then some groups have much less power than others. Further, the continuing presence of high-level employees of corporations and of the military suggests that Mills's concept of the military-industrial complex still holds some relevance (Bacevich, 2017).

Interlinkage of Economic and Political Power

Analysis of data from numerous advanced democratic nations, including the United States, demonstrates the significant relationship between economic inequality and political participation. Greater income inequality reduces interest in political issues, dampens political debate, and lowers voter participation among all citizens except the wealthy (Solt, 2008). When compared with past active protests and mass movements against the political power of wealth, "the democratic urge to rein in the dangerous ambitions of privileged elites has grown frail" (Gerstle & Fraser, 2005, p. 291). Several factors limit the extent to which governmental policy can be focused on inequality. These include the great polarization of voters, the lack of voter participation, the influence of high-income campaign contributors, and the inability of political institutions, most notably Congress, to address these issues (Bonica et al., 2013).

Those who have higher incomes can maintain their interest and involvement in politics because they have an inordinate effect on the political process, shaping policies that fit their own interests rather than those of the majority. This may be a partial explanation for the consistent relationship that has existed between socioeconomic status and voting. In the absence of effective power, the nonwealthy and uneducated may feel that the political process is out of their hands (Goubin, 2020). These findings give credence to arguments going back to Aristotle, de Tocqueville, and others who contend there is a close tie between economic equality and political democracy. The studies discussed earlier in this chapter show that office incumbents are most likely to come from high social classes. This class connection raises additional questions about the relationship between economic and political power. First, are **political action committees** (PACs) and lobbying groups so influential in the political process as to suggest dominance by one social class? Does money buy elections and votes? Second, and perhaps most important, are the upper class in general and its ruling "power elite" as united as Domhoff suggests?

Candidate Selection and Campaign Funding

Running for a federal political office is extremely expensive. The 2020 election was the most expensive in history, totaling $14.4 billion, more than doubling the cost of the 2016 election. Nine of the ten most expensive Senate elections in history and five of the ten most expensive in the House happened in 2020 (Evers-Hillstrom, 2021).

BOX 5.1 STATES' RIGHTS VERSUS THE FEDERAL GOVERNMENT

One of the reasons for the Civil War was disagreement about the power of individual states versus the power of the central federal government. This issue has not disappeared. States often differ in their laws over fundamental issues, such as gun control, Medicaid, and what constitutes a crime. As in the case of the criminalization of marijuana, sometimes these laws clash with federal law. For example, several states have legalized the sale of recreational marijuana, but it remains illegal at the federal level. Thus, banks may not lend money or open an account for those selling marijuana, even in states where it is legal. As a result, from the point of view of the state, individuals may have certain rights, but not according to federal law. When, if ever, should state law take precedence over federal law?

Short of actual occupancy in a political office, individuals or organizations can attempt to have political impact through direct influence of officeholders. In the recent past, direct lobbying has been carried out by various groups with financial power. Since the 1960s, there has been a significant increase in the number and activity of interest groups, an increased centralization of their headquarters in Washington, DC, a rise in the number of public-interest and single-issue interest groups, and more "formal penetration" on their part in governmental activities (Charnock, 2020). The number of PACs has spiraled upward in recent years, reaching 7,881 in 2020 (Federal Election Commission, 2020). Basically, PACs are interest groups that receive money from individuals sympathetic to their causes, so they can have an impact on federal elections.

PACs represent many different interest groups. Corporations, labor, assorted trade associations, and nonconnected specific-issues groups are among the organizations with PACs, and each follows different strategies. In 2019–2020, PACs spent over $4 billion dollars, with the largest PACs representing corporations (Federal Election Commission, 2020). So-called "super PACs" developed in 2010 as a result of a Supreme Court decision on campaign financing. These groups can raise unlimited amounts of money from organizations and individuals and then spend unlimited amounts in support of specific issues or candidates. In the 2020 election, 2,276 Super PACs spent over $2 billion (Open Secrets, 2021).

Contributions by PACs are part of the "soft money" candidates receive during their campaigns. Such funds also include money from individuals, unions, and corporations. Loopholes in federal legislation have fostered growth in the amount of soft money in political campaigns. More money has flooded in because of recent Court rulings. The Supreme Court's 2010 decision in *Citizens United v. Federal Election Commission* opened the door to unlimited spending by corporations and unions, arguing that these organizations have the same First Amendment rights to free speech as individuals. While they cannot give money directly to individual candidates, these organizations can use their own money to fund federal election campaigns that advocate issues and candidates that they prefer.

Photo 5.3 The Supreme Court ruling referred to as "Citizens United" highlighted the influence of large institutions such as corporations, unions, or lobbying groups in the election process.
Source: © Gene Crain/Shutterstock.

BOX 5.2 MONEY, POLITICS, AND JUSTICE

The infiltration of money into the political process has been an ongoing concern throughout US history. Alexander Hamilton (a founding father and Secretary of the Treasury under President Washington) and John Jay, the first Chief Justice, believed that the people who own the country ought to run it, whereas Thomas Jefferson and Theodore Roosevelt argued against and tried to stem the tendency toward a plutocracy, that is, government by the wealthy. It should come as no surprise then that the issue of unlimited and unrestricted campaign contributions would be a hot-button topic that would rally opposing groups to loudly argue their positions.

On January 21, 2010, these positions intensified when the US Supreme Court issued a ruling in the case of *Citizens United v. Federal Election Commission*, 130 S. Ct. 876 (2010). Briefly, the 5–4 majority opinion ruled that a section of the Bipartisan Campaign Reform Act (popularly known as the "McCain-Feingold Act"), which prohibited corporations and unions from spending money on media political ads during the final stages of campaigns, violated the First Amendment to the United States Constitution. Citing prior decisions which recognized that corporations have First Amendment rights, the Court concluded that the ban on such corporate spending was an impermissible ban on speech. The decision conflicted with laws in 24 states that banned corporations from using money from their general funds in campaigns. It also further polarized opinions. President Obama saw it as a victory for big companies and interest groups and a setback for ordinary Americans who have little leverage and little money.

The Supreme Court was clearly divided on the issue. Proponents viewed the decision as a victory for the First Amendment that in part says, "Congress shall make no law … abridging the freedom of speech." Even though corporations are not flesh-and-blood entities, under the law, they have the same rights and responsibilities as persons. Consequently, being allowed to spend one's money the way one wants is one aspect of the individual's (or corporation's) right to free speech. "Political speech is 'indispensable to decision making in a democracy, and this is no less true because the speech comes from a corporation rather than an individual'" (*Citizens United*, 130 S. Ct. at 904, quoting *First Nat'l Bank v. Bellotti*, 435 US 765, 777 [1978]; footnote omitted). Judges supporting the decision did not believe it would undermine public support for the government: "The appearance of influence or access, furthermore, will not cause the electorate to lose faith in our democracy" (*Citizens United*, 130 S. Ct. at 910, citing *Buckley v. Valeo*, 424 US 1, 46, 96 S. Ct. 612 [1976]).

Opponents of the decision worried about the potential flood of money that might lead to the buying of government positions by those with the most wealth. Former Supreme Court Justice Stevens, dissenting from the majority decision in *Citizens United*, argued that giving corporations the same status as individuals was wrong, that corporations and individuals are not the same. "In the context of election to public office, the distinction between corporate and human speakers is significant. Although they make enormous contributions to our society, corporations are not actually members of it" (*Citizens United*, 130 S. Ct. at 930 [Stevens, J., dissenting]). He also contended that the decision overturns past rulings that limited corporate spending: "The majority's approach to corporate electioneering marks a dramatic break from our past. Congress has placed special limitations on campaign spending by corporations ever since the passage of the Tillman Act in 1907" (*Citizens United*, 130 S. Ct. at 930 [Stevens, J., dissenting]). Finally, former Justice Stevens argued that lawmakers have a duty to guard against possibly negative effects of corporate spending in local and national elections. One of these effects, he feared, was a weakened stature for the Court: "The Court's ruling threatens to undermine the integrity of elected institutions across the Nation. The path it has taken to reach its outcome will, I fear, do damage to this institution" (*Citizens United*, 130 S. Ct. at 931 [Stevens, J., dissenting]).

Since *Citizens United*, costs for state and federal elections have skyrocketed. These include spending for Supreme Court positions in the states' court systems, which more than doubled since the 1990s to $56.4 million in the 2011–2012 election cycle. The economic tug-of-war for these elections primarily involved powerful interest groups on the right and left who sought to move the justice system in their direction. The late US Supreme Court Justice Ruth Bader

Ginsberg and former US Justice Sandra Day O'Connor worried that this trend can erode the average American's belief in the fairness of the justice system and confirm the belief of those who feel that those with money rule. A central question, of course, is whether the election of a given state court judge means that they will always cast decisions favorable to the interests that heavily funded the election. The majority in the *Citizens United* decision apparently would not envision a problem here. "The fact that speakers may have influence over or access to elected officials does not mean that these officials are corrupt" (*Citizens United*, 130 S. Ct. at 910); (Bannon and Reagan, 2013; Liptak, 2015; Sullivan and Adams, 2010).

The concern over the influence of PACs is based on the assumption that, *as a monolithic group*, contributors disproportionately influence federal policies. But it should be kept in mind that these groups vary widely in their specific interests and are not monolithic in this sense. In fact, the proliferation of varying interest groups might be viewed as an indication of pluralism at work. At the same time, however, there is some question about whether the attention paid to *specific* interest groups will hinder the ability of governing officials to effectively address problems that affect the *general* interest of US society (Cigler & Loomis, 2015).

Regarding the issue of PACs and their impact, studies suggest that PACs may affect who is elected. Studies conducted since *Citizen United* show that recent elections have been impacted by PACs, specifically advantaging Republican candidates. The potential explanation for this outcome is that the PACs that traditionally support Democrat candidates, such as labor unions, have faced declining funding over the years (Abdul-Razzak et al., 2020; Cox, 2021).

Do PACSs affect how elected officials vote? The research on this is more mixed. A study on climate change legislation showed that "every additional $10,000 a representative received from counter-movement industries significantly decreased odds of their taking the pro-environmental stance even when controlling for representatives' demographics, districts, Congressional polarization and time-period" (Ard et al., 2017, p. 1107). At the same time, a research study on 20 labor-related issues in the US House of Representatives, found that the amount of contributions from union-approved PACs was related to voting, but only on issues that had little media attention (Jones & Keiser, 1987). In other words, the less visible the issue, the greater the effect of contributions on voting behavior.

An analysis of the judgments of policy historians demonstrates that PACs do influence legislation, and that a few interest groups such as the AFL-CIO and the National Association of Manufacturers regularly influence behavior (Grossmann, 2012). The influence of PACs is particularly important on highly ideological issues, and it is likely that as our political environment becomes more ideologically polarized, PACs will increase their power over parties (Witko, 2006). It is not through the amount of the PAC contribution itself but through other mechanisms that economically powerful groups can influence voting patterns. Peoples and Gortari (2008) found that US representatives who received funds from the same *business* groups voted in a similar manner, but did not vote in the same way if they received money from the same *labor* organizations. An overview of current research studies on the relationship between monetary contributions and roll call voting found mixed results, with some studies suggesting that contributions have a major impact, while others find that they have little or no effect on public voting by congressional members (Hojnacki et al., 2012).

The impact of money on elections and voting continues as an issue largely because it pits those who are concerned about the corruption of politics against those who believe that everyone, including corporations and labor unions, should be allowed to spend their money as they wish. The Supreme Court ruling supporting First Amendment rights for corporations and other organizations served to bring this debate more fully into the public consciousness.

Ruling-Class Unity

Concerns about soft money and the power of PACs are related to suspicions that those with plentiful resources are unified and will exercise disproportionate control of the political process. Most of the data on elite cohesiveness for the past several decades indicates that the elite are broadly unified because of similarities in class background, membership patterns on corporate boards, and political behavior (Chu & Davis, 2015; Khan, 2012b).

Mills's and Domhoff's descriptions of the social backgrounds of the elite and the historical circumstances in which they rule suggest that they should be unified. Domhoff described their common membership in and interaction at exclusive clubs, attendance at elite schools, and frequent listing on the Social Register, while Mills described not only their social-psychological similarities but also the concentration and coalescence that occurred among the major institutions involved in the power elite. Domhoff detailed some evidence of intermarriages, unique schooling, and common leisure and social activities that point, he argued, to the existence of a cohesive upper class of which the public is conscious. Dye (2002) also concluded that there is general unity of opinion among the elite, even though there is some evidence of rising factionalism within it. And while there was an era of "high brow" culture, beginning during the Gilded Age, when elites separated themselves from the masses by their cultural knowledge and associations (e.g., attendance at the opera, support of classical music and art), increasingly the elites embrace a variety of cultural forms. "Such omnivorousness could be because elites are more open or inclusive, or omnivorousness may be the new symbolic boundary that marks elites, like snobbishness of old" (Khan, 2012b, p. 368).

More than simply sharing cultural interests and backgrounds, research continues to demonstrate that there are interlocking connections between elites and the corporations they represent, and these connections lead to common political behaviors among corporations (Barnes, 2017; Sapinski & Carroll, 2018). In early research, Useem (1984) directly addressed the issue of the political unity of what he calls the "inner circle" of business, looking at whether members of this group act on behalf of their own separate corporations or on behalf of the capitalist class as a whole. The inner circle he described is a network of leaders from large corporations who serve as top officers at more than one firm, who are politically active, and who serve the interests of the capitalist class as a whole rather than the narrow immediate interests of their individual companies.

Useem (1984) viewed capitalism in the United States as having moved from (1) "family capitalism" in which individual upper-class families dominated corporate ownership, through (2) "managerial capitalism" in which managers began to replace the dominance of upper-class owners around the turn of the twentieth century, to (3) "institutional capitalism" in which networks of intercorporate ties characterize the core of capitalism. The increasing control of corporations by their managers rather than owners and the increased concentration and interlocking in the corporate sector during this century have helped lay the basis for the development of this powerful circle.

Indeed, Dye's (2015) study of individuals in top institutional positions revealed that 4,000 individuals have formal control over half of the country's industrial, banking, communications, insurance, educational, legal, and cultural assets. The top 500 out of 6 million corporations control about 75 percent of the nation's gross domestic product, while "the 5 million corporations that receive less than $1 million in annual revenues account for less than 4 percent of the GDP" (p. 13). In 2021, four banks controlled almost 50 percent of all banking assets in the United States (Federal Reserve System, 2021), and in 2020, 25 top health companies controlled over three-quarters of all health insurance assets (Ng et al., 2020). Dye viewed this concentration of leaders of a few corporations in an "inner group" as cohesive, and, like Useem, found that multiple corporate interlockers were more likely than single directors to participate in governmental and other major organizations.

This inner circle is much more politically active than business in general because its members occupy several important positions at once, which (1) creates cohesiveness among its members; (2) helps mobilize economic and other resources; and (3) provides a powerful platform from which to express political positions. Moreover, its members are also closely tied to the upper class, which increases the circle's influence (Useem, 1984). One interesting recent study connected the cohesiveness of this inner circle with the failure of the United States to pass meaningful climate control policies. Hein and Jenkins (2017) argue that despite an increase in support for climate change mitigation policies by leaders in the public sector, including higher education and powerful nonprofits, a unified inner circle of upper-class corporate elites has successfully blocked such policies.

Some contemporary researchers suggest the possible beginning of a fragmentation of the inner circle, as once tightly connected boards have become increasingly disconnected from one another (Chu & Davis, 2015). Corporations have been under pressure to diversify their boards, and as the "inner circle" has been tainted by the controversies leading to the Great Recession, boards are composed of newcomers with fewer ties to other boards. "This suggests that the corporate elite is less able to act in a coordinated manner, and that the individual large shareholder has come to have much more power than the corporate board. The elite of the twenty-first century is so fractured, so ineffectual, that it is no longer able to act collectively to compel Congress to act" (Mizruchi, 2017). This has resulted in a greater political polarization—where elites might have voted to further the interests of the corporation, votes are now more aligned with political stances outside of the interests of the corporation. Ironically, this happens at a time when "social power and economic rewards have become increasingly concentrated in the hands of the few" (Khan, 2012b, p. 361).

A significant part of the reason for the tie between economic and political power lies in the interlocking between private and corporate wealth and political opportunity. It takes wealth, or at least access to wealth, to run a viable campaign for a major national political office. The connection between economic and political power may be deeper than this suggests, however, and may be based not on the characteristics of particular *individuals* but rather on the *structure and functioning* of the society.

The *structuralist* position suggests that, given the structure of a capitalist society, such as the United States, the government *must* act in a manner that supports the capitalist class and capitalism in general. This occurs regardless of the individuals who are in office. Political and economic institutions are so intertwined that the government, although it may be "relatively autonomous," is constrained to support and pass policies that maintain the capitalist economy. The state needs to provide a hospitable environment for investment and create a stable and smooth-running economy because it relies on the returns from the economy for its revenue. A stable economy also encourages political support for the government. In addition, the state provides programs (e.g., welfare, unemployment compensation) to deal with the fallout that comes from the operation of a capitalist system in which a relatively small number of corporations exercise inordinate influence. Inevitably, the state becomes involved in economic matters (Wilks, 2013). During the 2008–2009 economic crisis, for example, the US government provided hundreds of billions of dollars to large financial institutions—despite widespread public opposition—arguing that such support was needed to strengthen all aspects of the economy.

The preceding studies on campaign financing, holding office, and the capitalist economy indicate that both individuals and structural arrangements foster a relationship between economic and political power. Structural ties among institutions make it possible for some individuals to have access to positions of great power. According to some, however, these analyses overstate the role of the government in creating policy. This view suggests that many major policies are created outside the government, principally by the actions of corporations.

Summary

We began this chapter with a brief discussion on the importance and difficulty of conceptualizing power. We then moved to an analysis of pluralist, power-elite, and ruling-class views of the national power structure, and the data that bear on the validity of each.

There are clear relationships between socioeconomic position and voting, holding political office, and other forms of political participation. Those closer to the bottom of the class hierarchy are less likely than those in the middle and upper classes to vote, be elected to office, and be represented in powerful lobbying groups. Research indicates that those from higher socioeconomic levels, especially the upper class, are disproportionately represented in elite positions in a variety of institutional spheres. The tie between economic and political power, however, is more than just individual in nature; it is also structural. The fates of government and economy are linked—each needs the other. Consequently, a government in a society with a capitalist economy, for example, must support capitalism because its revenue and stability heavily depend on the smooth operation of that economy.

In the last few chapters, we have surveyed the forms of inequality along several axes: economic, status, and power. It is now time to examine in greater detail the most prominent explanations that have been given for social inequality in general. We begin in Chapter 6 with a discussion of classical explanations and then move on to an analysis of contemporary theories in Chapter 7.

Critical Thinking

1. Are information technology and the Internet creating new bases for power and domination? Is it the corporate rich who will claim these bases, or are new, powerful groups being created by these technological developments? Discuss your answer.
2. As globalization continues to open up nations to each other, do you think the soft power of a nation, that is, the respect for its culture, ideals, and values, will increasingly affect power arrangements between nations?
3. If the working and lower classes are underrepresented among those who vote, hold office, donate large sums of money to elections, and have effective lobbying power, how can we ensure representative or democratic government in the United States?

Web Connections

The Center for Responsive Politics lists the amount of money spent on federal elections, along with the amounts given by major individual and organizational donors. The center also gives information on the political affiliations of these donors. Visit www.opensecrets.org. Another source, the Joint Center for Political and Economic Studies, presents summary information on Black elected officials at every level of government. Its information also allows you to compare rates for Black men and women as well as differences in rates between states. Where does your state stand on electing Blacks to office? Visit www.joint-center.org.

Film Suggestions

Dark Money (2018). A documentary that views like a political thriller, it follows the effects of dark money (corporate money that is not traceable) on elections in Montana. It focuses on the effects of the Citizens United Supreme Court decision.

Divide and Conquer: The Story of Roger Ailes (2018). A documentary about the life of Roger Ailes who worked as a media consultant for multiple presidents and then went on to be the head of Fox News.

Fahrenheit 11/9 (2018). Michael Moore interviews American citizens to understand Donald Trump's victory. The film examines the media, the Electoral College, and the role of government.

Fourteen Women (2007). Explores the history of women in the Senate.

Legalize Democracy (2014). Critiques the current state of democracy in the United States.

RGB (2018). A documentary about Ruth Bader Ginsberg, the second woman to join the United States Supreme Court. The movie shows her rise and experiences on the Court.

PART 2

Causes of Inequality

6 Classical Explanations of Inequality

The discussions throughout Part 1 make it clear that multidimensional inequality is extensive in the United States, and, in a number of ways, it is becoming even more pronounced and disconcerting for many Americans. The widespread nature of social inequality makes explaining it all the more important. This chapter examines the broad classical explanations of Marx, Weber, Durkheim, and Du Bois, from which many modern thinkers have drawn. Karl Marx is discussed first because virtually all of his central ideas were formulated before any of the others and because subsequent theories are often viewed as reactions to Marx's work.

Karl Marx (1818–1883)

Few social scientists have had as great a political and economic impact as Karl Marx. His perspectives on society have been used by social scientists and ideologues, and his influence on modern sociology, and even society, has been pervasive. The ideas of all scholars are in large part shaped by the historical events and life situations they experience. This appears clearly in the case of Marx. Karl Marx was born on May 5, 1818, in the city of Trier, Prussia (now part of Germany). His family was of Jewish background and provided a bourgeois setting for Marx in his youth. His father and a neighbor, Ludwig von Westphalen, introduced him to the thinkers of the Enlightenment. Ludwig von Westphalen, in particular, became an intellectual companion with whom Marx discussed philosophy and literature. Marx later married von Westphalen's daughter, Jenny.

While studying at the universities of Bonn and Berlin, Marx became a friend of a group known as the Young Hegelians. The Young Hegelians helped convert Marx from the study of law to the study of philosophy. The increasing radicalism of his ideas encouraged his departure for Paris in late 1843. It was in Paris, a center of invigorating intellectual activity, that Marx began his close association and collaboration with Frederick Engels, the son of a manufacturer who acquainted Marx more fully with the real conditions of the working class. Marx's writing caused his expulsion from the city, and he moved from Paris to Brussels in 1845. By then, Marx already considered himself a socialist and revolutionary. He had aligned himself with several workers' organizations, and in 1848 he and Engels produced the *Manifesto of the Communist Party*.

After some moving around, Marx left for London in 1849, where he stayed for most of the remainder of his life. It was there that he produced most of his major writing. During his stay, his life and that of his family were marked by poverty, which was relieved only by his occasional employment as a European correspondent for the *New York Daily Tribune* and periodic help from his friend Engels. He became a leader of the International, a radical movement made up of individuals from several European countries, and in 1867 published the first volume of his monumental *Capital*. In the last decade of his life, Marx was already an honored figure among socialists and was able to live somewhat more comfortably than he did during his early London years. He died

DOI: 10.4324/9781003184966-8

Photo 6.1 Karl Marx's grave, alongside that of his wife Jenny, is in a cemetery in North London. Marx spent much of his adult life in London chronicling the state of the working class during industrialization in England.
Source: Photo by Charles E. Hurst.

on March 14, 1883, only one year after the death of his elder daughter and two years after the death of his wife, Jenny (G. S. Jones, 2016).

The Theoretical Context of Marx's Class Analysis

Marx subscribed to a materialist conception of social life. That is, he argued that activities are what characterize and propel human history. History consists of human beings going about producing and reproducing themselves in interaction with nature. Humans are a part of nature, and both nature and humans change as they interact, making them both a part of human history. History is really a process of "active self-making" (Simon, 1994, p. 98). It is *activity*, especially labor, that defines who we are. Consequently, a concentration on economic activity is fundamental for understanding history's process.

One of the most common misunderstandings of Marx's theory is the idea that he believed that everything is determined by the economic structure, that all other institutions are merely reflections of the economic system and are without causal influence. Although Marx considered the economic aspect the "ultimately determining element in history" and the "main principle," he did not think it was the only determining one. In a personal letter, while admitting that he and Marx had probably contributed to the confusion on this point, Engels put the matter succinctly:

> The economic situation is the basis, but the various elements of the superstructure … also exercise their influence upon the course of the historical struggles and in many cases preponderate in determining their *form*. There is an interaction of all these elements in which, amid all the endless host of accidents … the economic movement finally asserts itself as necessary. (Marx & Engels, 1970, p. 48 emphasis in original)

Thus, political, religious, and cultural factors play a role, though the "ultimately decisive" one is economic.

Labor is an expression of our nature. When freely engaged in, it allows us to realize our true human nature and satisfy our real basic needs (not manufactured ones). When freely done, labor is also an enjoyment because it is spontaneous. However, when forced or artificial, that is, alienated, it becomes more of a misery than an enjoyment. It twists our human nature. **Alienated labor** exists when private property and its owners hire or control others and define their labor for them. Instead of being for oneself, labor becomes a task that primarily benefits owners of property. One works to get food, shelter, and so on; that is, labor becomes a means to an end rather than an end in itself. Under capitalism, as in other class societies, the laborer and her or his labor belong to the capitalist. As a commodity, laborers have been hired at a price to work for the capitalist; for this period, the capitalist owns the workers and exploits them. It is out of the exploitation of the laborer by the capitalist that new value or profit is created because what is needed to reproduce the laborer (i.e., wage) is less than the value of what the laborer produces. It is this difference in value that defines exploitation and generates **surplus value** or profit for the employer. It is also private property and its control that defines classes and their relationship.

Historically, there have been several types of societies with class systems. According to Marx, the earliest societies were classless, being based on a "common ownership of land" (Marx & Engels, 1969, pp. 108–109). But all known subsequent societies have been class societies, and the engine of change in history has been class struggle. Private property spurs the development of classes. Although societies change and the specific names given to the various classes may change, the presence of dominant and subordinate classes remains. The particular form that relations take between the classes depends on the historical epoch and the existing economic mode of production. The **mode of production** refers to the particular type of economic system in operation, such as feudalism, capitalism, and so on. Within every mode of production are (1) means of production and (2) social relations of production. The means of production refer to the tools, machines, and other resources used in production, whereas the **social relations of production** refer to the property and power relationships among individuals in the economic system.

As we discussed in Chapter 3, Marx defined classes by their relationship to the means of production. Because of the classes' different relationships to private property (i.e., owners vs. nonowners), conflict is inherent in class society. Marx's theory is one of class struggle as class antagonism is built into the very structure of society. The existence of a given class always assumes the existence of another hostile class. "'Who is the enemy?' is a question that can be asked whenever Marx uses 'class'" (Ollman, 1968, p. 578). When the economic bases for classes are eliminated, classes themselves will disappear since the **proletariat** will be without the enemy, the capitalist.

Until then, in the process of class struggle, the proletariat develops from an incoherent mass (a class in itself) into a more organized and unified political force (a class for itself). The conditions that bring about this change are discussed in detail later.

Maintenance of the Class Structure

The system of inequality—class positions, the given relations of production, and the profits of capitalists—is maintained and protected by a variety of mechanisms. The state, of course, is the ultimate arbitrator and represents "the form in which the individuals of a ruling class assert their common interests" (Bottomore & Rubel, 1964, p. 223). "The executive of the modern State is but a committee for managing the common affairs of the whole bourgeoisie" (Marx & Engels, 1969, pp. 110–111). The state has used its force and legislation to maintain capitalist class relations (Marx, 1967, pp. 734–741). Struggles that do occur within the state are always class struggles.

A second mechanism used to maintain class relations is ideology, and the dominant ideology supports and legitimizes the position of the capitalist. "The ideas of the ruling class are in every epoch the ruling ideas: i.e., the class which is the ruling material force of society is at the same time its ruling intellectual force" (Marx & Engels, 1969, p. 47). Just as the ruling class has control over "material production," so too does it control "mental production," and the form these ideas take is clear: "The ruling ideas are nothing more than the ideal expression of the dominant material relationships" (Marx & Engels, 1969, p. 47). Of course, the ideas generated have been mentally separated in their association with the dominant class and hence can appear as eternal laws (such as the "free market") or rules generated by all of the society. Members of the ruling class themselves generally believe that. The ideas that support class relations are frequently promoted by bourgeois intellectuals, who are often nothing more than "hired prize-fighters" for capitalism (Marx, 1967, p. 15). Religion as an ideological institution similarly helps maintain the class system by preventing labor from seeing its real situation.

A third factor serving to bolster the set of economic relations is much less obvious than the two just mentioned. The capitalist structure itself strengthens its seeming inevitability by creating a working class that, because of custom and training come to view "the conditions of that mode of production as self-evident laws of Nature" (Marx, 1967, p. 737). The condition of workers freely hiring themselves out to capitalists who freely employ them to work in factories run for maximum efficiency makes capitalism appear as an entirely natural process and creates a dependency of workers on the system that makes it difficult for them to resist or rebel. As Miliband (1977) wrote, "The capitalist mode of production … veils and mystifies the exploitative nature of its 'relations of production' by making them appear as a matter of free, unfettered, and equal exchange" (p. 45).

Stages of Capitalism

According to Marx (1967), capitalism as a mode of production has gone through three principal stages: (1) cooperation, (2) manufacture, and (3) modern (machine) industry. Capitalism begins in the stage of cooperation when a large number of laborers are employed in one place working together to produce a given product. It is when workers are thus brought together that "the collective power of the masses" for the individual capitalist can be realized. Workers become more productive and efficient under these conditions, resulting in greater profit for the capitalist. This and each successive change in the mode of production are motivated by the desire to increase the surplus value of **labor power** and, therefore, the level of profit.

The period of manufacture begins in the sixteenth century and extends to the last part of the eighteenth century. Its characteristic is a strict and detailed division of labor among workers who have been brought together to cooperate in the production of the capitalists' products. Everyone has a specific function to perform; no one carries out all the tasks. Thus, with this change, there no longer exists a group of independent artisans cooperating, but rather a group of individuals performing minute tasks dependent on each other. "Its final form is invariably the same—a productive mechanism whose parts are human beings" (p. 338).

In manufacture, each person performs the same task over and over again until the job becomes routine and the laborer becomes a mere mechanism, but efficiency and perfection in production become reality. Skills that had been learned in apprenticeship become less necessary, and manufacture creates a set of unskilled laborers. The collective laborer, when organized in this fashion, increases production and as a result, increases the surplus value of their labor power to the capitalist. The profit for the capitalist goes up, and conditions for them could not be better. For the laborers, however, conditions worsen.

In the manufacture stage, the workers become alienated from their own labor. The work being done (1) is not an end in itself, but a *means* to an end; (2) is not voluntary but *forced*; (3) is not part of human nature (i.e., it is *external*); (4) is not work for the workers but for *someone else*; and (5) is *not spontaneous*. The object of their labor does not belong to the workers even though they have put a part of themselves into it. Rather, the product "becomes an object, takes on its own existence ... exists outside [them], independently, and alien to [them], and ... stands opposed to [them] as an autonomous power" (Bottomore & Rubel, 1964, p. 170). As appendages, workers become alienated from themselves, each other, and nature.

Under manufacturing, therefore, capitalists prosper as workers' conditions deteriorate, and the real nature of capitalism as a mode of production becomes clear. Capitalists prosper *because* laborers suffer. The two classes are not merely different levels but are inextricably interlinked in the capitalist mode. People and their labor power become commodities, things of use value to the capitalist, who owns and controls the instruments of production, the raw materials—everything. The laborers, in turn, have nothing but their own labor power to sell, and even that becomes twisted into a form suitable for maximum production.

In the machine or modern stage, like other forms of capitalist production, the development and use of machines are aimed at reducing the cost of commodity production for the capitalist by reducing the part of the day when workers are working for themselves and increasing that part when they are for the capitalist. That is, it is a way of increasing surplus value for labor. "The machine ... supersedes the workman" (Marx, 1967, p. 376). In modern industry, machines are organized into a division of labor similar to that which existed among laborers during the manufacture period. Since machines replace labor power, physical strength becomes less important, and capitalists seek to hire children and women. The result is a decrease in the value of the worker's labor power and a concomitant increase in the general exploitation of the family overall. When the value of the worker's labor power vanishes, laborers flood the market and reduce the price of labor power. Supply then outweighs demand for labor. In effect, machines are a means of controlling the collective laborer. "It is the most powerful weapon for repressing strikes, those periodic revolts of the working class against the autocracy of capital" (pp. 435–436).

Crises in Capitalism and Class Struggle

The increased competition for profit among capitalists generates crises at both the top and the bottom of the class structure, ultimately leading to the polarization of large capitalists versus the massive class of the proletariat. The initial result of the introduction of machinery is to increase profit, but problems arise. Employees are thrown out of work or work for low wages because they are not in demand. The proletariat increases in number and becomes more concentrated, and life conditions among members become equalized at a level of bare subsistence.

Competition among capitalists produces commercial crises, an "epidemic of over-production" whereby producers create more goods than the society needs, which in turn leads to increased concentration of capital since many go bankrupt (Marx & Engels, 1969, p. 114). A **crisis of overproduction** serves as an indication that the forces of production have become too strong for the property relations by which they are controlled ("fettered"). The capitalist responds by destroying productive forces and by trying to find new markets abroad, but these solutions are, at best, stopgap measures, and crises recur, each more serious than the previous. "Modern bourgeois society ... is like the sorcerer, who is no longer able to control the powers of the nether world whom he has called up by his spells" (p. 113). The means of production that the bourgeoisie originally brought into existence to benefit their own position and that permitted them to supplant feudalism now become the means that destroy them.

Bourgeois society becomes the stage for the impending class struggle between the capitalists and the collective laborer, between the bourgeoisie and the proletariat. As capitalism improved from simple cooperation through modern industry, the bourgeoisie became more powerful and entrenched, their ideology and ideas became dominant, and the organization of the state more evidently reflected their power. But so, too, did the proletariat develop as a class with the progress of capitalism. Initially, struggle against the bourgeoisie takes the form of individual protests, then protests by larger groups—not against the relations of production, but against the forces of production: workers smash tools, machines, and so forth in order to maintain their status as workers. At this point, they are still just a mass rather than an organized whole. But as conditions for them worsen—that is, as they become increasingly massed together on an equal basis in a minute division of labor under conditions of extreme alienation and misery—and as their livelihood becomes more uncertain, their actions become more those of a united class and less those characteristic of individuals competing among themselves. The appalling work conditions experienced by the proletariat forge it into a social class.

During the struggle that has its roots in the domination of the means of production and appropriation of its products (i.e., in a peculiar set of property relations), the proletariat becomes honed as a class, and the struggle takes on a greater political character. Ironically, the bourgeoisie has created the conditions that develop the class that revolts against it. As the decisive hour approaches, and the class and crisis nature of the society becomes increasingly evident, those in the bourgeoisie who see what is happening on the historical level also join the working class (Bottomore & Rubel, 1964, pp. 184–188).

Marx argued that a given social order is not replaced until all the forces of production that can be produced under it have been developed, and new relations of production (i.e., new social orders) do not appear until the material basis for their existence has been formed in the old society. This is essentially what happens, according to Marx when revolution occurs. Revolutions do not take place until the material conditions for their appearance are present. The mode of production shapes all other aspects of social life, and "at a certain stage of their development, the material productive forces of society come in conflict with existing relations of production … From forms of development of the productive forces these relations turn into their fetters" (Marx & Engels, 1969, pp. 503–504).

With proletarian revolution, the bases for the class system are removed and the proletariat is emancipated. In the interim, between the capitalist and classless society, a "dictatorship of the proletariat" exists, paving the way for a communistic society and the beginning of truly human rather than class history. Figure 6.1 summarizes some of the key elements of Marx's model.

Some Comments on Marx

Marx's theory has had a significant impact not only on the contemporary analysis of class structures but also on the study of society in general. That his work continues to generate discussion, as well as explanations and analyses built on his original ideas, is a tribute to the continued cogency and relevance of his theory. Marx's approach allows us to see at once the simultaneous existence of organization and conflict and their historical roots. He analyzes individual actions and emotions, as well as organizations and class structure, against the backdrop of societal settings and historical change.

The international character of modern **capitalism** that Marx predicted means that the impact of its internal crises and contradictions reverberate throughout the world. During the last three decades, "capitalism has intensified its grasp over the entire world, unleashing processes of economic

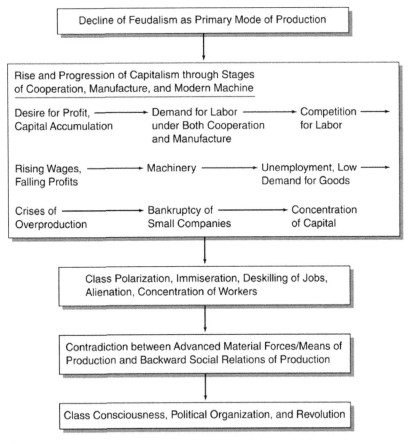

Figure 6.1 Core Elements in Marx's Theory of Class Struggle within Capitalism.

Photo 6.2 A woman operates a sewing machine in Bangkok, Thailand. The increased demand for inexpensive goods in the West has led to the growth of industrialization in less-developed countries.

Source: © 1000 words/Shutterstock.

change that intensify and render increasingly visible the links between the fate of people in the advanced capitalist countries and the rest of the world's population" (Gimenez, 2005, p. 11). During this time, many corporations have established plants and markets in foreign countries and have outsourced thousands of jobs. From a Marxist perspective, capitalism treats the world as a font of resources, a source of labor, and a large marketplace in which companies can sell their goods and services. While the "informal proletariat" composed of self-employed street workers and others like them is not the same group as Marx's factory proletariat, the growth in their numbers is still fostered by the movement of capitalist corporations into these economies (Choi, 2006). Capitalism has proved exceptionally resourceful in maintaining itself and forestalling widespread revolution. Being able to internationalize has provided capitalism with a mechanism for obtaining wider and wider markets and, therefore, has put off a crisis caused by its internal contradictions.

Although Marx's main predictions have not turned out exactly as he envisioned, many of the phenomena that he foresaw do exist to a degree. There has been a consistent trend toward more concentration of corporate power. There is also quite a bit of wealth inequality, and there are business ups and downs that capitalism follows. Moreover, every capitalist society has "class-based, working-class politics" to a certain degree (Collins, 1988). The US government responses to the 2008–2010 economic crisis, the 2016 Presidential election, and the more recent corporate tax cuts served to crystallize in the public's mind the differences in class interests of the capitalist and working classes.

Max Weber (1864–1920)

Many of those who followed Marx, and especially the major social theorists of the period, were engaged in a "debate with Marx's ghost" (Zeitlin, 1968). Among those most evidently aware of Marx's work and some of its shortcomings was Max Weber.

Weber is often considered to be the greatest sociologist in history. His "shadow falls long over the intellectual life of our era," wrote Mitzman (1970, p. 3). Much of what he contributed to social science still remains intact, and even those of his ideas that have proved weak or been discarded still provide a foundation from which further analysis can begin. Like Marx and other great theorists whose specific theories fit into a coherent whole, Weber's formulations regarding inequality must be considered in the context of his broader theory of the **rationalization** of the modern world. We will examine what Weber had to say about inequality, how US sociologists have interpreted his work in this area, and if and how he added to Marx's own analysis of class structure.

Max Weber's life was quite different from Marx's, but like Marx's, his life experiences clearly affected the propositions about society that he developed. Weber was born in Erfurt, Germany, in 1864, 16 years after the publication of *Communist Manifesto* and three years before the publication of the first volume of *Capital*. His family was upper middle class. His father was a fun-loving conformist who disliked and feared upsetting existing political arrangements. In sharp contrast, Weber's mother was an extremely religious person of Calvinist persuasion who often suffered the abuses of her much less moralistic husband, a fact that later became central in Max's repudiation of his father.

Despite its drawbacks for Weber, his parents' home was the site of frequent and diverse intellectual discussions featuring many of the well-known academicians of the day. From the beginning, Max was exposed to a potpourri of ideas. Though he was a sickly child, he was very bright, becoming familiar with the writings of a variety of philosophers before setting off at the age of 18 for the University of Heidelberg, where he studied law, medieval history, economics, and philosophy. At age 19, Weber left for Strasbourg to put in his military service. It was there that he developed a lifelong and deep friendship with his uncle Hermann Baumgarten, a historian, and his aunt, a devout Protestant, who was effective in putting her religious fervor into action. Consequently, Weber developed a greater respect for the religious virtues of his own mother and less of a regard for the worldly and cowardly qualities of his father.

A year later, he returned to live with his parents and to study at the University of Berlin, where he wrote his dissertation on medieval business. Carrying on a strictly disciplined and rigid life, he served as a barrister in the Berlin court system and as an instructor at the university. He wrote several works on agrarian history and agricultural laborers. These investigations included discussions of the social and cultural effects of commercialization and the role of ideas in economic behavior.

In 1893, Max Weber married Marianne Schnitget, a vibrant scholar in her own right. Marianne traveled with Max to America, where she met with social reformers Jane Addams and Florence Kelly. Marianne published several works on women, the law, and culture and was an active feminist and politician. After his death, she authored his biography (Lengermann & Niebrugge-Brantley, 1998).

After getting married and serving at the age of only 30 as a full professor of economics at the University of Freiburg, Max and Marianne left for Heidelberg, where he took a professorship, became more politically involved, and quickly developed a close circle of intellectual friends. During this period, Weber suffered a severe emotional breakdown and was able to do little of anything, even reading. He was only 33 years old at the time, and it was a number of years before his energy was restored. The breakdown may have been precipitated by a harsh confrontation with his father, very shortly after which his father died.

In the early 1900s, Weber's health was restored, and it was between this time and his death that Weber produced most of the works for which he is best known. He became enmeshed in German politics and volunteered for service during World War I, but later became disillusioned by the war and the German government's incompetence. Weber, unlike Marx, was accepted in

Photo 6.3 Max Weber.
Source: Keystone Press/Alamy Stock Photo.

polite society and was not a political radical, but he was generally a liberal and participated in the writing of the Weimar Constitution. There were many occasions when he fought bigotry and close-mindedness. Weber died of pneumonia on June 14, 1920, his broad knowledge leaving an unmistakable mark on social theory (Coser, 1971; Mitzman, 1970).

Rationalization of the World

Much of what Weber wrote had an undeniably unified theme. His discussions of bureaucracy, the Protestant ethic, authority, and even class, status, and party fit into his overall concern for social change and the direction in which he thought the Western world was moving. Thus, as is the case of Marx and many other nineteenth-century theorists, Weber's work on stratification must be understood within the context of his general perspective.

In contrast to Marx, who believed that capitalism and its accompanying denigration of the human spirit would eventually lead to a communistic and more humane society, Weber contended that alienation, impersonality, bureaucracy, and, in general, rationalization would be permanent societal features. Weber agreed with Marx that modern modes of technology have dehumanizing effects, yet he contended that bureaucracy and alienation are not temporary or peculiar to a passing period but are instead at the core of an increasingly disenchanted world. What the future promised in Weber's view was not a wonderfully free society in which people are reunited to themselves and nature, but rather an "iron cage"; what we have to look forward to is not "summer's bloom," but rather a "polar night of icy darkness and hardness." Bureaucratization and technical rationality are not likely to decrease but rather to increase under socialism.

A **bureaucracy** is characterized by its impersonality, hierarchy of rational-legal authority, written system of rules, clear division of labor, and career system. According to Weber, bureaucracy is technically more perfect than other methods of organization and is the most efficient and rational. "Precision, speed, unambiguity, knowledge of the files, continuity, discretion, unity, strict subordination, reduction of friction and of material and personal costs—these are raised to the optimum point in the strictly bureaucratic administration" (Gerth & Mills, 1962, p. 214). Business is carried out "without regard for persons," under "calculable rules." The lack of regard for persons is a central characteristic of all purely economic transactions. Since status honor and prestige are based on *who* a person is, the domination of the bureaucratic organization and a free market mean "the leveling of status 'honor'" and "the universal domination of the 'class situation'" (p. 215). The leveling of status strengthens the rule of bureaucracy by weakening status as a basis for position and encouraging the equal treatment of all, regardless of background.

Capitalism and bureaucracy support each other; both are impersonal. Bureaucracy hastened the destruction of feudal, patrimonial organizations and local privileges. Whereas feudalism was characterized by ties of personal loyalty and was grounded in small local communities, bureaucracy denies or destroys personal loyalty and demands loyalty to position, thereby equalizing individuals. Capitalist production requires it. Conversely, capitalism can supply the money needed to develop bureaucracy in its most rational form (Weber, 1968, p. 224). Bureaucracy and capitalism are characteristics of the contemporary modern society.

Bureaucracy and capitalism increase the prevalence of authority based on rational-legal, as opposed to charismatic or traditional grounds. In the rational-legal form, authority is based on the acceptance of rules regarding the right to issue commands as they apply to the formal position in the organization. Authority is attached to the office, not the person; it is impersonal.

Putting all of this together, we see that capitalism and the secularized Protestant ethic, class, bureaucracy, and rational-legal authority are mutually supportive and are integral parts of the increasingly rationalized modern society that Weber saw emerging. They stand in stark contrast to feudalism, the personalism of status honor, tradition and charisma, and premodern forms of organization. An adequate understanding of Weber's perspective on class and status, their relationship, and their distinction can be obtained only if his broader theory of historical development and its associated concepts are incorporated into the analysis. Keeping Weber's broader theory in mind, we turn to a discussion of his more specific ideas on inequality.

Tripartite Nature of Inequality

Weber argued that **power** can take a variety of forms. "Power," in general, refers to "the chance of a man or of a number of men to realize their own will in a communal action even against the resistance of others who are participating in the action" (Gerth & Mills, 1962, p. 180). A person's power can be shown in the *social order* through their status, in the *economic order* through their class, and in the *political order* through their party. Thus, class, status, and party are each aspect of the distribution of power within a community. For example, if we think about an individual's chances of realizing their own will against someone else's, it is reasonable to believe that the person's social prestige, class position, and membership in a political group will have an effect on these chances.

Social order refers to the arrangement of social honor (prestige) within a society. Different status groups (e.g., professors, construction workers) occupy different places along the prestige continuum. Economic order, in turn, refers to the general distribution of economic goods and services (e.g., owners and nonowners)—that is, to the arrangement of classes within a society. Finally, political order relates to the distribution of power among groups (e.g., political action committees, parties) to influence communal decisions. Weber's general scheme for inequality is presented graphically in Figure 6.2.

Although these are presented as three distinct and separate orders, it is a mistake to see them strictly as such. All of them are manifestations of the distribution of power and can and usually do influence each other, often in a quite predictable manner. The inclusion of the social and political dimensions is ordinarily seen as a "rounding out" of the economic determinism of Marx (Gerth & Mills, 1962, p. 47). But, as already pointed out, Marx was not a simple economic determinist; he viewed causal relationships in a more complex fashion. Moreover, Weber's own writings suggest that he did not view the three dimensions as being equally salient in capitalist society. Weber did not fully develop his political dimension, and the economic factor, as we shall see, outweighs the status element in the capitalist system of inequality. But at this point, it is necessary to examine each of Weber's three dimensions in greater detail.

Class

More so than Marx, Weber deliberately set out a number of formal definitions for his concepts (Weber, 1968). Weber's own conception of class parallels Marx's in several ways. Class, at its

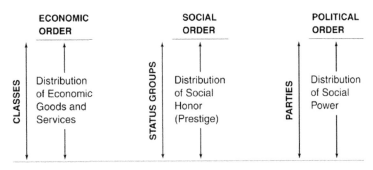

Figure 6.2 Weber's View of the General Distribution of Power.

core, is an economic concept; it is the position of individuals in the market that determines their class position. And it is how one is situated in the marketplace that directly affects one's life chances, "a common condition for the individual's fate" (Miller, 1963, pp. 44–45). Just as Marx indicated that capital begins when capitalist and laborer meet freely in the market when the laborer is free to sell his or her labor and form a relationship with the capitalist, Weber pointed out that persons are members of a class only if they have "the chance of using goods or services *for themselves* on the market" (p. 45, emphasis added). Consequently, enslaved individuals are not members of classes.

Weber distinguished three types of classes: property classes, commercial (acquisition) classes, and social classes. Individuals belong to the same class if they are in the same "class situation," which refers to the probability of individuals obtaining goods, position, and satisfactions in life, "a probability which derives from the relative control over goods and skills and from their income-producing uses within a given economic order" (Weber, 1968, p. 302).

Property classes are those who monopolize status privileges, such as education, and those who control the bulk of wealth, capital, and sales in the society. Such classes usually are composed of "rentiers," who get income from a number of sources, including people, land, factories, and bank securities. Those who are not privileged are those who are unfree or are paupers. Weber stressed the distinction between the top and the bottom classes but did mention that in each set of classes there are "middle classes" (Weber, 1968, pp. 302–303).

Commercial-class position is determined by "the marketability of goods and services," in other words, by the opportunity to exploit the market (Weber, 1968, p. 302). Merchants, industrial and agricultural employers, bankers, ship owners, professionals, and workers who have cornered certain skills are examples of entrepreneurs who are members of privileged commercial classes. In contrast, those who are unprivileged are usually laborers (skilled, semiskilled, and unskilled) (p. 304). Again, there are middle classes, but these are treated more as residual categories when compared with the other classes.

Social classes make up all class situations "within which individual and generational mobility is easy and typical" (Weber, 1968, p. 302). That is, a social-class structure is one in which there is fluidity and movement of individuals between class situations. Upward mobility is most likely, however, between adjacent classes. Examples of such social classes are the "working class as a whole," "the petty bourgeoisie," "the propertyless intelligentsia and specialists," and "the class privileged through property and education" (p. 305).

Class Consciousness and Class Struggle

According to Weber, classes of whatever kind need not be class conscious as Marx conceived them; they are not necessarily unified "communities." Class organization can occur in any one of the three types of classes, but **class consciousness** and class (communal) action are likely only under certain conditions. Weber argued that just because there are different property classes, for example, does not mean that they will necessarily engage in class struggle, although they may when circumstances are right. And when struggles do occur, they may not be over a basic change in the entire economy but may be more superficially over the distribution of wealth.

Class-conscious action is most likely if, first, "the connections between the causes and consequences of the 'class situation'" are transparent (Gerth & Mills, 1962, p. 184). If individuals can plainly see that there is a connection between the structure of the economic system and what happens to them in terms of life chances, class action is more likely. Weber believed this had happened among the proletariat. A second condition for class unification exists if there is an immediate opponent on whom the class can focus. Hence, workers will react against their immediate employers rather than those who are most distantly and perhaps even more profitably involved (such as stockholders). Third, class organization is also more likely if large numbers of individuals are in the same class position. The increasing growth of the proletariat would increase the chances of class action by them. Fourth, if all of the individuals are in one place and therefore are easier to organize, class unity is more probable. Finally, if their goals are directed and interpreted by a group of intelligentsia who are actually outside their class, class organization is more likely (Weber, 1947, pp. 427–428). These conditions are not inconsistent with those that Marx thought would forge a mass of individuals in the same class situation into a "class for itself." However, Weber cautions us about the belief that fully developed classes are never wrong—that is, "falsely conscious"—about their own interests. They can be.

Class struggles have changed in content throughout history, according to Weber. The focus of conflict has evolved from struggles over debt and credit in antiquity to struggles over the availability of consumer goods and their prices in the market during the Middle Ages to struggles over the price of labor in the modern world. Historically, class struggles begin when a credit market exists in which debtors pay high and often increasing rates of interest to the wealthy, who monopolize the credits (Miller, 1963, pp. 45, 48). But in each case, by definition, the struggle is of an economic character.

Status

Standing in theoretical and practical opposition to the market principle of class, which "knows no personal distinctions" and "knows nothing of 'honor,'" is the principle of status. Traditionally, status groups are ranked in terms of the "*consumption* of goods as represented by special 'styles of life,'" whereas classes are determined by their relations to the "production system and acquisition of goods" (Weber, 1963, p. 56; emphasis in original).

In addition, then, to being ranked in terms of market situation, individuals can be ranked on the basis of honor or prestige. A person's "status situation" consists of all aspects of his or her "life fate" that are determined by a "social estimation of honor" (Weber, 1963, pp. 49, 54). Status groups are based on a particular style of life, formal education, and/or inherited or occupational prestige. Certain groups may lay claim to (or, in other words, may usurp) a certain level of honor because of their hereditary background or family tree (such as the "First Families of Virginia"), because of their peculiar lifestyle, or because of their power. Thus, because of their formal education and occupational prestige, liberal arts professors might tend to socialize only among themselves and might have certain unwritten rules about how a member of the group should act or what kinds of goods and services are suitable for use in the status group and what kinds are not.

The stability of status groups is linked to political and economic conditions in a society and is one way in which the latter two aspects of inequality are related to the social dimension. The likelihood of a conventionally recognized status group developing into a "legal privilege, positive or negative, is easily traveled as soon as a certain stratification of the social order has in fact been 'lived in' and has achieved stability by virtue of a stable distribution of economic power" (Weber, 1963, p. 51; emphasis added). Weber is saying that status groups can be legalized and, therefore, become bases for political power differences when they have been around for some time and are buttressed by parallel differences in the distribution of economic resources. Where such stability exists, *caste groups* develop. Castes become supported by rituals (e.g., of purity), convention, and law. Separate castes may even develop their own religious beliefs. Usually, the status structure approaches this extreme form only when the fundamental differences between the groups are considered ethnic in nature (e.g., Jewish people). Caste is more than just simple ethnic segregation. The latter still permits each group in question to consider its own values (honor) to be high, but a caste system arranges these groups hierarchically, allotting one more honor than the rest. Any sense of dignity a lower-caste group might have would derive from its belief in a *future* beyond present conditions in which it would have an elevated status. In contrast, the privileged caste groups can and do derive their own sense of dignity from their *present and/or past* situation.

Weber stressed that class, status, and political power can be reciprocally related, with each affecting the others. Status can influence and even determine class (Weber, 1968, p. 306). However, his writing emphasized the effect of class on status in capitalist society. "Property as such is not always recognized as a status qualification, but in the long run it is, and with extraordinary regularity" (Weber, 1963, p. 49). Frequently, the richest person has the greatest prestige, and those in similar economic situations normally socialize with each other rather than with persons from different classes. Equality of status among individuals in unequal classes can "in the long run become quite precarious" (p. 49). Weber observed that although race, political power, and class have all been bases for status in the past, "today the class situation is by far the predominant fac-tor, for of course the possibility of a style of life expected for members of a status group is usually conditioned economically" (p. 53).

Despite the controlling importance of the class factor, Weber emphasized that status and class are not necessarily connected. Individuals who are low in class position can be high in prestige and vice versa. Analytically, status is opposed "to a distinction of power which is regulated exclusively through the market" (p. 54). If individuals who were high in class automatically received high status, "the status order would be threatened at its very root" (p. 55). Groups who base their high status on their lifestyle rather than only property are likely to feel threatened when the basis for honor shifts to the economic order.

Weber said very little about the conditions under which stratification by class or status pre-dominate. Weber maintained that "when the bases of the acquisition and distribution of goods are relatively stable, stratification by status is favored" (p. 56). If a status order is entrenched by virtue of monopolization of certain goods by particular groups, then the free-market principle is hindered; it cannot operate. Under these conditions, "the power of naked property per se, which gives its stamp to 'class formation,' is pushed into the background." But "every technological repercussion and economic transformation threatens stratification by status and pushes class situation into the foreground" (pp. 55–56). In contrast to commercial-class societies, which ordinarily operate in market-oriented economies, status societies are economically organized around religious, feudal, and patrimonial factors (Weber, 1968, p. 306). In capitalist societies, classes play a more important role than status (Giddens, 1973).

Parties

Political power generally is considered to be the third dimension of inequality included by Weber, though some interpret Weber to be saying that class, status, and party are each different forces around which the distribution of power can be organized (Giddens, 1973).

A **party** is an association that aims to secure "power within an organization [or the state] for its leaders in order to attain ideal or material advantages for its active members" (Weber, 1968, p. 284). Thus, Weber is not referring narrowly to what we think of as political parties (such as Democrats or Republicans) but to political groups more broadly conceived. Instead of parties being an outgrowth of class struggle, they can represent status groups, classes, or merely their own members and may use a variety of means to attain power. Well-organized interest groups would constitute parties in a Weberian sense.

Since parties aim for such goals as getting their programs developed or accepted and getting positions of influence within organizations, it is clear that they operate only within a rational order in which these goals are possible to attain and only when there is a struggle for power. Parties themselves, however, can be organized around a charismatic or traditional leader as well as being structured in a rational way with formal positions to which members are elected. Formally recognized political parties are not the only kind that exist; parties also can be organized around religious issues or those that concern the traditional rights of a leader in an organization (Weber, 1968, pp. 285–286).

Émile Durkheim (1858–1917)

In contrast to the theorists we have discussed, Émile Durkheim was not principally concerned with social inequality. Rather, he emphasized establishing sociology as a scientific discipline, uncovering the sources and forms of integration and moral authority, and tracking and understanding the place of individualism in modern industrial society (Giddens, 1978). Most of his works revolve around issues of integration and cohesiveness—that is, the question of order in society. Although liberal and reformist in outlook, Durkheim was a central founder of the functionalist school of thought in sociology, which views society as a social system tending toward equilibrium. The organic analogy of society is evident in his writing. Despite his preoccupations with questions of order and the evolutionary growth of societies, however, Durkheim had something to say about social inequality, and so a brief discussion is included here.

Émile Durkheim was born in 1858 in Alsace-Lorraine into a Jewish family which expected him to become a rabbi. Later, as a young man, he turned away from religion and became an agnostic, even though his study of the "elementary forms of religious life" is one of his major works. Durkheim wanted to study a subject that would directly address issues of moral and practical guidance for society, and he wanted to use a scientific approach in the analysis of issues. He turned to sociology as his discipline of choice and, to the disdain of many colleagues, became an imperialistic advocate of sociology rather than the other social sciences (Giddens, 1978). It is not surprising that topics related to order, development, and the relationship between the individual and the society would run as a common thread through Durkheim's body of work because of conditions in French society at the time. The early years of the Third Republic in France, when Durkheim was a young man, were marked by instability and conflicts between the political right and left.

Durkheim was actively involved in public affairs, including working toward restructuring the university system and helping early in the World War I effort by completing articles attacking Nationalist German writing (Coser, 1971). Durkheim's major sociological works did not begin to appear until the end of the nineteenth century. *The Division of Labor in Society*, the source we will be concerned with here, was completed in 1893, followed by *The Rules of Sociological Method* in 1895 and *Suicide* in 1897. Later, in 1912, he finished *The Elementary Forms of Religious Life*. Durkheim died in 1917 at the age of 59.

Durkheim and Inequality

In *The Division of Labor in Society*, Durkheim developed his theory of the movement of society from "mechanical" to "organic" solidarity. A society organized on mechanical solidarity is homogeneous, with a simple division of labor, and based on the similarity of the individuals in it. There is a strong collective conscience that serves as a principal source of moral cohesion. The individual ego is not prominent in this kind of society. In sharp contrast, societies organized around the organic form of solidarity are characterized by differences and interdependence in their division of labor. Social uniqueness, along with the increased individualism, can threaten the cohesiveness and stability of society. Corporate groups and the division of labor serve as means for integrating individuals in this kind of society. They stand midway, as it were, between the state and the individual.

In a fully developed organic society characterized by individualism, equal opportunity, specialization, and interdependence, inequality is to be expected because, at this point in evolution,

Photo 6.4 Émile Durkheim.
Source: Pictorial Press Ltd/Alamy Stock Photo.

Durkheim argued, it is based on differences in the *internal* abilities of individuals. A "normal" division of labor is based on internal differences between individuals, which include differences between men and women. Differences in the division of labor between men and women should persist, but other differences based on *external* qualities (e.g., race, inheritance), including classes, should decline and eventually disappear. As society evolves, differential rewards should, because of equal opportunity, directly reflect individual differences in abilities and differences in the social value of occupations. In short, Durkheim believed that as time moved on, modern society would be characterized by social inequalities between individuals based on their inner abilities rather than external characteristics. In a conflicting argument, however, while he argued that class and racial inequalities would diminish, he believed that social inequalities between men and women were justified due to internal differences between the sexes (Lehmann, 1995).

Until this point in evolution is reached, however, the division of labor can take on "abnormal" forms that prevent its appropriate and efficient functioning. Durkheim argued that this occurs when individuals' positions in it are forced or determined without moral regulation. Individuals must recognize the rights of others in the division of labor and their duties to society as well as to themselves. Ideally, each person must have the opportunity to occupy the position that fits their abilities (Grabb, 1984). When these conditions are not present, abnormal forms of the division of labor develop. Two of these are the **anomic** and **forced** forms of the **division** of labor.

In the first type, relations between people in the workplace are not governed by a generally agreed-on set of values and beliefs. Two of the developments that divided people were the split between "masters and workers," in which the organization is privately owned by the masters, and the arrival of large-scale industry in which workers were each given very narrow and differ-ent functions to perform. Both of these factors served to drive a wedge between employers and workers. With large industries, "the worker is more completely separated from the employer." And "at the same time that specialization becomes greater, revolts become more frequent" (Durkheim, 1933, p. 355). In smaller industries, in contrast, there is "a relative harmony between worker and employer. It is only in large-scale industry that these relations are in a sickly state" (p. 356). Large industry develops as markets grow and encompass groups not in immediate contact with each other. Producers and consumers become increasingly separated from each other. "The producer can no longer embrace the market in a glance, nor even in thought. He can no longer see its limits, since it is, so to speak, limitless. Accordingly, production becomes unbridled and unregulated" (p. 370); that is, a condition of **anomie** or normlessness exists. Economic crises develop, but industry grows as markets grow.

With the growth of industry and an increasingly minute division of labor, the individual worker becomes more "alienated," to use a Marxist term. Like Marx, Durkheim concluded that the worker becomes a "machine," performing mind-numbing, routine, repetitive labor without any sense of the significance of his or her role in the labor process: "Every day he repeats the same movements with monotonous regularity, but without being interested in them, and without understanding them" (p. 371). Although this description may sound intriguingly Marxist, Durkheim's view of the division of labor in modern society was quite different from that of Marx. Because of its nature, Durkheim viewed the division of labor as a central basis for integration in modern industrial society. It is only in certain abnormal forms that it becomes a problem. Basically, a complex division of labor is a necessity in *industrial* society. It is expected that, as societies develop, they become increasingly complex. In contrast, Marx viewed the division of labor as a source of basic problems in *capitalist* society. Class conflict was over fundamental issues in the property and social relationships involved in the division of labor. For Durkheim, class conflict was a surface symptom of an anomic state in which the employers and the workers were in conflict because of the absence of a common, agreed-on set of moral rules. The problems of modern society are not due to contradictions within capitalism "but derive from the strains inherent in the transition from mechanical to organic solidarity" (Giddens, 1978, p. 36). Marx saw regulation in capitalist society as stifling human initiative, whereas Durkheim saw moral regulation as necessary for individual liberty and happiness.

However, the mere presence of rules is not enough to prevent problems in the division of labor because "sometimes the rules themselves are the cause of evil. This is what occurs in class-wars" (Durkheim, 1933, p. 374). The problem here is that the rules governing the division of labor do not create a correspondence between individual talents or interests and work functions. The result is that the division of labor creates dissatisfaction and pain instead of integration and cohesiveness. "This is because the distribution of social functions on which [the class structure] rests does not respond, or rather no longer responds, to the distribution of natural talents" (p. 375). When the rules regulating the division of labor no longer correspond to the distribution of true talents among individuals, then the organization of labor becomes *forced* (the second type of division of labor referred to earlier). Durkheim argued that inequalities that were not based on "internal" differences between individuals were unjust. "External" inequality, which is based on inheritance, nepotism, or simple membership in some biological group, must be eliminated, according to Durkheim, because it threatens the solidarity of society. Superiority that results from differences in the resources of individuals is unjust. "In other words, there cannot be rich and poor at birth without there being unjust contracts" (p. 384). The sense of injustice associated with the significance of external inequalities becomes greater as labor becomes more separated from employers and the collective conscience becomes weaker.

Despite his realization of the injustices suffered by workers in the division of labor, Durkheim was not an advocate of class revolution. As mentioned, he did not believe that there is anything inherently wrong with a complex division of labor and, consequently, believed that only reformist change was needed to eliminate the problems associated with it. Durkheim felt that a complete revolution would destroy the delicate and complex membrane that made up society.

> I am quite aware when people speak of destroying existing societies, they intend to reconstruct them. But these are the fantasies of children. One cannot in this way rebuild collective life: once our social organization is destroyed, centuries of history will be required to build another. (quoted in Fenton, 1984, p. 31)

Durkheim suggested that deep, lasting change would take place gradually and through ameliorative reform rather than through drastic conflict. In this way also, he differed from Marx. Nor did he agree with Marx that the state was an instrument of oppression, but rather felt it could serve as an instrument of reform for a better society (Giddens, 1978). However, like Marx and in contrast to Weber, he had an optimistic view of future society. Fundamental class conflicts would be minimized once problems in the division of labor could be ironed out with appropriate policies and moral regulations over time.

W.E.B. Du Bois (1868–1963)

Neglected by the discipline for decades, it is only recently that W.E.B. Du Bois has been included among classical sociological theorists. This is likely for several reasons: First, though he was born only 50 years after Marx and was more or less a contemporary of Weber and Durkheim, he was speaking mostly from an American context and was often addressing the problems of the twentieth century. Marx, Weber, and Durkheim are often considered "classical theorists" because they are concerned with the "foundational moment arising from the internal transformation of European society" (Connell, 1997, p. 1513). At first glance, Du Bois' writings do not appear to address the same issues.

Second, while Du Bois was hailed as a powerful public sociologist, some wrongly believed that he never developed a complex sociological theory. Lewis Coser is quoted as stating that "[m]asters of sociological thought are those rare scholars who build theoretical systems, and Du Bois did not build such a system" (Morris, 2015, p. xv). Over half of his career was spent as an activist and a journalist, working outside of the walls of academia (Green & Wortham, 2015, p. 529); thus, many overlooked his strength as a social theorist. Further, his writing is beautiful and poetic, making it possible for some to overlook the complex theoretical constructions undergirding his writing.

Finally, and undeniably most importantly, persistent racism has precluded his recognition as a key figure in sociology (Green & Wortham, 2015; Morris, 2015).

> He was a black man writing mostly about black life at a time when most Americans cared little about black men—or women—or their lives. He studied, documented, and theorized about what many would rather ignore or sidestep: racism, that disturbing disease of American culture so readily denied and dismissed by those it infects. (Zuckerman, 2004, p. 7)

The racism of his time and the continuing racism in academia have limited the extent to which he has been embraced in the field.

There are very strong arguments for labeling Du Bois a classical theorist, particularly regarding issues of inequality. Classical sociological theory arose from the context of empire, colonialism, and the rise of the modern era. Du Bois' work fits centrally into that framework, as he teases out the national and global relationships between race, class, capitalism, and colonialism. Additionally,

Photo 6.5 W.E.B. Du Bois, 1907.
Source: National Portrait Gallery, Smithsonian Institution.

as with other classical theorists, he addressed the place of sociology as a discipline and how to combine theory with data collection and analysis. Du Bois can arguably be considered the founder of American empirical sociology, particularly with his groundbreaking work, *The Philadelphia Negro* (Green & Wortham, 2015; Morris, 2015). He outlined in various writings his blueprint for sociology as a discipline; for example, in several of his writings, he chastises sociologists for being armchair theorists or "car-window" sociologists who seek to understand the "snarl of the century" from casual observations while on holiday (Du Bois, 2007, p. 105). Finally, if by "classical," we mean foundational, there is no doubt that Du Bois provides us with foundational understandings of race, inequality, globalization, and urban ecology.

William Edward Burghardt Du Bois was born in 1868 in Great Barrington, Massachusetts, raised by his mother, a domestic worker. He speaks of his childhood as one remarkably free of an awareness of racial inequality:

> My schoolmates were invariably white; I joined quite naturally all games, excursions, church festivals … I was in and out of the homes of nearly all my mates, and ate and played with them. I was a boy unconscious of color discrimination in any obvious and specific way. (Du Bois, 1944, p. 28)

Recognized at an early age for his intelligence, his mostly White community raised money to send him to Fisk University, where he earned his first undergraduate degree. His time at Fisk represented his first experience with the South and Jim Crow racism (Morris, 2015, p. 16). It is here that he began refining his concept of **double-consciousness**, or "this sense of always looking at one's self through the eyes of others, of measuring one's soul by the tape of a world that looks on in amused contempt and pity" (Du Bois, 2007, p. 8). This double vision includes the conflicted phenomenon of seeing oneself simultaneously as an American and as an African American. At this point in his life, Du Bois became personally more aware of the felt realities of racism, and he thus pledged to focus his career on understanding and ameliorating discrimination facing people of color.

> From a section and circumstances where the status of me and my folk could be rationalized as the result of poverty and limited training, and settled essentially by schooling and hard effort, I suddenly came to a region where the world was split into white and black halves, and where the darker half was held back by race prejudice and legal bonds, as well as by deep ignorance and dire poverty.
>
> (Du Bois, 1944, p. 31)

After Fisk, Du Bois received his B.A. in History from Harvard, studying most notably with scholars such as William James, Josiah Royce, and George Santayana. Following his undergraduate work in 1892, he studied at the University of Berlin, where he was introduced to leading German scholars, including Max Weber and Gustav von Schmoller. His time in Berlin was immensely influential in forming his understanding of research in the social sciences, and he as well greatly influenced others, most notably Weber, to whom he introduced a more robust and complex understanding of race and racism (Morris, 2015). The social experience was also impactful—in Berlin, he found a cosmopolitan environment free of racial prejudice, which provided him the opportunity "of looking at the world as a man and not simply from a narrow racial and provincial outlook ... unveiled by the accident of color" (Du Bois, 1944, p. 35).

Following his return to the States, he completed his Ph.D.; he was the first African American scholar to earn a Ph.D. from Harvard. He taught for two years at Wilberforce University, followed by a year at the University of Pennsylvania as an "assistant in Sociology," where he wrote *The Philadelphia Negro*. Following his stint in Philadelphia, he accepted a professorship in History and Economics at Atlanta University, where he established a "Laboratory in Sociology." The aim of the laboratory was to understand the "problems facing American Negroes" via fieldwork and statistical analyses performed by both undergraduate and post-graduate students (Du Bois, 1903). It was during this period that he was dedicated to the development of an empirical sociology of enlightening others through the creation of a comprehensive catalog of the condition of African Americans in the United States.

> My faith in its success was based on the firm belief that race prejudice was based on widespread ignorance. My long-term remedy was Truth: carefully gathered scientific proof that neither color nor race determined the limits of a man's capacity or desert.
>
> (Du Bois, 1944, p. 41)

During this time and in much of his earlier career, he was often compared with the educator and African American leader Booker T. Washington in his approach to furthering the interests of Blacks in America. For Washington, that approach involved stressing industrial education, manual labor, and accommodation. Finding themselves at the bottom of the social hierarchy, Washington argued that it was there that African Americans must begin their work and education. Equality was a fight for the future (Morris, 2015, p. 8). Du Bois, in contrast, argued that Washington was supporting a system of segregation and that it was more essential to support the most talented of the race, whom he came to call the "talented tenth."

> Not the lifting of the lowly, but the unchaining of the unawakened mighty, will reveal the possibilities of genius, gift and miracle, in mountainous treasure-trove, which hitherto civilization has scarcely touched; and yet boasted blatantly and even glorified in its poverty.
>
> (Du Bois, 1944, p. 56)

Du Bois was to be disappointed with his time at Atlanta University, however, for although he and his colleagues produced a wealth of data on the condition of African Americans, they did not receive widespread recognition in the discipline. Though he certainly shed much truth on our understanding of Black America, that truth did not change minds and hearts.

Wanting to be engaged more in activism than in academic life, in 1909, Du Bois became one of the founders of the National Association for the Advancement of Colored People and the editor and publisher of the *Crisis*. Echoing Marx's focus on *praxis*, he stated:

> I faced situations that called—shrieked—for action, even before any detailed, scientific study could possibly be prepared. It was as though, as a bridge-builder, I was compelled to throw a bridge across a stream without waiting for the careful mathematical testing of materials. (Du Bois, 1944, p. 47)

It is also at this time that he began to consider himself a socialist: "But of one thing I am certain: I believe in the dictum of Karl Marx, that the economic foundation of a nation is widely decisive for its politics, its art and its culture" (Du Bois, 1944, p. 50).

Later in his career, Du Bois continued to become more radical and more focused on activist causes. He established and participated in various Pan African congresses aimed at fighting "**colonial imperialism**" (Du Bois, 1944, p. 24), and in 1945 represented the NAACP at the conference that established the United Nations. It was at one of the Pan African congresses that he met the future first president of Ghana, who invited him to the country. Becoming increasingly disillusioned with the NAACP and with the state of politics in the United States, Du Bois eventually moved to Ghana to edit the *Encyclopedia Africana*, where he died in 1968.

Race, Capitalism, and Class Inequality

In sociology textbooks, Du Bois is often relegated to the marginalized position of a "Black Sociologist" or is perhaps given a box in chapters on race as an historic commentator on issues of race and ethnicity. But as with Marx, Weber, and Durkheim, Du Bois was engaged in the work of understanding the central forces determining the modern era. Du Bois' research was closely related to Weber's method and attention, focusing on the relationship between agrarian populations and capitalism and stressing the power of ideas in affecting social behavior (Morris, 2015; Zuckerman, 2004). While for Weber, those ideas were located in the Protestant ethic, for Du Bois, it was the power of racism in forming social institutions and relationships (Zuckerman, 2004, p. 9). Studying under the economist von Schmoller, Du Bois was encouraged to engage in a close historical analysis of the relationship between history, culture, and economics (Morris, 2015, p. 152). As did Marx, Weber, and Durkheim, therefore, Du Bois was interested in understanding how capitalism flourished in European and American societies. For Du Bois, however, the key factor was "the colonization, exploitation, and domination of peoples of color" (Morris, 2015, p. 155). That is, he argued that we cannot understand the spread of capitalism globally as a system without recognizing that this growth and expansion were only possible through racial oppression.

Following his experience in the American South, the key question Du Bois was motivated to explore was the "Negro question." He summarized this question by stating that

> in the heart of the nation that had laughed about social prejudices and that had set itself the goal of erecting a state with the least conceivable class differences, there existed from the very beginning the worst of all caste differences that, unheeded, grew to a threatening girth, namely a slavery based on race and color. (Du Bois, 1944, p. 243)

The industrial development the United States enjoyed was "based on the blood and sweat of unpaid Negro labor in the seventeenth, eighteenth, and nineteenth centuries" (Du Bois, 1906, p. 284). How, in a society predicated on equality and the lack of social differentiation, do we find a system built on slavery?

Du Bois argued that a "shift in the ideology of the American people" led to the "struggle of the races." This struggle was caused by "(1) the growing inequality in the distribution of wealth, (2) the rise of imperialism, and (3) the color line" (Du Bois, 1906, p. 282). With the rise of large corporations, the gap between the rich and the poor increased dramatically, creating a wealthy class intent on centralizing power. "Private wealth of fabulous and almost incomprehensible proportions was accumulated next to which appeared the question of the poor, the lack of employment, homelessness and child misery" (Du Bois, 1906, p. 282). Additionally, the United States became a world power and became increasingly imperialistic. In its need for labor, it turned to regions inhabited by peoples of color, leading to the growth of the slave trade and the annexation of the Philippines, Puerto Rico, Panama, and Hawaii. The growth of inequality and imperialism created a conflict with notions of equality, the foundational ideology of the nation, according to Du Bois. This conflict needed to be reconciled.

The reconciliation was made possible by the hardening of the color line. By establishing a category of individuals who were distinguished by the color of their skin and designated as a caste, it was then an easier step to draw caste lines based on class: "Caste mentality produces caste mentality" (Du Bois, 1906, p. 284). To justify the enslavement of others in a system prided on equality, the other had to be defined as lesser. This perspective supported an ideology that, by nature, some are less worthy than others and thus can be exploited. Structures and processes established to maintain the color line also increased and concretized class differences.

In articulating the complex relationship between race and class, and in his other writings gender and nationality, Du Bois can be considered one of the first to articulate a theory of intersectionality (Hancock, 2005). He was greatly frustrated by socialist movements that ignored the significance of race in furthering and enabling class exploitation. Similarly, he was the first to draw attention to the class heterogeneity of the Black community and the important leadership opportunities this heterogeneity provided. Finally, he argued for the importance of building political movements based on these intersections:

> What is today the message of these black women to America and to the world? The uplift of women is, next to the problem of the color line and the peace movement, our greatest modern cause. When, now, two of these movements—woman and color—combine in one, the combination has deep meaning. (Du Bois, 1920, p. 105)

The Color Line: Race as Caste

Du Bois shared with the other classical theorists the concept that a social problem represents the mismatch between the goals of a society and the ability of an individual or group to achieve those goals. The key social problem for Du Bois was race; as he famously stated, "the problem of the Twentieth Century is the problem of the color line" (Du Bois, 2007, p. 1). That color line occurs because race in America had become a caste.

In unpacking the essence of race as a caste, Du Bois and Weber shared similar frameworks, perhaps due to the influence that Du Bois had on Weber's thinking about race. For both, castes represented rigid hierarchies based on "laws and rituals," separated and segregated, where members of the upper class are honored and command the respect of others (Morris, 2015, p. 164). For Du Bois, the creation of a racial caste system was and remains a political act aimed at centralizing political, social, and economic power (Morris, 2015, p. 39).

Du Bois argued that the United States originally was not built on a caste system—in fact, it was predicated on a model that rejected caste. A central dilemma in the founding of the United States, however, was the creation and availability of a labor supply to develop industry and to produce wealth. Slavery provided a solution to that problem, though one fraught with problems of discipline and control and the constant fear of rebellion. To address these concerns, slave codes were created restricting the movements and activities of slaves. This slave code was aimed to "fit a class distinguished by its condition more than by its race or color" (Du Bois, 1898, p. 4).

By the mid-eighteenth century, Du Bois argued that the presence of American-born, freed Blacks resulted in the beginning of communities and group life based on race. These groups were heterogeneous and, more ominously for the Whites in power, they held the potential for resurrection and rebellion. In response to these fears, the Slave Code became a Black Code, "replacing a caste of condition by a caste of race" (Du Bois, 1898, p. 4).

Following emancipation, the question of where to find a supply of cheap (or better yet free) labor only intensified, as the value of crops in the South gave rise to an agriculture industry sorely lacking workers. The race code provided solutions to this problem by creating laws and economic contracts that made the freed slaves economically dependent on White masters. For example, providing the precedent for and foreshadowing of the current environment described by Michelle Alexander in *The New Jim Crow* (2012), the criminalization of small offenses such as vagrancy forced freedmen and their children to work for former slave owners for free. A system in the South was established whereby convict labor could be hired out to those who paid the most. These owners then could treat the prisoners in nearly any manner they wished (Du Bois, 1906, p. 255). Thus, Du Bois argues that there was little difference between formal slavery and the new post-emancipation system (Morris, 2015, p. 39).

Photo 6.6 Sharecropper plowing, Montgomery County, Alabama.
Source: Library of Congress.

The movement from a code based on labor condition to a code based on race meant the development of a clear subordinated class held in lower regard and esteem by the wider population. With the criminalization and degradation of Blacks, "Americans begin to show not only open contempt for the 'bastard races,' but also a growing respect for snobbism and they gladly began to forget the color of their grandfathers' fingernails" (Du Bois, 1906, p. 283). White working-class individuals failed to recognize the similarity between the oppression of Blacks and the oppression that their parents and grandparents faced at the hands of capitalists and supported a system to exploit Black workers. From a Marxist framework, this involved the establishment of race consciousness over class consciousness, and as Du Bois argued,

> [A]s soon as the poison of the class mentality penetrates the life-spirit of a nation, then the standpoint of the privileged classes alone determines its judgment of good and evil … Class hierarchy grows today in America, in the land that was founded as a mighty protest against this folly that rules the world. It grows almost undisturbed, for its victims today are mostly blacks. (Du Bois, 1906, pp. 283–284)

Thus, slavery and subsequently the race code made possible the oppression of the working class by dividing White and Black laborers and the work they engaged in across color lines. Racial prejudice in Du Bois' model, therefore, was not primarily psychological but "a powerful weapon used by the dominant group to achieve and maintain power" (Morris, 2015, p. 131). For Du Bois, "the caste system was retrogressive because it prevented people from being judged on merits, restricted mass education and the franchise, and limited the effectiveness of labor unions to protect workers' rights" (Morris, 2015, p. 165).

A racial caste system for Du Bois is maintained via several structural mechanisms: (1) the spatial segregation of the races, limiting a sense of neighborliness and groupness between the races; (2) economic segregation, whereby some are able to create wealth and others are not, and work is segregated; (3) political relations, such that one race maintains control over political life and the administration of the government; and (4) intellectual or cultural interaction, or "the exchange of ideas through conversations and meetings" (Du Bois, 1906, p. 265).

In one of his more controversial statements, Du Bois argued that due to these structural mechanisms, Blacks were not part of the "social group" because of a lack of cultural development that "had not reached a sufficiently high grade of culture" (1898, p. 7). Because of the oppression they faced, Blacks did not develop sufficiently economically or in "mental training" and efficiency. Critics have suggested that Du Bois was "blaming the victim" and subscribing to a biologically based model of racial inferiority. But this was far from the reality of his argument: "systems of domination produce and are sustained by cultures of subordination that drastically curtail challenges from below and derail social development of the oppressed" (Morris, 2015, p. 39). If Blacks as a social group were underdeveloped, it was due to the oppression they faced.

Importantly, Du Bois also argued that Blacks were not part of the social group because they faced a population that did not want them to be part of the group and engaged in various mechanisms to exclude them. Thus, as a group, they were affected by both ignorance (cultural degradation) and prejudice. Du Bois suggested that it is important to recognize both factors but that politically this has been nearly impossible:

> If a Negro discusses the question, he is apt to discuss simply the problem of race prejudice; if a Southern white man writes on the subject, he is apt to discuss problems of ignorance, crime and social degradation; and yet each calls the problem he discusses the Negro problem, leaving in the dark background the really crucial question as to the relative importance of the many problems involved. (Du Bois, 1898, p. 9)

Du Bois' work, *The Philadelphia Negro*, successfully engages in such a multi-faceted study.

Urban Ecology

The Philadelphia Negro: A Social Study (Du Bois, 1899) represents an important work in the history of sociology and in our understanding of the theories of W.E.B. Du Bois, not only because it may represent the first and finest example of a sweeping empirical sociological study in the United States (Hunter, 2013b; Morris, 2015), but because it outlines brilliantly the relationship between race relations and the development of the physical and social infrastructure of the young nation. In the fall of 1896, having just left Wilberforce University, Du Bois arrived at the Seventh Ward of Philadelphia to begin an exhaustive study of the history and current state of the neighborhood. Du Bois and his assistant, Isabel Eaton, conducted a door-to-door canvas of the neighborhood, administering surveys and questionnaires, personal interviews, and analyzing archival data and statistics of the ward (McGrail, 2013).

Central to his study was an "ecological conundrum" (Hunter, 2013a, 2013b): Why were the rates of poverty and unemployment so high in the Seventh Ward when it was adjacent to the center of industry and employment in Philadelphia? The answer was that the Seventh Ward was its own social system, an urban enclave born of persistent racial exclusion, economic discrimination, and racial prejudice. "Here is a large group of people—perhaps forty-five thousand, *a city within a city*—who do not form an integral part of the larger social group" (Du Bois, 1899, p. 5; emphasis added).

Du Bois' analysis turned traditional urban ecological models on their heads. Most urban ecological models at the time, most notably those of Park and Burgess of the Chicago School, argued that the growth and development of a city stemmed from the nature of its core economic and social structures at the heart of the city. Du Bois argued something very different: that racial exclusion and the nation's history of slavery, along with the neglected *agency* of the Black community, profoundly affected the growth of cities, even a northern abolitionist city such as Philadelphia. "[T]he geography of opportunity—cultural, political, economic or otherwise—is tied to the racial geography of the city, fostering unevenness in the location and distribution of opportunity and residents" (Hunter, 2013a, p. 3).

Du Bois argued that the Seventh Ward of Philadelphia developed with clearly defended boundaries, maintained both from without via discrimination, and from within via the creation of Black social institutions. The ward was home to recent migrants from southern cities, including Baltimore, Memphis, Richmond, and Washington, DC, and as was the case with Black urban enclaves in most northern cities, the structure of the Seventh Ward has to be seen in the context of the racial geography of the nation as a whole. As Blacks moved north during the Great Migration, they established enclaves in northern cities that were bounded by borders maintained legally and culturally through racial practices and beliefs.

In his update on the state of the Seventh Ward, Marcus Hunter (2013a, pp. 7–8) argues forcefully that "Du Bois's urban approach, then, is one that conceptualizes the city's spatial organization as caused by racial historical events, namely those involving conflict." The migrants were coming into a city that did not want them: "The undeniable fact that most Philadelphia white people prefer not to live near Negroes limits the negro very seriously in his choice of a home and especially in his choice of a cheap home" (Du Bois, 1899, p. 295). We cannot, therefore, understand the persistent poverty of Black neighborhoods or the structure of our cities as a whole, including those in the north, without understanding how the United States as a nation wrestled with the "Negro Problem."

Equally central to Du Bois' argument, however, is the conclusion that the activities of Black residents in the neighborhood truly mattered as they had agency in the process of establishing the enclave. Black individuals actively created community through the establishment of social institutions such as churches, schools, and clubs, and these institutions further attracted newer migrants to

> **BOX 6.1 WHY NO REVOLUTION?**
>
> Famously Marx predicted that the proletariat would rise up and overthrow the capitalist systems, that the workers would be the "gravediggers of capitalism." Similarly, Du Bois stated that the "day of the colored races dawns" (Du Bois, 1906, p. 287), and he hoped that citizens would rise up to overthrow the color line. Du Bois was eventually pessimistic that this would ever happen, as are many contemporary Marxists. Why didn't the revolution happen? Also, as we will discuss more in Chapter 14, we are seeing an upsurge in political activity and rebellion. Will the current protests result in structural changes that will lessen the inequality in our society?

the city. Certainly, they were excluded from White neighborhoods through devices such as violence, racial covenants, and zoning restrictions, but Du Bois states that new migrants chose to live in the parts of the city where they could "easily form congenial acquaintances and new ties. The Negro who ventures away from the mass of his people and their organized life, finds himself alone, shunned and taunted, stared at and made uncomfortable" (Du Bois, 1899, p. 297). Black residents, heterogeneous in their class background, were "developing Black neighborhoods whose boundaries are based upon racial histories and the actions and attitudes of its residents" (Hunter, 2013a, p. 13). Thus, these institutions arose from the racial history of the city, yet they also worked to affirm it. Black residents were not merely reacting to racial histories, they were proactively creating histories. Du Bois' analysis is the first representation of a very "Black-centered" analysis of the growth and development of a city that recognizes the heterogeneity and vibrancy of the Black community (Hunter, 2013a).

Summary

It was mentioned at the outset of the chapter that a thorough understanding of what Marx, Weber, Durkheim, and Du Bois had to say about inequality depends on seeing and analyzing that work in the context of their broader theories and perspectives on society and human beings. Too often, as a reflection of our specialization and departmentalization, we wrench out only those segments of an individual's theory in which we have an immediate interest. This is not the way in which these theories were developed, and so taking them out of context can lead to distortions and, at best, only superficial understanding. Consequently, the specific observations made by these individuals on inequality should be couched in the broader frameworks of their overall perspectives and life experiences. Hopefully, this leads to a fuller comprehension of what each of these theorists was trying to convey.

It is clear from the discussion in this chapter that these men differed significantly in their views on human nature, the forms that inequality could take, and the bases and future of inequality. Weber saw human beings as self-seeking, whereas Marx viewed them in more selfless terms. Durkheim felt that individuals required regulation and guidance. Marx focused on economic classes, as did Durkheim in *The Division of Labor in Society*, whereas Weber examined economic classes as well as status groups, and to some extent, parties. Du Bois focused on the exploitation of people of color. Marx sought the source of inequality in an individual's relationship to the means of production, whereas Weber saw inequality arising from a number of sources, including market situation, lifestyle, and decision-making power. Durkheim argued that although inequality

Table 6.1 Summary of Basic Ideas on Inequality from Classical Theorists

	Theorists' Views on Inequality				
Theorist	Major Concern	Forms	Causes	Inevitability	Future
Marx	Classes in Capitalist Society	Historical Class Structures	Private Property	No	Revolution and Classless Society
Weber	Dimensions of Inequality and Shifts in Their Prominence	Class, Status, Party	Market Situation; Granting of Status Honor; Political Power	Yes	Rationalization of Society and Growing Salience of Class
Durkheim	Abnormal Forms of Division of Labor	Masters and Workers	Anomic and Forced Divisions of Labor	Mixed	Decline of Class Conflict in Industrial Society
Du Bois	Racial Inequality	Caste Race, Class	Political and Economic Power	No	Revolution and Destruction of the Color Line

continued to be based on biological and inheritance factors, he assumed that eventually, in organic society, most social inequality would be founded solely on individual differences in abilities. Weber and Durkheim did not see inequality as disappearing in the future, but Marx and Du Bois were more optimistic on this point.

Marx and Weber agreed that classes and class struggle are significant elements in societies. Both felt that capitalism has dehumanizing effects and is class-structured and that class is a predominant factor in modern society. They each outline similar conditions for class consciousness and protest. Weber, however, developed a more involved understanding of the nature of class. Du Bois argued that we cannot understand class without understanding race. In contrast to Marx and Weber, Durkheim argued that, because of its nature, industrial society contains less alienating and structured forms of inequality.

Table 6.1 highlights the central features of the main theorists covered in this chapter. The theories of Marx, Weber, Durkheim, and Du Bois were presented because their perspectives have helped to shape modern social science. Their impact has not always been obvious, but it has been pervasive.

Critical Thinking

1. Is class or social status more important in understanding the everyday conditions and choices of individuals in the United States?
2. Is a classless society possible or even approachable? If so, what problems, if any, would arise from the classlessness? If not, why not?
3. In light of current trends in poverty, income, and wealth inequality in the United States, which of these theorists seem to make the most sense? Why?
4. Taking into account that the United States is a capitalist society, do you think the federal government should or should not have a role in reducing inequality and poverty? Why?
5. What parts of Marx's theory still seem to apply today?

Web Connections

Marx, Weber, and Durkheim were among the giants of sociology during its classical period. To find out more about them and to read interviews that Marx and Engels had with various media representatives, go to the Marxist Archive, which also contains information on writers who followed in their footsteps. Comparisons of Marx with Weber and Durkheim can also be carried out by browsing and reading this website: www.marxists.org.

Film Suggestions

In Time (2011). A dystopian feature film that conveys Marx's social theory.

Up in the Air (2010). A feature film about a professional employment terminator (George Clooney) that illustrates many of Weber's ideas.

W.E.B. Du Bois: A Biography in Four Voices (1996). A documentary about the life and ideas of the classical theorist.

7 Contemporary Explanations of Inequality

Chapter 6 outlined how, at the onset of the modern age, the classical theorists provided a framework for explaining the inequalities that they were witnessing. They were generally thinking about structural changes in our society and how these brought about or increased inequality. For Marx, that inequality centered on class and the fundamental ways that capitalism structured the relationships between classes. Weber extended Marx's perspective by suggesting that status, honor, and political power are essential components of inequality. Durkheim emphasized the inequalities stemming from the division of labor, and Du Bois analyzed the complex relationships between race and class.

Contemporary theorists build on or borrow from each of these perspectives, recognizing the importance of the large-scale structural factors identified by the classical theorists but probing further about how these factors intersect with culture, interactional processes, individual identities, and definitions of self. Thus, within contemporary theory, conversations addressing inequality have posed a variety of questions: is inequality inevitable? Is inequality best explained by *individual* or by *structural* causes? What is the interaction between these individual and structural processes? What role does culture play? And finally, how do different kinds of inequality intersect?

Regardless of the direction or form their theory takes, many of those writing about social inequality begin with the idea that social inequality is about how the *categories* we use to describe people result in an unequal access to resources. As humans, we continually categorize the things around us—categories are how we think about the world and how we structure it. Thus, as we interact with other people, we recognize differences, and we place these differences into categories. Some people are tall, some are short. Some are smart, and some are, well, less so. Some are musical, and others cannot carry a tune. But how do we decide what the central categories are and which attributes or qualities belong in those categories? How do those categories lead to inequalities? How do they become ranked? Why are some categories more defining of who we are than others? And finally, how do these categories and the intersections between the categories structure our world and our individual sense of self?

This chapter outlines these more contemporary explanations for social inequality, focusing on broader or more generalized frameworks. Many of the other chapters in this text introduce theories explicating particular forms of inequality centered on class, gender, or race.

Inequality as Individual Difference

One of the more enduring arguments, stemming largely from Durkheim's work, is the idea that inequality is inevitable in any organized society due to individual differences in training and talent. This argument suggests that some people are simply more qualified and deserving and that these differences appropriately sort themselves out in a labor market. The imagery here is of society as a giant sorting machine involving things to sort (individuals), categories to sort them into,

DOI: 10.4324/9781003184966-9

processes for sorting them, and resources attached to these categories (Tilly, 2003). Sometimes the processes are based on the recognition of individual differences, other times they may be based on bias and prejudice. Regardless of the process, though, from this perspective individual differences are at the root of our understanding of inequality. In this section, we discuss this approach, beginning with functionalist theories of stratification, followed by more recent labor market theories.

Functionalist Theory of Stratification

Durkheim's belief that inequality in modern society is based primarily on differences in internal talents and the division of labor is echoed in the 1945 theory of Kingsley Davis and Wilbert Moore. Few theories of stratification have called forth the attention and criticism that the Davis–Moore theory has received. Though this theory is now quite dated and often contested, it provided a compelling framework that helped set the stage for a productive conversation across several decades among theorists of inequality.

Like Durkheim's theory, Davis and Moore's theory is based on a **functionalist** framework. The functionalist perspective views societies as social systems that have certain basic problems to solve or functions that have to be performed if the society is to survive. One of these problems concerns the motivation of society's members; if that motivation is absent, a society will not survive (Aberle et al., 1950, p. 103). If a society is to continue, important tasks must be specifically delineated and some means for their assignment and accomplishment created. And since certain goods of value are scarce, such as property or wealth, "some system of differential allocation of the scarce values of a society is essential" (p. 106). The result of this differential allocation (stratification) must be viewed as being legitimate and "accepted by most of the members—at least by the important ones—of a society if stability is to be attained" (p. 106).

The arguments in Davis and Moore's functionalist theory are quite easy to grasp and, on the surface, may appear to be commonsensical and even self-evident. One should keep in mind that the kind of thinking that is represented in their theory dominated sociology throughout the 1950s and much of the 1960s in the United States.

Davis and Moore (1945) indicated at the outset of their argument that they were trying to explain (1) the presence of stratification in all societies and (2) why *positions* are differentially ranked in the system of rewards in a society. Assuming that structure is at least minimally divided into different statuses and roles (i.e., a division of labor), Davis and Moore began by arguing that every society has to have some means to place its members in the social structure. A critical issue is the problem of motivating individuals to occupy certain statuses (full-time occupations) and to make sure that they are motivated to adequately perform the roles once they occupy those positions. Since some tasks are more onerous, more important for the society, and more difficult to perform, a system of rewards (inducements) is needed to ensure that these tasks are performed by the most capable individuals. "The rewards and their distribution become a part of the social order, and thus give rise to stratification" (p. 243). As with Durkheim's view of the ideal industrial society, Davis and Moore assumed that the society will run smoothly because the distribution of rewards to individuals will reflect the "internal inequalities" of their skills and capabilities.

Every society has a variety of rewards that it can use: (1) those "that contribute to sustenance and comfort" (money, goods of different kinds), (2) those related to "humor and diversion" (vacations, leisure), and (3) those that enhance "self-respect and ego expansion" (psychological rewards, promotion). Consequently, Davis and Moore are not simply talking about the distribution and system of economic rewards but all kinds of inducements that can promote motivation to perform tasks in the society. Not all positions have equal rewards attached to them, of course, and since that is the case, social inequality is "an unconsciously evolved device by which societies ensure that the most important positions are conscientiously filled by the most qualified persons"

(p. 243). According to this approach, since every society has tasks that are differentially important to its survival, every society is stratified.

Davis and Moore specified two criteria that determine the rewards that accrue to given positions: (1) the functional importance of the task; and (2) the "scarcity of personnel" capable of performing the task or the amount of training required (pp. 243–244). Together these determine the rank of a given position in the system of rewards—that is, in the stratification system. Consequently, "a position does not bring power and privilege because it draws a high income. Rather it draws a high income because it is functionally important and the available personnel is for one reason or another scarce" (pp. 246–247).

Societies differ in their stratification systems because they contain different conditions that affect either one or both of the principal determinants of ranking—that is, either functional importance or scarcity. The stage of cultural development and their situation with respect to other societies vary between societies, causing certain tasks to be more important in one society than in another and in personnel being scarcer for certain tasks than for others.

Figure 7.1 outlines the essential argument of the Davis–Moore thesis. What could be more logical? Certain tasks are more important than others, and some are more difficult to carry out. In order to make sure they are performed, more rewards are attached to them. Thus, people are motivated to perform them, and the society continues to function.

Critique of the Functionalist Theory of Stratification

For the first 40 years after its publication, Davis and Moore confronted a storm of criticism over their theory. A central problem of the Davis–Moore theory is how to establish the *functional necessity* of a task for a society. Further, their criteria for defining *functional importance* are not clear, and studies attempting to measure the effect of functional importance on reward structures have yielded, at best, mixed results (Wallace, 1997).

Another of the principal criticisms of the functional perspective is that it deals with highly abstract social systems (utopias) and has little to do with the operation of concrete societies (Dahrendorf, 1958). As it applies here, the criticism means that if stratification of rewards is the means by which a society ensures that the most qualified people fill the most important positions, then it is crucial that there be a free flow of talent throughout the society. But, in fact, as Tumin (1953) made plain, this is not the case in real societies. People in the lower strata usually have restricted opportunities, societies are not freely competitive, and people probably are not taking full advantage of the talent they may have. The roles of conflict and lack of opportunity must be considered when trying to understand the socioeconomic arrangement of real societies (Dahrendorf, 1958), and although Davis and Moore did mention the roles of power and wealth in determining and maintaining positions, they did not stress these as major determinants.

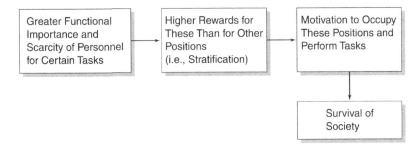

Figure 7.1 The Davis–Moore Theory of Stratification.

Finally, Tumin (1953) was the first major critic to point out that stratification can have numerous dysfunctions for society and the individual, a point ignored in the original Davis–Moore argument. Among the dysfunctions he noted are that stratification (1) inhibits the discovery of talent; (2) limits the extent to which productive resources can be expanded; (3) provides those at the top with the power to rationalize and justify their high position; (4) weakens the self-images among those at the bottom and thereby hinders their psychological development; (5) can create hostility and disintegration if it is not fully accepted by all in society; and (6) may make some feel that they are not full participants and, therefore, make them feel less loyal to the society. In a society where individuals can freely move up on the basis of their talent, would not the failures they suffer be felt even more acutely, knowing that they personally, and not the system, are to blame for their low position in the system of rewards? To what extent is the labor market structured to find those most talented?

Labor Market Theories of Earnings Inequality

The central place that individual differences and talents are sorted and ranked is in the labor market. If Davis and Moore are correct in their analysis of stratification, and if societal systems are functioning properly, labor markets should find those individuals most qualified for the jobs that are most important for a smoothly functioning society. A key question arising from their theory thus is whether labor markets actually operate in the efficient manner they assume. Labor market theories of inequality address this question and examine whether there are biases or imperfections in how individuals are sorted in the market.

The neoclassical labor market theory is based on the assumptions that: (1) a relatively free and open market exists in which individuals compete for positions; (2) position in that market depends heavily on the individual's efforts, abilities, experience, training, or **human capital**; and (3) there are automatic mechanisms that operate in the marketplace to ensure that imbalances between one's input (human capital) and one's rewards (wages) are corrected in a way that restores balance. From this perspective, human labor is seen as a good, similar to any other good in the marketplace (Sørensen, 2007).

In a society in which free competition exists, persons who contribute equal resources in the society receive a wage commensurate with their contributions. The more resources one offers and the greater one's value to any potential employer, the greater the demand for one's services and the higher the wages (Avent-Holt & Tomaskovic-Devey, 2014). Thus, factors such as one's education, training, skills, and intelligence are components that are crucial in explaining an individual's

---

BOX 7.1 WHY DOES LEBRON JAMES EARN SO MUCH?

In July 2018, the Los Angeles Lakers announced a four-year, $154 million deal with LeBron James, making him the highest paid professional basketball player in history and well on his way to becoming a billionaire. In writing about the deal, the *New York Times* stated that

> He has become a postseason staple—and a boon for the league, which has seldom, if ever, produced a player who so effortlessly combines strength and finesse, a 6-foot-8 forward who has the body of a bulldozer and the mind of a professor. (Stein & Cacciola, 2018)

How would Davis and Moore explain this salary? Would you agree? How would you explain why celebrity sports stars earn so much more than the average worker? Is that a good thing?

Photo 7.1 LeBron James.
Source: Wikicommons/Keith Allison.

wages. These are the elements that must be changed if one's wages are to change. We have seen, for example, a reduction in the wage gap between men and women in the past few decades, in part because of a reversal in the educational gap—women are now more highly educated than men, and this has reduced, though not eliminated, the gap in wages (Blau & Kahn, 2017). Of course, as we will see, the market often does not reward investments in human capital equally.

In addition to one's resources, the demand for one's skills is also important, and that demand depends on conditions in the marketplace. Demand for individuals, and therefore their wages, depends on the type of skills they possess and how talented they are at using them. Thus, a popular current explanation for wage differentials is the rise of skill-based technological change (SBTC), or the theory that our increased reliance on computer-based work has raised the demand for and productivity of highly skilled workers. Therefore, wages for these workers have risen faster than for those in non-technology-based fields (Hanley, 2014). The result has been an increasing polarization in wages, with a growing gap between high-paid workers and low-paid workers and a hollowing out of the middle. In sum, it is the combination of supply and demand in the market and one's resources (human capital investments) that determines one's wages in the open marketplace (Avent-Holt & Tomaskovic-Devey, 2014).

If an imbalance develops between what individuals contribute and the wages they receive, according to this theory, then supply and demand forces are set in motion to restore equilibrium in the market. For example, if wages for teachers are too low, the job will be viewed as undesirable and the supply of qualified teachers will go down. As the supply of teachers shrinks, demand for teachers increases. If greater demand for quality teachers occurs, there should be an increase in the wages employers are willing to pay these workers. In this way, equilibrium is restored. If the opposite occurs—that is, individuals are paid too much for the resource(s) they offer—a large supply of potential workers will appear, too large for the demand for them in the market. In order to ensure getting jobs, they will lower the wages for which they are willing to work. With the lower wages, employment expands, thus leading to a clearing of the labor market and a balancing between supply and demand. Again, equilibrium is restored (Avent-Holt & Tomaskovic-Devey, 2014). So, in addition to assuming a competitive market, this approach assumes that automatic mechanisms operate in the market to regulate it toward equilibrium.

If one accepts this argument, then what must be done to reduce earnings inequities is to attack the problems of human capital investment and the choices and returns associated with such investment. Solutions might stress more education and training opportunities as well as accurate and appropriate assessment of individuals' skills and economic payoffs for those skills.

Many current scholars, however, recognize that explanations of income and earnings distribution that rely on images of the free market and investments in human capital as the primary or sole factors in understanding economic inequalities are inadequate. Critics of the orthodox view assert that the market simply does not work the way that pure traditionalists say it does. Rather, the major reasons for inequality lie deep within the workings and cleavages of the capitalist economy—to quote Jonathan Rothwell, chief economist at Gallup, "Income inequality in the United States would fall drastically if people were compensated based only on their ability" (Rothwell, 2019). A number of observations about continuing difficulties in the market have made many analysts skeptical about the orthodox approach and its potential effectiveness in reducing inequality. Issues that critics argue neoclassical labor theory does not explain include: (1) the distribution of wages (who is paid what) within specific industries; (2) the structure of organizations; and (3) discrimination in the labor market. A central concern is that individual workers do not have free choices in the labor market and that the rewards they receive are often not commensurate with their human capital.

First, the model cannot account for the fact that wage differentiation persists *between* occupations, and even more so *within* occupations (Mouw & Kalleberg, 2010). For example, while this has decreased in recent years, it remains the case that there exists substantial gendered job segregation, meaning that men and women are not competing for the same jobs. Recent estimates suggest that occupational differences might account for as much as one-third of the differences in wages by gender (Blau & Kahn, 2017), and for all workers, occupational segregation is particularly important in explaining racial differences in wages (Mandel & Semyonov, 2016). In sum, occupational differences are increasingly important in explaining the wage gap, controlling for levels of human capital (Mouw & Kalleberg, 2010).

More perplexing, however, is the persistence of wage inequalities within occupations, even looking at very detailed occupational distinctions. Occupations are stratified both vertically and horizontally, such that gendered and racial disparities exist within particular occupations. For example, women in law firms are less likely to be partners, and the number of women and Black CEOs remains disproportionately low (Blau & Kahn, 2017). Even controlling for rank within occupations, however, wage differences persist.

The second critique of traditional models is that they do not recognize differences due to the structures of organizations (Sørensen, 2007). For example, larger organizations tend to pay higher wages and have greater wage inequality than smaller organizations (Avent-Holt & Tomaskovic-Devey, 2014, p. 382). As our economy becomes more concentrated and centralized and increasingly dominated by large firms, levels of inequality will rise.

Finally, traditional neoclassical models of labor markets do not account for persistent discrimination. First, they rely strongly on assumptions about the productivity of labor but fail to recognize that productivity itself is socially constructed: whether someone is seen as productive is highly influenced by their social status, such as whether they are male or female (Kalkhoff et al., 2020; Ridgeway, 1997). Second, models aimed at explaining wage inequality show that controlling for all expected factors, including education, experience, duration of labor, and occupational segregation, unexplained differences by race and gender separately and together persist, suggesting that discrimination continues and remains salient in explaining inequality (Blau & Kahn, 2017; Mandel & Semyonov, 2016).

Categorical Inequalities

In contrast to explanations for inequality based on individual characteristics, many dominant sociological theories have placed social structure, culture, and similar "social facts" at the center of their arguments. That is, they have tended to focus on the larger, macro world around us as the principal source for our individual fates and behaviors. In addition, many sociologists have recently come to recognize that neither individual differences nor structural explanations in isolation explain ongoing, persistent inequalities, but that

> We need to look across levels of analysis from the individual and interpersonal to the organizational to the macro-structural and cultural to discover how inequality processes at each level interpenetrate one another to create and sustain patterns of resource inequality. (Ridgeway, 2014, p. 2)

Inequality is created, embedded, and reproduced at all levels, including our individual cognitive structures, our relationships with one another, and the culture and structure of groups, organizations, and the wider society.

As we stated in Chapter 1, social inequality is not simply the idea that some people have more than others. Maybe one person was unexpectedly lucky and won the lottery, or inherited great sums of money, or perhaps another had terribly bad luck and ended up impoverished. In contrast, *social* inequality occurs when categories of individuals persistently and across many situations have less access to resources and opportunities than other groups. This is what Charles Tilly (1998) calls "**durable inequalities**."

All societies or groups categorize people—as cognitive psychologists tell us, thinking in terms of categories is one of the central ways that we make sense of our world (Allport, 1954). These categories might be based on who is family or who is not, on physical appearances, language differences, whether or not someone is funny, or whether or not you can roll your tongue into a cone. There are endless ways we can and do categorize people and recognize differences between groups; indeed, "we make as many distinctions among people as there are social locations" (Tomaskovic-Devey, 2014, p. 61).

The real question is why some differences between people become persistent and come to be the central frameworks by which we judge people. We don't, for example, assign bathrooms based on whether you can roll your tongue or not! And why do some categories imply moral worthiness and carry with them access to more resources? In short, how do categorical differences lead to inequalities? This next section will discuss various approaches to thinking about categorical inequality, including the relationship to individual statuses and identities, organizational and societal cultures, and social structure.

The Social Construction of Categories

Schwalbe (2008) suggests that, when we examine inequality over the long stretch of history, we find that unequal distributions of valuable resources among racial and ethnic groups in the early United States were often the result of "theft, extortion, and exploitation" (pp. 32–33). But it is the placement of groups of people into particular categories (e.g., less than human, biologically distinct) that are different from "us" (human, superior) that initiates and justifies the theft, extortion, and exploitation. In this sense, rather than being a natural inevitability, social inequality is a humanly manufactured "accomplishment." Categorizations of individuals such as male/female, gay/straight, citizen/noncitizen, abled/disabled, and Black/White/Hispanic/Asian are human creations and arise out of historical and cultural contexts (Ridgeway et al., 2009). For example, we will see clearly how changing historical and cultural situations produce changing classifications in the chapter on race when we discuss the shifting racial classifications of the US Census Bureau.

But what mechanisms spur the translation of simple nominal classifications, such as race and gender, into subjective rankings that evaluate a given race or gender as higher or lower in status than others? And how do particular characteristics get associated with those classifications? In some situations, there is a perfect match between categories, such as race and gender, and the distribution of resources. That is, some communities are perfectly racially segregated, such that some neighborhoods are purely White and others purely Black. In such situations, status inequalities arising through exploitation and the hoarding of opportunities by one group are easier (Tilly, 1998; Tomaskovic-Devey, 2014). Thus, when there is a clear and strong correlation between a recognized nominal trait like race or gender and possession of a valued resource (e.g., high salary), the nominal trait takes on a status value and becomes more salient in social situations (Ridgeway, 2014). "It does so because it transforms the situational control over resources and power into a status difference between 'types' of people that are evaluatively ranked in terms of how diffusely 'better' they are" (p. 3). As suggested earlier by Weber, status then takes on a moral character.

The status value associated with one's race or gender is further reinforced and becomes broadly accepted when repeated interactions take place among individuals with similar perspectives. Individual judgments made about the qualities possessed by others are shaped in interaction. This social influence, in turn, magnifies differences in the perceived qualities of individuals, with higher-status persons being "overvalued" and those of lower status "undervalued." Notable public persons receive high status from an individual simply because they get it from everybody else. Individuals then carry these beliefs into other situations and actions. As a result, status beliefs get disseminated throughout the society (Ridgeway et al., 2009).

Photo 7.2 Duct Taped Barbie.
Source: "Barbie provoking conversations on gender inequality" Craftivist collective is licensed under CC BY 2.0.

The classifications that become important and broadly accepted bases for social status are generally invented by those who have economic, political, or social power. Consequently, the categories/classifications often reflect their interests and result in dividing up the social world in a manner that privileges them. For example, *intelligence* is generally defined by psychological experts or persons in authority using the "intelligence quotient" or IQ, even though in recent decades, this measurement has come under attack from different, often less privileged, groups. Using this definition, only certain persons are defined as "intelligent." Through classifications like this (intellectual, racial, status, and so forth), we create "others" who simply do not measure up to the standards we have created. This process of "othering" creates and helps reproduce inequality (Schwalbe & Shay, 2014).

The concept of citizenship provides another example of how classifications are created. Classifying people on the basis of citizenship is a way of stating who belongs, who is recognized by the community, and who is deserving of the basic rights and resources provided to community members (Glenn, 2011). The category of citizenship is a powerful one, as it interacts with and informs other key statuses such as gender, race, and ethnicity. For example, when the United States took over territories from Mexico in the Southwest in 1848, the government announced that all residents in the region could move to Mexico or could choose either United States or Mexican citizenship (but not both). Thus, at a time when "full citizenship rested on white racial status, Mexicans, by implication, became 'white'" (p. 5). It was not until after 1930 that "Mexican" was a listed status in the US census. Similarly, the term *illegal immigrant*, used almost exclusively when speaking about non-European origin immigrants, is a form of othering that justifies inequalities and the lack of access to resources, such as education or work.

When their interests are at stake, groups will often compete for acceptance of their definitions or classifications. As we will see further in Chapter 10, at various times in history, groups have engaged in "racial projects" to define racial categories and associate positive or negative characteristics with the categories (Omi & Winant, 2015). Different groups may win, and some groups may win almost all of the time. Consequently, classifications may change or they may not:

> When one group wins, its vocabulary may be adopted and institutionalized while the concepts of the opposing groups fall into obscurity … The categories and meanings that they have created have direct consequences for the ways such phenomena are conceived, evaluated, and treated. (Spector & Kitsuse, 1977, pp. 8, 15)

Different definitions and classifications suggest different realities. When sociologists, as "professional experts," create measures of social class and, using data on income, education, and so on, define given individuals as "working class" or "middle class," or "upper class," they are, in effect, inventing these classes.

Individuals are "doing race" or "doing gender" when they engage in conversations or behaviors that create or reinforce differences between groups. In her engaging novel about the experiences of a Nigerian immigrant, Adichie provides advice to other immigrants about what it means to learn to be Black in America (Adichie, 2014, p. 273): "Dear Non-American Black, when you make the choice to come to America, you become black. Stop arguing. Stop saying I'm Jamaican or I'm Ghanaian. America doesn't care." She goes on to explain why immigrants might distance themselves from the label "black": "You say 'I'm not black' only because you know black is at the bottom of America's race ladder. And you want none of that." Part of the non-American Black experience, then, is learning how to be a Black woman or a Black man and learning what that categorization implies about your actions and how others perceive you.

Similarly, we learn what gender means by how it is done, that is, by how different individuals are defined and treated. It is in this defining and treatment that different genders are created, beginning early in life when boys and girls are treated differently. In this way, gender is socially constructed and is maintained through the recurrence of distinctions made in school, on the job, in the home, and in other institutions. We then define gender differences as inherent in each individual or as natural, and by treating individuals differently, we reproduce gender inequality (Lorber, 2001). It is in our daily interactions with others that gender is invented. Women and men are viewed as being *meant* for different roles and positions. Once constructed, inequalities are then reproduced.

Part of the interest in examining the dynamics of inequality in everyday life is related to a larger concern for understanding the real, active processes by which inequality is generated. A few more recent attempts have tried to tease out the interactions between the micro-level processes of inequality and the macro-level processes involved in the development and maintenance of structures of inequality. As we will see in subsequent chapters, they resonate with earlier and previously mentioned undertakings to *ground* theory, such as Omi and Winant's (2005) analysis of how racial categories are actually formed in historical context, for example, and West and Zimmerman's (1987) discussion of how individuals "do gender" in their everyday lives.

How Inequalities Persist

The social constructionist models discussed above show how categories are created, but they do not explain how these categories become durably unequal. That is, how do these categories remain unequal; how do these inequalities persist? Certainly, part of the answer is that once people have more, they do all they can to keep it. They hoard wealth and income and pass these resources on to their families, reproducing high-class status in the next generation. In addition to these material resources, however, families pass on symbolic and cultural resources to the next generation, ensuring the continuation of their class position. This is a process referred to as **social reproduction**.

Hoarding of Material Resources

One of the most detailed and grounded explanations of persistent inequality comes from Charles Tilly. Tilly (1998, 2003) cites two mechanisms that produce "durable" inequality: *exploitation* and *opportunity hoarding*. That is, inequalities happen because once individuals are able to gain any advantage, they use that advantage to maintain their power. For example, Shamus Khan (2012a) provides an in-depth ethnographic analysis of how private schools cultivate privilege among their students, ensuring that power and privilege remain in the hands of a few. Thus, inequality becomes established when people use their resources to extract something of value (e.g., resources, labor) from others (i.e., exploitation) or when they deprive the access of other groups or categories of people to valued resources (i.e., opportunity hoarding). Among other things, "valued resources" include weapons, labor, land, machines, capital, knowledge, and media control, that is, those items that provide their owner with power over others.

The categories selected for exclusion may be determined in part by social categories already existing in the wider society, for example, those involving gender or race. These categories may be borrowed for use in specific situations or organizations, as when socially defined gender roles are extended to work positions in a corporation. Means that are effective in maintaining dominance over women at home, for example, may be used in the workplace as well. For example, some have argued that women are best suited for caring for children in the home because of their innate abilities and thus are destined for jobs such as child care or nursing, both poorly paid occupations. Or racial categories and meanings that are established in earlier times to keep Black people or other minorities out of certain establishments (e.g., Jim Crow laws) may be extended later to new realms and forms of oppression (e.g., mass incarceration). This process of borrowing categories from other spheres of life is what Tilly refers to as *emulation* and is a further mechanism for sustaining inequalities and strengthening categorical distinctions.

The use of preexisting categories can serve to clarify, justify, and maintain unequal arrangements in the work setting. As with other classifications, social categories of groups simplify relationships among individuals at the same time that they often function to rank them.

> Categories matter ... [C]ategories facilitate unequal treatment by both members and outsiders ... The [c]ategories that matter most for durable inequality, however, involve both mutual awareness and connectedness; we know who they are, they know who we are, on each side of that line people interact with each other, and across the line we interact with them—but differently. (Tilly, 2003, p. 33)

Categories and the meanings attached to them come and go, as we see with historical shifts in racial classifications. How they come about and change depends heavily on the nature of the contact and interactions between the groups involved.

Adaptation also aids in the maintenance of inequality (Tilly, 2003). Once unequal relationships are established, daily routines or processes that support the systems of inequality are created. For example, in his study of total institutions, Goffman (1961) noted that one way inmates or residents adjusted to their controlled position was by becoming "model" inmates or residents, that is, by adjusting to and even accepting the role expected of them. Like emulation, such adaptation helps to sustain hierarchical arrangements. The four mechanisms of exploitation, opportunity hoarding, emulation, and adaptation, along with the systematic use of social categories, aid in the explanation of inequality structures and their durable nature.

Symbolic and Cultural Resources

As Tilly suggests, the processes of exploitation and hoarding involve the control of material resources. But this control is bolstered and supported through the control of symbolic and cultural resources as well (Lamont et al., 2014). The cultural resources provide not only the framework for justifying the inequality, but they ensure that these inequalities are reproduced in the next generation. Examples of such resources might include elements such as the transmission of skills, the validation of honor or prestige, or the communication of insider knowledge.

One of the most prominent theorists articulating the cultural and symbolic aspects of class reproduction is French sociologist Pierre Bourdieu. Bourdieu argues that culture is a mediating element between class structure/interests and everyday life and behavior and that it is a central way that class positions are maintained and reproduced. Foundational to his theory is the idea that individuals compete within different "fields" in a struggle for various kinds of capital. These fields constitute networks of relationships among positions (Bourdieu & Wacquant, 1992). Examples of fields include art, music, education, the law, or any arenas where individuals jockey for position and advantage. Think of the imagery of a playing field, as in soccer or football, where players struggle to get in a strong position where they can score and win the game.

What kinds of capital do people compete for? Originally, economists referred to capital as a stock of goods or accumulated wealth (the first use of the term referred to how many cattle someone owned). Adam Smith famously expanded the definition to include the labor of humans, an idea that, as we saw in Chapter 6, Marx found to be quite important. Thus, capital came to be seen as not only the hoarding of things, but it is also a productive force or something available to you to use in the manufacturing of goods (Hodgson, 2014). Capital is, therefore, something we can accumulate, but it is also something that can be converted or traded for other kinds of capital.

Contemporary sociologists recognize that there are many different types of capital that we compete for, including, among many others, human capital, or how much we have invested in ourselves in resources, such as education; physical capital, meaning our physical abilities, such as strength or beauty; or political capital, which refers to resources available to us to achieve political aims. Bourdieu focuses centrally on economic capital, such as money and wealth, **social capital**, referring to connections or networks we have that can help us gain economic capital and cultural capital, to be discussed below.

One of the main fields that Bourdieu often discusses is the field of education. Schools reproduce and legitimate inequalities by serving as the authority on who has the skills to be successful in their chosen field. By appearing to be objective and a source of knowledge, schools that produce both successful and failing students can justify the inequalities that follow. Since schools represent the interests of the dominant culture, Bourdieu argues, they value the **cultural capital** of the dominant class more than that of the lower classes.

Bourdieu (1977) suggested that higher education reinforces the value and status differences between the classes by honoring the cultural capital held by those in the higher classes. This capital—which consists of a group's cultural values, experience, knowledge, and skills—is passed on from one generation to the next. In organizing itself around the linguistic and cultural competence of the upper classes, higher education ensures that members of the upper classes are successful in school. That is, the language used, the cultural knowledge expected for success in school, and the values and behaviors honored are those of the upper class. This legitimates the class inequality that results because, on the surface, it appears that the inequality is largely the result of individual performance in a meritocratic, open educational system. In the words of one interpreter, "school serves as the trading post where socially valued cultural capital is parlayed into superior academic performance. Academic performance is then turned back into economic capital by the acquisition of superior jobs" (MacLeod, 2008, p. 14). The experiences in school and in the workplace of those in the working and lower classes, coupled with the general outlook and specific attitudes they have acquired because of their class milieu, lead them to believe that they cannot succeed in school, thus lowering their aspirations to do so (MacLeod, 2008). The result is stratification within the educational system, which then reinforces the class stratification in the wider society.

As a result of struggles within various fields, individuals come to occupy different classes that vary in the amounts and forms of their economic, social, and cultural capital. Some possess great amounts of wealth, extensive social networks, and fancy tastes and lifestyles and can use these resources to justify their possession of capital. Individuals in higher occupational positions tend to have more diverse and extensive social networks (social capital) that provide them with access to greater social resources. Moreover, since they tend to associate most often with similar kinds of individuals, most of the resources controlled by this group stay within it, helping to reproduce inequality (Erickson & Cote, 2009). The presence or absence of these resources forms a large part of the social context in which individuals live, and these objective conditions give rise to particular tastes, lifestyles, and ways of looking at the world. The upper class possesses a "taste of liberty and luxury," whereas the lower has "popular taste." "Distance from necessity" permeates the taste of the upper class, meaning that items in their culture are less directly functional and practical compared to the tastes of the lower class. A recent Budweiser commercial, for example, pokes fun of this distinction by mocking those ostentatious, upper-class consumers who insist on drinking craft beer and heralding the common people who enjoy a Bud.

An individual's **habitus** is a direct product of the person's structural situation; in fact, it is the psychological embodiment of the objective conditions in which one lives. Habitus refers to

Figure 7.2 A General Model of Bourdieu's Explanation of Social Reproduction.

a system of stable frameworks for viewing the world that provide the impetus for action. That is, we are socialized differently depending on where we are located within the social structure, and this socialization means that we are disposed to act one way versus another. Thus, different life conditions give rise to different forms of habitus, and those exposed to the same conditions will develop the same habitus (Bourdieu, 1990). The habitus, in turn, has a direct, constraining effect on the social action of individuals, which, coming full circle, contributes to reproducing the social structure. One of the strengths of Bourdieu's model is that he specifies the reciprocal relationship between structure and agency: we are not fully determined by our habitus, but it does provide the framework from which we decide to act.

Figure 7.2 gives a rough outline of Bourdieu's model. For example, an adolescent who lives within a structure with poor job opportunities, as evidenced by the experiences of their parents, will develop a view that chances of success are slight and that school makes no difference. This leads to behavior that accommodates them to a menial job, which in turn reinforces the existing job **opportunity structure**. Nothing changes.

Too often, class reproduction theories have ignored the separately lived and varied experiences of women and minority groups, an omission that can seriously limit the theories' ability to understand the habitus of these individuals and the reproduction of their economic situations. One of these lived variations concerns childbearing inside and outside marriage. In her analysis of childbearing outside of marriage, Sara McLanahan (2009) found that unmarried mothers, who often come from economically disadvantaged families and have lower-than-average educations, tend to have less stable partners and are likely to have weaker social support, more mental stress, and lower incomes than married mothers. The poorer resources and lower stability ultimately reduce their children's life chances and optimize the probability that their children will remain in a low economic position. Thus, low economic status leads to a habitus that provides less valuable cultural capital and ensures that social inequality is reproduced between generations.

Spatial Inequalities

Not surprisingly, material resources such as wealth and income make it possible for people to live in the best neighborhoods. Therefore, our class position is a key determinant of our spatial location. But it is also the case that the reproduction of poverty is closely related to where we are located. Thus, spatial location is another resource that those in power can limit access to and hoard, ensuring the continuation of inequalities. Ecological or socio-spatial factors, such as which neighborhood or city we are located in, are independent contributors to social inequality (Lamont et al., 2014). A socio-spatial approach argues that "space not only contains actions but also constitutes a part of social relations and is intimately involved in our daily lives" (Ryan et al., 2015, p. 19). Space has symbolic meaning, but societies also structure spaces that express the social relationships between us.

As we will see more fully in Chapter 11, spatial locations represent an interesting "in-between" contributor to inequality—they occur above the level of the individual but below the level of the wider society. They are the immediate place where broader "extralocal" forces, such as global economic processes or discriminatory frameworks, are played out (Sampson, 2012, p. 42). The racial segregation of neighborhoods reflects societal understandings of racial hierarchies, and at the same time, the streets are where racial social movements for change occur. Global recessions hit various neighborhoods in different ways, and resources such as education, cultural venues, and consumer goods are distributed differently across neighborhoods.

Neighborhoods and spaces literally "put people in their place." Streets have traditionally, for example, been gendered and racialized—women do not feel safe alone at night on the streets, and thus have no place there, and Black men are often seen as a danger on the streets. The suburbs of the 1950s were created with an image of both racial and gender relations (Spain, 2014). They were all White and were built with the assumption that women stayed in the home caring for the family while men commuted into the city to work. These spatial relationships then recreated the social roles that they were built on.

Sociologists have recognized for some time the importance of **neighborhood effects** or the independent power that neighborhoods have to affect our life chances. Research demonstrates that independent of family income or individual characteristics, neighborhoods that children grow up in affect their various outcomes, including education levels, health, future income, and the likelihood of risky behaviors, such as early childbearing or substance abuse (Sampson, 2012).

From a Marxist perspective, spaces are where elites are able to exert control and increase their power and wealth. In their discussion of a political economy of place, Logan and Molotch (2007) argue that human agents, and particularly elites, strategize to profit from places. "People dreaming, planning, and organizing themselves to make money from property are the agents through which accumulation does its work at the level of the urban place" (p. 12). The city becomes a "growth machine," where activities are focused on increasing rents and thus profits for the land owners. Neighborhoods that are strategic to the growth of the city are strengthened and maintained, those that are not, often those occupied by poor and minorities, are sacrificed.

In sum, spaces provide a mechanism through which inequalities are maintained and reproduced. For wealthy individuals, they provide a key venue for increasing wealth. At the same time, spaces can isolate those without resources, keeping them from access to the cultural, social, and economic capital necessary to thrive. Spaces are where we enact our identities and develop our sense of who we are and where we belong.

Identities, Interactions, and Inequalities

Our discussions above have focused mostly on the construction of categorical inequalities and on the structures that maintain these inequalities. As important, however, are the micro-level interactions that support these categories. These categories become central to how we view ourselves and how we interact with others. The categories that we embrace or that others have successfully imposed on us become our identities. "Identities are simply category labels that we use to name ourselves and the people around us" (Callero, 2018). These labels have several characteristics. First, they are embedded in and linked to the social structure; identities are socially situated. Second, the labels are not neutral names—they involve judgment and evaluation. And third, identities arise from interaction with others and combine in complex relationships with other identities.

Identities are located in social structures and are part of how we organize our social relations with one another (Bonilla-Silva, 1997; Risman, 2004). That is, identities are socially situated and, as such, are markers for where we belong—some identities belong in some places and not in others. For example, students belong in schools, but they do not belong in workplaces. Though you may be a student and a worker, when you are at work, you generally do not announce or display your student identity. Thus, social structures have rules about what identities can exist in a particular place or field and about the parameters of the category that the identity is labeling. We see this process clearly in our election processes, as the law formally wrestles with who can call themselves a "voter" via conflicts, such as the civil rights or suffrage movements, and informally in interactions when poll workers challenge potential voters who look like they do not belong. And as we will see in Chapter 10, the development of the concept of race was in great part about who was allowed to claim the identity "White."

Identities, therefore, involve social scripts or rules that result in a "rigging of the game," such that, in order to be allowed to play, we have to more or less abide by the existing rules and uphold inequalities: "to make an identity claim (or an identity imposition) stick, we have to know the rules of the game and how to use them" (Schwalbe, 2008, p. 166). These rules involve how those possessing certain identities may behave in a situation—for example, if you are occupying the identity of a mourner at a funeral, you shouldn't laugh. Why do we follow the rules? We are making the bet that the rewards for being allowed to occupy a particular identity are worth the cost of following the rules and sometimes sacrificing our own conceptions of ourselves and what is right (Schwalbe, 2008). As an example, men might listen to or tell sexist jokes as part of being in a location where male identities and masculinities are being performed, such as in a locker room. They may think that is wrong but say nothing because they fear that the cost of not being allowed to stay in that place and occupy that role will be too high. In doing so, they are maintaining the rules that surround this identity and its place in the social structure.

Our interactions with one another, both those like us and those not like us, reproduce inequalities, and are therefore not simply neutral processes of naming but representations of power. This is referred to as the process of "othering," whereby members of a dominant group create categories and determine the qualities that define who belongs in those categories (Schwalbe et al., 2000, p. 422). One form of othering, *oppressive othering*, "occurs when one group seeks advantage by defining another group as morally and/or intellectually inferior" (Schwalbe et al., 2000, p. 423). Defining groups as deficient justifies inequalities by a **legitimation process** that introduces a system that provides fewer benefits and rewards to another group. Thus, as we saw in Chapter 3, at various points in our history, those in power have defined those in poverty as being morally deficient and, therefore, not deserving of assistance. Non-White citizens have, at various times in our history, been defined as not sufficiently educated to be granted voting rights.

Another sort of othering is *defensive othering* or the "identity work done by those seeking membership in a dominant group, or by those seeking to deflect the stigma they experience as members of a subordinate group" (p. 425). This is the process whereby individuals in less powerful groups may participate in the othering of those in their own group, thereby furthering the stigma and working to distance themselves from that implied identity. For example, it is not uncommon for those receiving public assistance to complain about the number of welfare recipients who take advantage of the system and who do, therefore, not deserve welfare benefits (Hays, 2003).

Identities, therefore, not only involve named places in a social structure, but they also carry with them evaluations and judgments. This is the root of prejudice, or as Gordon Allport famously defined it, "an antipathy based on faulty and inflexible generalizations" (1954, p. 9). When psychologists and sociologists speak about how we interact with groups different from our own, they often distinguish between how we think about others, how we feel about others, and how we behave toward others (Dovidio et al., 2010, p. 61).

How we think about others involves stereotypes or those deeply ingrained attitudes that are held about different groups. These stereotypes, in turn, help to justify and sustain social inequalities, both in the interactional othering processes described above, as well as in social psychological processes involving how individuals view themselves and their capabilities and self-worth. Research suggests that **stereotype threat**, or individuals' worry that they will be judged negatively based on stereotypes, can lead to underperformance in work and school environments, thus, increasing inequalities. For example, images of ability and competence have limited the success and mobility of disabled workers. In an experimental study of blind subjects, Silverman and Cohen

(2014) found that blind individuals with higher levels of stereotype threat were more likely to avoid challenges, had a lower sense of well-being, and were less likely to be employed. When they think about the stereotype that they are incompetent, they become so. "Stereotype threat experiences threaten self-integrity, and people may defend their self-integrity by avoiding future situations that could arouse stereotype threat" (p. 1337). The power of these beliefs persists even when the evidence in each of these cases does not warrant such beliefs.

The beliefs and values that individuals hold derive, in large part, from the broader institutional and cultural frameworks in which they operate. These frameworks certainly operate consciously and explicitly, as in when individuals outwardly express bias or enact violence against particular groups in society, but at times the bias can be subconscious, as is the case with **implicit bias**. This is a cognitive process whereby stereotypes become ingrained in our mindset, and "individuals assign a collection of characteristics to others based on their appearance and race" (Russell-Brown, 2018, p. 185). Often "the mere presence of a person can lead one to think about the concepts with which that person's social group has become associated" (Eberhardt et al., 2004, p. 876). Thus, though this is not an intended or conscious process, hidden biases related to body size may lead physicians to misdiagnose illnesses in obese patients, or those in the criminal justice system, assuming criminality among Black men, may impose harsher sentences or be more likely to believe that a suspect is armed.

Our stereotypes or implicit biases about categories of people, therefore, affect our interactions with others, even at the smallest levels of interaction. We see this operating with **microaggressions**, or the "brief and commonplace daily verbal, behavioral, or environmental indignities, whether intentional or unintentional, which lie beneath visibility or consciousness and which communicate hostile, derogatory, or negative slights and insults toward targeted groups, persons, and/or systems" (Nadal et al., 2015, p. 147). These acts involve subtle ways that individuals might, often unknowingly, convey the idea that someone does not belong, is different, or is inferior. Examples of microaggressions include asking an Asian person where they are "really from" (signaling that they do not belong here); asking to touch a Black woman's hair (implying that it is different from normal hair); or referring to a Black candidate as "very articulate" (indicating surprise that a Black person can speak well). As Marilyn Frye (1983) famously argued in her essay on oppression, each of these aggressions is like a single bar of a birdcage: in and of itself, each bar does not provide an insurmountable barrier. But put together, all of the bars create an effective and limiting cage.

Often microaggressions are targeted at individuals based on the intersections of a number of identities, such as Muslim or African American women or Latino men, or at individuals whose complex identities do not "fit" traditional gendered stereotypes. Thus, Asian men are often targeted for being insufficiently masculine, Black women are seen as too assertive or angry and thus unfeminine, and Latina women are singled out in the workplace as not belonging (Nadal et al., 2015; Ridgeway and Kricheli-Katz, 2013). In fact, a recent study demonstrated that minority women are far more likely to be harassed in the workplace than minority men or majority men or women, indicating a kind of "double jeopardy" of sexual and ethnic harassment (Berdahl & Moore, 2006).

Theories of Intersectionality

As we discussed in the Introduction to this text, a central issue facing those studying inequality is how we address the reality that while various statuses and identities face unique forms of oppression, individuals occupy several positions in society simultaneously. In recent years, therefore, numerous feminist and race theorists have stressed that individuals in any particular group do not always have the same lived experiences as others, as various identities face unique forms of

BOX 7.2 WHAT'S IN A NAME?

What we name ourselves is not simply a personal decision, but it is social, political, and intrinsically tied to inequality. Personal identities are tied to group identities, and thus "what I call myself" is tied to "who are we, and where do we belong?" They are also intersectional, living at the intersections of our ethnic, racial, sexual, gender, and class identities.

The politics of naming have recently been seen clearly in controversy over what to call people of Latin American descent. As Daniel Hernandez of the *L.A. Times* recently noted, what to call individuals who trace their roots back to Latin America or Spain, is "a minefield of geography, color and language since we can be of any race and have few things in common beyond some degree of adherence to the Spanish tongue" (Hatzipanagos, 2018).

Nevertheless, in the interest of providing a gender-neutral term for characterizing this population, over the past couple of years, the term "Latinx" has gained popularity, so much so that it was recently added to Merriam-Webster's dictionary. Originally coined within the LGBTQ community to recognize gender inclusion, the term has become greatly popularized in the past few years. But not everyone is happy with the term. A number of native Spanish speakers argue that the term is insensitive to the Spanish language, a language that designates gender in many of its noun endings and does not generally use the letter "x."

As quoted in the *Washington Post* (2018), Sandra Velez comments: "Do they hate or revile their Hispanic/Latino ancestry so much they are willing (unwitting?) accomplices in erasing their own heritage? Because that's exactly what's happening" (Hatzipanagos, 2018). Others argue that the term Latinx was created in academic circles and by those born in the United States; it is "definitely *not* used by working-class immigrant adults, who probably have no idea that some of us brown folks are debating this at all" (Hernandez, 2017).

oppression (P. H. Collins & Bilge, 2016; Combahee River Collective, 2014; Crenshaw, 1989). Thus, when talking about women as a category, we need to recognize that women of color may have very different experiences from White women or that working-class men may experience masculinity differently than do upper-class men. The various dimensions of our lives intersect in powerful linkages that operate to affect the structure of societal inequalities and individual experiences of inequality in divergent ways.

This is what is meant by the importance of "intersectionality," or what Patricia Hill Collins (2002) calls "the matrix of domination." She continues in a later work by stating that "race, class, gender, sexuality, ethnicity, nation, ability, and age operate not as unitary, mutually exclusive entities, but as reciprocally constructing phenomena that in turn shape complex social inequalities" (Collins, 2015, p. 2). Our race, class, gender, gender identity, sexuality, nationality, and ability may all affect our position in society, both individually and in combination. As we have seen in several instances, for example, the occupational and earnings positions of women and men vary with their race. In their study of power at work, Elliott and Smith (2004) found that

> Men and women of various races and ethnicities experience increasing inequality in workplace power, relative to white men, but they experience it to different degrees and via different mechanisms … Evidence here suggests that a one-size-fits-all explanation hides more than it reveals. (pp. 384–385)

Since each group faces problems that are in part unique, the solutions to their domination need to vary as well.

As they first articulated the perspective, Black feminist scholars argued that researchers need to avoid what Adrienne Rich (1979) called "white solipsism"—the presumption that the experiences of Whites represent the norm. This concern arose in particular among feminists of color who believed that many second-wave feminists were generalizing the experiences of White women to all women. While people may have some experiences in common because they all share a gender, for example, they vary along other dimensions, such as race and social class. These dimensions intersect and affect each other in various and complex ways, with particular combinations having unique effects on life chances. As Browne and Misra (2003) put it, in speaking about the relationship of gender and race, "[r]ace is 'gendered' and gender is 'racialized' so that race and gender fuse to create unique experiences and opportunities for all groups—not just women of color" (p. 488). We could add that race and gender are also "classed," and class has been "gendered" and "racialized" in our history. That is, the particular pattern *itself* has an impact independent of the separate effects that might flow from one's gender, race, or class. Each of these patterns has particular cultural images or stereotypes associated with it. For example, Black, lower-class men are often seen as dangerous, Black women as unusually sexually active, White women as dependent and feminine, and so on (Browne & Misra, 2003).

There have been many renditions of intersectional theory, but they have in common the idea that a particular identity, such as gender, "is not an abstract and timeless essence, but an embodied and historical practice that is structured by other forms of inequality" (Williams, 2013, p. 614). When first introduced, intersectionality focused primarily on the intersection between racism and sexism. More recently, researchers have turned to a much broader range of oppressions, such as disability, citizenship, age, and sexuality (McBride et al., 2015). Intersectional theory has been used in many ways, including to describe the variable experiences of individuals based on their social location and specific contexts, to develop theoretical and methodological approaches to understanding gender, and finally, as a call for activism (Cho et al., 2013). Given this multiplicity of approaches to the question of intersectionality, there has been much debate on issues such as how we define it, what metaphor should be used to describe it (i.e., is it a web, a matrix, a road intersection), how many categories we should include, and whether it is static or dynamic. Additionally, intersectional approaches might focus on groups, on systems, or on processes (Cho et al., 2013).

In her foundational work, Leslie McCall (2005) suggests three possible approaches to intersectional research. The first is an *anti-categorical* approach. This approach emerged early in feminist discussion as a rejection of the viability of master, or overarching, categories. Examples include the works of writers such as Fausto-Sterling (2000), who critiqued the assumption that there are only two genders, and Omi and Winant (2005), who argue that rather than being a stable category, race is an ongoing project involving power structures and cultural representations (see Collins, 2015). While addressing very different topics, these works challenge "the singularity, separateness, and wholeness of a wide range of social categories" (McCall, 2005, p. 1778). Research from this approach questions our assumptions about categories and studies individuals and social settings without any assumptions about what category someone might fit into.

The second approach, an *intracategorical* approach, looks at experiences within a category, and, similar to the anti-categorical approach, it highlights the complexity of categories and the diversity within categories. McCall states that this approach arose in part because of the recognition of the failures of earlier research to capture the realities of lived experiences. For example, research on Black women was flawed because previous studies combined research on women taken from the experiences of White women and research on race stemming from understandings of Black men. Neither helped us understand the unique experiences of Black women (p. 1780). Therefore, by looking extensively into the variety of experiences of Black women as a category that exists at the intersection of other categories, we can develop more complex theoretical models. Another compelling example of this approach is the recent work by anthropologist Lila Abu-Lughod

(2013) which provides a rich detailing of the variety of experiences of Muslim women to demonstrate that the contemporary political assumption that Muslim women need to be "saved" by Westerners is problematic.

The final approach McCall discusses is an *intercategorical* approach, which compares the experiences of individuals across categories. Often this approach looks at relationships between social groups to understand broader forms of inequality. Thus, for example, McDonald (2011) looks at how the intersection of race and class affects aspirations, and Gengler (2012) examines how race, class, and gender define power relations in battered women's shelters. An intercategorical approach focuses on the margins and on the intersections to understand further the structure of inequality.

Often intercategorical approaches help us understand how systems operate either within a society or globally. Thus, Bose (2012) applies intersectional theory to understand how processes such as neoliberalism or globalization affect the experiences of women. She begins by recognizing that women's experiences vary greatly cross-culturally: "There is diversity across countries in their national-level gender inequalities based on intersecting axes of transnational, regional, cross-cutting, and unique national issues that structure gendered differences and concerns" (p. 70). But these variations help us understand cross-cutting themes and the relationships between the various systems and power relations.

Applying Intersectionality to Labor Market Theory

To return to a topic introduced earlier in the chapter, an assessment of labor market theories shows that one of the weaknesses with both the orthodox explanation and the labor market theories is that they both are unidimensional and non-intersectional. Understandably, given their origin and focus, they are rooted in economics and center on the economic sphere. Additionally, much of the research relies on generalizations about the types of work and the types of workers within a section of the economy—thus, there are often references to "women's work," or working-class jobs, with little attention to interactions between categories, such as gender, race, or citizenship (Flippen, 2014; McBride et al., 2015). An intersectional approach, however, recognizes that the experiences of workers in the labor market and thus explanations of inequalities cannot be easily characterized as being due to classification into one category but rather stem from the interactions between statuses. Similarly, individuals experience oppression across multiple institutions, such as work, family, and school, and thus a focus solely on the economic sphere provides a limited perspective on the lived experience of inequality.

An intersectional approach recognizes that what happens in the labor market is experienced differently across categories. As Rashawn Ray (2014) states, "lumping Black men and Black women together, or White men and White women together, does not allow for the divergent patterns across racial and gender groups to be ascertained" (p. 484). Thus, in understanding the experiences of Latinas, it is not enough to explain their wages due to the sector of work they find themselves in, but we must also consider whether or not they are said to be "undocumented" (Flippen, 2014). Intersectionality forces researchers to recognize that there is diversity in any category of worker and that individuals "within an intersectional space (i.e., of two overlapping categories) may be experiencing something completely different to those occupying one of the categories" (McBride et al., 2015, p. 335).

In discussing the limits of orthodox labor theory explanations for ethnic differences in occupation and wages, for example, Anthony Rafferty (2012) demonstrates the variability of success in the labor market by gender, ethnicity, and social class, after controlling for human capital. He finds a clear "ethnic penalty" in employment, meaning that members of some ethnic groups are more likely than native-born Whites to be overqualified for the jobs they occupy. Following the expected path of gaining more education and more training did not always result in higher-status jobs:

> Ethnicity, gender and social class when taken together therefore provide a more nuanced picture of ethnic differences in labour market outcomes, interrelating in varying ways both between and within ethnic groups and shaped by the material and cultural contexts in which individuals exert agency toward socio-economic goals. (p. 992)

Those facing the most difficulties were foreign-born individuals and those with less-developed social networks. Depending on their social context and background, some ethnic groups found particular niches within a market segment that did not reward them for their higher levels of education and training. Finally, intersectional research additionally suggests that a difficulty with traditional labor theory is that it ignores the impact of the globalization of markets.

Summary

The focus in this and Chapter 6 has been on general explanations of inequality. Each of the theories covered views the concept of inequality in a different way and is suggestive of different measures of it. Nevertheless, all of them are concerned with the distribution of scarce resources in society, principally political power, economic power, or both.

We began this chapter with a discussion of neo-classical explanations of inequality located in the individual, including an analysis of human-capital-based arguments addressing how individual differences are sorted out in labor markets. These explanations, however, do not examine the broader systemic causes of inequality.

The chapter turns then to the question of how inequality is related to "durable inequalities," or the categories that societies apply to people, and how those categories become socially constructed and ranked. Part of this process involves the reproduction of social inequality via the hoarding of material resources and the control of symbolic and cultural resources. These categories become closely tied to identities and micro-level interactions between people. The chapter concludes with an understanding of intersectionality.

Critical Thinking

1. What is wrong, if anything, with an argument that says that rewards are simply a reflection of one's skills and credentials as well as the importance of one's job?
2. Is it possible to categorize people without ranking them? If so, how? If not, why not?
3. What role do you think parent-child relationships play in the reproduction of social and economic inequality?
4. It has been argued that networks of interactions between countries and individuals have become faster, more complex, and widespread (Herkenrath et al., 2005). Will this lead to more or less inequality, or will it have no effect on it?

Web Connections

As suggested in this chapter, Pierre Bourdieu was one of the most influential social reproduction theorists. A summary of his ideas can be found at http://routledgesoc.com/profile/pierre-bourdieu.

Film Suggestions

Dear White People (2014). Based on real events, this is an account of life for Black students at the fictional Winchester College. It illustrates a range of microaggressions they face.

Inside Job (2010). A documentary on the mechanisms in economic, financial, and political policies that led to the 2008–2009 economic crisis.

The Corporation (2004). A documentary that investigates and reports on "the corporation" as the dominant institution of today, much like the Catholic Church and the Communist Party of the past. It also discusses how corporations are viewed as individuals under the US Constitution and what that means for their "character" and responsibilities.

Waiting for Superman (2010). A documentary that follows students through their education and demonstrates failures within the public school system.

PART 3
Winners and Losers

8 Sex and Gender Inequality

Throughout the first two parts of this book, we have talked about how important it is to view inequality from an intersectional perspective. We occupy several different statuses at one time, and all contribute in some way to inequality. Because the United States is a multicultural, multiracial society, the status of any of us is complicated by our race, class, gender identity, or sexuality, and these statuses intersect, creating a complex matrix of relationships and inequalities. Thus, the position of a woman or man, as well as the expectations of and interpretations associated with that category, often depend on whether they are a member of a particular minority group or social class.

In this part of the book, however, we are going to discuss in greater depth several statuses individually—**sex** and gender, sexuality, race and ethnicity, and nationality and religion. While understanding the intersectional nature of inequality is essential, so too is an in-depth analysis of the independent contributions of each of these statuses. To understand, for example, the unique position a queer Black woman occupies, we must understand fully how gender, race, and sexuality operate in creating and reproducing systems of inequality. We will begin that discussion here with a deep dive into the roots and dynamics of sex/gender inequality, followed by race and ethnicity.

Sex and race are **ascribed statuses** in the sense that there is a physical component to each of them. These physical components are given meaning within the context of a culture's values and beliefs and a society's economic and political arrangements. The result is that sexes and races are hierarchically arranged and differentially treated in society. Both sex and race are "categorical inequalities" (Ridgeway, 2011), meaning that a person's placement in one category or another can affect their access to societal resources. These categories become rigid, such that even though the biological realities of sex are far more complex than the binary we generally assume (Ainsworth, 2015), we are placed in one category or another, and that placement has lifelong implications for our material, social, and psychological well-being. We will begin our discussion by understanding the terms we use in this categorization.

Terms Relating to Sex and Gender

While the terms "**sex**," "**gender**," "**gender identity**," and "**gender expression**" are related to each other, they refer to different aspects of categorization. We typically use the word "sex" to refer to a classification given at birth based on a baby's biological characteristics (such as genitalia or DNA). Today in the United States, we tend to think of this as a binary categorization—the doctor either shouts, "It's a girl!" or "It's a boy!" The word "gender" is used to refer to a set of attitudinal, role, and behavior expectations that are socially and culturally defined and associated with each sex. "Gender identity" refers to how individuals conceptualize themselves as male, female, a combination of the two, or neither of them. Finally, "gender expression" refers to our outward appearance—the clothes, mannerisms, makeup, and other markers we use to perform a gender identity. When we talk about gender expression, we often talk about how masculine

DOI: 10.4324/9781003184966-11

or feminine someone is. Traditionally, Americans have viewed sex, gender identity, and gender expression as linked. In other words, a baby assigned "boy" at birth will go on to self-identify as male and act in masculine ways.

The problem with this traditional view of gender is that it ignores the wide variety of self-identities, gender practices, and even biological differences found in historical and contemporary societies around the world. One illustration of this complexity concerns individuals who have intersexed anatomies. The term **intersex** refers to a set of conditions in which a person is born with reproductive, chromosomal, or sexual characteristics that are not consistent with what we define as either the female or male category. For example, a person may have some cells that have XX chromosomes while other cells have XY chromosomes. This variation covers a wide array of sex-anatomy combinations and is thought to occur in as many 1 out of 1,000 children (Aydin et al., 2019).

Transgender people experience an incongruency between the gender they were assigned at birth and that with which they identify. For example, a person assigned male at birth may identify as a woman or vice versa. In contrast, the term **cisgender** refers to people who continue to identify as the gender they were assigned at birth. Many transgender people choose to align their gender expression with their gender identity through a transition. This may involve changing names, dress, mannerisms, and, in some cases, pursuing hormonal or surgical prescriptions to create consistency between their physical bodies and psychological identities. The term we use for people who identify as male but who were categorized as female at birth is transgender man (other common terms include "trans man" or "female to male" or FTM). We use the term transgender women for those who identify as female but who were categorized as male at birth (other common terms include "trans woman," "male to female," or MTF). Many transgender people do not challenge the idea that men should be masculine and women should be feminine. That is, they either accept the traditional gender categories or they conform to them to decrease the chance of experiencing discrimination or violence. They also define themselves as members of a gender they were not assigned at birth and therefore adopted many of those roles and attitudes traditionally associated with that gender.

Because transgender issues have only recently come to greater mainstream awareness, we have little data on how many transgender people there are. The most recent data from the Census Bureau's Household Plus survey indicates that 0.6 percent of Americans are transgender (US Census Bureau, 2021a). Health surveys from the Center for Disease Control conducted between 2017 and 2020 suggest that almost 1.4 percent of 13- to 17-year-olds from the United States identify as transgender (Ghorayshi, 2022).

Genderqueer people bend the rules associated with masculinity and femininity, refusing to conform to the gender binary. They may say that they are both male and female, or neither, or they may list genderqueer as their gender. People who are **gender fluid** move between genders. Being genderqueer or gender fluid is not necessarily linked to sexual orientation or gender expression. We do not know how many genderqueer or gender fluid people are currently in the United States.

There are several countries around the world that recognize more than two sexes and/or genders. For example, in India, the *hijras*, while male at birth, define themselves as neither men nor women but as a third gender. They adopt many aspects of a feminine gender presentation, but they are not stigmatized. Rather, they are thought to exemplify the Hindu belief that each person possesses both masculine and feminine elements. *Hijras* challenge and question the masculine/feminine dualism and embrace ambiguity (Bakshi, 2004). Prior to the arrival of Europeans, 130 American Indian tribes had members who were considered to be "two-spirit" people. Mostly men, they took on the social roles of women and often married men. They were held in high esteem and were not seen as homosexual but simply as a third gender. European colonists, however, found the practice to be unacceptable. The Spanish in California used particularly vicious methods to do away with the two-spirit people. The forced assimilation of Indian children in residential schools also instilled homophobic attitudes. Ultimately, most tribes began to move toward a two-gender system (Miller, 2006).

Intersex people have also caused society to question its assumptions about gender. Prior to the 1920s, intersex children received little attention and midwives, grandmothers, or other family members or community elders quietly made a decision about their gender assignment. After 1920, however, the medical establishment started taking surgical measures to make sure that a child's body looked like their assigned gender. They believed that people should be either male or female, and anything that did not fit the binary should be changed. Johns Hopkins University started a medical center to treat intersex people in the 1950s. Interestingly, the staff believed that gender was a result of socialization rather than nature. Therefore, if a child was young enough, they could easily learn to be either gender. The center tended to assign intersex children to be girls because they felt that it was harder to surgically create a boy than a girl (Intersex Society of North America, 2008). During this time, the public did not talk about intersex people and medical records were often hidden or destroyed.

Psychologists have also played a role in defining gender. In the 1980s, the American Psychiatric Association created a category in their *Diagnostic and Statistical Manual* (DSM) called "gender identity disorder" that referred to people who had a strong and consistent identification with a different gender from that to which they were assigned. The DSM-V, published in 2013, however, clearly states that being transgender is not, in and of itself, pathological. This view is reflected in a new name: **gender dysphoria**. The description of gender dysphoria emphasizes that the problem is not within the transgender person but is a result of societal prejudice and discrimination. In the run-up to the publication of the new DSM, some activists argued that there should be no category for transgender people at all, but others argued that without a diagnostic category, transgender people would not be eligible for hormones and other medical interventions under their health insurance policies.

Today we see changes in the ways gender is defined by governments—at the time of writing, up to 15 countries allow at least some nonbinary gender options on official documents. In 2017, Canada became the tenth country to officially include a third option on gender questions for people who do not identify on a binary. In Germany, parents of intersex babies can mark a third option on a birth certificate indicating that gender is indeterminate. Other countries (including Bangladesh, New Zealand, India, and Australia) allow adults to identify as a third gender on official documents. Argentina has now instituted some of the most open policies in the world, allowing transgender people to change their gender on official documents without the involvement of a judge or doctor. Government health care also covers all expenses related to transition. While the United States sometimes serves as a model to other countries for new policies, in the area of gender identification issues, it is clear that other countries are taking a strong lead. At the same time, 21 states and the District of Columbia allow residents to choose M, F, or X on their driver's license (Movement Advancement Project, 2021b).

Isn't It about Biology?

Biological explanations of gender inequality suggest that basic genetic, hormonal, or physical differences determine gender inequality. These are, however, inadequate for several reasons. First, a close examination of the differences between males and females shows that on most measures, the differences *within* categories are greater than the difference *between* categories (Epstein, 1988). Thus, with many so-called sex-typed behaviors, there is a greater range of behaviors among men than is seen when comparing men and women. Second, although there are some hormonal and physical differences between the sexes, these do not mandate that men will dominate women. These differences and any behaviors associated with them have to be culturally and socially

---

BOX 8.1 THE VIOLENT POLICING OF THE GENDER BINARY

Despite some progress in legal rights, 2021 looks to be the most deadly year for transgender and gender-nonconforming individuals, with at least 53 murders occurring in the year at the time of writing (Statista Research Department, 2021). Over 75 percent of those transgender individuals killed since 2013 were women of color, and over 85 percent were women. Nine victims were minors (Human Rights Campaign, 2021a).

How do we explain this increase? That is not an easy question since the problem is multidimensional, as many transgender and gender nonconforming people are facing various risk factors. At the cultural level, they are facing stigma for those who see them as a challenge to traditional binary definitions of gender. Transgender people of color are living at the intersection of several identities, facing isolation based in racism, sexism, and homophobia.

Often transgender and gender nonconforming individuals have been isolated by their families, who do not understand or accept their identities. This isolation leaves them vulnerable to violence from others and from themselves. In one study, over 81 percent report having thoughts of suicide (Herman et al., 2019). Transgender individuals face rejection from their partners after they come out, from their church communities, and from their workplace communities.

Additionally, transgender individuals are more likely to be economically isolated, similarly leaving them vulnerable. Many report workplace and housing discrimination, placing them in economically marginal situations (Herman et al., 2019). Finally, in the United States, we are facing a broader culture hostile to those who do not conform to binary gender expectations. In 2021, across the country, 25 anti-LGBTQ bills were enacted. Eight states passed anti-transgender laws, and over 130 anti-transgender bills were introduced across most states (Human Rights Campaign, 2021a).

What sort of policy solutions might address this situation? Why do you think at this time in history, violence against transgender individuals is so high?

---

interpreted (i.e., gendered). Finally, much of what we know about the differences between the sexes is filtered through our existing cultural assumptions about sex as a binary and the traits associated with that binary.

Note that our social understandings of gender have influenced our physical bodies and our biological knowledge: "(g)endered structures change biological function and structure. At the same time, biological structure and function affect gender, gender identity, and gender role at both individual and cultural levels" (Fausto-Sterling, 2019, p. 532). For example, scientists discovered the "sex chromosomes" early in the 1900s. Women carry two X chromosomes and men have one X and one Y (although it turns out there is variation in this as well). Science textbooks teach that the sex chromosomes determine whether we are male or female. In fact, this is a vast simplification and the term "sex chromosomes" is really a misnomer. The X and Y chromosomes only contain some of the genetic material that determines sex, and they also contain information about traits that have nothing to do with sex. Additionally, the development of sex is not entirely driven by chromosomes, hormones also contribute to sexual development. Richardson (2013) argues that we framed our scientific understanding of sex chromosomes in the way we did because it seemed to confirm the popular belief that there are two distinct genders.

One of the pitfalls of equating sex with gender has been to define the gender roles given to each sex as "natural," that by their nature, men and women perform specific roles and have particular characteristics. The old phrase "men are men and women are women" captures this belief. If, however, there is no fixed, necessary tie between gender and sex, then gender can be attached to anyone, male or female (Butler, 1999). Gender itself is not an entity or property of the individual, says Judith Butler; rather, it is "performative," a set of ritualistic, recurrent acts performed by individuals acting within a cultural and political system. Borrowing from Foucault and French feminists, Butler argues that concepts such as "woman" and "female" are created within a cultural framework that is also a system of power. Those who act in ways that are inconsistent with this framework are considered unintelligible or not normal (Butler, 1999; Lloyd, 2007).

Sex is just as culturally constructed as *gender*, contends Butler. Bodies have always been interpreted culturally and do not exist as social objects prior to their naming and interpretation. They appear to do so because culture is capable of producing "frames of reference which are so powerful that they congeal into the invariance and irreducibility of material reality" (Kirby, 2006, p. 23). The aim of a genealogy of the concept of gender is to uncover the acts that create and sustain it, and the social and political frameworks that underlie it and "police the social appearance of gender" (Butler, 1999, p. 44). Thus, gender is not a static, inherent quality but an accomplishment. The reality is that we are both biological and social beings, and as such, we need to "leave behind the social-versus-nonsocial, nature-versus-nurture oppositions, outlining an approach that intertwines sex, gender, orientation, bodies, and cultures without a demand to choose one over the other" (Fausto-Sterling, 2019, pp. 529–530).

Gender as Structure

Barbara Risman outlines a model for looking beyond individual-level theories and nature/nurture divides that argues that we should view gender as a multi-level "structure." In this model, gender involves "a dynamic, recursive causality between individual selves, interactional expectations, and macro cultural ideology and social organization" (Risman, 2018, p. 29). That means that the organization of our worlds based on gendered assumptions has implications for us as individuals, for how we interact with one another, and for the broader ways that we structure our societies. When sociologists talk about structure, they are referring to patterned ways of organizing behavior "that exist outside individual desires or motives" (Risman & Davis, 2013). For example, economics or politics are structures that affect how individuals interact at work, within families, and how they think about their relationship to the wider society. Gender is as systemic as politics and economics, and as a structure in its own right, it creates **gender stratification**, including who benefits, who has access to resources, and who has political and ideological power.

To say that gender is a powerful structure does not mean that we are fully determined by gender. Risman endorses Giddens' (1984) structuration theory which argues that humans create structures but that we can act back on them and change them as well. While the gender structure differentially offers opportunities and constraints based on sex categorization and therefore has great power over individuals and institutions, it does not fully determine either. We make choices, but those choices happen within structural constraints that have both material and cultural components.

Risman offers this model to move beyond explanations for gender inequality rooted solely in socialization. Socialization is important, but merely changing how individuals are socialized will not address the economic and political structures supporting inequality. Similarly, however, it is not enough to understand structured inequalities without addressing interactional and cultural components. Risman recognizes that gender structures are not homogeneous and that they are constructed differently in various cultures and at various times and places.

Let's take the fun example of children's toys. Why are toys in most stores displayed by gender (though there are noteworthy movements to change this—see Edwards, 2021)? Why does it even make sense to think that very young children want or need very different toys depending on their assigned sex? At the macro level, the gendering of toys is tied in with corporate profits—if we have to provide our children either boy blocks or girl blocks, for example, it means that if a family has both a boy and a girl they cannot share the toys; they need to buy twice as much! Toys divided by gender also affect how children interact with one another. Do they, for example,

Photo 8.1 The toys children play with can reinforce limiting gender stereotypes.
Source: © iStock.com/MattoMatteo.

engage in competition, or do they engage in imaginative play? And finally, through playing with toys, children develop a sense of who they are and who they can be based on gender. For example, a recent study of LEGO toys found that they were highly gender-typed, with LEGO City toys marketed to boys and LEGO Friends marketed to girls. Researchers found that "LEGO City encouraged boys to enact skilled professions, expertise, and heroism, but LEGO Friends focused on girls having hobbies; being apprentices; engaging in domestic, caring and socializing activities; and emphasizing beauty" (Dinella & Weisgram, 2018, p. 255).

The LEGO example is a good illustration of how the gender structure has implications at the individual, the interactional, and the macro level (see Figure 8.1). The *individual* level focuses on how we become and enact gendered selves, including socialization, the development of gender identities, and the construction of selves. At the *interactional* level, gender structures expectations we have of one another based on status, biases individuals may hold toward others and promotes

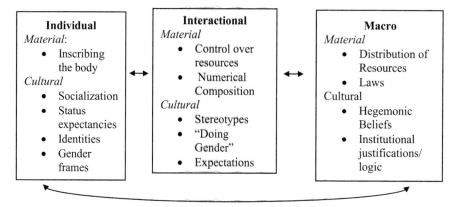

Figure 8.1 Risman's Gender Structure.
Source: Adapted from Risman, 2018.

the "othering" of categories of individuals. Finally, at the *macro level*, the gender structure contributes to organizational practices, laws, ideologies, and the distribution of resources (Risman, 2018, p. 40). This level involves larger-scale processes affecting how society is organized, how we structure our institutions, the rules and regulations guiding our everyday behaviors, our methods for allocating goods and resources across statuses, and, importantly, the ideologies that uphold these structures.

At each of these levels, as we saw in Chapter 7, inequalities are created and reproduced via both *cultural* and *material* processes. According to Risman, "(m)aterial processes are based upon physical bodies, laws, or geographical locations and how these impact social lives." Cultural processes are "ideological or socially constructed ideas that orientate peoples' perspectives and worldviews" (Scarborough & Risman, 2017, p. 2). Borrowing heavily from the model presented by Scarborough and Risman (2017), we'll be exploring here how the cultural and material resources play out at each level, followed by an analysis of the institutions of work, family, and education.

Cultural and Symbolic Processes

How we envision ourselves, what we expect of others, and how we structure the institutions around us are due in great part to the gendered culture surrounding us—whether we accept or reject the prevalent cultural models, our sense of who we are, and our decisions on how to act develop within the background of the wider culture. Below we will discuss three sociological theories addressing gendered culture that have implications for all three levels of analysis.

Gender Frames, Status, and Inequality

There is a decades-old riddle out there we remember hearing as children that goes like this: "A father and son were in a car accident where the father was killed. The ambulance brought the son to the hospital. He needed immediate surgery. In the operating room, a doctor came in and looked at the little boy and said I can't operate on him, he is my son. Who is the doctor?" To contemporary ears, and given the topic of this chapter, it might seem obvious that the surgeon is, of course, the boy's mother. But surprisingly, a very recent study indicates that this remains a salient riddle—fewer than one-third of college students participating in a study were able to guess correctly that the surgeon was a woman. In fact, *more* guessed that the surgeon was a same-sex male partner (Belle et al., 2021). How do we explain the persistence of such gender stereotypes? One explanation can be found in Cecilia Ridgeway's work on gender and status expectations.

Similar to Risman, Ridgeway (Ridgeway, 2009, 2014; Ridgeway & Correll, 2004) argues that gender serves as a cultural frame by which we organize our realities. Sex/gender provides a frame for us to both categorize and differentiate ourselves and others—it is how we can more or less instantly interpret people we encounter. It is why many jump to the conclusion that the surgeon in the riddle is a man! While there are various frames by which we distinguish ourselves and others, gender is a particularly powerful organizing principle because of the intimacy and frequency of our interactions. Class and race are highly salient statuses, but we are more likely to interact with other genders on a daily basis than with those of different classes and races (Ridgeway & Correll, 2004).

Our beliefs about the characteristics of each sex and appropriate gender roles help shape the positions individuals occupy in society, and in a recursive manner, the status of these positions legitimates gendered beliefs. As we saw in Chapter 4, gender is a status that carries with it expectations about competency and the appropriate rewards associated with the position—it divides people into "types," deserving differential levels of honor and respect. In this way, gender and the associated stereotypes serve as a basis for inequality between the sexes (Ridgeway, 2011). For example, in a recent study of political ambition among children, researchers found that "children not only perceive politics to be a male-dominated space, but with age, girls increasingly see political leadership as a 'man's world'" (Bos et al., 2021, p. 1). As they grow older, via "gendered political socialization," girls come to recognize that politics are meant for men, and as such, they do not envision themselves entering political careers.

Ridgeway argues that gender inequality can be explained by status expectancies or the idea that people expect others to differ in competency based on their status differences. "People form status beliefs that the 'type' of people who have more resources … are "better" than the "types" with fewer resources. Furthermore, because both advantaged and disadvantaged groups experience the apparent "superiority" of the advantaged "type," the resulting status beliefs are shared by dominants and subdominants alike, legitimating the inequality" (Ridgeway, 2014, p. 3).

The gender frames we use impact us at the individual level by giving us a model for characterizing and judging ourselves—as in, "am I a good woman?" or "as a man, I shouldn't be acting this way." As we will see in the next section on "doing gender," these frames also affect how we interpret one another and what are expectations of others are. Finally, when the gender frame becomes dominant, or hegemonic, as we will see with the concept of *hegemonic masculinity*, gender frames become reified into institutions and macro societal structures.

Doing Gender

In their foundational article, Candace West and Don Zimmerman (1987) reconceptualize gender from a view that sees it as a set of traits residing within individuals to something that people *do* in their interactions. Gender involves a display of behaviors, the "activity of managing situated conduct in light of normative conceptions of attitudes and activities appropriate for one's sex category" (p. 127). In our everyday interactions, each of us displays gender, including how we speak, dress, carry ourselves physically, or interact with others. We learn as young children how to display femininity or masculinity, though we certainly may not choose to at all times. By "doing gender," we reinforce the idea that there are essential differences between females and males. The act of accomplishing and displaying gender is a way of producing gender differences and reinforcing gender inequalities.

Transgender people often feel pressure to actively "do gender" in interactions. In their social interactions with gender-conforming individuals, especially at work, they need to negotiate the relationships between their biological sex, gender identity, and gender performance. While moving between gendered behaviors, transgender individuals become highly sensitive to gender discrimination because they experience differences in their treatment as they change their gender performances (Connell, 2010). Some give gender performances that are consistent with and expected of their biological sex, for example, a male exhibits masculine behavior. He will *do* the gender that is expected of him by gender-conforming colleagues, even though it is inconsistent with the gender with which he identifies. Others act with a mix of societally defined masculine and feminine behaviors or act openly in a manner consistent with their gender identity (Connell, 2010).

"Doing gender" theory was updated in 1995 to encompass class and race, arguing that both of these can also be seen as interactional "accomplishments." All three involve "doing difference" or enacting one's structural position in particular contexts, thereby reinforcing inequalities (West & Fenstermaker, 1995). More recently, Westbrook and Schilt (2014) have expanded on the concept by introducing the idea of "determining gender," an "umbrella term for the different subprocesses of attributing or, in some cases, officially deciding another person's gender" (p. 36). In their interactions, individuals engage in displays that indicate what gender they have determined someone to be, thereby announcing the appropriate expected behavior from that individual. Finally, others have highlighted Risman's point that we can act back on social structures by emphasizing that many of us engage in "undoing gender" (Butler, 2004), or "behaving in opposition to gender stereotypes, avoiding the use of stereotypes in evaluating others, or dismantling gender barriers" (Deutsch, 2007, p. 132).

Hegemonic Masculinity

Each of the above theoretical perspectives highlights micro-interactions (that is, interactions between individuals) but outline as well how these person-to-person interactions connect to the structure of society. All gender stereotypes and cultural narratives have implications for how we see ourselves and others, but some are so dominant that they are woven into the macro level of society. These are over-arching models, or hegemonic ideologies, about what it means to be masculine or feminine that serve as the underpinning for how we organize society. An example of this is Raewyn Connell's (1987) theory of gender inequality that focuses on masculinity, power, and consent. It draws, in part, on an understanding of gender as performative. Connell points out that across cultures and times, there have been many ways of expressing masculinity and femininity, but in any given culture at a particular time, one form of masculinity tends to be dominant. Called **"hegemonic masculinity,"** this set of behaviors and traits becomes the gold standard for proving manhood. In the current United States, hegemonic masculinity includes such traits as not showing emotion or weakness as well as being competitive and strong, taking risks, and being the breadwinner. Connell argues that these traits serve as an ideology that justifies male dominance over women. A particularly key aspect is heterosexuality, as it enables men to retain power in families. A recent survey of adolescents aged 10–19 reinforces Connell's ideas that society holds up one standard of masculinity. Of the boys in the survey, 35 percent said that society most values strength and toughness in boys. A full seven in ten said that they felt pressure to be physically strong and—of the adolescents aged 16 to 19—44 percent said that they feel pressure to resort to violence if they are provoked (Undem & Wang, 2018).

In Connell's model, ideal femininity is understood as being defined in relation to hegemonic masculinity. If "real men" are to be strong, real women should be weak. The corollary of the term hegemonic masculinity is "emphasized femininity." Emphasized femininity includes norms that encourage women to act in submissive ways with men, to be emotional caretakers, minimize abuse, concentrate on their physical appearance, and always desire a romantic partner (Korobov, 2011). Connell defines it as "the pattern of femininity which is given most cultural and ideological support ... patterns such as sociability ... compliance ... [and] sexual receptivity [to men]" (1987, p. 24). Again, the Undem and Wang (2018) survey provides evidence for this with seven out of ten girls aged 14–19 feeling judged as a sexual objects.

When people internalize ideas about hegemonic masculinity and emphasize femininity, domination appears to be natural. It begins to make sense that men should be in charge because they are strong and unemotional and that women, who are weak and driven by emotions, should be caretakers. In this way, hegemonic masculinity gets women to consent to their own domination because they too come to believe the images of men and women. It also achieves the consent of some men who cannot (or are not allowed to) live up to its standards. These men may not be able to achieve all the aspects of hegemonic masculinity (for example, they might be physically weak), but they still support the ideology because they see that it benefits them through the **"patriarchy** dividend" that all men receive to some degree. These men are said to have "complicit masculinity."

Note that hegemonic masculinity is not simply about the domination of women. Connell calls masculinities that do not support male domination "subordinate masculinities." Gay men can express masculinity, but it is a subordinate (and thus denigrated) form. This justifies homophobia and the exclusion of gay men from positions of power. Similarly, because ideas about hegemonic masculinity originate with people in power, poor and minority men are generally relegated to subordinate masculinities. Connell thinks that all forms of masculinity are culturally bound and that "[d]ifferent cultures and different periods of history construct gender differently. Striking differences exist, for instance, in the relationship of homosexual practice to dominant forms of masculinity" (Connell, 2015, p. 42). In other words, there are cultures whose definitions of hegemonic masculinity do not include heterosexuality.

Material Processes

Gender as structure is not only upheld by cultural practices but by material processes as well. Gender structures our institutions and how we organize our societies. For example, during a good part of our history, the binary assumption that men are productive, rational, and task oriented and that women are nurturing and caring led to the organization of labor such that work for a wage happened by men outside of the home, and the care of children, or reproductive labor, happened by women in the home. Our understanding of the characteristics of sex/gender influenced how we organized the institutions of work and family. This section will discuss these material processes, including the effects of gender on the body and on the legal system.

Inscribing the Body

Gendered cultural expectations do not simply affect how we act, but they are written on our bodies. As Risman argues, "boys and girls, men and women, and those who reject binary identities are all embodied, with real flesh and blood material objects—bodies—they have to interpret and display" (2018, p. 35). Gendered expectations affect how we move and carry ourselves—girls, for example, are taught to sit with their knees together and to take up as little space as possible. After a time, this embodied and gendered behavior becomes habitual and has a real effect on our neuromuscular system (Fausto-Sterling, 2019). A few examples include the fact that we can train our voices to be more masculine or feminine or that arduous athletic training can affect how frequently women menstruate.

Previous research on physical differences between males and females assumes that these are primarily due to the organization of the brain and to the presence of sex hormones such as estrogen and testosterone. But more recent research examines the feedback loops between the body (material processes) and cultural processes (Fausto-Sterling, 2019; Jordan-Young, 2011). At a societal level, cultural expectations about gender can affect the nature and extent of sex differences in a population. Sex differences vary across societies such that in some, they are more extreme, and in others, they are far less so. For example, research suggests that in societies that have a strong cultural preference for boys, such as China, boys are on average taller than in societies that do not have as strong a preference, controlling for other factors (Jordan-Young, 2011, p. 282). One possible explanation for this is that in such societies, the preference for boys means that boys are given more resources such as nutritional foods and better health care.

Another example can be found in differences in bone structure, a seemingly purely biological factor. "In the case of bone density and osteoporosis, some of the factors that underlie putatively innate biological sex differences include physical activity levels, especially weight-bearing work and exercise; diet, especially calcium intake; exposure to sunlight for vitamin D; and hormones—of these, only hormones have a plausible "biological" basis that is easy to conceptualize apart from gender" (Jordan-Young, 2011, p. 285). Bones develop differently across societies dependent on some of the material interventions—whether women or men engaged in strenuous work, or if they work outside, or if they are fed differently.

Gender and the Legal System

The other key material process is in the realm of laws. Laws not only stem from and reflect shared understandings of gender, but they also lead to differential access to resources and opportunities. Sports is a great venue for exploring this process. Our assumptions about the nature of biological differences by sex have affected our laws surrounding sports participation. For example, in the past few years, we have seen an increase in the number of laws at the state level regulating the participation of transgender youth in sports. Currently, ten states ban participation by transgender students in school sports, mostly K-12, for in some cases for college students as well (Movement Advancement Project, 2021b). These laws are based on strict binary constructions and ensure that sports competitions are fully sex-segregated (Sharrow, 2021). Assumptions about inherent biological differences between men and women underlie these rules—those proposing the laws argue that since men are naturally better at sports, allowing people born as men to compete as women would be an unfair advantage. But it is not clear that in all sports, cisgender males have an automatic large advantage. As we saw above, there are great variations between sex-based dichotomies in abilities across cultures. Additionally, while *on average*, men have an 8–12 percent advantage in performance compared to women, this varies by sport—in swimming, men's advantage is only 5 percent (Sandbakk et al., 2018).

Underlying these regulations are organizations that are similarly segregated: we have professional organizations in sports such as soccer or basketball divided by sex and involving differential rules for playing the game, organizing the leagues, and rewarding the athletes. For example, several collegiate and professional sports have limited the physicality of the game for women, assuming that they are more fragile. In ice hockey and lacrosse, women are not permitted to check other players with their sticks—in fact, men's lacrosse is considered a contact sport while women's is not. In this way, "societal construction of rules, and rules concerning physical contact specifically, serve to reify the notion of gender differences" (Wiser, 2014, p. 1658). As lacrosse started

---

BOX 8.2 TITLE IX AND ATHLETICS

The landmark legislation Title IX was passed in 1972. It states that no person can, on the basis of sex, be denied access to, denied benefits of, or discriminated against in any education program that receives federal funding. While the law was not intended specifically for athletics, it has had a huge impact on high school and college sports programs over the last three decades. Schools must offer the same number of athletic opportunities for males and females. This does not mean that there must be the same number of teams, but rather that schools must supply the same number of opportunities to play. Funding for different teams does not need to be equal, but it cannot be distributed in a discriminatory way (for example, giving female but not male teams substandard equipment to use would be a violation).

Title IX has had a significant impact, increasing the average number of women's college teams from 2.5 in 1972 to 8.32 in 2004 (Bell, 2008). At the same time, many argue that it has been ineffective in ending discrimination in athletics. For example, in the 2018–2019 season, the NCAA spent $4,285 for men's Division I and national championship participants but $1,700 less for female participants (Diaz, 2021). Women receive 86,000 fewer opportunities to participate in collegiate sports. Some people complain that Title IX denies men an opportunity to play certain sports. The argument is that football teams generally carry such large rosters, schools have to limit other types of men's sports to ensure that they are in compliance with Title IX. There is evidence, however, that the real reason other sports are sometimes cut is that football budgets are so high, they take all the available resources. In these cases, other sports are cut for both men and women. What do you think? Should Title IX be strengthened? Changed? Eliminated?

appearing at women's elite colleges in the early 1900s, the rules were based on raced and classed assumptions about how women should carry themselves.

There are many other ways that our expectations of the roles of men and women are codified into our legal system. As we'll see below, federal laws on workplace discrimination, parental leave, and violence against women or transgender individuals all provide a framework within which our interactions and identities play out. These frameworks connect to societal institutions such as family, education, and work, organizing the roles that coordinate our behaviors, transmitting cultural expectations, and often creating or reproducing inequalities.

Family

Family is a powerful site for reproducing and reflecting social inequalities at the individual, institutional, and macro levels. It is the place where we first develop our gender identities based on that first sex categorization—the importance of that is evident at the increasingly popular gender-reveal parties, where family and friends gather to announce the sex! At the interactional level, it is through our relationships with our parents and our siblings that we develop expectations of one another surrounding gender. And family is defined at the macro level by our overarching understandings and experiences of race, class, gender, nationality, and sexuality. Our laws determine what counts as a family, as we see currently in legislation on gay marriage and in the past with raced-based restrictions on marriage. Powerful ideologies such as hegemonic masculinities and essentialist notions of parenthood influence our actions in the home.

One of the first ways we develop gendered understandings is through the daily work of keeping house and caring for children. Despite changes in recent years in gender roles, a persistent fact of daily life is that women take on more of the burden of housework than men (Bianchi et al., 2012). According to the Organization for Economic Cooperation and Development, women in the United States spend almost four hours a day on unpaid work, compared with only 2.5 for men (OECD, 2021a). This has been replicated many times over the years, with recent findings that it persists over the life course (Horne et al., 2018) when both are unemployed (Aguiar et al., 2021), and during the COVID-19 pandemic (Zamberlan et al., 2021). Why does this gap persist, and why does it matter?

Several theories might explain the persistent gap in housework. One possibility surrounds gender socialization and the idea of "doing gender" outlined above. A central component of performing femininity has been for women to be nurturing and to take responsibility for the upkeep of the home. Little girls are given dolls and even toy vacuum cleaners to learn their appropriate roles. But haven't attitudes changed? Indeed, 2018 polling from the General Social Survey suggests that fewer than 5 percent of those polled strongly agreed that "preschool kids suffer if mother works," or that it is "better for man to work and woman to stay home," this down from 20 percent in 1975 (GSS Data Explorer, 2018).

Cultural expectations of motherhood certainly may play a role here as well. An ongoing model of ideal motherhood, particularly for middle- and upper-class women, has been that of "intensive mothering." This model argues that, despite expectations that women be in the labor force, whether or not our children succeed in the world depends on the intensive efforts of mothers; childrearing is viewed as primarily the responsibility of the mother (Hays, 1996). From early childhood, middle- and upper-class parents engage in what Annette Lareau (2011) has termed "concerted cultivation," the conscious preparation of their children in the skills and values they will need to be successful and to maintain their higher position in the social hierarchy. These expectations can be particularly difficult for single mothers in poverty, as they are facing expectations of motherhood that are both class-based and racialized (Fitz Gibbon, 2010).

These expectations of family roles are in contradiction with expectations for women at work. It should not be surprising, then, that women are more affected by household-related variables than are men. For example, Michelle Budig (2014) uncovered a "**motherhood penalty**" and "**fatherhood bump**" in her analysis of income data. This means that fatherhood is associated with higher wages, but motherhood is linked to lower wages. The fatherhood bump is particularly pronounced at higher levels of the income scale. Budig argues that this may be because employers see fathers as more responsible and warm (and therefore desirable as workers), but they see mothers as less committed to their careers.

In the United States, a strong attachment to work is expected and valued, and so the price paid by a new mother for taking even a short time-out can be significant. Many American women are aware of this and take as little time off as possible (Aisenbrey et al., 2009; Gangl & Ziefle, 2009). But when mothers are successful in higher managerial positions, they are often criticized as not being "feminine" enough, and this affects how they are evaluated. Since most high-level executive positions are assumed to require "masculine" qualities, men are not subjected to these criticisms (Benard & Correll, 2010).

Parents are caught in a structurally ambivalent position regarding gendered expectations of work and family. Despite the increasing assumption that women can be skilled workers and effective leaders and that men are often nurturing and supportive parents, the United States lacks the structural supports for us to be successful parents and workers. Among the 38 OECD countries (Organization of Economic Co-operation and Development), the United States is the *only* country that provides no paid maternity or paternity leave. Greece, for example, offers forty-three weeks of paid maternity leave; on average, OECD countries offer over eighteen weeks of paid leave. On average, fathers in OECD countries are eligible for seven paid weeks of leave (OECD, 2021b). Why does this matter? Generous family leave policies are related to improved child health outcomes, reduced infant mortality, increased labor force participation by women, and a safeguard for women's wages and incomes (Nandi et al., 2018).

How do these expectations of parenthood play out for transgender and queer parents? Queer and non-cisgender parents face assumptions about the biological or essential nature of parenting. How often have you heard people refer to "maternal instinct" or assume that "by nature" women know how to be mothers? The embedded assumption with these statements is that motherhood is directly linked to sex and that it is only performed by "female bodies" (Averett, 2021). This proves problematic for families with no bodies designated female from birth: either two male bodies or transgender parents. "(T)he incorporation of transgender people's reproductive endeavors shifts historical efforts to link pregnancy and childbirth to cisgender womanhood and cisnormative beliefs proposing that all people assigned female must identify as women" (Lampe et al., 2019, p. 866). As more people who identify as transgender engages in parenting, we shift our understanding of these roles.

BOX 8.3 WHY WAS COVID SO MUCH HARDER ON WOMEN?

Unlike other economic downturns, it has become increasingly clear that domestically and globally, women have been the most severely impacted by the pandemic (Alon et al., 2020; Bateman & Ross, 2020; United Nations, 2020). In the Great Recession of 2008, for example, job losses were much higher for men than for women, in great part because men are employed in industries that are usually the most highly affected by economic downturns, such as manufacturing or construction. But the economic downturn created by the pandemic has been much harder on women. Between February 2020 and January 2021, more than 2.5 million women left the labor force in the United States, compared with 1.8 million men (Shallal, 2021). Many of those have not done so voluntarily, despite the focus on the "great resignation" in the press: the unemployment rate for women increased by over 12 percentage points between February and April 2020, higher than that of men (Bateman & Ross, 2020). And the United Nations reports higher incidences of domestic violence toward women across the globe (United Nations, 2020).

What accounts for this? As is often the case, the pandemic highlights structural weaknesses regarding women's work and home life. First, women are highly disadvantaged in the labor market *vis a vis* the pandemic—they are overrepresented in industries such as restaurants and retail establishments, and they are less likely to be working in jobs that allow them to telecommute. Their jobs are more likely to be part-time or in the informal labor market, and as such, they are the first to be laid off, and they are often not eligible for support such as unemployment insurance (Alon et al., 2020).

Second, the lack of supports for women in balancing work and family obligations has been made increasingly evident. As we saw above, mothers spend far more time engaged in caring for children than do men; therefore, they carried the brunt of the burden when schools and childcare centers closed. For many women in the past couple of years, work outside the home became untenable.

Finally, the stress of lockdowns and worries about the pandemic have increased the incidences of domestic violence across the globe. At the same time that many women have been isolated with their abusers, social services that might have helped in the past are not available (United Nations, 2020).

Is this all bad news? Maybe there is a silver lining: businesses are beginning to be more flexible in how they organize work, and while their contributions still fall below those of mothers, fathers have increased their share of childcare and housework during the pandemic. Do you think this will change how we balance work and family? What policy changes would you recommend to solve these problems?

Education

One of the most interesting dynamics historically regarding gender and education has been the fact that women are now outpacing men at nearly all levels. Gender is linked to school completion, with 88 percent of girls graduating high school on time compared with 82 percent of boys. Looking at this intersectionally, the gap is greater among Black and Hispanic students (Reeves et al., 2021). A study by Kearney and Levine (2015) found that income inequality between the middle and lower class was linked to drop-out rates, at least among low SES boys. It appears that these boys use the middle class as their reference point for mobility, and when it seems unreachable (because the gap is so great), boys become discouraged about the possibility of education increasing their later wages. This causes them to drop out. Interestingly, girls do not react in the same way, although rates of teenage motherhood do move in tandem with inequality. There is also evidence to suggest that the predominance of female teachers influences young people's educational aspirations, encouraging young women more than men (Bailey & Dynarski, 2011).

The gender disparity in education carries on over to college. For most of American history, men attended and graduated from college at higher rates than women—the first year that the men and women had equal rates of college graduation was 1980. By 2018, about 57 percent of graduates were women (National Center for Education Statistics, 2020). When the data are broken down by race, we see that all groups follow the same pattern with women having higher graduation rates than men (see Figure 8.2). The disparity is particularly pronounced among Black people with 64 percent of bachelor's degrees awarded to women. Comparable numbers are 62 percent for American Indian/Alaskan Natives, 61 percent for Hispanics, 56 percent for Whites, and 55 percent for Asian/Pacific Islanders (National Center for Education Statistics, 2020). Interestingly, on average, transgender people obtain a higher level of education than do cisgender people. Their rate of graduate degrees is twice that of the general population, and they achieve bachelor's degrees at a rate that is 10 percent higher. This could be because transgender people try to get more education to compensate for workplace discrimination or it could be that people

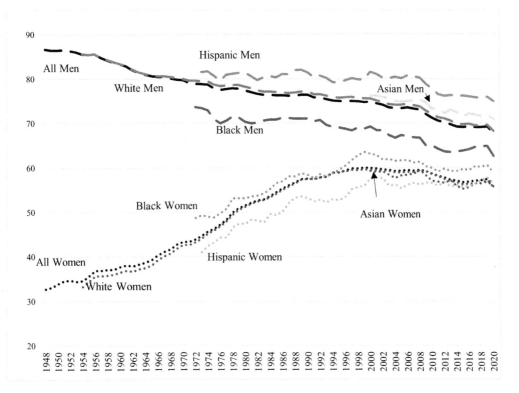

Figure 8.2 Bachelor's Degrees Received by Race and Gender, 2017–2018.
Source: National Center for Education Statistics (2020), https://nces.ed.gov/programs/digest/d19/tables/dt19_322.20.asp

who are more educated are more likely to identify as transgender. But, unlike the cisgender population, transgender women tend to be less educated than transgender men (Leppel, 2016).

The statistics in Figure 8.2 mask several underlying patterns. Just as with occupations, college students differ by gender in their fields of study, and their major has a significant impact on their future earnings. In 2017–2018, while 57 percent of bachelor's degrees went to women, less than 20 percent of computer science and engineering degrees were awarded to women. Conversely, almost 82 percent of degrees in education were awarded to women (and 71 percent of Sociology degrees!). These discrepancies only increase at the advanced degree level.

Within schools, gendered assumptions are significant and can negatively affect both boys and girls. Gender identity is strictly policed in schools; for example, 22 percent of LGBT youth reported being physically harassed for their gender expression (Kosciw et al., 2014). Research also points to how gender stereotypes affect children in school. For example, children tend to believe that girls are better in school than are boys. This can result in stereotype threat. As described in the last chapter, this term refers to a situation in which people perform poorly because they fear confirming a negative stereotype. In this case, it means that boys internalize the stereotype that they are bad at school and it causes them to do more poorly (Hartley & Sutton, 2013). Teachers have been shown to believe that girls are better at reading than boys, leading boys to have a worse self-concept in that subject (Retelsdorf et al., 2015). At the same time, girls are less likely to be perceived by teachers as competent in math, leading to stereotype threat in that area (Riegle-Crumb & Humphries, 2012).

These early differences in socialization and gendered educational environments play out very clearly in the lack of representation of women in STEM fields. Earlier research speculated that the difference was due to gender differences in academic preparation and achievement. But recent statistics demonstrate that while that gap has nearly closed at the high school level, the difference in persistence to graduation continues at the college level. A current study suggests that this difference is due partially to selection factors (i.e., women are slightly less likely to choose a major in STEM in part because they do not see themselves pursuing a STEM-based occupation) (Weeden et al., 2020). Additionally, experiences in the classroom also likely make a difference. One study found that college men are more confident than women in their abilities in STEM and more likely to identify themselves with STEM fields, and thus they are more likely to persist despite early academic failures (Penner & Willer, 2019).

When we think about colleges, we generally focus on students, but there is also research about how inequality impacts faculty members. For example, students show bias against their instructors through the words they use in their course evaluations, a central mechanism for evaluating faculty for promotion and tenure. This assumption that men are more intelligent or knowledgeable is echoed in the distribution by gender in academic fields. While women have made great progress in achieving parity in most academic fields, women are less likely to be represented in fields seen as requiring greater innate ability, such as physics and math (Leslie et al., 2015).

Gender and Work

A key site where the cultural and material processes of gender inequality operate is in the workplace. Our cultural expectations of gender determine what kinds of work people can perform based on their sex categorization or gender identity and how that work should be renumerated. This section will begin with a short history of gender and work, followed by an analysis of inequalities at the individual, interactional, and social levels.

A Brief History of Gender and Work in the United States

A common assumption is that women have only recently been working outside of the home. This, however, is far from the case. In the early history of the United States, as an agricultural, preindustrial colonial society, both women and men were directly involved in a variety of ways in production, but the nature of their labor was more often than not based on gender (Padavic & Reskin, 2002). The cultural norms of that time, as well as for the periods that followed, dictated that, first and foremost, women should be good wives and mothers; but, in fact, women were highly involved in the economy. They were raising stock, weaving, gardening, and even running businesses. While some women took over for their deceased or disabled husbands, most of the unmarried and widowed women went on the market as hired domestic workers. Women in slavery were expected to work alongside men in fields and factories, with a much less distinct sexual division of labor (Padavic & Reskin, 2002).

Until comparatively recently, women were attached to their families in a literal way, dependent on and subservient to their husbands or, in the case of slavery, to their owners. Thus, the idealized life of the female as someone removed from the harsh realities of the economy was strongly inconsistent with the actual circumstances of her life. Of course, even this ideal was never imagined for women of color, as this image of the protected "angel in the house" closely intersected with ideologies of race, class, and nation (Collins, 1998).

Through their economic activities, women contributed to the development of the first significant *industrial* organizations in the United States. The first textile factories, built around 1800 in Rhode Island and Massachusetts, recruited unmarried women from the farms of New England. Despite the promises of a proper place to work, conditions at these early factories left much to be desired. Even at Lowell Corporation in Massachusetts, among the most famous early

Photo 8.2 Portuguese mill girls who worked in the Lowell, Massachusetts mills. Ca. 1910–15.
Source: Everett Collection/Shutterstock.

textile mills, women worked an average of 13 hours a day, 73 hours a week, including 8 hours on Saturday (Kessler-Harris, 2003). Jobs in these early plants were gender segregated. Men held all supervisory positions as well as jobs in the mill yard, watch force, and repair shop; women were restricted to particular jobs operating equipment such as the looms and dressing machines. Men also were concerned about the entrance of women into the labor market because they felt that it would depress their wages. They fought to keep women out of the craft unions that later developed. Women held strikes in the 1830s and 1840s to protest reductions in wages, speedups in work pace, and increases in working hours (Dublin, 1993).

Between the end of the Civil War and 1900, the percentage of females in the workforce increased. In 1900, just over 20 percent (5 million) of all US women 15 years of age and older were employed as breadwinners, but only 15 percent of White females whose parents were born in the United States were, compared to 43 percent of Black females and 25 percent of White females with at least one foreign-born parent (US Department of Commerce and Labor, Bureau of Statistics, 1911). Many young women 10–15 years of age also worked outside the home. In 1900, almost 6 percent of White, native-born females did so, compared to over 30 percent of non-White females.

At the turn of the twentieth century, women made up a disproportionate number of workers in several occupations. For example, in 1900, they constituted 80–90 percent of all boarding and lodging housekeepers, servants, waiters, and paper box makers and over 90 percent of all housekeepers and stewards, nurses and midwives, dressmakers, milliners, and seamstresses. Men, on the other hand, dominated agricultural, common labor, bookkeeping, clerk/copyist, watch- and shoemaker, printer, dye works, and photography positions (US Census Office, 1903, Plate 90). Perhaps surprisingly, women comprised over 70 percent of the teachers and professors in colleges and over 50 percent of teachers of music, and men made up the majority of artists and teachers of art (Plate 90). Black females, however, were more likely to be wage earners than either native- or foreign-born White females.

Between 1930 and 1950, women's labor force participation shot up, with almost all of the increase driven by married women ages 30–45. In 1930, only 10 percent of married women worked, but this had risen to 25 percent by the end of the period (Goldin, 2014). The increase was driven by many factors, one of which was the reduction of the number of marriage bars (workplace policies that precluded employing a married woman) and the increasing availability of part-time work. Additionally, labor saving devices such as washing machines helped to reduce the work women needed to accomplish at home.

During the 1950s and 1960s, there was a surge in demand for labor that caused even more women to enter the labor force. They encountered obstacles, however, because they were locked out of many jobs, and those to which they were allowed entry (such as social work and teaching) had few chances for advancement. Additionally, many of the women who came of age during this time had not expected to work and, thus, did not prepare for it by getting higher education. The 1970s marked a significant turning point. Seeing their mother's experiences, more teenage girls began to expect that they might work in addition to being wives and mothers. As a result, they increased the amount of education they attained. For example, high school girls started taking more college preparatory classes and they also significantly closed the gap with boys in math and reading test scores. Women began to attend and graduate from college at rates similar to men. Not surprisingly, the marriage age for both college-graduating women as well as for those who attended but did not graduate rose. The fact that the contraceptive pill became more widely available in the 1970s also enabled people to marry later (Goldin, 2014). By 1994, a full 59 percent of women were in the labor force, but after that time, their participation began to level off (Lee, 2014).

As Figure 8.3 indicates, the gap between the labor force participation of women and men has been closing since the late 1940s. In 1950, men represented two-thirds of the labor force; by

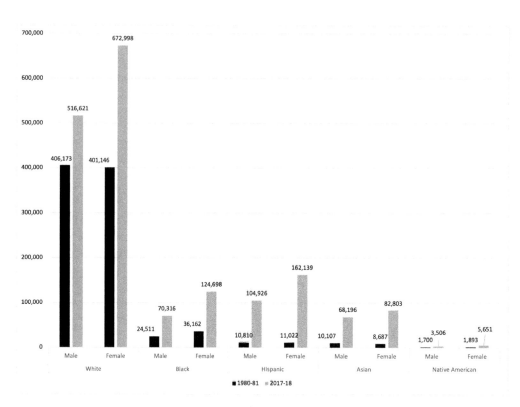

Figure 8.3 Number of Individuals over 16 in the Labor Force by Gender, Race, and Ethnicity.
Source: US Department of Labor (2020), https://www.dol.gov/agencies/wb/data/lfp/lfp-sex-race-hispanic

2000, the gap between women and men had fallen to only 7 percentage points (Toossi & Morisi, 2017). Among women, the labor force participation rate for Black women has been the highest, with Hispanic women historically reporting the lowest rates, though, by 2018, their rates begin to surpass those of White women. The rates of participation among Asian women have been nearly identical to those of Whites. Among men, conversely, Hispanics report the highest rates, with Black men reporting the lowest.

Over the last 50 years, women have made many gains in the workplace, including increasing their participation in paid labor, earning better salaries, and entering into fields historically dominated by men. At the same time, there is still occupational gender segregation and an income gap. There is also significant gender disparity in top leadership roles in the workforce. The first female CEO of any Fortune 500 companies was appointed in 1972, and the first woman of color leading a Fortune 500 company did not occur until 1999. While the number of female CEOs reached an all-time high of 41 in 2021, this still represents only 8.2 percent of the total (Hinchliffe, 2021).

Similarly, the gender gap in salaries has narrowed greatly over the years. In the early 1960s, women earned less than 60 percent than men; in 2021, women earned 82.6 percent of men's wages (US Bureau of Labor Statistics, 2021e). Interestingly, this gender gap does not just exist for cisgender men and women. One study that followed people before and after they made a gender transition found that transgender men increased their income slightly post-transition and transgender women saw their income drop significantly (Schilt & Wiswall, 2008).

In the United States, as in many countries, men spend more time in paid labor than do women (on average, about 5.33 hours per day compared to 4.0). At the same time, paid labor is not the only work that needs to be done in society; someone needs to care for children and the elderly and perform housework. When these forms of nonpaid work are taken into account, we see that women work about one and a half hours more per week than do men (World Economic Forum, 2021).

Explaining Work Inequality

Much of the explanation for gender inequality in work is connected to macro processes of how work is organized—these are the material processes of inequality. One of the reasons that women earn less than men is that they are clustered in particular occupations. Table 8.1 presents current information on the distribution of men and women over broad occupational

Table 8.1 Broad Occupational Distribution of Employed Persons 16 Years and Over, by Occupation and Sex: 2020

	Men					Women				
	Total	White	Black	Asian	Hispanic	Total	White	Black	Asian	Hispanic
Management, Professional	39.1	39.3	28.5	59.6	21.1	47.5	48.4	40.2	56.6	31.3
Service	12.5	11.8	17.6	10.6	17.6	18.8	17.6	25.3	17.3	27.9
Sales and Office	14.6	14.6	15.4	13.5	13.5	26.3	27.0	25.7	18.8	28.1
Natural Resources, Construction, Maintenance	16.0	17.5	11.2	5.0	26.3	1.1	1.2	0.7	0.6	2.2
Production, Transportation, Material Moving	17.7	16.9	27.1	11.4	21.4	6.2	5.8	8.1	6.7	10.4

Source: US Bureau of Labor Statistics (2021b), https://www.bls.gov/cps/cpsaat10.htm

Note: Numbers reflect the percentage of each category in the occupation.

Photo 8.3 For salary and image reasons, men seldom seek out occupations that have been dominated by women. About nine out of ten individuals in nursing are women.
Source: Rusty Watson at Unsplash.

categories. In general, women tend to be concentrated in white-collar and service occupations, while men are more spread out throughout the occupational spectrum. But among women, there are also significant variations. While White women are more likely than Black women to be managers or professionals, Black and Hispanic women are more likely to be found in service and blue-collar production positions.

Although Table 8.1 indicates some gender differences in occupation, as we examine more *detailed occupational* categories, the nature and extent of occupational segregation become clearer. A decline in occupational segregation has occurred in broad occupational categories, largely because of shifts in technology and organizational structures. But despite these general improvements, women still are found disproportionately in particular kinds of occupations. For example, women have increasingly moved into the ranks of managerial and professional occupations, but they tend to be concentrated among gender-typed occupations, such as teaching and nursing, and hold only a small percentage of positions as computer specialists, scientists, and engineers. Similarly, a man and a woman may both be in sales, but the woman is much more likely to be in clothing sales, while the man is involved in the selling of stocks and bonds. Craft occupations (carpentry, electrical contracting) and occupations that produce goods rather than services are another group of occupations in which women continue to be significantly underrepresented.

Despite the small movement toward gender desegregation, many aspects of current occupational profiles are quite similar to those that existed in earlier years. In 1940, almost all of the servants, stenographers/secretaries, housekeepers, and nurses were women, and they comprised more than half of the teachers, apparel and accessories operators, waitresses, and bookkeepers. As far back as 1870, women dominated in servants, clothing, certain kinds of teaching, and nursing occupations (Reskin & Roos, 2009).

Table 8.2 suggests that this gender-typing has continued. As one glances over the lists, it is easy to see that the positions in which women dominate tend to be those that demand "feminine" or "motherly" characteristics. Being able to work directly with people and to take

Table 8.2 *Broad Sample of Occupations in Which Women Represent at Least 90 percent or Less than 5 percent of Employed Labor Force: 2020*

Over 90 percent	Under 5 percent
Child Care Workers	Automotive Repair
Dental Hygienists	Boiler Operators
Dietitians and Nutritionists	Brickmasons and Welders
Hairdressers/Hairstylists/Cosmetologists	Carpenters
Medical/Dental Assistants	Construction Laborers
Medical Transcriptionists/Records	Crane and Tower Operators
Nurse Practitioners	Electricians
Preschool/Kindergarten Teachers	Firefighters
Receptionists and Information Clerks	Highway Maintenance Workers
Registered Nurses	Loggers
Secretaries and Administrative Assistants	Mapmakers and Surveyors
Skin Care Specialists	Pipelayers/Plumbers/Pipefitters
Speech-Language Pathologists	Roofers

Source: US Bureau of Labor Statistics (2021b), https://www.bls.gov/cps/cpsaat11.htm

care of others are qualities that are required in these occupations. In contrast, the positions held mostly by men are characterized by a different set of qualities; they require manual labor or physical attributes, often contain an element of danger, involve work with a product rather than a person, and demand technical or scientific skill. In essence, these two sets of occupations are distinguished by their "feminine" or "masculine" character. Why does this gender typing continue? It is due to a combination of the devaluing of traditionally "female" positions and the continued belief that men and women have different qualities by nature and are, therefore, meant for different jobs. Both of these notions have stalled the movement of women into most "male" blue-collar occupations and the movement of men into "female" occupations (England, 2010).

Many of the occupations dominated by women also do not have the protections afforded other positions. It was not until 2011, for example, that household workers were recognized by the International Labor Organization as being worthy of the same labor protections offered other workers (Boris & Fish, 2014). Nannies and maids often suffer long hours, low pay, few legal protections, and physical harassment, and often they are recent immigrants who fear deportation and thus are dependent on their employers for fair treatment (Parreñas, 2015).

There is little research on the employment, occupations, and income of transgender people. The most current research suggests that there is a statistical difference in wages between transgender and non-transgender individuals, with non-transgender individuals earning about 11.7 percent more than transgender individuals (Ciprikis et al., 2020).

Unemployment can be caused by many factors, but discrimination in the workplace might explain lower unemployment among transgender people. A 2019 study of the employment experiences of transgender individuals found that their unemployment rates were ten percent higher than the general population. This may be due to discrimination: a study asked respondents to report whether it was noticeable to other people that they were transgender. Those who responded "yes" had higher rates of unemployment than those who responded "no" (Leppel, 2019). Qualitative interviews with transgender workers bear this out: they report often facing hostility and a lack of acceptance (Dietert & Dentice, 2009). Eighteen states plus the District of Columbia have laws barring discrimination based on gender identity, but the laws vary widely in their scope. There are also over 200 cities with statutes barring discrimination

(ACLU, 2018b). While these laws represent progress in stopping employment discrimination, most Americans still do not live in places with these protections.

Gender segregation and the level of earnings associated with it are affected by what Petersen and Saporta (2004) called "the opportunity structure for discrimination" (p. 852). This refers to the variety of opportunities available to employers to discriminate against given categories of individuals. Using data collected over a nine-year period, Petersen and Saporta's research on a large organization revealed that employers were most likely to discriminate against women at the point of hiring rather than during their job tenure because discrimination is less detectable and less costly at this juncture. Once hired, women were more often placed in lower-level jobs and received lower wages than men, even though their educational levels were roughly similar. Thus, women went through a gatekeeping or filtering process that resulted in their being relegated to specific kinds of positions.

In her study of an industrial corporation, Kanter (1977) found that at the top is an inner cir-cle of individuals who have to be counted on to share a similar view of the organization and to behave in a manner consistent with that view. There are distinct pressures for homogeneity and conformity at the managerial level. A large part of the reason for this pressure to conform arises from the open nature of organizations and the managerial positions within them. Since position tasks are not well defined at that level and the organization operates in a "turbulent" environment with other organizations, the conclusion is that executives have to be able to trust one another and see one another's behavior as predictable. "Women were decidedly placed in the category of the incomprehensible and unpredictable" (p. 58).

More recent research in corporate law firms by Gorman and Kmec (2009) confirms Kanter's arguments. Their findings showed that women face a disadvantage when promotions near the top are being considered, and they attribute this disadvantage to an interaction of gender stereotyping and job characteristics. Specifically, they argue that assumptions about women's competence and appropriateness for particular tasks, together with the uncertainty and variety of the job itself and male dominance at the top, lead to lower chances for upward mobility for female members of law firms. This experience can further dampen the ambition and skills of women colleagues, reinforcing low mobility rates.

A recent study in the world of science similarly demonstrates the effects that expectations about the competencies of women affect their career trajectories. Administrators of the competi-tive program to gain access to the Hubble Space Telescope discovered that proposals by men were more successful than those by women. To test whether this was due to gender bias, they instituted a "dual-anonymization" system whereby all gender identifying items, including the names of any proposed team members, were stripped from the proposal. Researchers found that following this new submission process, proposal by *women* were more successful than those by men. Discussions with teams of reviewers indicated under the non-anonymized system, male reviewers frequently questioned the likely success of the proposals submitted by women (Johnson & Kirk, 2020).

Self-definitions and expectations combine with race, class, occupational segregation, and the internal market structure of organizations to limit mobility by women. For example, in a study of Hispanic schoolteachers in California, Flores and Hondagneu-Sotelo (2014) documented how social forces colluded to steer second-generation Hispanic American women into teaching rather than the higher-status occupations to which they had originally aspired. Limited funds made enrollment in most graduate programs out of reach, and most of the women could not afford to do the unpaid internships required by some professions. Importantly, many needed to help support their families as quickly as possible. Teaching jobs were plentiful for college-educated bilingual people and seemed to promise a measure of financial security. While teaching is certainly an important profession, it has limited mobility and income attached to it.

Global Trends in Gender Inequality

Each year, the World Economic Forum produces a gender gap report that ranks 156 countries on progress toward closing the gap between men and women along four dimensions, including economic participation and opportunity, education, health, and political empowerment (World Economic Forum, 2021). A score of 1 on the index means that a country is perfectly equal. A score of 0.5 means that women are at half the economic standing of men. Surprisingly, in 2021 the gender gap increased by 0.6 percentage points, falling to 0.68. Note that the 2021 report did not yet record the impact of the pandemic; it is expected that the gap will grow further due to global economic and political losses facing women.

In 2021 there was a wide range of gender inequality around the world. Iceland (which scored a 0.89) is the most economically equal country, and Afghanistan is the least (0.44). The United States ranks 30th, behind most of the European countries, at 0.76. The World Economic Forum estimates that, at the present rate, it will take 135.6 years to close the gap between men and women globally (World Economic Forum, 2021).

The dimension with the largest gap globally is political participation, with women holding only 26 percent of parliament seats and representing only 22 percent of ministers. The United States is among 81 countries that have never had a female head of state. The second-largest gap is in economic participation and opportunity. Although there has been progress toward closing the wage gap in the larger nations at the top of the index, in many countries, the gap remains substantial. Afghanistan has closed only 18 percent of the gap, Iraq, Syria, and Yemen are similarly below 30 percent.

Why does Iceland rank first? In the past several years, the country has made gender equality a priority, bringing the country to almost near gender parity. In 2000, Iceland passed the Act on Equal Status and Equal Rights of Women and Men, outlawing both direct and indirect discrimination against women. This act and several subsequent laws ban discrimination in pay, require at least 40 percent of company boards to be women, and provide the most generous parental leave policy in the world (each parent receives up to six months, but they can transfer one of those months to the other parent) (Werft, 2017).

Summary

This chapter has covered a lot of ground. We started with a discussion of the terms we use to describe sex and gender and how that has changed over the years. While Americans have traditionally recognized two genders, today, more of us identify as transgender, genderqueer, or gender fluid. We then explored the biological contributions to sex and gender, recognizing their interconnectedness.

We next examined the social construction of gender, framing our analysis with Risman's model of gender as structure. We talked about how gender as a structure operates at three levels–the individual, the interactional, and the institutional—and how these are created and reproduced by both cultural and material processes. We showed how, once categories are created, inequality becomes attached to them and is then maintained through a variety of interactional, cultural, and structural mechanisms.

Turning to current research, we outlined how gender operates in the three institutions of family, education, and work. We examined research on inequalities in each of these institutions and how these inequalities are related to cultural and material processes.

Beginning with family, we saw that our family roles demonstrate gendered expectations, affecting who does what work in the household and what parenting looks like. These differences have a powerful impact on our success in other realms, such as work and family.

Within the institution of education, both boys and girls are affected by stereotype threats in schools. From a very young age, children experience gender policing and consequences can be severe for those who do not act out their "proper" gender. A variety of microinequities involving language, popular media and stereotypes, and education also pervade relationships between genders.

Looking at work, we saw that, despite having been consistently involved in the economy since colonial times, women have regularly faced sex segregation and relegation to lower statuses in their employment. Occupational conditions today still reveal distinct inequalities between men and women. Women (1) are involved in a smaller range of occupations; (2) are less likely to be in positions of authority; (3) are more likely to work in smaller organizations in the peripheral sector of the economy; (4) are more likely to occupy positions with short career ladders; and (5) make less money than men even when they work full-time, year-round, and have comparable educational levels.

While we have made progress toward gender parity globally, there remain extreme differences between countries on variables such as labor participation, political participation, and health. These differences reflect how gender continues to be a powerful structure permeating all aspects of our lives.

Critical Thinking

1. Think about a specific occupation and its likely occupant (e.g., police officer, elementary school teacher, home builder). Does a specific gender come to mind? Why?
2. In your own life, how has gender limited you or allowed you to act a certain way or get involved in particular kinds of activities? What was it about your gender that created this effect?
3. What would be the social consequences if everyone accepted the belief that gender variation is a continuum rather than a dichotomy (i.e., if we believed that there are more than two genders)?
4. As technologies and the bases of the US economy change, will men and women become more equal economically? Support your answer.

Web Connections

The Global Policy Forum is a nonprofit, tax-exempt organization that consults with the United Nations on issues of international law and equity among nations. In the section on global inequality, there are recommended articles on gender inequality and comparisons of countries on the gender gap. Visit www.globalpolicy.org/socecon/index.htm. For information about transgender issues, visit the Williams Institute (http://williamsinstitute.law.ucla.edu).

Film Suggestions

Girls Can't Surf (2021). Shows women breaking into the male-dominated world of surfing.

I Am a Girl (2013). A documentary that follows six teenage girls from different countries (including the US, Cameroon, and Afghanistan) as they move toward adulthood. Their situations are remarkably different: for example, one is becoming a mother at 14, another is recovering from a suicide attempt, and one is not allowed to attend school.

No Box for Me (2019). A documentary about the lives and experiences of two intersexed people.

Minding the Gap (2018). This is a documentary following three teenage boys in Illinois. It illustrates the power and harm of hegemonic masculinity on their lives.

Always Jane (2021). A four-part documentary following a young trans woman in New Jersey.

9   **Sexual Orientation and Inequality**

In Chapter 8, we focused on how gender is related to a variety of inequalities. In this chapter, we examine the status inequality that is associated with sexual orientation. Perhaps you are wondering why we have chosen to talk about sexual orientation and gender identity separately. There are certainly many reasons to combine them. For example, both gay people and transgender/genderqueer people violate gender norms—gay people because they love people of the "wrong" gender, and transgender/genderqueer people because they identify with and/or express themselves as the "wrong" gender. It also makes sense to talk about LGBTQ people together because transgender people played a central role in the founding of the gay liberation movement and many advocacy groups continue to combine the groups under one umbrella. Similarly, social scientists have grouped LGBTQ people together in surveys, making it difficult to separate Q and T people from those who are LGB. At the same time, gender and sexual orientation are not the same; one's sexual orientation is distinct from one's gender identity.

The Complexity of Sexuality

Like race and gender, the categories we use to describe sexuality are not timeless, universal, or natural. Their construction has been the work of many entities including the state, medical professionals, religious groups, and activists. While there are multiple ways that sexuality could be (and is) categorized, our society has traditionally focused on the gender binary. Are we attracted to people of our own gender (homosexuality) or the other one (heterosexuality)? It is interesting to imagine a world in which we instead categorize sexuality by some other characteristic, like the kind of sexual activities we prefer to engage in (Crockett, 2020). Interestingly, there is a new category of sexuality that is not based on gender. **Demisexuality** refers to people who only feel sexual attraction after making an emotional connection with a person. Coined in 2006, there is little research on demisexual people, but it is a popular search term on Google and increasingly appears in the media (Iqbal, 2019).

Where did the categories of homosexual and heterosexual come from? They are **social constructions** found only in some societies during specific periods of time. Katz (2004) observes that knowledge of same-sex relations goes far back in history, but the terms "homosexual" and "heterosexual" that we moderns take for granted are only of nineteenth-century origin. They were

> a product of the transition to modernity … This sexual transformation involved such factors as the institutionalization of bourgeois middle-class values, the secularization of social medicine and state discourse on sexuality, the individualized concept of desire and identity, and the premium placed on reproduction within the nuclear family. (Herdt, 1997, p. 39)

DOI: 10.4324/9781003184966-12

The division of sexuality into the heterosexual/homosexual dichotomy is legitimized by the existence of other typologies such as male/female, public/private, instrumental/expressive, and rational/emotional, and the continued emphasis on these dichotomies as "natural" is what gives them a seemingly timeless and universal quality.

Today we see movement away from the sexuality binary. **Bisexuality**, a term appearing at the end of the nineteenth century, refers to an attraction to both men and women. It was not, however, until the 1970s and the rise of the gay liberation movement that the term came into common parlance (Rosenblum, 2017). Even today, there is some controversy about what the word should denote. Because "bi" means two, the word bisexuality suggests that there are just two genders. This is problematic for people who reject the gender binary and are attracted to multiple genders. Some bisexual advocacy groups have suggested that the term simply be redefined to mean attraction to more than one gender (Berg, 2020). A closely related alternative term, however, is *pansexuality* which refers to the potentiality of being attracted to all genders. Its name suggests more inclusivity by signaling that it incorporates attraction to transgender people and to people who identify outside the gender binary.

Adding the category of bisexuality/pansexuality expands our understanding of sexuality, but it still does not pick up the full complexity of the concept. For example, some researchers argue that there is a whole continuum of sexuality and that it is best categorized on a multi-point scale from *exclusively heterosexual* through *exclusively homosexual*, with options like "mostly heterosexual" in between. Polls conducted using these more nuanced categories reveal that, over time, increasing numbers of young people have changed from identifying as "exclusively heterosexual" to "mostly heterosexual" (Massey et al., 2021). At the same time, even a more nuanced categorization like this fails to recognize that sexuality includes at least three separate components: attraction, behavior, and identity. While many people are consistent across these three domains (for example, a man who is attracted to women, has sex with women, and identifies as straight), some people are not consistent. A woman might have sex with her husband but be attracted mostly to women and identify as bisexual. Research shows that there are also men who have occasional sex with other men but who identify as straight (Carrillo & Hoffman, 2018). Current sexuality categories cannot pick up these complexities.

Asexuality is an example of an orientation that is difficult to classify based on any of the measures described above. As a named identity, asexuality only traces back to the early 2000s (Cerankowski & Milks, 2014). It is generally defined as a "lack of sexual desire or attraction" (Scott & Dawson, 2015), but most writers on this topic note that asexuality does not necessarily mean a lack of intimacy or close emotional attachment. Asexuality is different from celibacy, in which people have sexual desire but choose not to act on it. The visibility of asexuality has been promoted by Asexual Visibility and Education Network (AVEN). There are also asexual characters on television including Raphael Santiago in Freeform's *Shadowhunters* and Todd Chavez in Netflix's *Bojack Horseman*.

In sum, we are currently in an exciting moment where, as a society, we are talking about reorganizing the categories of sexuality that have been in use for over one hundred years. Categories matter because they affect the lives, identities, and behaviors of both the people defined to be within the category as well as those defined as outsiders (Samuels, 2014). As we will see, they are also linked to inequality across a range of domains.

Intersectionality and Sexuality

In the last chapter, we described how the theory of hegemonic masculinity posits that sexuality is integral to the definition of masculinity (Connell, 1987; Connell & Messerschmidt, 2005). Men are told to behave in a masculine manner, while women are supposed to perform in a feminine manner, and heterosexuality is considered a part of their masculine and feminine performances. In other words, masculine men desire women and feminine women desire men. Additionally, men are expected to be dominant, and women to be submissive. In terms of sexuality, this means that men generally initiate sexual encounters, and their desires and pleasure tend to take priority. This may be part of the reason that rates of sexual abuse against women are so much higher than those against men (Cossins, 2000; Nurse, 2020).

Noted theorist Judith Butler (1999) agrees that gender and sexuality are inextricably linked. She describes a "heterosexual matrix" through which we view people. When we know someone's sex and gender, we simply assume their sexuality. In other words, if someone is male, they are automatically assumed to be straight. More recent research on the heterosexual matrix, however, finds that it works the other way too: when we know someone's sexuality, we assume their gender. As an example is Amélie Mauresmo, who was the first elite tennis player to come out as a lesbian in 1999. Prior to 1999, the media mostly focused on her ranking. After she came out, however, the coverage shifted to her muscles and other "masculine" attributes. In other words, her gender was assumed from her sexuality (Forman & Plymire, 2005; Tredway, 2014).

Similar to the connection people draw between gender and sexuality, race and sexuality have also become entwined. In other words, sexual orientation is read through a racial lens with homosexuality often racialized as White. In a study with college students, for example, Whitley et al. (2011) found that about 75 percent of both Black and White respondents associated the word "homosexual" with the word "white." Majorities also saw homosexuality as male. These associations are obviously problematic because they make lesbians and gay people of color socially invisible. Interestingly, it appears that Black, Hispanic, and Asian gay men become de-racialized, with fewer stereotypes about their own racial group applied to them than to their same-race heterosexual counterparts. In fact, people even start applying stereotypes about White people to Black and Hispanic gay men, effectively "whitening" them (Petsko & Bodenhausen, 2019). This racialization of sexuality has led activists to propose a new term for Black men who have sex with men. The term "same gender loving" is intended to recognize the intersectionality of race and sexuality. Similarly, a proposed new field of theory called *quare* studies focuses on the intersectional experiences of gay and lesbian people of color (Johnson, 2007). Decena's study with Dominican men in New York (2008) illustrates how "coming out" as gay intersects with ethnicity, socioeconomic status, and citizenship. Some of the men in his study strategically allowed their families to know that they loved other men without making an overt proclamation of being "gay." Coming out would not be liberating for them but rather would violate their sense of privacy and would make it seem as if they, rather than society, were the problem. Decena's study is an example of how the meanings of sexuality intersect with cultural images of gender, race, and class.

Population

It is impossible to know exactly what percentage of the population identifies as gay, lesbian, or bisexual because some people choose not to identify themselves out of fear for their safety. This alone tells us a great deal about the stigma attached to these categories. In addition, there are disagreements about the best way to count the gay/lesbian population. Measurement issues have revolved around how to define homosexuality and how to procure a representative sample.

Generally, four national data sets are used to estimate the size of the gay/lesbian population in the United States. The General Social Survey (GSS), the National Survey of Family Growth (NSFG), Gallup, and the US Census provide the best estimates. Unfortunately, the census does not directly ask about sexual orientation, only about whether a live-in partner of a respondent is of the same or opposite sex. Estimates from the census suggest that there were about 980,000 same-sex couples living together in the United States in 2019, up from about 887,456 in 2016. About 58 percent of them were married. There were more female than male couples and about 80 percent were White, similar to the percentage of White people in married different-sex couples (US Census Bureau, 2020b).

In 2016, the federal government sponsored research on the feasibility of adding one or more sexual orientation questions to the census. While the researchers concluded that it was possible to craft effective questions, the Trump administration did not act on their recommendation for the 2020 census (Fitzsimons, 2020). Instead, the census has asked sexual orientation questions on its Household Pulse Survey. In collaboration with multiple government agencies, the Pulse Survey was intended to be a rapid way to capture the impact of COVID-19 on people's lives. It is a national random sample rather than a census of the whole population. To identify sexual orientation, they asked, "Which of the following best represents how you think of yourself?" The possible responses were bisexual, gay/lesbian, straight, something else, or don't know. About 3.3 percent of the population identified as gay/lesbian with another 4.4 percent claiming a bisexual identity. Unfortunately, the rest of the questions the survey asked conflated sexual orientation and gender identity (with an LGBT category), but because transgender people were only 0.6 percent of the survey respondents, the data mostly reflect the gay/lesbian/bisexual population. LGBT people are younger, on average, than the general population and they are concentrated in western states including California, Colorado, Washington, Oregon, and Nevada with lower populations in the southern and midwestern states (US Census Bureau, 2021l).

The GSS, in contrast to the decennial census, asks direct questions about individual people's sexuality including, "Which of the following best describes you: gay/lesbian/homosexual, bisexual, heterosexual/straight?" In 2018, 1.7 percent of respondents picked the homosexual option and 3.3 percent chose bisexual. There is a clear upward trend since 2008 in the bisexual category, but not in the homosexual category (GSS, 2021). At the same time, the percentages of people identifying as LGB are lower than those found by the Pulse Survey. It is possible that this is a result of question wording, but it should also be noted that the data from the GSS are slightly older.

Like the GSS, Gallup collects data about individual people's sexual orientation. They have also conducted considerable research on how question wording affects responses (Meyer, 2019). Through 2017, they asked, "Do you personally identify as gay, lesbian, bisexual or transgender?" This question is problematic because it conflates sexual orientation and gender, resulting in a situation where people are unable to identify both their sexual orientation and their gender identity. Thus, in 2018, Gallup changed their question to: "Which of the following do you consider yourself to be: straight/heterosexual, lesbian, gay, bisexual, or transgender?" Respondents are allowed to select more than one answer, solving the gender/sexual orientation conflation issue. Gallup researched whether they should include more category options (like queer, asexual, and same gender loving), but experiments showed that a significant number of heterosexual people accidentally selected these options, probably because they were not familiar with them. The exclusion of these categories may cause some people to refuse to answer the question, however, Gallup decided that mistakes by the much larger group of people who identify as straight would be more damaging to the accuracy of their estimates (Meyer, 2019).

Gallup found that in 2017 about 4.5 percent of the population identified as LGBT. This was a significant increase from 2012 when 3.2 percent gave an affirmative response. In 2020, using the new question wording, 0.7 percent of Americans identified as lesbians and 1.4 percent as gay. A full 3.1 percent identified as bisexual. Adding in transgender respondents allows for a comparison with earlier years. There is a clear increase to about 5.6 percent of the population (Jones, 2021). Young people are driving the trend with 9.1 percent of respondents born between 1980 and 1999 ("millennials") identifying as LGBT, up from 5.8 in 2012. LGBT identity is even more common among Generation Z respondents (those born between 1997 and 2002), with 15.9 percent claiming it. These numbers are striking compared to baby boomers (people born between 1946 and 1964), among whom only 2 percent report being LBGT (Jones, 2021). Of course, it is hard to know if the younger generation really contains a higher percentage of LGBT people or whether they are simply more willing to identify themselves in a poll.

From the Gallup data, we know that women are more likely to identify as LGBT than are men (6.4 percent compared to 4.9). This is particularly true of bisexual identity with 4.3 percent of women choosing that option compared to just 1.8 percent of men (Jones, 2021). Past surveys have shown slight racial/ethnic differences as well with Hispanic people reporting the highest percentage of LGBT people (6.1), followed by people who are Black (5), Asian (4.9), and White (4.0) (Gallup, 2018).

The NSFG, conducted by the CDC, approaches the question of sexuality quite differently from the other surveys. It asks 18- to 44-year-olds about three elements of sexuality: behavior, attraction, and identity. Drawing on data collected between 2017 and 2019, the NSFG found that 20.8 percent of women report having engaged in sexual activity with another woman during their lifetime. This compares to just 7.3 percent of men. In terms of attraction, surveys conducted between 2015 and 2019 indicate that about 77 percent of women report being exclusively attracted to men, and 91 percent of men say they are only attracted to women. The data on identity is a little harder to parse because the NSFG asked half the respondents the question they have been using for years and the other half answered a new question with slightly different wording. Taking account of this, approximately 2.5 percent of respondents reported a gay/lesbian identity and 7.6 percent said that they were bisexual (CDC, 2021g). It is clear that Americans are much more likely to report same-sex attraction and behavior than they are a gay or bisexual identity.

Historical Inequality Based on Sexuality

Because homosexuality has long been stigmatized, we do not have much information about the experiences of gay men and lesbians historically. At the same time, there is some limited evidence of male and female same-sex romantic (although not necessarily sexual) relationships during colonial times. By the nineteenth century, however, we know from letters that close relationships between women were common and not seen as deviant. Many educated women chose not to marry, and some lived with other unmarried women. These arrangements were sometimes called "Boston marriages." There was also a tradition of "smashing" in women's colleges where women developed romantic crushes on each other.

During the 1920s, homosexuality was generally condemned, but there were places where acceptance began to grow. Greenwich Village in New York, for example, was a hotbed of alternative lifestyles. It was known as the artistic district, and gay men and lesbians were able to live there without attracting a lot of attention. Harlem (which was in the midst of an intellectual and cultural boom called the "Harlem Renaissance") was another place where there was more acceptance of homosexuality, although most people still did not talk about it publicly. In the 1930s, however, anti-gay activity began to increase across the country. For example, there were many police raids on places thought to be frequented by gay people. Laws were enacted that censored films or plays with homosexual content and New York made it illegal to sell liquor to gay people (Miller, 2006). Interestingly, it was not until World War II that the military banned homosexual people from service. Prior to that time, soldiers could be punished for engaging in sodomy but simply being homosexual was not a disqualification. During the war, the military began asking male recruits if they "liked girls." It was about this time that psychologists came to a consensus that homosexuality was a disorder and they added it to 1952 *Diagnostic and Statistical Manual* (DSM).

From the late 1940s until 1960, the federal government engaged in what came to be known as the "Lavender Scare," a campaign to uncover and fire gay federal workers. Senator

Joseph McCarthy was particularly committed to this cause, arguing that many gay people were Communists. He was so successful in making his case that two sets of congressional investigations were held to determine the extent of the problem and to decide what action should be taken. One of the reports concluded that gay people should not work for the federal government because they were "generally unsuitable" and constituted a security risk because they could be blackmailed. The report went on to state that homosexuals were a bad influence and could "pollute" an office if allowed to work there (Adkins, 2016). Thousands of people were fired, resulting in financial ruin for many, and some became so deeply depressed they committed suicide. Added to this, the FBI under the leadership of J. Edgar Hoover, as well as city police across the country, targeted gay men and lesbians.

> Homosexual acts were illegal in most states under existing anti-sodomy statutes … Furthermore, gays and lesbians were specifically excluded from laws and policies regulating fair employment practices, housing discrimination, rights of child custody, immigration, inheritance, security clearances, public accommodations, and police protection. (Button et al., 1997)

Starting in the late 1960s, child custody cases involving gay and lesbian parents came to public attention. Most of these cases involved couples from heterosexual marriages who had gotten divorced, and one of the parents had come out as homosexual. Courts consistently cited homosexuality as a reason to deny custody and visitation. To back up their decisions, judges claimed, completely without evidence, that gay people were more likely than heterosexuals to molest children. They also expressed concerns that a gay or lesbian parent would pass on their sexual orientation to their children. These discriminatory attitudes were bolstered by the fact that the American Psychiatric Association (APA) did not remove homosexuality as a mental illness from their DSM until 1973. By the mid-1980s, however, court opinions began to grant gay and lesbian parents custody and visitation rights (Rivers, 2010). This change was partly a response to activism, but it was also based on research indicating that children who grow up with lesbian or gay parents are well-adjusted and just as socially and academically competent as children of heterosexual parents. In fact, some research finds that they are less likely to engage in delinquent behavior (Gartrell & Bos, 2010). At the same time, many states continued to refuse to place children for adoption with gay couples.

The HIV/AIDS epidemic that began in the 1980s posed a serious challenge to the rights of LGB individuals. In the United States, the early cases of HIV/AIDS were clustered among gay men, leading researchers and policy makers to inaccurately name the disease "gay-related immune deficiency." By the end of 1985, there were 20,303 documented cases of AIDS worldwide (AVERT, 2015). Public misunderstanding and fears led to severe discrimination against those living with the disease. This, combined with a lack of government response, provided a catalyst for action in the gay community. In 1987, playwright and gay rights activist Larry Kramer founded the grassroots organization AIDS Coalition to Unleash Power or ACT UP. With the slogan "Silence=Death," the organization took a militant but nonviolent approach to protest. ACT UP demanded accelerated approval of AIDS drugs and soon became well known for protesting outside institutions such as the New York Stock Exchange and the Food and Drug Administration (Crimp, 2011).

Once progress had been made on AIDS, some gay activists turned their attention to the fight to legalize same-sex marriage. The first same-sex couple to file for a marriage license had done so in 1970 in Minnesota. They were denied the license and ultimately lost in court cases before the Minnesota Supreme Court and the US Supreme Court. Activists saw marriage as important not only for its symbolism of inclusion but also because it confers a wide variety of rights that have profound implications for inequality. These rights include hospital visitation if the partner is seriously injured, Social Security and pension benefits for a surviving partner, employer health insurance, and family leave if the partner is sick. As a whole, the federal government offers over 1,000 benefits based on marital status (Human Rights Campaign, 2015). Of these rights, Social Security survivor benefits are particularly important to families in terms of ensuring financial stability in case of the death of one partner. One analysis suggested that these benefits were worth up to $343,000 for a family in the years prior to marriage equality (Jurs, 2015). The denial of these important benefits was one of the reasons same-sex couples began to fight for the right to marry.

It should be noted that not all LGB people or groups were in favor of focusing activism on same-sex marriage. For example, critics argued that the institution of marriage had historically been a way for men to exert power over women. They felt that getting rid of the institution altogether would be a better solution than simply assimilating into it. Others felt that there were other issues (such as universal health care) that would help the LGB community more than marriage. Part of this critique involved the fact that most of the leaders of the movement were White middle- and upper-class men, and while marriage might be a priority for them, it was less so for poor people and people of color (Bernstein et al., 2018; NPR, 2010).

After 1970, multiple states passed bans preventing same-sex couples from marrying. The federal government became involved with the passage of the 1996 Defense of Marriage Act (DOMA). The fight over DOMA summarized below clearly illustrates how the fate of proposed legislation on sexual orientation has been strongly tied to (1) the extent to which it is seen as supporting or undermining traditional values and social order; and (2) how effectively and in what manner the issue is framed by proponents and opponents to the legislation. Public opinion polls have consistently shown that there is a contrast between Americans' reactions to gay and lesbian people's *morality*, on the one hand, and their rights to *civil liberties*, on the other. This may, in part, be explained by how each of these is interpreted. While *morality* relates to *individual behavior* and activates traditional heterosexual and religious beliefs of Americans, *civil rights* relates to gay and lesbian people as a *group*, does not refer to a specific behavior, and is not as easily linked to religious beliefs. Rather, the civil rights issue is more easily tied to ideas of equality and fairness (Loftus, 2001). The difference in respondents' attitudes in these two areas exposes contradictions within the value systems of many Americans.

Proponents of DOMA—aware of public opinion—tied the legislation directly to the moral dimension of public opinions on homosexuality. DOMA became a conflict that pitted religious values against those of a secular democracy and highlighted the issue of separation of church and state.

In arguing for its passage, the proponents of DOMA focused on the need to preserve traditional values of family and morality and on alleged attempts by the gay community to undermine "civilized" society. Traditional marriage was praised "as a 'cornerstone,' 'foundation,' 'bedrock,' and 'fundamental pillar' of any civilized society" (Lewis & Edelson, 2000, p. 202). In these ways, proponents sought to frame DOMA in *moral* rather than *civil rights* terms, knowing the public's perception of homosexuality as immoral. This effort was successful, at least in the short term.

The tide began to turn in the early 2000s as some states legalized same-sex marriage. By 2013, gay and lesbian couples could wed in twelve states and the District of Columbia. Until DOMA was overturned in 2013, however, same-sex marriages were not recognized at the federal level, the result being that people in long-term, same-sex relationships were not protected in the same ways that individuals in traditional marriages were. Today, gay men and lesbians have the same federal and state rights granted to persons in traditional marriages. While gay and lesbian married couples automatically became eligible for survivor benefits when the Court overturned DOMA, it was not until August of 2015 that the Justice Department grandfathered in same-sex couples who had been married in a state where it was legal but lived in states that did not recognize their marriages. This fix, however, did not help couples who had either chosen not to marry or who had been unable to afford to go to a state where gay marriage was legal. In 2021, the Justice Department and the Social Security Administration finally extended benefits to this group.

Same-sex marriage was legalized in all states in 2015 with the Supreme Court decision, *Obergefell v. Hodges*. This ruling stated that marriage is a fundamental right that is guaranteed by the Due Process and Equal Protection clauses of the 14th Amendment to the Constitution. Estimates suggest that 123,000 gay and lesbian couples got married in the year following the ruling, increasing the percentage of cohabitating couples who were married from 38 percent to 49 percent (J. M. Jones, 2016).

Inequality Based on Sexuality Today

As we will see in the next section, attitudes toward the LGB community are becoming more accepting over time. Yet inequality still exists. Why is this? Heterosexuality has long been viewed as natural and, therefore, normal, a view supported by dominant institutions, values, and behaviors. Traditional Judeo-Christian dogma views normal, moral, and legitimate sex as having a reproductive function and as belonging in monogamous marriages between men and women and views same-sex relations as sinful and abnormal (Herdt, 1997). These attitudes have existed over a long period of time, and, as a result, homophobia and structural discrimination are deeply baked into our society. Many theorists describe the United States (and many other countries) as **heteronormative**—meaning that heterosexuality is taken for granted and is therefore rarely questioned. Heteronormativity blinds many to how sexuality and inequality are linked.

An example of heteronormativity involves socialization. A study of mothers interacting with their children reveals that while they generally do not tell young children not to be gay, they inadvertently signal that heterosexuality is expected. For example, they assume their children are heterosexual and they project this identity onto their actions. This means that when a friendship develops between a young boy and girl, they are called "boyfriend" and "girlfriend," but similar terms are not used for same-sex friendship. A second example is that parents portray love and marriage as inextricably tied to heterosexuality. One mother, when her child asked what falling in love meant said, "Falling in love is when a man and a woman who are grown-ups have deep feelings for one another and want to spend all their time together" (Martin, 2009, p. 199). Most of these mothers would not say anything negative about gay men or lesbians but unthinkingly pass on the idea that heterosexuality is normal and natural to their children.

In this section of the book, we look at current inequalities based on sexual orientation. As with the chapters on race and gender, we divide the discussion into material and symbolic/cultural resources.

Material Resources

Stereotypes suggest that sexual minorities tend to be highly educated and affluent (Schneebaum & Badgett, 2019). The actual picture is more complex. Unfortunately, much of the data we have on material recourses conflates gender identity and sexual orientation. This is the case with recent data indicating that a higher percentage of LGBT people than others drop out of high school (9 percent compared to 6.8 percent). At the same time, LGBT people who graduate from high school are more likely to go on to further education but are less likely to actually complete a college degree (29.8 percent of LBGT people graduate from college compared to 31.6 percent of non-LGBT people). In other words, they are somewhat more likely to drop out of their higher education program (US Census Bureau, 2021l).

Income data are less complicated to parse. The Census tells us that LGBT people are much more likely to be in the lowest income category of below $25,000 a year (20 percent compared to 13.6 percent for non-LGBT people). This is partly a result of LGBT people being particularly hard hit economically during the COVID epidemic. They were more likely to report difficulty paying for housing, food insecurity, loss of employment, and difficulty paying expenses as a result of the pandemic (US Census Bureau, 2021l). Looking at the census, however, gay and lesbian couples who live together are somewhat less likely to be in the low-income category than are cohabitating heterosexual couples. This could indicate a true income difference, or it could simply reflect different propensities for gay and straight couples to live together.

An extensive study by the Williams Institute (Badgett et al., 2020) looked specifically at poverty prior to the pandemic. The researchers found that poverty rates are about the same for those who are lesbian or gay compared to their heterosexual counterparts, with women in both groups being much more likely to be poor than men. Notably, however, bisexual people are more likely to be in poverty than either homosexual or heterosexual individuals. This is particularly true of women: almost 30 percent of those identifying as bisexual are in poverty compared to about 18 percent of both lesbian and heterosexual women. Bisexual women in rural areas are at an even stronger disadvantage with 37 percent in poverty. As in the heterosexual population, LGB people of color experience poverty rates higher than White people.

There are several factors that influence levels of income inequality for LGB people. First, place matters. In states where people report more prejudicial attitudes, gay men earn less than their counterparts in less homophobic states. This appears to be directly related to the prejudice level of managers who determine salaries (Burn, 2020). A second factor is occupational segregation. Gay and lesbian workers tend to end up in somewhat different occupations than their straight counterparts. Occupational segregation varies by gender and education, however. Gay men are in more segregated occupations than are lesbians, and noncollege educated people are more segregated than those who hold a bachelor's degree (Finnigan, 2020).

Research suggests that gay and lesbian workers cluster in similar occupations in part because they are trying to avoid jobs where they perceive high levels of discrimination. This is less true of bisexual people, perhaps because it is easier to conceal their identity. Gay and lesbian workers also tend to choose jobs that are more gender-integrated (Finnigan, 2020). Interestingly, they are more clustered in jobs that require high levels of social perceptiveness and where there is task independence. Because homosexuality is stigmatized, gay people are often forced to pay close attention to how others are reacting to them. They need to read signs to help them decide whether or not it is safe to tell others they are gay. As a result, they become particularly suited to occupations (such as psychiatry) that involve social perceptiveness. Task independence means that a person's work is not dependent on others. Bus drivers have high task independence because they work alone and are not dependent on others to get the job done. In contrast, firefighters rely closely on each other. Task independence gives gay and lesbian people the freedom to decide how close they become to their coworkers and decreases the possibility that telling one person they are gay will be shared throughout the workplace. Task independence and social perceptiveness do appear to predict occupational segregation to some degree; the top five occupations with an overrepresentation of gay and lesbian people include psychologists, training/development specialists, social and community service managers, technical writers, and occupational therapists (Tilcsik et al., 2015).

Interestingly, it appears that working in female-dominated occupations has different health effects by gender and sexual orientation. Specifically, it results in higher levels of depression among heterosexual men but not among gay men. It is possible that this is because working in a female-dominated workplace is more of a threat to straight men's masculinity than it is to gay men. It is also possible that gay men face less discrimination while working among women than among men. Interestingly, lesbians experience more depression in female-dominated occupations than do straight women. This may be because they face discrimination in such workplaces (Ueno et al., 2018).

The US military is among the most masculine of institutions, yet there are a significant number of gay and lesbian soldiers. In 2015, a survey of military servicepeople found that 6.1 percent identify as gay, lesbian, bisexual, or transgender. There were more women than men in this group and the service branch with the highest proportion of LBGT people was the Navy (Meadows et al., 2018). While it is likely that there have always been gay men and lesbians in the military, we simply do not know because numbers were hard to estimate prior to 2011. Homosexual people were not allowed to enlist until 1994 and from 1994 until 2011, they could serve only so long as they did not reveal their homosexuality (under the "Don't Ask, Don't Tell" policy).

Cultural and Symbolic Resources

Discrimination plays a role in shaping LGB people's experiences from the time they are young. There is tremendous variation in when people begin to identify as a particular sexual orientation, but it appears that, on average, males began to feel sexual attraction toward others at about the age of nine-and-a-half and girls at about age ten. This is the same for both heterosexual and homosexual youth (Herdt & McClintock, 2000). Of course, gay and lesbian youth vary in whether and when to reveal their orientation to their families with research suggesting that only about 69 percent of lesbian and bisexual adult women have chosen to disclose their sexuality to their mothers. The equivalent number for fathers is 52 percent. Bisexual women are less likely to disclose to either parent than are lesbians (Baiocco et al., 2020).

There is often good reason LGB people fear coming out to their families. Those families who view homosexuality as a sin or abnormality sometimes reject their children. Others take their children to therapists who claim to be able to make people straight. Called "gay conversion therapy," this treatment regimen has been shown not only to be ineffective but to be dangerous as well. Some of the harms that result from gay conversion therapy and from parents trying to change adolescents' sexual identity on their own include depression, anxiety, suicide, suicidal ideation, less educational attainment and lower wages (Ryan et al., 2020). Although more than 20 states have outlawed it, it continues to be practiced in the remaining states and in some religious institutions who do not use state-licensed practitioners. The Williams Institute estimates that 20,000 youth who were ages 13–18 in 2018 will receive this treatment (Mallory et al., 2018).

The stigma placed on homosexuality exposes people to a wide array of stresses. The term "minority stress" refers to the tension people feel when they are a member of a stigmatized minority group. Some of this results from significant incidents of discrimination, violence, or rejection, but microaggressions can also cause it. Gay men and lesbians face slurs and often hear the expression "that's so gay" to refer to something negative. Minority stress can affect health and has been related to an increased rate of a range of conditions from the flu to more serious illnesses, such as cancer.

Schools are one place where LGB people experience a great deal of minority stress as they are often marginalized and stigmatized by fellow students. Results from a national survey indicated that harassment of LGB youth is common both in schools and online. For example, 32 percent of LGB students reported being bullied on school grounds. This compared to just 19 percent of heterosexual students. Similarly, 27 percent of LGB students and 14 percent of heterosexual students reported being harassed on social media. Girls were more likely than boys to report bullying both at school and electronically (Johns et al., 2020). Bullying of LGB students was particularly notable during the Trump administration. A study of 50,000 LGBT high school students found that 70 percent had witnessed bullying and harassment during the election or in its immediate aftermath. Of these students, 79 percent reported that these problematic occurrences had increased during and since the election (Berry, 2018).

Photo 9.1 Bullying is a major problem among youth, and it is more likely to occur in schools located in disadvantaged neighborhoods. Gay and lesbian youth are often easy targets. Research has suggested that boys are more likely to be victims of physical bullying, while girls are more likely to be victimized by indirect bullying such as teasing. Some data also indicate that victims are likely to be of lower social status in the school (Berger & Rodkin, 2009; Carbone-Lopez et al., 2010).

Source: © Mandy Godbehear/Shutterstock.

Minority stress sometimes has dire consequences for its victims. Reviews of research suggest that gay, lesbian, and bisexual youths are far more likely to have considered suicide. They are also more likely to attempt suicide (23 percent compared to 5 percent of heterosexual students). There is little difference by gender or race in attempted suicide among LGB youth (Johns et al., 2020).

As described above, some gay and lesbian people choose occupations where they believe there will be relatively low levels of discrimination. Unfortunately, this does not mean that they do not experience minority stress at work. In a large-scale study of 300,000 workers in federal agencies (which tend to have more inclusive policies than other workplaces), LGBT respondents reported poorer treatment, less fairness, and lower job satisfaction than did cisgender heterosexual workers. This was particularly the case for women and people of color (Cech & Rothwell, 2020). Many gay and lesbian workers choose not to reveal their sexual orientation at work, or they limit contact between their partners and children with their coworkers to avoid tension, especially in workplaces that have highly heteronormative cultures (Sawyer, 2018).

People of color who are also gay or lesbian often experience intensified minority stress because of their status as both sexual and ethnic/racial minorities (Frost et al., 2015). As an example of why this might be, think of a gay Asian man who faces discrimination from other Asians on the basis of his sexual orientation and racial discrimination from non-Asian gay people. In a survey conducted with 5,000 LGBT people of color, almost 60 percent said that they had experienced racial discrimination in the LGBT community, and more than 70 percent said that they had experienced homophobia/transphobia in their racial or ethnic community (Battle et al., 2012). In interviews, gay racial minority men describe experiencing racism, invisibility, exclusion, objectification, and sometimes sexual rejection in the gay community (Han & Rutledge, 2020).

Stereotypes about gay men and lesbians are deeply engrained in our society. Most often, they involve gender, with gay men portrayed as behaving in "feminine" ways and liking the same things many women enjoy. Lesbians are portrayed as masculine. People often do not recognize that these gender stereotypes shape their reaction to people, instead claiming that they have "gaydar" and simply know who is gay without being told. It turns out that gaydar is not real, it is simply the use of stereotypes to make assumptions—assumptions which more often than not turn out to be wrong (Cox et al., 2016).

One particularly damaging and pervasive stereotype about gay men is that they are more likely than heterosexual men to sexually abuse children. As Herek (2013) points out, this stereotype should not be surprising given a history of discredited groups being blamed for hurting vulnerable members of the majority group (for example, Black men being portrayed as rapists of White women). The child predator stereotype began as early as 1977 in the United States and was fueled by the erroneous linkage of homosexuality and pedophilia in the clergy sex abuse scandals of the early 2000s. In fact, multiple studies show that gay men are no more likely to abuse children than are straight men (Holmes & Slap, 1998; Jenny et al., 1994). While the acceptance of this stereotype has decreased markedly among Americans, it has not been entirely erased (Nurse, 2017).

It is important to note that gay and lesbian people are not the only ones to face minority stress based on sexual orientation. Bisexual people, for example, are in the unfortunate position of not being fully accepted by either the gay/lesbian or straight communities. Stereotypes portray bisexual people as confused and promiscuous (Zivony & Saguy, 2018). A study with college students even found that 15 percent felt that bisexuality was not a legitimate orientation. While this was less true of gay and lesbian respondents than heterosexuals, the attitude was present in both groups (Friedman et al., 2014). Bisexuality challenges the idea that orientation is innate and immutable, an idea that many straight and gay people believe. Additionally, when bisexual women partner with men or bisexual men partner with women, they may no longer feel welcome in the gay community. Some lesbians feel that bisexual women are secretly straight, and both lesbians and gay men sometimes suspect bisexual men of being secretly gay. The final result is that bisexual people are often relegated to a position of low status within a movement that is itself stigmatized by the larger heterosexual society (Matsick & Rubin, 2018).

Little research has been conducted to understand the links between inequality and asexuality, but one study found that Americans see asexual people as "less human" than either heterosexuals or homosexuals (MacInnis & Hodson, 2012). The study also found that respondents would be more willing to rent an apartment to a heterosexual person than either a homosexual or an asexual person.

This section of the book has illustrated that growing up gay, lesbian, bisexual, or asexual in a cultural and social setting in which there are strong expectations of heterosexuality can create deep stress for an individual. At the same time, the situation has improved in some notable ways. While the Internet can be an avenue of bullying, it can also allow LGB youths to feel less isolated. Such youths are able to gather information and connect with people like themselves who live far away. As we'll discuss in the next section, people's attitudes are shifting rapidly to become more accepting of both homosexuality and alternative gender expression. There is evidence that this decreasing discrimination against LGB people saves lives. For example, before same-sex marriage was legalized nationally, suicide rates of LGB youth decreased in states that legalized it. The rate for heterosexuals remained unchanged, suggesting that legalization caused the decrease among LGB youth. The authors speculate that the societal acceptance of homosexuality reflected in the legalization of same-sex marriage lessened emotional stress, which, in turn, decreased suicide rates (Raifman et al., 2017).

Public Opinion

The last 20 years have seen a remarkable change in public opinion toward sexual minorities. Survey data illustrate these changing attitudes. In 2002, only 38 percent of American adults felt that homosexuality was "morally acceptable." By 2008 they were evenly split on the morality of homosexuality, and by 2021 a full 69 percent saw homosexuality as morally acceptable. (Gallup, 2021b). Consistent with these polls, a general review of surveys done between 1977 and 2021 revealed a strong increase in the percentage of those who support the right of gay and lesbian people to adopt children and to be elementary or high school teachers (Gallup, 2021b).

It should be noted that opinions toward homosexuality are not monolithic; for example, there are differences in attitudes toward gay men and lesbians. Public opinion in the United States is similar to other nations in that feelings toward gay men are more negative than those directed toward lesbians (Bettinsoli et al., 2020). Researchers suggest that heterosexual male aversion to gay men may stem from a variety of factors including fear of sexual advances and the threat to masculinity that they are perceived to represent (Bortolin, 2010). The eroticization of lesbians and bisexual women in popular culture may allay homophobia against them (Yost & Thomas, 2012).

As noted above, we tend to see significant support for LGB equality when it is framed as an issue of civil rights. For example, when asked whether gay men and lesbians should have equal rights in terms of job opportunities, 93 percent of Americans reply affirmatively (Gallup, 2021b). By and large, the belief that civil liberties ought to be curtailed among gays and lesbians has steadily declined since the early 1970s. We see this support for civil liberties most dramatically in opinions about same-sex marriage. In 2001, 35 percent of Americans approved of legalizing same-sex marriage, while 57 percent opposed it. By 2015—when it was legalized—a majority of Americans (55 percent) supported it with only 39 percent opposing (Pew Research Center, 2015b). Today, the level of support is even higher with 70 percent of Americans in favor (Gallup, 2021b).

Not all Americans agree about whether the trend toward greater acceptance of lesbian and gay people is a positive one. Republicans, religious people, less-educated, and older adults are more likely than other groups to see the trend in a negative light (Kaufman & Compton, 2021). Americans are also less accepting of homosexuality than citizens of other Western countries. For example, the World Values Survey asks people in 79 countries about their attitudes toward social issues. Using a ten-point scale from "never justifiable" to "always justifiable," they ask respondents their opinion on homosexuality. The United States ranks 17th in acceptance of homosexuality (mean = 6.19), behind countries including Spain (7), Canada (7.68), Iceland (9.03), and Japan (6.71) (Inglehart et al., 2020). Religion appears to account for some of the difference between countries; the more religious the country, the less accepting of homosexuality (Horowitz, 2013). With some exceptions, countries that uphold strict gender norms also tend to be less accepting of homosexuality (Bettinsoli et al., 2020).

There are a number of other predictors of support for gay and lesbian rights. For example, people's views on the origin of homosexuality help to determine their feelings about same-sex marriage. Specifically, those who think homosexuality is a choice (rather than being something you are born with) are less supportive of marriage rights (Hoyt et al., 2019). Additionally, people who view marriage through a lens of **essentialism** (as an institution for one man/one woman that is natural and therefore invariant over time and place) are less likely to support same-sex marriage than those who see marriage as socially constructed (Duncan & Kemmelmeier, 2012).

Research consistently shows that men who identify as heterosexual are more homophobic than heterosexual women on a variety of dimensions. We see a similar phenomenon in many other countries as well (for a summary of the literature see Diefendorf & Bridges, 2020). Education, religion, and age are also related to homophobia, with more education being associated with lower degrees of prejudice. Religion drives attitudes toward homosexuality through at least three routes: religiosity, fundamentalism, and denomination. People who identify themselves as highly religious or as religious fundamentalists tend to be less supportive of homosexuality. In terms of denomination, Muslims and Protestants are less supportive than Catholics and Jewish people (Bratton et al., 2020). Among age groups, a greater proportion of those ages 65 and older hold prejudices, especially compared to those under 30 years of age. This may be partially accounted for by the generally lower education and greater religious traditionalism among older adults (Saad, 2012).

One factor that appears to reduce homophobia is contact with gay and lesbian people (Metin-Orta & Metin-Camgöz, 2020). This is not surprising because stereotyping often develops in the absence of regular contact between groups. An analysis of 41 studies revealed that contact reduces prejudice toward homosexual people, but it is more effective in reducing negative attitudes about lesbians than it is in reducing prejudice against gay men (Smith et al., 2009). Research has shown that contact also reduces prejudice against other groups, such as racial minorities. Contact is especially effective when it is between people of equal status who are pursuing a common goal (Pettigrew & Tropp, 2006).

Over the years, various studies have indicated that Black people are more hostile to homosexuality than White people (see, for example, Vincent et al., 2009). More recent research has revealed, however, that these attitudes are not linked to race per se but rather are a result of religiosity and region. Black people are more likely to be members of conservative Protestant denominations and to live in counties that are less accepting of homosexuality. While many religions today accept homosexuality, there continue to be conservative groups who do not. Members of these conservative groups also tend to spend more time in church-related activities, leaving them fewer opportunities for contact outside their group. When a person also lives in a conservative county, this further decreases the possibility of encountering ideas that are more positive toward gays and lesbians. White people who live in these counties and are members of conservative religious groups hold similar views to their Black counterparts (Adamczyk et al., 2016). There are also signs of change in the Black community, with Black college students less likely to identify as exclusively heterosexual than students from other groups. There are likely many reasons this is the case, but the intersectional approach of Black Lives Matter may be one factor (Massey et al., 2021).

Further complicating the relationship between race and attitudes toward homosexuality, Black people are more likely to recognize discrimination against LGB people and to support their civil rights than are members of other groups. In a national survey, 73 percent of Black people agreed that gay men and lesbians experience discrimination. This compared to 54 percent of White people, 66 percent of Hispanics, and 61 percent of people of mixed race. Black people are also more likely to express opposition to allowing businesses to refuse to serve LGB people on religious grounds (68 percent of Black people oppose compared to 64 percent of Hispanics and 60 percent of Whites) (Cox et al., 2017). It is likely that these views are a result of the empathy Black people feel due to the historic, albeit quite different, discrimination they themselves have faced (Gecewicz & Lipka, 2014).

As a final point about public opinion, it appears that attitudes toward LGB people are complicated by the intersectionality of statuses. In a large-scale study with college students from a public university in the Bible Belt, Worthen (2018) found that, in general, Native Americans have extremely accepting attitudes toward LGB people. Those Native American people who hold conservative Christian beliefs and strong patriarchal attitudes, however, are less accepting. A patriarchal attitude is also predictive of less acceptance of homosexuality among Hispanics (but not among Black or White people). Worthen also found that negative parental attitudes toward homosexuality predict college students' views—but only for heterosexual students. This study uncovers the complexity of attitudes and shows the need for more intersectional analyses. A second study looked at Asian American attitudes toward homosexuality and found that ethnicity intersected with religion, education, and generation in the United States. First-generation Asian Americans were much more likely to hold prejudicial attitudes than those in the second generation. Similar to other groups, education was associated with less prejudice and religiosity with more (Ju, 2021).

LGB People as Status Groups

As the surveys discussed above indicate, LGB people form status categories with low prestige or social honor. As such, they possess all the core attributes of status groups. Most notably, they are viewed by others as sharing certain lifestyle characteristics and being qualitatively different from outsiders. Being gay or lesbian, for example, is associated with having certain kinds of occupations (e.g., hairdresser) and dress (high fashion, artsy). However, their differences are defined as even deeper. Recall that in his depiction of status groups, Max Weber argued that extreme status separation between groups is most likely if the differences that separate them are thought of as being "ethnic" in nature. Consistent with this conception, scholar Stephen Murray has referred to the homosexual community as a "quasi-ethnic group" (1996, p. 4). This suggests that the differences must be viewed as fundamental, almost biological in nature, for caste-like arrangements to develop between groups. About half of US adults currently believe that homosexuality is biologically based (Gallup, 2021b). In their fight for political legitimacy and equal rights, the earliest gay-rights organizations in the United States (e.g., the Mattachine Society) characterized "homosexuals as a sexual minority, similar to other ethnic and cultural minorities" (Button et al., 1997, p. 25).

In addition to being viewed as qualitatively different in lifestyle, being seen as a different "kind" of people, separated from the rest of society, and occupying a distinctive place on a hierarchy of social honor or prestige, a status group is also perceived as having an internal social cohesion that unites them. That is, they are seen as sticking together and being mutually supportive of each other. As with most status groups, outsiders lump them all together, even though there is a wide diversity of people and experiences within the group. At the same time, given that sexual orientation divides gays and lesbians from, and is a primary basis for conflict with outsiders, it does help to unite them. This has resulted not only in the creation of informal friendship networks among sexual minorities but also in the development of neighborhoods with high concentrations of lesbians and gay men, separate institutions catering to a homosexual clientele, and political-rights organizations.

Finally, what marks LGB people as negatively defined status groups are fears of contamination and contact on the part of outsiders. Concerns about purity expressed by traditionalists and heterosexuals are indicative of concerted attempts to keep boundaries between heterosexuals and homosexuals intact. Publicly known association by a heterosexual with homosexuals, especially of a personal kind, creates the risk that some of the ostracism held for lesbians and gays may "rub off" on the individual.

Fear of contact with homosexual people can be so extreme that in legal cases in the United States and elsewhere, defendants have used a "gay panic defense," alleging that a gay person propositioned them, causing them to panic and attack (White, 2021). An example in the United States happened in 2018 when a gay panic defense was successfully used to bargain down a murder charge to the less serious charge of criminally negligent homicide. Other defendants have attempted a "trans panic" defense when they have become involved with transgender people who did not immediately reveal their status. In 2014, California banned both types of defenses, and fifteen more states have followed suit with legislation pending in another ten. Similar federal legislation has also been proposed (The LGBT+ Bar, 2021). The fact that panic defenses are considered legitimate enough to raise in court hints at a level of societal fear about personal contact between heterosexual and homosexual/transgender people. Similarly, 39 percent of LBGT people today live in states that allow adoption agencies to refuse to place children with them. In fact, 11 states expressly give agencies the right to discriminate based on their religious beliefs (Movement Advancement Project, 2021a). This refusal, at least in part, is based on stereotypes and fears of contagion.

Photo 9.2 Adoption and having children by surrogacy are becoming increasingly common for gay couples in the United States.
Source: Elvert Barnes/Wikicommons.

Negative beliefs about gay men and lesbians persist because they are consistent with prevailing stereotypes and help justify the hostile treatment of homosexual people. It is feared that unless gay and lesbian people are held in check, traditional morality and family structure as foundations of our society will become contaminated and seriously weakened. In the eyes of these opponents, social, cultural, and moral purity must be maintained, and contamination avoided at all costs.

The Law and Sexual Orientation

There are no federal laws that explicitly prohibit discrimination based on sexual orientation. Attempts have been made to use rights like equal protection, privacy, and free speech to protect LGB people, but these have not been particularly successful. As a result, Title VII of the 1964 Civil Rights Act has become important (Zimmer et al., 2000). This law prohibits employment discrimination because of an individual's race, color, religion, national origin, or sex. Arguments in favor of protection for sexual minorities (as well as for transgender and other non-gender-conforming people) under Title VII generally involve reference to the inclusion of "sex" in the law. Ironically, however, the word *sex* was inserted into Title VII at the last minute by a powerful anti-civil-rights representative who thought that, by adding it, the act would be voted down (Eskridge & Frickey, 1995). It passed anyway. It is still difficult to know exactly what Congress had in mind since *sex* was added to the legislation a day after it was presented. Consequently, there was little time for discussion of its meaning (Nathans, 2001).

Until recently, Title VII was not interpreted to protect people on the basis of sexual orientation. Instead, the courts and the Equal Employment Opportunity Commission (EEOC), the federal agency charged with enforcing Title VII, have historically interpreted "sex" to refer only to biology. This is partly because, over the years, confusion and inconsistency in conceptualizing and defining "sex," "gender," and "sexual orientation" have abounded in the courts. In a particularly notable case decided in 1978, *Smith v. Liberty Mutual Insurance Co.*, Smith was not hired as a mail clerk because he was seen as "effeminate" and, consequently, "not too suited for the job" (as quoted in Valdes, 1995, p. 138). A representative for the EEOC reported that Smith liked "playing musical instruments, singing, dancing and sewing." These were viewed as "interests … not normally associated with males" (p. 138). Smith argued that he had been denied employment because he had hobbies that were not consistent with the masculine role and, therefore, was a victim of gender stereotyping. That is, his argument had to do with the traditional connection made between sex and gender behavior. In contrast, the employer argued that he had not been hired because Smith was "suspected" of being gay. In other words, the employer drew a conclusion about Smith's sexual orientation based simply on his gender presentation. The court ended up drawing the same connection, noting that Title VII did not cover an individual's sexual orientation. Thus, it ignored the argument of Smith and the fact that the evidence demonstrated that the discrimination had been based, as Smith proposed, upon his *gender behavior* and not his *sexual orientation*. This shows how the court used the plaintiff's behavior as a measure of his sexual orientation and how stereotypical misinterpretations can result in legal defeats for lesbians, gay men, and others.

Another example of the narrow manner in which courts have interpreted Title VII is revealed in a 1979 case involving three gay plaintiffs who lost their jobs. The Ninth Circuit Court judge argued that in including sex as a basis for discrimination in Title VII, "Congress had only the traditional notions of '*sex*' in mind" and that it "applies only to discrimination on the basis of *gender* and should not be judicially extended to include sexual preference such as homosexuality" (as quoted in Zimmer et al., 2000, pp. 624–625 italics added).

It was not until 1989 that the courts began to recognize gender identity and expression as covered under Title VII. In the famous case of *Price Waterhouse v. Hopkins*, the US Supreme Court found that senior manager Ann Hopkins had been discriminated against because partners refused to promote her on the basis of her gender behavior. To them, Hopkins displayed many of the characteristics traditionally associated with masculinity. She was described by some partners as "macho," as having "overcompensated for being a woman," and in need of "a course at charm school" (Price Waterhouse v. Hopkins, 1989). In spite of her evidenced abilities and experience, Hopkins was passed over for partnership. In ruling against Price Waterhouse because of sex stereotyping, Justice Brennan stated that:

> [W]e are beyond the day when an employer could evaluate employees by assuming or insisting that they matched the stereotype associated with their group … An employer who objects to aggressiveness in women but whose positions require this trait places women in an intolerable and impermissible catch 22: out of a job if they behave aggressively and out of a job if they do not. Title VII lifts women out of this bind. (Price Waterhouse v. Hopkins, 1989, p. 251)

The disposition in the Ann Hopkins case opened the door for reinterpretation of Title VII for both gender nonconforming people as well as sexual minorities.

Two important cases established that both transgender and gay people are covered under the "sex" provision of Title VII. Starting in 2004 with the *Smith v. the City of Salem* decision, federal courts began to rule that transgender people are protected from employment discrimination. Even more recently, in *Baldwin v. the Department of Transportation*, the EEOC changed its stance about whether gay and lesbian people are also protected under the sex clause of Title VII. Decided in 2015, this case involved a man who was not hired for a permanent job because he was gay. The EEOC decided that discrimination against gay people is, in effect, discrimination based on gender—the worker's gender and the gender of his or her partner.

In the past, the use of Title VII to protect LGB people from discrimination has been problematic because it was simply a policy enforced by the EEOC. This meant that different administrations could put out executive orders telling the EEOC and the Department of Justice how to interpret it. For example, sexual orientation was included under the Obama administration but not during the Trump administration. A recent Supreme Court case, however, has made permanent the inclusion of sexual orientation and gender identity under Title VII. In *Bostock v Clay* (2020) the Supreme Court held that the sex provision of Title VII does protect gay, lesbian, and transgender people. Bostock was an amalgam of three cases where LGBT people were fired after revealing their sexuality or transgender status. The court ruled that they experienced sex discrimination because if their sexes had been different, they would not have been discriminated against. In other words, had the gay man, in one case, been a woman who loved men, she would not have been fired.

It should be noted that there are two important exemptions in Title VII. First, it does not apply to workers in companies with fewer than fifteen employees. Second, there is a religious exemption built into the law. Currently, it is not clear how much latitude the religious exemption gives employers to fire or not hire people based on sexual orientation or gender identity. Cases are being heard at lower court levels but will likely eventually reach the Supreme Court. For example, in *Starkey v. Roman Catholic Archdiocese of Indianapolis*, decided in August of 2021, a federal court ruled in favor of a Catholic school who fired a long-time guidance counselor for entering a same-sex marriage.

These court precedents and EEOC decisions about Title VII theoretically mean that most workers in the United States are protected from employment discrimination on the basis of sexual orientation and gender expression. This does not, however, protect against discrimination in other areas such as housing. President Biden has issued an executive order that extends the decision in Bostock to any area where discrimination on the basis of sex is illegal. This would include housing. As described, however, executive orders can be overturned by future administrations. Shoring up this executive order, however, are a number of local and state laws granting protections. For example, 22 states provide protection for both gender identity and sexual orientation in housing, and an additional 8 offer protection for one or the other (Movement Advancement Project, 2021b). At the same time, many states do not have these protections and there are some who have actively worked to limit or deny rights. For example, Arkansas has passed a bill preventing cities and localities from enacting anti-discrimination legislation that is stricter than any law at the state level. Since Arkansas has no anti-discrimination law protecting LGBTQ people, localities are now barred from doing so. Tennessee has a similar measure in place (Movement Advancement Project, 2018).

Full legal protection for sexual minorities has a long way to go. A recent poll revealed that about 35 percent of LBGTQ people have experienced employment discrimination in the past year. Sixty-five percent reported discrimination more generally (Gruberg et al., 2020). Health care is an area where many LBGTQ people experience discrimination. Recent legislation in a number of states that would allow health care providers to deny service based on religious convictions may provide further barriers for equal access. The year 2021 saw a record number of proposed laws regulating the lives of LBGT people. While most of the legislation involved trans people, at least two states passed bills that limit what teachers can say about homosexuality. North Dakota also passed a law allowing student groups at publicly funded schools to discriminate in who they allow to become members. This law will apply to a wide range of groups, but it is expected to disproportionately affect lesbian and gay students (Ronan, 2021).

Housing discrimination is a significant concern for LGB people, in part because gay men and lesbians are overrepresented among homeless people. In fact, sexual minority adults are more than twice as likely to have experienced homelessness during their lifetimes as their heterosexual counterparts (Choi et al., 2020). The risk of homelessness is particularly acute for LGB youth. One study in California found LGBT youth overrepresented in both foster care and unstable housing situations (Baams et al., 2019). While there are multiple reasons for the high number of

BOX 9.1 RELIGIOUS FREEDOM AND GAY WEDDINGS

In 2018, the US Supreme Court ruled in a case called *Masterpiece Cakeshop v. Colorado Civil Rights Commission*. The case stemmed from a 2012 incident when an engaged same-sex couple went to look at wedding cakes at Masterpiece Cakeshop. The owner refused to sell them a cake because he said that his religion precluded him from supporting same-sex unions. The couple filed a complaint with the Colorado Civil Rights Commission and the Commission agreed that discrimination had taken place. The Supreme Court ended up issuing a very narrow ruling that overturned the Commission's decision on the basis that they had been biased in the way they investigated and decided the case. Thus, the Supreme Court's decision had little impact on the larger issue of religious exemptions for people who sell custom work (flowers, cakes, or invitations, for example). It is expected that the Supreme Court will soon hear another case on this question. Religious freedom is central to American philosophy and practice. Others argue, however, that when one serves the public, one should not be allowed to discriminate. What if a religion, for example, encouraged its adherents to deny services to a racial or ethnic minority group? Is there a way to honor both religious freedom and equal rights for gay men and lesbians? How would you resolve this issue?

housing problems LGB people face, discrimination clearly plays a major role. The Department of Housing and Urban Development tested whether there was discrimination in the online housing market against gay men and lesbians. They sent out requests for information to people trying to rent out their apartments. Owners responded 15 percent less often to couples whose names suggested they were of the same gender (such as John and Jacob) than to couples with traditionally opposite gender names (Jennifer and John) (Friedman et al., 2013).

Because protections have been scattered and not enshrined in federal law until recently, in 2017, the Equality Act was introduced in Congress. This bill covers both sexual orientation and gender identity and protects much more than just employment, with provisions for housing, credit, educational access, and public accommodations. The House passed the bill in February of 2021, but, at the time of this writing, the Senate has failed to take it up.

Globalization and Sexuality

Looking around the world, we see a wide variety of reactions to people who are sexual minorities. There are many examples of countries where, like in the United States, discrimination against people who do not identify as heterosexual is present. In some areas of the world, homosexuality is even punished by death or imprisonment. At the same time, there are examples of countries that have been far more progressive on these issues than the United States. For example, when South Africa rewrote its constitution in 1996, it specifically outlawed discrimination on the basis of sexual orientation. In 1989, Denmark became the first country in the world to legally recognize same-sex unions. Ireland, a majority-Catholic country, approved same-sex marriage in 2015. They were the first country to achieve this using a referendum. In June of 2011, the United Nations adopted a resolution saying that rights for homosexual and transgender people were a "priority issue." This resolution was introduced by South Africa and approved by twenty-three countries from every region of the world including Cuba, Poland, Slovakia, Mexico, the United States, and Guatemala. Nineteen countries voted against the resolution, including Angola, Russia, and Pakistan (Human Rights Watch, 2011).

Between 1945 and 2005, there was a general trend of countries liberalizing their laws about sexuality. Specifically, they began to embrace a more individualistic perspective, allowing adults to make their own decisions about sex as long as those decisions were consensual. In fact, a full

90 percent of the policies about sexuality put in place during that time period expanded individual rights (Frank et al., 2010). Since 2005, however, more states have imposed restrictions on homosexuality than have liberalized their laws, resulting in a polarization in state responses. What accounts for these two poles? Research suggests that there are many factors at work. First, wealth and democracy strongly predict liberal laws. This is partly because people in poorer nations are more likely to associate sexuality with morality and democratic countries are more likely to frame sexuality as a rights issue (Adamczyk et al., 2018). In addition to wealth and democracy, the religiosity of a country and a Communist history predict restrictive laws as well as more negative public opinion toward LGB people (Hadler & Symons, 2018; L. L. Roberts, 2019). Russia is an interesting example. Although they liberalized their laws after the Cold War, the government has recently portrayed LGB rights as fundamentally at odds with its traditions and morals. They claim the gay rights movement is being imposed on them by Europe and the United States (Moss, 2021).

Given that societies often differ in their sexual mores, meanings, and classifications, when different cultures meet through globalization, it should not be surprising that clashes occur. We see this in some countries in Africa where the US government has actively promoted gay-rights policies. In fact, USAID has tied development money to gay rights, causing anger among some Africans who see it as a form of imperialism. As gay men and lesbians have become more visible in those countries due to US policies, discrimination and violence have increased. Making the situation even more complicated, Western religious groups have turned their attention to Africa in order to try and prevent the "mistakes" the United States has made in expanding gay rights (Onishi, 2015).

What about the impact of globalization on local gay cultures? Altman (2005) contends that homosexual communities in other industrialized nations model themselves after such communities in the United States. The language used and histories evoked are those that originate not in their own countries but in the United States. For example, police harassment of LGBT people sparked the Stonewall riots in the United States in 1969. Gay people in Europe sometimes cite it as giving birth to gay activism in their own countries even though such activism had begun earlier. This suggests the hegemonic position held by the United States in the world community.

Altman's argument that gay culture and identity are becoming homogenized across the world as a result of globalizing forces has been challenged by research, which describes a much more complicated picture of sexuality in varied settings. For example, while many gay male dating sites are available across the globe, people use them differently depending on where they live. They post different kinds of pictures and present different information about themselves. This is an example of both homogenization as people across the world access and use the same technology and heterogenization as they use it to suit their particular culture (Cserni, 2020). Adam et al. (1999) argue that, while there may be superficial similarities in tactics, terms, and symbols in gay movements across cultures, we must look to "local meanings of global tendencies" (p. 348). It is simply inaccurate to portray Western gay movements as the model to which others aspire (Jackson, 2009).

Summary

This chapter presented a brief overview of the inequities for people who are sexual minorities. Recent years have seen increases in our knowledge about gay, lesbian, and bisexual people, but we continue to know very little about asexual, demisexual, and pansexual people. It is clear that, while LGB people share many concerns, individuals' experiences vary greatly depending on their other statuses including race and class.

As a dishonored status group, LGB people have been singled out and stigmatized as individuals who do not fit dominant cultural ideas about appropriate behavior and lifestyles. Although sympathy and opinions in specific areas of civil rights have improved in recent years, significant proportions and subgroups within the United States continue to be hostile to people who are not heterosexual. Stereotypes persist, and this group continues to be a minority with distinct status-group attributes, yet without many of the legal protections afforded other minority groups. There is variation globally in attitudes toward and protections for LGB people. Globalization has had an impact on the meanings ascribed to sexuality and it has helped link gay and lesbian groups across national boundaries.

Critical Thinking

1. In what ways do race and class intersect with sexual orientation? What are some examples of how being gay might vary across classes and races?
2. Bullying appears to be a significant problem in many schools. What do you think can be done to curtail it?
3. The chapter gave some examples of heteronormativity. What examples can you provide?

Web Connections

For brief discussions of issues of concern to gay, lesbian, bisexual, and transgender groups, see the websites of the Human Rights Campaign (www.hrc.org). Visit also the National LGBTQ Task Force at www.thetaskforce.org/about/mission-history.html for reports on a wide range of issues related to LGBTQ rights.

Film Suggestions

Cured (2020). A documentary about the successful effort to remove homosexuality as a disorder from the American Psychiatric Association's Diagnostic and Statistical Manual in 1973.

I Carry You with Me (2020). A love story based on a true story about two Mexican men who fall in love and then navigate their relationship after one immigrates to the United States.

Forbidden: Gay and Undocumented (2016). This documentary is about a young gay man who was brought to the United States illegally by his parents when he was a child. The movie highlights his work as an activist in North Carolina at the beginning of the Trump presidency.

Out in the Night (2014). This documentary tells the story of a group of lesbians who were attacked by a man in New York City. Because he was wounded in the ensuing fight, the women were ultimately arrested, but four refused to plead guilty. The film explores the role of race, sexuality, and class in criminal justice.

Boy Meets Girl (2014). A love story about a trans woman exploring her bisexual identity in a small Kentucky town.

Pray Away (2021). A documentary about gay conversion therapy.

Unsettled (2019). This documentary follows gay refugees and asylum seekers from Africa and the Middle East as they try to come to the United States to escape being persecuted in their home countries.

10 Racial and Ethnic Inequality

In this chapter, we turn to look at how race and ethnicity are related to inequality in the United States. As you read, you may notice that the categories of gender and race/ethnicity have a lot in common. For example, both have been associated with biological differences and then imbued with social and cultural meanings that are used to justify inequality. The terms sex, gender, and race also have meanings that vary with the cultural, historical, and social context in which they are used. Consequently, none of these concepts has a fixed, unvarying definition. At the same time, we need to be careful about equating race and gender. Throughout this chapter, we'll see how the legacy of slavery and the continuing segregation of racial/ethnic minority groups has had a deep impact on the distribution of wealth, income, and status. Men and women are not segregated from each other in the same way, making their patterns of inequality different. Of course, while we focus on race/ethnicity in this chapter, we also acknowledge intersectionality whenever possible, pointing out, for example, how the experiences of men and women and those from different class backgrounds who share a race experience inequality differently.

The Meaning and Creation of Race

Sociologists often say that race is "socially constructed," but sometimes fail to be clear about what that means. As a result, people might think that social constructionists deny that there are physical differences related to family origins. That is not the case. Social constructionism acknowledges that people vary along a wide variety of dimensions, including some of the markers that we associate with race, such as skin tone, facial features, and hair texture. Humans developed these different features as they adapted to the different environments found around the world. For example, over many thousands of years, people developed lighter skin in the northern parts of the world. This is because humans need to receive a certain amount of sunlight to produce vitamin D. Light skin allows more sunlight to permeate the skin—which is helpful when people live in places where there is little sunlight most of the year.

While social constructionists acknowledge **phenotypical** difference, they also point out that there is no biological basis for race. There is tremendous physical variation within the groups we classify as races and there is no "race gene." While there have been past attempts to define race "scientifically" and to develop clear classifications, these have always been found to be faulty for one reason or another, and virtually all have fallen by the wayside. Some of the earliest attempts classified individuals by their ancestry rather than physical features. These classifications tended to conflate ethnicity, nationality, and physical characteristics (e.g., Jewish or Irish "race"). Other classifications identified and ranked groups in an **ethnocentric** fashion, separating the socially dominant group from others and ranking it highest. The features chosen to distinguish the races were those that appeared to separate the dominant from lower-ranking groups, groups that could then be exploited for their alleged inferiority. The attempted annihilation of the "Jewish race" by

DOI: 10.4324/9781003184966-13

the "Aryans" is an example of how racial categorizations can be based on and used for political rather than scientific reasons. As the social, economic, and cultural positions of groups changed, so did their race. While we usually think of a person's race as affecting their class position, in this case, *class* position helped to determine *race*. For example, with assimilation, Jewish, Irish, and Italian immigrants, once defined as "non-White," became "White."

The continual changing of racial categories in society and by governmental offices indicates that race is something that is created and anchored in the social, economic, and cultural conditions of the time. In the words of Omi and Winant (2005), it involves **racial formation**, which is a "sociohistorical process by which racial categories are created, lived out, transformed, and destroyed" (p. 109). Omi and Winant go on to argue that once racial categories are established, people engage in a process of **racialization** whereby they give the categories meaning by associating them with various characteristics or behaviors. For example, in the United States, the category of "Black" has come to be associated with poverty—even though there is a great deal of economic diversity within the group. Omi and Winant argue that racial formation and racialization are not just passive processes. Instead, we all participate to one degree or another. **Racial projects** are when people engage with the meanings of a racial category to argue for a particular distribution of resources. For example, a person is involved in a racial project when they argue that the United States is a meritocracy and affirmative action is unnecessary. Another racial project would be the argument that people of color face continuing discrimination and that we should continue affirmative action. Both arguments involve interpretations of race and the distribution of resources (and thus inequality).

Omi and Winant believe that, while anyone can engage in a racial project, not everyone has an equal chance of success. White people, who hold most power in society and have enshrined that power in institutions, have a large advantage when they use racial projects to justify why economic and power inequalities exist. The state is also an important player engaged in racial projects. For example, in Chapter 13, we will talk about state policies of mass incarceration as a racial project. It is important to note, however, that people and groups of color also engage in racial projects. For example, the civil rights movement was successful in reinterpreting racial injustice and winning some victories in terms of resources. In Chapter 14, we discuss #BlackLivesMatter as another racial project.

Interestingly, most White people do not think of "White" as a race. Rather, when speaking of race, the tendency is to think only of racial "minorities" as belonging to a race. Whiteness is invisible in this sense. "From an early age," observes Rothenberg (2008, p. 2), "race, for white people, is about everyone else." In Omi and Winant's terms, Whiteness is not racialized. The invisibility of Whiteness as a racial category fosters the illusion that being "White" is to be normal or the standard by which others are measured. Race is a term ordinarily used only in reference to other, non-White persons (Dye, 2002). The claim that White people are regular and normal and, therefore, representative of humanity allows Whiteness to be a central basis for power and privilege in society. The racial categories with which people are identified have direct consequences on their lives because society's social structures and the opportunities and blockages they create are shaped in part by the dominant group.

The Census and Racial Formation

The census is a particularly interesting example of the state engaging in racial formation. In the first census in 1790, Native American and Black people were separated out from others because of their political status, but it was not until 1820 that "race" or color was used in the census (Snipp, 2003). Throughout the rest of the nineteenth century, the racial classifications used by the Census Bureau were rooted in cultural, social, and intellectual developments going on in the wider society. The addition of "Chinese" and "Japanese" to the 1890 census racial classifications reflected growing concern on the part of the dominant group about their increasing numbers and their potential to compete with White workers on the West Coast. The added inclusion of "Octoroon" (one-eighth Black) and "Quadroon" (one-fourth Black) to the classifications symbolized the growing interest in and concern about racial purity at the end of the nineteenth century (Schaefer, 2015; Snipp, 2003). Interestingly, until 1960, Census Bureau workers decided people's race based on how they looked. This was clearly problematic and led to the Census Bureau changing its policy to allow individuals to self-identify (Snipp, 2003).

Over time, the Census Bureau has not just changed the number of categories and who determines race, it has also restricted or expanded the definitions of some categories, changing the number of people in them. For example, states often defined a person as Black if they had at least "one drop of Black blood." They used this definition as a means to restrict "Whiteness" and outlaw racial intermarriage (Brunsma & Rockquemore, 2002). Historical records also show an example of a category being broadened when the number of Puerto Ricans classified as White dramatically increased in early twentieth-century censuses of Puerto Rico's population. This occurred largely because of "boundary shifting," that is, the definition of "White" was broadened to include more people (Loveman & Muniz, 2007). These changes in turn reflect fluctuations in racial dynamics in the society at large.

When we examine historical fluctuations in the definition and meaning of race, it becomes apparent that racial classifications have served as indicators of which groups have political, economic, and social power and which do not. As described, however, nondominant groups sometimes fight for recategorization themselves. This can be seen in recent attempts to create a new ethnic category, Middle Eastern and North African (MENA). Since the 1920s, people of MENA descent have been categorized as White. This decision was made, in part, due to lobbying on the part of the groups themselves in the early 1900s. They did not want to be categorized as Asian because that would have made them ineligible for US citizenship under the Chinese Exclusion Act. Today, however, activists are calling for the establishment of the MENA category because they do not self-identify as White, and they experience discrimination like other minority groups. They point out that it makes little sense that Pakistani Americans can apply for minority small business loans because they are considered to be "Asian," but Iranians do not qualify because they are counted as "White" (Aidi, 2015).

In 2015, the Census Bureau tested a question that added MENA as a category and found that it enhanced the quality of the data (US Census Bureau, 2021f). The Office of Management and Budget, the agency that makes a final determination about census questions, ultimately decided against adding the category. Some critics charge that this decision was made because it would reduce the number of "White" respondents, and increase the number of people eligible for federal, state, and local benefits as members of a minority ethnicity. This illustrates the political nature of race and the census (Alshammari, 2020).

A second recently proposed change to the census involves the "Hispanic" ethnic identification. In today's census, Hispanic is not considered a racial category, but is listed as an ethnicity. An **ethnic group** includes people who have common ancestry and share a cultural heritage. It is more correct, however, to call Hispanics a **panethnic group**. Espiritu defines this kind of group as a "politico-cultural collectivity made up of peoples of several, hitherto distinct, tribal or national origins" (1994, p. 2). The "Hispanic" category is a panethnicity because it includes people from very different cultural backgrounds (Dominicans and Chileans, for example). The term "Hispanic" does not refer to a race because Hispanics can be of any race. For example, Hispanics from the Caribbean often look phenotypically Black, and there are Hispanics from Peru who look phenotypically Asian.

The creation of the Hispanic category was the result of work by state actors, ethnic leaders, and market groups (such as the television network Univision) during the 1970s (Mora, 2014).

The new category was useful for counting purposes, and it allowed the government to extend benefits to Hispanics as a minority group (Lee & Bean, 2004). While a Hispanic racial category was considered, the Census Bureau encountered resistance from a number of sources, including other minority groups who feared losing members (for example, there were concerns that Black Hispanics would check the "Hispanic" box rather than the "Black" box on the race question) (Mora, 2014). Not having Hispanic as an option in the race question is problematic, however, because many people see themselves as racially Hispanic. This causes them to either skip the race question, or to select the "some other race" option. For this reason, the census has been under pressure to use a combined race/origin question that would put Hispanic as a category alongside Black, White, and the other racial classifications. The census tested out a new combined format in 2015 and found that it lowered the percentage of Hispanics reporting "some other race" from 33 percent to 1 percent (Cohn, 2017). The Trump administration, however, delayed the decision about the change for so long that it could not be made in time for the 2020 census (Overberg, 2018).

Like the term "Hispanic," "Asian" is a panethnicity (although the census considers Asians to be a racial group). The term "Asian American" has been traced back to a student group in Berkeley in 1968. The organizers were inspired by the Black Power Movement and wanted to find a way to bring together students from China, Japan, and the Philippines. They believed that there were similarities between the groups in terms of immigration history and experiences of racial discrimination (Kandil, 2018). While the census incorporated the term for the first time in 1980, it took time for it to become popular. It should be noted, however, that although the term Asian is in widespread use today, there still is disagreement about which groups are included. In a 2016 survey, the vast majority of White, Black, and Hispanic respondents agreed that Chinese, Japanese, and Korean people are Asian but the percentages were much lower for Pakistanis and Indians (with, for example, 45 percent of White people saying that Pakistanis are "unlikely" to be Asian). Interestingly, Pakistanis and Indians self-identify as Asian but large percentages of Asians from other backgrounds (such as Chinese and Taiwanese people) said that those two groups were unlikely to be Asian (Lee & Ramakrishnan, 2017).

In the text above, we have described the census categories as though they are discrete, but of course, many Americans identify themselves as of more than one race. The census did not acknowledge this possibility until 2000, when they made it possible for people to check off multiple racial categories. The golfer Tiger Woods helped to call attention to this issue by calling himself a "Cabalinasian" (i.e., part Caucasian, Black, American Indian, Thai, and Chinese). In the 2010 census, about 2.5 percent of individuals in the United States identified themselves as multiracial. This number, however, increased by 264 percent by 2020, the largest gain of any racial/ethnic category (Pew Research Center, 2015a; US Census Bureau, 2021h). At this point, it is not clear how much of the increase resulted from a changing population and how much was caused by individual people changing their categories from one race to multiracial over time.

US Racial and Ethnic Relations: An Historical Sketch

Native Americans

When colonists arrived in North America, their relationships with Native peoples were sometimes cooperative because both groups were interested in trade and barter. The Europeans also relied on Native people for help with agricultural techniques (Lurie, 1982). But this cooperation was short-lived. An important lens through which to understand this change is settler colonization—a concept we introduced in Chapter 2. In traditional colonialism, one country goes into another to gain access to their natural and human resources. When Europeans arrived in North America, however, they were not just interested in the resources, they wanted to settle here permanently.

This meant that they had a vested interest in obtaining as much land as possible, regardless of who was living there first (Glenn, 2015). Because the British were farmers, they were most interested in good agricultural land. Those American Indians whose economies emphasized agriculture and who were located near the East Coast were the first to be overwhelmed by the colonists (Lurie, 1982).

In order for the Europeans to engage effectively in settler colonialism, they needed to find an ideology to rationalize taking away lands from indigenous people. Ideas and stereotypes of the "savage" that had developed in the sixteenth and seventeenth centuries provided colonists with a framework within which to interpret American Indians. Rather than color or racial distinction, religious and ethnocentric criteria were used initially to separate groups into superior and inferior categories. Specifically, distinctions were made between "Christians" and "heathens" and between "civilized" and "savage." Clearly, the American Indians were placed in the heathen and savage categories and this was used as a device to justify taking over their land (Fredrickson, 1981). Thus, distinct attitudes about this group were entrenched by the time the American Revolution occurred (Farley, 1988). These attitudes impeded the colonists' ability to see the wide cultural diversity among Native peoples. They lumped all of them into one category, creating a panethnicity. Still today, the term "Native American" includes people from many different tribes and thus different cultural backgrounds.

The tactics that Europeans used to take away indigenous lands are similar to those of settler colonialists around the world. Many Native peoples were killed by disease unwittingly brought by the settlers, but many others were simply murdered. A particularly horrifying case of this occurred in 1890 at Wounded Knee on the Pine Ridge Indian Reservation in South Dakota when the US government massacred at least 150 men, women, and children. Sometimes during violent confrontations, the Native peoples who were not killed were captured and sold into slavery both domestically and internationally.

Another tactic employed by the colonists was to drive native peoples off desirable land, sometimes forcing them to live in restricted areas. While this was common in colonial America, the process was made official in 1794 when the American government signed the first of 400 treaties with Native tribes. It is important to note that these treaties were signed between sovereign nations. In other words, the United States—even in the Constitution—recognizes American Indian tribal sovereignty. While a few of these treaties allowed the Native peoples to keep their land, the vast majority forced their relocation to land that was worth far less. Promises made to the tribes were repeatedly broken and many of the treaties were signed when the Native peoples were under great duress (Wang, 2015). Their removal from the lands was brutal, with many thousands dying in forced marches westward.

In the period roughly between 1880 and 1930, over 65 percent of the 138 million acres that had been held by American Indians moved to White ownership (National Park Service, 2021). The Dawes Act was a federal law that allowed tribal lands to be subdivided and parceled out to Native American families. Whatever was left after the families each got a share was given to settlers, often under the Homestead Act. The vast majority of these settlers were White, but newly freed Black people were also eligible. Facing discrimination in the Jim Crow Era South and a lack of housing options, some moved to tribal land (Miles, 2019).

One of the most pernicious ways Europeans tried to solidify control over Native peoples was by forcing them to assimilate to White American culture under the guise of "civilizing" them (Glenn, 2015). By the last decade of the nineteenth century, most American Indians were on reservations where they were forbidden to practice their religions. Their children were compelled to attend boarding schools run by White people, where they had to speak English and cut their hair (Brayboy & Lomawaima, 2018). Carving up reservation lands and giving parcels to nuclear families was also a form of forced assimilation. Prior to the Dawes Act, many tribes had family structures that were far more cross generational and communal and the idea of individual ownership of land was foreign (Glenn, 2015). Of course, while White Americans claimed to be interested in assimilating Native people, this only went so far. It was not until the 1920s that American Indians won citizenship and voting rights.

During the 1940s, the government began to close tribal rolls, preventing people from signing up as members. They also increased their seizure of Indian assets and dramatically cut federal benefits to the reservations. In 1952, the United States passed the Urban Indian Relocation Program. This program attempted to encourage (or force) Native peoples off the reservations and into cities. They were promised support to find good housing, education, and jobs. The reality, however, was much different. Few supports were offered and many of the families were swindled into paying very high rents for substandard housing. The promised vocational education did not appear until years after the program was launched. Ultimately, the program ended up increasing inequality (National Council of Urban Indian Health, n.d.). Simultaneously, the US government revoked the tribal status of over 100 tribal groups, granting themselves the right to take away the land that was in trust for Native use. Losing tribal status also meant that communities were no longer able to make use of the Indian Health Service and they were forced to give up other important government benefits as well (Glenn, 2015).

The history of Native Americans under settler colonization has been largely one of oppression and discrimination. At the same time, Native peoples have consistently fought back. For example, in 1969, citing the Treaty of Fort Laramie, a group of Native people took over the then-unused Alcatraz Island. In 1973, Native peoples occupied Wounded Knee for 71 days to protest inhumane living conditions on reservations. Native peoples, overcoming seemingly insurmountable odds, have maintained their languages, rituals, and traditions.

European Immigrants

As will be discussed in Chapter 11, the early European immigrants to the United States were Puritans from England. During the 1700s, many immigrants arrived from Ireland and Germany. Most of these early immigrants came seeking economic opportunities and many also sought religious freedom.

By the early 1800s, increasing numbers of people began arriving from southern and eastern Europe including Italian, Polish, and Greek people. These groups were initially categorized as non-White and suffered the consequences. There was widespread concern about maintaining the purity of the "White race" and a fascination with eugenics and **Social Darwinism**. Eventually, because of assimilation into American culture and economic mobility, many of these groups became classified as "White" (Barrett & Roediger, 2008; Brodkin, 2008). This shows again how racial classifications, rather than being scientifically based, are closely linked to the power and economic status of the groups involved.

African Americans

Land in early America was plentiful, but greater labor power was needed to take full advantage of its resources. The absence of large numbers of willing free laborers led to attempts to obtain forced labor that could be justified on ideological or philosophical grounds. American Indians were difficult to subdue and were a potential major threat because they were familiar with the countryside and could put up fierce resistance. On the other hand, large-scale, prolonged use of indentured White servants was unrealistic because they were freed after a period of servitude. This made the importation of non-White slave labor attractive. Slavery created a large labor pool of workers who did not know the land, and it helped to elevate all Whites to a higher status (Fredrickson, 1981).

Given the early colonists' views of Black people as evil, animalistic, uncivilized, and un-Christian, it is not surprising that they passed laws banning sexual mixing and intermarriage. Children of mixed parentage were considered Black (Fredrickson, 1981). Enslavement was a thorny issue that troubled some of the Founding Fathers (e.g., Washington, Hamilton) more so than others (e.g., Jefferson). The result was that the problem of what to do with slavery after the Revolution was put off again and again. Several thousand African Americans had fought in the Continental Army, but nevertheless, at the Constitutional Convention, it was decided that a Black man was only three-fifths of a person. Although Thomas Jefferson is associated with the belief that "all men are created equal," he owned 180 slaves when he died and thought of Black people as inferior to White: "I advance it therefore as a suspicion only, that the Blacks, whether originally a distinct race, or made distinct by time and circumstances, are inferior to the Whites, in the endowments both of body and mind" (quoted in Feldstein, 1972, pp. 52–53). Beliefs in the different endowments helped to justify slavery. After all, inhuman treatment could be tolerated if the members of a race were not considered fully human.

At the time of the first official census in 1790, the Black population was approximately 757,000, of whom almost 700,000 were slaves. Their numbers grew to almost 4.5 million by 1860, of whom 89 percent were slaves. Between 1790 and 1860, about 90 percent of all Black Americans in each census were slaves. Even though the slave trade was officially outlawed in 1808, it still flourished along the East Coast of the country. In 1790, 23 percent of all families had slaves, whereas by 1850, only 10 percent did. It should be noted, however, that a number of states had outlawed slavery by 1850, so the percentage of families with slaves in the slave-holding states was higher than 10 percent. Most families with slaves owned between seven and nine (US Census Bureau, 1979).

The system of inequality that developed between the races during the heyday of slavery up to the Civil War was essentially a caste system. In fact, similarities have been drawn between India's traditional, now outlawed, caste system and Black-White relations in the United States. In India, caste was both a system of inequality and a means of integration, with each caste assigned specific and unique functions. Those at the top were assigned the most honorific functions and were considered purer than those below. The lowest stratum, the Untouchables, were not part of the formal caste system itself; they were outside it (Bidner & Eswaran, 2015). Wilkerson (2020) points out that in the United States, Black people occupy the same position as the Untouchables, while White people are at the highest stratum (equivalent to the Brahmin). This caste system was obviously set in place early in US history when Africans were enslaved. Laws were passed that forbade Black people: (1) to intermarry with Whites; (2) to vote; (3) to testify against White people in legal cases; (4) to own firearms; (5) to use abusive language against Whites; (6) to own property unless permitted by a master; (7) to leave the plantation without permission or disobey a curfew; (8) to make a will or inherit property; and (9) to have anyone teach them to read or write, or give them books (Blackwell, 1985; Fredrickson, 1981).

The end of the Civil War, Emancipation, and Reconstruction did not end the misery for Black people, and, in fact, appear to have done little to change their caste relationship with Whites (Wilkerson, 2020). Legal, intellectual, economic, and population changes were occurring that provided support for continued discrimination. For example, White Americans in the South used **Jim Crow laws** to maintain their superior position. Increased labor competition from a continuously rising number of White immigrants from Europe made it difficult for Black people to find employment. Lynchings increased in the latter part of the nineteenth century and the migration of Black Southerners to the industrializing North during and after World War I resulted in severe clashes between Black and White workers, and in the years from 1917 to 1919, riots broke out in several cities. In the 1919 Chicago riot, Black people fought back against severe racism and lynching (Krugler, 2014).

In the 1920s, anthropologist Franz Boas spoke out forcefully against the racially based theories being propagated at the time, and by the 1930s and 1940s, other important scientists joined him in attacking the idea that Black people were inferior to White. Nazi racism also contributed to a re-examination of race domination in this country. This is ironic because the Nazis used the US racial caste system as a model for their own (Wilkerson, 2020). But discrimination continued, with Black people still encountering racism and exclusion within unions and industry. They also were segregated within the military and discrimination was so acute, there were a number of riots during World War II. At the same time, increasing organization and political power of African Americans during the late 1940s and 1950s helped to bring about some legislative changes and, eventually, the civil rights movement.

Wealth inequality between Black and White people has been perpetuated since early in US history, beginning with slavery and then by governmental policies that prohibited Black people from beginning certain kinds of businesses or entering particular markets. Agencies such as the Federal Housing Authority made loans and mortgages for Black people more difficult to obtain, and there was a lack of opportunity to take advantage of the wealth-accumulation benefits of lower capital gains taxes, home mortgage deductions, and Social Security benefits. Joe Feagin (2006) calls this enshrinement of racism in the American system at its founding **systemic racism**. As we will see, the legacy of this history continues in present-day structures and outcomes.

Asian Americans and Pacific Islanders

The preceding historical sketch reveals how extensive racial inequality has been in US society. In addition to the groups already mentioned, Asian Americans have suffered the effects of stereotyping and unfair treatment. Chinese laborers were recruited in the 1850s to come to the United States to build railroads as well as to work in the mines and factories. Although they were only a small part of the US population, they made up a full 20 percent of the labor force in California in 1870 (Center for Global Education, 2020). Near the end of the nineteenth century, some Japanese immigrants obtained labor jobs but were disliked by unions and employees of other races. They were lumped in with the Chinese as part of the "yellow peril," the fear that Asians would take over. At about the same time, in 1898, the United States annexed Hawaii by force, overturning their monarchy. This take-over was prompted by White plantation owners who did not want to pay US import taxes on products such as sugar and who were worried about the power of the monarchy over their profits.

As we discuss at length in the next chapter, the United States essentially cut off any immigration from Asia with the Chinese Exclusion Act of 1882. Filipino people, however, were not covered by this act because the Philippines had been annexed to the United States. As a result, many Filipino people were able to come to the West Coast starting in the 1920s to fill positions in the canneries and factories. The faced severe discrimination, which worsened after the market crash of 1929. Violent mobs attacked Filipino farmworkers in cities including Watsonville, Salinas, San Francisco, and San José. In 1933 California passed a law banning marriages between Filipinos and Whites (Equal Justice Initiative, n.d.).

The events at Pearl Harbor that initiated the entry of the United States into World War II exacerbated negative feelings toward Japanese Americans. Under Executive Order 9066, people on the West Coast with virtually any Japanese ancestry were rounded up and moved into concentration camps. This was not done to either German or Italian Americans, even though the United States was at war against Germany and Italy as well as Japan. This strongly suggests a heavy influence of racism. The 113,000 Japanese people sent to these camps without the benefit of trial could take only personal items, leaving behind and then losing most of their property.

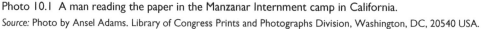

Photo 10.1 A man reading the paper in the Manzanar Internment camp in California.
Source: Photo by Ansel Adams. Library of Congress Prints and Photographs Division, Washington, DC, 20540 USA.

After the war, terrorism and bigotry against Japanese Americans continued, although no instances of espionage by them were ever proved. Even while in the camps, they remained loyal to their adopted country.

Mexican Americans

The first Mexicans in what would later become the United States were not immigrants. They were Mexican citizens, living in territory that was part of Mexico. In 1836, however, Texas declared itself an independent republic—although Mexico did not recognize it as such. The United States annexed the land in 1845 and demanded that Mexico cede the territory. The resultant Mexican American War lasted two years and only ended when the United States conquered the capital of Mexico City. As part of the Treaty of Guadalupe Hidalgo, Mexico ceded much of the land that later became the states of Texas, California, Arizona, New Mexico, Utah, and Colorado. About 75,000 Mexicans were living on this land and were given a choice between moving to Mexico and remaining where they lived. If they stayed, they could choose either United States or Mexican citizenship. Their rights to their land and their language were protected by the treaty. Even those who became US citizens, however, quickly found that their citizenship did not mean equal rights. In the last half of the nineteenth century, Mexican Americans frequently had their land taken away by European settlers (Weber, 2006). What was a dual-language system in California quickly became English-only (Summers Sandoval, 2009).

Photo 10.2 Dolores Huerta, an iconic labor activist during the 1960s and 1970s.
Source: US Department of Labor.

At the time of the signing of the Treaty of Guadalupe Hidalgo, only "free whites" were allowed to become US citizens. Because the treaty did not mention race yet allowed Mexicans to become citizens, it essentially treated them as White. The fact that the race of Mexicans was not clearly spelled out in the treaty, however, opened the door for numerous legal challenges by nativist organizations. Confusion and anti-Mexican sentiment in some localities and states also meant that whether citizenship was actually approved for Mexicans varied greatly. Mexicans were consistently portrayed as outsiders, even though many of their families had been on land that later became the United States for generations. The issue was only settled in 1940 when citizenship rights were extended to people who traced their descent to the Western hemisphere (Molina, 2014).

Racial and Ethnic Inequality Today

Although we have made some progress in reducing inequalities by race and ethnicity, there is much work to be done. This section will outline the present state of racial and ethnic inequalities, beginning with how differentials in income can be explained by occupational stratification, and then moving to a discussion of cultural and symbolic resources.

Chapter Two presented data showing how the average income in the United States varies dramatically by race and ethnicity. Part of the reason relates to how occupations are distributed across groups. Table 8.1 showed the current broad occupational distributions for Black, Asian, Hispanic, and White men and women. We saw that the greatest concentration of White, Black, and Asian men is in the managerial/professional category, while Hispanic men are most often working in natural resources/construction. Among women, the greatest concentrations of all groups are in the managerial/professional occupations.

But these general categories mask real discrepancies among more detailed classifications of occupations. In Table 10.1, we see that Black people are most underrepresented in certain high-level professional and upper-level skilled white-collar positions involving authority or decision-making, and they are overrepresented in various private and governmental service and aide occupations. The positions in which Black people are typically underrepresented require

Table 10.1 Sample of Specific Occupations in Which Black and Hispanic People Are Significantly Overrepresented and Underrepresented: 2020

Underrepresented	(%)	Overrepresented	(%)
Black People			
Farmers and Ranchers	0.7	Barbers	28.2
Aircraft Pilots	3.4	Home Health Aides	37.4
Veterinarians	0	Security Guards	31.1
Dieticians/Nutritionists	1.4	Postal Service Clerks	38.4
Dentists	1.4	Taxi Drivers	27.7
Web Developers	3.7	Bus Drivers	37.0
Editors	0.7	Industrial Truck and Tractor Operators	25.5
Chemical Engineers	1.5	Parking Attendants	34.0
Drywall/Ceiling Tile Installers	1.0	Nursing Assistants	35.2
Hispanic People			
Writers/Authors	2.4	Drywall/Ceiling Tile Installers	73.1
Statisticians	2.0	Roofers	53.2
Lawyers	5.8	Maids and Housekeeping Cleaners	46.1
Chemists/Material Scientists	2.2	Tree Trimmers	45.5
Farmers and Ranchers	4.3	Carpet/Tile Installers	53.2
Postsecondary School Teachers	6.2	Construction Laborers	46
Occupational Therapists	6.5	Cement Masons/Finishers	53.3
Advertising/Promotions Managers	3.5	Sewing Machine Operators	36.9
Aircraft Pilots	5	Insulation Workers	54.5
Pharmacists	3.4	Dishwashers	37.6

Source: Bureau of Labor Statistics (2021a), www.bls.gov/cps/cpsaat11.pdf.

specialized training or high levels of education. Their overrepresentation lies in certain mid- to lower-level service jobs, such as security guards, barbers, and bus drivers. Government jobs have been crucial to the economic survival of many Black families since Reconstruction. Today, one in five Black workers holds a job in the public sector. This is because the government is required to be more transparent, and it has more protections in place against discrimination. The Black-White wealth gap is considerably smaller between workers with public sector jobs than it is in the private sector. Public sector jobs often pay higher wages than comparable private sector work and have better pension/retirement benefits. Unfortunately, many public sector jobs disappeared during the 2008 Recession. We saw a similar phenomenon during the pandemic, with one million public sector jobs lost between September 2019 and September 2020. Over 200,000 of the lost jobs were held by Black people (Madowitz et al., 2020).

The fact that Hispanic people are overrepresented in construction and agriculture jobs leads to instability because those occupations tend to be seasonal. These occupations, along with food services, where Hispanics also tend to be overrepresented, are also greatly affected by economic shocks. In other words, when there is a recession, consumers stop building new homes and eating out (Zamarripa, 2020). The pandemic hit the food services sector particularly hard with a loss of 6 million jobs between February and April of 2020. While the industry has recovered, in July 2021, it was still about a half-million jobs down from its pre-pandemic levels (National Restaurant Association, 2021). Additionally, as a group, Hispanic workers are the most concentrated of any group in jobs that cannot be performed from home, endangering their safety and making it extremely difficult to manage work and childcare (Gould et al., 2020).

You may have noticed that Native Americans are not listed in the occupational charts. This is because the Bureau of Labor Statistics does not provide their data. In an analysis with census data, however, researchers found that American Indians/Alaska Natives are occupationally segregated from White people and are disproportionately concentrated in low-wage work. This difference holds even with statistical controls for education and other demographic characteristics (Liebler et al., 2018).

As described, one result of occupational segregation is that the racial and ethnic groups earn different incomes. An analysis of Bureau of Labor Statistics data conducted in 2017 showed that the average of the salaries of the 20 occupations with the highest percentage of White people was $119,767. The equivalent figure for Black people was $31,130 and $31,764 for Hispanics. The average for occupations with the highest percentages of Asians was $104,272 but that figure masks a particularly high variance (e.g., the occupations on this list include both medical scientists and manicurists) (Fox, 2017). Research suggests that about 39 percent of the gap between White and Black, and White and Hispanic, workers can be explained by occupational segregation. On average, Asian people earn more than Whites and half of this disparity is a result of occupational segregation. There is no evidence that occupational segregation by race is decreasing over time (Weeden, 2019).

There seem to be at least three ways that occupational segregation results in income disparities. First, minorities are either less likely to be hired for jobs or they are segregated into low-wage jobs that are dominated by other minorities. This phenomenon, called **crowding**, increases competition in the minority-dominated occupations and reduces wages (Bahn & Cumming, 2020). A recent study of hiring in the high-paying tech industry found that Black, Hispanic, and White people are equally likely to apply for jobs, but that Black and Hispanic workers are less likely to get a callback, interview, and offer than are their White counterparts, leading to crowding in other industries (Parasurama et al., 2020).

The second-way occupational segregation results in income differences is that jobs in which there are a high concentration of minority employees have lower wages attached to them. This is true regardless of the qualifications of the workers or the characteristics of the place of employment. In other words, there is a causal relationship between the racial composition of jobs and their wages (Hamilton et al., 2011). The final connection between occupational segregation and income inequality is that minority workers tend to lose ground in wages to White workers as they get older and move through their careers (Maume, 2004; Willson, 2003). The initial lower levels of wages for these workers, coupled with their cumulative disadvantage, make it difficult to accumulate wealth or develop an inheritance for their children. Black and Hispanic workers are also less likely to be in occupations that provide benefits such as pensions and retirement funds, making retirement difficult (Sullivan et al., 2019).

Researchers have identified a set of processes in organizations that limit the mobility of minority workers. **Tokenism**, for example, is when a White-dominated company or institution admits a very limited number of people of color in an effort to prove that they are inclusive. Research finds that these "tokens" become highly visible and their performance is scrutinized more than that of the majority group. This leads to considerable stress (Kanter, 1977). In a study of Black and Latino police officers, Stroshine and Brandi (2011) found evidence that both men and women experience the negative effects of tokenism. **Pigeonholing** (Cose, 1993) is another phenomenon that affects mobility for minorities. It is when people of color are steered into positions within organizations that are defined as appropriate for them. In the professional realm, these are often the "diversity management" jobs or jobs that serve high numbers of minority clients. These jobs tend to have limited power and mobility associated with them (Hall & Stevenson, 2007).

A phenomenon related to pigeonholing is **cultural taxation** or "identity taxation." These terms are normally used in reference to faculty jobs in higher education but can easily be applied more broadly. Cultural taxation (Padilla, 1994) is when people of color are asked to take on extra work to add diversity on committees or when they are asked to provide extra support services for students of color. Hirshfield and Joseph (2012) coined the term "identity taxation," which is broader than cultural taxation. They defined it as when "faculty members shoulder any labor—physical, mental, or emotional—due to their membership in a historically marginalized group within their department or university, beyond that which is expected of other faculty members in the same setting" (p. 214). Both cultural and identity taxation result in a situation where minorities (including gay, lesbian, and gender-nonconforming people) do not have time or energy left to do the work they need for promotion.

One of the particular problems Black workers face as they move up the occupational hierarchy is the pressure to "act white" in order to be viewed as professional and reduce the possibility of discrimination. This pressure is quite real. One study found that White people, and to a lesser extent Black people, view Black workers who adapt their behavior to mirror the dominant group as more professional than those who behave in ways associated with being Black. The dominance of White people at upper levels of management gives them considerable power to define the workplace culture and appropriate norms (McCluney et al., 2021).

Hispanic people face a somewhat different set of pressures that prevent them from moving up the occupational hierarchy. Interviews with agricultural employers suggested that they use monolithic cultural reasons to justify hiring Hispanics into low-level manual agricultural jobs. They view Hispanics as appropriate for these kinds of jobs because they believe they are more willing to do hard physical labor than are White workers who, they say, seldom even apply for such jobs. Moreover, employers rationalize low pay and poor conditions by saying that the workers are better off than they would be in their family's country of origin. A steady flow of immigrants and use of race-neutral rhetoric on the part of employers ensure a low-wage ethnic working force, continued profit for White employers, and maintenance of a racialized division of labor (Maldonado, 2009).

Cultural and Symbolic Resources

In the United States, it is clear that being White makes many of the daily aspects of life easier, while being a member of a minority group often makes everyday living more problematic. Like women, racial and ethnic minorities have been subjected to a host of everyday indignities. These indignities are independent of class position. Language, which reflects cultural values, helps to undergird the system of social inequality as it pertains to minorities, and yet because it is so much a part of our everyday lives, we seldom step back and look at it in any depth. The derogatory terms used to describe different ethnic and racial groups reveal the stigma against them. Sometimes terms referring to these groups are used to describe some disliked or despised behavior (e.g., "an Indian giver," to "Jew down," to "gyp"). Language is a powerful tool for shaping the attitudes toward and general beliefs about groups, and what makes it exceptionally influential is that it is part of the matrix of everyday life and derogatory terms are often used without intentional thought being given to their implications.

Embedded in this language are stereotypes of different racial and ethnic groups. Jokes and humor aimed at labeling and denigrating minorities have a long history in the United States, going back to the early seventeenth century when the first slaves arrived in the country. As new ethnic groups emigrated to the country, jokes that reinforced negative images of them increased. Such jokes helped to justify the stereotypes and poor treatment many immigrant groups received (Hughes, 2003).

In the absence of real knowledge about specific groups, stereotypes provide a means by which individuals develop ideas about the characteristics of other groups. Many Americans, for example,

BOX 10.1 INDIAN RESERVATIONS AND INEQUALITY

In the 1830s, the Supreme Court ruled that native tribes were sovereign nations and had the right to their own government. Today the United States recognizes 574 tribal groups and there are 326 reservations. Reservations are land set aside for tribes, but not all tribes have reservations and some have more than one. Reservation lands were won in court battles after Native lands were taken by force from tribes. Reservations are generally inferior land to the land that the tribes lost.

Land ownership is a complicated matter on reservations. Some of the land is "owned" by individual tribe members but is held in trust by the federal government. This is referred to as "trust land." There is also land that is simply owned by individuals (called "fee land"). Trust land has implications for inequality because it can only be owned by tribal members or by the tribe as a whole. This preserves the land as tribal land. The people who own the land are allowed to will it to their own family members (as long as they are tribe members) or sell it to someone in the tribe. This type of arrangement makes the land exempt from property tax but it is problematic because families cannot sell it on the free market and thus cannot build equity (which is a primary way many other American families increase their wealth).

Because reservations are both within the United States and outside of it, special rules apply. The US government provides health care through the Indian Health Service and American Indians can receive welfare benefits. Life on reservations can be hard because there are high rates of unemployment. The Indian Health Service is underfunded and cannot provide adequate care for all the people who need it, thus rates of diseases and mental health issues are high.

have not had personal or extended contact with Native Americans. Yet many schools and professional sports teams have adopted names and mascots that are supposed to represent Native American qualities. There has been, however, substantial pushback to this in recent years. Both the Washington Redskins and the Cleveland Indians have announced changes to their names. At the time of this writing, however, the Atlanta Braves plan to retain their name and continue to use a tomahawk logo. These terms and images are important because they shape our ideas about the supposed distinctiveness of Native Americans (King & Springwood, 2001). They also damage the chances of accurately understanding the diversity and real qualities of Native Americans.

One reason for stereotypes is the lack of personal, concrete familiarity that individuals have with persons in other racial or ethnic groups. Lack of familiarity encourages the lumping together of unknown individuals. This happens early in life. Babies who are primarily exposed to people of one race tend to be able to individualize them, but simply view faces from other races as one category. Familiarity encourages images of variation and individuality, while unfamiliarity fosters images of sameness (Ferera et al., 2021).

BOX 10.2 CHURCH AND RACE

As described, contact between the races is limited in the United States. One of the places we see this is in churches. In a recent report, sociologist Michael Emerson (2020) found that only 16 percent of churches had memberships that were at least 20 percent racially diverse. While this is up from 6 percent in 1998, it indicates that the vast majority of Americans worship in segregated churches. Looking at the denominational level, Catholics and Evangelical Christians are the most likely to attend a multiracial parish, with mainline Protestants considerably less so. What do you think? Why are churches so segregated? What might be the impact?

The media, especially movies and television, have also perpetuated stereotypes of African Americans and other minorities. For example, African Americans have been portrayed as lazy, slow-thinking, and subservient, and American Indians as savage and hostile (Marger, 1997). By ignoring heterogeneity among the more than 500 American Indian tribes through its presentation of the generic Indian and suggesting that American Indians are relics of the Old West, the media have contributed to the distortion in White Americans' image of American Indians. A study found that over 95 percent of the first 200 images that appeared while doing Google and Bing searches for the terms "Native American" and "American Indian" were historical (Leavitt et al., 2015). One researcher points out that, while Americans generally recognize minstrel shows as being racist, children are actively socialized to "play Indian" (Robertson, 2015).

The images of Asian Americans are also contradictory and problematic. A recent study of Asian/Pacific Islander (API) characters in popular movies found that, not only were they portrayed less than their presence in the population, API women were sexualized, tired stereotypes were utilized, and a full quarter of API characters were killed during the film, generally by violent means (Yuen et al., 2021). At the same time, Asian Americans are often seen as the "model minority." This myth can cause pressure on individual Asian people when they are held to a higher standard than others. In fact, it appears that the stereotype of the model minority is so strong, Asians who are not highly successful experience negative outcomes. For example, while highly educated Asian Americans tend to earn more than similarly educated White people, those Asians with low levels of education tend to earn less than similar Whites, suggesting that the incongruity between the model minority myth and reality results in those individuals being seen as defective (Kim & Sakamoto, 2014). The model minority myth is also problematic as it implicitly denigrates other minorities by suggesting that their cultures are somehow inferior in relation to the "model."

There are many additional, subtle, taken-for-granted advantages that are attached to the status of being White. In their everyday experiences in school, Black undergraduates have typically been tokenized, stereotyped, and assumed to have gained college admission through affirmative action rather than through their own efforts. In 2019, 65 percent of Black respondents said that they had been treated with suspicion in the last year and 60 percent reported being treated as though they were not smart. The equivalent numbers for Hispanic respondents were 37 and 48; for Asian respondents 34 and 36; and for White respondents 25 and 26 (Pew Research Center, 2019a). Hispanics often have their citizenship questioned and are treated coldly (Rivera et al., 2010; Watkins et al., 2010). As described in Chapter 7, Asians report that they are often asked where they are from and that a truthful response such as "Ohio" does not suffice. In many cases, the question is not about where the person is from but is rather about the ethnic origins of the person's family. Frequent repetition of the question suggests to the person that they are seen as a foreigner and outsider (see "26 Questions Asians Have for White People" (Buzzfeed, 2015) for a humorous treatment of the topic).

One of the classic statements about everyday, taken-for-granted White privileges comes from Peggy McIntosh (2004). Among the 46 she lists are how being White allows her to do the following:

- freely choose a place that she wants and can afford to live in
- go shopping, feeling secure that she will not be harassed or followed
- be fairly sure that her voice will be heard even in a non-White group
- rely on her skin color to protect her from being seen as financially unreliable
- feel that her children will receive an education that acknowledges the contributions of her race and in which teachers treat her children fairly

- talk with her mouth full and not have people put this down to her color
- not worry about acknowledging the views of non-White people
- consider a wide variety of options in her life without worrying about whether her race would be a factor in limiting them

Since its publication in the 1980s, McIntosh's list has proved extremely useful for uncovering the ways privilege invisibly manifests itself in the day-to-day experience of many White people. Some academics and practitioners, however, argue that McIntosh's work should not be considered in isolation, as it insufficiently recognizes that Whiteness is socially constructed. It also fails to acknowledge intersectionality. We know, for example, that a poor White man from a rural area may not experience privilege in the same way that a rich urban White man might (Lensmire et al., 2013). Acknowledging privilege can make Whites feel that they are doing something good, but it does little to confront racism, particularly at the structural level (Cabrera, 2017). Another argument is that the term *White privilege* is a euphemism that obscures the dominance and violence that create and maintain it (Leonardo, 2004). At the same time, the White privilege list can be an important step in interrogating the advantages that come with being categorized as White.

Class, Color, and Race

Most people think of race as a biologically fixed category that cannot be affected by class. But as we saw earlier, races are socially constructed, and how one identifies with a given race and is placed in a racial category by others can depend on one's class position. Because of this, there is remarkable fluidity in racial identity. Saperstein and Penner (2012), for example, examined race and ethnicity data gathered between 1979 and 1998. Interviewers were asked to assign respondents a racial category based on observations at 19 different points in time. Respondents were also asked to identify their own racial category twice during the period.

Looking at the interviewer-assigned racial categories, it was found that over 20 percent of the sample changed races over the time period, some multiple times. While this fluidity was primarily between the White, Asian, and Hispanic categories, there was also movement into and out of the Black category. Similarly, self-identification (which was only measured in 1979 and 1998) changed over time. Importantly, both self- and interviewer-assigned racial and ethnic categorizations were strongly correlated with class markers including unemployment, welfare use, poverty, and incarceration. In other words, unemployment or welfare use resulted in a higher likelihood that a person would be considered Black.

Race and class forces collide in the phenomenon of colorism. Colorism is when "people attribute higher status and grant more power and wealth to one group, typically those designated as white, and believe that that is the right thing to do. Then for the same reasons, people attribute higher status and grant more power and wealth to people of one complexion, typically light skin, within the groups designated as non-white" (Hochschild & Weaver, 2007, p. 646). Colorism starts early; for example, African American adolescents with darker skin are more likely to be suspended than those who are lighter-skinned (Hannon et al., 2013). Interviews with dark-skinned Black women reveal that from the time they are children, they experience bullying, discrimination, and stereotyping that portrays them as aggressive (Hall, 2017). In adulthood, Black people with darker skin tend to have lower educations, incomes, and occupational statuses than those who have lighter skin (Monk, 2014). Colorism also appears to be related to how intelligent Black and Hispanic people are perceived to be by White people (Hannon, 2015).

Colorism is far more complex than simply discrimination against Black and Latino people with dark skin. For example, recent research suggests that colorism affects White Americans as well, with people with lighter skin being less likely to get arrested than those with darker skin. In this study, skin tone did not predict the likelihood of arrest for Black people, although Black people of all skin tones were at an increased risk of arrest compared to White people. The researchers speculate that this is because, in the location of their study, 95 percent of police officers were White. As described above, ingroup members tend to see outgroup members as homogenous, so when White police officers interact with Black citizens, they just see them as "Black" rather than making distinctions in skin tone. With their own ingroup, however, they see variation in skin tone and it impacts their decisions (Branigan et al., 2017). A second example of the complicated nature of colorism involves political candidates. Black voters tend to prefer Black female candidates who have dark skin and Afrocentric features over those with lighter skin and less Afrocentric looks. Researchers believe this is because they see these characteristics as signaling a connection with the Black community (Burge et al., 2020; Lemi & Brown, 2019).

Similar to racial and ethnic categorization, skin tone assessment appears to be affected by class and status markers. In one study, when respondents were prompted to believe that a Black person was well-educated, they later remembered the person as being lighter in skin tone than if they were prompted to think the person was not educated (Ben-Zeev et al., 2014).

The shading of one's skin is not only significant in the United States; throughout history, it has been socially important around the globe. In her international analysis of what she calls a "yearning for lightness," Evelyn Nakano Glenn (2008) found rising demand for skin lighteners in all parts of the world, including Southeast and East Asia, India, and many countries in Latin America and Africa. In the United States, skin color made a difference early in history. Slaves with lighter skins were treated better than those with darker skin or full African ancestry, later giving rise to groups, such as "blue vein societies," associations of more prosperous freed Black people whose blue veins could be seen because of their lighter skins. These organizations mirrored the "blue blood" societies among wealthy Whites. This continued past emancipation when some Black groups used either a **brown-bag** or a fine-tooth comb test to screen potential new members. Those whose skin was darker than a brown grocery bag were deemed ineligible as were those whose hair could not pass easily through a fine-tooth comb (Stalnaker-Shofner, 2020).

The fact that skin color and social class interact may make growing class discrepancies within minority communities and between Whites and other groups even more significant. Saperstein and Penner (2012) point out that the "whitening" of successful or well-educated people of color can contribute to inequality because it widens the chasm between groups. In other words, if successful people of color become White, the people who remain in the minority category will appear to be very different from Whites, hardening racial categories.

Colorism is important because of its relationship to inequality. Bonilla-Silva (2004) also believes that it is a central marker in a new racial system emerging in the United States. He argues that increased multiethnicity, immigration, and globalization are among the forces leading the United States into a three-tiered racial system with "Whites," "Honorary Whites," and "Collective Blacks." The category of "White" is expanding to include some light-skinned and highly assimilated Latinos. "Honorary Whites" include a variety of racial/ethnic groups that generally have been thought of as separate from "Whites" (e.g., Japanese Americans, Arab Americans, Asian Indians). The third category, labeled "Collective Black," includes not only African Americans, but newer, generally poorer East Asian immigrants, "dark-skinned and poor Latinos," and "reservation-bound Native Americans" (pp. 225–227). This suggested classification clearly shows the interaction of economic and racial/ethnic forces.

Theories of Racial and Ethnic Inequality

As is the case for sex and gender inequality, there have been a variety of attempts to explain racial inequality, ranging from biological to cultural and structural.

Biological Explanations for Racial Inequality

Attempts to anchor an adequate explanation for racial inequality in biology have been numerous and have also been widely criticized. Even if biological differences could be demonstrated, their relevance for social and economic inequality between the races would still be problematic, given the fact that many studies demonstrate that individual characteristics do not fully explain such inequality. The whole idea of racial differences in biology is also problematic based on its assumption that different races can be accurately, indisputably, and objectively identified. As we have seen, this is not the case.

Although biological explanations of racial and ethnic differences have largely been discredited, some scientists are still engaged in discussion about the link between genetics and race. Once the human genome was charted in 2000, it opened the door to research looking for a link between race and propensities for disease or criminality. While scientists claim their work to be race-neutral, social scientists have again pointed out that the empirical work that is being done relies on socially constructed categories of race. In other words, it assumes that "White" is a real category and attempts to find specific gene combinations linked to that category. This type of research also has the potential to mislead the public into false causational thinking. For example, it may appear that being Black causes a higher risk of cancer, but in reality, Black people are simply more likely to live near toxic waste dumps that cause cancer (Collins, 2015; Duster, 2015).

Like the debate over genetics, people sometimes argue for the existence of biological race by noting that racial groups have different rates of some diseases. For example, sickle cell anemia in the United States is more common among people with dark skin. It turns out that the reason has little to do with race but rather is linked to where people's ancestors came from. Scientists have learned that the mutation that causes sickle cell also helps to prevent malaria. This was greatly advantageous in areas of the world with high rates of malaria. While darker skin was common in most of these areas, the mutation was also found in regions where lighter-skinned people lived (for example, in Greece and Southern Italy). Conversely, some areas where darker-skinned people lived, such as Southern Africa, did not have high rates of the mutation because there was not a lot of malaria. Most of the slaves who were brought to the United States were from Western Africa where rates of the mutation were high (Fish, 2013).

Class-Based Explanations of Racial Inequality

One of the most controversial and prominent discussions on the intersection of race and class involves arguments about their relative effects on the life chances of individuals. Scholars differ on which they think is most important. Here we discuss theorists who think that class is the main driver of racial inequality. We start with the sophisticated class-based theories of race relations in the United States that were developed by Oliver C. Cox in the late 1940s.

Cox (1948, 1976) viewed race relations and inequality in the United States as a product of economic exploitation. Forcibly bringing slaves to the United States was essentially a way of getting labor so that White people could exploit the natural resources of the country. Racism as an ideology was not the root of exploitation; rather, it followed from it and was used to justify the economic exploitation of Black people. Racism, therefore, is a relatively recent phenomenon. Given its character and economic basis, "racial antagonism is essentially political-class conflict." Racial antagonism is used by employers to divide Black and White workers, and racial ghettos are maintained because they facilitate control over Blacks and perpetuate a self-defeating lifestyle. Black people may want to assimilate, but it is not in the interests of dominant Whites for them to do so.

What is attractive about Cox's arguments is that he intermingled elements of racism, colonialism, class inequality, and capitalism in a comparative framework. Racial inequality is bound up with the development and expansion of European empires and the rise of capitalism and its labor needs. Trade is the lifeblood of international capitalism. The need to control potential markets and sources of raw materials strengthens the tendency of capitalism to colonize and exercise political control in the world economic system. Loans, raw materials, markets for manufactured goods, and imperialism each play a part in creating and fastening ties (chains) between dominant and subordinate nations in the worldwide capitalist system (Cox, 1959, 1964). Race prejudice is then used to justify imperialism.

Edna Bonacich (1980) attempted to integrate and synthesize many of the arguments in class-based theories of race inequality. She comments that employers look for cheap labor, and that often involves looking outside national boundaries. Pick up a piece of clothing from a well-known and expensive brand and notice where the item has been sewn. The labels frequently cite places such as Honduras and the Dominican Republic. Wages are lower in less-developed countries because of fewer regulations and a traditionally lower standard of living. Members of the domestic working class then see themselves as competing with cheap laborers in Third World countries and may (1) react with nationalist and racist fervor against such groups, or (2) see both themselves and other working-class groups from around the world as victims of capitalist development. Which of the two reactions is pursued by the domestic working class depends in part on the extent to which capitalists can control the colonized working class and manipulate the domestic working class, on how visible the experience of competition with outside cheap labor is in the domestic working class, and on how proletarianized this class is itself (Bonacich, 1980).

William Julius Wilson (1982) also argues the primacy of class over race in determining the life chances of Black people but he does not write from a Marxist perspective. He believes that, while political and economic changes in society have opened up more potential opportunities for Black people, these changes have also helped create urban joblessness. Black people have been particularly affected, for example, by trends that continue today but began decades ago: the shift from a manufacturing to a service economy, a broadening split between low-wage and high-wage labor markets, and by the movement of industries out of the central cities (Bonacich, 1980; W. J. Wilson, 2012).

Wilson does not argue that race is irrelevant today, but he thinks that its effect is mostly due to the continuing impact of historical racism. Thus, historical discrimination has a more significant impact on Blacks' lives today than does contemporary discrimination. He thinks that current economic and political forces are the most important for understanding events and behaviors within the Black community. Wilson reiterated his thesis in 2015, arguing that, while race remains important, globalization, technological innovation, and decreases in medium-skilled jobs are key factors in Black employment prospects (American Sociological Association, 2015).

Race-Based Explanations of Inequality

In sharp contrast to those who stress the primacy of economic-class factors in explaining the socio-economic condition of Black people, others emphasize the greater and, in some cases, increasing significance of race. They suggest that the gains that Black people have made relative to White people have been exaggerated or overestimated. For example, Black gains seem large when starting with a baseline of slavery, but appear much smaller when contemporary Black people are compared to Whites (Feagin & Elias, 2013; Shams, 2015). On a day-to-day basis for adults, race often overrides class in its importance. For example, a longitudinal study of residential migration among Black and White people suggests that racial factors are more important than wealth in explaining the slow rate of Black movement into heavily White neighborhoods (Crowder et al., 2006). In other words, movement into White neighborhoods is slowed much more by racist practices than it is by a lack of ability to pay for homes.

Wilson's thesis that class matters more than race was put to an empirical test by Douglas Massey and Nancy Denton (1993), who found that the residential segregation of Black people is key in limiting their mobility. While Wilson argued that middle-class Black people leave inner-city neighborhoods, Massey and Denton showed that Black people of all classes have little ability to move out of minority-majority neighborhoods. They find that other ethnic and racial groups have improved their fortunes by moving to more integrated neighborhoods where there are jobs, but Black people remain trapped in poor neighborhoods with little access to employment. Massey and Denton concede that economic factors do matter, but they find that race drives segregation and that segregation is a major factor in economic mobility.

Another challenge to theories that posit that class matters more than race comes from critical-race theorists. Critical-race theorists make a wide range of arguments but, in general, share the conviction that (1) while Whiteness is invisible to Whites, it is a position from which Whites view themselves as well as others; (2) it is a privilege of which Whites are unaware; and (3) society and cultural norms and institutions are organized in ways that privilege Whiteness (Frankenberg, 1997; Lucal, 1996). That is, the way institutions work and how laws are structured in society are rooted in racism. This means that racism is not only, or even primarily, a psychological property of the individual (Feagin, 2006). Critical-race theorists draw inspiration from the work of W.E.B. Du Bois who identified race as the central organizing principle of American society.

It should be clear that from a **critical-race perspective**, viewing racism as an individual phenomenon masks its structural nature and prevents its eradication. Moreover, since White people are generally unaware of how social arrangements benefit them above others, they do not see a reorganization of society as necessary. They assume its neutrality and argue for a colorblind perspective in which all are able to operate freely within the existing structure, thus leaving success solely up to the individual.

Defining racism in individualistic rather than structural terms allows people to ignore the institutional context within which individuals of different races are embedded, and to deflect attention from the issue of White privilege. It also enables White people to point to obviously racist others, failing to acknowledge their own role in recreating the system through seemingly "race neutral" decisions about living in segregated neighborhoods or attending private majority-White schools (Bonilla-Silva, 2021). Just as poverty is viewed by most as a problem of the poor, that is, *their* problem, the race problem is seen as a problem about minorities. The result is that most studies of racism examine the oppression and discrimination minorities encounter and do not include the privileges that dominant groups enjoy and that foster racial inequality. Additionally, traditional theories see racism as resulting from individual prejudice. The result is that remedies for racism emphasize enlightenment, education, and training to change the prejudiced individual rather than reorganizing the institutional structures that privilege the dominant group.

BOX 10.3 CRITICAL RACE THEORY AND SCHOOLS

One of the most divisive political topics to emerge in the last few years involves the teaching of critical race theory (CRT) in the nation's schools. Although very few elementary or high schools actually teach CRT (it's almost exclusively taught at the college level), conservatives have used the issue to mobilize their base. They argue that CRT makes White students feel guilty and that it divides the races. Opponents of this position point out the importance of teaching the truth of racism in our country's history. CRT also provides a much-needed platform for the voices and experiences of people of color, which are often marginalized. What do you think? How should issues of race be taught in the schools?

Eduardo Bonilla-Silva is a well-known critical-race theorist who has developed a sophisticated theory of race inequality (1997). He argues that racial stratification happens when a powerful group of people can benefit from the development of a racial order. Slavery is an obvious example of this—White people had a strong economic incentive to create a racial hierarchy to justify exploiting the labor of Africans. But Bonilla-Silva does not think that racism is simply rooted in the past: it is based in the material reality of today and it is inherent in the structures of our current institutions. White people today still benefit from keeping minority groups subordinate. This racial order gives them greater access to everything from jobs, to college admissions, to prestige. Bonilla-Silva focuses on the effects of "racial ideologies," which are the stories that the dominant group tells about the hierarchy to justify it and to make it appear natural. Racial ideology is not exactly the same as prejudice because prejudice exists in individual consciousness. Bonilla-Silva is clear that racial ideology is a product of cultural processes. He also notes that racial ideologies are not static; they sometimes have to change to take account of cultural shifts. This could happen because the composition of racial groups changes or because a minority group wages a large-scale campaign for change.

Bonilla-Silva (1997) argues that today Americans have developed a "color-blind" racial ideology to justify the racial order. The first strand of this ideology is the belief that there used to be racial inequality in the United States but that now there is a meritocracy and people earn what they have. The second strand says that any segregation of the racial groups today (such as residential segregation) is not a result of racism. Instead, it is just natural because "birds of a feather flock together." The third strand seeks to explain obvious racial differences that exist, such as the overrepresentation of Whites in high-paying jobs, by turning to culture ("Black people just don't want to work as hard"). Finally, colorblind racism deals with any claims of racism by minimizing what happened and blaming the victim ("That person is just being hypersensitive, it wasn't a big deal" or "They are just playing the race card").

Omi and Winant (2015), discussed at length above, are also critical-race theorists. They argue that race was built into America from its very founding. The Constitution itself demarcated non-Whites as less than Whites when they were not granted citizenship. As described above, in 1787, the Constitutional Convention passed the 3/5 compromise. This part of the Constitution counted Blacks as 3/5 of a person for the purposes of deciding representation in the Congress. Blacks could not vote, but this compromise gave the slave-holding states more power in the Congress since they could inflate their population figures without giving any power to slaves. Like other critical theorists, Omi and Winant see these examples as evidence that race is the primary area of struggle in America. Disparate racial projects struggle for dominance and, while those supported by Whites generally win, people of color can sometimes make progress.

What do critical race theorists think about the possibility of eradicating racism? Feagin and Elias (2013) believe that White people use their power to create race and to build it into our societal structures. As a result, they argue that it will be difficult, if not impossible, to overcome persistent racism in our country. Bonilla-Silva, and Omi and Winant, however, argue that social movements have the potential to effect change. Bonilla-Silva (2021) also points to "contradictions" where not all White people, due to class or gender or sexual orientation, benefit equally from White privilege. This could allow for alliances across racial lines and, ultimately, social change. At the same time, he cautions that the presence of such contradictions in no way guarantees change as even poor White people value and benefit from not being at the bottom of the racial hierarchy.

Summary

Historical and contemporary evidence documents the inequality that has existed between White people and various minority groups, including African Americans, American Indians, Asian

Americans, and Hispanic Americans. The exploitation of African Americans for their labor and American Indians and Mexican Americans for their land was justified by racist ideologies, stereotypes, and the force of law. Many minority groups have incomes, earnings, and occupational statuses that are lower than those of Whites, and their poverty rates are higher. Differences in family composition, educational levels, and labor-force participation do not fully account for these economic discrepancies. African Americans and other minorities also experience day-to-day microinequities. Biases in language, education, and the media constitute many of these, but there are some, such as those noted by McIntosh (2004), that occur in a variety of settings.

Several theories have been developed to explain racial and ethnic inequality, ranging from models that are based on biology, to those based on social class, and those based on race and racism. In general, the latter two are more sophisticated and focus on the centrality of differential power and economic domination in accounting for racial inequality. These theories and research evidence show how the variables discussed in the last several chapters–class, gender, and race—are intertwined and influence each other.

Critical Thinking

1. How do historical events continue to play a role in racial and ethnic inequality today? Can the effects of these events ever be erased? How?
2. Does the degree of darkness or shade of color play a role in the inequality between individuals that is independent of race? Explain and give examples.
3. Critical-race theory argues that racism is primarily structural in nature. What does this mean, and what kinds of examples can you provide to demonstrate this?
4. Why, and to whom, are Native American names and mascots for sports teams harmful? Who do they benefit? How?

Web Connections

Segregation is still widespread in the United States. To get an idea of how racial/ethnic groups are distributed within major US cities, go to www.nytimes.com/interactive/2015/07/08/us/census-race-map.html?_r=0.

Film Suggestions

Asian Americans (2020). Winner of a Peabody award, this five-hour documentary delves deeply into the history of Asians in America.

Driving While Black (2020). A documentary about how restrictions on travel have had a devastating impact on African Americans' ability to get ahead in the United States.

I Am Not Your Negro (2016). Written by James Baldwin and narrated by Samuel L. Jackson, this documentary looks at the history and present of life in America for Black people.

Sweetheart Dancers (2019). A story about a Two Spirit couple who want to participate in the traditional Native American Sweetheart Dance. A good look at part of Native American culture.

Latino Vote: Dispatches from the Battleground (2020). This documentary follows the effort to get out the Latino vote in the battleground states of Texas, Nevada, Pennsylvania, and Florida during the run-up to the 2020 election.

Immigration, Place, and Religion

In 1923, Ernest Burgess famously proposed his concentric zone theory of urban growth that used Chicago as a model for understanding how groups sort themselves in a city. In this model, each new group arriving in the city

> has the effect of a tidal wave inundating first the immigrant colonies, the ports of first entry, dislodging thousands of inhabitants who overflow into the next zone, and so on and on until the momentum of the wave has spent its force on the last urban zone. (Burgess, 1923, p. 88)

Burgess' model was quintessentially American, and in the end, quite optimistic. He describes a city where Russian Jews, Italians, Poles, Lithuanian Catholics, and Black people struggle to find their place, ultimately succeeding in creating a mosaic of social worlds within the city. There were many things that were wrong with Burgess' model, most notably the focus on assimilation and the failure to recognize the forces of racism at the heart of the sorting process, but it spurred the beginning of our thinking of how groups move through space and the effects of those movements on their futures and life chances. He was right in noting that this sorting of groups is at the heart of the American experience, and that it is inextricably linked with inequalities.

The first few chapters of this book outlined the types of resources—status, income, wealth, and power—that groups vie for, and the durable inequalities that derive from the categories in which people are placed. The focus in the chapters on gender, sexuality, and race was on how these inequalities affect particular groups. In this chapter, we talk about the importance of place in affecting the ability of groups, particularly those defined by immigration status and religion, to garner the resources necessary to thrive.

Burgess' model shows that since early in the history of the United States, immigration, place, and religion have been closely tied together. This is partly because ethnicity and religion often drive where people live. For example, many settlers in the early colonies were Puritans fleeing religious persecution in their home countries. Later waves of immigrants tended to congregate in ethnic enclaves where they shared a language, culture, and religion. Burgess alludes to this when he talks about groups of Russian Jews or Lithuanian Catholics living close together. Even today, immigrants often live in particular areas where churches are the center of community life.

Immigration and religion are also tied together because public acceptance of immigrant groups varies based on their religion. For example, during the nineteenth century, there was strong opposition to Catholics being allowed to come to the United States, and more recently, the Supreme Court upheld a travel ban that was originally framed as excluding Muslims. Religion may evoke such strong reactions because of its association with "Americanness." Every few years, Pew asks respondents what it means to be "truly American." While the percentage has decreased since 2016 in both parties, 46 percent of Republicans and 25 percent of Democrats cite "being

DOI: 10.4324/9781003184966-14

Christian." Majorities in both parties also list "speaking English" and "sharing US cultures and traditions" (Connaughton, 2021).

In this chapter, we look at how immigration, religion, and place affect inequality. While there are many areas of intersection, we also consider their impact separately, beginning with a description of the experiences of a number of immigrant groups in the United States and how they struggled to find a place. We then look at the relationship between religion and inequality, with a focus on how religion is sometimes used to justify inequalities. We conclude the chapter with a discussion of the key role of place in producing and reproducing inequalities.

Immigration in American History

Historically, the waves of immigrants who arrived in the United States from Europe during the nineteenth and early twentieth centuries were victims of religious, economic, and social discrimination. From the start of the country, 35 (over a third) of the Pilgrims who arrived on the *Mayflower* were part of a Puritan sect that was not accepted by the Church of England. In 1630, thousands more Puritans began fleeing England because they were being persecuted for their beliefs. Economic issues also drove immigration. For example, starting in 1845, a fungus destroyed much of Ireland's potato crop, causing widespread starvation and leading millions to emigrate to the United States. Later waves of immigrants included Germans, followed by people from southern and eastern Europe.

Immigration policy was the responsibility of individual states until the 1880s, when the US Supreme Court ruled that it was a federal matter. This new federal power combined with high levels of **nativist** sentiment led the United States to pass a very restrictive immigration policy in 1924. The law set up national quotas and created the first limits on immigration from Europe. Quotas were based on the number of foreign-born people from each country who were in the United States in 1880, ensuring that Irish, German, and British immigration levels were kept high and levels from Southern and Eastern Europe were low (Passel & Rohal, 2015). People from Asia and the Middle East were not able to come to the United States and the number of immigrants allowed from Africa was set very low.

By the 1960s, there were calls to change the national quota system. In 1965, a new immigration law was passed, dropping country-level quotas and prioritizing family reunification and skilled workers. Up to three-quarters of visas began going to families of people already in the United States and most of the rest went to skilled workers. Refugee visas were capped at 6 percent. Other key changes since 1965 include the creation of the categories of "diversity immigrants" and "Temporary Protected Status" for immigrants from countries in crisis (for example, due to a natural disaster or a civil war).

These changes have had a significant impact on the composition of the population of the United States. In 1970, about 5 percent of residents were foreign-born, mostly from Europe. Today the percentage of foreign-born is about 13.7, with most originating from Latin America and Asia (Budiman, 2020). As we will see in the snapshot of the history of Mexican and Asian immigrants below, US policy regarding who is allowed to immigrate has often centered on changes in the need for labor.

Mexican Immigrants

As we discussed in Chapter 10, Mexico was forced to cede large swaths of land to the United States after the conclusion of the Mexican American War in 1848. One of the provisions of the treaty allowed the Mexicans living in these areas to become US citizens. Although it has been contested many times, Mexicans have—at least officially—never been denied the possibility of citizenship. In fact, Mexican immigration was much less restricted than Asian immigration. We see this in the 1924 immigration law. It excluded Asians but did not place a quota on immigration from Mexico. The lack of a restriction was primarily because large employers wanted to hire Mexican workers at will (Molina, 2014).

Immigration from Mexico has waxed and waned, depending on the demand for labor and the laws in place at any given time. Generally, Mexican workers have been used and then dispensed with when no longer needed. A notable, but little known, example occurred during the Great Depression when approximately one million people of Mexican descent— 60 percent of them US citizens—were rounded up and sent to Mexico (Balderrama & Rodriguez, 2006). Policies changed again in 1942 when the United States needed laborers and started the Bracero Program to provide short-term contracts (generally 60–90 days) to Mexican workers. By the time the program was shut down in 1965, over 4.6 million contracts had been given to 2.5 million men, mostly to work in agribusiness (Mize, 2016). The Mexican government has also responded to its own labor needs by working with the US government to stem illegal migration. For example, in the 1950s, the United States and Mexican governments worked in concert to send many thousands of Mexicans back to Mexico under the program "Operation Wetback."

As has been the case with other racial/ethnic minorities, negative stereotypes of Mexican immigrants have been used over time to argue for limiting immigration or citizenship. For example, in the 1930s, there was a debate about "birthright citizenship." At the time, this kind of citizenship allowed people who were born on US soil and those who were born outside the country but whose fathers were citizens to obtain citizenship. In 1933, legislation was introduced that would allow American mothers to bestow their citizenship status on children born outside the country as well. The ensuing debate was about both race and gender. There was fear that the change would allow more non-Whites to become citizens, and many people were opposed to the idea of increasing the number of citizens of Mexican descent. These fears were fueled by stereotypes of Mexicans, including the inaccurate portrayal of Mexican women as having too many children and therefore needing charity (Molina, 2014).

Asian Immigrants

There were not many Asian people living in the United States prior to 1850 but their numbers began to increase as Chinese men immigrated to look for gold in California. Chinese people also began working in a number of industries, including garment production and agriculture, and they provided much of the labor that built the railroads (Office of the Historian, 2016). As Chinese people began to find success in the United States, however, they came to be seen as an economic, cultural, and religious threat. Images of Chinese people as opium-smoking, devious, and dangerous were summarized in the term "yellow peril," popular in the second half of the nineteenth century (Kawai, 2005).

The Chinese Exclusion Act, passed in 1882, forbade immigrants from China from coming to the United States. Originally set to expire after ten years, the law was renewed several times and was even extended to include Chinese people living in the newly annexed Hawaii and the Philippines from coming to the mainland. Other parts of the law made it illegal for legal residents to return to the United States if they left to visit China. The Exclusion Act was repealed in 1943 but it was not until 1952 that the United States created a quota for Asian immigrants. As described, important changes were made in US immigration laws in 1965 that weakened the old quota system and enabled the proportion of immigrants coming from Asia and Latin America to grow significantly.

Immigration Today

The United States is home to more immigrants than any other country in the world. In 2018, 44.8 million people living in the United States were foreign-born. While Mexico has long supplied the largest number of immigrants, China and India have recently surpassed it. Today the largest share of immigrants in the country are from Asia (Budiman, 2020).

Generally, greater social and economic inequality in a country encourages the poorer citizens to move to less unequal countries. Thus, the movement is often from less- to more-developed countries, such as the United States (Docquier & Rapoport, 2012). Many of these new immigrants have less education and fewer high-level skills than native citizens. In 2018, for example, 27 percent of immigrants to the United States had not completed high school, compared to 8 percent of the native-born. At the same time, our immigration policies also advantage highly educated and specially trained immigrants. About 32 percent of all immigrants, compared to 33 percent of the native-born, had a bachelor's degree or higher. It should be noted, however, that education varies by region of immigration, with immigrants from South Asia being particularly likely to have a higher degree (Budiman, 2020).

Immigrants are disproportionately represented in a number of key occupations. Healthcare is a good example with more than 2.6 million immigrant workers. A full 28 percent of physicians working today in the United States were born outside the country (Batalova, 2020). Immigrants also participate actively in creating businesses. About 55 percent of the billion-dollar start-ups in 2018 were founded by immigrants (Anderson, 2018).

Regarding average income, immigrants lag somewhat behind those born in the United States at every age. On average, the median income of an immigrant household in 2019 was $63,550 compared to $66,040 for native-born households (Batalova et al., 2021). Their concentration in certain kinds of jobs such as textiles, cooking, tailoring, and other service positions helps account for their lower earning. Additionally, as we saw in Chapter 3, immigrants are generally not eligible for any type of welfare, although green card holders (permanent legal residents) are eligible in some circumstances. Importantly, however, income rises with length of residence in the United States and the children of immigrants tend to do better in terms of education and income than do people whose families have been in the United States for three generations or more (The CAP Immigration Team & Nicholson, 2017).

Refugees arrive in the United States as a more disadvantaged group than other types of immigrants. A refugee is a person who has been displaced by their country of origin and applies for legal status while still outside the United States (this is different from asylum seekers who, at least up until the pandemic, applied to stay here once they have arrived). Prior to the pandemic, it took an average of two years for a refugee to be cleared to come here. It is not yet clear what long-term effect the pandemic will have.

In the past, the United States was the country that accepted the most refugees, but that has begun to change. In 2016, 85,000 refugees resettled here but President Trump decided to lower the cap and by his last full year in office, only 11,411 refugees were allowed to enter the country (Budiman, 2020; Finnegan, 2021). At the time of this writing, the Biden administration plans to increase the cap to 62,500 but is not on track to do so. The administration did admit about 60,000 Afghans after the Taliban reasserted control of the country in August of 2021. These immigrants, however, were not admitted as refugees but rather were given "humanitarian parole," which essentially allows them a short-term visa to be in the country.

Because refugees generally come from war-torn countries and have spent time in camps, they arrive here with little wealth. Unlike other immigrants, refugees are granted some financial help upon arrival and are fast-tracked for permanent residency. While their median income is lower than the native-born, average income rises strongly over time in the country and is about equivalent to the national average after ten years. Poverty levels end up being about one percentage point higher than the national average, even though employment rates are actually higher (Bier, 2019). At the same time, these statistics mask a great deal of variation. For example, during the 1970s, the United States admitted many Southeast Asian refugees fleeing the Vietnam War, the genocide committed by the Khmer Rouge Dynasty in Cambodia, and mass bombings in Laos. The United States did not yet have a resettlement program and the new arrivals were scattered around the country, oftentimes to impoverished communities. The volunteer agencies who stepped up to help were neither given clear instructions nor did they have the necessary funding to set up the refugees for success. Consequently, even today, these Southeast Asian immigrants lag behind other refugee groups in terms of education and income (SEARAC/AAAJ, 2020).

Settlement, Ethnic Enclaves, and Assimilation

As in the past, immigrant groups tend to settle in particular places in our country. The two major cities with the largest percentage of foreign-born residents are Miami, Florida (40.9 percent) and San Jose, California (38.6 percent). Immigrants tend to choose cities with many economic opportunities and a large creative class. Those cities with lower percentages of immigrants are disproportionately in the Rustbelt (Batalova et al., 2021). The government helps to create ethnic communities when it resettles people from a particular country into the same region. This happened, for example, when the United States accepted refugees from war-torn Somalia. Between 2000 and 2016, the vast majority were resettled in Minnesota (particularly in Minneapolis, Saint Paul, and Saint Cloud) and in Texas (in Houston, Dallas, and Fort Worth) (Rush, 2016).

As Burgess noted at the top of the chapter, when immigrants arrive in the United States, they sometimes settle near other people from their home countries. We generally call these areas "ethnic enclaves." Logan et al. (2002) define an enclave as a neighborhood where there is a high concentration of immigrants, where most residents are poor, and where there are not a lot of amenities. As immigrants find stable jobs, learn English, and make connections, they generally move out of enclaves to other neighborhoods that are better off and where there is a lower immigrant concentration. Ethnic enclaves were an important feature of urban areas in the nineteenth century, but many still exist today. Chinatowns are often held up as the prime example, but many other ethnic groups have enclaves. Perhaps you are familiar with Polish enclaves in Chicago or the famous Cuban enclave, Little Havana, in Miami. While European enclaves have declined in significance in some cities, new enclaves have emerged. For example, the *New York Times* reported that while a bustling German enclave in New York is now mostly historical memory, Staten Island has become home to many Sri Lankans and large numbers of Ghanaians live in the Bronx (Semple, 2013).

There is mixed evidence about the economic effect of ethnic enclaves, mainly because their impact varies by ethnic group and gender. One study, for example, found that living in an enclave appears to slow English language acquisition (and therefore job prospects) for Chinese and Mexican immigrants (Beckhusen et al., 2013). Another study found that Hispanic enclaves are not always a way station. While some residents do increase their income and move out, many end up staying. It is possible that those who stay are disproportionately undocumented and do not leave the enclave because they fear increased scrutiny of their status (Alba et al., 2014). At the same time, enclaves appear to have important social benefits because they provide immigrants with social networks and sources of advice on how to navigate their new country. Whether an enclave has a positive or negative impact on wages appears to vary depending on a wide range of group and individual factors including the size and average skill level of the enclave, and the nationality and gender of the person (Pedace & Rohn Kumar, 2014).

The manner and extent of adaptation of US immigrants have varied, and group assimilation has not followed the same paths or resulted in the same experiences. Part of the reason for the lack of smooth assimilation of some immigrant groups is that Americans have varying attitudes about immigrants from different regions of the world. Specifically, they hold more negative attitudes toward immigrants from Latin America, the Middle East, and Africa than they do about those from Europe or Asia (Passel & Rohal, 2015).

The fact that different groups of immigrants arrive with different histories, skills, and education interacts with factors in the United States. This includes what sort of welcome they receive as well as whether they arrive at times of economic boom or during a recession. This variation has resulted in "segmented assimilation," in which the experience of adaptation varies depending on the human capital of the immigrant group, the strength of its family structure, and the reception it receives in the host country (Portes & Rumbaut, 2005). Some groups, such as Chinese immigrants, form economic enclaves that develop into a source of support and income for new immigrants. Other groups arrive in the United States with fewer community resources on which to draw. Refugees can have a particularly hard time because they enter the country with higher rates of war trauma, posttraumatic stress disorder, and depression (Rasmussen et al., 2012). As described, they face economic challenges as well since, on average, they have less wealth and education than other immigrants and their social networks in the United States tend to be poorer (Capps & Newland, 2015).

The Impact of Immigration

Between 2016 and 2020, economic crises and the increased popularity of more conservative political ideologies led many countries—including the United States—to become more concerned and restrictive about their immigration policies. Even the traditionally more liberal Scandinavian countries embraced some anti-immigration arguments. The pull of these conservative ideologies in Europe appears to be waning, however, resulting in calls to return to higher levels of immigration (Temko, 2021). COVID-19 has complicated the situation because of border closures and restrictions on movement. Time will tell what Europeans decide to do with their immigration policy once the pandemic has fully lifted.

Here in the United States, there has been a great deal of discussion about the impact of immigration on native employment and wages. An extensive report by the National Academies of Sciences, Engineering, and Medicine found that, in the long run, immigrants do not reduce the wages or employment opportunities of native-born people (Blau & Mackie, 2017). This is partly because in communities with large numbers of immigrants, native workers tend to shift away from manual labor jobs toward higher-paying positions that require more education or better communication skills (Constant, 2014). New immigrants may, however, reduce employment opportunities for earlier generations of immigrants and they may also reduce the number of hours teenage workers are employed (Blau & Mackie, 2017). Additionally, there is evidence to suggest that increased Hispanic immigration may lead to interethnic competition for low-skill jobs in the agricultural, manufacturing, and construction sectors in some areas of the country (Shihadeh & Barranco, 2010).

While most of the conversation about economics and immigration focuses on its potential impact on low-skilled workers, it is also possible—although not common—for high-skilled immigrants to displace native workers. H-1B temporary visas allow companies to hire a foreign national for up to three years. Sometimes employers use these visas to hire low-wage workers for jobs when they cannot find enough native workers. Often, however, companies hire highly trained workers for technology jobs. The law says that employers are not allowed to replace any American workers, but a loophole allows them to do so if the job pays $60,000 a year or more and the foreign worker has at least a master's degree. Because the average pay of IT workers, particularly in the high-tech California Bay Area, is greater than $60,000, it makes fiscal sense to use H-1B foreign workers instead of American citizens. In the past, companies such as Disney and Southern California Edison have fired their American workers and replaced them with H-1B visa holders (Campbell, 2016). Complicating this picture, however, research finds that when H-1B visas are limited, many companies do not hire native workers (Peri et al., 2015). Multinationals instead offshore jobs, resulting in fewer employment opportunities in the United States (Glennon, 2020). Proponents of the H-1B visas also argue that the program has brought workers into areas where there are not enough native workers, boosting the economy. It has allowed companies to hire highly talented people from other countries, improving their output.

Various studies have tried to ascertain whether immigrants cost more than they bring into the economy. The findings suggest that, on average, first-generation immigrants cost more than they contribute in taxes (mainly because they tend to be low-earning and have dependents who require public education) but, by the second generation, they put more into the economy than they take out (Blau & Mackie, 2017). The Trump administration commissioned a report in 2017 to calculate the cost of refugees (not immigrants more generally). The Department of Health and Human Services found that, over the last ten years, refugees have put approximately $63 billion more into the economy than they have taken out. The report was never officially released (Hischenfeld Davis & Sengupta, 2017).

One rarely discussed economic advantage of immigration involves the Social Security system. Legal immigrants pay into the system but tend to take out less than do native workers. This is partly because immigrants who arrive in the United States later in their lives may not work long enough to qualify for payments, although they are required to pay into the system (Sevak & Schmidt, 2014). Many undocumented workers also pay social security. In 2016, they contributed an estimated $13 billion in payments into the system (and 3 billion dollars into Medicare) (N. Roberts, 2019). Some believe that a small number of undocumented workers (perhaps 700,000) have obtained false birth certificates and may be able to access Social Security when

Photo 11.1 An Immigration and Naturalization Service truck patrols the US border in Arizona. With increasing economic uncertainty, immigration issues have received more attention.
Source: © iStock.com/Phototreat.

they retire. The vast majority, however, will never be able to claim benefits. This is because they use false social security numbers that are not linked to their own names. Others pay their taxes through an Individual Tax Identification Number (ITIN) which is linked to their name but does not enable them to claim Social Security. Instead, all of that money will be added to the general trust, which is paid out to aging Americans (Goss et al., 2013).

Other surprising ways that immigration affects the US economy include the fact that, by working for low wages, immigrants allow some struggling businesses to survive, increasing the jobs available in the community (Peri, 2014; Waters et al., 2014). Immigrants have helped to revive dying rural towns. One study of 2,767 rural areas found that 68 percent had suffered population declines since 1990, with an average decrease of 24 percent. Had it not been for an influx of immigrants, these areas would have contracted by an average of 30 percent (Mathema et al., 2018). When there are immigrant workers in an industry, it may buffer native workers from economic downturns because the immigrant workers are generally let go first during a recession, essentially protecting the native workers' jobs (Dancygier & Walter, 2015). It also appears that when immigrants send money back home, it can have a positive impact on economic growth in their countries of origin. In fact, these remittances constitute about 4 percent of the GDP of low-income nations (Ratha, 2018).

Undocumented Immigration

Most immigrants in the United States come into the country legally, but there are also a substantial number of people who have either entered the country illegally or have overstayed visas. Estimates suggest that in 2019, there were about 11 million people living illegally in the country. Mexicans make up the largest share of these unauthorized immigrants (5.3 million or 48 percent) (Migration Policy Institute, 2021). Central Americans, however, make up a growing share of illegal entries. What is particularly notable about the new Central American immigrants is the disproportionate representation of children unaccompanied by their parents. The largest number of unaccompanied children caught crossing the border happened in 2014, when over 68,000 were taken into custody but the numbers spiked again in 2021 due to ongoing violence and severe economic hardship exacerbated by the pandemic. In February of 2021 alone, more than 9,400 unaccompanied minors from Central America were caught crossing the border (Dickerson, 2018; Romo, 2021).

Rates of illegal entry into the United States are affected by factors in both the United States and immigrants' country of origin. As described, many citizens from El Salvador, Guatemala, and Honduras have come here driven by violence and extreme poverty in their home countries. Gang violence is particularly problematic there. A recent study finds that some of this violence is gender-based, involving the rape of girls and women and violence against LGBTQ people (Dotson & Frydman, 2017). US policies also affect rates of illegal entry. For example, when the Bracero Program ended, the number of unauthorized immigrants from Mexico increased substantially because there were tight caps on other types of legal immigration (Massey & Pren, 2012). Initially, many of the people who entered illegally did so to work during the harvest season. They would then return home during the winter. In 1986, however, increased security was imposed at the border and, in response, many undocumented workers simply stayed in the United States rather than risk crossing back and forth as they had in the past (Massey et al., 2015).

When we talk about undocumented immigrants, we often think about people from Mexico and Central America. While these groups are the majority among the undocumented in terms of sheer numbers, it should be noted that Asians make up about 15 percent of the population. Most of these immigrants are from India, China, and the Philippines (Migration Policy Institute, 2021).

Unauthorized immigrants have higher poverty rates than those who have entered the country legally. They also have fewer ways to work themselves out of poverty. For example, it is much more difficult for people without documents to attend college. Nineteen states allow unauthorized immigrants to attend public colleges at in-state tuition rates. While Michigan as a state does not have this policy, the University of Michigan system made the decision to extend in-state tuition to undocumented students. Seven states allow them to receive state financial aid. Unauthorized immigrants, however, cannot receive federal financial aid and three states prohibit them outright from in-state tuition rates. An additional two states do not allow them to enroll in public universities at all (NCSL, 2021).

Employers are not allowed to hire people who do not have paperwork showing that they have a right to work in the country. If a person is hired but is later discovered to be here illegally, the employer is required to fire them. One problem is that an employer might fire a worker for some reason other than the fact that they are undocumented (for example, because they are pregnant or have complained about working conditions) but the employer claims that they were fired for being undocumented. Thus, even though undocumented workers theoretically have the same protections against discrimination as other workers, in practice, they cannot take advantage of those protections.

An area that has not been well addressed in terms of undocumented immigration and inequality involves "mixed status" families. In these 2.3 million families, some of the children are citizens and others are not (this can happen when older children were born outside the United States and the younger children were US-born). Mixed-status families can have some children with health insurance and some without, or some who can go to college and some who cannot afford to do so. This can cause painful inequalities within families as well as psychological distress for both family members who are documented as well as undocumented (Logan et al., 2021).

Undocumented Childhood Arrivals

Estimates suggest that there are about 3 million people in the United States today who were brought to this country illegally as children (Ortega et al., 2018). They are often called the "Dreamers" after a bill that was introduced in Congress in 2001 that would have provided them with a path to citizenship. While the bill passed the House in 2012, it failed to pass the Senate.

BOX 11.1 IMMIGRANT DETENTION

As described in Chapters 8 and 9, LGBTQ people face a host of stresses in daily life. These stresses are particularly acute, however, for those being held in immigration detention centers and prisons. Prior to 2015, transgender people were often housed with people of the gender they were assigned at birth, rather than the gender they were living. In 2015, ICE agreed to a set of reforms and began housing transgender people together. ICE contracted with a private prison in Colorado to provide this service starting in 2017, but the facility was later shut down due to medical negligence that resulted in the death of at least one person and the denial of basic medical care to many others (Fowler, 2020). Additionally, LGBT people experience extremely high rates of sexual violence in immigrant detention. In 2017, LGBT people were only 0.14 percent of the population in ICE detention but made up 12 percent of the victims of sexual assault (Gruberg, 2018). Gay, lesbian, and transgender people who are harassed in either immigration or correctional custody are sometimes put in solitary confinement to protect them. Many negative and sometimes permanent psychological effects are associated with this, including an increase in panic attacks, hallucinations, and sensitivity to external stimuli (Hananel, 2018).

In response, Obama used an executive order to create the Deferred Action for Childhood Arrivals (DACA) program. It allowed about 800,000 people (under the age of 31) who were brought illegally to the United States as children to receive two-year (renewable) temporary residency permits.

DACA provides certain limited rights, including work authorization but not eligibility for federal financial aid. In some states and in some colleges, however, DACA students are eligible for financial aid. DACA does not ensure that its recipients can receive in-state tuition even if they meet the residency requirements. This is the case in Georgia, for example, although at the time of this writing, the state legislature is considering a bill that would set tuition for DACA students at 100 to 110 percent of in-state tuition. The bill would also require public colleges to give priority to in-state non-DACA recipients (R. Williams, 2021). Other states, such as Ohio, allow DACA students to pay in-state tuition if they meet the other residency requirements.

In 2017, President Trump signed an executive order rescinding the DACA program. To date, however, the issue is tied up in the courts and current DACA recipients are allowed to renew their status, although no new applications are being accepted. In 2021, Senator Durbin introduced the Dream Act of 2021, which would provide a path to citizenship for some children who were brought into the country illegally. At the time of this writing, the bill is in committee. In some ways, it is surprising that Congress has been unable to pass this kind of legislation before because there is wide support (74 percent) among the public for allowing the Dreamers to stay in the country (Krogstad, 2020).

Public Opinion Toward Immigration

Over time in the United States, there has been a gradual trend of increasing support for immigration. For example, the Cato Institute (2021) found that 23 percent of Americans would like to see more immigration. This is up from 10 percent in the mid-1990s. Gallup asks respondents whether they think immigration is good or bad. In 2001, 62 percent said that it was good but, by June of 2021, the figure was 75. While there were some minor downticks over the period, in general, the trend was upward (Gallup, 2021a). Younger people, those with higher educations, and Democrats are more likely to have positive attitudes about immigration (Pew Research Center, 2018). There has been a lot of research about whether people who are at risk of being displaced from their job by immigrant workers are more likely to have negative attitudes toward immigration. It appears that the answer is no. Concern about immigration is often symbolic, representing people's fears about cultural or economic change in the nation as a whole (Hainmueller & Hopkins, 2014).

There is variability in attitudes toward immigration among both Hispanics and Asians. As in the general population, younger Hispanics and those who are Democrats express more favorable attitudes. Perhaps not surprisingly, foreign-born Hispanics tend to feel more positively about immigration than do those who are native-born (Stringer, 2018). Support for immigration is fairly high among Asian people but there are dramatic differences by country of origin. For example, when asked if there should be a path to citizenship for undocumented immigrants, a full 86 percent of the Hmong respondents agreed compared to only 44 percent of Chinese people (Ramakrishnan et al., 2016).

In recent years, the public has debated the pros and cons of illegal immigration. Interestingly, surveys show that Americans overestimate the percent of the immigrant population that is undocumented. In 2018, over half of Americans thought that most immigrants were here illegally when the actual number was one quarter (Pew Research Center, 2018). An innovative study of perceptions among White Americans found that they associate illegality with Mexican origin and with low-status jobs in the informal economy. When an immigrant is highly educated, they are perceived to be here legally. The study also found that respondents strongly associated ille-gality with violent crime, perhaps linked to former President Trump's rhetoric about immigrants as criminals (Flores & Schachter, 2018). Given these perceptions, it is perhaps surprising that there is not widespread agreement with other negative stereotypes of unauthorized immigrants. For example, 77 percent of Americans disagree with the idea that unauthorized immigrants take away jobs from others (Pew Research Center, 2020b).

Recent Immigration Policies

Although Americans tend to view immigration favorably, we do not have a coherent or functional system of laws that enable people to come to this country in a reasonable amount of time. At the time of this writing, the immigration system is in disarray; the pandemic has increased the already lengthy queue for people seeking to come to the United States. The Biden administra-tion has not yet provided a consistent vision for immigration, retaining a number of Trump-era restrictions on US entry. This is important because, as described, the US Supreme Court has held that the federal government, under the Supremacy Clause of the Constitution, has the power to regulate immigration. While states can make decisions tangentially related to immigration, they cannot regulate it.

The vagueness of what "tangentially related to immigration" means has led to a number of conflicts between localities/states and the federal government. For example, since the 1980s, sev-eral cities have declared themselves "sanctuary cities" and refuse to help federal efforts to deport immigrants. The Trump administration threatened legal and economic sanctions against these cities. At the same time, some legislation affecting immigrants at the state level has been allowed. For example, 16 states and DC now allow a person to get a driver's license if they have proof of identity (which can include a foreign passport) or can prove residency in the state. Applicants do not need to prove citizenship.

On his first day in office, Joe Biden sent the US Citizenship Act to Congress. This bill would provide a pathway to citizenship to many people currently in the country illegally, although not to those with criminal records. It is designed to catch up on the backlog of permanent residency applications. At the time of this writing, the bill is in the Immigration and Citizenship Committee of the House.

Much of our discussion above focused on the ethnicity of immigrants and how their nationality and the way in which they immigrated affected their reception in the country and their levels of success. But from the founding of the United States, immigration has been tied for many to the expression of religion. Ethnic enclaves are often also religious enclaves, and religious identifica-tion affects how successful a group is in gaining status, power, and wealth.

Religion and Inequality

Religion has been important across many cultures and time periods as a determinant of inequal-ity. Today, recent violent incidents have sensitized more Americans to the religious division of Islam, Judaism, and Christianity. At least in the short term, these incidents solidify the bounda-ries that separate these religious communities as some individuals "look down on" members of different religions. The religious differences are often viewed with ethnic overtones, suggesting that Muslims, Christians, and other religious groups are made up of different *kinds* of people, and confirming Weber's belief that status communities are perceived as groups of people who are *inherently* different. This situation can lead to the reinvigoration of religion as an important basis of status honor or dishonor, and a justification for denying religious groups access to economic and symbolic resources.

Religious Diversity in the United States

Prior to European settlement, the native peoples of North America had deep religious traditions and customs that shaped their way of life and how they viewed the world. Of course, native peoples were not one homogeneous group; their beliefs and practices varied by tribe. As described in Chapter 10, the early European settlers used the fact that Native Americans were not Christians to justify "othering" them as heathens. They could then rationalize removing them from their lands, committing violence against them, and forcibly removing their children to residential schools. Many of the native peoples were coerced or threatened into converting to Christianity by the missionaries.

There were several different religions among the early European settlers, but the largest group were Congregationalists, followed by Presbyterians and Anglicans. There were also small numbers of Catholics, Jews, and Mennonites (Davidson & Pyle, 2011). Historians disagree over when the first Muslim person arrived in North America. It may have been in 1527 when a Moroccan guide named Estevanico of Azamor arrived in Florida (The Pluralism Project, 2018). The first large wave of Muslims to come to the United States were brought as slaves from Africa. In fact, estimates suggest that 10–15 percent of the African slaves were Muslim (Public Broadcasting Service, 2014). During the 1800s, diversity grew as other denominations of Protestants gained members and American religions such as the Church of the Latter-day Saints were founded. Immigration also brought more Catholic and Jewish people into the country and the first group of free Muslim immigrants (mostly from the Eastern Mediterranean) arrived between 1880 and 1914 (Pipes & Durán, 2002).

During the early 1900s, the continuing immigration of Catholic and Jewish people made their numbers much more significant. The influx of these groups caused a backlash that led to the passage of the 1924 immigration bill, severely limiting immigration from non-Protestant areas of the world. As described, however, the 1965 immigration changes once again opened the door to countries all over the world and the numbers of Catholics (generally from Mexico and Central America), Muslims (primarily from the Middle East and Africa), and Jewish people (from Eastern Europe) began to increase.

In 2020, a survey about Americans' religious identification found that 70 percent identify as Christian with the largest groups being Evangelical Protestant, mainline Protestant, and Catholic. Muslim, Jewish, and Mormon people each represent only about 1 percent of the general population. A full 23 percent of the population say that they do not have a particular religion (PRRI, 2020). While there clearly is religious diversity in the United States, it is moderate compared to other countries. We are ranked 68th out of 232 countries in terms of religious diversity (Cooperman & Lipka, 2014).

Religion and the Legitimation of Inequality

French sociologist Emile Durkheim argued that religion is integrative for society because its beliefs and rituals take individuals out of their secular private lives and bring them together to form a community. It is out of the social gathering of individuals in a religious setting that feelings of a superior force or power outside individuals first arise. Thus, Durkheim argued that the worship of supernatural forces in religious rituals is really an adoration of the powers of society:

> In the divine, men realize to themselves the moral authority of society, the discipline beyond themselves to which they submit, which constrains their behavior even in spite of themselves, contradicts their impulses, rewards their compliance, and so renders them dependent and grateful for it. (Sahlins, 1968, pp. 96–97)

Given this description, it should come as no surprise that images of the supernatural world often mirror the social structure of society. Swanson (1964) showed concretely in his study of non-Western societies that a social hierarchy on Earth is reflected in a social hierarchy in the supernatural realm. For example, in societies in which older people occupied positions of importance, ancestors were a subject of worship, and in societies in which there was a great deal of social inequality, religion helped to legitimate the differences between the top and the bottom.

Particular branches of Christianity have also legitimated people's beliefs about inequality, for example, in their dictum that self-denial, continuous effort, and hard work result in success. This kind of spirit is what is embodied in Weber's concept of the "Protestant ethic." Hard work and religious beliefs were intermingled by many famous preachers early in US history. Cotton Mather, a charismatic Puritan preacher of the late seventeenth century, lectured that people's occupations were "callings" and not to be ignored. If individuals do not engage in their occupations, but rather remain idle (slothful), poverty will befall them. Riches are the result of industry, and poverty the result of individual laziness. Those who are poor should expect no help from others since it is their own behavior that has resulted in their dismal situation.

Advocates of Dutch Calvinism justified slavery by viewing Black people as sinners and considered slavery a just condition for their sins and inferiority in the eyes of God. In the United States prior to Emancipation, a special slave catechism was used in many churches to justify domination by masters, to encourage work, and to attribute lack of work to personal laziness. White pastors told Black people that God created the masters over them and that the Bible tells them that they must obey (Fishel & Quarles, 1967). There are additional elements in Christianity that have been used to support the continual subordination of women to men, including the biblical argument about the origins of woman out of man and the injunctions to obey one's husband in marriage. The impact of religion on beliefs about inequality has continued. Members of dominant religions, especially White people who espouse Evangelical Protestantism and Catholicism, are more likely than members of minority religions such as Judaism or those who are not religious to support the inequality status quo, believing that poverty is a result of individuals' flaws rather than a consequence of luck or structural defects (Zauzmer, 2017).

Civil religion is used to justify the "American way of life." It is a mixture of religious and political ideology in which the US social structure and culture are seen as favored by God. God and Americanism go hand in hand in this ideology because this is a nation "under God," and its institutions are sanctified by the Almighty. At civil ceremonies and during certain public occasions, such as the opening of Congress, presidential inaugurations, and the Pledge of Allegiance, it is suggested that God is the benefactor of the United States. The "American way" that is seen as blessed incorporates the values of individualism, freedom, capitalism, and equality of opportunity, which make up a core part of the ideology supporting inequality. Some televangelists conjoin Christianity and Americanism in a manner that makes them not only mutually supportive but almost indistinguishable. In this ideology, to attack Americanism becomes tantamount to committing a serious sin. Americanism is supposed to be accepted, not criticized nor undermined.

More recently, the "prosperity gospel," arising within American Evangelical and Pentecostal denominations post-1940 emphasizes a belief consonant with key American principles, including a personally engaged God who demonstrates individuals' salvation by conferring wealth and health. Consistent with capitalist views of consumerism and materialism, individual effort and hard work are rewarded with prosperity and ultimately salvation. A belief in the prosperity gospel is negatively associated with socioeconomic status, perhaps because wealthier individuals do not believe that divine intervention is necessary to achieve success (Schieman & Jung, 2012).

Karl Marx viewed religion under capitalism as having many of the effects on inequality just discussed. People are expected to put up with inequality; religion lulls them into a false sense of complacency. That is, it makes them *falsely conscious* of their real situation. It blinds them to the real causes of their predicament (i.e., class exploitation, not personal sin). In this way, socioeconomic inequality is seen as legitimate by those who blame only themselves or look forward to another life when conditions will be better for them.

Of course, Marx realized that historically, before capitalism, religion had been used to support the oppressed; even in our own time, religions have not always supported the status quo. Martin Luther King Jr and the Southern Christian Leadership Conference used religious ideas to try to improve conditions of Black people in the United States (Harris, 1999). Catholic bishops have fought on the side of the poor against many Latin American dictatorships (Hale, 2020). Faith has been central to many localized social movements in the United States such as tenant organizing in Chicago (Jeung, 2007). Pope Francis has been very vocal in speaking against inequality, tweeting on April 28, 2014, that "[I]nequality is the root of social evil," and in a speech in Bolivia in 2015, he stated: "Working for a just distribution of the fruits of the earth and human labor is not mere philanthropy. It is a moral obligation. For Christians, the responsibility is even greater: it is a commandment" (Huddleston, 2015). Despite these instances in which religion has opposed inequality, historically, it has been more closely associated with its legitimation and maintenance.

Religion and Inequality in Society

Sociologists have long studied the relationship between religion and wealth. Weber described how Protestant ethics paved the way for the emergence of capitalism (Weber, 1905). Other scholars have found significant differences in wealth, income, and education between religious groups. Interestingly, however, religion is generally not given much space in textbooks on inequality, possibly because some people see it as something that is chosen rather than as innate or even socially assigned (Davidson & Pyle, 2011). Most Americans, however, simply adopt the religion of their parents, suggesting that religion is more of an ascribed than an achieved status. For example, about 80 percent of people raised by two Protestant parents identify as Protestant themselves. The same is true for 62 percent of Catholics raised by two Catholic parents (Pew Research Center, 2016c).

At the end of the twentieth century, four religious groups were ranked high in terms of wealth, prestige, and power. These included Episcopalians, Unitarians, Presbyterians, and Jewish people (Davidson & Pyle, 2011). Research today suggests that Jewish people have the highest average incomes, followed by Hindus, Episcopalians, Presbyterians, and atheists/agnostics. Race, however, interacts with religion, with two of the poorest denominations being historically Black (National Baptist Convention and the Church of God in Christ) (Masci, 2016).

Many factors have been put forth to explain inequality between religious groups, the first involving history and inheritance. Mainline Protestants have held greater wealth, power, and prestige in the United States since its founding. For example, three denominations of Protestants (Anglicans, Congregationalists, and Presbyterians) made up only 9 percent of the population but were 95 percent of the signatories to the Declaration of Independence. These denominations, along with Episcopalians, maintained a disproportionate share of the wealth, power, and prestige throughout the 1800s (Davidson & Pyle, 2011). Wealth and power are passed down through families and this has advantaged today's mainline Protestants. A second reason for group differences is that religion indirectly influences wealth through particular ways of living. Conservative Protestants, for example, tend to emphasize early marriage, high fertility, and women staying out of the labor market, all of which have a negative impact on wealth attainment. Conservative Protestants also tend to discourage secular higher education, particularly for girls. In contrast, the Jewish faith places a large emphasis on education and Mormons are increasingly emphasizing higher education as well (Davidson & Pyle, 2011; Keister, 2011; Keister and Sherkat, 2014). A third reason for group differences involves race. Religious groups tend to be racially homogeneous and race, as we learned in Chapter 10, is a key determinant of access to resources (Davidson &

Pyle, 2011). Finally, beliefs matter. Conservative Protestants often believe that money belongs to God and are more likely to give to their churches than are other groups. They also are more likely to see money as evil and as an impediment to knowing God, thus they are less likely to see saving for retirement as important (Keister, 2008).

Looking outside the United States, we see interesting links between religion and inequality. For example, the more income inequality in a country, the greater the average level of religiosity. This correlation is strong, but the direction of causation has been difficult to establish. Research does show that in unequal societies, poor people tend to be religious for the comfort it provides in financial hardship. Rich people also tend to be religious in these countries because it enables them to legitimize their place in the economic hierarchy (Solt et al., 2011). This essentially supports Marx's argument about religion. At the same time, it also appears that people in religious countries prefer to give private charity than to support the poor through the state. This makes inequality appear higher in those countries because most measures of inequality do not include the value of charitable contributions, either as decreasing the income of the giver, or increasing that of the receiver (Elgin et al., 2013). Finally, it appears that some strong religious movements across the globe have resisted the centralization of the state, limiting its ability to redistribute wealth. They have also actively worked against attempts to organize the working class, making it more difficult for them to articulate their interests (Jordan, 2016).

Religion and Discrimination

Religious tension is not new in America. Since Colonial times, both Catholic and Jewish people have been seen as inherently different and inferior to Protestants. For example, anti-Catholic sentiment was central to the nativist movement in the nineteenth century. **Anti-Semitism** was particularly virulent after World War I. The Ku Klux Klan actively targeted Jewish people, and newspapers ran denigrating and stereotyped images of them. Harvard University went so far as to place a quota on Jewish admissions. Harvard's president then argued that the quota was in the Jewish students' best interest because if there were fewer of them, the other students would have less reason to be antisemitic (American Jewish Historical Society, 2018).

BOX 11.2 AMISH AND INEQUALITY

Amish people provide an interesting example of the overlap between immigration, place, and religion. Although they are Christians, they were persecuted for their beliefs in Europe and came to the United States almost two centuries ago hoping to be able to freely practice their religion. The Amish live in a traditional way in rural communities (mostly in Ohio and Pennsylvania). They do not use electricity or motor vehicles and they dress very conservatively. Religion and their church are deep at the heart of their communities.

Compared to mainstream society, the Amish have very little economic inequality. Because Amish children only attend school through the 8th grade, it decreases the possibility of occupational stratification. Occupational stratification is also limited because most of the Amish choose to farm their land. Additionally, the Amish are dedicated to taking care of each other. They do not accept government welfare, Social Security, or Medicare (although they do pay taxes) but their churches aid members who are having economic difficulty. Interestingly, there are several different orders of Amish and there is some level of inequality in income between them, with more liberal orders having a higher average income (Moledina et al., 2014). Today, more Amish are working in tourism-related industries, perhaps leading to greater economic inequality in the future (Kraybill & Nolt, 2004).

Photo 11.2 Stereotyping a group often results in all its members being thought of as the same and, therefore, deserving of the same treatment by dominant groups. The September 11, 2001, attacks on the Twin Towers of the World Trade Center in New York City provided an impetus to stereotyping and increased attacks on Muslims, as witnessed by this Minneapolis picketer on the 2010 anniversary of 9/11.
Source: © Peter Marshall/Alamy Stock Photo.

While discrimination against Catholics has decreased dramatically in the United States, Jewish people continue to be targets of harassment and discrimination for their faith. This may be because Catholics are Christians and are thus seen as less "other." FBI records show that, in raw numbers, Jewish people are the targets of the most religious hate crime in the United States with 683 reported incidents in 2020 alone (FBI, 2021b). The Antidefamation League collected data on 2024 antisemitic incidents in the same year (ADL, 2021). Muslims also experience discrimination in America with 110 hate crimes against them reported in 2020 (FBI, 2021b). The Pew Research Center asks respondents to rank how warmly they feel about various religious groups. Muslims are consistently ranked lower than other groups, along with atheists (Mohamed, 2021).

On a more positive note, Americans' feelings toward Muslims appear to have improved over time. Responses to the "feeling thermometer" have increased since 2014 (from 40 percent reporting "warm" feelings to 49 percent in 2019) (Pew Research Center, 2017b, 2019b). Non-Muslims' knowledge about Islam and their levels of contact with Muslim people are also increasing over time. As we see with public opinion toward other minorities, familiarity with a group is linked to more positive views (Pew Research Center, 2019b). At the same time, the media do not appear to be helping to foster positive attitudes toward Muslims. In a meta-analysis of studies looking at this topic, a number of key themes emerge. First, the amount and kind of media coverage changed after 9/11, becoming far more negative. Second, the media tends to focus its coverage of Muslims on terrorism, war, and immigration—all topics that make them seem threatening. Third, coverage of Muslim women focuses on the ways Islam is perceived to be oppressing them. Little room is given for actual Muslim voices in the coverage (Ahmed & Matthes, 2017).

Contrary to popular perception, Muslims are an extremely diverse group—they are of many ethnicities, races, and backgrounds. The types of Islam they practice are diverse as well. Data on Muslims are hard to come by because the US Census does not ask the religion of respondents. The Pew Foundation, however, conducted a large-scale study in 2017. They found that, while only about 42 percent of Muslims in the United States are native-born, a very high percentage (82) of all Muslims are citizens. About a quarter of US Muslims have families who have been in the United States for at least three generations—many of those are African Americans, but it should be noted that 40 percent of American Muslims identify themselves as White. Muslims tend to have about the same rate of college education as the non-Muslim population but have a higher rate of people in poverty (40 percent reported an annual income of less than $30,000 compared to 32 percent of the US population more generally). Muslims are about five percent more likely to be without a job than the general population (Pew Research Center, 2017a).

The experiences of immigrants, whether due to their race, ethnicity, mode of immigration, or religion demonstrate that as groups move into a society, they are sorted in particular places and enclaves. How important is the type of place groups are sorted into? What are the long-term and often generational impacts of the type of place we occupy? This last section will broadly address the relationship between place and inequality.

Place and Inequality

One of the surprises from the 2016 Presidential election was the strength of the rural vote, leading commentators to increasingly speak of the rural/urban divide within our electorate, signaling a change from earlier moments when what mattered most was whether a voter was from the North or the South. This divide was seen even more strongly in the 2020 election, perhaps due to divergent attitudes about pandemic prevention methods (Siegler, 2020). But the story is far more complicated than simply whether a voter is a rural or an urban resident. The polarization between the homogeneous, White rural communities and small towns, versus the diverse larger cities is a powerful manifestation of the result of the sorting of groups, as are the insecurities and fears about the outcomes of that sorting. Place matters in social phenomena such as voting, but the importance of place reaches far beyond simply population density or even regional differences such as North or South. Think for a moment of the United States as a large geographical grid on which different groups travel and reside in particular places. If you could see this grid from above, what would it look like? Social patterns of enclaves, segregation, inclusion, and exclusion would become evident, demonstrating that inequalities distribute themselves unevenly across space.

Perhaps the clearest and most consequential manifestation of spatial inequalities is residential segregation by income, race, and ethnicity. Income segregation has increased since 2000, mirroring the increase in income inequality (Reardon et al., 2018). *Where* people live is associated with their status lifestyles. The United States has neighborhood clusters, many of which are clearly and intentionally connected with specific groups occupying different status levels. The elegant mansions of the so-called blue blood estates neighborhoods in places such as Beverly Hills and Scarsdale hold those at the top of the status ladder, while many neighborhoods in West Philadelphia and Watts are disproportionately dwelling places of African American and single-parent families. That these distinct cultural pockets exist should not be surprising: If they have ample resources, the neighborhoods people choose to live in are those with residents whose political and cultural values are similar to their own (Bishop, 2009). As we can see in Figure 11.1, income groups are not spread evenly across the country, with concentrations of the affluent in the Northeast, California, Florida, and the Northwest.

We must not forget, however, that living in a particular community or neighborhood is not always the result of free choice. Resources and status help dictate where we live. Constraint also enters the picture when people try to keep "undesirables" out of their neighborhoods through mortgage-loan practices, building restrictions, and zoning procedures. Increasingly, we find new

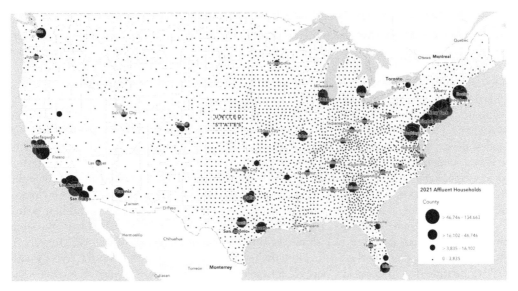

Figure 11.1 Affluent Neighborhoods, 2021.

Note: The "Affluent households" hategory includes those households in each county with a median income over $173,200 and a median net worth of $577,500.

Source: www.arcgis.com. Portions of this image include intellectual property of ESRI and its licensors and are used herein under license. Copyright © 2022. All rights reserved.

housing developments for the affluent that are surrounded by walls and maintained by armed guards at secured entrances. These communities are often planned and monitored by electronic surveillance devices, and constitute another, perhaps more blatant, form of segregated neighborhood.

Photo 11.3 This gated community in California is an example of the increasing economic segregation in the United States.

Source: © slobo/Getty Images.

As noted earlier in this text, Weber made a point of identifying exclusionary tactics as devices used by higher-status groups to keep their position intact. Privacy and security, and, most important, seclusion from others, mark these "walled communities." Turf wars are perpetrated not only by those at the bottom of the status system but also by those at its pinnacle. The control of physical space is one reflection of inequalities in our society.

It should come as no surprise, therefore, that the wealthy are the most segregated group, resulting in what Michael Sandel (2012) has referred to as the "skyboxification" of society. "At a time of rising inequality, the marketization of everything means that people of affluence and people of modest means lead increasingly separate lives" (p. 203). Sandel uses the apt analogy of skyboxes in sports stadiums to demonstrate how the wealthy have walled themselves off from the rest of society. Sports stadiums, most especially ballparks, were at one time the great equalizers where the wealthy and the poor together would enjoy watching their city's baseball team. That is no longer the case, as the poor sit in the "cheap seats" while the wealthy watch from above in their boxes.

Despite this income segregation, racial/ethnic diversity has certainly increased in many of our cities and towns, but as Figure 11.2 shows us, this diversity is unevenly distributed. Diversity is greatest on the coasts and in the South. Nonetheless, there remain patches across the country with little or no diversity. In Garfield County, Montana, there is a 3 percent chance that two people drawn at random will be from different racial or ethnic backgrounds. In Los Angeles County, California, that percentage rises to 87 percent. Not surprisingly, 91 percent of residents in Garfield County voted for Donald Trump in 2016, whereas 72 percent of those in Los Angeles County voted for Clinton, and many precincts in the city of Los Angeles reached levels of 94 percent support for Clinton (Bloch et al., 2018). This urban/rural disparity is not simply because cities are occupied by more minorities. As was especially true in the 2016 election, the more diverse the neighborhood, the more likely it was to vote Democratic (Florida, 2017). As we saw in Chapter 5, the dispersion of diversity, then, has important political consequences.

Fundamentally, while levels of *racial* segregation have declined slightly since their peak in the 1970s, they remain high and continue to have consequential effects. Many cities are

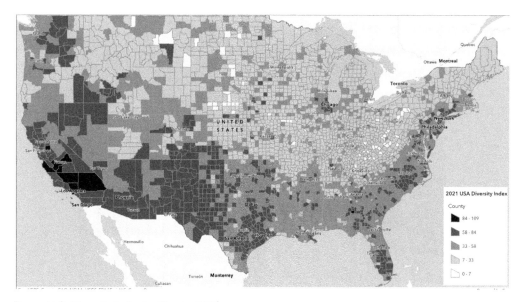

Figure 11.2 Diversity Index by County, 2021.

hypersegregated. Farrell (2008) comments, "The divide between the urban core and suburban ring remains a substantial if not defining component of segregation and racial distinctions between suburban communities are increasing" (p. 467). Segregation of Asian and Hispanic immigrants is present but less extreme than that of Blacks (Parisi et al., 2011).

Residential segregation itself is largely a result of inequality processes. Early in the twentieth century, Black people moved in large numbers from the South to the North, frequently recruited by employers who were fighting unions and who wished to use them as strikebreakers. This only intensified racist feelings and fear among Whites, leading to the creation of **restrictive covenants** in neighborhoods and **blockbusting** by real estate dealers who hoped to profit from the Black migration. Later, the movement of industry out of cities and increasingly poor opportunities for stable employment impoverished these areas. These developments led to the consequent concentration of Black people into isolated, overcrowded, poor neighborhoods, often called ghettos. Black writers in the 1940s began using this term to point out the structural and legal factors that forced Blacks into these neighborhoods and kept them there. They were comparing these processes with the Nazi ghettos (Duneier, 2017).

BOX 11.3 THE STIGMA OF PLACE: APPALACHIA

Neighborhoods and communities conjure up different perceptions and evaluations—stereotypes have been attributed to Californians, New Englanders, the Old South, the New South, Midwesterners, and Appalachians. Some of these regions, perhaps most notably Appalachia, are groups that are consistently ranked lower in markers of inequality such as income, wealth, and prestige.

As a strip in the eastern part of the United States, Appalachia covers parts of 13 states, bordered on the north by southern New York State; on the south by parts of Mississippi, Alabama, and Georgia; on the west by the eastern sections of Kentucky and Tennessee; and on the east by the western portions of Pennsylvania, Virginia, and the Carolinas. It includes all of West Virginia.

Recent census analyses indicate that, while there are variations within Appalachian subregions, wages lag behind the national average. Appalachian per capita income is only about 85 percent that of non-Appalachian regions (Pollard & Jacobsen, 2021). Part of the reason appears to be related to differences in the distribution of employment fields; the economic returns from mining and farming are significantly lower than those from services and manufacturing. Central Appalachia, where most of the mining occurs, also happens to be the poorest segment of Appalachia (Pollard & Jacobsen, 2021). At the same time, many counties in Appalachia are more economically diversified than the United States average and there is an effort by youth to stay in the region (Appalachian Regional Commission, 2014; Semuels, 2015).

Appalachia is often viewed as a region with different values from the mainstream. Individualism, a love of and dependence on family and an attachment to home, a belief in personal liberty and independence, fatalism and resignation, a belief in the essential equality of all individuals, a disdain for and suspicion of formal education, and the centrality of personal religion all have been characteristics frequently associated with Appalachians (e.g., Batteau, 1984; Erikson, 1976), despite the great variety in the region.

The mountain people frequently have been portrayed as being physically, socially, and culturally isolated from the outside world, and conversely, as having close relationships among themselves, especially within families. These subcultural characteristics have often been interpreted as the principal causes for the unusually high rates of poverty found in Appalachia. This constitutes a form of victim blaming, however, because evidence suggests that it has not been subcultural values or isolation as much as the nature of the region's ties to the outside that have exacerbated and perpetuated the high poverty rate. In sum, what exists in Appalachia is an interesting confluence of economic and status factors that must be understood within their historical context. Most importantly, our traditional image of Appalachians, while not consistent with much empirical evidence, has encouraged us to label Appalachians as a separate status group with low prestige.

Can you think of other regions that have been stigmatized?

Fewer neighborhoods since the 1990s are entirely African American, but they remain majority-minority neighborhoods due to the in-migration of low-income Hispanics. When comparing levels of segregation of *minority* urban populations from majority White, levels of segregation have only declined about four percentage points, and this segregation continues to have a negative impact on residents, particularly as it is combined with income segregation (Jargowsky, 2018). As Massey and Denton indicated in their classic study *American Apartheid* (1993), the effects of racial segregation are magnified by class segregation. Because levels of poverty are higher within Black and Hispanic communities, segregation by race and ethnicity results in the concentration of poverty. While there have been improvements, "to the extent that reductions in racial segregation have played out in large central cities, the benefits of these reductions may be limited if they occurred within fiscally strapped central cities or within aging, deteriorating suburbs" (Jargowsky, 2018, p. 22).

The current extreme racial segregation of Black people is not one of choice; in contrast to Whites, most Black people prefer a decidedly mixed neighborhood (Krysan et al., 2009). Rather, it has been the actions of government, real estate agencies, banks, and the construction industry that have shaped and maintained segregation through their loan and mortgage policies, gatekeeping of neighborhoods, and construction requirements. Sometimes the style of discrimination is soft and nuanced, as found in these comments by real estate agents who guide Whites away from certain areas:

> Black people do live around here, but it has not gotten bad yet; [or] "That area is full of Hispanics and blacks that don't know how to keep clean"; or [This area] is very mixed. You probably wouldn't like it because of the income you and your husband make. I don't want to sound prejudiced. (Farley & Squires, 2005, p. 36)

What is important about such segregation is that it means that the tools and avenues needed to succeed are largely out of reach of isolated minorities; access to decent education, health care, and employment is severely limited. The possibility of investing in a desirable home that will increase in value over time, laying a foundation for future wealth, is also almost nonexistent. These conditions perpetuate the low socioeconomic position of residents and freeze the positions of those middle-class persons who live there. As a structural fact, these conditions are beyond the power of any person to change (Farley & Squires, 2005; Massey & Denton, 1993).

Why does segregation matter? As we discussed in Chapter 7, the neighborhood someone grows up in, regardless of their individual characteristics, has a major impact on their future success in school, their income, their health, and the life chances of their children. For example, as the poverty level of a neighborhood increases, regardless of child and family characteristics, children's educational achievement worsens. This happens because, "as an important developmental context, neighborhoods provide social and institutional resources that vary in their levels of availability and quality" (Morrissey & Vinopal, 2018, p. 193).

Neighborhood disadvantages are sustained and reproduced across generations. Pointing to the persistence of poverty within families, "two-thirds of African Americans who were raised in the poorest 25 percent of American neighborhoods are raising their own children in similarly disadvantaged neighborhoods" (Iceland et al., 2013, p. 117). This lack of mobility guarantees that many of the ill effects faced by the parents will be felt as well by their children.

One of the central reasons for immobility is that those raised in poor neighborhoods, controlling for other factors including education, family background and structure, and race, will earn substantially less over their lifetimes than those raised in wealthier neighborhoods. Incredibly, in 2015, the lifetime income differential for those born in a bottom-quartile neighborhood compared with those born in a top-quartile neighborhood was $910,000 (Rothwell & Massey, 2015). This difference is mostly due to variances in school quality.

As we will discuss in Chapter 12, poor neighborhoods adversely affect health and well-being. Living there increases residents' likelihood of developing hypertension, obesity, diabetes, and depression (Diez Roux & Mair, 2010). These effects might be due to the lack of healthy food options in poor urban neighborhoods, the isolation felt in poor rural neighborhoods, or proximity to environmentally toxic areas (Burton et al., 2013).

Finally, both economic and racial segregation in a city are costly not only for the individuals living in segregated neighborhoods, but for all residents of the region. A study of Chicago from the years 1990 to 2000 found that

> higher levels of economic segregation are associated with lower incomes, particularly for Black residents. Further, higher levels of racial segregation are associated with lower incomes for Blacks, lower educational attainment for Whites and Blacks, and lower levels of safety for all area residents. (Acs et al., 2017, p. 4)

On a broader scale, not only do neighborhoods and communities affect our life chances, but so do regions. One important recent finding about social mobility is that there are strong variations by region of the country. For example, there is comparatively low mobility in the Southeast region and high mobility in the Mountain West and the rural Midwest. The researchers use two cities to illustrate this regional difference. In Charlotte, North Carolina, the chances of a child from the lowest quintile of the income distribution making it to the top quintile is 4.4 percent. The equivalent number in San Jose, California, is 12.9 percent. The researchers find five features that distinguish high from low mobility areas. High mobility areas tend to have less income inequality, less residential segregation, more stable families, better schools, and stronger social capital (Chetty et al., 2014). As groups are sorted into particular places based on characteristics including national origin and religion, inequalities are maintained and reproduced.

Summary

In this chapter, we looked at three areas that are very much linked to inequality: immigration, religion, and place. Though seemingly unconnected, the experiences of immigrants represent dynamic intersectional processes that play out in the spaces they occupy. Place matters as groups are sorted and sort themselves by race, ethnicity, gender, sexuality, and religion. As Burgess suggested back in 1923, as groups create enclaves, they create social worlds that are impacted by the structural factors affecting the society as a whole, including how we distribute material, symbolic, and cultural resources. These social worlds provide comfort and sustenance, but they are also the targets of discrimination and exclusion.

Critical Thinking

1. Think about where you live. How does your neighborhood affect your perception of others? How has your neighborhood either helped you be more successful in school, or perhaps made school more difficult?
2. How have our changing definitions of what it means to be an "American" affected our treatment of immigrant groups?
3. How do religious groups affect the growth and stability of cities and towns? Think about your city and the number and diversity of churches, temples, and religious community centers. What role do these play in the health of the city?

Web Connections

The Immigration History Center at the University of Minnesota has a lot of online resources, including maps of ethnic enclaves and immigrant stories. Check out their website at https://cla.umn.edu/ihrc/research.

Film Suggestions

Bisbee '17 (2018). Using a compelling mix of fictional (recreations) and nonfictional (interviews with relatives) elements, this film explores a massive deportation of Mexican and German striking miners from Bisbee, Arizona, in 1917. They were taken in cattle cars and dumped in the New Mexican desert.

American Muslim (2019). A documentary following the daily life of a diverse group of Muslims in New York City.

Chinatown Rising (2019). Explores Chinatowns as ethnic enclaves and as places of resistance.

I Was Born in Mexico But (2013). A creative interview-based film about a young woman who was born in Mexico and brought here illegally by her parents when she was three years old. It was not until she was a teenager that she found out her citizenship status.

Targeting El Paso (2020). A documentary that looks at how El Paso became ground zero for Trump administration's immigration policies. It also covers the mass shooting at a Walmart by a White supremacist.

PART 4

Consequences of Social Inequality

12 Inequality, Health, and the Environment

In Part 1 of this book, we looked at some of the resources that are unequally divided in our society. These included income, wealth, political power, and status. Then we turned to look at the causes of inequality and we conducted an examination of the categories—such as gender and immigrant status—that help to determine how resources are allocated. In this section of the book, we look at the consequences of inequality. We focus on health and crime because these are areas where inequality exerts particularly strong effects. We recognize, however, that it is overly simplistic to say that health or crime is a consequence of existing inequalities. It is the reverse as well, with each having the potential to cause inequality. This operates at an individual level when, for example, a sick person is forced to take time off work, jeopardizing future promotions. It also operates at a societal level as when the criminal justice system perpetuates racial inequalities.

While we have discussed intersectionality at multiple points throughout this text, we have not yet presented a lot of examples because we thought it was important to consider each category of stratification on its own. Now, however, we focus on some of the complicated ways those categories interact in terms of health and crime.

Physical Health

There is nothing more basic to life than physical health, and it is evident that individuals rate their own health status differently, depending on their race, gender, and income as well as the intersections between those categories. As we see in Figure 12.1, individuals who are poor are much more likely than nonpoor people to consider their health as below average. Similarly, a slightly greater percentage of women than men classify their health in that way. In terms of race and ethnicity, Native Americans as well as Black and Hispanic people, are more likely than White and Asian people to rate their own health as only fair or poor. An intersectional analysis, however, shows a much more complicated picture. For example, while women report having worse health than men, the gender gap is greater for Black and Hispanic people than for Whites. Similarly, we know that income is positively associated with self-assessed health, but a deeper analysis shows that this is not the case for Black women (Brown et al., 2016). One final example involves nativity. Foreign-born Black and White people report better health than their native-born counterparts. This relationship is reversed, however, in the case of Asian and Hispanic people (Hummer & Gutin, 2018).

Looking more closely at the gender gap in health, women tend to live longer than men but suffer from more illnesses, some of which, such as arthritis, are related to their longer lifetimes (Read & Gorman, 2010). Women have higher rates of disability, of acute conditions such as respiratory and digestive problems and infections, as well as higher rates of chronic conditions. Women over the age of 65 are more likely than men of the same age to report difficulty in their daily activities. Among chronic conditions, the rates for *nonfatal* varieties are especially higher for women. These include various digestive problems, anemias, osteoporosis, arthritis, migraine

DOI: 10.4324/9781003184966-16

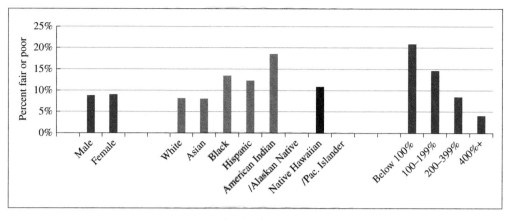

Figure 12.1 Percent of Respondents Assessing Health Status as Fair or Poor, by Sex, Race, Ethnicity, and Poverty Status, 2018.

Source: National Institute of Health (2021). Table 16, https://www.ncbi.nlm.nih.gov/books/NBK569311/table/ch3.tab16/

headaches, urinary infections, and varicose veins. The rates for fatal chronic conditions, such as heart disease, are higher for men (AARP, 2009; Federal Interagency Forum on Aging-Related Statistics, 2012). Looking intersectionally, however, we see that not all women have worse health than men. Aside from racial/ethnic differences, we also see that lesbians not only report better health than women of any other sexual orientation but also better than the reported health of straight, gay, and bisexual men (Gorman et al., 2015).

Social Context and Physical Health

Why are there group differences in health outcomes? While it is tempting to focus on individual behaviors or risk factors, it is important to acknowledge that the social and economic *context* in which people live has a causal effect on their health that is independent of the effects of the *personal* status of the individuals. For example, neighborhoods that are characterized by physical deterioration, environmental problems, lack of access to medical care and healthy food, and social disorder, along with the fear that they create, play a significant role in the poorer mental and physical health statuses found among their residents (Galster, 2012). Further evidence of the impact of neighborhood conditions on health comes from a social experiment that randomly selected people living in public housing to receive a voucher allowing them to move to a wealthier neighborhood. Ten years later, the researchers found that the group who moved had lower rates of obesity and diabetes than the group who had remained in their original location (Ludwig et al., 2011).

Like neighborhoods, the wider community also affects health. For example, regions with lots of jobs in mining, quarrying, oil and gas tend to have lower average life expectancy than do communities with other kinds of jobs. Not surprisingly, people who live in communities with more primary health care services live longer than do those who live with limited services. High population density has deleterious effects on individuals' health, but living in a place where the population is growing has a positive impact. It should also be noted that residents of communities with high concentrations of immigrants tend to have better health. This may be because of higher levels of cohesion or more community support for healthy behavior (Dobis et al., 2020).

While there is solid evidence that social and economic conditions explain a large part of group differences in health, people often have trouble understanding this argument when it comes to race/ethnicity. Even scientific researchers become confused. When they examine whether there are racial/ethnic differences in various health markers, they will often find them. They may then see race as "causing" the disparity, although it is usually the different social and economic conditions under which the groups live that are responsible (Collins, 2015; Fujimura, 2015). For example, as we discussed in Chapter 2, racial/ethnic minorities tend to have lower average levels of income and wealth than do White people. This has a negative impact on their health. Similarly, discriminatory housing policies have forced minorities, particularly Black Americans, to disproportionately live in neighborhoods marked by insufficient social infrastructure and instability, again having negative repercussions on health.

Do poverty and neighborhood fully explain the health disparities between the racial/ethnic groups? Some studies find that the answer is yes. For example, although Black people have higher rates of hypertension and diabetes than White people, Black and White men living in the same neighborhood in Baltimore had similar rates (Thorpe et al., 2015). At the same time, other studies find that class and neighborhood do not completely explain health disparities, particularly when it comes to differences between Black people and other groups. This suggests there is another factor at work—and that factor is likely racial discrimination and microaggressions. Being rich or living in a well-resourced neighborhood is not a protection from racism. In fact, well-off people of color frequently have to spend a great deal of time in majority-White environments, increasing their exposure to discrimination and minority stress. This kind of stress leads to deleterious health outcomes (Smith, 2021; Turner et al., 2017).

Like African Americans, Hispanic immigrants have high average levels of poverty and live in segregated areas, yet their health tends to be better than that of the native born (although they report it to be worse). As described, there are some health benefits to living in ethnic enclaves—where immigrants are more likely to reside than are the native born. A second possible reason for the native/foreign-born health disparity involves the length of exposure to negative health conditions and racism in the US native-born people may simply suffer more due to longer exposure (Viruell-Fuentes, 2007; Viruell-Fuentes et al., 2012). It will be important to track immigrant health over the next few years because immigration policy has changed over time and that may affect health. In the past, immigrants were generally resettled in large urban areas, and many lived in ethnic enclaves. Today, however, increasing numbers of immigrants are being resettled to areas with few others from their home countries (Viruell-Fuentes et al., 2012).

Individual Factors in Physical Health

Of course, health outcomes are not simply a function of social context; individual-level factors also play a role. As described, low socioeconomic status contributes to earlier mortality and probability of sickness. This is partly because poor people receive less preventive care. Poor people are also concentrated in dangerous jobs and they are more likely to do shift work, which has been linked to a host of negative health outcomes, including diabetes, heart disease, depression, and cancer (Brown et al., 2020; Kecklund & Axelsson, 2016). The number of work hours affects health as well. People who have to work many hours (often at multiple jobs) disproportionately suffer ill health (Bannai & Tamakoshi, 2014).

Many studies find that the link between socioeconomic status and morbidity is causal, and that lower status is more likely to lead to sickness than sickness is to lead to lower status (National Center for Health Statistics, 2010; Warren, 2009). At the same time, causality does go both ways. One study found that severe health crises significantly drain the economic resources of couples, particularly as they get close to retirement age. The wealth of African American couples was especially hard hit by health crises (Thompson & Conley, 2016).

Some influences on health are behavioral. For example, smoking, poor diet, lack of exercise, and obesity are all linked to health problems. Research suggests that they are also more prevalent among lower socioeconomic groups. A variety of explanations, all of which derive from a low-status position, have been given for the higher rates of these unhealthy behaviors. First, poverty is associated with higher stress, leading to unhealthy habits as a means of coping. In a powerful book about the experience of being poor, Linda Tirado (2014) argues that poor people disproportionately smoke because it is an accessible way to feel good in a very stressful life. Well-off people have the option of using other means to feel good, such as massages or vacations, but these are simply out of reach for the poor. Additionally, low-income people are sometimes targeted by companies that market unhealthy products. For example, for at least 40 years, tobacco companies targeted advertising to low-income consumers, particularly African Americans and women of all races (Brown-Johnson et al., 2014).

Lifestyle decisions are not the only individual-level route through which poverty influences health. We also know that compared to the nonpoor, lower-status individuals generally experience more traumatic events in their lives that affect their health and are more likely to be limited in their daily activities because of **chronic health problems** (Hatch & Dohrenwend, 2007). Continuous **economic hardship** throughout one's life appears to increase the chances for being functionally disabled, having a chronic condition, and experiencing recurrent physical symptoms (Kahn & Pearlin, 2006).

Looking at gender disparities in health, Read and Gorman (2010) suggest that while biology plays some role, we must also look to differences in work and leisure, health care, lifestyles, and gender expectations. Riskier behaviors and greater exposure to serious violence contribute to men's lower life expectancy. Women also tend to engage in healthier lifestyles, to seek more preventive care, and to be more attentive to their bodies and therefore more sensitive to symptoms. Thus, they take more continuous care of their health problems than men do. Finally, women are better at reporting minor health problems, which might help minimize the seriousness of those problems later in life and help account for their longer life expectancy.

At the same time that women take better care of themselves, their lower occupational and earnings status raises their vulnerability to illness, as do the greater family stresses and intimate violence they face (Read & Gorman, 2010). However, even when their initial health is the same, women become healthier and have fewer physical limitations the longer and more continuously they are employed than women who are either intermittently employed or not in the labor force (Hergenrather et al., 2015).

BOX 12.1 SLEEP DEPRIVATION, HEALTH, AND INEQUALITY

There are a number of jobs that require unusually long and/or irregular hours. This is especially true of being a prison guard. Because there must be staff members on duty at prisons twenty-four hours a day, they require mandatory overtime (MOT) to cover unfilled shifts. In other words, if there are not enough people to cover a given shift, staff members from the shift that preceded it are forced to stay on the job until they can be relieved. This results in insufficient and unpredictable sleep, both of which have been linked to poor health outcomes and lowered life expectancy. Here's what one guard said,

> You are not mentally prepared to work for at least 16 hours. I like to know ahead of time when I am working overtime. It is hard to work 16 hours and then get up again the next morning prepared to deal with the inmate population. You have to be able to quickly diffuse situations. I have trouble sleeping, so I am already not getting the required amount of sleep. MOT makes

it worse. I also have not brought enough food to have two meals, so I begin feeling sluggish. Imagine the effects after 16 hours of dealing with various personalities. Tempers flare. Things that would not normally bother you are enhanced ten times and incidents get out of control quickly. (As quoted in Spinaris, 2019.)

Some argue that the stress and difficult conditions prison guards work under are justified by their high rate of pay. Contrary to popular belief, however, on average correctional officers only make about $46,000 per year working in state-level facilities (US Bureau of Labor Statistics, 2021a).

While we tend to think about how an individual's work hours and income affect their own health, it turns out that spousal employment matters too. For example, Kleiner and Pavalko (2014) found men's health suffers when their wives work long hours, but women's health improves when their husbands do. The researchers speculate that this may be because men substitute housework for exercise when their wives work a lot. In contrast, women's health may improve when their husbands work long hours because the family's financial situation improves, allowing them to take better care of their health. Another study found that women's health suffers the most when they work long hours, do a disproportionate share of the housework, and feel that the household division of labor is unfair (Thomas et al., 2018). In terms of earnings, increases in a person's own earnings are positively related to health, but the effects of increases in *spousal* earnings appear to be more complicated. For example, one study found that among heterosexual married couples, a woman being the breadwinner in the household is linked to poorer physical health outcomes for the husband (Springer et al., 2019). It appears that men are most likely to suffer when their wives become more involved and successful in the world of work, a sphere which, traditionally, has been portrayed as a man's province.

Protective Factors

When talking about health and inequality, it is easy to focus on poor health. But many people—across all social groups—have excellent health. What are some of the factors that enhance health? Study after study has found that strong social group membership has deep effects on both physical and psychological health. This is likely because groups provide support, but also because they enhance members' self-esteem and because group membership gives people a heightened sense of personal control in their lives (Greenaway et al., 2015). The importance of social groups on health extends to racial identity. For example, African Americans who have a strong positive racial group identity are less depressed when faced with financial hardship (Hughes et al., 2014).

Related to social group membership, holding multiple roles appears to confer health benefits. Specifically, people who combine work and family tend to have better mental health than people who just focus on one role, although single parents often have high stress levels that can have adverse health consequences (for a review of the literature, see Engels et al., 2021). Sociologically, it makes sense that multiple roles lead to higher well-being since roles provide people with their identities. On the other hand, involvement and responsibility in *too many* areas can increase a person's feeling of loss of personal control and thereby increase stress and depression symptoms (Mirowsky & Ross, 2003).

Obviously, some conditions and life events may help prepare and strengthen individuals for stressful conditions. For example, in the early 1980s, Elder and Liker (1982) analyzed data from middle-class women who were young adults during the Great Depression. They found that those women who had suffered serious economic loss during the Depression felt less helpless and more assertive and in control of their lives fifty years later than the women who did not experience such losses. Working-class women, on the other hand, who entered the Depression with fewer resources to begin with and experienced serious reductions in economic resources, felt less assertive and had a greater sense of being victimized. What this suggests is that life's obstacles are more easily overcome and can even have long-term beneficial effects when those experiencing them have had, at the outset, ample resources on which to build a strong life.

Health in Cross National Perspective

How does the United States compare to other countries in terms of health? There are many ways this could be measured, but it is common to look at life expectancy and infant mortality because both are well documented and—obviously—extremely important. Overall, the United States has a fairly high infant mortality rate of 6 per 1,000 live births. Many other countries, including Japan, and Cuba, have lower rates of infant death. Within the United States, the infant mortality rate among children of Black mothers is more than twice that of Whites (10.8 per 1,000 live births compared to 4.6). The rate for Hispanic children is 4.9, and that for Asians is even lower (3.6). Native Americans/Alaskan Natives have the second highest rate of 9.4 (CDC, 2021c).

In 2020, the average life expectancy for all Americans was 77.3 years, lower than that of most other industrial countries, including Japan, Australia, Canada, and most of western Europe (Arias et al., 2021; The World Bank, 2021). Across groups in the United States, women live longer than men (80.2 years compared to 74.5 years). In terms of race, White people born in 2020 had an average life expectancy of 77.6 years. The equivalent figure for Black people was 71.8, and 78.8 for Hispanics (Arias et al., 2021). Current data were not available for Asians and American Indians, but slightly older research found a life expectancy of 86.5 and 76.9, respectively (Kaiser Family Foundation, 2014).

Psychological Health

Consider for a moment how important physical health is in anyone's life. It affects one's chances in employment, social activities, travel, and relationships with others. Psychological health is also a basic element of a meaningful life, but are the chances for such health evenly distributed among groups in US society? In 2019, 51.5 million adults in the United States had some diagnosable mental illness. This represented almost 20 percent of the population. Of those, 13.1 million had serious mental illnesses, defined as disorders that substantially reduce the ability to carry out major activities. Mixed race people, those between the ages of 18 and 25, and women report the highest rates of mental illness in general and serious mental illness in particular (NIMH, 2021).

As we describe below, many studies have found a link between lower socioeconomic status and poor mental health. But the nature of the relationship is complex, and the direction of causality is a source of controversy. One argument is that individuals who become mentally ill lose their jobs (and their incomes) and then are socially selected or **drift** into a lower class as a result. The alternative view is that the characteristics of a class position create conditions that foster mental health or illness. This is the **social causation** position. Both positions may apply in different circumstances, and the nature of the relationship may vary depending on the specific illness in question.

But, as with physical health, there appears to be little question that economic conditions affect the degree of an individual's psychological distress and whether they receive treatment for it. To have "serious psychological distress," a person must have experienced symptoms of mental illness plus feelings of distress such as worthlessness, sadness, nervousness, or hopelessness for a period of one year. A study of adults in New York City confirmed higher rates of "serious psychological distress" among racial/ethnic minorities, women, and the poor. Individuals with incomes below the poverty line had rates that were over five times those of persons with incomes that were at least 600 percent above the poverty level (Choden et al., 2018).

Why does poverty have such a devastating impact on mental health? In a recent review of the literature published in *Science*, the authors find that poverty is associated with income instability, causing stress. It is also associated with poor living conditions that make it difficult to sleep and to avoid environmental contaminants. Low-income pregnant women suffer stress and malnourishment that can impact both their own physical and mental health as well as that of their children across their lifetimes (Ridley et al., 2020).

Recent research suggests that impoverished people have an elevated risk for developing post-traumatic stress disorder (PTSD), particularly if they live in disordered or high crime areas (Lane et al., 2017). PTSD is an anxiety disorder precipitated by one or more traumatic incidents. People with PTSD can have a range of symptoms, including flashbacks and hypersensitivity to stimuli. An Attorney General's National Task Force (2012) found that children who are exposed to multiple kinds of trauma have a greatly elevated risk for PTSD and other mental disorders. A group that is particularly likely to experience trauma leading to mental health issues is American Indians. A study on reservations found that a full 78 percent of residents had been exposed to at least one major trauma as a child. These traumas were linked to higher rates of depression, PTSD, and suicide attempts (Brockie et al., 2015).

The greater feelings of distress found in lower socioeconomic groups have been linked to greater feelings of vulnerability, powerlessness, and alienation, while people in higher social class positions have a greater feeling of mastery and control (Brender-Ilan, 2012; Mirowsky & Ross, 2003). Feelings of self-mastery and control over one's life appear to be an important set of mediating influences on mental health. Feelings of powerlessness are related to higher levels of chronic depression (Wiersma et al., 2011). The importance of mastery over one's life for mental health is further implied by findings that show that job insecurity, over which individuals have little control, increases depressive feelings (Meltzer et al., 2010). Unemployment, like job insecurity, is linked to higher rates of mental illness. Although they could not prove causation, a meta-analysis of studies of young people found that unemployment is associated with worse mental health outcomes (Bartelink et al., 2020). Another study, however, found that the effect does appear to be causal, with even short spells of unemployment resulting in negative mental health outcomes among citizens of four countries (including the United States) (Cygan-Rehm et al., 2017).

As with all the topics in this chapter, here we consider intersectionality between identity categories and mental health. A large-scale study of over 15,000 US adolescents considered the role of social class, immigration status, gender, and race on depression. All four exert effects with non-immigrant Latinas and Native American girls who are low income having the highest depression scores. White non-low-income males had the lowest depression scores (Evans & Erickson, 2019).

Access to Healthcare

Medical costs are a major cause of economic and health inequality. Most people pay for healthcare using insurance, either provided by their employer or by the federal government. The United States is an outlier among industrialized countries, however, in its heavy reliance on employer-provided coverage and its failure to cover all citizens. Other countries achieve universal health coverage in various ways: some through a single payer system where the government reimburses physicians for all care (Canada and Taiwan), others through mandating that everyone procure insurance through either a private or public insurer (Germany and Japan along with others), or, in the United Kingdom, through a socialized system whereby the government owns and runs the health service.

In addition to low rates of coverage, the healthcare system in the United States is an outlier in its expense. One way to look at this is to consider the percentage of the gross domestic product consumed by healthcare. We spend a full 17.1 percent of our GDP on healthcare, while Canada spends 10.7 percent, Switzerland 11 percent, and Germany 11.2 percent (The Commonwealth Fund, 2020).

The American system today is substantially different from that prior to 2014, when the major provisions of the Affordable Care Act (ACA) took effect. The goal of the ACA was to increase the number of people with health insurance and to improve the quality of care while also decreasing costs. The law requires more private companies to provide insurance to their employees. People without employer coverage are able to buy subsidized coverage on state and federal exchanges. Significantly, the ACA allowed states to expand Medicaid coverage to anyone whose income puts them under 138 percent of the poverty line. The federal government initially paid for 100 percent of the expansion, but that rate dropped to 90 percent in 2020. States have the option of declining the expansion. Today, all but 12 of the states have expanded their Medicaid programs.

In addition to expanding the number of options for affordable health insurance, the ACA prohibits health insurers from removing sick people from coverage or rejecting people with pre-existing conditions. Children can stay on their parents' medical insurance up to the age of 26. Another provision requires insurers to provide mental health as well as substance abuse services. Finally, the ACA incentivized individuals to get health insurance by allowing the federal government to levy a fine on the uninsured.

The provisions of the ACA led to tremendous gains in insurance coverage. Looking just at the period between 2013 and 2016, the percentage of the nonelderly uninsured dropped from 20.5 to 12.2. These figures are particularly important because nonelderly adults were (and continue to be) the most uninsured group. Many elderly people and poor children were already covered by government insurance prior to the advent of the ACA. Among the racial/ethnic groups, Hispanics experienced the greatest gains in insurance coverage over the period, and among social classes, those earning between 100 percent and 199 percent of the poverty line gained the most (Foutz et al., 2017). Rates of insurance are much higher in states that opted into expanded Medicaid coverage. Those that refused to opt in are primarily located in the Southeast and Midwestern regions of the country.

Today about 10 percent of Americans are without insurance. This is up from a small dip in coverage that happened in 2019 and 2020. This dip, at least in part, was because the federal government rescinded the fine that uninsured people were initially required to pay under the ACA. The removal of that fine was problematic because healthy people were more likely to opt out of insurance, making it more financially difficult for insurance companies to cover the costs of the less-healthy people who remained in the pool. As a result, premiums went up in 2019, making it more difficult for people to afford coverage. The situation changed again in 2021 with the pandemic and the new administration. Although 6 percent of Americans lost coverage due to job loss during the pandemic, about two-thirds of them were able to obtain other coverage. The federal government held a special enrolment period in 2021 that enabled many people to sign up for the exchanges. Finally, the federal government increased funding for Medicaid due to the pandemic, but states who accepted the extra money were not allowed to drop anyone from their rolls (Collins et al., 2021).

While the ACA has been successful at increasing the rates of coverage, it has not yet solved all the problems with the health care system. In particular, poor and minority people are still less likely to be insured. In the first half of 2021, for example, about 22 percent of those who earned less than $25,000 per year were still uninsured (see Figure 12.2). The rate decreased to 2 percent among those earning $200,000 or more per year. Hispanics had the highest uninsured rate (26 percent), compared to Black people at 11 percent, Whites at 7 percent, and Asians at 6 percent. Part of the reason for the high percentage of uninsured Hispanics is that the ACA specifically

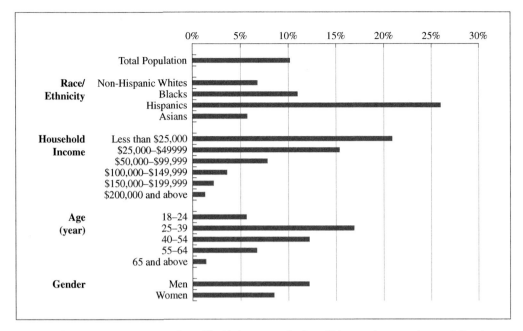

Figure 12.2 Percent of Persons without Health Insurance, by Race/Ethnicity, Income, Age, and Gender, July 2021.

Source: US Census Bureau (2021g) Household Pulse Survey June 2021. Week 31, Table 3. https://www.census.gov/data/tables/2021/demo/hhp/hhp31.html

excludes people who are undocumented from receiving subsidies to pay for insurance and it does not allow them to obtain Medicaid. In terms of age, although they do not appear in the chart, people aged 65 and over have the highest insurance rate because most qualify for Medicare. We see that about 12.2 percent of nonelderly adults are uninsured. Children age 12–18 are at about half that rate, with younger children doing somewhat better (Collins et al., 2021; Georgetown University Health Policy Institute, 2021).

Unfortunately, the ACA does not address the problem of rising premiums or deductibles. In a recent national survey, Collins et al. (2021) found that one-third of insured respondents said that paying their medical costs was a hardship. It is clear that this is a problem that will need to be addressed. Medical bills can create economic hardship for upper-income Americans but can be absolutely devastating for those in the middle or lower classes.

Given the differences in health conditions between groups, one might expect to find parallel differences in the preventive use of physicians and other health care providers. In general, the differences are in the expected direction, but not always. For example, Asian and Native American women are less likely to have had a Pap smear in the last three years than are White or Black women (Artiga et al., 2016). This is surprising because Asian people have a relatively high rate of insurance and good health on average. But research suggests that young Asian women do not have a lot of knowledge about cervical cancer and many do not have a regular physician who would suggest getting routine Pap smears (Gor et al., 2011). There are particularly striking differences in receipt of prenatal care by race. About 82 percent of White mothers but only 67 percent of Black, 63 percent of American Indian, 72 percent of Hispanic, and 52 percent of Native Hawaiian/Alaskan Native mothers received it. Prenatal care is also stratified by education level. About 88 percent of college graduates obtain prenatal care, but the same is only true of 63 percent of those who have not completed high school (Osterman & Martin, 2018). Among the consequences of lower rates of preventive care among the poor and minorities are greater numbers of emergency-room visits and higher rates of hospitalizations (Moore et al., 2017).

There is no widespread agreement on a single reason as to why poor people and racial/ethnic minorities receive less than adequate health care. Perhaps it is simply that those in lower socio-economic positions choose not to seek care for their health problems. This does not appear to be the case, however. A study with low-income Americans found that they wanted to seek medical care but were precluded from doing so because of high co-pays, lack of information about what procedures would cost before they agreed to them, and an inability to get time off of work (Lewis et al., 2017). Access to hospitals also matters. Between 2003 and 2020, over 100 rural hospitals closed. This increased barriers for care, particularly for the elderly and poor (GAO, 2021).

Poor people and people of color sometimes face discrimination when they receive care, making them less enthusiastic about returning. Some physicians hold stereotypes that can affect the diagnosis and treatment of these patients. When patients perceive discrimination from a health care provider, they are more likely to experience psychological distress, including depression, lowered self-esteem, and anxiety (Schmitt et al., 2014). In 2017, 32 percent of Black respondents to a survey reported experiencing discrimination in a healthcare setting and 22 percent reported that they or family members had put off care out of fear of discrimination (Bleich et al., 2019). Another study found that people with mental health issues who are both racial/ethnic minorities and LGBT experience particularly acute discrimination in health care settings (Holley et al., 2016). Researchers have found that physicians believe—incorrectly—that poor patients are more likely to sue them. This can cause doctors to treat poor patients differently or refuse to accept Medicaid patients (McClellan et al., 2012).

Other explanations offered for disparities in health care treatment include lack of access and affordability. Thomas (2014) found that healthcare providers are disproportionately leaving poor urban areas to move to more affluent suburbs. Specifically, over half of the urban areas that the federal government designated as having a physician shortage are in high-poverty neighborhoods. Region matters too. About 60 percent of rural counties have no physician who is licensed to treat opioid addiction with medication. The equivalent number for urban areas is 24 (Rural Health Research Gateway, 2018).

In some cases, individuals' access to effective care may be compromised by language barriers. Although many clinics and hospitals have translation services available, they are insufficient to meet the needs of a large and diverse group of immigrants. Consequently, children sometimes "broker" care for their parents—translating both language and culture during appointments. This is a difficult job, as medical terminology is complex, and children may not know the highly specialized words in either language. Brokering can also be difficult when parents feel embarrassed by the health issue, when the prognosis is extremely upsetting, or when directions for care are very detailed (Katz, 2014).

The ACA was extremely helpful for people who have mental health issues. In a survey that compared 2013 to 2017, respondents who reported poor mental health in 2017 were more likely to report having coverage and a regular source of treatment. They were also less likely to report not being able to afford treatment (Thomas et al., 2017). At the same time, only about 65 percent of Americans with serious mental illnesses received treatment in 2019 (NIMH, 2021). Why would people who could afford treatment for mental illnesses not obtain it? It turns out that there are many obstacles besides the financial. For example, many areas of the United States have severe shortages of mental health professionals. One study found that the majority of US counties do not have enough mental health professionals to meet their population's needs and that the problem is particularly acute in rural areas. Additionally, Medicaid payment rates for mental health are much lower than for medical or surgical procedures and, consequently, providers are unwilling to take on Medicaid patients (Maxwell et al., 2020).

In some cases, the stigma of mental illness can prevent people from seeking treatment. Men tend to be less willing to seek care, although there are racial and ethnic variations among them. In an analysis that included Black, White, and Mexican American men, it was found that Mexican Americans were the least likely of the three groups to seek care. Homosexual men were more likely to seek care than heterosexual men and older men were more likely than younger men. An intersectional analysis of the data revealed that White men with higher incomes were more likely to seek care than their poorer counterparts, but it is the opposite for Black men (Parent et al., 2018). In a meta-analysis of studies on stigma, researchers also found that military personnel and health care providers were particularly likely to say that stigma prevents them from seeking treatment (Clement et al., 2015).

COVID-19 and Inequality

The COVID-19 pandemic is a tragedy that has led to millions of deaths, economic hardship, and social upheaval. We focus on it both because the pandemic has had a profound effect on inequality and because inequality has shaped the course of the pandemic. For example, inequality has been found to be related to the risk of contracting the disease, the risk of being hospitalized and dying, and the chances of receiving vaccination and treatment. The coronavirus has also caused inequality to increase, the impact of which is likely to be felt far into the future.

To date, few researchers have considered COVID in terms of intersectionality. This is unfortunate, because categories of oppression have combined in ways that lead some people to have much greater risk of illness and death than others. Hankivsky and Kapilashrami (2020) comment, "intersectionality shows that risks and impacts (of COVID) are shaped by a *web of intersecting factors*, including age, sex, gender, health status, geographic location, disability, migration status, race/ethnicity, and socioeconomic status (SES)."

COVID-19 Infections

While anyone can contract COVID-19, particular groups of people have been at heightened risk. These tend to be the same groups—the poor, people of color, the disabled, and the elderly—who disproportionately suffer from many different health problems. Once again, the explanation for these disparities is largely structural: these groups are more likely to live and work in conditions that increase the risk for contracting the coronavirus and other transmissible illnesses. For example, research shows that housing density matters. The more crowded the living space, the higher the transmission risk (Gyamfi-Bannerman & Melamed, 2020). This is why congregate living facilities like homeless shelters and prisons have had extremely high rates of infection. Disabled people are more likely to live in congregate settings and this partially explains their higher risk for COVID (CDC, 2021b). Poor people are also more likely to live in crowded living conditions and to be incarcerated. Hispanic people (who have 1.9 times the chance of contracting COVID than do White people) also tend to live in larger and more intergenerational households than members of other racial/ethnic groups (3.24 people on average compared to 2.42 people in non-Hispanic households), making it more difficult to contain the spread of illness between household members (US Census Bureau, 2020a). While good data are not available, researchers speculate that household size also partly explains why Native Americans contract COVID at 1.7 times the rate of White people (Williamson, 2021).

Workplaces are another area of increased risk. Low-income workers are less likely to be able to do their jobs remotely and are more likely to have to take public transportation to those jobs. Hispanic, Black, and Native American people are also less likely to have the kind of internet access that allows for working at home. While only 12 percent of White people are "smartphone-only

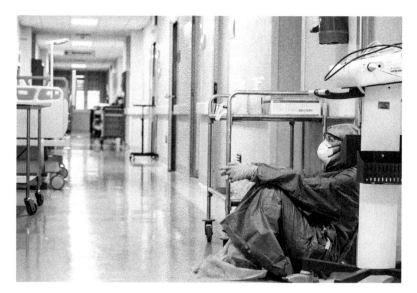

Photo 12.1 Healthcare workers have been overwhelmed by the number of people sick with COVID.
Source: Alberto Giuliani/Wikimedia Commons.

Internet users," the equivalent figure for Latinos is 25 percent,17 percent for Black people, and 33 percent for Native Americans (Atske & Perrin, 2021; Morris & Howard, 2019). Not only did not having a computer make working or going to school from home difficult, but it also limited access to accurate information about the disease. Racial/ethnic disparities in COVID cases are also, at least in part, a result of the occupational segregation that we discussed in Chapter 10. Latinos and Native peoples are particularly likely to have jobs, like restaurant and construction work, that must be performed on-site. Hispanic people also disproportionately work in meat and poultry processing plants, sites that have had huge outbreaks of the coronavirus (Thompson, 2020). During April and May of 2020, for example, at least 16,223 workers in meat and poultry processing plants were infected (CDC, 2020).

Mortality from COVID-19

At the time of this writing, the world is approaching 5 million deaths from COVID-19. These deaths are not spread proportionately across countries. For example, Bulgaria has recorded about 315 deaths per 100,000 people. Other countries with high death tolls include Brazil (285 per 100,00) and Mexico (221 per 100,000). The United States, however, is not far behind with a rate of 219 per 100,000. This translates to more than 1 in 500 Americans dying from COVID-19 (Johns Hopkins, 2021).

What determines a country's death rates? It certainly has something to do with the control measures that have (and have not) been put in place during the course of the pandemic and it can also be explained by disparities in reporting since some countries were less willing to attribute deaths to COVID. Older populations tend to have higher death rates, as do populations with high numbers of pre-existing conditions and high rates of obesity (Wise, 2021). Inequality has played an important role, with low-income countries struggling more to provide health care to sick people as well as to vaccinate their own populations. Countries also vary in terms of their capacity to deal with an influx of very sick people. Even in the United States, our health system became overwhelmed numerous times, making it difficult for very ill people to be able to access the care they needed.

Turning to look at the death rate from the coronavirus within the United States, there are clear links with categories of inequality. As described above, class and race are linked to health status and, in turn, many diseases are associated with an elevated risk of serious COVID-19. These diseases are called comorbidities and they include chronic kidney disease, diabetes, chronic pulmonary disease, obesity, and heart disease (CDC, 2021a). People of color and the poor are more likely to have many of these pre-existing conditions (Selden & Berdahl, 2020). Smoking, as described above, is also concentrated among the poor and is associated with poor outcomes from COVID (CDC, 2021a).

By far, the primary predictor of serious illness and death from COVID is age. In fact, a full 27 percent of deaths occurred in the 85 and older group of Americans (CDC, 2021f). It should be noted, however, that White people tend to live longer than other racial/ethnic groups, so there are more elderly White people, increasing the number of deaths in the group (Selden & Berdahl, 2020). At the same time, Black and Hispanic people have died at disproportionately high rates. In a rare intersectional analysis of deaths from COVID-19 in Georgia and Michigan, researchers found that men died at higher rates than women in all racial/ethnic groups but that the disparity varied between groups. Black men had the highest rate of death, followed by Black women, White men, White women, Asian/Pacific Islander men, and Asian/Pacific Islander women (Rushovich et al., 2021). Data were not available for Hispanic people, but other studies have shown them to have death rates higher than any other group, at 2.3 times those of White people (CDC, 2021d).

Avoidance of Medical Care

One of the unfortunate effects of the pandemic has been to discourage people from receiving medical services for illnesses other than COVID-19. Research suggests that a full 40 percent of Americans postponed medical care during 2020. Thirty-two percent put off routine/preventative care and 12 percent delayed emergency/urgent care. Again, we see striking differences by racial/

BOX 12.2 DISABILITY AND HEALTH CARE RATIONING DURING COVID

As described, disabled people are at elevated risk of contracting COVID, becoming seriously ill, and dying. Michael Hickson was one of those victims. In 2017, he was driving to his job as an auto insurance claims adjustor when he suffered cardiac arrest. Although the paramedics managed to keep him alive, he had a traumatic brain injury and became quadriplegic. In June of 2020, he was admitted to the hospital with COVID-19. Due to his pre-existing conditions, he became very ill, and doctors decided to remove him from life support, without the agreement of his wife or five teenage children. The family has filed a discrimination claim which is being heard by the Federal Office of Civil Rights. Key to the case is an audio recording in which a doctor seems to explain that the decision to stop treatment was because of Mr. Hickson's low quality of life.

While we do not know exactly what happened in Mr Hickson's case, we do know that disabled COVID patients have been denied care in some circumstances. A large-scale investigation in Oregon found multiple cases of people with disabilities being denied care or pressured to sign DNR (do not resuscitate) orders. It became clear that the lives of people with disabilities were counted as "lesser than" and that increased their risk of serious illness and death (J. Shapiro, 2020).

ethnic and socioeconomic groupings. Black and Hispanic people were more likely than White people to avoid needed emergency/urgent care, as were disabled people and those with pre-existing health conditions (Czeisler et al., 2020).

Regular screenings are a crucial tool in catching cancer before it becomes too advanced to treat. Like other medical procedures, these screenings decreased dramatically during the pandemic. A study of colorectal, breast, and prostate screenings found that the pandemic led to a deficit of more than 9 million screenings nationally. This obviously has long-term implications for the mortality and health of the population. Interestingly, the greatest decline in screenings was in the highest SES group, resulting in a narrowing of the gap between economic groups (Chen et al., 2021).

The huge number of deaths from COVID-19 in the United States, combined with the impact of postponed medical care, has dramatically affected life expectancy. On average, the population has lost 1.3 years. The impact has disproportionately affected Black and Hispanic people, causing reductions of 2.10 and 3.05 years, respectively (Andrasfay & Goldman, 2021). CDC data allow us to look at 2020 life expectancy intersectionally. Black men fare the worst, with an average life expectancy of 68 years. Black women now have a life expectancy of 75.7 years (Arias et al., 2021). As described above, COVID-19 is not the only explanation for variations in life expectancy by social group, but it has had a significant impact.

BOX 12.3 A VACCINATION SUCCESS STORY

The first COVID-19 vaccine became available to the public early in 2021. As of this writing, the majority of eligible Americans have been vaccinated. But Native Americans have notably higher rates than average. There are several reasons for their success. First, the Biden administration allowed tribes to handle their own vaccine distribution. This meant Native peoples could distribute vaccines according to their own cultural traditions. Second, tribal members were able to receive information about the vaccine from trusted members of their own group. Third, community values in Native groups made it easier for people to understand that vaccines were about protecting others, not just oneself (Silberner, 2021).

Opioid Epidemic

The opioid epidemic and the COVID-19 pandemic are, obviously, very different from each other. But opioid misuse, like COVID outcomes, is related to inequality. Opioids include prescription pain relievers, heroin, and some synthetic drugs like fentanyl. Opioids have been in use for thousands of years across the globe, but in the 1990s, US doctors began to prescribe them to people for chronic conditions like back pain. Prior to this time, prescriptions were generally only given to people for short periods of time to help them deal with pain from acute conditions (post-surgery or in the immediate aftermath of a serious injury). The pharmaceutical companies, however, were interested in increasing profits and undertook to convince doctors that opioids were safe for long-term use. The scientific basis for their claim was weak at best; the safety data actually came from hospitalized short-term opioid users. In addition to this misleading data, pharmaceutical companies showered doctors with gifts and trips to encourage them to use their products. Their pitch came at an opportune moment because the medical community had recently declared that pain was a "fifth sense" (along with sight, hearing, smell, and taste) that needed to be actively managed and controlled. Opioids seemed like a perfect solution.

Doctors began to dramatically increase the number of prescriptions they wrote for opioids, leading to widespread addiction. The National Institute on Drug Abuse (2021b) reports that between 8 percent and 12 percent of people prescribed an opioid for a chronic condition during this period became addicted. By the early 2000s, rates of addiction and overdose were climbing and today are at record levels. To illustrate, in 1999, fewer than 20,000 Americans died by drug overdose. By 2019, number had increased to over 70,000 (National Institute on Drug Abuse, 2021a). 2020 was an even worse year with 93,000 deaths (CDC, 2021e). Experts believe that the 2020 increase was largely a result of COVID and its attendant isolation and grief. The pandemic also caused access to addiction and other mental health treatment to be limited just at the same time people were using drugs to cope with increased anxiety and depression.

It should be noted that the numbers of deaths reported above are for all overdose deaths, not just those caused by opioids. But the majority (70 percent in 2019) were opioid-related (National Institute on Drug Abuse, 2021a) with most of those deaths caused by fentanyl (Baumgartner & Radley, 2021). While it can be taken by itself, fentanyl is more often mixed with heroin (or sometimes with cocaine) and it is difficult for users to gauge how much is in what they are ingesting. Some argue that these deaths are unrelated to prescription opioids. This is misleading, however, because researchers have found that about 80 percent of heroin users became addicted because of a prescription for pain relief (National Institute on Drug Abuse, 2021b). When they are no longer able to obtain—or no longer able to afford—prescription drugs, they sometimes begin using illegal substitutes.

In order to understand the course of the opioid epidemic, it is vital to consider location and inequality. Appalachian areas in states including West Virginia, Pennsylvania, Kentucky, and Ohio have suffered—and continue to suffer–particularly high rates of addiction and overdose death. This is not an accident; residents in these areas have notably high rates of chronic pain due to working in dangerous conditions in mines and factories. Their pain is real, as was their doctors' desire to help them. Pharmaceutical companies took advantage of this situation and targeted doctors in these areas. Making things worse, the region lacked a strong public health infrastructure to address the crisis and had few drug rehabilitation services available (Appalachian Regional Commission, 2021).

The fact that the early years of the opioid epidemic were concentrated in Appalachia meant that many of the deaths were among White people. This led to the perception that the typical opioid user was White. Racialization of drugs is not new, but in the past, most illegal drugs have been associated with marginalized groups—those perceived to be a threat to White interests. For example, in the late 1800s, opium was associated with Chinese Americans and was used as a rationale for limiting their immigration. It was not a coincidence that this association coincided with concerns that Chinese laborers were competing for limited numbers of low-wage jobs (Ahmad, 2000). Additionally, there is compelling evidence that the punitive war on drugs, begun by the Nixon administration, was an attempt to control Black Americans during the civil rights struggle as well as young people considered to be "hippies" (Alexander, 2012; LoBianco, 2016).

Often when drugs become racialized, politicians and the public support harsher punishments. For example, once crack cocaine was associated with Black Americans in the 1980s, mandatory minimum sentences for possession were increased dramatically. With opioids, however, the public has been much more likely to favor treatment over harsh sentencing. This is likely because of its racialization as White. Research comparing the reactions of the media and politicians to the upsurge in crack use in the 1980s (which was racialized as Black) and the opioid epidemic confirms that crack was discussed as a criminal justice issue, while opioids have much more often been portrayed as a medical issue (Kim et al., 2020; Shachar et al., 2020).

Regardless of public perceptions, a wide range of Americans use opioids today. In a complex intersectional analysis, Persmark et al. (2020) found that—by far—the group with the highest level of opioid misuse is White low-income men between the ages of 18 and 29. Unexpectedly, however, the second-highest group is high-income Black women ages 18–29. The next four groups are White men of various incomes, followed by young low-income Hispanic and then Black men. The author speculates that the high rate of use among Black young high-income women could be a result of racism and sexism. Research has consistently shown that doctors are less likely to prescribe pain drugs to Black people because they believe that they are more likely to become addicted and because they believe (wrongly) that Black people are biologically able to tolerate more pain (Hirsh et al., 2020; Hoffman et al., 2016). In the last twenty years, doctors have become more aware of this research and may have reacted by prescribing more to the Black people (young, high-income women) they perceived to be least likely to become addicted.

Research suggests that the most effective type of treatment for opioid addiction is drug-assisted therapy alongside traditional talk therapy. But race plays a role in who is able to access which particular treatment. For example, Black people are disproportionately prescribed methadone which requires a daily visit to a clinic for supervision. Other drugs, like buprenorphine, have been made available by prescription and can be taken in one's own home. These drugs are disproportionately given to White people (Hansen et al., 2016). This is partly because there are more physicians licensed to prescribe buprenorphine in White areas, but it is likely also linked to stereotypes about the moral character of Black people.

Lead Poisoning

Lead poisoning is an issue that many people associate with the 1970s and 1980s, but, in fact, it continues to be a problem today, particularly for the poor. In 2018, there were a half million children diagnosed with dangerously high lead levels in their blood (CDC, 2018). How does this happen? In the past, gasoline was made with lead and children either inhaled or ingested enough of it to cause poisoning. Sales of leaded gas for on-road vehicles became illegal in the United States in 1996. Today the primary problem is lead paint. Most houses before the 1950s were painted with lead-based paint. The lead was added to make the paint more water-resistant, durable, and vivid. Children get lead poisoning from eating chipped paint or inhaling dust in old houses. While people of all backgrounds are susceptible, the problem has disproportionately hit poor communities because the houses in these neighborhoods are older and more run-down. The poor are also less likely to have their children tested for lead exposure and/or to have access to information about lead poisoning.

While its use decreased from the 1950s to the 1970s, lead paint was not outlawed for houses until 1978, although the government ordered a phase-out starting earlier in the decade. Even with these restrictions, there are millions of homes that still have lead paint. An interactive map showing the percentage of housing stock built before 1950 can be found at (https://www.arcgis.com/apps/mapviewer/index.html?webmap=d1d812d709214603b74aa3a263e81f6f). An example of a spike in lead poisoning occurred in New Orleans after Hurricane Katrina (Rabito et al., 2012). As people returned to their badly damaged homes, they were forced to renovate, uncovering lead paint.

Lead exposure can lead to a large range of negative health outcomes, including lowered IQ, behavioral problems (such as decreased attention span), and reduced educational attainment (WHO, 2015). There are also a wide range of physical symptoms that result from lead exposure, up to and including death. While controversial, some scientists have linked increases in the crime rate during the 1960s and 1970s with high levels of lead exposure in children who came of age during those years (Drum, 2015). Regardless of whether this association is true or not, we know that when children are lead-poisoned, the inequalities can last a lifetime.

Another tragic example of lead poisoning and **environmental injustice** plagues the former manufacturing boomtown of Flint, Michigan. In the 1950s, Flint was the second largest General Motors (GM) auto manufacturer in the United States. As the deindustrialization of America began in the 1980s and continued through the 1990s, GM closed and relocated some of its manufacturing plants. This left many Rustbelt cities, including Flint, reeling. The 2014 American Community Survey found that even 20 years after the GM plant closings, Flint still had not recovered (US Census Bureau, 2014a, 2014b). In 2019, 38.8 percent of the city lived below the poverty level (US Census Bureau, 2020c).

Because of these high poverty rates, there is a low tax base to support city services. This has caused budget problems for many years, and ultimately the state took over the management of the city, giving a great deal of power to a governor-appointed city manager. In April 2014, the manager (in consultation with state-level workers and agencies) approved a switch in the city's water source from the more expensive Lake Huron, which is Detroit's water source, to the local Flint River (Graham, 2016). Although river water is more corrosive than lake water, the switch was done without using any type of corrosion inhibitor, causing the pipes to begin to leach lead into the water (Roy, 2016). Marc Edwards, a professor and water engineer, began an independent study of the water quality in the summer of 2014 (Graham, 2016). His team found blood-lead-level spikes as early as that summer, just months after the switch (Bliss, 2016).

Through the Freedom of Information Act, Edwards was able to obtain a July 2015 internal report from the Michigan Department of Health and Human Services that alerted officials that lead poisoning rates "were higher than usual for children under age 16 living in the City of Flint during the months of July, August, and September, 2014" (Bliss, 2016). Edwards continued on with his study and in the fall of 2015 found that the water in Flint had many times the recommended EPA limit for lead particles (Graham, 2016).

After the EPA warned Michigan officials in February 2015, Governor Snyder and the emergency manager commissioned two state agencies to conduct further studies (Maddow, 2015). However, there were methodological problems in how the tests were conducted, and the details of the results were withheld from Flint citizens. By the fall of 2015, however, reports from pediatricians of high lead levels in children could no longer be ignored (Bliss, 2016; Roy, 2015). It was clear that although Flint residents were paying some of the highest water bills in the United States, they were slowly being poisoned (Roy, 2016). The governor authorized the switch back to Detroit water in October 2015, but lead poisoning cases continued to emerge. It was not until January 2016, that the governor finally took action to address the effects of the lead poisoning. This was 20 months after the water switch and at least several months after he knew about the toxic lead levels (Bliss, 2016; Graham, 2016).

Today the government maintains that Flint's water is safe to drink. Some residents, however, continue to distrust the water and are upset that a program that handed out free bottled water to residents has been discontinued (Chavez, 2018). In November of 2021, however, a historic class-action suit was finalized by a federal judge. It will provide 626 million dollars in compensation to residents who were affected by lead poisoning.

Unfortunately, Flint is only the tip of the iceberg in terms of lead. Reuters analyzed records of childhood lead levels from across the country and found nearly 3,000 zip codes that had higher average levels than Flint did at the height of its crisis. The source of the lead varies—in some places, it is a result of old paint, and in others, it is discarded industrial waste (Pell & Schneyer, 2016). It is likely a high percentage of children, many of whom were already struggling with poverty, will grow up with the consequences of lead poisoning.

Climate Change

Like lead poisoning, climate change illustrates the connections between health, the environment, and inequality. Climate change refers to alterations in temperature and weather patterns caused by humans burning greenhouse gases (such as oil and coal). While these gases are burned all over the world, developed countries burn a disproportionate share. Specifically, the ten countries/regions that emit the most greenhouse gas are responsible for over two-thirds of emissions worldwide. In order, these include China, the United States, the EU, and India. Part of the reason that India and China emit so much greenhouse gas is because of their huge populations. Looking at emissions on a per capita basis, Canada and the United States emerge as the highest (Ge et al., 2020).

In addition to directly emitting greenhouse gases, developed countries tend to consume products that result in climate change and they encourage less-developed countries to produce those goods. For example, Brazil has destroyed large swaths of its rainforest in order to use the land for other purposes. Notably, they recently became the second largest producer and exporter of soybeans in the world, growing them on land that was once rainforest (Gilbertie, 2021). Brazil also makes money from the rainforest through its export of Amazonian wood. The United States is one of the primary importers of this wood. Even though the United States has regulations about the sources of imports, it is difficult to track wood's origin and illegal imports can easily enter the country (Spring, 2020).

Brazil decreased the rate of deforestation between 2004 and 2014, but has increased it substantially since. For example, it increased 34 percent between 2018 and 2019, and another 9.5 percent by 2020 (Silva Junior et al., 2021). There is compelling evidence to suggest that the continued destruction of the Amazon may result in increasingly intense droughts and severe heat waves that will have worldwide effects (Garcia-Navarro et al., 2015). These potential environmental disasters will be difficult for poorer nations to escape, as they will not have the resources to take care of their people or safeguard their economies in the way that wealthier nations can. For example, India is dependent on the monsoon for drinking water and for water for agriculture. The Intergovernmental Panel on Climate Change believes that climate change is already resulting in a more erratic monsoon season. Too little rain can result in famine, and too much rain can quickly cause flooding and crop damage. If India sees a number of erratic seasons in a row, it is likely to force impoverished rural people into the cities, causing chaos and even deeper poverty (*The Economist*, 2015).

Climate change has numerous effects on human health. Big storms and hurricanes are becoming more common, and large swathes of the affected areas often lose power. Those who cannot leave their homes due to disability, poverty, or age, are in real danger when they cannot heat or air-condition their homes. Heat waves related to climate change are increasing as well. For example, in June of 2021, the Pacific Northwest experienced a week-long heat wave. There were over 600 excess deaths that week, largely among the elderly, those without homes, and people who work outdoors. Because temperatures are climbing, more people are anticipated to die of heat-related ailments in the future. Poor people, who have less access to air conditioning in their homes, are particularly at risk for heat-related ailments (Popovich & Choi-Schagrin, 2021).

The last few summers have seen huge wildfires in the western part of the country. These have had significant health consequences for people near the fires, but the smoke has spread as far as the East Coast. Smoke exposure is linked to a range of health issues that include aggravated heart and lung disease and respiratory ailments. The groups that are most at risk are those with pre-existing heart or lung disease, older people, children, people with diabetes and asthma, and pregnant people (EPA, 2018). Climate change is also associated with increases in some pathogens that can harm humans. For example, "valley fever" is caused by a fungus called Coccidiodes that lives in the soil in the Southwestern United States as well as in parts of Mexico and South and Central America. It can make people sick when they breathe in its spores. This problem is moving northward with climate change and is expected to increase the number of cases by 50 percent by 2100 (NSF, 2019).

Low income and minority communities are particularly at risk from climate change because they are more likely to be built in areas prone to flooding. As we discussed in Chapter 2, much of poor people's wealth is tied up in their homes. When those homes lose value because of the increasing danger of flooding, this has a significant impact on their owners' ability to survive. In terms of health, returning to homes that have been flooded is dangerous because of an increase in mold and its associated health risks. There is also increased risk of injuries and chemical hazards because stored chemicals may have leaked from their containers (CDC, 2019).

BOX 12.4 THE IMPACT OF CLIMATE CHANGE ON HEALTH

Climate change is projected to have many effects on the mental and physical health of individuals as well as communities. For example, a recent study with 10,000 young people from 10 different countries (including the United States) found that 45 percent reported experiencing anxiety and depression due to climate change that impacted their daily life (Hickman et al., 2021). Figure 12.3 illustrates the wide range of health impacts climate change may have.

Figure 12.3 An Illustration of How Climate Change Impacts Physical, Mental, and Community Health.

Source: Clayton, S., Manning, C. M., Speiser, M., & Hill, A. N. (2021). Mental health and our changing climate: Impacts, inequities, responses. American Psychological Association and ecoAmerica. https://ecoamerica.org/mental-health-and-our-changing-climate-2021-edition/

Summary

This chapter has focused on how inequality shapes health, and how health shapes inequality. We looked at mental and physical health outcomes to see how they are stratified by socioeconomic status, race/ethnicity, gender, age, sexuality, and immigrant status. It turns out that when groups have different health outcomes, it is largely the result of social and economic context, but individual-level factors like smoking, use of preventative care, and differences in the likelihood of possessing health insurance also play a role.

One point should be made about the research conducted on these health and inequality. Although significant relationships have been found between race, gender, sexuality, and SES, on the one hand, and health, on the other hand, we do not want to suggest that these are the only variables or always the most important variables in explaining variations. Rather, the question of interest has been whether inequality in its various forms plays any role in producing various health outcomes. It seems apparent that it does. Indirectly, the organization of a competitive capitalist society and, more directly, the system of inequality that it creates, result in individuals and families being placed in different positions regarding access to and possibilities of gaining the "good things" in life. The role of poverty and inequality in affecting life chances extends beyond US borders into the world as a whole. Income inequality and poverty are implicated in physical and mental health between nations. In many ways, then, the effects of inequality reach inside the intimate lives of individuals in the United States and elsewhere.

We concluded the chapter with four case studies that illustrated the links between health and inequality. COVID-19 and the opioid epidemic spread through the population in ways shaped by inequality and have had a disproportionate impact on low-status groups. Both will impact inequality in the future. Lead poisoning and climate change illustrate how environmental health is linked to individual health and—again—how categories of inequality affect outcomes.

Critical Thinking

1. To what extent should individuals be held responsible for their health and actions if these are shaped by their opportunities and circumstances?
2. Why do you think that research results regularly show that women have higher rates of mental illness and distress than men in the United States?
3. What effect do you think a requirement for everyone to have health insurance has had on the health of the US population? Does it reduce, increase, or simply maintain the overall level of health in the country? Why?
4. As competition for them increases, how can access to desirable spaces and land be made equitable? What role, if any, should the government play in this process?

Web Connections

Health, United States, a volume published yearly by the National Center for Health Statistics, contains a wealth of longitudinal and cross-sectional information on the life expectancy, mortality, and health conditions of the US population, including information on all the states. Check it to see how your income, age, and educational group compare on health measures, as well as how your state compares to others. Go to www.cdc.gov/nchs/index.htm

Film Suggestions

Heroin(e) (2017). Oscar-nominated film about the opioid epidemic featuring interviews with people who became addicted as well as with judges and social workers.

One Nation Under Stress (2019). Narrated by Sanjay Gupta, this film looks at stress and its impact on Americans' lives.

Totally Under Control (2020). Follows the COVID epidemic as it spreads across the United States as well as the political and public health dilemmas the nation faces.

Heal (2017). This film does a deep dive into the American healthcare system and provides suggestions for reform.

Unnatural Causes: Is Inequality Making Us Sick? (2008). A seven-part series on socioeconomic status, race, and health.

13 Inequality, Crime, and Criminal Justice

In this chapter, we turn to look at how crime and criminal justice shape and are shaped by inequality. We consider the ways that inequality at both the individual and community levels can lead to crime as well as how crime contributes to inequality. The system of criminal justice is also a focus of inquiry because it draws disproportionately from poor and minority populations and has itself been linked to the perpetuation of inequality.

Perspectives on Crime and the Law

At first glance, "crime" appears to be a simple concept. When someone breaks the law, they have committed a crime—case closed. While this is technically true, such a simple definition glosses over a whole host of issues. Why do we have particular laws? Which of our laws are enforced and which are ignored? How is the behavior of various individuals interpreted in terms of legality? These kinds of issues lead some sociologists to say that crime is "socially constructed." In other words, while there are some crimes such as murder, that have a fairly clear definition, we also have laws that are vague and selectively enforced. For example, there are many places with laws against "loitering." It is not at all clear what loitering is and how it differs from the legally permissible "waiting." Loitering is dependent on both the social context and the interpretation of particular people's behavior.

Social theory provides us with a number of different perspectives to understand the purpose of crime and the law. A "harm perspective" posits that each society's definition of crime (and the laws that attempt to regulate it) are based on an assessment of social harm. Acts such as murder that are very harmful, are more likely to be criminalized and penalized than are less harmful acts. Loitering, for example, is not terribly harmful so the penalties applied to it are low and the law is only enforced on occasion. A functionalist perspective on crime, like the harm perspective, acknowledges that some acts cause harm, but it also sees a certain level of crime as a natural, healthy, and normal part of society. For example, crime can result in important innovations (think of Rosa Parks refusing to give up her seat on the bus and the societal changes it helped spark). Emile Durkheim, a famous functionalist, believed that crime and the law are a way for a society to create solidarity because they draw boundaries between members and nonmembers. He argued that laws reflected the collective conscience of the society.

Karl Marx, who wrote from a conflict perspective, had a strikingly different view of crime and the law. He thought that the wealthy use crime and laws to control the poor and benefit themselves. For example, acts common in the lower classes are more likely to be criminalized and punished. In support of this argument, people sometimes point to differences in sentencing and enforcement of **white-collar** and **street crimes**. White-collar crimes—which tend to be committed by the wealthy—are rarely punished. This is true even though the level of social harm is immense: over $300 billion are lost each year and, in 2020, there were 4,764 documented cases of workers dying from occupational injuries, many of which were linked

DOI: 10.4324/9781003184966-17

to illegal and unsafe working conditions (Cornell Law School, 2016; US Bureau of Labor Statistics, 2021i). In contrast, poor people are prosecuted for a wide variety of offenses and some laws seem designed to target them. For example, a survey of 187 cities found that, over the last fifteen years, there has been a dramatic increase in laws that criminalize behaviors common to the poor such as living in vehicles (43 percent of cities) and sleeping in public (18 percent of the cities had a total ban and 27 percent banned it in particular places like parks) (Bauman, 2019).

W.E.B. Du Bois' perspective on crime and law bears some similarities to Marx's because both believed that the primary function of laws was to control poor people (Gabbidon, 2001). Du Bois, however, extended the argument to racial minorities. He argued that, "The rich are always favored somewhat at the expense of the poor, the upper classes at the expense of the unfortunate classes, and whites at the expense of Negroes" (Du Bois, 1899, p. 249). As one example, he pointed to the convict leasing system. This set of laws, enacted after Emancipation, forced prisoners to work for free on the former slave plantations. Localities began criminalizing many new petty offenses and selectively locking up Black people so that they could be forced to labor for the wealthy landowners.

The Measurement of Crime

In the United States, we generally measure crime rates with the FBI's Crime Index, which includes both property crimes (burglary, larceny-theft, motor vehicle theft, and arson) and violent crimes (murder, forcible rape, robbery, and aggravated assault). One of the problems with this list of **index crimes** is that it does not include any serious, very costly white-collar or **corporate crimes**. Since the latter are largely crimes perpetrated by middle- or upper-class individuals, it would be a mistake to look only at index crimes to reach a conclusion about the relationship between socioeconomic status and crime. If we did, it would bias the conclusion against individuals in the lower social and economic classes.

Crime data from the FBI have another drawback: they reflect only those crimes which are reported to the police. We know this severely underrepresents the true level of crime because data from the National Crime Victimization Survey (NCVS) show that many victims choose not to contact the police. The NCVS asks a national sample of Americans ages 12 and over if they have been the victim of a crime in the last six months. It also asks a number of follow-up questions about the crime and whether it was reported to the police. The NCVS consistently shows that less than half of all crime is reported. Crimes such as rape and household theft are particularly unlikely to be reported with a report rate of only 34 and 27 percent, respectively (Gramlich, 2020).

BOX 13.1 WEARING SAGGY PANTS

In 2018, lawmakers in South Carolina proposed a law banning the wearing of saggy pants. This follows on the heels of a similar proposal in Mississippi in 2017 and the successful passage of laws in communities in Florida and New Jersey (Ballesteros, 2018). While most of the laws and proposed laws call for fines instead of jail time, in Tennessee, two teenagers were jailed on obscenity charges when they wore saggy pants in public (Mazza, 2017). Some people say that these laws simply enforce common decency. Others say that they are not about decency, but are intended to target Black people (who are associated with the style, although they are not the only people to wear it). What do you think of these laws? Should saggy pants be illegal?

Research suggests that rates of reporting are linked in complicated ways with categories of inequality. A study of nonsexual violent assaults found when an offender is White and the victim Black, the crime is much less likely to be reported than if the races are reversed. Interestingly, these racial differences appear to be less significant in more egalitarian communities (where Black and White people are less residentially segregated and more economically equal) (Xie & Lauritsen, 2012). Police misconduct also has an impact on citizen's willingness to report crimes. One study found that, after a high-profile police killing of an unarmed Black man in Milwaukee, there was a dramatic decrease in crime reports for a year, particularly from Black people (Desmond et al., 2016). Similarly, Black women are less likely to report physical and sexual violence than are White women because of distrust in the legal system and fear of a violent police response if the perpetrator is Black (Decker et al., 2019).

People who are in the country illegally are particularly unlikely to report crime to the police because they fear being deported. Specifically, only 17 percent of victims who are undocumented report the crime, compared to an average of 40 percent for people here legally (Comino et al., 2020). There is good reason for unauthorized immigrants to fear deportation since, in 2018, the Trump administration changed longstanding policy and allowed people who were at court for non-immigration issues (for example, as a witness to a crime or as a victim) to be arrested on immigration charges. In 2021, the Biden administration reversed this policy, arguing that it endangered public safety. It is not clear, however, that unauthorized immigrants are aware of the new policy and may continue to fear reporting crime. Immigrants who are here legally may also fear making reports because it could put family members who are not documented at risk (ACLU, 2018).

Criminality

We can think about the effect of inequality on crime in two ways. First, inequality in a society or region (at the macro level) could impact the crime rate. For example, areas with more income inequality might have higher (or lower) crime rates than more egalitarian areas. Inequality also might impact crime at a more individual (micro) level. Perhaps, for example, inequalities between men and women or between immigrants and the native-born lead to different levels of criminality. Here we look at each of these levels in turn, moving from the macro to the micro.

Economic Inequality and Crime at the Macro Level

Sociologists have long believed that inequality leads to crime. Why might that be? There are at least three possibilities. First, a rational choice perspective would suggest that when there is a lot of inequality, there are—by definition—a lot of poor people and a lot of rich people. The poor people have limited opportunities for mobility, providing an incentive to steal from the rich people. A second possibility (called *strain theory*) is that, in situations of inequality, poor people may feel envy and anger at the rich people, prompting crime. Jacobs and Richardson (2008) comment: "Resentment is more likely among the relatively deprived in an affluent society than it is among the absolutely deprived in an impoverished society" (p. 31). A final possibility, known as social disorganization theory, posits that when there is a high level of inequality, poor and rich people tend to live in separate neighborhoods. The poor neighborhoods do not have the resources to maintain effective institutions, leading to family breakdown, decrepit housing, and few employment opportunities. The fact that there is little to bind individuals to the community can—in some cases—result in a lack of the social controls needed to minimize crime (Atems, 2020).

There is ample research suggesting that inequality and crime are connected at the macro level, but the relationship is complicated by the fact that there are differences by crime type and context. For example, Choe (2008) found that inequality in an area increases property crime, but not violent crime (except rape). Other researchers have also concluded that inequality has a stronger impact on property crime than on violent crime (Rufrancos et al., 2013). McVeigh (2006) found that inequality is more likely to lead to crime if individuals in different classes interact with each other. Inequality also has a stronger impact on crime if people do not attribute it to merit. In other words, when people believe that others' wealth is unearned, it fosters a sense of injustice that can lead to criminal behavior. Finally, Burraston et al. (2018) found that both the level of absolute deprivation as well as the level of inequality affect the level of crime, but that inequality has a stronger effect in areas with medium levels of poverty than in areas with high levels, perhaps because there is more opportunity for poor people to see their relative disadvantage in more mixed socioeconomic areas.

But what about poverty? Does it have an impact on the crime rate, independent of inequality? It appears that the answer is yes. As social disorganization theory predicts, areas with high levels of concentrated poverty, high unemployment, many single-parent families, and residential segregation tend to have more crime than other areas (Burraston et al., 2018; Sampson & Bean, 2006). Interestingly, areas with high number of immigrants have lower crime (Han & Piquero, 2021). It is possible that immigrant communities are more socially organized, creating institutions and networks to help each other (Nielsen et al., 2005).

Like poverty, unemployment in an area can drive crime independent of inequality. In a longitudinal study, Phillips and Land (2012) examined data from 1978 to 2005 on the commission of seven index crimes at the county, state, and national levels. Their results are interesting because they indicate that unemployment has divergent effects. It tends to lower some kinds of property crime because unemployed people are at home more often, effectively guarding their houses. On the other hand, unemployment has the potential to increase nonhome property crime because it enhances criminal motivation (because unemployed people need money). Similarly, Fallahi et al. (2012) analyzed national employment data and found that, in the short term, unemployment is linked to increases in motor vehicle theft but decreases in burglary. Another study found a relationship between the employment level in an area and violent crime. An analysis of 2,462 US counties indicated that high levels of employment (even if it is less than full-time) lower the violent crime rate (Lee & Slack, 2008).

Inequality and Crime at the Micro Level

A great deal of research has been conducted to determine whether particular social groups, such as poor people, commit more crimes than others. It turns out that poverty, in and of itself, does not directly lead individual people to commit crime. Instead, there is an indirect relationship through circumstances associated with poverty. We know, for example, that poor children are more likely to end up in foster care, and foster care is linked to increased and more chronic offending (Yang et al., 2017). Poverty is also linked with exposure to lead-based paint, another predictor of delinquency (Doleac, 2017). While family poverty, in itself, does not appear to predict violent crime, it does predict living in a neighborhood with concentrated poverty and, as discussed above, this increases the chance of criminal involvement (Sampson et al., 2005). It additionally limits job opportunities, making drug dealing a more attractive option for poor youth (Dunlap et al., 2010). The chances of experiencing traumatic events are higher in impoverished neighborhoods, and trauma is linked to delinquency (Yun et al., 2021).

Perhaps not surprisingly, research suggests that employed people are less likely to engage in crime than are the unemployed. In one study, each additional quarter (three months) of unemployment increased the risk of arrest for a property crime by 3.5 percent among people who already had a criminal record (Siwach, 2018). What may be more surprising, however, is that not all jobs are equally effective at deterring crime. High-quality, stable jobs are much more effective than are those that are menial, low-paying, and unstable. In fact, LaBriola, 2020) finds that low-quality jobs do not exert a deterrent effect at all, but high-quality jobs do. Among teenagers, work also decreases crime, but only to a point. Teenagers who work fewer than 20 hours a week are less likely to engage in delinquency, but after 20 hours, work appears to be associated with higher delinquency (Bachman et al., 2011; Staff & Uggen, 2003). Further research is needed to figure out why the deterrent effect of employment appears to dissipate at 20 hours for teenagers but not for adults.

Probably the most debated—and mischaracterized—relationship between individual characteristics and crime involves race. The statistics presented later in the chapter show that Black people are more likely to be arrested for most crimes than are their counterparts in other groups (see Table 13.3 later in this chapter). Research indicates, however, that this difference in rates is not due to cultural differences, but rather to differences in the structural contexts in which the groups live and to police being particularly likely to surveil and arrest Black people. We discuss the link between race and discriminatory criminal justice treatment later in the chapter. Here we focus on the structural context argument. It might feel familiar to you. This is because we introduced it in the last chapter to explain racial health disparities. In both cases, it appears that it is not so much that race determines outcomes, but rather that race is linked to living conditions which, in turn, are related to outcomes. That is to say that the causes of Black crime are similar to the causes of crime by any group, but Black people are exposed more forcefully and thoroughly to social contexts that encourage criminal behavior, such as poverty, poor jobs, social isolation, and unemployment (this argument about race and social context is sometimes called the **racial invariance hypothesis**) (Galster & Santiago, 2015). This setting results in fewer opportunities and less attachment of Black people to the wider society. Higher crime rates follow, as do victimization rates, and since it is Black people who are concentrated in these areas, it is their rates that spiral upward.

There is strong evidence showing that any individual exposed to an isolated and impoverished environment over time is vulnerable to criminal behavior and victimization (Kposowa et al., 1995; Sampson & Wilson, 1995). At the same time, however, new scholarship suggests that we should be open to the idea that the unique history and cultures of different racial/ethnic groups might strengthen or weaken the relationship between environment and crime (Unnever, 2016). For example, the long history of discrimination against Black people in America simply makes their experiences incomparable to those of White people. Experiencing this kind of subordination can lead to extreme stress that is linked to crime for a small group of Black people (Unnever & Owusu-Bempah, 2018).

Future research will allow us to better understand how structural conditions interact with history and culture to produce variations in crime. It will also be important to further study how community conditions play a role in crime. Living in a poor family located in a community that is also suffering economically intensifies the effects of family and neighborhood disadvantage on crime. Thus, it is not just one's immediate poverty but also the surrounding context that contributes to violence and other types of crime (Hay et al., 2007; Peterson & Krivo, 2009). To understand differences in crime and victimization rates between rich and poor, as well as between the racial/ethnic groups, we need to appreciate the social context and history that generate such differences.

Hispanic people have lower rates of contact with the criminal justice system than Black people, and Asians have lower rates than any other group. One reason for this is that the population of both Hispanics and Asians contain significant numbers of immigrants. Foreign-born people report engaging in less crime than people born here. This is supported by their lower arrest rate across all age groups and is true for both immigrants who are here legally as well as illegally (Ewing et al., 2015; The Sentencing Project, 2017). Research suggests, however, that crime rates do increase slightly in the second and third generations (Bersani, 2014). As mentioned above, the lower crime rate may partly be because first and second-generation immigrants are more likely to live in ethnic enclaves (Han & Piquero, 2021).

Explaining the fact that men commit far more crimes than women is, in some ways, more difficult than explaining racial/ethnic differences. This is because men and women are not isolated from each other in the way that racial groups often are. There are a number of theories involving inequality that have been put forward. For example, Messerschmidt (1993) argued that crime is a way of expressing masculinity, especially when other routes are blocked (see Chapter 8 for a detailed description of the theory of hegemonic masculinity). Crime is not part of what is defined as feminine, so girls have less incentive to engage in it. Messerschmidt's theory is intersectional because he includes race and its interaction with gender as a key component. He posits that, because of discrimination, minority males have a particularly difficult time achieving standards of hegemonic masculinity and so may resort more often to crime.

A second theory that tries to explain the gender crime gap points to the fact that males tend to have more delinquent peers, encouraging criminality. In addition, it appears that young men are more likely to be influenced by those delinquent peers than are young women (Stults et al., 2021). John Hagan and his colleagues (Hagan et al., 1985, 1987) put forward a third theory based on power and inequality. They hypothesized that in families where wives and daughters have little power, there is less freedom and risk-taking on the part of women. Hence, daughters will be significantly less likely than sons to commit delinquent acts. The data the researchers collected supported their hypotheses and revealed that the gender differences in delinquency declined as one went down the class hierarchy. In other words, gender differences were greatest in the upper class. This may be because sons in this class have greater power relative to their mothers and criminal activity does not incur as great a punishment risk for them as it does for daughters. This theory connects gender differences in delinquency to power differences in the family, which in turn are a reflection of power differences in the workplace. In more recent updates to their theory, Hagan and his colleagues (Hadjar et al., 2007) add gender dominance ideology as a factor. They posit that families who subscribe to traditional gender roles are more likely to closely monitor daughters. Thus, there will be higher rates of delinquency among sons.

Feminist researchers point out that criminology has historically overlooked the experience of girls and women by focusing exclusively on males and by failing to recognize that gender itself might determine crime patterns. Meda Chesney-Lind and Lisa Pasko (2013) draw on a wide range of research to conclude that a notably high percentage of the girls and women who are arrested for crimes have been victims of sexual abuse and assault. This has been found to be the case for transgender men as well (Rogers & Rogers, 2021). The trauma that they have experienced leads them into situations where crime becomes a survival strategy. For example, girls who are the victims of incest or abuse are more likely to run away from home and then steal or engage in prostitution to support themselves. Importantly, simply running away can be enough to result in incarceration. This is because running away is considered a status offense, an act that is legal for adults, but not for children. While the law says that youth are not supposed to be incarcerated for status offenses, many states violate this law. There is also an exception for when youth violate a court order. This could happen when an abused girl runs away and is ordered by a court to stay there. If she runs away again, she can legally be incarcerated (Baumle, 2018).

Victimization

The sections above illustrate how inequality is linked to both the crime rate as well as to circumstances that affect individual people's propensity to commit crime. Here we look at its relationship to crime victimization. Table 13.1 presents violent victimization by race, gender, and income. It shows that income is highly correlated with victimization, with poorer people significantly more

Table 13.1 Estimated Rates of Violent Victimization, Excluding Simple Assault, by Race/Ethnicity, Sex, and Residence: 2020

Victim Characteristics	Violent Crime Victimization Rate
Race	
White	5.3
Black	7.5
Hispanic	5.5
Asian/Native Hawaiian/Other Pac. Islander	1.8
Other**	18.7
Sex	
Male	5.1
Female	6.2
Household Income	
Less than $20,000	11.4
$20,000–$49,999	5.8
$50,000–$99,999	5
$100,000–$199,999	3.4
$200,000 or more	2.8

** Includes Native Americans/Alaskan Natives and people of two or more races.

Source: Morgan and Thompson (2021). *Criminal victimization, 2020,* https://bjs.ojp.gov/sites/g/files/xyckuh236/files/media/document/cv20.pdf

likely to become victims of violent crime. We also see that people of color are at elevated risk, particularly Native Americans and those of mixed race. Although men and women have close to the same rate, men are more often the victims of crimes such as assault, robbery, and homicide, while women are more often the victims of sexual assault and intimate partner violence (Lauritsen & Heimer, 2008). It should also be noted that there are important intersections between categories. For example, Black women have higher rates of victimization than either White or Hispanic women (Lauritsen et al., 2014).

Social conditions affect the number of crimes committed against members of demeaned status groups. **Hate crimes** are violent or property crimes against a person or group of people primarily because of their race, religion, disability (mental or physical), sexual orientation, gender identity/expression, or ethnicity/national origin. One characteristic that distinguishes them from other crimes is the nature of the motivation. Hate crimes have a symbolic function in that they are directed as a *warning* against groups of low status. Consequently, who the specific victims are may be irrelevant to the perpetrator(s) since they serve only as a representative of the group. As warnings, hate crimes are aimed at reinforcing the existing social hierarchies and keeping groups in their place. Thus, they lead to intimidation and fear reaching into the entire group, not just the individual victim.

Knowledge about the extent, causes, and consequences of hate crimes is incomplete for several reasons. First, there has been little systematic research on them. Second, states vary in the groups that they include as potential victims, making rate comparisons difficult and conclusions about total numbers suspect. Third, some states simply do not report any hate crimes at all; a survey by the Associated Press looking at six years of data, found this to be the case in 17 percent of all law enforcement districts (Cassidy, 2016). Finally, like many other crimes, hate crimes are underreported.

Despite deficiencies, FBI data are generally used to reach conclusions about hate crimes in the United States as a whole. In 2020, 8,263 hate crime incidents were reported, involving 11,129 victims. This was the highest level in over a decade. About 62 percent of all the reported crimes were racially motivated. Race crimes were followed by biases based on sexual orientation, religion, gender expression, and disability, respectively. Extreme concerns about racial and ethnic purity, immigration, job competition, residential infiltration, and the sanctity of marriage and Christianity often lie behind these biases. Target groups are viewed as threats to the living standards of perpetrators, who see their own way of life as under siege from contaminating elements. About 55 percent of the perpetrators were White, and 21 percent were Black. The race of about 16 percent was unknown (FBI, 2021c).

Table 13.2 shows the number of hate crimes reported to the FBI by bias type. The percentages do not total to 100 because the FBI reports so many different categories, it would be unwieldy to include them all. Notably, the table does not include a category the FBI calls "anti-lesbian, gay, trans, bisexual." This category is used when hate is expressed against a group of people who have different sexual identities. The number of hate crimes against these groups is large (306), especially when considered in combination with the numbers of individual hate crimes against sexual minorities and transgender individuals.

Biases against many of the groups in Table 13.2 are longstanding. As we saw in Chapter 8, abusive acts against Black people were permitted during slavery, and the creation of the Ku Klux Klan (KKK) after the Civil War helped keep racist fires burning. Current White supremacist groups in the United States include various segments of the KKK, neo-Nazi and skinhead groups, and some

Table 13.2 Number of Incidents and Victims of Hate Crimes by Bias Motivation: 2020

Motivation	No. of Incidents	Percent of the Total
Race/Ethnicity		
Anti-White	869	10.5
Anti-Black	2,971	34.7
Anti-Asian	279	3.4
Anti-American Indian/Alaska Native	96	1.2
Anti-Hispanic or Latino	517	6.3
Religion		
Anti-Jewish	683	8.3
Anti-Islamic (Muslim)	110	1.4
Sexual Orientation		
Anti-Gay Male	673	8.1
Anti-Lesbian	103	1.2
Anti-Bisexual	17	0.01
Gender		
Anti-Transgender	213	2.6
Anti-Gender Non-Conforming	53	0.6
Disability		
Anti-Physical	53	0.6
Anti-Mental	77	0.9
Multiple-Bias Incidents	211	2.6

Source: FBI (2021b), https://crime-data-explorer.fr.cloud.gov/pages/explorer/crime/hate-crime

extreme Christian groups, such as Christian Identity and the Christian Defense League. At the time of this writing, there were at least 838 such groups operating in the United States, up from about 600 in 2000 (Southern Poverty Law Center, 2021). Prejudice against gay men and lesbians also has deep historical roots, principally highlighted by laws against sodomy in place as early as the 1600s in the United States, and which required the death penalty or severe mutilation as punishment. Such laws continued in many states until 2003, when the US Supreme Court declared them unconstitutional. Among other elements, feelings of superiority and concerns about competition over resources demonstrate the role of status inequality in the production of hate crimes.

There have been a number of particularly tragic hate crimes in recent years. In 2019, 23 people were killed and another 23 wounded in a shooting in a Walmart in a majority-Latino neighborhood in El Paso, Texas. In 2018, 11 Jewish people worshipping at the Tree of Life Synagogue in Pittsburgh were murdered by a gunman. In 2020, hate crimes against Asian Americans increased by 76 percent, fueled by racist rhetoric falsely linking Asian people to the COVID-19 pandemic(Barr, 2021).

It is hard to compare the number of hate crimes in the United States with other countries because of differing definitions. Additionally, many countries do not collect data or do not disaggregate them to identify the victims or the seriousness of the crimes. The Organization for Security and Co-operation in Europe, however, collected data from 42 states in Europe, Eurasia, and North America and documented many hate crimes against refugees, Roma people, and Muslims. In the United Kingdom, hate crimes increased 18 percent between 2019 and 2020. The vast majority of the 125,848 reported incidents were based on race or xenophobia. The situation was similar in Germany with hate crime reports increasing 19 percent between 2019 and 2020. In the United States, the increase was 30 percent (OSCE/ODIHR, 2021).

Hate crimes legislation is not without its critics on both the left and the right of the political spectrum. One critique says that acts such as assault are already illegal, making enhancements to the law unnecessary. Others argue that it is too difficult to figure out the intent in a criminal situation. How can you tell if someone committed a crime because of hate or if it was for some other reason? For example, in 2021, an Asian man was stabbed while walking down the street in New York City. Because the assailant did not say anything, prosecutors did not charge it as a hate crime, although it was widely perceived to be one (Hong & Bromwich, 2021). Sometimes a free speech argument against hate crime legislation is made, arguing that while assault should not be condoned, expressing hate should be considered protected under the First Amendment. Some progressive activists also oppose hate crime laws because they believe they do little to deter crime. Others see the laws as a way to placate oppressed people without addressing the systemic roots of inequality. Finally, an argument has been made that we should be working to dismantle the massive prison-industrial complex rather than consigning people to more time in prisons that do little to rehabilitate them (Black and Pink, 2009; Reddy, 2011).

The Criminal Justice System

In recent years, the public has paid increasing attention to the criminal justice system as a contributor to inequality in society. From protests over police shootings of unarmed Black people to discussions about how the bail system hurts poor people, the public seems to have engaged with the idea that the criminal justice system is not bias-free. Research on this topic, however, is somewhat complicated. The criminal justice system has a number of stages, beginning with the definition of crime, and continuing with labeling of individuals as potential criminals, arrest procedures, court procedures, and sentencing. Because there are so many stages of the process, so many different jurisdictions, and because of the complexity of factors that determine outcomes, it can be hard to isolate the impact of bias at any specific place or at any given historical moment.

Photo 13.1 Thousands of people protest against the police in New York City. Minorities who live in poor neighborhoods are more likely than others to view police and other governmental authorities with suspicion and to feel they are treated unfairly in the justice system.
Source: © iStock.com/Leonardo Patrizi.

At the same time, there is strong and consistent evidence of bias—particularly against racial and ethnic minorities—at all points in the process (Hinton et al., 2018). More importantly, however, bias appears to accrue over the criminal justice stages so that even if there is not a large disparity at any one point in time, the cumulative effect on a given individual is large (Kurlychek & Johnson, 2019).

One of the most important theories that has been used to understand bias in the criminal justice system involves racial threat. First proposed by Blalock (1967), this theory suggests that groups compete for economic and political resources. When a minority group appears to be gaining ground relative to White people, White people in power use the criminal justice system to contain that threat. This can be either at the macro or micro level. In other words, racial threat could lead to more punitive or biased laws, and it could also play out in individual arrest or sentencing decisions by police or judges. Generally, studies define threat by the percentage of the population that is non-White, but sometimes researchers consider whether or not minority group representation is growing in an area (Dollar, 2014).

School-to-Prison Pipeline

When we think about the institutions that make up the criminal justice system, we often think about the police, courts, and prisons. But what about schools? Research suggests that there are a number of policies that link schools and prisons. One example is zero-tolerance policies that set predetermined sanctions (often suspension or expulsion) for certain infractions such as drug possession, bullying, or having a gun. More than two-thirds of American schools hire police officers called School Resource Officers (SROs) to be on school grounds. Research on whether SROs make schools safer is limited and the results have been mixed (Lindsay et al., 2018). There is evidence to suggest, however, that schools with SROs report larger numbers of non-serious incidents to police, resulting in more children coming into contact with juvenile courts for matters that previously would have been handled within the schools (Na & Gottfredson, 2013).

The term "school-to-prison pipeline" links punitive policies to contacts with the criminal justice system. For example, research shows that children who have been suspended or expelled from school have much higher rates of later arrest than do similar children who have not faced these disciplinary actions. They also have stronger feelings of anxiety and depression (Lewis et al., 2012; Merikangas et al., 2010). This is of real concern since the number of suspensions and expulsions is high. During the 2015/2016 school year, 2.7 million students served out-of-school suspensions and 120,000 were expelled (Rafa, 2019). Consistent with the racial threat theory, the larger the percentage of Black students in a school, the higher the rate of suspensions, controlling for a range of variables including the school's crime rate and poverty (Hughes et al., 2017).

While there may be some very serious infractions that warrant removing children from schools, the reality is that many suspensions and expulsions are for fairly minor incidents. A study in Texas found that only a small percentage of cases (3 percent) were so serious that the suspension or expulsion was mandatory under the rules. The other 97 percent were discretionary, meaning that the schools could select a range of responses. Students who were suspended or expelled through discretionary actions were three times more likely to become involved with the criminal justice system in the next year compared to students who did not receive these disciplinary actions (Morgan et al., 2014). A large-scale investigation by the General Accounting Office (2018) found that Black students were dramatically overrepresented in suspensions and expulsions, even when controlling for the poverty level of the schools attended. Boys and disabled students were also overrepresented in the group of students with disciplinary actions.

The pandemic and the resultant move to online education complicated the picture of the school-to-prison pipeline. There are no data on suspensions and expulsions during this period, but anecdotal evidence suggests that some children were barred from online participation for behavioral problems. Even more concerning, estimates suggest that about 3 million children simply disappeared from school after March 2020. These include children who did not have internet access or who were unable to learn in that format (Coffey, 2021). While some returned when in-person school resumed, thousands did not (Mitropolous, 2021). It is likely that pandemic-related educational losses will have a deep impact on both crime and on inequality more generally in the years to come.

On a more positive note, recent years have seen movement to stop schools from being a pipeline to prison. Between 2013 and 2018, for example, there were 36 bills introduced in states to reform school disciplinary policies. There were only seven that increased or mandated penalties. Partially in response to the Black Lives Matter movement, several major school districts, including Minneapolis, Denver, and Portland, Oregon, have moved to remove SROs (Sheasley, 2021). Reforms in school discipline could have significant results. For example, one study found that if racial disproportionalities in school-based discipline were eliminated, it would decrease the racial gap in arrests by a full 16 percent (Barnes & Motz, 2018).

Arrests

An arrest is generally the first official step in the criminal justice process. As discussed above, however, arrests provide very limited information. They only tell us about crimes that have been reported and for which a suspect has been identified and located. Police officers also have some discretion in whether to make an arrest, introducing a possible element of bias. For example, in a meta-analysis of 27 different datasets, Kochel et al. (2011) found that Black people are about 30 percent more likely to be arrested than are White people in comparable situations. Low-income teenagers are also more likely to experience an arrest than their better-off counterparts (Mowen & Brent, 2016). This is likely because police officers hold particular stereotypes of delinquents that result in lower-class persons being arrested more often (Tapia, 2010). In essence, police have certain expectations of criminal behavior and these images lead them to more frequently monitor and arrest people of color and those in the lower class, regardless of the frequency of their actual criminal behavior. A recent study of drug arrests supports this argument, finding that police are more likely to use proactive strategies (like pedestrian or vehicle stops) with Black people and reactive strategies (responding to a citizen's complaint) with White people. In other words, Black people are more likely to be arrested when police officers decide they are suspicious but White people more often get arrested when someone reports them to police, and the police must respond (Gaston, 2019).

In Chapter 11, we talked about the importance of place in determining people's outcomes. Place strongly affects the likelihood of arrest as well. In a study of drug arrests, Gaston (2019) found that police make assumptions about who belongs where. When White people are in predominately Black neighborhoods, they are more likely to be arrested for drugs. The reverse is also true; a police officer assesses a Black person in a White neighborhood to be "out of place" and is more likely to stop them. Because there are more White areas than Black, and because businesses and government offices are more likely to be in White areas, Black people end up being more at risk for law enforcement contact.

A second example of the importance of place in determining arrests concerns the general socioeconomic status of a neighborhood and how it influences the attention paid to it by authorities. For example, during the 1990s and early 2000s, several cities, led by New York, began to engage in "aggressive order policing." This type of policing requires officers to intervene in situations of minor disorder in communities (for example, loitering or public drinking) on the theory that it will prevent a slide into more serious types of crime. The idea for aggressive order policing was taken from the broken windows theory by Kelling and Wilson (1982). This theory posits that when police clamp down on small infractions in a neighborhood, residents will feel less fearful of crime. Kelling and Wilson extrapolated this to argue that aggressive order policing would ultimately reduce not just fear but crime as well. Aggressive order policing has been highly criticized because it focuses police attention on poor neighborhoods and leads to "stop and frisk" policies that result in poor and minority youth having a disproportionate number of contacts with the police (Howell, 2009). While stop-and-frisk has been declared unconstitutional, police in New York continue to make many discretionary stops and racial disparities persist (Speri, 2021).

Policies such as aggressive order policing affect the relationship between official rates of crime/delinquency, race, and social class, complicating efforts to draw conclusions about the

BOX 13.2 CAHOOTS AS AN ALTERNATIVE TO POLICE

Over the last several years, there have been calls to "Defund the Police." While some activists do support the abolition of the police force, the expression more commonly reflects a desire to redirect some of the money spent on police to other methods of crime control. For over thirty years, a city in Oregon has been doing exactly that. When 911 operators in Eugene receive a call, they assess the potential for violence, and when it is moderate or low, they redirect the call to a program called CAHOOTS (Crisis Assistance Helping out on the Streets). CAHOOTS responds to the call with an unarmed team composed of a medic and a social worker. The situations they respond to vary widely, from mental health crises to public intoxication to family disputes. In 2019, CAHOOTS responded to 24,000 calls, saving the city over 15 million dollars, and only requiring police backup in 150 cases. CAHOOTS responders are trained in how to deescalate situations, deal with people who are under extreme stress, and provide referrals to needed services. In 30 years, there have been no deaths or serious injuries (A. Shapiro, 2020). What do you think of this type of "defunding the police?" Should other cities adopt such programs?

Table 13.3 Percentage of All Arrests and Arrests for Selected Crimes, by Gender and Race: 2020

Offense Charged	Male	Female	White	Black	Native American/ Alaska Native	Asian
All Arrests	72.6	27.4	67.7	27.1	1.8	0.92
Homicide	86.7	13.3	41.8	54.3	1.2	0.87
Sex Offenses	96.6	3.4	69.1	24.7	1.2	1.6
Robbery	85.3	14.7	39.4	56.4	1.4	0.9
Assault	72.8	27.2	62	32.9	1.8	1.2
Burglary	82	18	67.3	28.5	1.6	0.8
Larceny-Theft	59.4	40.6	66.4	28.5	1.9	1.2
Motor Vehicle Theft	78.2	21.8	66.5	28.9	2.3	0.7
Drug Offenses	72.6	27.4	69.2	26.1	1.6	0.1
Prostitution	42.4	57.6	51.7	39.6	0.5	6

Source: FBI (2021a). Arrestees download. https://crime-data-explorer.app.cloud.gov/pages/downloads

Note: Percentages do not add up to 100 percent for the racial/ethnic categories because Native Hawaiian, Pacific Islanders, and those of unknown race are excluded. Hispanics are not considered a racial group by the FBI and are included under the other categories.

relationships between them. This should be kept in mind when thinking about the data presented in Table 13.3. We can see that, in 2020, about 73 percent of those arrested across all crime categories were men. The highest arrest rate for women was in the category of prostitution (58 percent of those arrested for this crime were women). In recent years, arrest rates for women have increased. In terms of race, while most of those arrested in 2020 were White people (68 percent), Black people were disproportionately represented in the arrest rates for all index crimes. A small percentage of arrests, generally 2–3 percent per group, involved American Indians, Alaskan Natives, and Asians.

Bail

People who are arrested for very serious crimes must stay in jail until their case is resolved. For less serious crimes, however, people are often allowed to live at home prior to trial. They are either released "on their own recognizance" or they must pay bail to secure their release. Being released on one's own recognizance simply means that a person promises to be present for trial. Bail is an amount of money—set by a judge—that an accused person can pay to obtain their release. If they show up at trial, the money is returned to them. If a person does not have enough money to pay bail, they can go to a bail bonds company and borrow the money. These companies generally charge a fee of around 10 percent of the amount of the bail. They also require collateral (such as a deed for a house or a car) in case the accused fails to come to trial. The reason the bail system exists is so that people can continue to work, take care of their families, and also prepare for their trial.

Bail has recently come under criticism for its links with inequality. For example, a study of bail decisions in Miami and Philadelphia found that judges were less likely to release Black than White arrestees pretrial. The study suggests that this happens because bail judges harbor stereotypes of Black people that make them overestimate the risk they pose to society (Arnold et al., 2018). A study in New Jersey found evidence of racial and ethnic bias in the requirement to pay bail, how high the bail was set, and how able the defendant was to meet the bail. Specifically, Black and Hispanic people were more likely than Whites to be required to pay bail rather than being released on their own recognizance. Black people were also assigned somewhat higher bail than the other two groups, and both Blacks and Hispanics were less able than Whites to pay the bail amount (Sacks et al., 2015).

Bail has also been criticized because people with money are allowed to go free and poor people are forced to stay in jail. Pretrial detention has been linked to a host of negative outcomes, including job loss, an inability to prepare for trial, family hardship, and an increase in guilty pleas. The reason guilty pleas increase is that, in order to get out of jail, people agree to plea bargains that they might otherwise reject. A plea bargain is an offer made by the prosecutor to reduce the charges in exchange for a guilty plea. One reason that people who stay in jail are more likely to be convicted is that they sometimes have to appear in court in jail uniforms, biasing judges and juries (Dobbie et al., 2018).

A number of states and local jurisdictions are currently working on bail reform. Washington DC was one of the first to mostly eliminate cash bail in 1992. In 2017, 94 percent of defendants were released without cash bail and a full 88 percent showed up for trial. New Jersey has also taken significant steps to reduce the use of cash bail (The Marshall Project, 2020). In 2021, Illinois became the first state to eliminate cash bail altogether (Evans & Oceguaera, 2021).

Criminal Sentencing

Criminal sentencing goes to the heart of questions about the fairness of the justice system. Sentencing policy in the United States is complicated, however, because there is wide variation between states. Some of this variation is linked to inequality; the larger the proportion of Black people in a state population, the more strict the sentencing guidelines. Recent research shows that this is likely a result of racial threat and the greater political power of White people. When there are large numbers of Black citizens in a state, White people tend to favor more punitive policies. In turn, politicians are more likely to enshrine White people's policy preferences into law, even when they directly contradict the preferences of minorities (Duxbury, 2021).

Inequalities exist on an individual level in criminal sentencing as well, with those who are lower in status faring worse than others. Even when the type of offense and previous criminal record are taken into account, lower-income individuals have been found to be more likely to be sentenced to prison and to receive longer sentences. After examining results from many studies, Reiman and Leighton (2012) concluded that, generally, "for *the same crime*, the system is more likely to investigate and detect, arrest and charge, convict and sentence, sentence to prison and for a longer time, a lower-class individual than a middle- or upper-class individual" (p. 162).

It is quite clear that social class and sentencing are linked. But what about race and sentencing? It turns out that this question is complicated and requires an intersectional analysis that includes gender and age. In other words, it is not possible to isolate racial differences because women and men of the same race receive different average sentences, and the same is true of different age groups. For example, an analysis conducted in Wisconsin indicates that Black people are more likely to be sentenced to incarceration than White or Hispanic people, but that is only true of men. In terms of sentence length, Black men receive lower average sentences than other groups, but this is because many are locked up for minor offenses that do not result in sentences—or even arrests–for people from other racial groups. Reflecting the importance of age, Hispanic men between the ages of 30 and 39 received the longest sentences of any group (Freiburger & Sheeran, 2020).

An analysis of all Pennsylvania misdemeanor and felony convictions between 2003 and 2010 showed that, in general, Black and Hispanic people receive higher sentences than do Whites and men receive longer sentences than do women. In terms of age, defendants between 18 and 20 and older defendants (over 50) generally receive more lenient sentences than people 21–50 years old. It should be noted, however, that Black and Hispanic male teenagers do not get a break on sentencing while White teenagers of both genders and Black and Hispanic female teenagers do. The authors of the study point out that Hispanics in all age groups are sentenced more harshly than equivalent White people. The authors think this might be because the Hispanic population is increasing in Pennsylvania, causing a rise in racial threat (Steffensmeier et al., 2017).

There is evidence that racial and ethnic disparities in sentencing vary by crime type, with especially long sentences meted out to Black people for drug crimes (Warren et al., 2012). This may be because drug offenses are considered minority crimes, and consequently result in stiffer punishment for Blacks and Hispanics (Steffensmeier & Demuth, 2000). Steen et al.'s (2005) work suggests that sentencing varies across crime types because of racial stereotyping about "normal" crime and dangerousness. Black males fare worse in drug-crime sentencing because it is perceived to be a Black crime and because Black people are seen as more dangerous.

Not much is known about the sentencing of American Indians, but it appears that they are more likely to be incarcerated and to receive long sentences than similarly situated White, Hispanic, or Black people. This is particularly the case for young Native Americans (Franklin, 2013). At the same time, there are strong differences in sentencing by region, reflecting different levels of cooperation between the federal government and tribal authorities (Ulmer & Bradley, 2018).

As described above, it is very difficult to tease out the separate effects of race and gender, because they are intersectional. In general, however, studies suggest that women receive more lenient sentences than men (see, for example, Doerner, 2015; Starr, 2012). There are several reasons this may be the case. First, it is possible that judges look paternalistically on women, seeing them as weak and in need of protection (Franklin & Fearn, 2008). It may also have to do with the fact that women are more often caretakers of children or elderly adults (Steffensmeier et al., 2017). It should be noted that, while the research supports the idea that women receive more leniency in court, it also suggests that there is variation based on the type of crime, the circumstances, and the race of the defendant. Crimes in which women act in stereotypically masculine ways, for example, may result in higher sentences. This hypothesis is supported by the fact that women are less likely to be sentenced to prison than men for property or drug crimes, but not for violent crimes (Rodriguez et al., 2006). Similarly, women who have lengthy criminal histories are given longer average sentences than equivalent men, but that relationship between criminal history and gender is reversed in the case of short criminal histories. One possible explanation is that judges see criminality as a masculine attribute and women who engage in a lot of it violate gender norms (Tillyer et al., 2015). Women accused of violent crimes are also more likely than men to be referred for psychiatric evaluations, adding further evidence that women who violate gender norms are seen as pathological (Thompson, 2010).

Photo 13.2 The negative effects of imprisonment go far beyond the isolation, monotony, and regimentation experienced by inmates. They also include strained family relationships, disenfranchisement, and dampening of future economic prospects.

Source: Skyward Kick Productions/Shutterstock.

BOX 13.3 MISSING NATIVE WOMEN

One of the major media stories in 2021 involved Gabby Petito, a White woman who disappeared on a road trip with her fiancé. She was later found dead in Wyoming. While this was clearly a tragedy, scant attention has been paid to thousands of cases of missing Native American women. The 1,500 cases in the federal system in 2021 are likely a severe undercount of the problem (US Department of the Interior, 2021). In a 2017 study, the Urban Indian Health Institute found that there were over 5,700 reports of missing Indigenous women and girls in 2016, but only 116 of those cases appeared in Department of Justice records. And less than 5 percent of these cases were documented in the media (Lucchesi & Echo-Hawk, 2017). New solutions are being explored, including the creation of a Missing and Murdered Unit in the Bureau of Indian Affairs. The hope is that this new unit will both focus attention and foster interagency collaboration to find solutions.

While little research has been conducted on citizenship status and sentencing, one study found that there is an impact of citizenship, but that the direction of the relationship depended on region. In some districts, being a noncitizen resulted in shorter sentences and in some, the sentences were more lengthy (Hartley & Armendariz, 2011). Further complicating matters, among Hispanics, people who are arrested for a drug offense and are undocumented are the most likely to be sentenced to incarceration, followed by those who are not citizens but are here legally, followed by citizens. Interestingly, among Black people, those who are undocumented have an equal chance of incarceration as a documented noncitizen, suggesting that Hispanic undocumented immigrants are seen as more of a threat. At the same time, the sentences that both undocumented and documented Hispanic noncitizens receive are shorter on average than those handed down to Hispanic citizens. Researchers speculate that this might be because judges see people who are here illegally as a flight risk, so incarceration is used to prevent them from leaving. But judges then assume that this group will be deported after they serve their sentence, causing them to implement lower sentences (Valadez & Wang, 2017).

Mass Incarceration

Incarceration in the United States has grown enormously over the last thirty years. Since 1985, the number of adults in prisons and jails in the United States has increased more than 500 percent to about 2 million persons in 2019, giving the United States the highest rate of incarceration in the world (The Sentencing Project, 2021).

In Table 13.4, we present the rate of incarceration in the United States compared to selected other countries. The United States is ranked first in the world, both in terms of the total size of its prison population, as well as in the rate at which we incarcerate people. The term **mass incarceration** is used to point out America's exceptionally high rate of imprisonment. When academics use it, they also mean to reference the larger social context in which incarceration occurs. For example, Christopher Wildeman (2012) says the term refers "to the current American experiment in incarceration, which is defined by comparatively and historically extreme rates of imprisonment and by the concentration of imprisonment among young, African American men living in neighborhoods of concentrated disadvantage."

There has been a great deal of debate about the origin and purposes of mass incarceration. We review some of the prominent theories below, but it is important to note that the war on drugs—originally declared by President Richard Nixon in 1971—has had a huge impact on increasing incarceration. While Nixon claimed to be concerned about the effects of drug use on individuals, families, and communities, there is evidence to suggest that, from its inception,

Table 13.4 Incarceration Rates of Selected Countries per 100,000 People

Rank	Country	Rate
1	United States/2019	629
2	Rwanda/2021	580
3	Turkmenistan/2021	576
8	Panama/2021	438
15	Brazil/2020	381
27	Costa Rica/2021	298
47	South Africa/2021	235
73	Poland/2021	189
90	Mexico/2021	170
116	England and Wales/2021	133
127	Egypt/2021	118
139	France/2021	103
174	Denmark/2021	72
206	Japan/2020	37

Source: World Prison Brief (2021). *Prison rates.* https://www.prisonstudies.org/highest-to-lowest/prison_population_rate?field_region_taxonomy_tid=All

the war on drugs was politically motivated. In an interview, John Ehrlichman, who was Nixon's domestic policy chief, said,

> We knew we couldn't make it illegal to be either against the war or black, but by getting the public to associate the hippies with marijuana and blacks with heroin, and then criminalizing both heavily, we could disrupt those communities. We could arrest their leaders, raid their homes, break up their meetings, and vilify them night after night on the evening news. Did we know we were lying about the drugs? Of course, we did. (Baum, 2016)

Regardless of the intent of the War on Drugs, its effects have been enormous, particularly on people of color and the poor.

BOX 13.4 THE PANDEMIC AND INCARCERATION

COVID-19 hit US prisons hard. According to the COVID Prison Project, by the end of November 2021, there were over 560,000 recorded cases among incarcerated people and prison staff and over 2,900 people had died. To try to stem infection, some states and the federal government chose to release small numbers of prisoners early. In general, those who were released were nearing the ends of their sentences and/or had not committed crimes against people. Even more important in terms of reducing the size of the overall prison population, fewer people were admitted in 2020 than in the preceding years. The Vera Institute for Justice calculated that there was an overall decrease in the prison population by about 14 percent. Even with these measures, however, rates of infection remained high. Perhaps this should not be surprising given how crowded prisons remain. California, for example, is still operating at 112 percent of capacity (Kang-Brown et al., 2021; Widra, 2021).

Table 13.5 Percentage Distribution of State and Federal Prison Inmates and General Population by Gender and Race: 2020

Race/Ethnicity	Prison Inmates		General Population, Both Men and Women
	Male	Female	
White, Non-Hispanic	29.2	47	57.8
Black, Non-Hispanic	34	17.7	12.1
Hispanic	23.6	18.6	18.7
Asian American	1.3	0.8	5.9
American Indian/Alaska Native	1.5	2.5	0.7

Source: Carson (2021). *Prisoners in 2020*, Table 10 and US Census Bureau (2021c). Quickfacts.

Note: People who identified as two or more races, other, or unknown are not included on the chart. Rounding also contributes to totals not equaling.

Our nation's prisons (both state and federal) disproportionately hold men and people of color. A full 93 percent of inmates are male and about 30 percent of the population is White, 33 percent Black, and 23 percent is Hispanic. Table 13.5 shows a much more complicated intersectional analysis of the race and gender of people sentenced to state correctional institutions. The table is difficult to read because it tells us the percentage of males and females who fall into each racial/ethnic category. For example, it tells us that out of all the males in prison, 29 percent are White (while White people make up 58 percent of the US population). But among female prisoners, a full 47 percent are White. This makes it clear why intersectional analysis is so important. White women are much more likely to be locked up than White men, but this relationship is reversed for Black and Hispanic people. Table 13.5 also shows that Black men make up about 34 percent of the male population in prison but only 12 percent of the general population. Black women are overrepresented as well, but by much less (17.7 percent compared to 12 percent).

Race and gender are not the only category of inequality related to the risk of incarceration. Income and education are important as well. One large-scale study found that, of people who were incarcerated between 2009 and 2013, 56 percent had no earnings at all two years prior to their arrest. Of those who were working, average wages were only $12,780 (Looney & Turner, 2018). For reference, in 2010, the average income was about $39,959 (Khimm, 2011). Incarcerated people also tend to come from families that are poor. Boys born to families in the lowest 10 percent of the income distribution had a 9.6 percent chance of being incarcerated as adults. This compares to a rate of 0.49 percent for those from the top 10 percent (Looney & Turner, 2018). In terms of education, a full 30 percent of incarcerated people have not completed high school, while the comparable figure for the general population is 14 percent (Tofig, 2017).

Much has been written about the reasons for mass incarceration and its effects. Several important scholars have linked it to the maintenance of inequality in society. In a widely read book, Michelle Alexander (2012) argued that mass incarceration is the "New Jim Crow." This new system, like slavery and Jim Crow before it, ensures that Black people remain economically and socially subservient. Unlike the prior systems, however, the New Jim Crow appears, on its face, to be racially neutral. Loïc Wacquant (2009) makes a similar argument, tracing what he calls "hyper-incarceration" to slavery and Jim Crow. He focuses more on class, however, seeing neoliberalism as justifying the reduction of the welfare state and the loss of jobs in urban centers. Hyper-incarceration becomes the new system to control the poor.

One other driver of the incarceration boom may involve mental health. Many state mental health residential facilities were closed in the 1960s over concerns about their terrible conditions.

The emptying of these asylums correlates with the increase in prison populations. While studies on whether these two phenomena are causal are equivocal, it makes some sense that they are connected (Kim, 2016). Communities were simply unable to provide enough services for the people who left the facilities. This likely led to an increase in homelessness as well as crime and arrests (Markowitz, 2006). While this cannot entirely account for mass incarceration, it may have played a part. Unfortunately, even though the wave of deinstitutionalization was nearly 50 years in the past, the same problems remain: there are simply not enough mental health services available in communities and our nation's prison system has taken over as a major provider of these services (Ford, 2015). It is estimated that about a third of all state and federal inmates have been diagnosed with a mental health condition. Three times as many prisoners qualify as having serious psychological distress than do people in general population (Bronson, 2017). While it was a correlational analysis and so cannot be taken as causal, states that have fewer mental health services available have higher rates of incarceration. In fact, in 2015, six of the ten states with the least access to mental health services were in the top ten states in terms of rates of incarceration (Mental Health America, 2016).

Impact of a Criminal Record on Individual-Level Inequality

Incarceration has a deep impact on inequality through its effects at the individual level. For example, a criminal record makes it very difficult to get a job, particularly for Black people. Research in Milwaukee found that even with identical resumés, not only were job applicants with criminal records less likely than noncriminals to be called back for interviews, but Black *noncriminals* even got fewer callbacks than Whites with *criminal* records. Whether Black or White, having a criminal record decreases the chances for employment, but this is especially true for those who are Black (Pager, 2003).

Imprisonment also erodes the employment skills and related human capital of incarcerated people, making them less likely and less eager to seek employment after being in prison (Apel & Sweeten, 2010). It seems logical to assume that this affects wages. Obviously, wages (or potential wages) are lost during the period of imprisonment, making life more difficult for children who are dependent on their incarcerated parents' income. Adding to this problem, families of prisoners incur costs for traveling to visit, expensive collect calls, and monetary fines attached to their loved one's convictions (Harris et al., 2010; Wakefield and Uggen, 2010).

How does having been incarcerated affect wages once people are released? The research findings are actually mixed on this question. Most studies find a negative impact but others find no or even a positive impact (see, for example, Kling, 2006; Western & Pettit, 2010). These divergent findings appear to be a function of the variation in incarceration's impact on different groups at different historical moments. A recent large-scale study finds that race is particularly salient. The wage impact of incarceration on White and Hispanic people appears to be low or nonexistent, while Black people take a significant wage hit as a result of incarceration (Apel & Powell, 2019). These effects further reduce the chances of building up wealth for the next generation and help reproduce inequality.

Incarceration reduces a person's political power because 48 out of 50 states in the United States do not allow prison inmates to vote. Additionally, many of these states severely limit individuals with felonies from voting even after they have served their sentences. As a result, in 2020, about 5.7 million citizens were not allowed to vote due to having felonies on their records. This included 1 in every 16 Black people (Uggen et al., 2020). Many of the disenfranchisement rules were passed after the Civil War during Reconstruction, when Black people were a potential political force. States in which non-Whites made up a large percentage of the prison population are those most likely to have the most restrictive disenfranchisement laws (Behrens et al., 2003).

Notably, in 2018, Florida voters passed Amendment 4, overturning their disenfranchisement law. Florida had been one of only three states that permanently disenfranchised all former felons. In response to the success of Amendment 4, the state government passed a law disallowing anyone who owes fines or fees to the state from voting. This likely affects a significant percentage (estimates suggest more than three-quarters) of people with felony records, overriding the will of the people to allow them the vote (Mower & Taylor, 2020).

Many people in our nation's prisons are parents. In 2019, more than 5.7 million children under the age of 18 had one or both parents incarcerated during some portion of their childhood—this represents 1 in 12 children (Gotsch, 2018). The incarceration of a mother is particularly damaging because it often results in a child being placed in foster care, but the incarceration of either parent has been linked to problems for children including: mental health issues, a drop in educational achievement, and a weakening of the bond with the parent (Anne E. Casey Foundation, 2016; Nurse, 2002; Pew Research Center, 2016b). This means that mass incarceration will have societal effects for many years to come.

Impact of Mass Incarceration on Societal Level Inequality

When most people think about the effects of incarceration, they think about the individual-level effects like those described above. Research has found, however, that there are also community and macro-level effects. The prison system tends to draw from particular impoverished urban neighborhoods, resulting in what Laura Kurgan and Eric Cadora (2006) called "million dollar blocks." This name reflects the fact that the state is paying at least a million dollar a year to imprison people from these blocks. These neighborhoods suffer as their residents bounce in and out of the prison system.

Sociologist Todd Clear finds that low levels of incarceration do not appear to strongly impact an area's crime rate, moderate levels decrease it, and high levels actually increase crime because of their impact on social cohesiveness and informal social control (Clear et al., 2003). He says, "Concentrated incarceration in those impoverished communities has broken families, weakened the social-control capacity of parents, eroded economic strength, soured attitudes toward society, and distorted politics; even, after reaching a certain level, it has increased rather than decreased crime" (2009, p. 5). Rates of both sexually transmitted disease and teenage pregnancy also increase as incarceration increases in a region (Nowotny et al., 2020).

Beyond simply forbidding prisoners to vote, strict disenfranchisement rules may also have a dampening effect on voting rates of Black people and lower socioeconomic groups in general, further weakening the impact of these groups on political outcomes and policies (Bowers & Preuhs, 2009). Such laws can affect who gets elected to the US Congress and the presidency (Uggen et al., 2016).

Summary

In this chapter, we looked at the relationship between inequality, crime, and criminal justice. Official statistics reveal a relationship between being male, a minority, or poor and the probability of being arrested. Part of this association stems from the school-to-prison pipeline, which funnels low-status children into the criminal justice system. The bulk of the studies on arrests and sentencing also suggests a bias against groups of lower socioeconomic standing and people who are racial/ethnic minorities. A variety of data, then, raise questions about the fairness of the criminal justice system. The definition of the crime problem in terms of FBI Crime Index offenses, the special treatment given to white-collar crime, official reporting of crimes, and the type of punishment also strongly suggest that justice is not evenly meted out in US society.

Moreover, the findings of a relationship between income inequality and crime rates suggest that inequality helps produce crime and that reductions in inequality may produce reductions in crime. Hate crimes, motivated by biases against particular demeaned status groups, also reflect the social inequalities in society.

Critical Thinking

1. What must be done to change the living conditions in low-income neighborhoods that help generate street crime?
2. Historically, why has ordinary street crime received more attention from authorities than white-collar and corporate crimes when evidence suggests they result in greater costs for individual victims and society than street crime?
3. What are the most pressing inequalities in terms of criminal justice in our country? What are some ways we can begin to tackle them?

Web Connections

The Sentencing Project regularly collects and reviews information on prison populations, state laws, sentencing issues, and criminal justice in general. It is a good place to find data summaries on a variety of law enforcement topics. Go to www.sentencingproject.org.

Film Suggestions

Time (2020). Winner of the best director award at Sundance, this documentary follows Sibil Fox Richardson as she works to get her husband released from prison.

The Sentence (2019). This documentary looks at the impact of mandatory minimum sentences with a focus on one woman's story.

Southwest of Salem: The San Antonio Four (2016). This documentary follows the case of four Latina lesbians who were wrongfully convicted of raping two girls. It explores the homophobia and racism in the legal system.

Prison Kids (2015). Provides a view into the juvenile justice system through the stories of four different young people.

13th (2016). A powerful movie about how America has used the prison system to control and contain Black people.

PART 5

Social Change

14 Social Inequality and Social Movements

In societies where extensive social inequality not only exists but is also perceived as being unjust, it is not unusual for people to demonstrate their feelings against it. The large-scale Black Lives Matter protests began in 2015 and the #MeToo movement are good contemporary examples. Systems of inequality instigate social movements aimed at altering them, and conversely, the success of social movements is measured in terms of their impact on those systems. The extent to which either of these relationships is actualized, as you will see, depends on structural, cultural, and historical conditions in the society at the time. Economic shifts, prevalent ideologies, political policies, and unique historical events all impress themselves on the shapes of inequality and social movements.

Consistent with our multidimensional focus, following a discussion of social movement theory, this chapter will explore social movements related to class, race, and gender that aim explicitly at reducing inequality and improving the life chances of the groups in question, as well as a brief analysis of those social movements aimed at maintaining status and privilege. The purpose here is not to provide an exhaustive history of these movements, but rather to demonstrate systematically how each of them grew out of conditions relating to the structure of social inequality at the time, and how that structure affected the ebb and flow, goals, and tactics of those movements.

What Are Social Movements?

Inequality has never been popular, particularly for those at the losing end of the equation. But it has not always spurred collective action. At various moments in history, citizens have protested unfair treatment, but these protests have not always risen to the level of an organized social movement. For our purposes, social movements can be defined as "collective challenges, based on common purposes and social solidarities, in sustained interaction with elites, opponents, and authorities" (Tarrow, 2011, p. 9). As such, they are more than episodic moments of discontent—they involve a leadership structure, members, resources, and coordinated efforts. The rise of extended and cohesive social movements marks a particular moment in history, beginning in the late eighteenth century with the expansion of nation-states and the growth of capitalism (Staggenborg, 2015; Tilly & Wood, 2015).

As nation-states developed in the eighteenth and nineteenth centuries, so did the rise of electoral politics. The spread of democracy has been key to the rise of social movements, as the "empowerment of citizens through contested elections and other forms of consultation combines with protections of civil liberties such as association and assembly to channel popular claim making into social movement forms" (Tilly & Wood, 2015, p. 11). Electoral politics encourage the rise of special interest groups, whose favor is courted by candidates and parties. These groups often overlap, intersect, interact, and sometimes compete for the attention of candidates, resulting in increasingly identifiable social movements.

DOI: 10.4324/9781003184966-19

The shift to capitalistic modes of production is also central to the rise of social movements as we know them today. As feudal serfs leave the spatially and legally bounded environment of working for landlords and begin to engage in wage labor, they are freer to interact with other workers and participate in political activity (Staggenborg, 2015, p. 5). Significantly, the rise of capitalism also brings an increase in disaffected members of the bourgeoisie and the rise of the middle class; these groups engage in coalition building with workers over common concerns, or at least common enemies such as the landed aristocracy (Tarrow, 2011, p. 75). The middle-class members bring with them resources and connections to wider-ranging networks, making social movements more feasible.

Social movements have a variety of aims, categorized by Tilly and Wood as claims that are about products, identity, or standing (Tilly & Wood, 2015, p. 13). Movements focused on products are those that oppose current or proposed actions taken by the movement's target, such as efforts by anti-vaccination activists to protest federal vaccine requirements. Identity claims establish the cohesion of a particular group, emphasizing its solidarity and "we-ness," as exemplified by the #MeToo movement. Finally, standing claims address perceived slights or grievances of one group compared to others, as seen in the gay rights movement's efforts to guarantee the same marriage rights for LGBTQ individuals as were available to heterosexual couples, or the racial grievances expressed by the Proud Boy organizations. Though at their origin, movements may be centered on a particular claim, at various points in their histories, movements may shift their claims and focus on new sets of concerns.

Some social movement theorists argue that differences in the nature of claims between movements mark a change from **"old" social movements** that mostly focused on class issues and the redistribution of wealth, and "new" social movements, where participants were not "seeking to gain political and economic concessions from institutional actors, to further their 'interests' in conventional terms. Rather they sought recognition for new identities and lifestyles" (Polletta & Jasper, 2001, p. 286). These so-called new social movements focused on "quality of life issues," and included among others the anti-war movements of the 1960s, the feminist movement, the LGBTQ rights movement, and the environmental movement. New social movement theory arose when scholars recognized that the Marxist theories of social change that were based on an industrial economy and which focused on the needs of workers did not explain the rise of movements in a postindustrial age (Pichardo, 1997). As we will see below, as these movements arose from a society structured very differently from an industrial economy; the movements themselves started to be structured differently, as they "prefer to remain outside of normal political channels, employing disruptive tactics and mobilizing public opinion to gain political leverage" (p. 415). These movements reflect the networked society within which they have arisen, and as such, mobilize a variety of physical and digital networks, working at the intersections of various identities (Castells, 2015; Wang et al., 2018).

Current social movement theorists, however, argue that the distinction between social movements and normal political channels such as political parties is no longer very clear—indeed, it may never have been. The labor movement has generally been connected with the Democratic Party, and the Tea Party with Republicans (Kincaid, 2017). Political leaders and parties have become quite adept at leveraging the organizational and emotional power of social movements.

How Do Social Movements Arise?

Regardless of their aims or structure, how do social movements arise? Early in the history of social movement theory, scholars recognized that it is not simply the case that when conditions are at their worst, workers revolt. While they do not all agree on primary causes, however, they have focused on three central factors (McAdam, 2017). First, social movements need the political

---

BOX 14.1 HOW HAS SOCIAL MEDIA CHANGED SOCIAL MOVEMENTS?

Social movements have always relied on the media to coordinate their efforts, gain new supporters, and publicize their activities. The rise of social media has amplified these efforts, and in many
respects, changed the nature and operations of social movements. Current social movements use
social media for "mobilizing offline protests or online actions through weak ties, sustaining online
communities and collective identities to be used for political mobilization, and proliferating sympathetic movement frames and messaging to counter mainstream narratives about movement issues"
(Caren et al., 2020, p. 448).

Social media outlets allow social movements to skirt barriers imposed on communications by
mainstream media or governments, as we saw with the Arab Spring protests (Charrad & Reith,
2019) and the January 6th insurrection at the Capitol (Timberg et al., 2021). They have also been
useful in building solidarity for a cause, as we saw with the #SayHerName movement that brought
attention to the police killings of Black women, and in building a common social identity and culture
surrounding an issue, as in the case of global youth movements surrounding climate change (Nasrin
& Fisher, 2021).

But there might be a downside to the interpenetration of social media into social movements.
As quickly as social media can create buzz and excitement around a hashtag, it can also spur
instantaneous and cohesive opposition to that movement. We saw this clearly with the rise of the
#BlackLivesMatter movement, which gave rise to the counter movement to deracialize police brutality
with #AllLivesMatter (Gallagher et al., 2018).

Additionally, the anonymity and ease of creation of social media platforms allow the rise of movements centered on behaviors and attitudes that would be otherwise socially unacceptable, and allow
for the practice of covert mobilization, as we saw with the January 6th insurrection. The ease of
posting across platforms allows for "(t)he strategic deployment of a 'softer side' of narratives that
cast the far right as an oppressed minority against a pluralistic, multicultural majority, while within
more anonymous platforms they employ offensively vitriolic racist and sexist rhetoric" (Caren et al.,
2020, p. 151).

Do you think that social media has been a good thing for social movements? What standards, if
any, should be imposed on social media?

---

opportunity to rise and thrive, since "lacking standing in institutional politics, their bargaining
position relative to established polity members is weak" (p. 194). At their onset, claim-makers
are on the outside of the status quo and are therefore reasonably powerless. But as power relations
change, opportunities begin to develop. This change can come from a variety of sources, including demographic shifts, environmental or economic crises, political realignments, or precipitating
events. For example, the #NeverAgain gun control movement was developed by high school
students who were survivors of a mass shooting at the Marjory Stoneman Douglas High School.
This tragic moment provided the political opportunity for their voices to be heard.

Second, once the political environment has changed, making room for the rise of a social
movement, there must also exist the organizational or "mobilizing structures through which
emergent movements seek to organize and press their claims" (McAdam, 2017, p. 194). Social
movements need some vehicle by which they can organize, mobilize resources, and catalyze
change. These vehicles often include existing social networks or institutions—thus, the Civil
Rights movement took advantage of the network of Black churches as it began to mobilize, and
the anti-war movement of the 1960s developed in great part from student organizing efforts at
residential colleges (McAdam, 2003).

Finally, the claims made by social movements need to be framed and interpreted in ways that
gain resonance. As McAdam explains, social movements involve both emotional and cognitive

components. First, people need to feel angry and believe that they have been harmed; and second, they must by some measure cognitively understand that there is hope to remedy the situation and see a path towards remedial action.

The recent increase in activity of right-wing movements has prompted a theoretical rethinking of how and when social movements arise. Unlike social movements from the left, right-wing movements are those that act "on behalf of relatively advantaged groups with the goal of preserving, restoring and expanding the rights and privileges of its members and constituents" (McVeigh, 2009, p. 32). Compared with others, these movements are not coming from a place of less privilege and reduced resources, and thus their focus has been more on threats to political and status-based power. Status-based arguments are those that go "beyond economic interest and open up the possibility of political action centered in issues of honor, prestige, and values" (Kincaid, 2017, p. 4). At the same time, they maintain attention to material concerns: "modern right-wing political movements work to incorporate aspects of both symbolic politics and status-based concerns over lifestyle, values, and prestige while simultaneously blending these issues with concerns over the control of material resources" (Kincaid, 2017, p. 5).

Right-wing movements are connected to inequality in several ways. Rising inequality reduces levels of cohesion and trust in a society, creating tensions between economic groups and raising concerns about status and power. It increases our level of intolerance of others, and leads to the "erosion of prosocial behavior" (Jay et al., 2019, p. 421). Additionally, inequality increases the level of anxiety for all economic groups—it becomes clear that everyone can lose their standing, and "those who are wealthier may rapidly become more fearful when they perceive that the economic context becomes unpredictable and unstable" (Jetten et al., 2017, p. 76). During times of greater economic inequality and stability, fear of immigrants and "out-groups" increases (Jay et al., 2019).

As we will see from the discussion below, right-wing movements have not been the first or only movements to mobilize emotion. In her recent book on the Movement for Black Lives, Woodly argues that we are "in the grips of a politics of despair" that has been decades in the making (2021, p. 6). Several trends contribute to this political moment, including "(1) rising inequality, (2) declining political trust, (3) declining interpersonal trust, (4) declining civic knowledge, (5) declining and stratified political participation, and (6) declining political efficacy" (p. 6). Within this politics of despair lies the hope and potential for contemporary social movements to reengage the public in political participation. Social movements can "remind members of the polity that there is a public sphere where politics can and must take place if democracy is to be both authorized by and responsive to the people" (p. 18).

The rest of this chapter outlines these dynamics in movements focused on class, race, and gender. These are certainly not the only social movements that have had significant impacts on our cultural, social, and political environments. For example, as we discussed in Chapter 9, the LGBTQ rights movement has achieved important gains in policies such as marriage equality. The movements discussed in this chapter are illustrative, however, of central processes and dilemmas facing social movements addressing inequality. While several of the more recent movements appear very different in their aims and structure compared with the older movements, they share the common goals of addressing inequalities and bringing about social change. They also owe much of their inspiration, energy, and tactics to those movements preceding them.

The Labor Movement

Raymond Hogler et al. (2015) contend that the viability of a continuously strong labor movement has been made problematic in the United States by cultural values associated with the founding of the country. Beliefs in individualism, small government, a Protestant ethic, free markets and free labor, and the sanctity of private property have made it difficult for the labor movement to prosper on a consistent basis. Nevertheless, many of the rights and advances enjoyed by workers today are due to the historic efforts of labor unions.

The Historical Development of the Labor Movement: The Industrial Revolution

Although the first recorded strike in the United States was in 1768 by New York journeyman tailors, the large-scale development of trade unionism occurred during the Industrial Revolution with the establishment of the American Federation of Labor (AFL) in 1886 (Nicholson, 2004). The poor conditions and deprivations experienced by industrial workers in the latter part of the nineteenth and early part of the twentieth centuries created dissatisfaction and feelings of hostility. Even though there was some improvement in wages after 1880, hours were long, wages remained low, and working conditions were dangerous. There were few, if any, protections against the hazards of chemicals, machinery, and inhalants from work in the mines and mills, nor the dangers in working on the railroads, construction, and logging.

In the waning decades of the nineteenth century, the social organization of the economy was undergoing rapid change, and these changes had implications for both employers and employees. Industrialization brought in its wake a more simplified, detailed division of labor, increasing the need for less-skilled laborers. This **scientific management**, sometimes called Fordism, divided the work process into its smallest components in order to increase efficiency and output on the shop floor. Machines often fomented dissatisfaction among skilled craftworkers and encouraged antagonism between the unskilled industrial workers. As machines rapidly took the place of workers, control over the workplace more frequently fell into the hands of owners and their foremen. These shifts in technology helped to stimulate the growth of the labor movement.

Along with technological changes, productivity rose rapidly, but so did the demand for labor. Immigrants flooded into the United States from a variety of countries. Consequently, the late nineteenth century was also a period in which the size of company workforces increased. The industrial working class grew significantly, but it was composed of individuals from sharply contrasting social and cultural backgrounds. As the demand for labor grew, and immigrants flooded into the country to take lower positions in the mines, mills, and factories, the labor force in the North was almost as segregated by nationality in 1900 as the southern market was by race (Green, 1980). Moreover, as the century came to an end, the proportion of women and African Americans involved in industry also increased. In 1900, almost a quarter of all women were in the labor force.

Not surprisingly, early efforts of unionization met with strong resistance from business owners. The heterogeneous nature of the working class at this time created divisions that hindered the solidarity of workers, and owners capitalized on this. When conflict arose with their employees, immigrants and Black workers were often used as strike-breakers. Additionally, spies were employed to monitor labor activities and legal actions were encouraged against militant workers and organizations. The informal political alliance between business and government was reflected in the frequent use of police or military might in putting down worker protests; in numerous strike actions between 1890 and 1920, state militia and federal troops were used against workers.

Finally, the rise of **welfare capitalism** helped to minimize solidarity among workers. Briefly, welfare capitalism included special savings plans and bonuses, homeownership aid programs, stock-purchasing options, and group insurance plans. Most significant among the programs offered were employee representation plans or work councils and unions controlled by the company. These plans presumably gave workers a meaningful voice in the operation of the organization, but did not enhance the ability of labor to organize effectively in its own interests.

Early unionizing efforts were characterized by racial and ethnic conflict. Some labor leaders had no wish at all to bring non-Whites into the organized labor movement, but rather were

Photo 14.1 Unions fought for and won an end to child labor in the United States.
Source: Glasshouse Images/Alamy Stock Photo.

primarily interested in advancing the interests of White, skilled craftworkers. Exclusionary practices, including explicit policies prohibiting the admission of non-Whites, were not uncommon among many AFL unions (Green, 1980). Samuel Gompers, who founded the American Federation of Labor in 1881, was against the inclusion of non-White, nonskilled workers. In 1905, Gompers proclaimed to a group of union members in Minneapolis that "Caucasians" were "not going to let their standard of living be destroyed by Negroes, Chinamen, Japs, or any others" (quoted in Green, 1980, p. 46).

In contrast to the American Federation of Labor, which sought to unionize skilled White craftworkers, other organizers felt that it was crucial to organize all industrial workers. Among those groups that supported the organization of all workers, some had socialist or communist leanings. The Socialist Party of America, founded in 1901 under the leadership of the charismatic Eugene Debs, also favored an organizational umbrella that would cover the mass of workers in industry. A few years later, the Industrial Workers of the World (IWW), and several decades later, the Congress of Industrial Organizations (CIO) also actively sought the membership of Black and all industrial workers.

From the Depression to the Present

The 1920s and the early 1930s were not kind to US workers. Bernstein (2010) labeled the 1920–1933 period "the lean years" for workers. A litany of the problems for workers included the stagnation of the union movement during the period (union membership fell from 5 million in 1920 to 3.5 million in 1929) and the absence of any effective industry-wide collective-bargaining tools. Employers could hire whom they wanted, and workers had little recourse in the matter. Older workers found it more and more difficult to hold on to their jobs, as farm migrants and women increasingly entered the urban labor force. Mechanization displaced workers and up to a third could not find work again. Moreover, the shift to more mechanized professional positions did not help workers who did not have the qualifications for such positions.

The effects of the Great Depression on employment were disastrous. In the middle of 1930, almost 4.5 million were without jobs. By early 1931, an estimated 8.3 million were unemployed, but the number was to rise even further to 13.6 million by the end of that year, and to 15 million by early 1933. At that time, about one-third of all wage/salary workers were completely out of work. Many others were only working on a part-time basis (Bernstein, 2010).

Needless to say, the Depression changed political dynamics inside and outside the labor movement. It made many workers and unions recognize the need for state help and intervention and it spurred questions about the ability of the present economic and political systems to deal with catastrophic problems, especially as it became clear over the bitter years of the 1930s that it was not the lack of individual efforts but rather broader social forces that were behind much of the misery being experienced (Piven & Cloward, 1979). At the same time, however, most citizens still had faith in the US system and did not see socialism or communism as a viable alternative. Nor did they think of themselves as a cohesive working class fighting capitalism (Aronowitz, 1973; Zieger, 1986).

In the early part of the twentieth century, labor had received little help from the federal government. Several critical events strengthened labor's hand during the 1930s. One was the rising prospect of war in Europe. US companies that had armament contracts with European countries could not afford major labor unrest to disrupt production. A second event, mentioned above, was the passage of the Wagner Act, which legalized the right of workers to organize and bargain collectively under the protection of the National Labor Relations Board (NLRB). The NLRB had the power to monitor business compliance with the law. This law, bitterly fought by business, resulted in a rapid upsurge in union membership (see Figure 14.1). In the mid- and late 1930s, union membership tripled, reaching about 9 million by 1939 (Zieger, 1986). The New Deal and

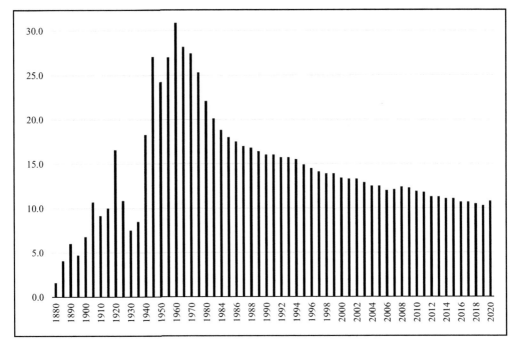

Figure 14.1 Percentage of US Work Force Holding Union Membership, 1880–2020.

Source: Data from 1880 to 1984 are from the Harvard Business School (2021), *Trade Union Membership.* https://www. hbs.edu/businesshistory/courses/resources/historical-data-visualization/Pages/details.aspx?data_id=37. Data from 1985 to the present are from the Bureau of Labor Statistics (2021c), *Union Members Summary.* https://www.bls.gov/webapps/legacy/cpslutab1.htm

events during the 1930s left in their wake a triumvirate of power: big government, big business, and big labor. During and after World War II, union membership was still high and growing, and unions were an effective force for improving working conditions for their members.

Despite this growth in union power, by the end of the 1930s, the ideological tide had already begun to shift against organized labor. As a result, the Taft-Hartley Act of 1947 was able to pass. It renewed many of the powers that businesses had lost by the Wagner Act, including allowing states to pass laws stating that employees cannot be required to join a union or to pay dues. As we will see, this ruling gave rise to later "right to work" laws. It also curbed the power of unions to strike, required an anti-Communist pledge from workers, and redefined labor's rights in much narrower terms (Piven & Cloward, 1979; Zieger, 1986). Union membership generally grew during the 1950s, reaching its peak in 1960. However, differences of opinion within the labor community surfaced over Vietnam and the civil rights and women's movements of the 1960s, leading to declines in membership.

The Russian Revolution, America's involvement in World War I, and the accompanying patriotic fervor that swept the nation legitimated political and coercive attacks on socialist organizations and the IWW. As a result, the power of the left in organized labor declined. In the patriotic context of the postwar period, organized labor, in general, was a victim of attacks from industry. With the restrictive immigration laws of the 1920s reducing the inflow of unskilled labor, industry's source of fresh workers was weakened, meaning that there were fewer workers to bring into the unions. By the late 1920s, labor unrest had calmed down even though the cost of living was increasing, erasing many of the gains that had been made by some workers (Zieger, 1986).

During the conservative 1980s and early 1990s, unions were again under attack, membership declined, and union leadership appeared weaker than in the earlier heyday of organized labor. More specifically, the breach of traditional understandings between unions and management, coupled with vigorous business attacks on unions since the 1970s, helped to weaken unions. In addition, globalization, and rapid employment growth in new areas coupled with higher unemployment in traditional occupations, the lack of national unity among unions, and a hostile political climate certainly contributed (Clawson & Clawson, 1999; Farber & Western, 2016). Today, only 10.8 percent of wage and salary workers in the United States are union members (this rate is up 0.5 percent since 2019, though this may be due to a greater rate of job loss of non-unionized workers than unionized workers during the pandemic). The rate among public employees is much higher than that found among workers in the private sector (34.8 versus 6.3 percent), and it is much higher in traditionally more liberal regions such as the Northeast, Midwest, and Pacific West, than in more conservative areas such as the South and Mountain West. Finally, men are slightly more likely to belong to unions than women, and Black workers are more likely than White, Asian, or Hispanic workers (US Bureau of Labor Statistics, 2021c).

During the pandemic, there has been a substantial increase in unionizing activity and labor unrest: Liz Shuler, president of the AFL-CIO, stated that "I've been traveling a lot to picket lines all over the country in the last couple of months, been in so many different states and across all industries. But the one thing that's been really consistent is the sentiment of the working people who are out there taking the risks is that they are absolutely fed up" (Sainato, 2021). With workers quitting at record rates, unions are feeling emboldened, leading to greater unionizing efforts, seen most notably in the success of the first union vote in a Starbucks facility. The pandemic years have also seen thousands of workers striking, representing manufacturing (John Deere, Volvo), food production (Frito-Lay, Nabisco, Kellogg's), higher education (New York University, Columbia University, Harvard), and fast-food chains (McDonald's, Wendy's Burger King) (Sainato, 2021).

Importantly but not surprisingly, the decline of union membership is occurring at a time of conservatism, increasing globalization, and open markets, when transnational corporations have gained more economic and political leverage. The weakness of labor against business does not bode well for a decline in economic inequality. Indeed, a study by Western and Rosenfeld (2011) finds that the decline in unions accounts for between a fifth and a third of the growth in inequality from 1973 to 2007. "The decline of American labor and the associated increase in wage inequality signalled the deterioration of the labor market as a political institution" (Western & Rosenfeld, 2011, p. 533).

Perhaps the labor movement has come full circle and will again mobilize to restore worker power. It is helpful that most of the public are sympathetic, with approval of labor unions at 68 percent in 2021, its highest since 1965. Approval was at its lowest in 2009 at 48 percent (Brenan, 2021). At the same time, most do not feel that union members who work in the public sphere, such as teachers, police officers, and firefighters, should be allowed to strike. In light of local and state budgetary problems, unionization and collective bargaining by public employees have become a hot issue. In the past few decades, we have seen an increase in states adopting "right to work" laws limiting the ability of unions to require membership. Currently, 27 states have enacted such laws. Research suggests that the passage of these laws has had the political effect of creating a negative environment for unions, while at the same time increasing income inequality by lowering labor's power and resources (VanHeuvelen, 2020).

The Civil Rights Movement

While the labor movement was consequential in focusing attention on inequality and injustices, scholars agree that the civil rights movement of the 1950s and 1960s represented a watershed moment in social movements and "fertilized the ground in which numerous American social movements took root and flowered into widespread collective action" (Morris, 1999, p. 528). At the cusp of the movement in the early 1940s, following protests of the police killing of an unarmed soldier in Baltimore, Congressman Adam Clayton Powell, Jr., one of only two Black representatives serving in Congress, stated: "It is up to the colored people now to save democracy in America, for it seems there is on one left in America who knows what democracy is" (Williams, 2015, p. x). These words have held powerful resonance from that moment up to present struggles for social justice.

As was the case in the labor movement, there had been many instances of protest against racial injustice before the civil rights movement. Revolts by slaves against their masters, the Underground Railroad, the massive growth of the National Association for the Advancement of Colored People (NAACP) membership to almost half a million during World War II, and the demands that led Roosevelt to establish a Fair Employment Practices Committee all provide evidence of racial protest and a push for racial equality before the purported beginning of the civil rights movement (Morris, 1999; Williams, 2015).

Anti-lynching efforts beginning with Reconstruction were emblematic of these early efforts, brought to popular audiences with Billie Holiday's iconic song "Strange Fruit," referencing Black bodies hanging from Southern trees. Journalist Ida B. Wells is perhaps best known for exposing the prevalence of lynching and linking it to White supremacy in the late 1800s. Wells argued that "lynching was intricately linked to the protection of white economic power. It was an unofficial tool of the state to thwart black economic advancement" (Francis, 2018).

In the late nineteenth and early twentieth centuries, Black people had few resources with which to launch a massive civil rights campaign. First, racist ideologies discouraged support from Whites. Second, most Black Americans were fully but exploitatively integrated into the Southern economic and political structure. There were few economic opportunities open to them, and Jim Crow laws kept them in their assigned place. Finally, the federal government did little to alleviate the oppressive conditions under which Black people lived. Congress stood by as they were disenfranchised and treated violently in the South.

An indisputable specific date for the beginning of the civil rights movement cannot be given, though the traditional argument is that it began in the period between 1953 and 1955, during which the Supreme Court's historic *Brown v. Board of Education* decision was made, and systematic bus boycotts began in Baton Rouge, Louisiana, and Montgomery, Alabama. Contemporary scholars, however, refer to a "long" civil rights movement that goes back much further, with the most active phase beginning during the WWII era and rising in both the North and the South (Williams, 2014; Williams, 2015).

The Changing Context of Racial Inequality

After World War I, it was clear that changing economic and political conditions would strengthen the power position of Black Americans. Among these economic changes was a decline in the centrality of agriculture in the Southern economy coupled with increasing industrialization of the urban South. This agrarian decline was fostered, in part, by declines in immigration and agricultural exports during the war. Accompanying the decline in immigration was an increase in the demand by northern industry for laborers from the South. Both "King Cotton" and industry needed workers, but changing circumstances created a shift in demand from agriculture to industry. Called the "Great Migration," before and after the war, there was massive African American migration to the North and to cities to seek employment in industries (McAdam, 2010).

Southern agriculture suffered again during the Great Depression of the early 1930s. An overproduction of cotton due to decreased demand led to a drastic decline in its price, which spelled disaster for many Southern farmers. In Mississippi, at that time, perhaps the greatest stronghold of White supremacy, farmers lost their land at about twice the national rate (Bloom, 2019). Later, during the 1940s, as mechanization also became more and more essential in agriculture, some farmers left agriculture behind, and the average size of land-holdings increased. This meant that more Black as well as White farmworkers were economically displaced and needed to seek employment in the industries of northern and southern cities (Piven & Cloward, 1979). Southern agriculture also had to diversify its products to feed the soldiers in military camps during World War II (Bloom, 2019). All these circumstances served to shake up the foundations of the traditional economy in the South.

The changed geographic and economic base of Black Americans helped to develop their voting power and the institutional bases needed for the civil rights movement (McAdam, 2010). Cities provided greater opportunities for them to get organized, to receive more education, and to lay the basis for an expanded Black middle class. The growth of these strengths within the Black community was important in the genesis of the civil rights movement. There is good evidence that, despite the importance of external resources to the movement, its origins and development can be traced to reliance on institutions indigenous to the Black community (Hunter, 2013b; Morris, 2015).

Black colleges, churches, and civic and fraternal institutions provided not only economic resources but also the communication network and most of the leaders needed to organize the movement. Martin Luther King Jr., for example, was influential as a movement leader not only because of his charisma but also, crucially, because of the personal and organizational backing he received (Clayton, 2018). The influence of the Southern Christian Leadership Conference (SCLC) during most of the movement's career suggests the relevance of religious institutions.

Local colleges also provided most of the students who, early in the 1960s, were involved in the civil disobedience actions that helped bring about legislative changes.

External support of protests generally comes after the protests themselves. These additional resources are a *product* rather than a *cause* of protest (McAdam, 2010). The patronage that did come later from outsiders appears to have been given less out of feelings of conscience and injustice than out of concern to keep the movement moderate, weaken the radical element, and exercise some control over the direction of the movement (Jenkins & Eckert, 1986). The nonviolent sit-ins of college students and others in the South in the early 1960s, for example, brought much financial and other support from outside, northern groups. The violent protests later in the 1960s in northern and western cities, on the other hand, produced a White backlash, partly because of the violence, but also because of the switch in focus of problems from the rural South to the urban ghettos of the North.

Establishment forces were further weakened by many people's negative reaction to the increased stridence and militancy of White Southerners' reaction to African American protests for equality. This helped to isolate the South, especially the Deep South, from the rest of the nation. On the other side, changing economic and social conditions created a split in the "Solid South" between the interests of business and agriculture. The traditional social and political structure had been grounded in a particular kind of economy. A weakening in the basis of that agricultural economy threatened the survival of sociopolitical arrangements that primarily benefited the rich landowner and discriminated against African Americans. "Racial patterns and racial consciousness have as their foundation particular class structures, and they develop and change as these structures themselves change" (Bloom, 2019, p. 3).

Class and economic factors were implicated in the shifting allegiances to racial inequality, but *racist ideology* was still an underlying element in accounting for not only social and economic inequality in the South but also reactions to Black peoples' attempts to eliminate it. The continued significance of racism was manifested in the support given by lower-class as well as upper-class White Southerners to the discriminatory treatment of Black people. Upper-class White Southerners who had vested local economic interests fought the hardest against voting rights for Black Americans because to afford this right would have been tantamount to surrendering power to them. Although the voting regulations effectively prohibited many lower-class Whites as well as Blacks from voting, the former went along with their upper-class peers in supporting the laws. The Southern aristocracy played on racist images of Black people and used the image of competition between Blacks and Whites as a means to obtain the support of lower-class Whites and to reassert White supremacy following the Civil War (Gates, 2020).

In addition to the changes in the US economy and social-cultural factors that strengthened Black unity, other historical events and conditions helped to lay the groundwork for the civil rights movement that was to come in the 1950s. Migration to the North not only meant a greater probability of voting but also led to Black politicians holding office in several major cities (Bloom, 2019). Politicians with presidential aspirations became increasingly concerned about potential Black political defections and, as a result, often courted the Black vote.

Despite this courtship, governmental policies continued to underrepresent the interests of Black people. But they also, perhaps inadvertently, strengthened their position. As we saw in the history of the labor struggles, the New Deal's policies had an impact. Similarly, the public works programs of the New Deal provided Black people with an alternate source of income outside the relatively narrow range of private positions open to them. Having another source of income meant less dependence, and created a source of power with which to fight oppression (Bloom, 2019; Piven and Cloward, 2012). This federal source of work and the increased demand for labor in industry helped to drive wages up—wages that dominant agricultural groups were increasingly hesitant to pay (Bloom, 2019).

World War II brought further changes. Unionization of Black workers became less difficult than had been the case only a decade earlier. Employment conditions improved, especially with the wartime economy. National unity was a preferred emphasis, discouraging protest. But there was an emphasis among some of the "Double V": Victory abroad against fascism, and victory for democracy at home (Johnson, 2010, p. 207).

After the war, several political events occurred that affected efforts for racial equality. As we saw in the work of W.E.B. Du Bois, liberation struggles abroad against colonialism heartened many Black leaders who became convinced that change was possible (Morris, 2015). These events, coupled with the racist overtones of Nazism against which the United States had fought, meant that continued racial inequality at home could prove to be an embarrassment. Harry Truman, in running for the presidency in 1948, had to present a platform that showed a strong desire for civil rights if he was to defeat opponents who also were courting the vote of those Black Southerners who had migrated to the cities of the North. As part of this, he ordered the desegregation of the military. The economic and political context had shifted to the extent that Truman was advised to court Black voters even at the risk of turning away Southern Democrats (Piven & Cloward, 1979).

A final political element in the late 1940s that affected civil rights efforts came out of the developing "cold war" with the former Soviet Union. "Red-baiting" was fashionable, and civil rights groups and leaders were not immune to accusations of being communist (Rocksborough-Smith, 2018). White supremacists argued that communists were behind the movement for Black equality. McCarthyism understandably frightened Black people, and the majority of Black leaders took a gradual and calm approach. All of the conditions discussed thus far comprise the context in which the Supreme Court made its momentous *Brown v. Board of Education* decision in 1954.

A Brief History of the Civil Rights Movement

The *Brown v. Board of Education* decision was a true watershed in the effort for civil rights. It declared segregation in education to be unconstitutional. In concluding his argument, Chief Justice Earl Warren stated simply, "We conclude that in the field of public education the doctrine of 'separate but equal' has no place. Separate educational facilities are inherently unequal" (National Archives, 2016). This decision had a powerful effect on Black people and on Southern Whites. The movement for equality was given a boost, but at the same time, a White countermovement was established to fight these advances. While Black people were jubilant about the decision, the South's White elite were not about to accept it without a fight. Many said unequivocally that they would not comply with the law in this case (Morris, 1986, p. 27). Even though the decision by the Court to desegregate had been unanimous, it had not come to this decision easily. In order to get the unanimous ruling, Warren had to agree on a policy of gradual implementation of the desegregation policy. The qualification of gradualism left room for Southern dissenters to fight enforcement, and it led to frustration on the part of Black Americans who wished speedy implementation of the law.

There was no strong push on the part of the government for the implementation of the law; the dominance by conservative elements of the major political parties in Congress meant no rapid enforcement would be forthcoming. The FBI's J. Edgar Hoover still saw racial unrest as being communist-inspired (Bloom, 2019). In the South, White churches and the press generally opposed the ruling, and local White Citizens' Councils were set up to fight desegregation. In 1956, the membership in these councils approached 250,000 (Piven & Cloward, 1979).

In the mid-1950s, notable bus boycotts by Black citizens occurred in Baton Rouge, Montgomery, and Tallahassee. Perhaps the most famous of these was initiated by Rosa Parks in Montgomery in December of 1955. Parks was an active NAACP participant who first became involved in protests in Detroit. She had been put off a bus previously for refusing to move to the back. This time, she had gotten on a crowded bus and refused to surrender her seat to a White man and, at the next bus stop, she was arrested for violating the local bus ordinance (Williams, 2015). News of her arrest spread, and a bus boycott was organized by a group of local Black leaders. Assuming that it would be best to appoint an outsider as its leader, they appointed a hesitant, young, middle-class, nonviolent, and intellectually sophisticated Black minister to lead the boycott.

The Reverend Martin Luther King Jr. was well educated, a newcomer to the area, and had attended theological school in the North. He was stunned by the blatant racism that seemed to be so out of place in a period when Black people had become more educated and urbanized. His critiques about the state of the world at the time were wide ranging, focusing on concerns about "militarism, materialism, and racism" (Yanco, 2014). As a result, he was actively involved in anti-war and anti-poverty movements, though of course it is his work against racial injustice that we are most familiar.

Dr King's best-known early work in civil rights was with the Montgomery Improvement Association, where he led a nonviolent boycott of the bus system. Local Black churches provided sites for meetings and arranged for alternative modes of transportation. The boycott went on for over a year, and during that time, White resistance tried a range of tactics to bring it to an end. Legal tactics such as arrests and jailings for minor or fictitious infractions of local laws were used. Economic sanctions also were tried; some activists deeply involved in the boycott lost their jobs. Finally, violent tactics were used: Many beatings occurred, and four Black churches and the homes of King, his associate Ralph Abernathy, and another supporter were bombed. In the last analysis, however, the nonviolent boycott prevailed, and the US Supreme Court declared Alabama's bus segregation laws unconstitutional.

The nonviolent, long-suffering, patient approach of the boycott contrasted in the national media with the harsh White reaction. Many outside the South were appalled at the tactics used by the White resistance. In contrast, King's "neo-Gandhian persuasion" seemed reasonable and acceptable as a means for obtaining equal rights. Above all, it was nonviolent and embraced the Christian beliefs of turning the other cheek and not condemning individual racists. It blamed the system of segregation rather than the individuals who enforced it (King, 1958). As a result of the boycott, King and his approach to injustice gained worldwide attention. Out of the boycott, other civil rights groups were organized, most notably the SCLC under King's leadership.

A familiar pattern of Black-White confrontation began to develop as a result of the early boycotts. Basically, the sequence would begin with nonviolent Black protests, followed by a militant White response, which in turn often led to federal intervention. It did not take long for Black leaders to figure out how to get the attention of federal officials who had been unreliable and largely unresponsive in the past in enforcing rights that were theirs under the Constitution.

In the early 1960s, sit-ins were held throughout the South as a way of protesting segregation of public facilities. Similar protests were held in northern cities to demonstrate sympathetic support of the civil rights protestors. One of the most famous of the sit-ins occurred in early February 1960 in Greensboro, North Carolina. Four Black students sat down at a Woolworth's lunch counter and asked for coffee and donuts. When refused, they kept their seats until the store closed. The next day, more students did the same thing, but White officials remained implacable, and it was only after repeated sit-ins that Greensboro allowed such service six months later. This sit-in inspired similar protests throughout the South and afforded a means by which college students could become meaningfully involved in the civil rights movement. Adults also joined in these protests. Not only sit-ins at lunch counters but sleep-ins in the lobbies of motels, swim-ins at pools, play-ins at recreational areas, kneel-ins at churches, and read-ins at libraries followed. Boycotts also were carried out against merchants who refused desegregation (Sitkoff, 1981). Local White reactions were often swift and violent. Kickings, pistol whippings, dog attacks, jailing, and even acid throwing were among the repressive means used against the protestors. But still, the sit-ins continued.

One result of these demonstrations was that they showed Southerners the depth of Black feelings about these matters. They were also powerful in bringing to the attention of the nation the injustice of widespread legal segregation practices. Largely as a result of the active concern of Black college youths, their impatience with years of waiting, and the seemingly futile legal maneuverings of the more conservative approaches in the civil rights movement as typified by the NAACP, other, more militant types of organizations (such as the Student Nonviolent Coordinating Committee [SNCC]) began appearing in the early 1960s (Morris, 1999; Sitkoff, 1981).

In 1961, the Congress of Racial Equality (CORE), founded in 1942, organized a "freedom ride" from Washington, DC, to New Orleans to see if states and municipalities were complying with the federal law against discrimination in interstate bus terminals. These rides went into the Deep South where White resistance was strongest. As with other peaceful protests, these rides too evoked violent White resistance. Beatings and deaths of protestors, for example, took place in several Alabama cities, including Birmingham and Montgomery. Again, much of the violence was broadcast through the media.

It was only when waves of public sympathy came that the federal government acted to protect the protestors and enforce the law. When there was no publicity, little was done; violations of the law were left unpunished. It became clear to protestors that to receive public attention and sympathy and to prod the government to act, it was more effective to elicit a violent response. One of the most brutal reactions to the nonviolent demonstrations of King and the SCLC occurred in Birmingham in the spring of 1963. Sit-ins, marches, and similar techniques had been used to protest local segregation. After these had been going on for a time, the local police commissioner, Eugene "Bull" Connor, came down violently on the protestors. His violent response was seen by millions on television. Officials used dogs, high-pressure hoses, cattle prods, clubs, and even a police tank to beat down the protestors. President Kennedy and his brother Robert, who had wanted "cooling-down" periods by Black protestors and a more gradual approach to desegregation, sent federal representatives to help reach a compromise between King and local officials. But the protestors would not back down. Finally, the SCLC obtained desegregation of some public facilities, a promise of nondiscriminatory hiring, and the formation of a biracial committee in Birmingham (Sitkoff, 1981).

As successful protests became more frequent, more working-class Black people were drawn into the movement. Greater competition among the major Black organizations (SCLC, SNCC, CORE, NAACP) occurred with each group vying for the dominant position. They sponsored massive demonstrations throughout the country. A national March on Washington occurred in August 1963, sponsored by numerous civil rights, union, and church organizations and involving well over 200,000 individuals. During the summer of 1964, hundreds of individuals worked in Mississippi to increase voter registration, and three workers were brutally murdered. President Kennedy began to press for a civil rights law in 1963, and shortly thereafter, the Civil Rights and Voting Rights Acts were passed under President Johnson. This national legislative response helped to delegitimize the need for protest, especially in the eyes of northern Whites.

Despite the passage of these laws, several other changes had occurred that helped alter the nature of the Black movement from the nonviolent protest tactics of King to cries for "Black Power" and Black "Freedom." First, the slow, compromising approach of the federal government to the problems experienced by Blacks on a day-to-day basis, coupled with the patient nonviolent method of King, convinced some in the civil rights movement of the need for more drastic action on their own behalf. The consistently violent reactions by Whites to the nonviolent protests over the years widened the gap between factions within the civil rights movement in the early 1960s.

Second, the focus of the civil rights movement had been on the South, but the migration of many Black people into the cities of the North and West led to a shift in goal emphasis within the movement. The problems of Black city dwellers became the focus: poverty, employment, housing, poor schools, and so on. The civil rights movement has been interpreted by some as largely a movement by and for middle-class individuals, while the focus of the Black movement on problems of city residents appeared to demonstrate a greater concern for the Black working and lower classes. In total, the shift in the movement was from an emphasis on integration, political and social rights, and nonviolence to one on Black separatism, economic needs, and more militant tactics (Bloom, 2019).

At the heart of many of these later organizations and efforts was a connection between injustices against Blacks and the system of capitalism. An example of such an organization was the Mississippi Freedom Democratic Party (MFDP), established in great part due to the work of Ella Baker, Fannie Lou Hamer, and Robert Moses. "Organizations like the MFDP argued that egalitarian democracy was connected to dismantling the anti-Black state and its enablers, and that the most revolutionary way to dismantle the totalitarian state was to protest for the right to vote and for equal and fair political representation" (Francis & Wright-Rigueur, 2021, p. 448). A central focus of the MFDP was on state-sanctioned violence, revealing a "racist police state" (p. 448), brutally attacking and repressing Black individuals.

Violent riots occurred during the "long hot summers" of the 1960s in many major cities, including Chicago, Cleveland, Milwaukee, Dayton, San Francisco, Detroit, Newark, New Haven, Boston, Buffalo, and others. During this period, nearly 2000 rebellions occurred across the country. These rebellions were in response to "long-simmering community issues over police brutality, racial inequality, segregation, and discrimination" (Francis & Wright-Rigueur, 2021, p. 451).

The civil rights movement has led to a variety of important social and cultural changes in US society. It helped to break down Jim Crow and segregation laws, sparked programs to help the disadvantaged, and inspired hope for social progress. It certainly stimulated and provided major parts of the strategic and tactical frameworks for other rights movements such as those on behalf of women and LGBTQ individuals. Perhaps most significantly, the battles for civil rights in the 1950s and 1960s changed American culture by fostering more liberal and fair-minded attitudes. In this way, the civil rights movement of the 1960s has continued to influence most Americans today (Griffin & Bollen, 2009; Isaac, 2008), and is certainly present in current movements for racial justice such as the Black Lives Matter movement.

The Black Lives Matter Movement

While the Civil Rights Movement arguably entered a phase of quiescence following the 1970s and into the beginning of this century, movements toward racial justice have seen a resurgence with movements such as the Black Lives Matter movement and #SayHerName. These and other contemporary social justice movements, all build on past efforts and further the often invisible work of organizing that continues in the background (Clayton, 2018). Indeed, "'black lives matter' represents a civic desire for equality and a human desire for respect, the intellectual roots of which lie deep in the history of Black American thought" (Lebron, 2017). Despite this legacy of past movements, however, the Black Lives Matter movement (now expanded to the Movement for Black Lives or M4BL) is very different in structure and origin from those preceding it. Established by three Black and queer women in the era of social media, the movement is avowedly intersectional, and reflects our decentralized, networked society.

In 2012, Trayvon Martin, an unarmed 17-year-old Black boy, was shot and killed by George Zimmerman while walking in a Florida neighborhood. Prosecutors in the case argued that Zimmerman was suspicious of Martin because he was "an unfamiliar tall black teenager in a hoodie walking around Mr Zimmerman's gated community" (Alvarez, 2015). Zimmerman ignored a police dispatcher's advice to leave the teenager alone and forced a confrontation with Martin, eventually shooting and killing him. Zimmerman was acquitted of second-degree murder, successfully pleading

Photo 14.2 The past few years have seen a resurgence of activism centered on issues of police shootings and persistent racism.
Source: Tverdokhlib/Shutterstock.

self-defense (Alvarez, 2015). This event sparked national outrage centering on issues of racial profiling and racial injustice. The viral #BlackLivesMatter movement was created in response. The term was coined when Black activist Alicia Garza tweeted:

> The sad part is, there's a section of America who is cheering and celebrating right now. and that makes me sick to my stomach. We GOTTA get it together y'all. Stop saying we are not surprised. That's a damn shame in itself. I continue to be surprised at how little Black lives matter. And I will continue that. Stop giving up on black life. Black people. I love you. I love us. (Quoted in Woodly, 2021, p. 21)

Her friend Patrisse Khan-Cullors re-tweeted Garza's heartfelt statement, adding the hashtag "BlackLivesMatter." With this, seemingly instantaneously, a social movement was born.

The strategies and goals of the Black Lives Matter movement are greatly informed by an intersectional approach to understanding oppression and injustice (Garza, 2015; Shor, 2015). Specifically, the organizers take an *intracategorical* approach to their work (see Chapter 7), in that through underscoring and understanding the diversity of experiences of Black individuals based on statuses, such as gender, class, sexuality, gender expression, citizenship, and ability, they can better move toward achieving racial justice. In her explanation of the goals of the movement, Garza states:

> Progressive movements in the United States have made some unfortunate errors when they push for unity at the expense of really understanding the concrete differences in context, experience, and oppression. In other words, some want unity without struggle. As people who have our minds stayed on freedom, we can learn to fight anti-Black racism by examining the ways in which we participate in it, even unintentionally, instead of the worn out and sloppy practice of drawing lazy parallels of unity between peoples with vastly different experiences and histories. (2015)

The origin of BLM comes from "rejection of respectability politics, use of social media as an organizing vehicle, and the centering of Black feminist politics" (Francis & Wright-Rigueur, 2021, p. 452).

The approach of the movement borrowed directly from the Black Liberation movement, and more specifically from the efforts of the SNCC from the 1960s (Shor, 2015). It originally employed a decentralized, community-based structure that brought together loosely organized chapters across the country. As the movement has matured, similar to other social movements, it has developed a slightly more centralized structure (Gyamfi & Konadu, 2021). As did SNCC organizer Ella Baker, Garza and her colleagues sought to break away from the more traditional, male-dominated civil rights organizational structure in which the work of women and LGBTQ individuals in the movement was greatly marginalized and made invisible. Garza explains that

> [t]he narrative of this movement's beginnings counter the typical origins of black leadership, which are often personified via cisgender, heterosexual black men. If people were looking for a remake of Martin Luther King Jr., Jesse Jackson or Al Sharpton, they'd be disappointed, and rightfully so. (Garza, 2015)

At times the movement has come into conflict with older generations of organizers, as was seen in December of 2014 when Black Lives Matter members stormed the stage after the Reverend Al Sharpton refused to allow any younger speakers during a rally protesting the killings of young Black men (Shor, 2015).

The movement has garnered a fierce social media presence, at least in part because of its dedication to inclusion. The movement has become even more relevant as police shootings and violence against Blacks gain media attention. The deaths of Tamir Rice, Freddie Gray, Eric Garner, Michael Brown, Sandra Bland, and George Floyd have been highlighted as examples of the many Black people who have been killed at the hands of the police under questionable circumstances. Most recently, the death of George Floyd prompted large-scale Black Lives Matter protests across the country. At the beginning of the protests, the movement was quite popular, with 67 percent of those polled registering approval. By the end of the protests, support had fallen to 55 percent (Horowitz, 2021).

The #BlackLivesMatter movement has seen significant backlash from people who argue that it ignores the value of White people who are also victims of violence, and that it has inspired acts of violence. A careful analysis of the protests over the years, however, showed that "during the 12,839 racial justice protests in 2020, only 4 percent included property damage" (Goff & McCarthy, 2021). The #AllLivesMatter platform was created by people concerned that White victims were left out. Similarly, the #BlueLivesMatter platform was focused on valuing and remembering the lives of police officers lost in the course of their work. Critics of All Lives Matter, however, argue that Black Lives Matter is intended to highlight the systematic disparity in the way Blacks and Whites are treated under the law. Critics also point out that All Lives Matter fails to recognize that the Black Lives Matter movement is not suggesting that White lives do not matter, but rather that Black lives have been limited by institutionalized inequalities that Whites do not face in the same ways (Garza, 2015).

The Black Lives Matter movement represents an important new wave of civil rights activism. Although there has been significant backlash to the movement, it has placed racial inequality and violence squarely in the public consciousness.

The Women's Movement

In both the civil rights and early labor movements, women experienced discrimination and inequality, and their interests were rarely central to the movements. Women needed their own movement to advance their interests. Like the civil rights movement, the women's movement has had an uneven history. Its unevenness is reflected in the fact that there were two or three separate branches in the history of the movement, each wrestling with its own conception of equality for women. The trajectories of each strand and their points of conflict with each other represent the difficulty of addressing intersectional inequalities. Some activists strongly supported an approach that had a laser-like focus on sex or gender discrimination alone, others, particularly those involved in the labor and civil rights movements, favored an approach that recognized the simultaneous discriminations of sex, race, sexuality, and class (Cobble et al., 2014). As was the case with the other movements we have surveyed, internal conditions interacted with external circumstances to determine the nature of the movement. Many of those conditions were related to structures of economic, racial, and sexual inequality in the society.

The women's movement in the United States began in the late 1700s and early 1800s and has continued, although not always actively and publicly, to this day. The earliest organized efforts by women in the United States involved attempts to increase their educational rights and to fight for the abolition of slavery, and it was during involvement in the abolitionist movement of the 1830s that some women began expressing an acute awareness of their own low political status. As proved to be the case with their involvement in other historical movements, women were not given significant status or voice in the abolitionist movement. Indeed, while this movement was fighting for an end to slavery, women were being prevented from joining some abolitionist organizations and were muzzled in their attempt to speak in public on the issues. Women had to create their own antislavery organizations because they were being excluded from many of the men's organizations (Ryan, 2013). Women experienced similar issues in the early labor union movement. While demanding rights and social justice for workers, many unions were at the same time barring women from membership. In those cases where women were members, few held leadership positions.

In 1867, Sojourner Truth, a crusader for both women's and African Americans' rights, wrote of the neglect of women's rights among those who advocated such fights for African Americans:

> There is a great stir about colored men getting their rights, but not a word about colored women; and if colored men get their rights and not colored women theirs, you see the colored men will be masters over the women, and it will be just as bad as it was before. (Truth, 1867)

Time and again, it became clear to many women that they would have to have their own organizations and movement if equal rights were ever to be achieved.

Two of the women who had attended the antislavery convention in London were Elizabeth Cady Stanton and Lucretia Mott. They were convinced of the need for an organization exclusively for women's rights and to that end they organized a meeting in Seneca Falls, New York, in July of 1848. About 300 men and women attended, including Frederick Douglass and Susan B. Anthony. The attendees approved a "Declaration of Sentiments" based loosely on the wording of the Declaration of Independence. Among other things, this document argued for the basic equality of men and women and stressed that historically men had dominated over women in religious institutions, employment opportunities, and family and political life. Included among the declarations was a demand for the right to vote. Although this last demand has been said to signal the beginning of the suffrage movement, most of the women at the Seneca Falls meeting were more concerned with issues in their immediate experience: control of property and earnings, rights over children, rights to divorce, and so forth. From 1848 to the Civil War, women's conventions were held almost every year in different cities of the East and Midwest (Ryan, 2013).

The Early Social Context and Directions

The social environment within which women were advocating greater freedoms and rights was not hospitable. This was reflected not only in women's marginal status in male abolitionist and labor organizations but also in the reactions within other dominant institutions. Religious institutions and the media railed against the embryonic women's movement. It was as if natural and supernatural orders were being violated by the attempts to gain women's rights equal to those of men. In order to spread the word, women had to rely on some abolitionist papers and their own journals (Bey, 2017). Late in the nineteenth century, Stanton and others produced *The Woman's Bible*, a systematic critique to demonstrate that the traditional Bible was a major source of the subjugation of women.

The formation of the movement also was affected by the forces of early industrialization. Not being allowed to learn skills, women who needed to work were relegated to either household or low-paying work, while wealthier (usually White) women were not expected to work but rather to appear and act as "ladies," or the "angel in the house" (Bey, 2017). This class division among women had an impact on the membership and goals of the early women's organizations. It was largely middle- and upper-class women who initiated the early movement and who fashioned its goals to fit their problems and desires, such as the desire for education in the professions and civil service, and property and voting rights. At the same time, they pushed for lower numbers of hours for female factory workers (Cobble et al., 2014). Although the latter appeared as a form of protection for women, it was also seen by many men as a way to minimize work competition from women. In sum, the religious and cultural milieu, along with the conditions of industrialization and slavery, helped to shape the form of the early women's movement as well as reactions to it.

After the Civil War, when the 14th and 15th Amendments on Black rights were being debated, women were told that attempts to include them in these amendments would only diffuse the focus that was being placed on rights for Blacks alone. The incorporation of women as well as men into the amendments, they were told, would hinder their passage (Tobias, 2018). The thrust for a separate women's movement accelerated, and basically two strands developed. One, under Elizabeth Cady Stanton and Susan B. Anthony, formed the National Woman Suffrage Association. It emphasized a variety of rights for women and viewed the vote as a means to obtaining them. The other, exemplified by the American Woman Suffrage Association under Lucy Stone and others, focused only on the vote. Eventually, the emphasis on the vote won out in the movement and the two organizations merged into the National American Woman Suffrage Association (Tobias, 2018). It was during this period that the term **feminism** came onto the public scene. It would have been unthinkable to use such a term during the "woman movement" of the nineteenth century. Feminism suggested a radical change in all relations with men and also attracted smaller numbers of followers than the earlier "woman movement" (Cott, 1987).

In this *first wave* of the feminist movement, two of the most active groups pushing for the enfranchisement of women were the Congressional Union and the group derived from it, the National Woman's Party (NWP). Both were at the forefront of the movement between 1910 and 1920. The NWP was viewed as having a single objective, and any diversion from its pursuit was considered harmful. The rigid adherence to this philosophy resulted in insensitivity to the unique goals and problems of subgroups within the female population. As Cott observed perceptively:

> Only women holding culturally hegemonic values and positions—that is, in the United States, women who are White, heterosexual, middle class, politically midstream—have the privilege (or deception) of seeing their condition as that of "woman," glossing over their other characteristics. (1986, p. 58)

Many suffragist groups of the time were imbued with the racism of the broader culture and did little to combat it.

After the enfranchisement of women was accomplished in 1920, the movement for women's rights changed drastically. Rather than completely dying, the movement fractured internally, in large part because the attainment of the franchise had meant different things to different organizations and individuals. In essence, some women saw enfranchisement as an end in itself, while others viewed it as a means to reach more important goals, such as an Equal Rights Amendment (ERA) for women. Still, others believed that the movement ought to focus on the needs of low-income women and women of color.

The ERA was the goal of the NWP, while the more conservative National American Woman Suffrage Association fought against the ERA, formed the League of Women Voters, and worked for the active citizenship of women. The idea of universalistic legislation covering women's rights also was opposed by the Women's Bureau of the Department of Labor and several women's organizations aligned with the labor movement. They feared that the legalization of equality with men would remove the protections women received under the protectionist legislation of the 1920s, which limited women's involvement in the labor force. Frieda Miller, director of the Women's Bureau, stated that "identity of treatment is not the same as equality" (Cobble et al., 2014, p. 42).

It is this latter branch of the woman's movement that is often overlooked in the history of feminism. Many histories look only to those activists centered solely on sex/gender discrimination, such as the suffrage movement or efforts to pass the ERA, while in truth, there were many activists working throughout the history of the feminist movement from within other movements. Dorothy Cobble calls these women "social justice feminists," arguing that from the beginning, they brought an intersectional approach to women's rights. Many of these began their work within labor unions, learning their tactics, employing their ideology, and at times sharing resources. Mary Anderson, the first director of the US Women's Bureau in 1920, argued that "to insist only upon women's legal rights no matter what happened to other rights could result in greater inequality" (Cobble et al., 2014, p. 11). As Cobble notes, "from the 1930s to the 1960s, the struggle for the rights of low-income women and women of color surged forward as the labor and civil rights movements gained ground" (p. 4).

The movement thus was splintered by the multiple ties of many women to other social movements. Once the 19th Amendment had passed, many women moved on to other causes, such as temperance, birth control, union organizing, and addressing poverty (Tobias, 2018). Black women and working women had concerns other than those held by educated middle- or upper-class women, and some eventually formed their own organizations. Black women, for example, did not put the passage of the ERA and goals of the birth control movement anywhere near the top of their agenda: "For them, racial concerns overwhelmed those of sex" (Giddings, 1984, p. 184). Lynching, for example, was a problem that hit much closer to home for them.

From Limbo to Resurgence

From 1945 to the 1960s, the women's movement was fragmented. On the one hand, women had experienced greater opportunities during the war, and did not want to give up those advances. By the same token, though, they recognized that men returning from the war needed their jobs, and women had a difficult time competing with the leadership experiences men had during the war (Cobble et al., 2014; Tobias, 2018). In the years immediately after World War II, the social and cultural environment was not hospitable to protest from any minority group. It was a conservative cultural period—one that sanctified the traditional male and female roles. Thus, even if some women wanted to protest, there were few effective avenues through which to do so, and their protests would not have had the support of the federal government. You will recall that during this postwar expansion period, social inequality, in general, was an issue that was minimized.

In light of its persistence through the difficult climate of the postwar period, the NWP served as the organization of abeyance for the women's movement. It provided tactics, social networks, and an identity to spur the resurgence of the activist phase of the *second wave* of feminism in the 1960s and 1970s. The National Organization for Women (NOW), which was founded in 1966, used many of the tactics of the NWP, such as political pressure and lobbying. Activists kept pressure

> ## BOX 14.2 SHOULD THE UNITED STATES FINALLY PASS THE ERA?
>
> As is discussed in this chapter, the ERA was first proposed by the National Women's Party in 1923. The most recent version of the proposed constitutional amendment is as follows: "Equality of rights under the law shall not be denied or abridged by the United States or any State on account of sex." Did you assume that this right already existed? If so, you are in good company: About 80 percent of Americans believe that equal rights based on sex or gender were guaranteed by law decades ago (Puckett-Pope, 2020). But that is not the case! Despite the fact that currently 73 percent support the ratification of the ERA (AP-NORC, 2020), it has not yet happened. In 1972, the ERA passed both the House and Senate, but it was not ratified by the needed 38 states, due to strong opposition from conservative groups (led in part by Phyllis Schlafly, portrayed in the FXs series in 2020 entitled *Mrs. America*). In January of 2020, Virginia became the 38th state to ratify the ERA, but the deadline to approve the measure expired in 1982. The House voted in February of 2020 to do away with the deadline, but it is not clear that it has the authority to do that.
>
> Historically, there has been opposition to the ERA from the right and the left. Those on the right argue that it undermines traditional family values, while those from the left argue that it does not go far enough to recognize the intersectional nature of inequalities. What do you think? Should we finally pass the ERA?

on the government, thereby encouraging President Kennedy's decision to form a Presidential Commission on the Status of Women, and to include "sex" in Title VII of the 1964 Civil Rights Act. This was strongly opposed by the some of the more conservative and segregationist members of the NWP, with Nina Horton Avery of the NWP hoping for members of Congress who would "use their brains and energies to prevent a mongrel race in the US and who will fight for the rights of white citizens in order that discrimination against them may be stopped" (Cobble et al., 2014, p. 58). Theirs was, however, not the majority voice in the movement.

Although the 1945–1960 period was not marked by significant advances in the women's movement, several other social, cultural, and economic changes were occurring that created the structure necessary for a resurgence of the movement in the 1960s. These included increased employment in a wider range of occupations for women, smaller families, and higher levels of educational attainment. In other words, by the time the 1960s arrived, women were more educated, had more earnings, and many had significant experience in the labor force. This experience brought women face-to-face with their limited occupational opportunities. Added to this was the fact that the civil rights movement was peaking in the early 1960s and ideas about equality and sexual freedom were becoming more popular. All these events and conditions made the context ripe for a resurgence of the women's movement.

During the 1960s and 1970s, some feared that the women's movement would deflect from continuing racial issues and would focus primarily on White middle-class women. The concerns that Betty Friedan expressed in *The Feminine Mystique*, those of the alienated suburban housewife, seemed far removed from the real everyday problems of most women of color and poor women. Additionally, many Black women considered White women to be simply another part of the White enemy and believed their own problems to be both more serious and qualitatively different. They resented White feminists' equating sexism with racism and promoting the idea that Blacks and women experience a "common oppression" (Nachescu, 2008, p. 47). Consequently, during this period, most activist Black women did not identify with the priorities of the White women's movement, and did not join it (Breines, 2007). Further souring feelings between Black and White women was the fact that the women's movement was seen as having benefited from the earlier and costly efforts of the civil rights movement (Giddings, 1984).

In June 1966, a meeting of state commissions on the status of women convened in Washington, DC (Cobble et al., 2014). It was here that the NOW was created, largely because of the belief that the Equal Employment Opportunity Commission, which had developed out of the Civil Rights Act of 1964 and was supposed to deal with sex discrimination, was doing little about the problems of women in the labor market. Race and sex again appeared to be working at cross-purposes. NOW's early emphasis on equal rights, which was attractive to many middle- and upper-class women, turned off Black women, lesbians, and those who were members of unions (Rosen, 2006). Conversely, when NOW leaders desired membership in the Leadership Conference on Civil Rights, they were denied with the argument that women's problems did not constitute a civil rights issue (Cobble et al., 2014).

The civil rights movement and the newly resurgent women's movement of the 1960s intertwined race and sex issues in other ways as well. Experience in civil rights activities provided many women with knowledge about tactics and organizing problems and gave them a sense of their own capabilities. At the same time, however, their participation made it clear, as it had been made clear to women involved in the abolitionist movement, that they needed to develop their own organizations and movement. Women, Black and White, were not accorded high status in the civil rights movement, especially in the later Black Power stage. This is despite the fact that, though largely unrecognized, Black women had performed many varied leadership roles (Barnett, 1993).

Young women's experiences in the student New Left movement also left much to be desired. While the movement preached fewer restrictions on sexuality, the men generally treated the women who were members as objects available for the taking. Women had few positions of power in the New Left. The experiences of many younger women in both the Black Power and New Left movements helped motivate them to create a network of feminists committed to their own unique cause.

Despite its successes, the women's movement has continued to encounter an array of fearsome obstacles. The political, economic, and social conditions of the 1980s generated a strong antifeminist countermovement. By the end of the 1970s, many average citizens had been told by the media that women had reached their goals. Added to this message was another that portrayed "feminists as anti-male, lesbian, humorless, and politically correct ideologues" (Anderson, 1997, p. 313).

Nevertheless, a *third wave* of feminism dominated by younger women continued into the 1980s and 1990s, and emphasized (1) intersectionality, particularly the influence of queer studies; (2) the representation of a variety of perspectives and theoretical approaches rather than grand narratives; and (3) an inclusivity in definitions of feminisms (Evans & Chamberlain, 2015; Snyder, 2008). Instead of pursuing equality through political action, third-wave feminists often focus on personal empowerment in the cultural sphere, through music, fashion, genderqueer behaviors, and other multiple identities (Aronson, 2003; Diamond, 2009; Wrye, 2009).

Some suggest that in the early years of the twenty-first century, a *fourth wave* of feminism emerged that reaches outward to others, stressing the importance of an "internal sense of gender equality," a spirituality that views all humans as part of one community, and actions that aid the whole world and its downtrodden populations (Diamond, 2009, p. 218). The focus of the fourth wave has been on issues such as violence against women; online feminism; humor; and intersectionality and inclusion (Chamberlain, 2017). Some argue that the fourth wave is now in full swing:

> Over the past few years, as #MeToo and Time's Up pick up momentum, the Women's March floods Washington with pussy hats every year, and a record number of women prepare to run for office, it's beginning to seem that the long-heralded fourth wave might actually be here. (Grady, 2018)

As evidenced by the #MeToo movement, the fourth wave owes its rise to social media. The #MeToo movement first gained substantial traction in October 2017 through a viral Twitter post made by actress Alyssa Milano, calling for women to respond "me too" if they had experienced sexual assault or harassment. Since its original posting, #MeToo has become popular in countries outside the United States as well, with deviations such as #BalanceTonPorc, translated from the French as "snitch out your pig" (Fox & Diehm, 2017). The #MeToo movement also played a significant role in the second women's march on Washington. This march, spurred by former President Donald Trump's inauguration, was joined by #MeToo protesters in speeches against the mistreatment of women in society.

As with Black Lives Matter, #MeToo is an intersectional movement. The phrase "me too" originated from Black social activist Tarana Burke in 2006. Burke co-founded Just Be Inc., a nonprofit aimed at supporting the health and well-being of young women of color. In her work, Burke realized the pervasiveness of sexual assault and abuse (Garcia, 2017). Men, such as actors Terry Crews and Jimmy Bennett, have also responded to the #MeToo movement. In an August 2018 tweet, Burke supported male survivors' place in the movement, stating,

> I've said repeatedly that the #metooMVMT is for all of us, including these brave young men who are now coming forward … My hope is that as more folks come forward, particularly men, that we prepare ourselves for some hard conversations about power and humanity and privilege and harm. (Kai, 2018)

Support for the Contemporary Feminist Movement

Since the 1970s, support for the women's movement and feminism has increased, though public opinion is complex. Most Americans appear to support many of the specific ideas associated with the equality of men and women. At least 97 percent of Americans in 2020 believe that women should have equal rights with men, and but only 41 percent of women believe that the women's movement has helped them (Horowitz & Igielnik, 2020). In 2020, 61 percent of women and 40 percent of men considered themselves "feminist"—and a full 68 percent of women under 30 identified as feminist and 74 percent of college-education women (Barroso, 2020).

Photo 14.3 Events such as the Women's March of 2016 demonstrate the rise of intersectional social movements.
Source: Photo by Heather Fitz Gibbon.

It has been argued that using the imagery of "waves" of feminism makes the diversity within the various women's movements less visible, and makes it appear that the movement has been monolithic (Springer, 2002). Since the so-called first wave, there have been movements focused on the concerns of a diversity of women, addressing issues of race, class, ethnicity, and sexuality. However, the women's movement has traditionally been seen as a White middle-class one that does not address the needs of all women (Rosen, 2006). One veteran feminist observes that most of the achievements of the women's movement have not really affected poor women: "I think living in poverty is an unresolved problem of the women's movement" (Bolgar, 2009, p. 198). The diversity within the movement with respect to race, sexuality, gender expression, class-specific goals, and assumptions about the nature of men and women has provided a source of strength. But under the pressures of a countermovement against feminism, these divisions could widen and splinter the movement. What can be a source of strength can also be a source of damaging division.

Summary

All of the social movements discussed were focused on reducing social inequalities of one sort or another. But as has been noted before, such grievances are not sufficient for either the development or continuance of a social movement. The surrounding social structure must generate openings and opportunities for movements to develop and prosper. Conditions such as social unrest and economic upheaval create potential economic and political opportunities that lead to the appearance of social movements.

The cultural context also affects the life and structure of a social movement. You have seen how a variety of societal values and ideologies have been reflected in the character of labor, women's, and civil rights movements. Racist, sexist, and class values and their intersection deeply influenced the shape of and membership in each movement, creating internal divisions and pressures toward homogeneous organizations.

In addition to structural opportunities and cultural milieu, the resources available to a group affect the development of a movement. Of course, whether an aggrieved group can obtain such resources also depends on the structure of opportunities and the cultural milieu.

Finally, the presence of opportunities, resources, and a favorable cultural milieu fosters the development of power and a sense of a *cognitive liberation* in which groups of aggrieved individuals redefine their situation and their potential for successful solutions (McAdam, 2010). On the other hand, when groups have few opportunities and no resources, and the culture is adverse, the chances of a new revolutionary consciousness and a successful social movement are slim indeed. Until equity is achieved, however, movements for class, racial, and gender equality are likely to continue in the United States, if only sporadically.

Critical Thinking

1. Given the current economic difficulties in the United States at large, what do you think the prospects are for a resurgence of a vibrant labor movement? Explain your answer.
2. What effect, if any, do you think the conservative movements that have arisen in the United States since the early 1980s will have on the country?
3. What kinds of new inequalities are emerging from which movements might develop? What conditions might maximize or minimize the chances for these movements?
4. Why has it been difficult for those in the labor, civil rights, and women's movements to join forces?
5. To what extent would you describe the Black Lives Matter movement as an intersectional movement?

Web Connections

Visit the AFL-CIO's website at www.aflcio.org to learn about issues of importance to unions. To read about the goals of the feminist movement in the 1960s and 1970s, go to http://womenshistory.about.com/od/feminism. The story of the civil rights movement as told by its veterans can be read at www.crmvet.org. The Black Lives Matter website (http://blacklivesmatter.com) provides a detailed history of the movement and its political underpinnings, as well as a dynamic representation of current activities and changes in the movement. Compare the tactics in this movement to that represented on the AFL-CIO website above.

Film Suggestions

Stay Woke: The Black Lives Matter Movement (2016). Chronicles of the rise of the movement and interviews with its founders.

Mission Blue (2014). We did not cover the environmental movement in this chapter but if you are interested, check out this documentary about Sylvia Earle, who has been called the "Joan of Arc" of the oceans.

Equal Means Equal (2016). Shortlisted for an Oscar, this documentary looks at women's rights in the US today and includes interviews with a number of the icons of the feminist movement.

Selma (2014). This film depicts a three-month period in 1965 in which Dr Martin Luther King Jr led a march from Selma to Montgomery, Alabama. Though they faced violent opposition, the march ultimately ended in the signing of the Voting Rights Act of 1965.

Whose Streets? We Will Not Go Quietly (2017). A documentary about the Ferguson Uprising that was sparked by the police killing of Michael Brown.

Women of the Movement (2022). A series chronicling a series of women active in the civil rights movement, beginning with Mamie Till-Mobley, the mother of Emmett Till.

15   Policy Alternatives

In Chapter 1 of this book, we asked the question, "Is inequality inevitable?" Having spent fourteen chapters outlining the magnitude and scope of inequality as well as the systemic structural and cultural processes that produce it, we want to end this book on a more optimistic note by concluding that while some inequalities will always exist, there are steps that we can take to lessen their magnitude.

Other countries provide strong evidence that inequality can be reduced when there is a will to do so. Since its independence from South Africa in 1990, for example, Namibia has significantly lowered the gap between rich and poor by investing in education, dropping its poverty rate from 53 percent to 23 percent (Lawson, 2017). South Korea has also taken bold steps to reduce inequality, including increasing the minimum wage by 16.4 percent, raising the corporate tax rate, and expanding welfare spending. President Moon Jae-in stated in 2017:

> As of now, my Administration is pursuing bold measures to change the economic paradigm in order to deal with economic inequalities that stand in the way of growth and social cohesion ... This is what we call a "people-centered economy." (Lawson & Martin, 2018)

And Iceland famously passed a law in 2018 requiring corporations to prove that they are paying men and women the same. To quote Matthew Martin, Development Finance International's director:

> What's most striking is how ... combatting inequality isn't about being the wealthiest country or the one with the biggest economy. It's about having the political will to pass and to put into practice the policies that will narrow the gap between the ultra-rich and the poor. (Inman, 2018)

In this chapter, we outline a few of the more prominent policy proposals currently being discussed by policy makers and scholars of inequality. Some are quite controversial and extensive, while others are more widely accepted. The policies outlined here are obviously not exhaustive, and they focus mostly on economic inequalities. These proposals can be grouped into four categories: (1) spreading the wealth—policies aimed at redistributing wealth and income; (2) developing the capacity for self-sufficiency; (3) addressing spatial inequalities; and (4) expanding and guaranteeing political representation.

Redistributive Policies

As you may recall, in Chapter 7, we argued that one of the explanations for the persistence and reproduction of inequality is that once people have control of resources, they do what they can to maintain that control, either via hoarding or through the exploitation of others. From this perspective, one approach to reducing inequality is to spread the wealth—to redistribute resources from those at the top to those at the bottom. Not surprisingly, redistributive policies are some of

DOI: 10.4324/9781003184966-20

the most controversial, as some argue that they inhibit the free market and provide disincentives for work and innovation. Nonetheless, some of these approaches have gained in popularity in recent years. The proposals we cover here include the universal basic income (UBI), changes in the wage structures, and the expansion of the earned income tax credit (EITC).

Universal Basic Income

One idea getting much attention right now is the UBI. This program gives each household enough money to remain above the poverty line, with no strings attached. Depending on the variant of the program proposed, the amount is pegged to the number of individuals in the family, but to neither income nor wealth. In other words, every person receives a check from the government. Generally, the payments replace all other government assistance programs, and their amount is often tied to fluctuations in the gross domestic product (GDP). A commonly suggested amount in the United States is about $1,000 a month: "enough to live on—*somewhere* in America, at least—but not nearly enough to live on well" (Heller, 2018). Various countries have piloted such programs, including Finland, which discontinued it due to cost, Canada, the Netherlands, Scotland, and Iran (Heller, 2018).

In the United States, since 2018, at least 20 pilots of UBI programs have been instituted (Holder, 2021). The most recent city to pilot such program is Atlanta, offering 300 residents $500 a month, particularly targeting the poorest women in the city. Mayor Keisha Lance Bottoms explains the program by stating that "We are seizing this moment to realize Dr. Martin Luther King Jr.'s vision for addressing economic security and pervasive poverty" (McDade, 2022).

Some of the excitement for the UBI is coming from those concerned about disruptions stemming from the automation of labor in the tech industry. The proposal has received support from people at very different ends of the political spectrum, including Elon Musk and conservative Charles Murray (Levinson, 2017), and most recently was a cornerstone of Andrew Yang's 2020 presidential bid. Worried about the effects of the tech industry on its citizens, the City of Stockton, California, announced in 2018 that it would give 125 residents $500 per month for 18 months. Stockton Mayor Michael Tubbs, stated that: "We have a bunch of folks starting off life already behind, born into communities that don't have a lot of opportunity … I want Stockton to be [a place people] want to live in" (Crane, 2018).

Evaluations of the Stockton program demonstrated early success. The funds helped mitigate income volatility among recipients, and contrary to the concerns of some opponents, the money was used for basic essentials such as food, and to pay off debt and cover unexpected expenses. Further, the funds did not dissuade recipients from working—in fact, in some cases, the money made it easier for people to work because it provided stability allowing them to take on new employment. Researchers found that employment among the participants increased by 12 percent (Lowrey, 2021).

One of the attractions of the UBI is the fact that since it is universal, it does not involve an evaluation of whether recipients deserve the aid. Proponents argue that too often racism is at the heart of how we evaluate social welfare programs and those who benefit from them. As we saw in Chapter 3, societies have frequently made decisions about whom to help based on whether they are deemed "worthy." Often worthiness is determined by assessing who is a stranger and who belongs. "When genuinely redistributive schemes are perceived to disproportionately benefit [strangers], the resentment of those who fund them tends to block their expansion and even to jeopardize their viability" (Parijs & Vanderborght, 2017, p. 252).

While gaining some support, the UBI is highly controversial and would likely be difficult to implement. The strongest criticism is that the costs of this program would be too prohibitive; estimates place costs at between $1.5 trillion and $3.9 trillion per year (Feldstein, 2016;

Heller, 2018), representing at least 9 percent of GDP. Other concerns continue to center on worries about the behavioral effects of automatic payments, the concern being that the cash payments might encourage idleness and provide a disincentive for work. Stockton's initial findings (described above) seem to disprove this point, but there is other limited evidence as well supporting the argument that UDI does not lead to individuals working less. In 1997, the Eastern Band of Cherokee Indians began distributing the profits from their casino to all members of the tribe. Each person receives between $4,000 and $6,000 per year. Researchers from Duke University found that this program did not reduce the hours people worked. They also found that the program increased the educational attainment of the children in households that received money and decreased mental health problems (Marinescu, 2017). Critics, however, argue that the sample sizes are far too small for us to know if the program was a success (Editorial Board, Wall Street Journal, 2021).

Given the potential costs of the UBI, some have suggested implementing a similar but more targeted variant called the negative income tax. Under this program, everyone is guaranteed a certain amount of income. People who fall above that line pay taxes proportional to their income, but never enough to put them below the line. People whose income is below the threshold receive a check for the amount of the gap. Note that this program is different from the UBI because it does not provide money to everyone, only those who do not have enough income to lift them out of poverty. As poor people's income increases, the benefit would decrease. This program is obviously considerably less costly than the UBI and it could, in theory, replace welfare programs such as TANF (Feldstein, 2016).

A negative income tax was proposed during the Johnson administration in the 1960s but was reduced to a series of experiments under the Nixon administration. The experiments occurred in parts of New Jersey, Pennsylvania, Washington, and Colorado. Canada ran a similar experiment. Although there were methodological problems with the experiments, their findings indicated that there might be a very small decrease in the number of hours worked when the benefit is high. At the same time, the NIT appears to increase the level of education attained by children of recipients and to improve health. It does not appear to have an effect on marriage or fertility (Marinescu, 2017).

Another variant of the UBI is a child tax credit (CTC). The CTC is something many other rich industrial nations use to lower inequality (Matthews, 2017). In Denmark, for example, parents receive a check for each child. The amount decreases as the child ages but in 2018, parents of children up to the age of 2 received about $680 per quarter. The United States currently employs a CTC, but it is very limited. The CTC system we currently have in place allows poor families to receive part of their credit in a tax refund, but they must earn income to receive the credit. In other words, families who owe less in tax than their credits can get a check for part of the difference.

A much-heralded component of the American Rescue Plan administered in the summer of 2021 was an expansion of the CTC, where parents with household incomes under $150,000 received up to $3,600 per child. This was a temporary, one-year measure aimed at COVID-19 relief, though many have suggested that this should become permanent (at the time of writing, this is under negotiation in President Biden's Build Back Better plan). Research from the Columbia University Center on Poverty and Social Policy suggested that the implementation of the CTC would reduce child poverty overall by over six percent, but would have the greatest effect on children of color, reducing poverty among Black children by 12 percent, and Hispanic and Native American children by about 10 percent (Center on Poverty and Social Policy, Columbia University, 2021). Critics of the program argue that it will actually harm children, as it provides parents with disincentives to work (Meyer & Corinth, 2021). Some Americans and key Congressional leaders therefore argue that it should be paired with work requirements (Philbrick, 2022).

Changes to the Wage Structure

A fairly straightforward approach to reducing inequality, although perhaps as controversial as the UBI, is to either pay those at the bottom of the ladder more, or those at the top less. The former approach is represented by increasingly popular measures to raise the minimum wage, and the latter approach involves caps on CEOs' compensation packages. We talked about the minimum wage policies in Chapter 3, so here we will concentrate on policies involving the top of the income structure.

As an alternative or a supplement to raising the minimum wage, some have proposed capping the earnings of those at the top. To that end, the cities of Portland, Oregon, and San Francisco, California have each passed increased corporate taxes on companies whose CEOs earn more than 100 times the pay of the median worker. In Portland, companies with CEOs earning more than 100 times face a ten percent tax increase. Those whose CEO compensation is more than 250 times the median wage face a 25 percent increase. The revenues are targeted to programs that help the homeless (Woolf, 2016). In San Francisco, the increased tax ranges from 0.1 percent to 0.6 percent. City officials expect that this tax will result in $140 million in additional revenues (Anderson, 2020).

Surprisingly, these types of proposals do not just come from Democrats. In 2015, then-Congressman Mick Mulvaney wrote an amendment to a highway bill that stipulated that the Export-Import Bank would not support a company whose CEO compensation is 100 times or more than the median salary (Schroeder, 2015).

Caps to CEO earnings have gained some popularity following the tax cuts for the wealthy included in the federal tax reform bill of 2017. Critics of the reform bill suggest that

> Lower top tax rates did not make top income earners more productive but instead increased their incentives to bargain for higher compensation. American chief executives have reaped salaries that are multiples higher than their counterparts at companies in similar sectors and of comparable sizes in continental Europe, where top tax rates have remained largely unchanged. (Omi & Menendian, 2014, p. 18)

In other words, lowering the tax rate on wealthy people does not make them better workers, it makes them want more income since they can keep more of it. Capping their compensation would be one way to address this problem. Nonetheless, such proposals remain few and have not gained widespread support.

Changes to Taxation Policies

Several policies have emerged recently focus on changes to how we tax individuals and corporations. One of the more successful US anti-poverty programs is the earned income tax credit (EITC). As we saw in Chapter 3, it is credited with lifting families out of poverty, increasing the labor force participation rate, and decreasing early marriage child-bearing among women in poverty (Michelmore & Lopoo, 2021).

Given this success, a proposal popular with both Republicans and Democrats is to increase the reach of the EITC. The credit was increased with the American Recovery Act during the pandemic, but the Biden administration is looking to extend that and expand it for families without qualifying children living at home. Currently, except for the poorest workers, the EITC supports families with children, and disproportionately goes to single mothers. Critics of the expansion suggest that it would increase marriage penalties and divorce bonuses for low-income couples (Steuerle, 2021).

Proposals such as those expanding the EITC are popular and enjoy more bipartisan support than other assistance programs because of the focus on work: "Its popularity stems in no small part from the fact that the EITC is not just a handout, but a program that induces more people into the workforce and encourages them to work more, by bolstering their wages" (Lowrey, 2018).

On the tax revenue side, similar to the policies described above taxing corporations with highly paid CEOs, several local governments have proposed or approved increased taxes to create programs to reduce inequality. Portland, Oregon has increased taxes on top earners to pay for "pre-school for all;" Arizona voters approved Proposition 208 in 2020, which increased taxes on incomes above $250,000 to augment funding for education; and Colorado passed a provision to increase **payroll taxes** to pay for a paid medical and family leave program (Wakamo, 2020).

Some policy makers have additionally argued for a wealth tax or a billionaire tax, as was proposed by Elizabeth Warren and Bernie Sanders in the 2020 Presidential election and more recently by Senate Democrats working to pass President Biden's Build Back Better plan (Weisman, 2021). As discussed in Chapter 3, the reality is that wealthy Americans pay proportionally very little in taxes: "The notion that America, even if it may not collect as much in taxes as European countries, at least does so in a progressive way, is a myth. As a group, and although their individual situations are not all the same, the Trumps, the Bezoses and the Buffetts of this world pay lower tax rates than teachers and secretaries do" (Saez & Zucman, 2019). Proposals to remedy this include a two percent tax on the net worth over $50 million and three percent for a net worth above $1 billion (Bokat-Lindell, 2019), and efforts to close loopholes in the collection of taxes at the highest levels. Critics of a wealth tax suggest that it may serve as an impediment to economic growth (Brannon, 2020) and that it may in fact be unconstitutional, though this is highly disputed (Johnsen & Dellinger, 2018).

BOX 15.1 SHOULD WE PAY REPARATIONS TO BLACK AMERICANS?

One of the much-discussed proposals to address social inequalities is to pay reparations to Black Americans for the psychological, social, physical, and economic harms of slavery. There are many conceptions of what reparations might look like, but definitions include a "system of redress for egregious injustices" (Perry, 2020) or "the full acceptance of our collective biography and its consequences" (Coates, 2014).

Currently, there is a bill awaiting a House vote to create a commission to study the possibility of reparations. HR 40, the Commission to Study Reparation Proposals for African Americans Act, was first introduced by the late representative John Conyers of Michigan in 1989—he went on to re-introduce it each year until his retirement in 2017. The bill was passed for the first time by the Judiciary Committee of the House in 2021, but it has yet to be put up for a vote in the House (King, 2021). The current bill, introduced by Representative Sheila Jackson Lee, proposes seeks "to address the fundamental injustice, cruelty, brutality, and inhumanity of slavery in the United States and the 13 American colonies between 1619 and 1865 and to establish a commission to study and consider a national apology and proposal for reparations for the institution of slavery" (Jackson Lee, 2021).

Reparations are not new to the United States—the government has provided reparations three times: To Native Americans for removing them from their lands, to Japanese Americans for their unjust internment during World War II, and via the Marshall Plan to Jewish survivors of the Holocaust. Black Americans, however, have received nothing—in fact, in some states, White slaveholders were paid reparations for the loss of their "property" (enslaved individuals) following the Civil War, while those who were enslaved received nothing (Perry, 2020).

Those arguing for reparations cite many deciding factors, both material and symbolic. Materially, proponents point to many factors, among them the first and foremost the physical harm to enslaved peoples, their families, and their descendants. A second key factor is the racial wealth gap, precipitated by the fact that while slaveowners accrued wealth literally on the backs of enslaved individuals, while Black families were unable to build intergenerational wealth. This was due to various ongoing processes, including the theft of lands of Black families during reconstruction and decades of discriminatory and segregationist housing policies.

Symbolically, proponents argue for the need for the United States to come to a reckoning with its past. Ta-Nehisi puts this quite eloquently:

> What I'm talking about is more than recompense for past injustices—more than a handout, a payoff, hush money, or a reluctant bribe. What I'm talking about is a national reckoning that would lead to spiritual renewal. Reparations would mean the end of scarfing hot dogs on the Fourth of July while denying the facts of our heritage. Reparations would mean the end of yelling 'patriotism" while waving a Confederate flag. Reparations would mean a revolution of the American consciousness, a reconciling of our self-image as the great democratizer with the facts of our history. (Coates, 2014)

What form should reparations take? Proposals are varied: some suggest they should go directly to individuals who are descendants of the formerly enslaved in the form of individual payments, tuition remission, student loan forgiveness, down payments for home purchases, or small business loan start-up funds (Perry, 2020). Others believe that reparations should be at the societal level, going to various funds to support the development of resources, grants, and public institutions aimed at rebuilding Black wealth and infrastructure.

While the federal bill on a reparations commission is under discussion, several local governments have begun to consider plans. Over 80% of Detroit voters approved the creation of a reparations commission in November of 2021 to determine how the city might address issues of racial injustice (C. Williams, 2021). And the city of Evanston, Illinois recently distributed $11 million in reparations, to be used as housing grants (Heyward, 2021).

About 62 percent of Americans oppose reparations, not surprisingly divided along racial lines, with 72 percent of White Americans in opposition, compared with 14 percent of Black Americans (Hunt & Reichelmann, 2021). Opponents to reparations point to the cost of such programs, to the difficulty in determining who is owed reparations, and to the idea that no one now living is responsible for the practice of slavery.

What do you think?

Developing the Capacity for Self-Sufficiency

As opposed to the policies above that, for the most part, focus on redistributing wealth, the policies in this section are designed to increase individual and family capacity for maintaining self-sufficiency. These policies are based on a model of asset-building designed to decrease inequalities in the various forms of capital discussed in Chapter 7, including human, economic, and cultural capital. Policies we discuss here include those that encourage savings, the building of wealth, and educational reform.

Reducing the Wealth Gap

As we saw in Chapter 2, inequality is not simply measured by differences in income but also by discrepancies in wealth. This wealth gap cuts across racial groups, but it is most pronounced between Blacks and Whites. One study, for example, found that Black families have $5.04 in wealth for every $100 owned by White families (Thompson, 2018). This wealth gap perpetuates inequalities across generations by limiting the ability of families to move to better neighborhoods, save for college, and provide for their retirement. Low levels of wealth held by the middle and working class, combined with a historically low savings rate, helped make them more vulnerable to the economic dislocations of the Great Recession (Weller & Helburn, 2009, p. 3).

One method countries can use to help people build assets is to create individual development accounts (IDAs). These special savings accounts work very much like workplace retirement funds in that deposits made by an individual are matched by the IDA program—in other words, for every dollar a person saves, they get back two dollars. To open an IDA, an individual must be low income, usually falling below 200 percent of the poverty line. Withdrawals from the savings account can only be used to purchase assets such as buying a house, paying for college, or opening a small business. While the primary goal of the IDA programs is to build the assets necessary for individuals to succeed, a secondary goal is to help people to establish a habit of saving (Boshara, 2005). IDA programs are small but fairly common in the United States today. The federal government funds many of them through a program called Assets for Independence which is managed by the Department of Health and Human Services. An agency that is selected to be a provider must match the federal dollars they get with an equal amount of money from other sources. A variant of IDAs is to provide incentives for savings in the form of tax credits. While demonstrating moderate success, critics argue that these programs can be costly and difficult to administer. Current IDA programs are not large, and thus have had a minimal impact on poverty as a whole.

Educational Reform

In earlier chapters, we discussed how important the acquisition of cultural capital is in upward mobility. Scholars and policymakers correspondingly argue that an investment in education, and particularly in early childhood education, would do a great deal to reduce societal inequalities. "Differences in early education and school quality are among the most important components of the persistence in income disparities across generations" (Omi & Menendian, 2014, p. 17). For example, researchers found that having a higher quality kindergarten experience has a significantly positive effect on how much you earn as an adult, whether you attend college, how much you save, and whether you own a home (Chetty et al., 2011).

Some liberal policymakers argue for increasing spending on education, particularly early childhood education, and implementing universal early preschool programs. While currently 43 states provide publicly funded preschool, the levels of support differ widely—for example, Washington, DC spends $15,748 per child while Mississippi spends less than $2,000 per child (Sanches & Nadworny, 2017).

Some proposals suggest increasing our funding levels for higher education. For example, during his recent Presidential bids, Vermont Senator Bernie Sanders famously endorsed free college education for all. His plan, called "College All," would provide students with family incomes of less than $125,000 free college tuition, cut student loan interest rates, and provide increased funding for work-study programs. At the announcement for the program, Sanders stated:

> Our economy will not survive in the future unless we have the best-educated work force in the world … Our job, if we are smart, is to do everything possible to make it easier for people to pay for their education—not harder. (Kreighbaum, 2017)

Free college for all is gaining traction in some sectors—in January 2017, New York Governor Andrew Cuomo implemented a tuition-free program for all families in New York earning below $125,000, and Rhode Island's Governor promised residents two tuition-free years of public college (Kreighbaum, 2017). Congressional Democrats initially included a proposal for free community college for families earning less than $125,000 in the Build Back Better plan, but this proposal was eliminated from subsequent drafts of the bill.

Because free college for everyone would be expensive, some people argue that it is simply not feasible. They point to other ways that we could help students better afford tuition costs. For example, some have suggested increasing the funding for the federal Pell Grant program. Pell Grants help low-income undergraduate students pay for college. As the name implies, Pell Grants are not loans and do not need to be repaid if a student completes their program. Pell is a huge program: a full 32 percent of undergraduate students received it in the 2017–2018 school year (The College Board, 2018). Pell Grants address issues of both economic and racial inequality as over half of Black and Hispanic undergraduates qualify for and receive these grants (The Education Trust, 2015). Although Pell Grants have helped many students, nine out of ten still need to take out student loans to pay for school (Douglas-Gabriel, 2015). Expanding the program could reach more students and could decrease the need for student loans.

Conservatives, like liberals, stress education as an important means to reduce inequality. Their focus, however, has been more on ways to provide families with information regarding the quality of schools and school choice. Legislators have emphasized performance-based funding, and the use of vouchers to support families in finding the best education to fit the needs of their children. Performance-based funding is when the government ties school funding to some measure, usually test scores. A school whose students do not meet the required average test score gets less funding. In theory, this would encourage schools to work harder to educate their students. Conservatives also support better targeting the Pell Grant program to those who truly need it, and linking education at all levels more directly to the needs of employers (Holtz-Eakin, 2016).

Addressing Spatial Inequalities

As we learned in Chapter 11, one of the prime contributors to inequality is residential segregation. Racial segregation, combined with economic segregation, limits mobility and reproduces poverty across generations. Reducing racial and economic segregation, therefore, would go a long way toward reducing economic inequalities.

Encouraging Home Ownership

A central means of reducing levels of racial and economic segregation is through the support of home ownership. Home-ownership programs provide residents with choices, thus enabling greater social mobility. Today, however, about two-thirds of these kinds of supports go to families in the top 20 percent of taxpayers in the form of home-ownership tax subsidies (Urban Institute, 2017). There are several proposed programs aimed at remedying this gap. First, we could create more credits for first-time homebuyers, paid for by limiting mortgage interest tax deductions. As described in Chapter 3, the Trump administration did place new limits on these kinds of deductions, but people can still deduct up to $750,000. This is obviously a huge loss in tax revenue that could be used to provide credits for new homebuyers.

A second idea is the establishment of community land trusts, where a community-based organization buys tracts of land and provides long-term leases for low-income residents. When the residents go to sell the home, they receive a portion of the profits, with the rest remaining with the community trust, enabling them to provide more low-income loans (Axel-Lute, 2018).

Third, we could change the Section 8 housing program. In the past, the low-income recipients received vouchers to help them rent homes or apartments. This could be changed to allow them to use the vouchers to purchase their first home rather than simply making rent payments (Olsen, 2007). One component of President Biden's housing policy proposal involves providing down-payment assistance to first-time homebuyers and greatly increasing the housing voucher program for rental assistance (Campisi, 2021).

Another innovative program that could be extended is the Moving to Opportunity (MTO) program, first introduced by the federal Department of Housing and Urban Development in the 1990s. One of the few true experiments in social policy, MTO asked the question of whether moving families from poor neighborhoods to middle-class neighborhoods would improve outcomes for children. The program created an experiment that divided 4,604 families into three groups. One group was offered a rental assistance voucher that could only be used in a neighborhood with low poverty levels, the second group was given a voucher to be used in any neighborhood they would like, and the third group was not given a voucher (Chetty et al., 2016).

There have been many studies over the years of the MTO project, and most concluded that results were quite positive. If children were moved at a young age, they were significantly more likely to attend college, live in better neighborhoods as adults, and they were less likely to become single parents. Chetty argues that, "The findings imply that offering vouchers to move to lower-poverty neighborhoods to families with young children who are living in high-poverty housing projects may reduce the intergenerational persistence of poverty and ultimately generate positive returns for taxpayers" (Chetty et al., 2016, p. 855).

Expanding and Guaranteeing Political Representation

None of the policies outlined above can come to fruition without a political system that includes an educated, involved electorate with full access to voting rights. One of the greatest threats to any effort to reduce inequality is a political system that limits the voices of some and gives more power to others to define political agendas and contribute to social change. This issue has become especially salient in the last few election cycles.

The Voting Rights Act of 1965 was a keystone of the civil rights movement, lessening discrimination in the electoral process and improving minorities' access to the polls. In 2013, however, key provisions of the act were struck down by the Supreme Court, including provisions that required states to request approval from the federal government for any planned changes to their voting policies. This change, "severely weakened the federal government's oversight of discriminatory voting practices" (Human Rights Campaign, 2018).

As we saw in Chapter 5, several states introduced discriminatory electoral practices that limited the voting rights of minority citizens after the 2013 changes to the Voting Rights Act, and more recently, following the 2020 Presidential election. To date, nineteen states have enacted over thirty-three laws limiting access to voting (Brennan Center for Justice, 2021). These laws include the restriction of early voting, limits on mail-in ballots, and in some cases, expanding the rights of state legislatures to reject final vote counts and limiting the authority of election officials.

In recent years, several federal bills have been introduced to address voting rights, including the John Lewis Voting Rights Expansion Act, H.R. 4, passed by the House in 2021 (but at the time of writing, the bill has been introduced to the Senate, but it had not voted) (Sewell, 2021). The act would restore and modernize many of the provisions of the original voting rights act, including requiring elections officials to publicly announce all voting changes at least 180 days before an election; and allowing the expansion of the federal government's authority to send federal observers to "any jurisdiction where there may be a substantial risk of discrimination at the polls on Election Day or during an early voting period" (Human Rights Campaign, 2021b).

The Freedom to Vote Act, drafted by Senator Joe Manchin of West Virginia, was introduced to the Senate, but at the time of writing has not gained support. The general thrust of this bill is to develop national standards for voting, including enacting an automatic voter registration system through the DMV, standardizing how many early in-person voting days are allowed (at least 15), offering same-day voter registration and no-excuse mail voting, instituting rules for when and how to count mail-in votes, and ensuring that all voters have access to online voter registration (Brennan Center for Justice, 2022).

Photo 15.1 Voting by mail was particularly popular during the COVID outbreak.

Source: Tiffany Tertipes at Unsplash.

BOX 15.2 WHICH ORGANIZATIONS ADDRESS SOCIAL INEQUALITY?

There are a number of organizations whose central purpose is to address issues of exclusion and inequality. For those looking to make a difference, connecting with these organizations would be a good place to start.

American Civil Liberties Union (ACLU) (www.aclu.org/)

The ACLU is a nonprofit whose main purpose is to "defend and preserve the individual rights and liberties guaranteed by the Constitution and laws of the United States." It is a non-partisan organization, having taken action against both Republican and Democratic administrations. They focus on several civil rights and personal liberty issues, such as criminal justice reform, free speech, disability rights, immigrants' rights, juvenile justice, LGBT rights, national security, privacy, racial justice, religious liberty, voting rights, and reproductive freedom.

Southern Poverty Law Center (SPLC) (www.splcenter.org/)

The SPLC uses "litigation, education, and other forms of advocacy" to combat bigotry and defend marginalized communities. They are well known for monitoring the spread and actions of hate groups through the "Extremist Files" and the "Hate Map." The organization also provides resources such as teaching kits to educators who wish to make their schools and other institutions more equitable, as well as resources for the educators themselves to learn how to promote justice in these institutions.

National Organization for Women (NOW) (https://now.org)

Dedicated to "achieving full equality for women through education and litigation," NOW was established at the height of the second-wave Women's Movement. The organization's concerns include focusing on issues of economic justice, discrimination, reproduction, LGBTQ rights, women's health and body images, and issues facing women globally.

American Immigration Council (AIC) (www.americanimmigrationcouncil.org/)

The AIC is a nonprofit that defends the rights of American immigrants through "research and policy analysis, litigation and communications, and international exchange." The organization believes that all people have the right to a fair chance at legal immigration, and that the United States should welcome those in search of safety and greater opportunity.

> **ProPublica (**www.propublica.org/**)**
> ProPublica is an independent, nonprofit newsroom that publishes investigative journalism on matters of public interest, with a focus on issues of politics, criminal justice, education, and technology. Pro-Publica's mission is "to expose abuses of power and betrayals of the public trust by government, business, and other institutions, using the moral force of investigative journalism to spur reform through the sustained spotlighting of wrongdoing."
> **New Leaders Council (**www.newleaderscouncil.org/**)**
> New Leaders Council provides training and education to young people to equip them with the tools necessary to create significant change. Their six-month training program prepares participants to "run for office, manage campaigns, create start-ups and networks of thought leaders" with the hope that they will take these skills back to their communities. The organization has 50 chapters across the country.

Summary

This chapter has presented a number of different kinds of policies aimed at reducing inequality. They fall into several different categories: policies that redistribute income or wealth, those that help people build assets for a more successful future, those that address spatial inequality, and those that increase political representation. The list of policies we came up with is just a beginning, however, because there are many other exciting ideas that we were not able to include. As you reach the end of this book, know that you have the tools to explore issues of inequality on your own. Among many other possibilities, you can do this through working with some of the organizations listed in Box 15.2, through voting, or through engaging in research about some aspect of inequality.

Critical Thinking

1. Which of the solutions provided above make the most sense to you? Why?
2. What kinds of solutions haven't we talked about that would be important?
3. Do you think that the burden of solving problems of inequality should rest with the government or should they be market-based solutions?

Web Connections

Various think tanks provide resources for examining solutions to inequality. For addressing issues of spatial injustices, such as housing inequalities and poverty, the Urban Institute (https://urban.org) provides valuable reports. Similarly, the Pew Foundation is an evidence-based research center providing statistics on inequality and policy solutions (www.pewresearch.org/).

Film Suggestions

Free Money: The Case for Universal Basic Income (2018). This documentary argues for UBI by exploring a wide range of current programs.

Reparations (2021). Documents the struggle for Black Americans to receive atonement for slavery.

Inequality for All (2013). Raises awareness of the growing inequality in this country and provides policy recommendations from Robert Reich.

Welcome to Change (2018). This documentary explores a unique charter school in San Francisco that is specifically designed to support at-risk youth.

70 Acres in Chicago (2014). Examines the aftermath of the razing of the Cabrini Green projects in Chicago and explores the possibilities of developing mixed-income housing.

Glossary of Basic Terms

absolute mobility a shift in economic resources without a simultaneous change in an individual's position relative to others.

alienated labor the structural condition whereby workers are separated and estranged from the products and processes of their labors, and eventually from themselves and humankind.

anomic division of labor a condition whereby the divisions and conflicts between workers and owners result in a lack of solidarity and common purpose.

anomie a state of normlessness. As used by Durkheim, the term refers to an abnormal condition in society where the usual norms no longer hold sway and people feel a sense of unease and alienation.

anti-semitism negative feelings or prejudice toward Jewish people.

ascribed qualities qualities conferring status that are mostly inherited or beyond an individual's control, such as race, ethnicity, or class at birth.

asexuality a sexual orientation defined by the absence of sexual desire.

benefits cliff the situation when a small increase in wages leads to reduction in public benefits, thus keeping them poor.

bisexuality a sexual orientation denoting the possibility of attraction to both men and women, although some define it to refer to the possibility of attraction to all genders.

blockbusting when real estate agents convince Whites that minorities are moving into the neighborhood; the Whites then sell their houses for low prices, and the real estate agents resell the houses at higher prices to minority families.

bourgeoisie in Marxist terms, the upper class. They are the owners of the means of production and they hire labor.

brown-bag test criterion used to screen individuals from membership in a group or organization if their skin color is darker than a brown grocery bag.

bureaucracy an organization run by non-elected officials with clear rules and formal standards.

capital gains money obtained through the sale of property or investments.

capitalism an economic system based on private ownership, competition, and open markets.

caste system a closed social ranking system dividing categories of individuals in which position is ascribed and which is legitimated by cultural and/or religious institutions.

chronic health problems health problems that continue over a long period of time.

circulation mobility mobility that reflects the cultural and social openness of a society.

cisgender an adjective describing people whose gender identity matches the sex they were assigned at birth.

class defined variously as individuals or groups who (1) occupy the same position on hierarchies of occupational prestige, income, and education; (2) are in the same relation to the system of production; or (3) are in the same relation to the system of production and are also class conscious.

class consciousness the full awareness within a group of its class position and relationship with other classes, along with action based on this awareness.

colonial imperialism political and economic domination by a region achieved by exploiting the labor of peoples in colonial or quasi-colonial regions.

colorism when people attribute higher status to those who have lighter skin.

commodity as Marx uses the term, this is an object that satisfies human need and is exchanged for something else. Labor is an example of a commodity.

contingent workforce includes people who work on a nonpermanent basis as contractors, freelancers, or consultants.

corporate crime crime committed by corporate officials for the immediate benefit of their corporation rather than themselves.

crises of overproduction the inability of capitalism to sell all that it produces, largely because of the inconsistency between low, impoverished wages and advanced technology.

critical-race perspective views racism and race relations as rooted and hidden in the structure and historical social arrangements of society rather than as issues of individual prejudice.

crowding because minorities are less likely to be hired for some jobs, they become segregated into low-wage jobs that are dominated by other minorities.

cultural capital a group's cultural values, experiences, knowledge, and skills passed on from one generation to the next.

cultural taxation when minorities are expected to take on extra work on diversity issues without extra compensation.

demisexuality a sexual orientation in which attraction to others is based on a close emotional attachment rather than on gender or appearance.

diffuse status a characteristic such as race or gender that leads people to expect a particular level of competence across a range of social contexts (this is contrasted with **specific status**, see below).

double consciousness the sensation of viewing and judging oneself through both one's own eyes and those of the dominant group. The term was coined by W.E.B.

Du Bois in reference to the African American experience.

drift hypothesis in the study of the relationship between mental illness and social class, the argument that illness causes one's downward mobility through the class system.

durable inequalities when categories of individuals persistently and across many situations have less access to resources and opportunities than other groups.

Earned Income Tax Credit a government initiative to encourage work by allowing low-income workers, especially those with children, to pay less tax and increase their refunds.

economic hardship spending more than 40 percent of one's income on debt payment.

endogamy refers to marriage within one's own social group.

environmental equity/justice concerns the extent to which groups have equal access to public land resources and equal exposure to environmental hazards.

essentialism the idea that people are born with a certain unchanging, underlying "essence" that can include sexual orientation or gender identity.

estate tax a tax charged when a person dies and passes on their wealth. Only very large inheritances are subject to this tax.

ethnic group a group distinguished on the basis of its native cultural and linguistic characteristics.

ethnocentrism belief that one's culture is the best and should be used as a standard to rate other cultures.

eugenics movement people who believe that the human race could and should be improved by selecting for particular characteristics. They advocate selective breeding or preventing some people from having children.

fatherhood bump the increase in pay, promotions, and benefits associated with fatherhood.

feminism the belief in social, political, economic, and personal equality among the sexes.

forced division of labor where the division of labor does not arise naturally based on skills and talents, but rather by force exerted by those in power.

functionalist theory of stratification the argument that stratification is a necessary device for motivating talented people to perform society's most difficult and important tasks, and that it arises from scarcity of talent and the differential social necessity of tasks.

gender a set of attitudinal, role, and behavior expectations, which are socially and culturally defined, associated with each sex.

gender dysphoria refers to the feeling that one's true gender is not consistent with that assigned at birth.

gender expression how a person uses their external appearance to signal their gender. This can include such things as dress or mannerisms.

gender fluid refers to people who do not subscribe to the gender binary. Their gender is not fixed.

gender identity a person's own perception of their gender.

genderqueer people whose feelings and behaviors are not confined by the gender binary.

gender stratification the degree to which access to valued resources is restricted because of gender.

gerrymandering drawing political boundaries to advantage one political party.

Gini index a societal-level measure of inequality that ranges between 0 and 1, with 0 indicating complete equality and 1 indicating complete inequality. The measure tells us how different the actual distribution of income is in a society compared to a society where everyone gets exactly the same percent of income.

globalization *economically*, the acceleration of international trade and flow of financial capital; *politically*, the opening of national borders to foreign goods and services; and *socially*, the free flow and exchange of cultural ideas and structural arrangements among nations.

habitus Bourdieu's term for a system of stable dispositions to view the world in a particular way.

hate crime a violent or property crime that is motivated at least in part by a bias against the victim's race, religion, disability, sexual orientation, gender, ethnicity, or national origin.

hegemonic masculinity the dominant model of masculinity present in a culture at a particular time.

heteronormative a worldview that assumes heterosexuality is the normal and natural state.

homophily the phenomenon where people seek out and interact with only with who are similar to themselves.

Horatio Alger 1832–1899 a novelist who wrote stories about poor boys entering the middle- and upper-class through hard work and determination.

human capital the investments one makes in oneself (i.e., education, acquisition of skills, and experience).

hypersegregation when cities are extremely segregated across several measures of segregation.

ideology a set of ideas or beliefs that justify a particular system of stratification.

implicit bias internalized stereotypes of marginalized groups that unconsciously direct our feelings and actions.

income deficit how far below the poverty level one's income falls.

index crimes eight crimes that FBI uses to calculate the crime index. They include homicide, rape, robbery, burglary, aggravated assault, larceny, motor vehicle theft, and arson.

in-kind benefits noncash outlays given to recipients of government programs, such as food stamps, medical assistance, and job training.

inner circle a network of leaders from large corporations who serve as top officers at more than one firm, who are politically active, and who serve the interests of the capitalist class as a whole.

institutional view of social welfare belief that since poverty is often beyond the control of individuals, and one of government's legitimate roles is to help those in need, welfare should be available to help people out of poverty.

intergenerational mobility a change in economic or social hierarchical position between generations.

interlock when a member of a board of directors on one corporation also serves on the board of another corporation.

intersectionality the idea that one's race, sex, ethnicity, and social class (among other identities), when combined, create distinctive social positions that have effects that are independent of the separate effects of each component taken separately.

intersex term used to describe a variety of conditions in which a person is born with a reproductive or sexual anatomy that does not seem to fit the typical definitions of female or male.

intragenerational mobility vertical economic or social movement within one's own lifetime.

Jim Crow laws enacted during the nineteenth and early twentieth centuries, these laws legalized segregation and stripped Blacks of political power.

labor power the mental and physical capacities exercised by individuals when they produce something of use.

legacy college and university preferences given to the children of alumni.

legitimation process the means and manner by which social inequality is explained and justified.

linked fate the idea that those candidates closest matching someone's identity are more likely to represent their interests.

lookism discrimination based on how well people conform to beauty standards.

mass incarceration historically and comparatively high rates of imprisonment in a society. The term is also sometimes used to refer to the race and class disproportionalities associated with high levels of incarceration in the United States.

mass society a society in which the vast majority of the population is unorganized, largely powerless, and manipulated by those at the distant top.

means of production the material (e.g., machines) and nonmaterial techniques used to produce goods and services in an economy.

means tested social welfare programs that determine eligibility by setting particular income and asset levels.

microaggressions or microinequities everyday ways in which, because of their social ranking, individuals are ignored, put down, highlighted, or demeaned.

minority stress the stress associated with being a member of a stigmatized minority group. It is a result of prejudice and discrimination and is associated with a host of negative health outcomes.

mode of production the particular type of economic system in a society, including its means of production (e.g., technology) and social/authority relations among workers and between workers and owners. Capitalism and feudalism are two modes of production.

motherhood penalty the decrease in wages, promotions, and benefits associated with motherhood.

nativism placing priority on the interests of native-born people over immigrants.

neighborhood effects ways that the neighborhood a person lives in plays a role in determining their behaviors and outcomes.

net worth one's wealth minus one's debts.

new social movements social movements centered on issues of identity and lifestyle.

occupational structure how different occupations are distributed in a society. For example, one society might have a lot of jobs in agriculture while another focuses on technology.

old social movements social movements mostly focused on class issues and the redistribution of wealth.

opportunity structure characteristics of the cultural, social, political, legal, occupational, economic, and other institutions that affect the chances of social mobility either positively or negatively.

panethnic group a collectivity who, historically, were considered to be from distinct groups but today are, for political and cultural reasons, grouped together. Examples include Hispanics, Asians, and Native Americans.

pansexuality a sexual orientation denoting the possibility of attraction to people of all gender identities.

party an association aimed at or specifically organized to gain political power in an organization or society (Weber).

patriarchy a complex of structured interrelationships in which men dominate women.

payroll tax taxes charged on people's earned income. Employers usually withhold these taxes from employees' paychecks.

phenotype observable characteristics of organisms that can be a result of genetics, environment, or both. It can include physical characteristics (such as hair color) or behaviors.

pigeonholing steering members of a particular category (e.g., racial or gender) into positions deemed appropriate for them.

pluralism the view stressing that power is distributed throughout society among various groups rather than concentrated.

political action committee (PAC) a group that organizes around a broad or narrow common interest to influence political policy in its favor.

poverty line the amount of income considered adequate to provide the basic necessities of life. In the United States, the government calculates this amount using pretax income. Anyone whose income falls below the line is considered poor.

power the ability of a person to achieve what they want despite resistance from others.

power elite a small group or set of groups that dominate the political process and masses in a society.

prestige the social ranking accorded a position or occupation; a synonym for status honor.

proletariat the working class.

public assistance programs cash and in-kind government programs for the poor that are means tested (i.e., require that individuals prove their eligibility) and to which there is a social stigma attached.

racial formation a term coined by Omi and Winant to refer to the ways that race categories are socially constructed by various political and social forces over time.

racial invariance hypothesis the idea that causes of crime are the same for all racial groups but that the groups are differentially exposed to those causes.

racial project a term coined by Omi and Winant that is part of their larger theory of **racial formation** (see above). People engage in racial projects when they interpret or explain racial dynamics with the intention of justifying the distribution of resources along particular racial lines.

racialization social and psychological process by which social phenomena such as poverty and welfare are connected with a particular racial group.

rationalization the increasing bureaucratic, technological, and impersonal character of the modern world (Weber).

redistributive policies policies that seek to redistribute resources from those at the top to those at the bottom.

reference group the often abstract group of people with whom we compare ourselves. For example, the authors' reference group would be liberal arts professors.

regressive taxes require that all people pay the same rate of tax. For example, sales tax is regressive because everyone in a locality pays the same amount. It is called regressive because it requires poor people to spend a greater proportion of their income on it than rich people.

relative mobility a shift in one's position on the economic ladder in comparison to another person or group.

residual view of social welfare the belief that since poverty is caused by personal flaws, welfare programs should be minimal, with low benefits and strict eligibility requirements to discourage their use.

restrictive covenant an agreement on how land can or cannot be used. In this book, the term refers to an agreement, often contained in a deed, that land will not be sold to or occupied by non-White people.

ruling class the broad Marxist view that the upper class, or an active arm of it, generally dominates the political process in society to protect its interests.

scientific management a system of control used by management in which labor tasks are simplified and standardized by being broken down into their smallest elements.

sedimentation the reproduction and perpetuation of lower levels of wealth over generations for given groups.

settler colonialism a model of colonialism based on the taking and settling of the lands of indigenous peoples rather than on the exploitation of labor.

sex a category usually determined based on the physical or chromosomal features of a newborn.

social capital the size and nature of networks of social relationships possessed by a person or group.

social causation thesis in the study of the relationship between mental illness and social class, the argument that social class position is causally related to the probability of mental illness.

social closure excluding people from a social group in order to deny them valuable resources.

social constructionism a perspective that explains how social phenomena are socially created through definitions, classifications, and categorizations used by individuals.

Social Darwinism the theory that natural selection and survival of the fittest apply to people as well as to other animal species. This theory has been used to justify colonialism and slavery.

social insurance government programs, such as Social Security, for which individuals who have worked for a certain period of time are automatically eligible and seen as deserving of aid.

social order the arrangement of social honor (prestige) within a society.

social relations of production the nature of property and power relationships among workers, between workers and managers/supervisors, and between owners and nonowners in an economic system.

social reproduction the process by which structural conditions (like class) reproduce themselves.

social stratification a condition in which the ranking system among groups or categories of individuals is firmly established, resulting in a set of social layers separated by impermeable boundaries.

socioeconomic status a person's position on several continuous social and economic hierarchies, such as education, income, occupation, and wealth.

specific status a characteristic that leads people to expect a particular level of competence, but only in limited and relevant circumstances. For example, a mathematician is only expected to be competent in math, not sports (contrast this term with **diffuse status**, see above).

stages of capitalism capitalism's movement through phases of cooperation, manufacture, and modern industry (Marx).

status the relative ranking of individuals and groups on the basis of *social* and evaluated characteristics; contrasts with **class** (see above), which is largely an *economic* ranking.

status attainment the study of the factors and processes that account for the educational, occupational, and economic attainment of individuals.

status-based politics politics based on someone's status or position in society. Examples include politics based on race or gender.

stereotype threat individuals' worry that they will be judged negatively based on stereotypes, leading to underperformance in work and school environments.

street crimes crimes listed by the FBI's Crime Index, including burglary, larceny-theft, motor vehicle theft, arson, murder, forcible rape, robbery, and aggravated assault.

structural mobility mobility that is due to shifts in the occupational distribution or changes in technology.

subjective class one's perception of one's own social class.

subprime mortgages housing loans given to people whose credit is not good enough to get a conventional mortgage. They usually charge higher rates of interest than conventional mortgages.

surplus value profit for the employer or business owner.

systemic racism discriminatory practices and ideologies that were built into social institutions (such as the economy and the educational system) from early in a country's history.

tokenism recruiting one or a small number of minorities as a symbolic gesture of inclusion.

transgender referring to individuals who do not self-identify with the gender they were assigned at birth.

underclass a small, urban, largely unemployed, chronically poor, welfare-dependent group of individuals living in impoverished neighborhoods whose children often wind up in the same position. Today this term is regarded by many as problematic because of its association with Blacks in the inner city.

welfare capitalism special benefits used by management to minimize solidarity among workers.

white-collar crime crimes committed by individuals of high status or corporations using their powerful positions for personal gain.

References

Aaronson, D., & Mazumder, B. (2008). Intergenerational economic mobility in the United States, 1940 to 2000. *Journal of Human Resources, 43*(1), 139–172.

Aronson, P. (2003). Feminists or "postfeminists"? Young women's attitudes toward feminism and gender relations. *Gender & Society, 17*(6), 903–922.

AARP. (2009). *Chronic condition prevalence in the 50+ US population.* American Association of Retired Persons Public Policy Institute.

Abdul-Razzak, N., Prato, C., & Wolton, S. (2020). After citizens United: How outside spending shapes American democracy. *Electoral Studies, 67,* 102190. https://doi.org/10.1016/j.electstud.2020.102190

Aber, L., Butler, S., Danziger, S., Doar, R., Ellwood, D. T., Gueron, J. M., Haidt, J., Haskins, R., Holzer, H. J., Hymowitz, K., Fellow, W. E. S., Mead, L., Mincy, R., & Reeves, R. V. (2015). *Members of the AEI/Brookings working group on poverty and opportunity.* Brookings Institution.

Aberle, D. F., Cohen, A. D., Davis, M. J., & Sutton, F. X. (1950). The functional prerequisites of a society. *Ethics, 60,* 100–111.

Abu-Lughod, L. (2013). *Do Muslim women need saving?* Harvard University Press.

ACLU. (2018). *Freezing out justice: How immigration arrests at courthouses are undermining the justice system.* American Civil Liberties Union. https://www.aclu.org/sites/default/files/field_document/rep18-icecourthouse-combined-rel01.pdf

Acs, G., Pendall, R., Treskon, M., & Khare, A. (2017). *National trends and the case of Chicago, 1990–2010.* Urban Institute.

Adam, B. D., Duyvendak, Jan Willem, & Krouwel, A. (1999). Gay and lesbian movements beyond borders? National imprints of a worldwide movements. In B. D. Adam, J. W. Duyvendak, & A. Krouwel (Eds.), *Global emergence of gay and lesbian politics* (pp. 344–372). Temple University.

Adamczyk, A., Boyd, K. A., & Hayes, B. E. (2016). Place matters: Contextualizing the roles of religion and race for understanding Americans' attitudes about homosexuality. *Social Science Research, 57,* 1–16.

Adamczyk, A., Kim, C., & Schmuhl, M. (2018). Newspaper presentations of homosexuality across nations: Examining differences by religion, economic development, and democracy. *Sociological Perspectives, 61*(3), 399–425. https://doi.org/10.1177/0731121417724563.

Adichie, C. N. (2014). *Americanah.* Anchor Books.

Adkins, J. (2016). "These people are frightened to death:" Congressional investigations and the lavender scare. *National Archives, 48*(2). https://www.archives.gov/publications/prologue/2016/summer/lavender.html

ADL. (2021). *Audit of antisemitic incidents 2020.* Anti-Defamation League. https://www.adl.org/audit2020

Adler, W. T., & Thompson, S. A. (2018, November 7). "Blue wave" wasn't enough to overcome republican gerrymanders. *The New York Times.* https://www.nytimes.com/interactive/2018/11/07/opinion/midterm-elections-2018-republican-gerrymandering.html

Aguiar, J., Sequeira, C. F., Matias, M., Coimbra, S., & Fontaine, A. M. (2021). Gender and perception of justice in housework division between unemployed spouses. *Journal of Family Issues, 42*(6), 1217–1233. https://doi.org/10.1177/0192513X20942823.

Ahler, D. J., Citrin, J., Dougal, M. C., & Lenz, G. S. (2017). Face value? Experimental evidence that candidate appearance influences electoral choice. *Political Behavior, 39*(1), 77–102.

Ahmad, D. L. (2000). Opium smoking, anti-Chinese attitudes, and the American medical community, 1850–1890. *American Nineteenth Century History, 1*(2), 53–68.

Ahmed, S., & Matthes, J. (2017). Media representation of Muslims and Islam from 2000 to 2015: A meta-analysis. *International Communication Gazette, 79*(3), 219–244.

Aidi, H. (2015, February 2). Middle Eastern Americans push census change. *Al Jazeera America.* http://america.aljazeera.com/opinions/2015/2/middle-eastern-americans-push-census-change.html

Ainsworth, C. (2015). *Sex redefined.* MacMillan.

Aisenbrey, S., Evertsson, M., & Grunow, D. (2009).

Is there a career penalty for mothers' time out? A comparison of Germany, Sweden and the United States. *Social Forces*, 88(2), 573–605.

Akerlof, G. A., & Kranton, R. E. (2010). *Identity economics*. Princeton University Press. https://www.degruyter.com/document/doi/10.1515/9781400834181/html

Alba, R., Deane, G., Denton, N., Disha, I., McKenzie, B., & Napierala, J. (2014). The role of immigrant enclaves for Latino residential inequalities. *Journal of Ethnic and Migration Studies*, 40(1), 1–20.

Alexander, M. (2012). *The new Jim Crow: Mass incarceration in the age of colorblindness* (Revised edition). New Press.

Alfani, G. (2020, October 15). Pandemics and inequality: A historical overview. *VoxEU. Org*. https://voxeu.org/article/pandemics-and-inequality-historical-overview

Alkire, S., Apablaza, M., Chakravarty, S., & Yalonetzky, G. (2017). Measuring chronic multidimensional poverty. *Journal of Policy Modeling*, 39(6), 983–1006. https://doi.org/10.1016/j.jpolmod.2017.05.020.

Allegretto, S., & Reich, M. (2018). Are local minimum wages absorbed by price increases? Estimates from internet-based restaurant menus. *ILR Review*, 71(1), 35–63. https://doi.org/10.1177/0019793917713735.

Allport, G. W. (1954). *The nature of prejudice*. Addison-Wesley Publishing.

Alon, T., Doepke, M., Olmstead-Rumsey, J., & Tertilt, M. (2020). *The impact of COVID-19 on gender equality* (Working Paper No. 26947). National Bureau of Economic Research. https://www.nber.org/system/files/working_papers/w26947/w26947.pdf

Almås, I., Cappelen, A. W., Sørensen, E. Ø., & Tungodden, B. (2022). Global evidence on the selfish rich inequality hypothesis. *Proceedings of the National Academy of Sciences*, 119(3). https://doi.org/10.1073/pnas.2109690119

Alshammari, Y. H. (2020, April 1). Why is there no MENA category on the 2020 US census? *Aljazeera America*. https://www.aljazeera.com/news/2020/4/1/why-is-there-no-mena-category-on-the-2020-us-census

Altman, D. (2005). The globalization of sexual identities. In M. B. Zinn, P. Hondagneu-Sotelo, & M. A. Messner (Eds.), *Gender through the prism of difference* (pp. 216–226). Oxford.

Altonji, J., Contractor, Z., Finamor, L., Haygood, R., Lindenlaub, I., Meghir, C., O'Dea, C., Scott, D., Wang, L., & Washington, E. (2020). *Employment effects of unemployment insurance generosity during the pandemic*. Tobin Center for Economic Policy, Yale University. https://tobin.yale.edu/sites/default/files/covid-19%20response/CARES-UI_identification_vF(1).pdf

Alvaredo, F., Chancel, L., Piketty, T., Saez, E., & Zucman, G. (2018). The elephant curve of global inequality and growth. *AEA Papers and Proceedings*, 108, 103–108. https://doi.org/10.1257/pandp.20181073

Alvarez, L. (2015, February 24). US won't file charges in Trayvon Martin killing. *The New York Times*. http://www.nytimes.com/2015/02/25/us/justice-dept-wont-charge-george-zimmerman-in-trayvon-martin-killing.html

American Jewish Historical Society. (2018). *Harvard's Jewish problem*. Jewish Virtual Library. https://www.jewishvirtuallibrary.org/harvard-s-jewish-problem

American Society of Plastic Surgeons. (2021). *2020 national plastic surgery statistics*. https://www.plasticsurgery.org/documents/News/Statistics/2020/plastic-surgery-statistics-full-report-2020.pdf

American Sociological Association (2015). William Julius Wilson says his arguments on race and class still apply. *Footnotes*, 43(6), 3.

Anderson, M. L. (1997). *Thinking about women*. Allyn & Bacon.

Anderson, S. (2018). *Immigrants and billion-dollar companies*. National Foundation for American Policy. https://nfap.com/wp-content/uploads/2019/01/2018-BILLION-DOLLAR-STARTUPS.NFAP-Policy-Brief.2018-1.pdf

Anderson, S. (2020, November 4). San Franciscans vote overwhelmingly to rein in overpaid CEOs. *Inequality.Org*. https://inequality.org/great-divide/san-francisco-ceo-pay-tax/

Andrasfay, T., & Goldman, N. (2021). Reductions in 2020 US life expectancy due to COVID-19 and the disproportionate impact on the Black and Latino populations. *Proceedings of the National Academy of Sciences*, 118(5). https://doi.org/10.1073/pnas.2014746118

Andreoni, J., & Petrie, R. (2008). Beauty, gender and stereotypes: Evidence from laboratory experiments. *Journal of Economic Psychology*, 29(1), 73–93.

Anne E. Casey Foundation. (2016). *A shared sentence: The devastating toll of parental incarceration on kids, families, and communities*. Anne E. Casey Foundation. http://www.aecf.org/resources/a-shared-sentence/

Apel, R., & Powell, P. (2019). Level of criminal justice contact and early adult wage inequality. *RSF: The Russell Sage Foundation Journal of the Social Sciences*, 5(1), 198–222. https://doi.org/10.7758/rsf.2019.5.1.09

Apel, R., & Sweeten, G. (2010). The impact of incarceration on employment during the transition to adulthood. *Social Problems*, 57(3), 448–479.

AP-NORC. (2020). *The Equal Rights Amendment and discrimination against women*. https://apnorc.

org/projects/the-equal-rights-amendment-and-discrimination-against-women/

Appalachian Regional Commission. (2014). Economic diversity in Appalachia: Statistics, strategies, and guides for action. ARC. https://www.arc.gov/wp-content/uploads/2020/06/EconomicDiversityinAppalachiaCompilationofAllReports.pdf

Appalachian Regional Commission. (2021). Health disparities related to opioid misuse in Appalachia. *Creating a Culture of Health in Appalachia*. https://healthinappalachia.org/issue-briefs/opioid-misuse/

Ard, K., Garcia, N., & Kelly, P. (2017). Another avenue of action: An examination of climate change countermovement industries' use of PAC fonations and their relationship to Congressional voting over time. *Environmental Politics, 26*(6), 1107–1131.

Arias, E., Betzaida, T.-V., Ahmad, F., & Kochanek, K. (2021). *Provisional life expectancy estimates for 2020*. Centers for Disease Control and Prevention. https://doi.org/10.15620/cdc:107201

Arnold, D., Dobbie, W., & Yang, C. S. (2018). Racial bias in bail decisions. *The Quarterly Journal of Economics, 133*(4), 1885–1932.

Aronowitz, S. (1973). *False promises: The shaping of American working class consciousness*. McGraw-Hill.

Artiga, S., Foutz, J., Cornachione, E., & Garfield, R. (2016). *Key facts on health and health care by race and ethnicity*. Henry J. Kaiser Family Foundation. https://www.kff.org/report-section/key-facts-on-health-and-health-care-by-race-and-ethnicity-section-2-health-access-and-utilization/

Asante-Muhammad, D., Collins, C., Hoxie, J., & Nieves, E. (2017). *The Road to Zero Wealth: How the Racial Wealth Divide is Hollowing out America's Middle Class*. Institute for Policy Studies and Prosperity Now.

Associated Press. (2020, July 20). *Explaining AP style on Black and White*. AP News. https://apnews.com/article/archive-race-and-ethnicity-9105661462

Atems, B. (2020). Identifying the dynamic effects of income inequality on crime. *Oxford Bulletin of Economics and Statistics, 82*(4), 751–782. https://doi.org/10.1111/obes.12359

Atske, S., & Perrin, A. (2021). *Home broadband adoption, computer ownership vary by race, ethnicity in the US*. Pew Research Center. https://www.pewresearch.org/fact-tank/2021/07/16/home-broadband-adoption-computer-ownership-vary-by-race-ethnicity-in-the-u-s/

Attorney General's National Task Force. (2012). *Defending childhood: Protect, heal, thrive*. Attorney General's National Task Force on Children Exposed to Violence. https://www.hopeforchildrenfoundation.org/community/blog-2/

Aurand, A., Emmanuel, D., & Yentel, D. (2018). *A shortage of affordable homes*. National Low Income Housing Coalition.

Aussenberg, R. A. (2018). *Errors and fraud in the Supplemental Nutrition Assistance Program*. Congressional Research Service. https://sgp.fas.org/crs/misc/R45147.pdf

Autor, D. (2019). *Work of the past, work of the future* (Working Paper No. 25588). National Bureau of Economic Research.

Autor, D. H., Manning, A., & Smith, C. L. (2016). The contribution of the minimum wage to US wage inequality over three decades: A reassessment. *American Economic Journal: Applied Economics, 8*(1), 58–99. https://doi.org/10.1257/app.20140073

Avent-Holt, D., & Tomaskovic-Devey, D. (2014). A relational theory of earnings inequality. *American Behavioral Scientist, 58*(3), 379–399.

Averett, K. H. (2021). Queer parents, gendered embodiment and the de-essentialisation of motherhood. *Feminist Theory, 22*(2), 284–304. https://doi.org/10.1177/1464700121989226

AVERT. (2015, July 20). *History of HIV and AIDS overview*. Global Information and Education on HIV and AIDS. https://www.avert.org/professionals/history-hiv-aids/overview

Avery, D. (2020, November 8). Congress will have record number of LGBTQ lawmakers next session. *NBC News*. https://www.nbcnews.com/feature/nbc-out/congress-will-have-record-number-lgbtq-lawmakers-next-session-n1246487

Axel-Lute, M. (2018). *Is the housing market the answer to the racial wealth gap?* Shelter Force. https://shelterforce.org/2018/10/29/is-the-housing-market-the-answer-to-the-racial-wealth-gap/

Aydin, B. K., Saka, N., Bas, F., Bas, E. K., Coban, A., Yildirim, S., Guran, T., & Darendeliler, F. (2019). Frequency of ambiguous genitalia in 14,177 newborns in Turkey. *Journal of the Endocrine Society, 3*(6), 1185–1195. https://doi.org/10.1210/js.2018-00408

Baams, L., Wilson, B. D. M., & Russell, S. T. (2019). LGBTQ youth in unstable housing and foster care. *Pediatrics, 143*(3), e20174211. https://doi.org/10.1542/peds.2017-4211

Bacevich, A. (2017, August 12). Trump hasn't drained the swamp—he's put the military in charge of it. *The Spectator*. https://www.spectator.co.uk/2017/08/trump-hasnt-drained-the-swamp-hes-put-the-military-in-charge-of-it/

Bachman, J. G., Staff, J., O'Malley, P. M., Schulenberg, J. E., & Freedman-Doan, P. (2011). Twelfth-grade student work intensity linked to later educational attainment and substance use: New longitudinal evidence. *Developmental Psychology, 47*(2), 344–363.

Badgett, M. V. L., Choi, S. K., & Wilson, B. D. M. (2020). LGBT poverty in the United States. In J. A. Reich (Ed.), *The state of families:*

Law, policy, and the meanings of relationships (pp. 385–387). Routledge.

Bahn, K., & Cumming, C. S. (2020). *Factsheet: US occupational segregation by race, ethnicity, and gender*. Washington Center for Equitable Growth. http://www.equitablegrowth.org/factsheet-u-s-occupational-segregation-by-race-ethnicity-and-gender/

Bailey, M. J., & Dynarski, S. M. (2011). *Gains and gaps: Changing inequality in U.S. college entry and completion*. National Bureau of Economic Research. http://www.nber.org/papers/w17633

Baiocco, R., Pistella, J., & Morelli, M. (2020). Coming out to parents in lesbian and bisexual women: The role of internalized sexual stigma and positive LB identity. *Frontiers in Psychology, 11*, 609885. https://doi.org/10.3389/fpsyg.2020.609885

Baker-Sperry, L., & Grauerholz, L. (2003). The pervasiveness and persistence of the feminine beauty ideal in children's fairy tales. *Gender & Society, 17*(5), 711–726.

Bakshi, S. (2004). A comparative analysis of hijras and drag queens: The subversive possibilities and limits of parading effeminacy and negotiating masculinity. *Journal of Homosexuality, 46*(3–4), 211–223.

Balderrama, F. E., & Rodriguez, R. (2006). *Decade of betrayal: Mexican repatriation in the 1930s* (Rev. ed). University of New Mexico Press.

Ballesteros, C. (2018, February 21). South Carolina lawmakers want fines and community service for people who wear their pants too low. *Newsweek.* https://www.newsweek.com/democrats-south-carolina-want-fine-residents-who-sag-their-pants-815233

Bannai, A., & Tamakoshi, A. (2014). The association between long working hours and health: A systematic review of epidemiological evidence. *Scandinavian Journal of Work, Environment & Health, 40*(1), 5–18.

Bannon, A., & Reagan, L. (2013). *New politics of judicial elections 2011–12*. Brennan Center for Justice. http://www.brennancenter.org/publication/new-politics-judicial-elections-2011-12

Barnes, J. C., & Motz, R. T. (2018). Reducing racial inequalities in adulthood arrest by reducing inequalities in school discipline: Evidence from the school-to-prison pipeline. *Developmental Psychology, 54*(12), 2328–2340. https://doi.org/10.1037/dev0000613

Barnes, R. C. (2017). Structural redundancy and multiplicity within networks of US corporate directors. *Critical Sociology, 43*(1), 37–57.

Barnett, B. M. (1993). Invisible southern Black women leaders in the civil rights movement: The triple constraints of gender, race, and class. *Gender & Society, 7*(2), 162–182.

Barr, L. (2021, October 25). Hate crimes against Asians rose 76% in 2020 amid pandemic, FBI says. *ABC News.* https://abcnews.go.com/US/hate-crimes-asians-rose-76-2020-amid-pandemic/story?id=80746198

Barrett, J. E., & Roediger, D. (2008). How White people became White. In P. S. Rothenberg (Ed.), *White privilege: Essential readings on the other side of racism* (3rd ed., pp. 35–40). Worth Publishing.

Barroso, A. (2020). *61% of U.S. women say "feminist" describes them well; many see feminism as empowering, polarizing.* Pew Research Center. https://www.pewresearch.org/fact-tank/2020/07/07/61-of-u-s-women-say-feminist-describes-them-well-many-see-feminism-as-empowering-polarizing/

Barry, K. M., Farrell, B., Levi, J. L., & Vanguri, N. (2016). A bare desire to harm: Transgender people and the equal protection clause. *Boston College Law Review, 57*, 507–566.

Bartelink, V. H. M., Zay Ya, K., Guldbrandsson, K., & Bremberg, S. (2020). Unemployment among young people and mental health: A systematic review. *Scandinavian Journal of Public Health, 48*(5), 544–558. https://doi.org/10.1177/1403494819852847

Bartels, L. M. (2008). *Unequal democracy: The political economy of the new gilded age.* Princeton University Press.

Batalova, J. (2020, May 13). *Immigrant health-care workers in the United States*. Migration Policy Institute. https://www.migrationpolicy.org/article/immigrant-health-care-workers-united-states-2018

Batalova, J., Hanna, M., & Levesque, C. (2021, February 9). *Frequently requested statistics on immigrants and immigration in the United States.* Migration Policy Institute. https://www.migrationpolicy.org/article/frequently-requested-statistics-immigrants-and-immigration-united-states-2020

Bateman, N., & Ross, M. (2020). *Why has COVID-19 been especially harmful for working women?* Brookings Institution. https://www.brookings.edu/essay/why-has-covid-19-been-especially-harmful-for-working-women/

Batteau, A. (1984). The sacrifice of nature: A study in the social production of consciousness. In P. Beaver, & B. Purrington (Eds.), *Cultural adaptation to mountain environments* (pp. 94–106). University of Georgia Press.

Battle, J., Patrana A., & Daniels, J. (2012). *Social justice sexuality project, 2010 cumulative codebook.* City University of New York Graduate Center.

Baum, D. (2016, April). Legalize it all. *Harper's Magazine.* https://harpers.org/archive/2016/04/legalize-it-all/

Bauman, T. (2019). *No safe place: The criminalization of homelessness in US cities*. National Law Center on Homelessness and Poverty.

Baumgartner, J. C., & Radley, D. C. (2021). *The drug overdose toll in 2020 and near-term actions for addressing it*. The Commonwealth Fund. https://doi.org/10.26099/gb4y-r129

Baumle, D. (2018). Creating the trauma-to-prison pipeline: How the US justice system criminalizes structural and interpersonal trauma experienced by girls of color. *Family Court Review, 56*(4), 695–708. https://doi.org/10.1111/fcre.12384

Beaumont, P. (2021, February 3). Decades of progress on extreme poverty now in reverse due to COVID. *The Guardian.* http://www.theguardian.com/global-development/2021/feb/03/decades-of-progress-on-extreme-poverty-now-in-reverse-due-to-covid

Beaver, K. M., Boccio, C., Smith, S., & Ferguson, C. J. (2019). Physical attractiveness and criminal justice processing: Results from a longitudinal sample of youth and young adults. *Psychiatry, Psychology and Law, 26*(4), 669–681. https://doi.org/10.1080/13218719.2019.1618750.

Beckhusen, J., Florax, R. J. G. M., de Graaff, T., Poot, J., & Waldorf, B. (2013). Living and working in ethnic enclaves: English language proficiency of immigrants in US metropolitan areas. *Papers in Regional Science, 92*(2), 305–328.

Behrens, A., Uggen, C., & Manza, J. (2003). Ballot manipulation and the "menace of Negro domination": Racial threat and felon disenfranchisement in the United States, 1850–20021. *American Journal of Sociology, 109*(3), 559–605.

Bejarano, C., Brown, N. E., Gershon, S. A., & Montoya, C. (2021). Shared identities: Intersectionality, linked fate, and perceptions of political candidates. *Political Research Quarterly, 74*(4), 970–985. https://doi.org/10.1177/1065912920951640

Bell, R. C. (2008). A history of women in sport prior to Title IX. *The Sport Journal, 10*(2). http://thesportjournal.org/article/a-history-of-women-in-sport-prior-to-title-ix/

Bell, W. (1987). *Contemporary social welfare.* MacMillan Publishing Company.

Bellafiore, R., & Mauro, M. (2019). *Does America have a progressive tax code?* Tax Foundation. https://taxfoundation.org/growing-percentage-americans-zero-income-tax-liability/

Belle, D., Tartarilla, A. B., Wapman, M., Schlieber, M., & Mercurio, A. E. (2021). "I can't operate, that boy is my son!": Gender schemas and a classic riddle. *Sex Roles, 85*(3–4), 161–171. https://doi.org/10.1007/s11199-020-01211-4

Benard, S., & Correll, S. J. (2010). Normative discrimination and the motherhood penalty. *Gender & Society, 24*(5), 616–646.

Ben-Moshe, L., & Magaña, S. (2014). An introduction to race, gender, and disability: Intersectionality, disability studies, and families of color. *Women, Gender, and Families of Color, 2*(2), 105–114.

Ben-Zeev, A., Dennehy, T. C., Goodrich, R. I., Kolarik, B. S., & Geisler, M. W. (2014). When an "educated" Black man becomes lighter in the mind's eye. *Sage Open, 4*(1), 1–9.

Berdahl, J. L., & Moore, C. (2006). Workplace harassment: Double jeopardy for minority women. *Journal of Applied Psychology, 91*(2), 426–436.

Berg, A. (2020, September 23). The evolution of the word "bisexual"—and why it's still misunderstood. *NBC News.* https://www.nbcnews.com/feature/nbc-out/evolution-word-bisexual-why-it-s-still-misunderstood-n1240832

Berger, C., & Rodkin, P. C. (2009). Male and female victims of male bullies: Social status differences by gender and informant source. *Sex Roles, 61*(1–2), 72–84.

Berger, J., & Ward, M. (2010). Subtle signals of inconspicuous consumption. *Journal of Consumer Research, 37*(4), 555–569.

Berger, N., & Fisher, P. (2013). *A well-educated workforce is key to state prosperity.* Economic Analysis and Research Network. https://www.epi.org/files/2013/A%20well-educated%20workforce%20is%20key%20to%20state%20prosperity.pdf

Berkhout, E., Galasso, N., Lawson, M., Morales, P. A. R., Taneja, A., & Pimentel, D. A. V. (2021). *The inequality virus: Bringing together a world torn apart by coronavirus through a fair, just and sustainable economy.* Oxfam International.

Bernstein, I. (2010). *The lean years: A history of the American worker, 1920–1933.* Haymarket Books.

Bernstein, M., Harvey, B., & Naples, N. A. (2018). Marriage, the final frontier? Same-sex marriage and the future of the lesbian and gay movement. *Sociological Forum, 33*(1), 30–52.

Berry, K. (2018). LGBT bullying in school: A troubling relational story. *Communication Education, 67*(4), 502–513. https://doi.org/10.1080/03634523.2018.1506137

Bersani, B. E. (2014). An examination of first and second generation immigrant offending trajectories. *Justice Quarterly, 31*(2), 315–343. https://doi.org/10.1080/07418825.2012.659200

Bérubé, M. (2006). Foreword: Another word is possible. In R. McRuer (Ed.), *Crip theory: Cultural signs of queerness and disability* (pp. vii–xii). New York University Press.

Bettinsoli, M. L., Suppes, A., & Napier, J. L. (2020). Predictors of attitudes toward gay men and lesbian women in 23 countries. *Social Psychological and Personality Science, 11*(5), 697–708. https://doi.org/10.1177/1948550619887785

Bey, M. (2017). Black women, Black ink: The "word" of Black feminism. In H. V. Williams (Ed.), *Bury my heart in a free land: Black women intellectuals in modern US history* (pp. 3–26). ABC-CLIO.

Bhattarai, A. (2021, June 21). Retail workers are quitting at record rates for higher-paying work: "My life isn't worth a dead-end job." *Washington Post.* https://www.washingtonpost.com/business/2021/06/21/retail-workers-quitting-jobs/

Bhutta, N., Bricker, J., Chang, A. C., Dettling, L. J., Goodman, S., Moore, K. B., Reber, S., Volz, A. H., & Windle, R. A. (2020). Changes in US family finances from 2016 to 2019: Evidence from the survey of consumer finances. *Federal Reserve Bulletin, 106*(5), 1–42.

Bhutta, N., Chang, A. C., Dettling, L. J., & Hsu, J. W. (2020). *Disparities in wealth by race and ethnicity in the 2019 Survey of Consumer Finances.* Federal Reserve. https://www.federalreserve.gov/econres/notes/feds-notes/disparities-in-wealth-by-race-and-ethnicity-in-the-2019-survey-of-consumer-finances-20200928.htm

Bianchi, S. M., Sayer, L. C., Milkie, M. A., & Robinson, J. P. (2012). Housework: Who did, does or will do it, and how much does it matter? *Social Forces, 91*(1), 55–63. https://doi.org/10.1093/sf/sos120

Bidner, C., & Eswaran, M. (2015). A gender-based theory of the origin of the caste system of India. *Journal of Development Economics, 114*, 142–158.

Bier, D. J. (2019, February 12). *Encouraging findings of the Trump administration's report on refugees and asylees.* Cato Institute. https://www.cato.org/blog/encouraging-findings-trump-admins-report-refugees-asylees

Birchfield, V. L. (2012). *Income inequality in capitalist democracies: The interplay of values and institutions.* Penn State Press.

Bird, R., & Newport, F. (2017). *What determines how Americans perceive their social class?* Gallup Polls. http://news.gallup.com/opinion/polling-matters/204497/determines-americans-perceive-social-class.aspx

Bishop, B. (2009). *The big sort: Why the clustering of like-minded America is tearing us apart.* Houghton Mifflin Harcourt.

Black and Pink. (2009). *A compilation of critiques on hate crimes legislation.* Black and Pink. http://www.againstequality.org/wp-content/uploads/2009/10/critiques-on-hate-crimes.pdf

Blackwell, J. E. (1985). *The Black community: Diversity and unity.* Harper & Row.

Blalock, H. M. (1967). *Toward a theory of minority-group relations.* Wiley.

Blau, F. D., & Kahn, L. M. (2017). The gender wage gap: Extent, trends, and explanations. *Journal of Economic Literature, 55*(3), 789–865.

Blau, F. D., & Mackie, C. (2017). *The economic and fiscal consequences of immigration.* Division of Behavioral and Social Sciences and Education, National Academies of Science. https://www.nap.edu/catalog/23550

Blau, P. M., & Duncan, O. D. (1967). *The American occupational structure.* Wiley.

Blazina, C., & Desilver, D. (2021). *A record number of women are serving in the 117th Congress.* Pew Research Center. https://www.pewresearch.org/fact-tank/2021/01/15/a-record-number-of-women-are-serving-in-the-117th-congress/

Bleich, S. N., Findling, M. G., Casey, L. S., Blendon, R. J., Benson, J. M., SteelFisher, G. K., Sayde, J. M., & Miller, C. (2019). Discrimination in the United States: Experiences of Black Americans. *Health Services Research, 54*(S2), 1399–1408. https://doi.org/10.1111/1475-6773.13220

Bliss, L. (2016). *Government response to Flint's water crisis comes far too late.* CityLab. http://www.citylab.com/cityfixer/2016/01/flint-lead-water-national-guard-too-late/423822/

Bloch, M., Katz, J., & Quealy, K. (2018). An extremely detailed map of the 2016 presidential election. *The New York Times.* https://www.nytimes.com/interactive/2018/upshot/election-2016-voting-precinct-maps.html, https://www.nytimes.com/interactive/2018/upshot/election-2016-voting-precinct-maps.html

Bloom, J. M. (2019). *Class, race, and the civil rights movement* (2nd ed.). Indiana University Press.

BLS. (2021a). *Employed persons by detailed occupation, sex, race, and Hispanic or Latino ethnicity, Table 11.* Bureau of Labor Statistics.

BLS. (2021b). *Table 1101: Quintiles of income before taxes, Consumer expenditure surveys, 2020.* Bureau of Labor Statistics.

Bokat-Lindell, S. (2019, September 26). Do we need a wealth tax? *The New York Times.* https://www.nytimes.com/2019/09/26/opinion/wealth-tax-warren-sanders.html

Bolgar, H. (2009). A century of essential feminism. *Studies in Gender and Sexuality, 10*(4), 195–199.

Bonacich, E. (1980). Class approaches to ethnicity and race. *Insurgent Sociologist, 10*(2), 9–23.

Bonica, A., McCarty, N., Poole, K. T., & Rosenthal, H. (2013). Why hasn't democracy slowed rising inequality? *Journal of Economic Perspectives, 27*(3), 103–124.

Bonilla-Silva, E. (1997). Rethinking racism: Toward a structural interpretation. *American Sociological Review, 62*(3), 465–480.

Bonilla-Silva, E. (2004). From bi-racial to tri-racial: Towards a new system of racial stratification in the USA. *Ethnic and Racial Studies, 27*(6), 931–950.

Bonilla-Silva, E. (2021). What makes systemic racism systemic? *Sociological Inquiry, 91*(3), 513–533. https://doi.org/10.1111/soin.12420

Boris, E., & Fish, J. N. (2014). "Slaves no more": Making global labor standards for domestic workers. *Feminist Studies*, 40(2), 411–443.

Bortolin, S. (2010). "I don't want him hitting on me": The role of masculinities in creating a chilly high school climate. *Journal of LGBT Youth*, 7(3), 200–223.

Bos, A. L., Greenlee, J. S., Holman, M. R., Oxley, Z. M., & Lay, J. C. (2021). This one's for the boys: How gendered political socialization limits girls' political ambition and interest. *American Political Science Review*, 1–18. https://doi.org/10.1017/S0003055421001027

Bose, C. E. (2012). Intersectionality and global gender inequality. *Gender & Society*, 26(1), 67–72.

Boshara, R. (2005). *Individual development accounts: Policies to build savings and assets for the poor.* Brookings Institution. https://www.brookings.edu/research/individual-development-accounts-policies-to-build-savings-and-assets-for-the-poor/

Bositis, D. A. (2007). Black political power in the new century. In R. D. Bullard (Ed.), *The Black metropolis in the twenty-first century* (pp. 221–242). Roman & Littlefield Publishers, Inc.

Bottomore, T. B. (2006). *Elites and society.* Routledge.

Bottomore, T. B., & Rubel, M. (1964). *Karl Marx: Selected writings in sociology and social philosophy.* McGraw-Hill.

Boudette, N. E. (2018, November 27). GM to idle plants and cut thousands of jobs as sales slow. *The New York Times.* https://www.nytimes.com/2018/11/26/business/general-motors-cutbacks.html

Bourdieu, P. (1977). Cultural reproduction and social reproduction. In J. Karabel, & A. H. Halsey (Eds.), *Power and ideology in education* (pp. 487–510). Oxford University Press.

Bourdieu, P. (1990). *The logic of practice.* Stanford University Press.

Bourdieu, P., & Wacquant, L. J. D. (1992). *An invitation to reflexive sociology.* Polity Press.

Bowers, M., & Preuhs, R. R. (2009). Collateral consequences of a collateral penalty: The negative effect of felon disenfranchisement laws on the political participation of nonfelons. *Social Science Quarterly*, 90(3), 722–743.

Bowles, S., & Gintis, H. (2002). Schooling in capitalist America revisited. *Sociology of Education*, 75, 1–18.

Brady, D. (2019). Theories of the causes of poverty. *Annual Review of Sociology*, 45, 155–175.

Brady, D., Finnigan, R. M., & Hübgen, S. (2017). Rethinking the risks of poverty: A framework for analyzing prevalences and penalties. *American Journal of Sociology*, 123(3), 740–786. https://doi.org/10.1086/693678

Brady, D., & Parolin, Z. (2020). The levels and trends in deep and extreme poverty in the United States, 1993–2016. *Demography (Springer Nature)*, 57(6), 2337–2360. https://doi.org/10.1007/s13524-020-00924-1

Brady, H. E., Schlozman, K. L., & Verba, S. (2015). Political mobility and political reproduction from generation to generation. *The ANNALS of the American Academy of Political and Social Science*, 657(1), 149–173.

Branigan, A. R., Wildeman, C., Freese, J., & Kiefe, C. I. (2017). Complicating colorism: Race, skin color, and the likelihood of arrest. *Socius: Sociological Research for a Dynamic World*, 3, 237802311772561. https://doi.org/10.1177/2378023117725611

Brannon, I. (2020, September 29). A wealth tax is not a solution for income inequality. *Forbes.* https://www.forbes.com/sites/ikebrannon/2020/09/29/a-wealth-tax-is-not-a-solution-for-income-inequality/

Bratton, T. M., Lytle, R., & Bensel, T. (2020). Attitudes of Muslim Americans toward homosexuality and marriage equality: Moving beyond simply understanding Christian public opinions. *Sociological Inquiry*, 90(4), 765–793. https://doi.org/10.1111/soin.12334

Brayboy, B. M. J., & Lomawaima, K. T. (2018). Why don't more Indians do better in school? The battle between US schooling & American Indian/Alaska native education. *Daedalus*, 147(2), 82–94.

Breines, W. (2007). Struggling to connect: White and Black feminism in the movement years. *Contexts*, 6(1), 18–24.

Brenan, M. (2021, September 2). *Approval of labor unions at highest point since 1965.* Gallup.Com. https://news.gallup.com/poll/354455/approval-labor-unions-highest-point-1965.aspx

Brender-Ilan, Y. (2012). How do income and its components and perception relate to alienation? *Journal of Applied Social Psychology*, 42(2), 440–470.

Brennan Center for Justice. (2021, October). *Voting laws roundup.* https://www.brennancenter.org/our-work/research-reports/voting-laws-roundup-october-2021

Brennan Center for Justice. (2022, January). *The Freedom to Vote Act.* https://www.brennancenter.org/our-work/research-reports/freedom-vote-act

Brockie, T. N., Dana-Sacco, G., Wallen, G. R., Wilcox, H. C., & Campbell, J. C. (2015). The relationship of adverse childhood experiences to PTSD, depression, poly-drug use and suicide attempt in reservation-based native American adolescents and young adults. *American Journal of Community Psychology*, 55(3–4), 411–421.

Brodkin, K. (2008). How Jews became White. In P. S. Rothenberg (Ed.), *White privilege: Essential readings on the other side of racism* (3rd ed., pp. 41–53). Worth Publishing.

Bronson, J. (2017). *Indicators of mental health problems reported by prisoners and jail inmates, 2011–12* (NCJ 250612). Bureau of Justice Statistics.

Brown, D. K. (2001). The social sources of educational credentialism: Status cultures, labor markets, and organizations. *Sociology of Education, 74,* 19–34.

Brown, J. P., Martin, D., Nagaria, Z., Verceles, A. C., Jobe, S. L., & Wickwire, E. M. (2020). Mental health consequences of shift work: An updated review. *Current Psychiatry Reports, 22*(2), 1–7. https://doi.org/10.1007/s11920-020-1131-z

Brown, S. L. (2010). Marriage and child well-being: Research and policy perspectives. *Journal of Marriage and Family, 72*(5), 1059–1077. https://doi.org/10.1111/j.1741-3737.2010.00750.x

Brown, T. H., Richardson, L. J., Hargrove, T. W., & Thomas, C. S. (2016). Using multiple-hierarchy stratification and life course approaches to understand health inequalities: The intersecting consequences of race, gender, SES, and age. *Journal of Health and Social Behavior, 57*(2), 200–222. https://doi.org/10.1177/0022146516645165

Browne, I., & Misra, J. (2003). The intersection of gender and race in the labor market. *Annual Review of Sociology, 29,* 487–513.

Brown-Johnson, C. G., England, L. J., Glantz, S. A., & Ling, P. M. (2014). Tobacco industry marketing to low socio-economic status women in the US. *Tobacco Control, 23*(0), 139–146. https://doi.org/10.1136/tobaccocontrol-2013-051224

Brucker, D. L., Mitra, S., Chaitoo, N., & Mauro, J. (2015). More likely to be poor whatever the measure: Working-age persons with disabilities in the United States. *Social Science Quarterly, 96*(1), 273–296.

Brunsma, D. L., & Rockquemore, K. A. (2002). What does "Black" mean? Exploring the epistemological stranglehold of racial categorization. *Critical Sociology, 28*(1–2), 101–121.

Budig, M. J. (2014). *The fatherhood bonus and the motherhood penalty.* Third Way and Next. http://www.thirdway.org/search?q=budig

Budiman, A. (2020). *Key findings about US immigrants.* Pew Research Center. https://www.pewresearch.org/fact-tank/2020/08/20/key-findings-about-u-s-immigrants/

Burge, C. D., Wamble, J. J., & Cuomo, R. R. (2020). A certain type of descriptive representative? Understanding how the skin tone and gender of candidates influences Black politics. *The Journal of Politics, 82*(4), 1596–1601. https://doi.org/10.1086/708778.

Burgess, E. W. (1923). The growth of the city: An introduction to a research project. *Proceedings of the American Sociological Society, 18,* 85–97.

Burn, I. (2020). The relationship between prejudice and wage penalties for gay men in the United States. *Industrial and Labor Relations Review, 73*(3), 650–675. https://doi.org/10.1177/0019793919864891

Burraston, B., McCutcheon, J. C., & Watts, S. J. (2018). Relative and absolute deprivation's relationship with volent crime in the United States: Testing an interaction effect between income inequality and disadvantage. *Crime & Delinquency, 64*(4), 542–560. https://doi.org/10.1177/0011128717709246

Burton, L. M., Lichter, D. T., Baker, R. S., & Eason, J. M. (2013). Inequality, family processes, and health in the "new" rural America. *American Behavioral Scientist, 57*(8), 1128–1151.

Butler, J. (1999). *Gender trouble.* Routledge.

Butler, J. (2004). *Undoing gender.* Routledge.

Button, J. W., Rienzo, B. A., & Wald, K. D. (1997). *Private lives, public conflicts: Battles over gay rights in American communities.* CQ Press.

Buyuker, B., D'Urso, A. J., Filindra, A., & Kaplan, N. J. (2021). Race politics research and the American presidency: Thinking about white attitudes, identities and vote choice in the Trump era and beyond. *Journal of Race, Ethnicity, and Politics, 6*(3), 600–641. https://doi.org/10.1017/rep.2020.33

Buzzfeed. (2015, September 27). 26 questions Asians have for White people. *BuzzFeed.* http://www.buzzfeed.com/dayshavedewi/26-questions-asians-have-for-white-people

Cabrera, N. L. (2017). White immunity: Working through some of the pedagogical pitfalls of "privilege. *Journal Committed to Social Change on Race and Ethnicity, 3*(1), 78–90.

Cai, Z., & Heathcote, J. (2022). College tuition and income inequality. *American Economic Review, 112*(1), 81–121.

Caliendo, M., & Lee, W. S. (2013). Fat chance! Obesity and the transition from unemployment to employment. *Economics & Human Biology, 11*(2), 121–133.

Callero, P. (2018). *Being unequal: How identity helps make and break power and privilege.* Rowman & Littlefield.

Calnitsky, D. (2018). Structural and individualistic theories of poverty. *Sociology Compass, 12*(12), e12640. https://doi.org/10.1111/soc4.12640

Cammenga, J. (2021). *State and local sales tax rates, 2021.* Tax Foundation. https://taxfoundation.org/2021-sales-taxes/

Campbell, A. F. (2016, December 6). There's a clear way to fix the H-1B visa program. *The Atlantic.* https://www.theatlantic.com/business/

archive/2016/12/fixing-h-1b-visa-loophole/509639/

Campbell, A. F. (2018, November 29). "Inhumane": A laid-off GM worker in Ohio responds to massive job cuts. *Vox*. https://www.vox.com/2018/11/29/18117931/gm-worker-layoffs-reaction

Campbell, A. L. (2007). Parties, electoral participation, and shifting voting blocs. In T. Skocpol, & P. Pierson (Eds.), *The transformation of American politics* (pp. 68–102). Princeton University Press.

Campisi, N. (2021, November 19). Can't afford a home? Here's how Biden's affordable housing proposal could help. *Forbes Advisor*. https://www.forbes.com/advisor/mortgages/cant-afford-a-home-heres-how-bidens-affordable-housing-proposal-could-help/

Capps, R., & Newland, K. (2015). *The integration outcomes of US refugees*. Migration Policy Institute. https://www.google.com/url?sa=t&rct=j&q=&esrc=s&source=web&cd=3&ved=0ahUKEwjgprDboqTcAhWkz4MKHQK2Bj0QFgg-MAI&url=https%3A%2F%2Fwww.migrationpolicy.org%2Fsites%2Fdefault%2Ffiles%2Fpublications%2FUsRefugeeOutcomes-FINALWEB.pdf&usg=AOvVaw1HhN_z9yNCc6_5f5Za9Lzl

Carbone-Lopez, K., Esbensen, F.-A., & Brick, B. T. (2010). Correlates and consequences of peer victimization: Gender differences in direct and indirect forms of bullying. *Youth Violence and Juvenile Justice*, 8(4), 332–350.

Carels, R. A., Young, K. M., Wott, C. B., Harper, J., Gumble, A., Hobbs, M. W., & Clayton, A. M. (2009). Internalized weight stigma and its ideological correlates among weight loss treatment seeking adults. *Eating and Weight Disorders—Studies on Anorexia, Bulimia and Obesity*, 14(2–3), 92–97.

Caren, N., Andrews, K. T., & Lu, T. (2020). Contemporary social movements in a hybrid media environment. *Annual Review of Sociology*, 46(1), 443–465. https://doi.org/10.1146/annurev-soc-121919-054627

Carli, L. L., & Eagly, A. H. (2007). Overcoming resistance to women leaders. In B. Kellerman, D. L. Rhode, & S. D. O'Connor (Eds.), *Women and leadership: The state of play and strategies for change* (pp. 127–148). Wiley.

Carnevale, A. P., Werf, V. D., Quinn, M., Strohl, M. C., & Repnikov, J. (2018). *Our separate and unequal public colleges*. Georgetown University Center on Education and the Workforce.

Carr, D. (2005). Political polls. *Contexts*, 4(1), 31–32.

Carrier, J. G., & Kalb, D. (Eds.). (2015). *Anthropologies of class: Power, practice, and inequality*. Cambridge University Press.

Carrillo, H., & Hoffman, A. (2018). From MSM to heteroflexibilities: Non-exclusive straight male identities and their implications for HIV prevention and health promotion. In A. G. Perez-Brumer, R. Parker, & P. Aggleton (Eds.), *Rethinking MSM, trans and other categories in HIV prevention* (pp. 105–118). Taylor & Francis.

Carson, E. A. (2021). *Prisoners in 2020—Statistical tables* (NCJ 302776; p. 50). US Department of Justice.

Carson, J. L., Crespin, M. H., Finocchiaro, C. J., & Rohde, D. W. (2007). Redistricting and party polarization in the US House of Representatives. *American Politics Research*, 35(6), 878–904.

Carter, P. L. (2005). *Keepin' it real: School success beyond Black and White*. Oxford University Press.

Cassell, D. K., Salinas, R. C., & Winn, P. S. (2005). *The encyclopedia of death and dying*. Facts On File.

Cassidy, C. A. (2016, June 15). Patchy reporting undercuts national hate crimes count. *Associated Press*. http://www.bigstory.ap.org/article/8247a1d2f76b4baea2a121186dedf768/ap-patchy-reporting-undercuts-national-hate-crimes-count

Castells, M. (2015). *Networks of outrage and hope: Social movements in the internet age*. John Wiley & Sons.

Cato Institute. (2021, April 27). *72% of Americans say immigrants come to the United States for jobs and to improve their lives*. https://www.cato.org/blog/poll-72-americans-say-immigrants-come-us-jobs-improve-their-lives-53-say-ability-immigrate

Cauthen, K. (1987). *The passion for equality*. Rowman & Littlefield.

CBO. (2020). *The distribution of household income, 2017*. Congressional Budget Office. https://www.cbo.gov/system/files/2020-10/56575-Household-Income.pdf

CBPP. (2019). *Policy basics: The earned income tax credit*. Center for Budget and Policy Priorities.

CBPP. (2020, April 14). *Policy basics: Introduction to Medicaid*. Center on Budget and Policy Priorities. https://www.cbpp.org/research/health/introduction-to-medicaid

CBPP. (2021a, March 31). *Policy basics: Temporary assistance for needy families*. Center on Budget and Policy Priorities. https://www.cbpp.org/research/family-income-support/temporary-assistance-for-needy-families

CBPP. (2021b, June 7). *Tracking the COVID-19 recession's effects on food, housing, and employment hardships*. Center on Budget and Policy Priorities. https://www.cbpp.org/research/poverty-and-inequality/tracking-the-covid-19-recessions-effects-on-food-housing-and

CBPP. (2021c, October 4). *A quick guide to SNAP eligibility and benefits*. Center on Budget and Policy Priorities. https://www.cbpp.org/research/

food-assistance/a-quick-guide-to-snap-eligibility-and-benefits

CDC. (2018). *Lead*. https://www.cdc.gov/nceh/lead/default.htm

CDC. (2019, October 15). *Water, sanitation, and hygiene-related emergencies and outbreaks*. https://www.cdc.gov/healthywater/emergency/extreme-weather/building-damage.html

CDC. (2020, December 10). *Risk of exposure to COVID-19: Racial and ethnic health disparities*. https://www.cdc.gov/coronavirus/2019-ncov/community/health-equity/racial-ethnic-disparities/increased-risk-exposure.html

CDC. (2021a, May 13).*Underlying medical conditions associated with high risk of severe COVID-19: Information for healthcare providers*. https://www.cdc.gov/coronavirus/2019-ncov/hcp/clinical-care/underlyingconditions.html

CDC. (2021b, June 21). *COVID-19 information for people with disabilities*. https://www.cdc.gov/ncbddd/humandevelopment/covid-19/people-with-disabilities.html

CDC. (2021c, September 8). *Infant mortality*. https://www.cdc.gov/reproductivehealth/maternalinfanthealth/infantmortality.htm

CDC. (2021d, September 9). *Risk for COVID-19 Infection, hospitalization, and death by race/ethnicity*. https://www.cdc.gov/coronavirus/2019-ncov/covid-data/investigations-discovery/hospitalization-death-by-race-ethnicity.html

CDC. (2021e, October 6). *Provisional drug overdose data*. National Center for Health Statistics. https://www.cdc.gov/nchs/nvss/vsrr/drug-overdose-data.htm

CDC. (2021f, October 13). *COVID-19 provisional counts: Weekly updates by sex and age*. https://www.cdc.gov/nchs/nvss/vsrr/covid_weekly/index.htm

CDC. (2021g, November 8). *Key statistics from the National Survey of Family Growth*. National Center for Health Statistics. https://www.cdc.gov/nchs/nsfg/key_statistics/s-keystat.htm

Cech, E. A., & Rothwell, W. R. (2020). LGBT workplace inequality in the federal workforce: Intersectional processes, organizational contexts, and turnover considerations. *Industrial and Labor Relations Review, 73*(1), 25–60. https://doi.org/10.1177/0019793919843508

Center for Global Education. (2020). *Asian Americans then and now*. Asia Society. https://asiasociety.org/education/asian-americans-then-and-now

Center on Poverty and Social Policy, Columbia University. (2021). *Poverty reduction analysis of the American Family Act*. https://www.povertycenter.columbia.edu/news-internal/2019/3/5/the-afa-and-child-poverty

Centers for Medicare and Medicaid Services. (2021). *June 2021 Medicaid & CHIP enrollment data highlights*. https://www.medicaid.gov/medicaid/program-information/medicaid-and-chip-enrollment-data/report-highlights/index.html

Cerankowski, K. J., & Milks, M. (Eds.). (2014). *Asexualities: Feminist and queer perspectives*. Routledge.

Cerny, P. G. (2017). The limits of global governance: Transnational neopluralism in a complex world. In R. Marchetti (Ed.), *Partnerships in international policy-making: Civil society and public institutions in European and global affairs* (pp. 31–47). Palgrave Macmillan UK.

Chae, J. (2019). What makes us accept lookism in the selfie era? A three-way interaction among the present, the constant, and the past. *Computers in Human Behavior, 97*, 75–83. https://doi.org/10.1016/j.chb.2019.03.012

Chamberlain, P. (2017). *The feminist fourth wave*. Springer.

Chang, C. (2014, August 12). *Separate but unequal in college Greek life*. The Century Foundation. https://tcf.org/content/commentary/separate-but-unequal-in-college-greek-life/

Charnock, E. J. (2020). *The rise of political action committees: Interest group electioneering and the transformation of American politics*. Oxford University Press.

Charrad, M. M., & Reith, N. E. (2019). Local solidarities: How the Arab Spring protests started. *Sociological Forum, 34*, 1174–1196. https://doi.org/10.1111/socf.12543

Chavez, N. (2018, April 7). Michigan will end Flint's free bottled water program. *CNN*. https://www.cnn.com/2018/04/07/us/flint-michigan-water-bottle-program-ends/index.html

Chen, J., & Cottrell, D. (2016). Evaluating partisan gains from Congressional gerrymandering: Using computer simulations to estimate the effect of gerrymandering in the US House. *Electoral Studies, 44*, 329–340.

Chen, R. C., Haynes, K., Du, S., Barron, J., & Katz, A. J. (202s1). Association of cancer screening deficit in the United States with the COVID-19 pandemic. *JAMA Oncology, 7*(6), 878–884. https://doi.org/10.1001/jamaoncol.2021.0884

Chen, S. (2013, August 15). Million-dollar mausoleums. *Wall Street Journal*. http://www.wsj.com/articles/SB10001424127887323477604578654084003664860

Cherlin, A. J. (2016, August 25). The downwardly mobile for Trump. *The New York Times*. https://www.nytimes.com/2016/08/25/opinion/campaign-stops/the-downwardly-mobile-for-trump.html

Chesney-Lind, M., & Pasko, L. (2013). *The female offender: Girls, women, and crime* (3rd ed.). Sage Publications.

Chetty, R., Friedman, J., Saez, E., Turner, N., & Yagan, D. (2020). *The determinants of income segregation and intergenerational mobility: Using test scores to measure undermatching* (Working Paper No. 26748). National Bureau of Economic Research. https://doi.org/10.3386/w26748

Chetty, R., Friedman, J. N., Hilger, N., Saez, E., Schanzenbach, D. W., & Yagan, D. (2011). How does your kindergarten classroom affect your earnings? Evidence from Project Star. *The Quarterly Journal of Economics, 126*(4), 1593–1660.

Chetty, R., Grusky, D., Hell, M., Hendren, N., Manduca, R., & Narang, J. (2017). The fading American dream: Trends in absolute income mobility since 1940. *Science, 356*(6336), 398–406.

Chetty, R., Hendren, N., Jones, M., & Porter, S. R. (2018). *Race and economic opportunity in the United States.* The Equality of Opportunity Project.

Chetty, R., Hendren, N., & Katz, L. F. (2016). The effects of exposure to better neighborhoods on children: New evidence from the moving to opportunity experiment. *American Economic Review, 106*(4), 855–902.

Chetty, R., Hendren, N., Kline, P., & Saez, E. (2014). Where is the land of opportunity? The geography of intergenerational mobility in the United States. *The Quarterly Journal of Economics, 129*(4), 1553–1623. https://doi.org/10.1093/qje/qju022

Chetty, R., Hendren, N., Kline, P., Saez, E., & Turner, N. (2014). *Is the United States still a land of opportunity? Recent trends in intergenerational mobility* (Working Paper No. 19844). National Bureau of Economic Research. http://www.nber.org/papers/w19843

Cho, S., Crenshaw, K. W., & McCall, L. (2013). Toward a field of intersectionality studies: Theory, applications, and praxis. *Signs, 38*(4), 785–810.

Choden, T., Gu, Y., Guynh, S., Hoenig, J., & Norman, C. (2018). *Serious psychological distress among adults in New York City, 2002–2015* (No. 102; EPI Data Brief). New York City Health.

Choe, J. (2008). Income inequality and crime in the United States. *Economics Letters, 101*(1), 31–33. https://doi.org/10.1016/j.econlet.2008.03.025

Choi, S. K., Harper, G. W., Lightfoot, M., Russell, S., & Meyer, I. H. (2020). *Homelessness among LGBT adults in the US.* Williams Institute. https://williamsinstitute.law.ucla.edu/publications/lgbt-homelessness-us/

Choi, W. K. (2006). Proletarianization, the informal proletariat, and "Marx" in the era of globalization. *Annual Meeting of American Sociological Association*, Montreal, August.

Chu, J. S. G., & Davis, G. F. (2015). *Who killed the inner circle? The decline of the American corporate interlock network* (SSRN Scholarly Paper No. 2061113). Social Science Research Network. http://papers.ssrn.com/abstract=2061113

Cigler, A. J., Loomis, B., & Nownes, A. (Eds.). (2015). *Interest group politics* (9th ed.). Congressional Quarterly.

Ciprikis, K., Cassells, D., & Berrill, J. (2020). Transgender labour market outcomes: Evidence from the United States. *Gender, Work & Organization, 27*(6), 1378–1401. https://doi.org/10.1111/gwao.12501

Clawson, D., & Clawson, M. A. (1999). What has happened to the US labor movement? Union decline and renewal. *Annual Review of Sociology, 25*, 95–119.

Clayton, D. M. (2018). Black Lives Matter and the civil rights movement: A comparative analysis of two social movements in the United States. *Journal of Black Studies, 49*(5), 448–480. https://doi.org/10.1177/0021934718764099

Clayton, S., Manning, C. M., Speiser, M., & Hill, A. N. (2021). *Mental health and our changing climate: Impacts, inequities, responses.* The American Psychological Association and ecoAmerica. https://ecoamerica.org/mental-health-and-our-changing-climate-2021-edition/

Clear, T. R. (2009). *Imprisoning communities: How mass incarceration makes disadvantaged neighborhoods worse.* Oxford University Press.

Clear, T. R., Rose, D. R., Waring, E., & Scully, K. (2003). Coercive mobility and crime: A preliminary examination of concentrated incarceration and social disorganization. *Justice Quarterly, 20*(1), 33–64.

Clement, S., Schauman, O., Graham, T., Maggioni, F., Evans-Lacko, S., Bezborodovs, N., Morgan, C., Rüsch, N., Brown, J. S. L., & Thornicroft, G. (2015). What is the impact of mental health-related stigma on help-seeking? A systematic review of quantitative and qualitative studies. *Psychological Medicine, 45*(01), 11–27.

Coates, T.-N. (2014, May 22). The case for reparations. *The Atlantic.* https://www.theatlantic.com/magazine/archive/2014/06/the-case-for-reparations/361631/

Cobb, J. (2016, April 17). Learning to talk About class. *The New Yorker.* https://www.newyorker.com/magazine/2016/04/25/learning-to-talk-about-class

Cobble, D. S., Gordon, L., & Henry, A. (2014). *Feminism unfinished: A short, surprising history of American women's movements.* W. W. Norton & Company.

Coccia, A. F. (2021). *Tackling the benefits cliff: Smoothing benefits phase-outs to drive economic security for Ohio's children.* Children's Defense Fund Ohio. https://cdfohio.org/cdf_oh_blog/8231-2/

Coffey, L. T. (2021, September 15). School during the pandemic: The children who disappeared. *Today*. https://www.today.com/specials/schoolduringpandemic/

Cohen, D., Shin, F., Liu, X., Ondish, P., & Kraus, M. W. (2017). Defining social class across time and between groups. *Personality and Social Psychology Bulletin, 43*(11), 1530–1545.

Cohn, D. (2017). *Census may change questions on race, Hispanic origin for 2020*. Pew Research Center. https://www.pewresearch.org/fact-tank/2017/04/20/seeking-better-data-on-hispanics-census-bureau-may-change-how-it-asks-about-race/

Colker, R. (2004). Homophobia, AIDS Hysteria, and the Americans with Disabilities Act. *Journal of Gender, Race and Justice, 8*, 33–53.

Collins, P. H. (1998). It's all in the family: Intersections of gender, race, and nation. *Hypatia, 13*(3), 62–82.

Collins, P. H. (2002). *Black feminist thought: Knowledge, consciousness, and the politics of empowerment*. Routledge.

Collins, P. H. (2015). Science, critical race theory and colour-blindness. *The British Journal of Sociology, 66*(1), 46–52.

Collins, P. H., & Bilge, S. (2016). *Intersectionality*. Polity Press.

Collins, R. (1988). *Theoretical sociology*. Harcourt College Pub.

Collins, S. R., Aboulafia, G. N., & Gunja, M. (2021). *As pandemic eases, what's state of coverage affordability in US?* The Commonwealth Fund. https://www.commonwealthfund.org/publications/issue-briefs/2021/jul/as-pandemic-eases-what-is-state-coverage-affordability-survey

Collins, S. R., Gunja, M. Z., & Aboulafia, G. N. (2021). *US health insurance coverage in 2020: A looming crisis in affordability*. The Commonwealth Fund. https://www.commonwealthfund.org/publications/issue-briefs/2020/aug/looming-crisis-health-coverage-2020-biennial

Combahee River Collective. (2014). A Black feminist statement. *Women's Studies Quarterly, 42*(3/4), 271–280.

Comino, S., Mastrobuoni, G., & Nicolò, A. (2020). Silence of the innocents: Undocumented immigrants' underreporting of crime and their victimization. *Journal of Policy Analysis and Management, 39*(4), 1214–1245. https://doi.org/10.1002/pam.22221

Congressional Research Service. (2021). *Membership of the 117th Congress: A Profile*. https://crsreports.congress.gov/product/pdf/R/R46705

Connaughton, A. (2021). *In both parties, fewer now say being Christian or being born in US is important to being "truly American."* Pew Research Center. https://www.pewresearch.org/fact-tank/2021/05/25/in-both-parties-fewer-now-say-being-christian-or-being-born-in-u-s-is-important-to-being-truly-american/

Connell, C. (2010). Doing, undoing, or redoing gender? Learning from the workplace experiences of transpeople. *Gender & Society, 24*(1), 31–55.

Connell, R. W. (1987). *Gender and power: Society, the person and sexual politics*. Cambridge University Press.

Connell, R. W. (1997). Why is classical theory classical? *American Journal of Sociology, 102*(6), 1511–1557.

Connell, R. W. (2015). Masculinities and globalization. In M. B. Zinn, P. Hondagneu-Sotelo, and M. A. Messner (Eds.), *Gender through the prism of difference* (5th ed., pp. 41–52). Oxford University Press.

Connell, R. W., & Messerschmidt, J. W. (2005). Hegemonic masculinity: Rethinking the concept. *Gender & Society, 19*(6), 829–859. https://doi.org/10.1177/0891243205278639

Connolly, W. E. (1969). *The challenge to pluralist theory*. Lieber-Atherton.

Constant, A. F. (2014). Do migrants take the jobs of native workers? *IZA World of Labor*. https://doi.org/10.15185/izawol.10

Cook, J. A., & Jonikas, J. A. (2002). Self-determination among mental health consumers/survivors: Using lessons from the past to guide the future. *Journal of Disability Policy Studies, 13*(2), 88–96.

Cookson, P. W., & Persell, C. H. (2010). Preparing for power: Twenty-five years later. In A. Howard, & R. Gaztambide-Fernandez (Eds.), *Educating elites: Class privilege and educational advantage* (pp. 13–30). Rowman & Littlefield.

Cooperman, A., & Lipka, M. (2014). *US doesn't rank high in religious diversity*. Pew Research Center. http://www.pewresearch.org/fact-tank/2014/04/04/u-s-doesnt-rank-high-in-religious-diversity/

Corak, M. (2013). Income inequality, equality of opportunity, and intergenerational mobility. *Journal of Economic Perspectives, 27*(3), 79–102.

Cornell Law School. (2016). *White-collar crime*. Legal Information Institute at Cornell Law School. https://www.law.cornell.edu/wex/white-collar_crime

Cose, E. (1993). *Rage of a privileged class: Why are middle-class Blacks angry? Why should America care?* HarperCollins.

Coser, L. A. (1971). *Masters of sociological thought: Ideas in historical and social context*. Harcourt Brace Jovanovich.

Cossins, A. (2000). *Masculinities, sexualities, and child sexual abuse*. Kluwer Law International.

Cott, N. F. (1986). Feminist theory and feminist movements: The past before us. In J. Mitchell, & A. Oakley (Eds.), *What is feminism?* (pp. 49–62). Pantheon.

Cott, N. F. (1987). *The grounding of modern feminism*. Yale University Press.

Courtney-Long, E. A., Carroll, D. D., Zhang, Q. C., Stevens, A. C., Griffin, S., Armour, B. S., & Campbell, V. A. (2015). Prevalence of disability and disability type among adults—United States, 2013. *Morbidity and Mortality Weekly Report*, 64(29), 777–783.

Cox, C. (2021). *Campaign finance in the age of super PACs* (SSRN Scholarly Paper No. 3794817). Social Science Research Network. https://doi.org/10.2139/ssrn.3794817

Cox, D., Lienesch, R., & Jones, R. P. (2017). *Who sees discrimination? Attitudes about sexual orientation, gender identity, race, and immigration status: Findings from PRRI's American Values Atlas*. Public Religion Research Institute. https://www.prri.org/research/americans-views-discrimination-immigrants-blacks-lgbt-sex-marriage-immigration-reform/

Cox, O. C. (1948). *Caste, class and race: A study in social dynamics*. Monthly Review Press.

Cox, O. C. (1959). *The foundations of capitalism*. New York: Philosophical Library.

Cox, O. C. (1964). *Capitalism as a system*. Monthly Review Press.

Cox, O. C. (1976). *Race relations: Elements and social dynamics*. Wayne State University Press.

Cox, W. T. L., Devine, P. G., Bischmann, A. A., & Hyde, J. S. (2016). Inferences about sexual orientation: The roles of stereotypes, faces, and the gaydar myth. *The Journal of Sex Research*, 53(2), 157–171. https://doi.org/10.1080/00224499.2015.1015714

Crabbe, R., Pivnick, L. K., Bates, J., Gordon, R. A., & Crosnoe, R. (2019). Contemporary college students' reflections on their high school peer crowds. *Journal of Adolescent Research*, 34(5), 563–596. https://doi.org/10.1177/0743558418809537

Crane, R. (2018, July 9). Stockton, California to give $500 in basic income to some residents. CNN. https://money.cnn.com/2018/07/09/technology/stockton-california-basic-income-experiment/index.html

Crenshaw, K. (1989). Demarginalizing the intersection of race and sex: A Black feminist critique of antidiscrimination doctrine, feminist theory and antiracist politics. *University of Chicago Legal Forum*, 139–167.

Crimp, D. (2011, December 6). Before Occupy: How AIDS activists seized control of the FDA in 1988. *The Atlantic*. https://www.theatlantic.com/health/archive/2011/12/before-occupy-how-aids-activists-seized-control-of-the-fda-in-1988/249302/

Crockett, J. (2020). "Damn, I'm dating a lot of White guys:" Gay men's individual narratives of racial sexual orientation development. In J. G. Smith, &

C. W. Han (Eds.), *Home and community for queer men of color: The intersection of race and sexuality* (pp. 1–27). Lexington Books.

Crowder, K., South, S. J., & Chavez, E. (2006). Wealth, race, and inter-neighborhood migration. *American Sociological Review*, 71(1), 72–94.

CRRJ. (2016). *Bringing families out of "cap"tivity: The path toward abolishing welfare family caps*. Center on Reproductive Rights and Justice, School of Law, University of California.

Cserni, R. T. (2020). Limitations of existing cultural globalization perspectives: A case study of the influence of technology on sexualities. *Sociology Compass*, 14(3), e12763. https://doi.org/10.1111/soc4.12763

Cubanski, J., & Neuman, T. (2018). *The facts on Medicare spending and financing*. Kaiser Family Foundation. https://www.kff.org/medicare/issue-brief/the-facts-on-medicare-spending-and-financing/

Cygan-Rehm, K., Kuehnle, D., & Oberfichtner, M. (2017). Bounding the causal effect of unemployment on mental health: Nonparametric evidence from four countries. *Health Economics*, 26(12), 1844–1861. https://doi.org/10.1002/hec.3510

Czeisler, M. É., Marynak, K., Clarke, K. E. N., Salah, Z., Shakya, I., Thierry, J. M., Ali, N., McMillan, H., Wiley, J. F., Weaver, M. D., Czeisler, C. A., Rajaratnam, S. M. W., & Howard, M. E. (2020). Delay or avoidance of medical care because of COVID-19–related concerns—United States, June 2020. *Morbidity and Mortality Weekly Report*, 69(36), 1250–1257. https://doi.org/10.15585/mmwr.mm6936a4

Dahl, A. (2018). *Empire of the people: Settler colonialism and the foundations of modern democratic thought*. University Press of Kansas.

Dahl, R. A. (1961). *Who governs?: Democracy and power in an American city*. Yale University Press.

Dahrendorf, R. (1958). Out of utopia: Toward a reorientation of sociological analysis. *American Journal of Sociology*, 64, 115–127.

Dahrendorf, R. (1970). On the origin of inequality among men. In E. O. Laumann, P. M. Siegel, & R. W. Hodge (Eds.), *The logic of social hierarchies* (pp. 3–30). Markham.

Dancygier, R., & Walter, S. (2015). Globalization, labor market risks, and class cleavages. In P. Beramendi, S. Hausermann, H. Kitschelt, & H. Kriesi (Eds.), *The politics of advanced capitalism* (pp. 133–156). Cambridge University Press.

Darrah-Okike, J., Rita, N., & Logan, J. R. (2021). The suppressive impacts of voter identification requirements. *Sociological Perspectives*, 64(4), 536–562. https://doi.org/10.1177/0731121420966620

Datta Gupta, N., Etcoff, N. L., & Jaeger, M. M. (2016). Beauty in mind: The effects of physical attractiveness on psychological well-being and distress. *Journal of Happiness Studies*, 17(3), 1313–1325.

Davidai, S., & Gilovich, T. (2015). Building a more mobile America—One income quintile at a time. *Perspectives on Psychological Science*, 10(1), 60–71.

Davidson, J. D., & Pyle, R. E. (2011). *Ranking faiths: Religious stratification in America*. Rowman & Littlefield Publishers.

Davis, K., & Moore, W. E. (1945). Some principles of stratification. *American Sociological Review*, 10, 242–249.

de Brey, C., Musu, L., McFarland, J., Wilkinson-Flicker, S., Diliberti, M., Zhang, A., Branstetter, C., & Wang, X. (2019). *Status and trends in the education of racial and ethnic groups 2018* (NCES 2019-038). National Center for Education Statistics.

De Camargo, C. R., & Whiley, L. A. (2020). The mythologisation of key workers: Occupational prestige gained, sustained … and lost? *International Journal of Sociology and Social Policy*, 40(9/10), 849–859. https://doi.org/10.1108/IJSSP-07-2020-0310

de Tocqueville, A. (1966). *Democracy in America* (M. Lerner and J. P. Mayer, Eds.; G. Lawrence, Trans.). Harper & Row.

Decena, C. U. (2008). Tacit subjects. *GLQ: A Journal of Lesbian and Gay Studies*, 14(2–3), 339–359.

Decker, M. R., Holliday, C. N., Hameeduddin, Z., Shah, R., Miller, J., Dantzler, J., & Goodmark, L. (2019). "You do not think of me as a human being": Race and gender inequities intersect to discourage police reporting of violence against women. *Journal of Urban Health*, 96(5), 772–783. https://doi.org/10.1007/s11524-019-00359-z

DeLeire, T. (2000). The Wage and Employment Effects of the Americans with Disabilities Act. *The Journal of Human Resources*, 35(4), 693–715.

DeParle, J. (2021, July 28). Pandemic aid programs spur a record drop in poverty. *The New York Times*. https://www.nytimes.com/2021/07/28/us/politics/covid-poverty-aid-programs.html

Derenoncourt, E., & Montialoux, C. (2020). Minimum wages and racial inequality. *The Quarterly Journal of Economics*, 136(1), 169–228. https://doi.org/10.1093/qje/qjaa031

Desmond, M. (2016). *Evicted: Poverty and profit in the American city*. Crown.

Desmond, M., Papachristos, A. V., & Kirk, D. S. (2016). Police violence and citizen crime reporting in the Black community. *American Sociological Review*, 81(5), 857–876.

Desmond, M., & Western, B. (2018). Poverty in America: New directions and debates. *Annual Review of Sociology*, 44(1), 305–318. https://doi.org/10.1146/annurev-soc-060116-053411

Deutsch, F. M. (2007). Undoing gender. *Gender & Society*, 21(1), 106–127. https://doi.org/10.1177/0891243206293577

Diamond, D. (2009). The fourth wave of feminism: Psychoanalytic perspectives. *Studies in Gender and Sexuality*, 10(4), 213–223.

Diaz, J. (2021, October 27). The NCAA's focus on profits means far more gets spent on men's championships. *NPR*. https://www.npr.org/2021/10/27/1049530975/ncaa-spends-more-on-mens-sports-report-reveals

Dickerson, C. (2018, August 16). Who tracks migrant children who enter the US alone? Don't ask us, 4 agencies say. *New York Times*. https://www.nytimes.com/2018/08/16/us/trump-immigration-unaccompanied-minors.html

Diefendorf, S., & Bridges, T. (2020). On the enduring relationship between masculinity and homophobia. *Sexualities*, 23(7), 1264–1284. https://doi.org/10.1177/1363460719876843

Diermeier, M., Goecke, H., Niehues, J., & Thomas, T. (2017). *Impact of inequality-related media coverage on the concerns of the citizens* (Working Paper No. 258; DICE Discussion Paper). Düsseldorf Institute for Competition Economics.

Dietert, M., & Dentice, D. (2009). Gender identity issues and workplace discrimination: The transgender experience. *Journal of Workplace Rights*, 14(1), 121–140.

Diez Roux, A. V., & Mair, C. (2010). Neighborhoods and health. *Annals of the New York Academy of Sciences*, 1186(1), 125–145.

Dinella, L. M., & Weisgram, E. S. (2018). Gender-typing of children's toys: Causes, consequences, and correlates. *Sex Roles*, 79(5–6), 253–259. https://doi.org/10.1007/s11199-018-0943-3

Dionne, E. J. (2004, June 13). E pluribus unum? *Akron Beacon Journal* (B2).

DiPrete, T. A. (2007). Is this a great country? Upward mobility and the chance for riches in contemporary America. *Research in Social Stratification and Mobility*, 25(1), 89–95.

Dobbie, W., Goldin, J., & Yang, C. (2018). The effects of pre-trial detention on conviction, future crime, and employment: Evidence from randomly assigned judges. *American Economic Review*, 108(2), 201–240.

Dobis, E. A., Stephens, H. M., Skidmore, M., & Goetz, S. J. (2020). Explaining the spatial variation in American life expectancy. *Social Science & Medicine*, 246, 112759. https://doi.org/10.1016/j.socscimed.2019.112759

Docquier, F., & Rapoport, H. (2012). Globalization, brain drain, and development. *Journal of Economic Literature*, 50(3), 681–730.

Doerner, J. K. (2015). The joint effects of gender and race/ethnicity on sentencing outcomes in federal courts. *Women & Criminal Justice*, 25(5), 313–338.

Doherty, C., Kiley, J., & Johnson, B. (2017). *The partisan divide on political values grows even wider*. Pew Research Center.

Dolan, K. (2005). How the public views women candidates. In S. Thomas, & C. Wilcox (Eds.), *Women and elective office: Past, present, and future* (pp. 41–59). Oxford University Press.

Doleac, J. L. (2017). *New evidence that lead exposure increases crime*. Brookings Institution. https://www.brookings.edu/blog/up-front/2017/06/01/new-evidence-that-lead-exposure-increases-crime/

Dollar, C. B. (2014). Racial threat theory: Assessing the evidence, requesting redesign. *Journal of Criminology*, *2014*, 1–7. https://doi.org/10.1155/2014/983026

Domhoff, G. W. (1971). *The higher circles*. Vintage.

Domhoff, G. W. (1998). *Who rules America?: Power and politics in the year 2000*. Mayfield.

Domhoff, G. W. (2006). Mills' The Power Elite 50 years later. *Contemporary Sociology*, *35*, 547–550.

Domhoff, G. W. (2009). The power elite and their challengers: The role of nonprofits in American social conflict. *American Behavioral Scientist*, *52*(7), 955–973.

Dotson, R., & Frydman, L. (2017). *Neither security nor justice: Sexual and gender-based violence and gang violence in El Salvador, Honduras, and Guatemala*. Kids in Need of Defense. https://supportkind.org/wp-content/uploads/2017/05/Neither-Security-nor-Justice_SGBV-Gang-Report-FINAL.pdf

Douglas-Gabriel, D. (2015, March 18). House Republicans want to cut back grants for poor college students. *Washington Post*. https://www.washingtonpost.com/news/wonk/wp/2015/03/18/house-republicans-want-to-cut-back-grants-for-poor-college-students/?utm_term=.7ad101bb384b

Dovidio, J. F., Hewstone, M., Glick, P., & Esses, V. M. (2010). Prejudice, stereotyping and discrimination: Theoretical and empirical overview. In F. Dovidio, M. Hewstone, & P. Glick (Eds.), *The Sage handbook of prejudice, stereotyping and discrimination* (pp. 3–28). Sage.

Drum, K. (2015, February 12). Lead and crime: The Brennan Center weighs in. *Mother Jones*. http://www.motherjones.com/kevin-drum/2015/02/lead-and-crime-brennan-center-weighs

Du Bois, W. E. B. (1898). The study of the Negro problems. *The Annals of the American Academy of Political and Social Science*, *11*(1), 1–23.

Du Bois, W. E. B. (1899). *The Philadelphia Negro: A social study*. University of Pennsylvania.

Du Bois, W. E. B. (1903). The laboratory in sociology at Atlanta University. *The Annals of the American Academy of Political and Social Science*, *21*(3), 160–163.

Du Bois, W. E. B. (1906). The Negro question in the United States. *CR: The New Centennial Review*, *6*(3), 241–290.

Du Bois, W. E. B. (1920). *Darkwater: Voices from within the veil*. Dover Publications.

Du Bois, W. E. B. (1944). My evolving program for Negro freedom. *Clinical Sociology Review*, *8*(1), 27–57.

Du Bois, W. E. B. (2007). *The souls of Black folk*. Oxford University Press.

Dublin, T. (1993). Women, work, and the family: Female operatives in the Lowell Mills, 1830–1860. In N. F. Cott (Ed.), *Industrial wage work* (Vol. 7/1, pp. 33–42). K. G. Saur. https://doi.org/10.1515/9783110969450.33

Duncan, M. L., & Kemmelmeier, M. (2012). Attitudes toward same-sex marriage: An essentialist approach. *Analyses of Social Issues and Public Policy*, *12*(1), 377–399.

Duneier, M. (2017). *Ghetto: The invention of a place, the history of an idea*. Farrar, Straus and Giroux.

Dunlap, E., Johnson, B. D., Kotarba, J. A., & Fackler, J. L. (2010). Macro-level social forces and micro-level consequences: Poverty, alternate occupations, and drug dealing. *Journal of Ethnicity in Substance Abuse*, *9*(2), 115–127. https://doi.org/10.1080/15332641003772611

Dunn, A. (2018). Is the US economic system fair? Republicans, Democrats divided. *Pew Research Center*. http://www.pewresearch.org/fact-tank/2018/10/04/partisans-are-divided-over-the-fairness-of-the-u-s-economy-and-why-people-are-rich-or-poor/

Durante, F., Fiske, S. T., Kervyn, N., Cuddy, A. J. C., Akande, A., Debo, Adetoun, B. E., Adewuyi, M. F., Tserere, M. M., Ramiah, A. A., Mastor, K. A., Barlow, F. K., Bonn, G., Tafarodi, R. W., Bosak, J., Cairns, E., Doherty, C., Capozza, D., Chandran, A., Chryssochoou, X., & Storari, C. C. (2013). Nations' income inequality predicts ambivalence in stereotype content: How societies mind the gap. *British Journal of Social Psychology*, *52*(4), 726–746. https://doi.org/10.1111/bjso.12005

Durkheim, E. (1933). *The division of labour in society*. Free Press.

Duster, T. (2015). The molecular reinscription of race in science, law and medicine: A post-genomic surprise. *The British Journal of Sociology*, *66*(1), 1–27.

Duxbury, S. W. (2021). Who controls criminal law? Racial threat and the adoption of state sentencing law, 1975 to 2012. *American Sociological Review*, *86*(1), 123–153. https://doi.org/10.1177/0003122420967647

Dye, T. R. (2002). *Who's running America? The Bush restoration*. Prentice Hall.

Dye, T. R. (2015). *Who's running America? The Obama reign*. Routledge.

Easley, J. (2018). Spatial mismatch beyond Black and White: Levels and determinants of job access among Asian and Hispanic subpopulations. *Urban Studies*, 55(8), 1800–1820. https://doi.org/10.1177/0042098017696254

Eberhardt, J. L., Goff, P. A., Purdie, V. J., & Davies, P. G. (2004). Seeing Black: Race, crime, and visual processing. *Journal of Personality and Social Psychology*, 87(6), 876–893.

Economic Policy Institute. (2021). *The productivity–pay gap*. https://www.epi.org/productivity-pay-gap/

Edin, K., & Kefalas, M. (2011). *Promises I can keep: Why poor women put motherhood before marriage* (Revised). University of California Press.

Edin, K., & Shaefer, H. L. (2015). *$2.00 a day: Living on almost nothing in America*. Houghton Mifflin Harcourt Publishing.

Editorial Board, *Wall Street Journal*. (2021, March 22). Universal basic income hype. *Wall Street Journal*. https://www.wsj.com/articles/universal-basic-income-hype-11616453781

Edwards, J. (2021, October 11). New California law will force retailers to have "gender neutral" toy sections. *Washington Post*. https://www.washingtonpost.com/nation/2021/10/11/california-law-gender-neutral-children-toy-section/

EEOC. (2002). *Enforcement guidance: Reasonable accommodation and undue hardship under the Americans with Disabilities Act*. United States Equal Opportunity Commission. https://www.eeoc.gov/policy/docs/accommodation.html

EEOC. (2009). *Fact sheet on the EEOC's final regulations implementing the ADAAA*. United States Equal Opportunity Commission. https://www.eeoc.gov/laws/regulations/adaaa_fact_sheet.cfm

Eggleston, J., Hays, D., Munk, R., & Sullivan, B. (2020). *The wealth of households: 2017*. Current Population Reports. https://www.census.gov/content/dam/Census/library/publications/2020/demo/p70br-170.pdf

Eisinger, J., Ernsthausen, J., & Kiel, P. (2021, June 8). *The secret IRS files: Trove of never-before-seen records reveal how the wealthiest avoid income tax*. ProPublica. https://www.propublica.org/article/the-secret-irs-files-trove-of-never-before-seen-records-reveal-how-the-wealthiest-avoid-income-tax

Ekins, E. (2019). *Findings from the Cato Institute 2019 Welfare, work, and wealth national survey*. Cato Institute. https://www.cato.org/publications/survey-reports/what-americans-think-about-poverty-wealth-work#

Elder, G. H. Jr, & Liker, J. K. (1982). Hard times in women's lives: Historical influences across forty years. *American Journal of Sociology*, 88(2), 241–269.

Elgin, C., Goksel, T., Gurdal, M. Y., & Orman, C. (2013). Religion, income inequality, and the size of the government. *Economic Modelling*, 30(Supplement C), 225–234. https://doi.org/10.1016/j.econmod.2012.08.017

Elliott, J. R., & Smith, R. A. (2004). Race, gender, and workplace power. *American Sociological Review*, 69(3), 365–386.

Emerson, M. (2020, January 8). New 2020 statistics on multiracial churches. *Multiethnic.Church*. https://multiethnic.church/released-new-2020-statistics-on-multiracial-churches/

Engels, M., Wahrendorf, M., Dragano, N., McMunn, A., & Deindl, C. (2021). Multiple social roles in early adulthood and later mental health in different labour market contexts. *Advances in Life Course Research*, 100432. https://doi.org/10.1016/j.alcr.2021.100432

England, P. (2010). The gender revolution: Uneven and stalled. *Gender & Society*, 24(2), 149–166.

EPA. (2018, November 12). *How smoke from fires can affect your health*. United States Environmental Protection Agency. https://www.epa.gov/pm-pollution/how-smoke-fires-can-affect-your-health

Epstein, C. F. (1988). *Deceptive distinctions: Sex, gender, and the social order*. Yale University Press.

Equal Justice Initiative. (n.d.). *White mobs attack Filipino farmworkers in Watsonville, California*. Retrieved August 17, 2021, from https://calendar.eji.org/racial-injustice/jan/19

Erickson, B., & Cote, R. R. (2009). Social capitals and inequality: The reproduction of gender and occupational prestige differences through individual social networks. *American Sociological Association Annual Meetings, Social Capital Regular Session*. July 11.

Erikson, K. T. (1976). *Everything in its path*. Simon and Schuster.

Eskridge, W., & Frickey, P. (1995). *Cases and materials on legislation: Statutes and the creation of public policy*. West Publishing Company.

Espiritu, Y. L. (1994). *Asian American panethnicity*. Temple University Press.

ESRI. (2020). *USA 113th Congressional Districts* [Map]. https://wooster.maps.arcgis.com/apps/mapviewer/index.html?webmap=9e9bb293b2b9467e9a9790b8d9b5c840

ESRI. (2021a). *Affluent neighborhoods, 2021* [Map]. https://wooster.maps.arcgis.com/home/webmap/viewer.html?webmap=d8691411ee104551b35da0661ee1e100

ESRI. (2021b). *Diversity, 2021* [Map]. https://wooster.maps.arcgis.com/home/webmap/viewer.html?webmap=03294a7d409448b58b5cb83e3060186c

Evans, C. R., & Erickson, N. (2019). Intersectionality and depression in adolescence and early adulthood: A MAIHDA analysis of the national longitudinal study of adolescent to adult health, 1995–2008. *Social Science & Medicine, 220*, 1–11. https://doi.org/10.1016/j.socscimed.2018 .10.019

Evans, E., & Chamberlain, P. (2015). Critical waves: Exploring feminist identity, discourse and praxis in western feminism. *Social Movement Studies, 14*(4), 396–409.

Evans, E., & Oceguaera, R. (2021, February 23). *Illinois criminal justice reform ends cash bail, changes felony murder rule.* Injustice Watch. https://www. injusticewatch.org/news/2021/illinois-criminal- justice-reform-cash-bail-felony-murder/

Evans, M., Kelley, J., & Peoples, C. D. (2010). Justifications of inequality: The normative basis of pay differentials in 31 nations. *Social Science Quarterly, 91*(5), 1405–1431.

Evers-Hillstrom, K. (2021, February 11). *Most expensive ever: 2020 election cost $14.4 billion.* OpenSecrets News. https://www.opensecrets. org/news/2021/02/2020-cycle-cost-14p4-billion- doubling-16/

Ewing, W. A., Martinez, D., & Rumbaut, R. (2015). *The criminalization of immigration in the United States.* The American Immigration Council.

Fain, P. (2019, May 23). *Feds release broader data on socioeconomic status and college enrollment and completion.* Inside Higher Ed. https://www. insidehighered.com/news/2019/05/23/feds- release-broader-data-socioeconomic-status-and- college-enrollment-and-completion

Fairdosi, A. S., & Rogowski, J. C. (2015). Candidate race, partisanship, and political participation: When do Black candidates increase Black turnout? *Political Research Quarterly, 68*(2), 337–349.

Fallahi, F., Pourtaghi, H., & Rodríguez, G. (2012). The unemployment rate, unemployment volatility, and crime. *International Journal of Social Economics, 39*(6), 440–448.

Fanger, S. M., Frankel, L. A., & Hazen, N. (2012). Peer exclusion in preschool children's play: Naturalistic observations in a playground setting. *Merrill-Palmer Quarterly, 58*(2), 224–254.

Farber, H., & Western, B. (2016). Can increased organizing reverse the decline of unions in the United States: Lessons from the last quarter- century. In P. V. Wunnava (Ed.), *The changing role of unions: New forms of representation.* Routledge.

Farley, J. E. (1988). *Majority-minority relations.* Prentice Hall.

Farley, J. E., & Squires, G. D. (2005). Fences and neighbors: Segregation in 21st-century. *America. Contexts, 4*(1), 33–39.

Farrell, C. R. (2008). Bifurcation, fragmentation, or integration? The racial and geographical structure of US metropolitan segregation, 1990–2000. *Urban Studies, 45*(3), 467–499.

Fausto-Sterling, A. (2000). *Sexing the body: Gender politics and the construction of sexuality.* Basic Books.

Fausto-Sterling, A. (2019). Gender/sex, sexual orientation, and identity are in the body: How did they get there? *The Journal of Sex Research, 56*(4–5), 529–555.

FBI. (2021a). *Documents and downloads: Arrestees.* Crime Data Explorer. https://crime-data-explorer. app.cloud.gov/pages/downloads

FBI. (2021b). *Hate crime.* Federal Bureau of Investigation: Crime Data Explorer. https://crime- data-explorer.fr.cloud.gov/pages/explorer/crime/ hate-crime

FBI. (2021c, August 30). *Hate crime statistics.* US Department of Justice. https://www.justice.gov/ hatecrimes/hate-crime-statistics

Feagin, J. R. (2006). *Systemic racism: A theory of oppression.* Routledge.

Feagin, J. R., & Elias, S. (2013). Rethinking racial formation theory: A systemic racism critique. *Ethnic and Racial Studies, 36*(6), 931–960.

Featherman, D. L., & Hauser, R. M. (1978). *Opportunity and change.* Academic Press.

Federal Election Commission. (2020, September 18). *Statistical summary of 18-month campaign activity of the 2019–2020 election cycle.* FEC.Gov. https:// www.fec.gov/updates/statistical-summary-18- month-campaign-activity-2019-2020-election- cycle/

Federal Interagency Forum on Aging-Related Statistics. (2012). *Older Americans 2012: Key indicators of well-being.* http://www.agingstats. gov/main_site/data/2012_documents/docs/ entirechartbook.pdf

Federal Reserve System. (2021, September 30). *Large commercial banks.* https://www.federalreserve.gov/ releases/lbr/current/default.htm

Feldstein, M. (2016, August 23). Here's how to reduce inequality and poverty in America. In *MarketWatch.* National Public Radio. https://www. marketwatch.com/story/heres-how-to-reduce- inequality-and-poverty-in-america-2016-08-23

Feldstein, S. (Ed.). (1972). *The poisoned tongue: A documentary history of American racism and prejudice.* William Morrow.

Fenton, S. (1984). *Durkheim and modern sociology.* CUP Archive.

Ferera, M., Pun, A., Baron, A. S., & Diesendruck, G. (2021). The effect of familiarity on infants' social categorization capacity. *PLOS ONE, 16*(3), e0247710. https://doi.org/10.1371/journal. pone.0247710

Feuer, A. (2021, April 6). Fears of White people losing out permeate Capitol rioters' towns, study finds. *The New York Times.* https://www. nytimes.com/2021/04/06/us/politics/capitol-riot- study.html

Finn, P. J. (2012). Preparing for power in elite boarding schools and in working-class schools. *Theory Into Practice, 51*(1), 57–63.

Finnegan, C. (2021, October 7). Biden admits historic low number of refugees, outside of Afghan evacuees. *ABC News*. https://abcnews.go.com/Politics/biden-admits-historic-low-number-refugees-afghan-evacuees/story?id=80438027

Finnigan, R. (2020). Rainbow-collar jobs? Occupational segregation by sexual orientation in the United States. *Socius: Sociological Research for a Dynamic World, 6*. https://doi.org/10.1177/2378023120954795

Fish, J. M. (2013, March 19). Sickle cell anemia isn't evidence for the existence of races. *Psychology Today*. http://www.psychologytoday.com/blog/looking-in-the-cultural-mirror/201303/sickle-cell-anemia-isn-t-evidence-the-existence-races

Fishel, L. H., & Quarles, B. (1967). *The Negro American: A documentary history*. William Morrow.

Fitz Gibbon, H. (2010). Learning to mother: The definition of motherhood by participants in a welfare reform parenting class. *International Journal of Sociology of the Family, 36*(1), 49–63.

Fitzsimons, T. (2020, March 24). 2020 census: What LGBTQ Americans should know. *NBC News*. https://www.nbcnews.com/feature/nbc-out/2020-census-what-lgbtq-americans-should-know-n1167656

Flanagan, C. A., & Kornbluh, M. (2019). How unequal is the United States? Adolescents' images of social stratification. *Child Development, 90*(3), 957–969. https://doi.org/10.1111/cdev.12954

Fleischer, D. Z., & Zames, F. (2001). *The disability rights movement: From charity to confrontation*. Temple University Press.

Flippen, C. A. (2014). Intersectionality at work: Determinants of labor supply among immigrant Latinas. *Gender & Society, 28*(3), 404–434.

Flores, G. M., & Hondagneu-Sotelo, P. (2014). The social dynamics channelling Latina college graduates into the teaching profession. *Gender, Work & Organization, 21*(6), 491–515.

Flores, R. D., & Schachter, A. (2018). Who are the "illegals"? The social construction of illegality in the United States. *American Sociological Review, 83*(5), 839–868. https://doi.org/10.1177/0003122418794635

Florida, R. (2017). *The new urban crisis: How our cities are increasing inequality, deepening segregation, and failing the middle class—and what we can do about it*. Basic Books.

Floyd, I., Pabetti, L., Meyer, L., Safawi, A., Schott, L., Bellew, E., & Magnus, A. (2021). *TANF policies reflect racist legacy of cash assistance*. Center on Budget and Policy Priorities. https://www.cbpp.org/research/family-income-support/tanf-policies-reflect-racist-legacy-of-cash-assistance

Foley, J. (2021, December 15). Big Wall Street bonus pools may be hard to drain. *Reuters*. https://www.reuters.com/breakingviews/big-wall-street-bonus-pools-may-be-hard-drain-2021-12-15/

Forbes. (2021). *The Forbes 400 2020: The richest people in America*. https://www.forbes.com/forbes-400/

Ford, M. (2015, June 8). America's largest mental hospital is a jail. *The Atlantic*. https://www.theatlantic.com/politics/archive/2015/06/americas-largest-mental-hospital-is-a-jail/395012/

Forman, P. J., & Plymire, D. C. (2005). Amélie Mauresmo's muscles: The lesbian heroic in women's professional tennis. *Women's Studies Quarterly, 33*(1/2), 120–133.

Foster, A. C., & Rojas, A. (2018). Program participation and spending patterns of families receiving government means-tested assistance. *Monthly Labor Review*, January, 1–22.

Foutz, J., Squires, E., Garfield, R., & Damico, A. (2017). *The uninsured: A primer—Key facts about health insurance and the uninsured under the Affordable Care Act*. Kaiser Family Foundation. https://nationaldisabilitynavigator.org/wp-content/uploads/news-items/KFF_Key-Facts-about-Health-Insurance-and-the-Uninsured_Dec-2017.pdf

Fowler, L. (2020, February 28). A long journey awaits transgender migrants in detention. *High Country News*. https://www.hcn.org/articles/justice-a-long-journey-awaits-transgender-migrants-in-detention

Fox, J. (2017, August 16). The jobs most segregated by gender and race. *Bloomberg*. https://www.bloomberg.com/view/articles/2017-08-16/the-jobs-most-segregated-by-gender-and-race

Fox, J. (2018, February 7). It's beginning to look a lot like the Gilded Age. *Bloomberg*. https://www.bloomberg.com/opinion/articles/2018-02-07/it-s-beginning-to-look-a-lot-like-the-gilded-age

Fox, K., & Diehm, J. (2017, November 9). #MeToo's global moment: The anatomy of a viral campaign. *CNN*. https://www.cnn.com/2017/11/09/world/metoo-hashtag-global-movement/index.html

Fox, L. (2020). *The Supplemental Poverty Measure: 2019* (No. P60-272; Current Population Reports). United States Census Bureau.

Francis, M. M. (2018). The strange fruit of American political development. *Politics, Groups, and Identities, 6*(1), 128–137. https://doi.org/10.1080/21565503.2017.1420551

Francis, M. M., & Wright-Rigueur, L. (2021). Black Lives Matter in historical perspective. *Annual Review of Law and Social Science, 17*, 441–458.

Frank, D. J., Camp, B. J., & Boutcher, S. A. (2010). Worldwide trends in the criminal regulation of sex, 1945 to 2005. *American*

Sociological Review, 75(6), 867–893. https://doi.org/10.1177/0003122410388493

Frankenberg, R. (1997). *Displacing whiteness*. Duke University Press.

Franklin, C. A., & Fearn, N. E. (2008). Gender, race, and formal court decision-making outcomes: Chivalry/paternalism, conflict theory or gender conflict? *Journal of Criminal Justice*, 36(3), 279–290.

Franklin, T. W. (2013). Sentencing Native Americans in US federal courts: An examination of disparity. *Justice Quarterly*, 30(2), 310–339.

Franko, W. W. (2017). Understanding public perceptions of growing economic inequality. *State Politics & Policy Quarterly*, 17(3), 319–348. https://doi.org/10.1177/1532440017707799

Fredrickson, G. M. (1981). *White supremacy: A comparative study in American and South African history*. Oxford University Press.

Freiburger, T. L., & Sheeran, A. M. (2020). The joint effects of race, ethnicity, gender, and age on the incarceration and sentence length decisions. *Race and Justice*, 10(2), 203–222. https://doi.org/10.1177/2153368717739676

Friedman, M. R., Dodge, B., Schick, V., Herbenick, D., Hubach, R. D., Bowling, J., Goncalves, G., Krier, S., & Reece, M. (2014). From bias to bisexual health disparities: Attitudes toward bisexual men and women in the United States. *LGBT Health*, 1(4), 309–318.

Friedman, S., Reynolds, A., Scovill, S., Brassier, F. R., Campbell, R., & Ballou, M. (2013). *An estimate of housing discrimination against same-sex couples*. US Department of Housing and Urban Development, Office of Policy Development and Research. http://papers.ssrn.com/sol3/papers.cfm?abstract_id=2284243

Frost, D. M., Lehavot, K., & Meyer, I. H. (2015). Minority stress and physical health among sexual minority individuals. *Journal of Behavioral Medicine*, 38(1), 1–8.

Frye, M. (1983). *The politics of reality: Essays in feminist theory*. Crossing Press.

Fujimura, J. H. (2015). A different kind of association between socio-histories and health. *The British Journal of Sociology*, 66(1), 58–67.

Gabbidon S. L., Higgins, G. E., & Potter H. (2011). Race, gender, and the perception of recently experiencing unfair treatment by the police: Exploratory results from an all-Black sample. *Criminal Justice Review*, 36(1), 5–21.

Gallagher, R. J., Reagan, A. J., Danforth, C. M., & Dodds, P. S. (2018). Divergent discourse between protests and counter-protests: #BlackLivesMatter and #AllLivesMatter. *PLOS ONE*, 13(4), e0195644. https://doi.org/10.1371/journal.pone.0195644

Gallup. (2018). *In US, estimate of LGBT population rises to 4.5%*. Gallup Polls. https://news.gallup.com/poll/234863/estimate-lgbt-population-rises.aspx

Gallup. (2021a). *Immigration*. Gallup.Com. https://news.gallup.com/poll/1660/Immigration.aspx

Gallup. (2021b). *LGBT rights*. Gallup Polls. https://news.gallup.com/poll/1651/Gay-Lesbian-Rights.aspx

Gallup and NAIS. (2017). *NAIS-Gallup report on NAIS graduates: Seeking critical collegiate experiences and consistent progression in higher education*. Gallup Polls. https://resources.finalsite.net/images/v1566939827/sageridgeorg/ydvpnbul648btl6hzqls/NAIS_Gallup_Report_on_NAIS_Graduates.pdf

Galster, G., & Santiago, A. (2015). Neighborhood ethnic composition and outcomes for low-income Latino and African American children. *Urban Studies*, 54(2), 482–500.

Galster, G. C. (2012). The mechanism(s) of neighbourhood effects: Theory, evidence, and policy implications. In M. van Ham, D. Manley, N. Bailey, L. Simpson, & D. Maclennan (Eds.), *Neighbourhood effects research: New perspectives* (pp. 23–56). Springer Netherlands.

Gangl, M., & Ziefle, A. (2009). Motherhood, labor force behavior, and women's careers: An empirical assessment of the wage penalty for motherhood in Britain, Germany, and the United States. *Demography*, 46(2), 341–369.

Gans, H. J. (1996). From "underclass" to "undercaste": Some observations about the future of the post-industrial economy and its major victims. In E. Mingione (Ed.), *Urban poverty and the underclass* (pp. 39–152). Blackwell Publishers.

GAO. (2018). *Discipline disparities for Black students, boys, and students with disabilities*. United States Government Accountability Office. https://www.gao.gov/products/gao-18-258

GAO. (2021). *Rural hospital closures: Affected residents had reduced access to health care services*. US Government Accountability Office. https://www.gao.gov/products/gao-21-93

Garcia, S. E. (2017, October 20). The woman who created #MeToo long before hashtags. *The New York Times*. https://www.nytimes.com/2017/10/20/us/me-too-movement-tarana-burke.html

Garcia-Navarro, L., Fisher, T., Amaria, K., & Migaki, L. (2015, November 12). *Why deforestation happens (and why it's hard to stop)*. National Public Radio. http://apps.npr.org/lookatthis/posts/brazil/

Gartrell, N., & Bos, H. (2010). US national longitudinal lesbian family study: Psychological adjustment of 17-year-old adolescents. *Pediatrics*, 126(1), 28–36.

Garza, A. (2015). *Herstory: Black Lives Matter*. Black Lives Matter. http://blacklivesmatter.com/herstory/

Gaston, S. (2019). Producing race disparities: A study of drug arrests across place and race. *Criminology*, *57*(3), 424–451. https://doi.org/10.1111/1745-9125.12207

Gates, H. L. G. (2020). *Stony the road: Reconstruction, white supremacy, and the rise of Jim Crow.* Penguin.

Gaztambide-Fernandez, R. A. (2009). *The best of the best: Becoming elite at an American boarding school.* Harvard University Press.

Ge, M., Friedrich, J., & Vigna, L. (2020). *Four charts explain greenhouse gas emissions by countries and sectors.* World Resources Institute. https://www.wri.org/insights/4-charts-explain-greenhouse-gas-emissions-countries-and-sectors

Gecewicz, C., & Lipka, M. (2014). *Blacks are lukewarm to gay marriage, but most say businesses must provide wedding services to gay couples.* Pew Research Center. http://www.pewresearch.org/fact-tank/2014/10/07/blacks-are-lukewarm-to-gay-marriage-but-most-say-businesses-must-provide-wedding-services-to-gay-couples/

Gengler, A. (2012). Defying (dis)empowerment in a battered women's shelter: Moral rhetorics, intersectionality, and processes of control and resistance. *Social Problems*, *59*(4), 501–521.

George, M. (2013). Seeking legitimacy: The professionalization of life coaching. *Sociological Inquiry*, *83*(2), 179–208.

Georgetown University Health Policy Institute. (2021, September 15). The poorest children are the ones that lost health insurance during the pandemic. *Center For Children and Families.* https://ccf.georgetown.edu/2021/09/15/the-poorest-children-are-the-ones-that-lost-health-insurance-during-the-pandemic/

Gerstle, G., & Fraser, S. (2005). Coda: Democracy in America. In S. Fraser, & G. Gerstle (Eds.), *Ruling America: A history of wealth and power in a democracy* (pp. 286–292). Harvard University Press.

Gerth, H. H., & Mills, C. W. (Eds.). (1962). *From Max Weber: Essays in sociology.* Oxford University Press.

Gertz, G. (2020). *Did Trump's tariffs benefit American workers and national security?* Brookings Institution. https://www.brookings.edu/policy2020/votervital/did-trumps-tariffs-benefit-american-workers-and-national-security/

Ghorayshi, A. (2022, June 10). Report reveals sharp rise in transgender young people in the U.S. *The New York Times.* https://www.nytimes.com/2022/06/10/science/transgender-teenagers-national-survey.html

Giddens, A. (1973). *The class structure of the advanced societies.* Harper and Row.

Giddens, A. (1978). *Emile Durkheim.* Penguin Books.

Giddens, A. (1984). *The constitution of society: Outline of the theory of structuration.* University of California Press.

Giddings, P. (1984). *When and where I enter: The impact of Black women on race and sex in America.* Bantam.

Gilbert, D. L. (2018). *The American class structure in an age of growing inequality* (10th ed.). Sage Publications.

Gilbertie, S. (2021, January 25). The world's two largest soybean exporters have depleted their supplies. *Forbes.* https://www.forbes.com/sites/salgilbertie/2021/01/25/the-worlds-two-largest-soybean-exporters-have-depleted-their-supplies/

Gilens, M., & Page, B. I. (2014). Testing theories of American politics: Elites, interest groups, and average citizens. *Perspectives on Politics*, *12*(3), 564–581.

Gimenez, M. E. (2005). Capitalism and the oppression of women: Marx revisited. *Science & Society*, *69*, 11–32.

Gimpelson, V., & Treisman, D. (2018). Misperceiving inequality. *Economics & Politics*, *30*(1), 27–54.

Glenn, E. N. (2008). Constructing citizenship: Exclusion, subordination, and resistance. *American Sociological Review*, *76*(1), 1–24.

Glenn, E. N. (2011). Constructing citizenship: Exclusion, subordination, and resistance. *American Sociological Review*, *76*(1), 1–24.

Glenn, E. N. (2015). Settler colonialism as structure: A framework for comparative studies of US race and gender formation. *Sociology of Race and Ethnicity*, *1*(1), 52–72. https://doi.org/10.1177/2332649214560440

Glennon, B. (2020). *How do restrictions on high-skilled immigration affect offshoring? Evidence from the H-1B program* (Working Paper No. 27538). National Bureau of Economic Research. https://www.nber.org/papers/w27538

Goedert, N. (2014). Gerrymandering or geography? How Democrats won the popular vote but lost the Congress in 2012. *Research & Politics*, *1*(1), 1–8.

Goff, K., & McCarthy, J. D. (2021, October 12). Critics claim BLM protests were more violent than 1960s civil rights ones. That's just not true. *Washington Post.* https://www.washingtonpost.com/politics/2021/10/12/critics-claim-blm-was-more-violent-than-1960s-civil-rights-protests-thats-just-not-true/

Goffman, E. (1959). *The presentation of self in everyday life.* Doubleday.

Goffman, E. (1961). *Asylums.* Doubleday Anchor Books.

Goffman, E. (1967). *Interaction ritual: Essays on face-to-face interaction.* Anchor Books, Doubleday.

Goldin, C. (2014). A grand gender convergence: Its last chapter. *American Economic Review*, *104*(4), 1091–1119.

Gor, B. J., Chilton, J. A., Camingue, P. T., & Hajek, R. A. (2011). Young Asian Americans' knowledge and perceptions of cervical cancer and the human papillomavirus. *Journal of Immigrant and Minority Health, 13*(1), 81–86. https://doi.org/10.1007/s10903-010-9343-7

Gordon, H. L., Walker, L. S., Gur, S., & Olien, J. L. (2018). Obesity and gender as status beliefs. *Social Science Research, 71*, 11–18. https://doi.org/10.1016/j.ssresearch.2017.12.004

Gorman, B. K., Denney, J. T., Dowdy, H., & Medeiros, R. A. (2015). A new piece of the puzzle: Sexual orientation, gender, and physical health status. *Demography, 52*(4), 1357–1382. https://doi.org/10.1007/s13524-015-0406-1

Gorman, E. H., & Kmec, J. A. (2009). Hierarchical rank and women's organizational mobility: Glass ceilings in corporate law firms. *American Journal of Sociology, 114*(5), 1428–1474.

Goss, S., Wade, A., Skirvin, J. P., Morris, M., Bye, K. M., & Huston, D. (2013). *Effects of unauthorized immigration on the actuarial status of the Social Security trust funds* (Actuarial Note No. 151). Social Security Administration.

Gotsch, K. (2018, April 24). *Families and mass incarceration*. The Sentencing Project. https://www.sentencingproject.org/publications/6148/

Goubin, S. (2020). Economic inequality, perceived responsiveness and political trust. *Acta Politica, 55*(2), 267–304. https://doi.org/10.1057/s41269-018-0115-z

Gould, E. (2020). *State of working America wages 2019: A story of slow, uneven, and unequal wage growth over the last 40 years*. Economic Policy Institute. https://www.epi.org/publication/swa-wages-2019/

Gould, E., Wilson, V., & Perez, D. (2020, August 20). *Latinx workers—Particularly women—Face devastating job losses in the COVID-19 recession*. Economic Policy Institute. https://www.epi.org/publication/latinx-workers-covid/

Grabb, E. G. (1984). *Social inequality: Classical and contemporary theorists*. Holt Rinehart & Winston.

Grady, C. (2018, July 20). The waves of feminism, and why people keep fighting over them. *Vox*. https://www.vox.com/2018/3/20/16955588/feminism-waves-explained-first-second-third-fourth

Graham, D. A. (2016, January 9). What did the Governor know about Flint's water, and when did he know it? *The Atlantic*. http://www.theatlantic.com/politics/archive/2016/01/what-did-the-governor-know-about-flints-water-and-when-did-he-know-it/423342/

Gramlich, J. (2020). *What the data says (and doesn't say) about crime in the United States*. Pew Research Center. https://www.pewresearch.org/fact-tank/2020/11/20/facts-about-crime-in-the-u-s/

Green, D. S., & Wortham, R. A. (2015). Sociology hesitant: The continuing neglect of W.E.B. Du Bois. *Sociological Spectrum, 35*(6), 518–533.

Green, J. R. (1980). *The world of the worker*. Hill and Wang.

Greenaway, K. H., Haslam, S. A., Cruwys, T., Branscombe, N. R., Ysseldyk, R., & Heldreth, C. (2015). From "we" to "me": Group identification enhances perceived personal control with consequences for health and well-being. *Journal of Personality and Social Psychology, 109*(1), 53–74. https://doi.org/10.1037/pspi0000019

Greenwood, D. N., & Dal Cin, S. (2012). Ethnicity and body consciousness: Black and White American women's negotiation of media ideals and others' approval. *Psychology of Popular Media Culture, 1*(4), 220–235.

Griffin, C., Szmigin, I., Bengry-Howell, A., Hackley, C., & Mistral, W. (2013). Inhabiting the contradictions: Hypersexual femininity and the culture of intoxication among young women in the UK. *Feminism & Psychology, 23*(2), 184–206. https://doi.org/10.1177/0959353512468860

Griffin, L. J., & Bollen, K. A. (2009). What do these memories do? Civil rights remembrance and racial attitudes. *American Sociological Review, 74*(4), 594–614.

Grossmann, M. (2012). Interest group influence on US policy change: An assessment based on policy history. *Interest Groups & Advocacy, 1*(2), 171–192. https://doi.org/10.1057/iga.2012.9

Gruberg, S. (2018, May 30). *ICE's rejection of its own rules is placing LGBT immigrants at severe risk of sexual abuse*. Center for American Progress. https://www.americanprogress.org/issues/lgbtq-rights/news/2018/05/30/451294/ices-rejection-rules-placing-lgbt-immigrants-severe-risk-sexual-abuse/

Gruberg, S., Mahowald, L., & Halpin, J. (2020, October 6). *The state of the LGBTQ community in 2020*. Center for American Progress. https://www.americanprogress.org/issues/lgbtq-rights/reports/2020/10/06/491052/state-lgbtq-community-2020/

Grue, J. (2016). The social meaning of disability: A reflection on categorisation, stigma and identity. *Sociology of Health & Illness, 38*(6), 957–964.

GSS. (2021). *GSS data explorer*. NORC at the University of Chicago. https://gssdataexplorer.norc.org/trends/Gender%20&%20Marriage?measure=sexornt

GSS Data Explorer. (2018). *Gender and marriage*. https://gssdataexplorer.norc.org/trends/Gender%20&%20Marriage?measure=fepresch

Guyton, J., Langetieg, P., Reck, D., Risch, M., & Zucman, G. (2021). *Tax evasion at the top of the income distribution: Theory and evidence* (No. w28542). National Bureau of Economic Research. https://doi.org/10.3386/w28542

Gyamfi, B., & Konadu, K. (2021). Black Lives Matter: How far has the movement come? *The Conversation*. http://theconversation.com/black-lives-matter-how-far-has-the-movement-come-165492

Gyamfi-Bannerman, C., & Melamed, A. (2020, June 18). Socioeconomic status and crowded housing linked to COVID-19. *New York-Presbyterian Health Matters*. https://healthmatters.nyp.org/crowded-homes-poor-neighborhoods-linked-to-covid-19/

Hadjar, A., Baier, D., Boehnke, K., & Hagan, J. (2007). Juvenile delinquency and gender revisited: The family and power-control theory reconceived. *European Journal of Criminology, 4*(1), 33–58.

Hadler, M., & Symons, J. (2018). World society divided: Divergent trends in state responses to sexual minorities and their reflection in public attitudes. *Social Forces, 96*(4), 1721–1755.

Hagan, J., Gillis, A. R., & Simpson, J. (1985). The class structure of gender and delinquency: Toward a power-control theory of common delinquent behavior. *American Journal of Sociology, 90*, 1151–1178.

Hagan, J., Simpson, J., & Gillis, A. R. (1987). Class in the household: A power-control theory of gender and delinquency. *American Journal of Sociology, 92*, 788–816.

Hahl, O., & Zuckerman, E. W. (2014). The denigration of heroes? How the status attainment process shapes attributions of considerateness and authenticity. *American Journal of Sociology, 120*(2), 504–554.

Hainmueller, J., & Hopkins, D. J. (2014). Public attitudes toward immigration. *Annual Review of Political Science, 17*(1), 225–249.

Hajnal, Z., Lajevardi, N., & Nielson, L. (2017). Voter identification laws and the suppression of minority votes. *The Journal of Politics, 79*(2), 363–379.

Hakobyan, S., & McLaren, J. (2016). Looking for local labor market effects of NAFTA. *Review of Economics and Statistics, 98*(4), 728–741. https://doi.org/10.1162/REST_a_00587

Hale, C. (2020). Catholic Church advocacy in Latin America. In P. A. Djupe, M. J. Rozell, and T. G. Jelen (Eds.), *The Oxford encyclopedia of politics and religion* (Vol. 1–2). Oxford University Press.

Hall, D., & Cooper, D. (2012). *How raising the federal minimum wage would help working families and give the economy a boost.* Economic Policy Institute. https://files.epi.org/2012/ib341-raising-federal-minimum-wage.pdf

Hall, D., & Stevenson, H. (2007). Double jeopardy: Being African-American and "doing diversity" in independent schools. *The Teachers College Record, 109*(1), 1–23.

Hall, J. C. (2017). No longer invisible: Understanding the psychosocial impact of skin color stratification in the lives of African American women. *Health & Social Work, 42*(2), 71–78. https://doi.org/10.1093/hsw/hlx001

Hamermesh, D. (2011). *Beauty pays: Why attractive people are more successful.* Princeton University Press.

Hamilton, D., Austin, A., & Darity, W. Jr. (2011). *Whiter jobs, higher wages: Occupational segregation and the lower wages of Black men* [Briefing Paper]. Economic Policy Institute.

Han, S., & Piquero, A. R. (2021). Is it dangerous to live in neighborhoods with more immigrants? Assessing the effects of immigrant concentration on crime patterns. *Crime & Delinquency*, 00111287211007736. https://doi.org/10.1177/00111287211007736

Han, C. W., & Rutledge, S. E. (2020). They don't date any dark people: The queer case of gay racism. In J. G. Smith, & W. Han (Eds.), *Home and community for queer men of color: The intersection of race and sexuality* (pp. 31–48). Lexington Books.

Hananel, S. (2018, May 30). *LGBT immigrants in detention centers at severe risk of sexual abuse.* Center for American Progress. https://www.americanprogress.org/press/release/2018/05/30/451380/release-lgbt-immigrants-detention-centers-severe-risk-sexual-abuse-cap-analysis-says/

Hancock, A.-M. (2005). W.E.B. Du Bois: Intellectual forefather of intersectionality? *Souls, 7*(3–4), 74–84.

Hankivsky, O., & Kapilashrami, A. (2020, May 15). Intersectionality offers a radical rethinking of COVID-19. *The BMJ.* https://blogs.bmj.com/bmj/2020/05/15/intersectionality-offers-a-radical-rethinking-of-covid-19/

Hanley, C. (2014). Putting the bias in skill-biased technological change? A Relational perspective on white-collar automation at general electric. *American Behavioral Scientist, 58*(3), 400–415.

Hannon, L. (2015). White colorism. *Social Currents, 2*(1), 13–21.

Hannon, L., DeFina, R., & Bruch, S. (2013). The relationship between skin tone and school suspension for African Americans. *Race and Social Problems, 5*(4), 281–295.

Hansen, H., Siegel, C., Wanderling, J., & DiRocco, D. (2016). Buprenorphine and methadone treatment for opioid dependence by income, ethnicity and race of neighborhoods in New York City. *Drug and Alcohol Dependence, 164*, 14–21. https://doi.org/10.1016/j.drugalcdep.2016.03.028

Hanson, A., Brannon, I., & Hawley, Z. (2014). Rethinking tax benefits for home owners. *National Affairs.* https://www.nationalaffairs.com/publications/detail/rethinking-tax-benefits-for-home-owners

Harris, A., Evans, H., & Beckett, K. (2010). Drawing blood from stones: Legal debt and social inequality in the contemporary United States. *American Journal of Sociology, 115*(6), 1753–1799.

Harris, F. C. (1999). *Something within: Religion in African-American political activism.* Oxford University Press.

Harris Polls. (2014). *Doctors, military officers, firefighters, and scientists seen as among America's most prestigious occupations.* Harris Insights and Analytics. http://www.harrisinteractive.com/NewsRoom/HarrisPolls/tabid/447/mid/1508/articleId/1490/ctl/ReadCustom%20Default/Default.aspx

Hartley, B. L., & Sutton, R. M. (2013). A stereotype threat account of boys' academic underachievement. *Child Development, 84*(5), 1716–1733.

Hartley, R. D., & Armendariz, L. F. (2011). Border justice? Sentencing federal narcotics offenders in southwest border districts: A focus on citizenship status. *Journal of Contemporary Criminal Justice, 27*(1), 43–62.

Harvard Business School. (2021). *Trade union membership.* https://www.hbs.edu/businesshistory/courses/resources/historical-data-visualization/Pages/details.aspx?data_id=37

Hatch, S. L., & Dohrenwend, B. P. (2007). Distribution of traumatic and other stressful life events by race/ethnicity, gender, SES and age: A review of the research. *American Journal of Community Psychology, 40*(3–4), 313–332.

Hatzipanagos, R. (2018, September 14). "Latinx": An offense to the Spanish language or a nod to inclusion? *Washington Post.* https://www.washingtonpost.com/news/post-nation/wp/2018/09/14/latinx-an-offense-to-the-spanish-language-or-a-nod-to-inclusion/

Hauser, O. P., & Norton, M. I. (2017). (Mis) perceptions of inequality. *Current Opinion in Psychology, 18*, 21–25. https://doi.org/10.1016/j.copsyc.2017.07.024

Hay, C., Fortson, E. N., Hollist, D. R., Altheimer, I., & Schaible, L. M. (2007). Compounded risk: The implications for delinquency of coming from a poor family that lives in a poor community. *Journal of Youth and Adolescence, 36*(5), 593–605.

Hays, S. (1996). *The cultural contradictions of motherhood.* Yale University Press.

Hays, S. (2003). *Flat broke with children: Women in the age of welfare reform.* Oxford University Press.

Hechter, M. (2004). From class to culture. *American Journal of Sociology, 110*(2), 400–445.

Hein, J. E., & Jenkins, J. C. (2017). Why does the United States lack a global warming policy? The corporate inner circle versus public interest sector elites. *Environmental Politics, 26*(1), 97–117. https://doi.org/10.1080/09644016.2016.1244966

Heller, N. (2018, July 2). Who really stands to win from universal basic income? *The New Yorker.* https://www.newyorker.com/magazine/2018/07/09/who-really-stands-to-win-from-universal-basic-income

Hennessy, J. (2009). Morality and work-family conflict in the lives of poor and low-income women. *The Sociological Quarterly, 50*(4), 557–580.

Herdt, G. H. (1997). *Same sex, different cultures: Gays and lesbians across cultures.* Westview Press.

Herdt, G. H., & McClintock, M. (2000). The magical age of 10. *Archives of Sexual Behavior, 29*(6), 587–606.

Herek, G. M. (2013). Facts about homosexuality and child molestation. *Professor Herek's Blog.* http://psychology.ucdavis.edu/faculty_sites/rainbow/html/facts_molestation.html

Hergenrather, K. C., Zeglin, R. J., McGuire-Kuletz, M., & Rhodes, S. D. (2015). Employment as a social determinant of health: A systematic review of longitudinal studies exploring the relationship between employment status and physical health. *Rehabilitation Research, Policy, and Education, 29*(1), 2–26.

Herkenrath, M., König, C., Scholtz, H., & Volken, T. (2005). Convergence and divergence in the contemporary world system: An introduction. *International Journal of Comparative Sociology, 46*(5–6), 363–382.

Herman, J. L., Brown, T. N. T., & Haas, A. P. (2019). *Suicide thoughts and attempts among transgender adults.* Williams Institute. https://williamsinstitute.law.ucla.edu/wp-content/uploads/Suicidality-Transgender-Sep-2019.pdf

Hernandez, D. (2017, December 17). The case against "Latinx." *LA Times.* http://www.latimes.com/opinion/op-ed/la-oe-hernandez-the-case-against-latinx-20171217-story.html

Hertel-Fernandez, A., Mildenberger, M., & Stokes, L. C. (2018). Legislative staff and representation in Congress. *American Political Science Review, 113*(1), 1–18.

Hertz, T. (2005). Rags, riches and race: The intergenerational economic mobility of Black and White families in the United States. In S. Bowles, H. Gintis, & M. O. Groves (Eds.), *Unequal chances: Family background and economic success* (Vol. 2005, pp. 165–191). Russell Sage and Princeton University Press.

Hess, A. J. (2021, January 29). How the coronavirus pandemic may be causing support of labor unions to rise. *CNBC.* https://www.cnbc.com/2021/01/29/support-of-labor-unions-is-at-65percen-theres-whats-behind-the-rise.html

Heyward, G. (2021, September 25). Reparations for Black residents are becoming a local issue as well as a national one. *The New York Times.* https://www.nytimes.com/2021/09/25/us/reparations-african-americans-usa.html

HHS. (2020). *Characteristics and financial circumstances of TANF recipients fiscal year 2019.* US Department of Health and Human Services. https://www.acf.hhs.gov/sites/default/files/documents/ofa/fy19_characteristics_final.pdf

HHS. (2021). *Characteristics and financial circumstances of TANF recipients fiscal year 2020.*

US Department of Health and Human Services. https://www.acf.hhs.gov/ofa/data/characteristics-and-financial-circumstances-tanf-recipients-fiscal-year-2020

Hickman, C., Marks, E., Pihkala, P., Clayton, S., Lewandowski, E., Mayall, E., Wray, B., Mellor, C., & van Susteren, L. (2021). A global survey of climate anxiety in children and young people and their beliefs about government responses to climate change. Lancet Planetary Health.

Highton, B. (2017). Voter identification laws and turnout in the United States. Annual Review of Political Science, 20(1), 149–167.

Hinchliffe, E. (2021, June 2). The female CEOs on the Fortune 500 just broke three all-time records. Fortune. https://fortune.com/2021/06/02/female-ceos-fortune-500-2021-women-ceo-list-roz-brewer-walgreens-karen-lynch-cvs-thasunda-brown-duckett-tiaa/

Hinton, E., Reed, C., & Henderson, L. (2018). An unjust burden: The disparate treatment of Black Americans in the criminal justice system. Vera Institute of Justice.

Hirschfield, P. J. (2015). Lethal policing: Making sense of American exceptionalism. Sociological Forum, 30(4), 1109–1117. https://doi.org/10.1111/socf.12200

Hirsh, A. T., Anastas, T. M., Miller, M. M., Quinn, P. D., & Kroenke, K. (2020). Patient race and opioid misuse history influence provider risk perceptions for future opioid-related problems. American Psychologist, 75(6), 784–795. https://doi.org/10.1037/amp0000636

Hirshfield, L. E., & Joseph, T. D. (2012). We need a woman, we need a Black woman': Gender, race, and identity taxation in the academy. Gender and Education, 24(2), 213–227.

Hischenfeld Davis, J., & Sengupta, S. (2017, September 18). Trump administration rejects study showing positive impact of refugees. New York Times. https://www.nytimes.com/2017/09/18/us/politics/refugees-revenue-cost-report-trump.html

Hochschild, A. R. (2018). Strangers in their own land: Anger and mourning on the American right. The New Press.

Hochschild, J. L., & Weaver, V. (2007). The skin color paradox and the American racial order. Social Forces, 86(2), 643–670. https://doi.org/10.1093/sf/86.2.643

Hodge, R. W., Siegel, P. M., & Rossi, P. H. (1964). Occupational prestige in the United States, 1925–63. American Journal of Sociology, 70, 286–302.

Hodgson, G. M. (2014). What is capital? Economists and sociologists have changed its meaning: Should it be changed back? Cambridge Journal of Economics, 38(5), 1063–1086.

Hoffman, K. M., Trawalter, S., Axt, J. R., & Oliver, M. N. (2016). Racial bias in pain assessment and treatment recommendations, and false beliefs about biological differences between blacks and whites. Proceedings of the National Academy of Sciences, 113(16), 4296–4301. https://doi.org/10.1073/pnas.1516047113

Hogler, R. L. (2015). The end of American labor unions: The right-to-work movement and the erosion of collective bargaining. Praeger Publishing.

Hogler, R. L., Hunt, H. G., & Weiler, S. (2015). Killing unions with culture: Institutions, inequality, and the effects of labor's decline in the United States. Employee Responsibilities and Rights Journal, 27(1), 63–79.

Hojnacki, M., Kimball, D. C., Baumgartner, F. R., Berry, J. M., & Leech, B. L. (2012). Studying organizational advocacy and influence: Re-examining interest group research. Annual Review of Political Science, 15(1), 379–399.

Holder, S. (2021). The US cities giving residents direct cash payments. Bloomberg City Lab. https://www.bloomberg.com/news/articles/2021-12-28/the-u-s-cities-giving-residents-direct-cash-payments

Holley, L. C., Tavassoli, K. Y., & Stromwall, L. K. (2016). Mental illness discrimination in mental health treatment programs: Intersections of race, ethnicity, and sexual orientation. Community Mental Health Journal, 52(3), 311–322.

Holmes, W. C., & Slap, G. B. (1998). Sexual abuse of boys: Definition, prevalence, correlates, sequelae, and management. JAMA, 280(21), 1855–1862.

Holtz-Eakin, D. (2016). Reducing poverty the Republican way. Pathways: A Magazine on Poverty, Inequality, and Social Policy, Winter, 4, 14–17.

Hong, N., & Bromwich, J. E. (2021, March 18). Asian Americans are being attacked. Why are hate crime charges so rare? The New York Times. https://www.nytimes.com/2021/03/18/nyregion/asian-hate-crimes.html

Horne, R. M., Johnson, M. D., Galambos, N. L., & Krahn, H. J. (2018). Time, money, or gender? Predictors of the division of household labour across life stages. Sex Roles, 78(11), 731–743. https://doi.org/10.1007/s11199-017-0832-1

Horowitz, J. (2016). Dimensions of job quality, mechanisms, and subjective well-being in the United States. Sociological Forum, 31(2), 419–440.

Horowitz, J. M. (2013). Americans less accepting of homosexuality than other westerners—Religion May be one reason. Pew Research Center. http://www.pewresearch.org/fact-tank/2013/06/12/americans-are-less-accepting-of-homosexuality-than-canadians-western-europeans-and-religion-may-be-one-explanation/

Horowitz, J. M. (2021). Support for Black Lives Matter declined after George Floyd protests, but has remained unchanged since. Pew Research Center. https://

www.pewresearch.org/fact-tank/2021/09/27/support-for-black-lives-matter-declined-after-george-floyd-protests-but-has-remained-unchanged-since/

Horowitz, J. M., & Igielnik, R. (2020). *A century after women gained the right to vote, majority of Americans see work to do on gender equality.* Pew Research Center's Social & Demographic Trends Project. https://www.pewresearch.org/social-trends/2020/07/07/a-century-after-women-gained-the-right-to-vote-majority-of-americans-see-work-to-do-on-gender-equality/

Horowitz, J. M., Igielnik, R., & Kochhar, R. (2020). *Trends in US income and wealth inequality.* Pew Research Center's Social & demographic Trends Project. https://www.pewresearch.org/social-trends/2020/01/09/trends-in-income-and-wealth-inequality/

Horwitz, S. R., Shutts, K., & Olson, K. R. (2014). Social class differences produce social group preferences. *Developmental Science, 17*(6), 991–1002.

Hotchkiss, J. L. (2004). A closer look at the employment impact of the Americans with Disabilities Act. *The Journal of Human Resources, XXXIX*(4), 887–911.

Hout, M. (1988). More universalism, less structural mobility: The American occupational structure in the 1980s. *American Journal of Sociology, 93,* 1358–1400.

Hout, M. (2008). How class works: Objective and subjective aspects of class since the 1970s. In A. Lareau, & D. Conley (Eds.), *Social class: How does it work?* (pp. 25–64). Russell Sage Foundation.

Howell, B. (2009). Broken lives from broken windows: The hidden costs of aggressive order-maintenance policing. *New York University Review of Law & Social Change, 33,* 271–329.

Hoynes, H. W. (2014). A revolution in poverty policy. *Pathways, Summer,* 23–27.

Hoyt, C. L., Morgenroth, T., & Burnette, J. L. (2019). Understanding sexual prejudice: The role of political ideology and strategic essentialism. *Journal of Applied Social Psychology, 49*(1), 3–14. https://doi.org/10.1111/jasp.12560

Huang, C., & Cho, C. (2017, October 30). *Ten facts you should know about the federal estate tax.* Center on Budget and Policy Priorities. https://www.cbpp.org/research/federal-tax/ten-facts-you-should-know-about-the-federal-estate-tax

Huddleston, T. (2015, September 14). 5 Pope Francis quotes on capitalism, inequality, poverty. *Fortune Magazine.* http://fortune.com/2015/09/14/pope-francis-capitalism-inequality/

Hughes, B. B., Hanna, T., McNeil, K., Bohl, D. K., & Moyer, J. D. (2021). *Pursuing the sustainable development goals in a world reshaped by COVID-19.*

Frederick S. Pardee Center for International Futures and United States Development Programme. https://sdgintegration.undp.org/sites/default/files/Foundational_research_report.pdf

Hughes, C., Warren, P. Y., Stewart, E. A., Tomaskovic-Devey, D., & Mears, D. P. (2017). Racial threat, intergroup contact, and school punishment. *Journal of Research in Crime and Delinquency, 54*(5), 583–616. https://doi.org/10.1177/0022427816689811

Hughes, M., Kiecolt, K. J., & Keith, V. M. (2014). How racial identity moderates the impact of financial stress on mental health among African Americans. *Society and Mental Health, 4*(1), 38–54. https://doi.org/10.1177/2156869313509635

Hughes, M. K. (2003). Through the looking glass: Racial jokes, social context, and the reasonable person in hostile work environment analysis. *Southern California Law Review, 76,* 1437–1482.

Human Rights Campaign. (2015). *An overview of federal rights granted to married couples.* http://www.hrc.org/resources/an-overview-of-federal-rights-and-protections-granted-to-married-couples/

Human Rights Campaign. (2018). *Voting Rights Advancement Act.* http://www.hrc.org/resources/voting-rights-advancement-act/

Human Rights Campaign. (2021a). *An epidemic of violence.* HRC Digital Reports. https://reports.hrc.org/an-epidemic-of-violence-fatal-violence-against-transgender-and-gender-non-confirming-people-in-the-united-states-in-2021

Human Rights Campaign. (2021b, October 8). *John Lewis Voting Rights Advancement Act.* HRC. https://www.hrc.org/resources/voting-rights-advancement-act

Human Rights Watch. (2011, June 17). *Historic decision at the United Nations.* https://www.hrw.org/news/2011/06/17/historic-decision-united-nations

Hummer, R. A., & Gutin, I. (2018). Racial/ethnic and nativity disparities in the health of older US men and women. In M. K. Majmundar and M. D. Hayward (Eds.), *Future directions for the demography of aging: Proceedings of a workshop.* National Academies Press. https://www.ncbi.nlm.nih.gov/books/NBK513079/

Hunt, M. O., & Reichelmann, A. V. (2021). *How we repair it: White Americans' attitudes toward reparations.* Brookings Institution. https://www.brookings.edu/blog/how-we-rise/2021/12/08/how-we-repair-it-white-americans-attitudes-toward-reparations/

Hunter, M. A. (2013a). A bridge over troubled urban waters. *Du Bois Review: Social Science Research on Race, 10*(01), 7–27.

Hunter, M. A. (2013b). *Black citymakers: How The Philadelphia Negro changed urban America.* OUP USA.

Hurst, C. E., & McConnell, D. L. (2010). *An Amish paradox: Diversity and change in the world's largest Amish community*. John Hopkins University.

Husler, B., Shaul, C., & Vazquez, S. (2021). *Idaho multicultural buying power*. Idaho Department of Labor. https://www.labor.idaho.gov/dnn/Portals/0/Publications/Idaho_MultiCultural_Buying_Power_2021.pdf

Hussar, B., Zhang, J., Hein, S., Wang, K., Roberts, A., Cui, J., Smith, M., Mann, F. B., Barmer, A., Dilig, R., Nachazel, T., Barnett, M., & Purcell, S. (2020). *The condition of education 2020* (NCES 2020-144). US Department of Education.

Iacurci, G. (2021, January 5). Scammers have taken $36 billion in fraudulent unemployment payments from American workers. *CNBC*. https://www.cnbc.com/2021/01/05/scammers-have-taken-36-billion-in-fraudulent-unemployment-payments-.html

Iceland, J., Sharp, G., & Timberlake, J. M. (2013). Sun Belt rising: Regional population change and the decline in Black residential segregation, 1970–2009. *Demography*, *50*(1), 97–123.

Igirlnik, R. (2020). *Few in US owned stocks outside of 401(k)s in 2019, fewer said market had a big impact on their view of economy*. Pew Research Center. https://www.pewresearch.org/fact-tank/2020/09/25/few-in-u-s-owned-stocks-outside-of-401ks-in-2019-fewer-said-market-had-a-big-impact-on-their-view-of-economy/

Inglehart, R., Haerpfer, C., Moreno, A., Welzel, C., Kizilova, K., Diez-Medrano, J., Lagos, M., Norris, P., Ponarin, E., & Puranen, B. (Eds.). (2020). *World values survey: Round seven country-pooled datafile 2017–2020*. JD Systems Institute. https://www.worldvaluessurvey.org/WVSOnline.jsp

Inman, P. (2018, October 9). Developing nations "making strides in cutting rich-poor gap." *The Guardian*. https://www.theguardian.com/inequality/2018/oct/09/worlds-poorest-nations-making-strides-cutting-rich-poor-gap

Intersex Society of North America. (2008). *What's the history behind the intersex rights movement?* http://www.isna.org/faq/history

Iqbal, N. (2019, September 7). No lust at first sight: Why thousands are now identifying as "demisexual." *The Guardian*. http://www.theguardian.com/society/2019/sep/07/no-lust-at-first-sight-day-i-finally-realised-i-was-a-demisexual

IRS. (2020, October 21). *The tax gap*. https://www.irs.gov/newsroom/the-tax-gap

Isaac, L. (2008). Movement of movements: Culture moves in the long civil rights struggle. *Social Forces*, *87*(1), 33–63.

Jack, A. A. (2019). *The privileged poor: How elite colleges are failing disadvantaged students*. Harvard University Press.

Jackson, P. A. (2009). Capitalism and global queering: National markets, parallels among sexual cultures, and multiple queer modernities. *GLQ: A Journal of Lesbian and Gay Studies*, *15*(3), 357–395.

Jackson Lee, S.(2021, April 14).*H.R.40—117th Congress (2021–2022): Commission to Study and Develop Reparation Proposals for African Americans Act* (2021/2022) [Legislation]. https://www.congress.gov/bill/117th-congress/house-bill/40/

Jacobs, D., & Richardson, A. M. (2008). Economic inequality and homicide in the developed nations from 1975 to 1995. *Homicide Studies*, *12*(1), 28–45.

Jahoda, A., Wilson, A., Stalker, K., & Cairney, A. (2010). Living with stigma and the self-perceptions of people with mild intellectual disabilities. *Journal of Social Issues*, *66*(3), 521–534.

Jardim, E., Long, M., Plotnick, R., van Inwegen, E., Vigdor, J., & Wething, H. (2017). *Minimum wage increases, wages, and low-wage employment: Evidence from Seattle* (Working Paper No. 23532). National Bureau of Economic Research. https://doi.org/10.3386/w23532

Jargowsky, P. A. (2018). The persistence of segregation in the 21st century. *Law & Inequality: A Journal of Theory and Practice*, *36*, 207–230.

Jay, S., Batruch, A., Jetten, J., McGarty, C., & Muldoon, O. T. (2019). Economic inequality and the rise of far-right populism: A social psychological analysis. *Journal of Community & Applied Social Psychology*, *29*(5), 418–428. https://doi.org/10.1002/casp.2409

Jedwab, R., Johnson, N. D., & Koyama, M. (2020). *The economic impact of the Black Death* (Working Paper II-WP-2020–14). Institute for International Economic Policy, The George Washington University.

Jenkins, J. C., & Eckert, C. M. (1986). Channeling Black insurgency: Elite patronage and professional social movement organizations in the development of the Black movement. *American Sociological Review*, *51*, 812–829.

Jenny, C., Roesler, T. A., & Poyer, K. L. (1994). Are children at risk for sexual abuse by homosexuals? *Pediatrics*, *94*(1), 41–44.

Jetten, J., Mols, F., Healy, N., & Spears, R. (2017). "Fear of falling": Economic instability enhances collective angst among societies' wealthy class. *Journal of Social Issues*, *73*(1), 61–79. https://doi.org/10.1111/josi.12204

Jeung, R. (2007). Faith-based, multiethnic tenant organizing: The Oak Park story. In P. Hondagneu-Sotelo (Ed.), *Religion and social justice for immigrants*. Rutgers University Press.

Johns, M. M., Lowry, R., Haderxhanaj, L. T., Rasberry, C. N., Robin, L., Scales, L., Stone, D., & Suarez, N. A. (2020). Trends in violence victimization and suicide risk by sexual identity among high school students—Youth Risk Behavior Survey,

United States, 2015–2019. *MMWR Supplements*, 69(1), 19–27. https://doi.org/10.15585/mmwr.su6901a3

Johns Hopkins. (2021, September 27). *Mortality analyses*. Johns Hopkins Coronavirus Resource Center. https://coronavirus.jhu.edu/data/mortality

Johnsen, D., & Dellinger, W. (2018). The constitutionality of a national wealth tax. *Indiana Law Journal*, 93(1), 111–137.

Johnson, E. P. (2007). "Quare" Studies, or (almost) everything I know about Queer Studies I learned from my grandmother. In K. E. Lovaas, & M. M. Jenkins (Eds.), *Sexualites and communication in everyday life* (pp. 69–85). Sage Publications.

Johnson, K. (2010). *Reforming Jim Crow: Southern politics and state in the age before Brown*. Oxford University Press.

Johnson, S. K., & Kirk, J. F. (2020). Dual-anonymization yields promising results for reducing gender bias: A naturalistic field experiment of applications for Hubble Space Telescope time. *Publications of the Astronomical Society of the Pacific*, 132(1009), 034503. https://doi.org/10.1088/1538-3873/ab6ce0

Jones, G. S. (2016). *Karl Marx*. Harvard University Press.

Jones, J. M. (2016). *Same-sex marriages up one year after Supreme Court verdict*. Gallup Polls. https://news.gallup.com/poll/193055/sex-marriages-one-year-supreme-court-verdict.aspx

Jones, J. M. (2021, February 24). *LGBT identification rises to 5.6% in latest US estimate*. Gallup Polls. https://news.gallup.com/poll/329708/lgbt-identification-rises-latest-estimate.aspx

Jones, W., & Keiser, K. R. (1987). Issue visibility and the effects of PAC money. *Social Science Quarterly*, 68(1), 170–176.

Jordan, J. (2016). Religion and inequality: The lasting impact of religious traditions and institutions on welfare state development. *European Political Science Review*, 8(1), 25–48. https://doi.org/10.1017/S1755773914000381.

Jordan-Young, R. M. (2011). *Brain storm: The flaws in the science of sex differences*. Harvard University Press.

Ju, D. H. (2021). Factors shaping Asian Americans' attitudes toward homosexuality. *Ethnic and Racial Studies*, 1–24. https://doi.org/10.1080/01419870.2021.1884732

Jurs, M. (2015). *How much is the right to marry worth when it comes to Social Security?* Financial Engines. http://blog.financialengines.com/2015/06/09/marriage-equality-and-social-security/

Kahlenberg, R. (2010, September 30). Elite colleges, or colleges for the elite? *New York Times*. https://www.nytimes.com/2010/09/30/opinion/30kahlenberg.html

Kahn, J. R., & Pearlin, L. I. (2006). Financial strain over the life course and health among older adults. *Journal of Health and Social Behavior*, 47(1), 17–31.

Kai, M. (2018, August 21). *Tarana Burke warns against derailing #MeToo*. https://theglowup.theroot.com/there-is-no-model-survivor-tarana-burke-warns-against-1828474115

Kaiser Family Foundation. (2014). *Life expectancy at birth by race/ethnicity*. https://www.kff.org/other/state-indicator/life-expectancy-by-re/

Kaiser Family Foundation. (2021). *Who could get covered under Medicaid expansion?* https://www.kff.org/medicaid/fact-sheet/uninsured-adults-in-states-that-did-not-expand-who-would-become-eligible-for-medicaid-under-expansion/

Kakwani, N., Wang, X., Xu, J., & Yue, X. (2020). Assessing the social welfare effects of government transfer programs: Some international comparisons. *Review of Income and Wealth*. https://doi.org/10.1111/roiw.12500

Kalkhoff, W., Melamed, D., Pollock, J., Miller, B., Overton, J., & Pfeiffer, M. (2020). Cracking the black box: Capturing the role of expectation states in status processes. *Social Psychology Quarterly*, 83(1), 26–48. https://doi.org/10.1177/0190272519868988

Kandil, C. Y. (2018, May 31). *After 50 years of "Asian American," advocates say the term is "more essential than ever."* NBC. https://www.nbcnews.com/news/asian-america/after-50-years-asian-american-advocates-say-term-more-essential-n875601

Kang-Brown, J., Montagnet, C., & Heiss, J. (2021). *People in jail and prison in 2020*. Vera Institute of Justice. https://www.vera.org/publications/people-in-jail-and-prison-in-2020

Kanter, R. M. (1977). Some effects of proportions on group life: Skewed sex ratios and responses to token women. *American Journal of Sociology*, 82, 965–990.

Kasakove, S., & Thrush, G. (2022, January 7). Federal rental assistance is running out, with tenants still in need. *The New York Times*. https://www.nytimes.com/2022/01/07/us/federal-rental-assistance-evictions.html

Katz, J. N. (2004). "Homosexual" and "Heterosexual." In R. S Kimmel, & Plante R. E. (Eds.), *Sexualities: Identities, behaviors and society* (pp. 44–46). Oxford University Press.

Katz, M. B. (1996). *In the shadow of the poorhouse: A social history of welfare in America*. Basic Books.

Katz, M. B. (2013). *The undeserving poor: America's enduring confrontation with poverty* (2nd ed.). Oxford University Press.

Katz, V. (2014). Children as brokers of their immigrant families' health-care connections. *Social Problems*, 61(2), 194–215.

Kaufman, G., & Compton, D. (2021). Attitudes toward LGBT marriage and legal protections post-Obergefell. *Sexuality Research and Social Policy*,

18(2), 321–330. https://doi.org/10.1007/s13178-020-00460-y

Kaufman, J. A., Salas-Hernández, L. K., Komro, K. A., & Livingston, M. D. (2020). Effects of increased minimum wages by unemployment rate on suicide in the USA. *Journal of Epidemiology and Community Health*, 74(3), 219–224. https://doi.org/10.1136/jech-2019-212981

Kawai, Y. (2005). Stereotyping Asian Americans: The dialectic of the model minority and the yellow peril. *Howard Journal of Communications*, 16(2), 109–130.

Kearney, M. S., & Levine, P. B. (2012). *Why is the teen birth rate in the United States so high and why does it matter?* National Bureau of Economic Research. https://www.nber.org/system/files/working_papers/w17964/w17964.pdf

Kearney, M. S., & Levine, P. B. (2015, March 3). *Income inequality, social mobility, and the decision to drop out of high school.* Brookings Papers on Economic Activity, Washington D.C.

Kecklund, G., & Axelsson, J. (2016). Health consequences of shift work and insufficient sleep. *BMJ*, 355, 365.

Keister, L. A. (2008). Conservative protestants and wealth: How religion perpetuates asset poverty. *American Journal of Sociology*, 113(5), 1237–1271. https://doi.org/10.1086/525506

Keister, L. A. (2011). *Faith and money: How religion contributes to wealth and poverty.* Cambridge University Press.

Keister, L. A., & Moller, S. (2000). Wealth inequality in the United States. *Annual Review of Sociology*, 26, 63–81.

Keister, L. A., & Sherkat, D. E. (Eds.). (2014). *Religion and inequality in America: Research and theory on religion's role in stratification.* Cambridge University Press.

Keller, W., & Olney, W. (2017). *Globalization and executive compensation* (No. 23384). National Bureau of Economic Research.

Kelling, G. L., & Wilson, J. Q. (1982). Broken windows: The police and neighborhood safety. *The Atlantic*, 249(3), 29–38.

Kendall, D. E. (2002). *The power of good deeds: Privileged women and the social reproduction of the upper class.* Roman & Littlefield Publishers, Inc.

Kendall, D. E. (2011). *Framing class: Media representations of wealth and poverty in America.* Rowman & Littlefield.

Kerrissey, J. (2015). Collective labor rights and income inequality. *American Sociological Review*, 80(3), 626–653.

Kessler Foundation. (2015). *The Kessler Foundation 2015 National Employment and Disability Survey: Report of main findings.* https://kesslerfoundation.org/sites/default/files/filepicker/5/KFSurvey15_Results-secured.pdf

Kessler-Harris, A. (2003). *Out to work: A history of wage-earning women in the United States.* Oxford University Press.

KFF. (2020, December 16). *Total number of Medicare beneficiaries.* Kaiser Family Foundation. https://www.kff.org/medicare/state-indicator/total-medicare-beneficiaries/

Khan, S. R. (2012a). *Privilege: The making of an adolescent elite at St. Paul's School.* Princeton University Press.

Khan, S. R. (2012b). The sociology of elites. *Annual Review of Sociology*, 38(1), 361–377. https://doi.org/10.1146/annurev-soc-071811-145542

Khimm, S. (2011, October 20). The median US wage in 2010 was just $26,363. *Washington Post.* https://www.washingtonpost.com/blogs/ezra-klein/post/the-median-us-wage-in-2010-was-just-26363-government-reports/2011/10/20/gIQAdabX0L_blog.html

Kiger, P. J. (2021). Minimum wage in America: A timeline. In *The History Channel.* The History Channel. https://www.history.com/news/minimum-wage-america-timeline

Kim, C., & Sakamoto, A. (2014). The earnings of less educated Asian American men: Educational selectivity and the model minority image. *Social Problems*, 61(2), 283–304.

Kim, D. Y. (2016). Psychiatric deinstitutionalization and prison population growth. *Criminal Justice Policy Review*, 27(1), 3–21.

Kim, J., & Chatterjee, S. (2019). Student loans, health, and life satisfaction of US households: Evidence from a panel study. *Journal of Family & Economic Issues*, 40(1), 36–50. https://doi.org/10.1007/s10834-018-9594-3

Kim, J. W., Morgan, E., & Nyhan, B. (2020). Treatment versus punishment: Understanding racial inequalities in drug policy. *Journal of Health Politics, Policy and Law*, 45(2), 177–209. https://doi.org/10.1215/03616878-8004850

Kincaid, J. D. (2017). Theorizing the radical right: Directions for social movements research on the right-wing social movements. *Sociology Compass*, 11(5), e12469. https://doi.org/10.1111/soc4.12469

King, C. R., & Springwood, C. F. (Eds.). (2001). *Team spirits: The Native American mascots controversy.* University of Nebraska Press.

King, E. B., Rogelberg, S. G., Hebl, M. R., Braddy, P. W., Shanock, L. R., Doerer, S. C., & McDowell-Larsen, S. (2016). Waistlines and ratings of executives: Does executive status overcome obesity stigma? *Human Resource Management*, 55(2), 283–300.

King, M. (2021, April 15). Reparations bill approved out of committee in historic vote. *Politico.* https://

www.politico.com/news/2021/04/15/reparations-bill-committee-historic-vote-481811

King, M. L. Jr. (1958). *Stride toward freedom: The Montgomery story*. Harper & Row.

Kirby, V. (2006). *Judith Butler: Live theory*. Continuum.

Kleiner, S., & Pavalko, E. K. (2014). Double time: Is health affected by a spouse's time at work? *Social Forces, 92*(3), 983–1007.

Kling, J. R. (2006). Incarceration length, employment, and earnings. *The American Economic Review, 96*(3), 863–876.

Knell, M., & Stix, H. (2020). Perceptions of inequality. *European Journal of Political Economy, 65*, 101927. https://doi.org/10.1016/j.ejpoleco.2020.101927

Knuckey, J., & Kim, M. (2020). The politics of White racial identity and vote choice in the 2018 midterm elections. *Social Science Quarterly, 101*(4), 1584–1599. https://doi.org/10.1111/ssqu.12809

Ko, L. (2016). Unwanted sterilization and eugenics programs in the United States. In *Independent Lens*. Corporation for Public Broadcasting. http://www.pbs.org/independentlens/blog/unwanted-sterilization-and-eugenics-programs-in-the-united-states/

Kochel, T. R., Wilson, D. B., & Mastrofski, S. D. (2011). Effect of suspect race on officers' arrest decisions. *Criminology, 49*(2), 473–512.

Kochhar, R., & Cilluffo, A. (2018). *Key findings on the rise in income inequality within America's racial and ethnic groups*. Pew Research Center. http://www.pewresearch.org/fact-tank/2018/07/12/key-findings-on-the-rise-in-income-inequality-within-americas-racial-and-ethnic-groups/

Koffmar, L. (2015, April 28). *Genetic variation is a necessity*. Phys.Org. https://phys.org/news/2015-04-genetic-variation-necessity.html

Konish, L. (2021, August 11). Where the push to bring Supplemental Security Income benefits up to federal poverty level stands. *CNBC*. https://www.cnbc.com/2021/08/11/where-a-push-to-bring-ssi-benefits-up-to-federal-poverty-level-stands.html

Konnikova, M. (2014, February 21). 18 US presidents were in college fraternities. *The Atlantic*. https://www.theatlantic.com/education/archive/2014/02/18-us-presidents-were-in-college-fraternities/283997/

Korobov, N. (2011). Young men's vulnerability in relation to women's resistance to emphasized femininity. *Men and Masculinities, 14*(1), 51–75.

Kosciw, J. G., Greytak, E. A., Palmer, N. A., & Boesen, M. J. (2014). *2013 National School Climate Survey: The Experiences of Lesbian, Gay, Bisexual and Transgender Youth in Our Nation's Schools*. GLSEN.

Kotkin, J. (2010). Ready set grow. *Smithsonian, July/August*, 61–67.

Kovalski, M. A., & Shelner, L. (2020). *How does unemployment insurance work? And how is it changing during the coronavirus pandemic?* Brookings Institution. https://www.brookings.edu/blog/up-front/2020/07/20/how-does-unemployment-insurance-work-and-how-is-it-changing-during-the-coronavirus-pandemic/

Kposowa, A. J., Breault, K. D., & Harrison, B. M. (1995). Reassessing the structural covariates of violent and property crimes in the USA: A county level analysis. *British Journal of Sociology, 46*, 79–105.

Kraus, M. W., Côté, S., & Keltner, D. (2010). Social class, contextualism, and empathic accuracy. *Psychological Science, 21*(11), 1716–1723.

Kraus, M. W., Piff, P. K., & Keltner, D. (2011). Social class as culture: The convergence of resources and rank in the social realm. *Current Directions in Psychological Science, 20*(4), 246–250.

Kraybill, D. B., & Nolt, S. M. (2004). *Amish enterprise: From plows to profits* (2nd ed.). Johns Hopkins University Press.

Kreighbaum, A. (2017, April 4). Sanders, Democratic colleagues introduce new free-college bill. *Inside Higher Education*. https://www.insidehighered.com/news/2017/04/04/sanders-democratic-colleagues-introduce-new-free-college-bill

Kriesberg, L. (1979). *Social inequality*. Prentice-Hall.

Krogstad, J. M. (2020). *Americans broadly support legal status for immigrants brought to the US illegally as children*. Pew Research Center. https://www.pewresearch.org/fact-tank/2020/06/17/americans-broadly-support-legal-status-for-immigrants-brought-to-the-u-s-illegally-as-children/

Krogstad, J. M., & Fry, R. (2014). *More Hispanics, Blacks enrolling in college, but lag in bachelor's degrees*. Pew Research Center. http://www.pewresearch.org/fact-tank/2014/04/24/more-hispanics-blacks-enrolling-in-college-but-lag-in-bachelors-degrees/

Krugler, D. F. (2014). *1919: The year of racial violence: How African Americans fought back*. Cambridge University Press.

Krysan, M., Couper, M. P., Farley, R., & Forman, T. A. (2009). Does race matter in neighborhood preferences? Results from a video experiment. *American Journal of Sociology, 115*(2), 527–559.

Kurgan, L., & Cadora, E. (2006). *Million dollar blocks*. Spatial Information Design Lab, Columbia University. http://spatialinformationdesignlab.org/projects/million-dollar-blocks

Kurlychek, M. C., & Johnson, B. D. (2019). Cumulative disadvantage in the American criminal justice system. *Annual Review of Criminology, 2*(1), 291–319. https://doi.org/10.1146/annurev-criminol-011518-024815

Kuwabara, K., & Thébaud, S. (2017). When beauty doesn't pay: Gender and beauty biases in a peer-to-peer loan market. *Social Forces*, 95(4), 1371–1398. https://doi.org/10.1093/sf/sox020

LaBriola. (2020). Post-prison employment quality and future criminal justice contact. *The Russell Sage Foundation Journal of the Social Sciences*, 6(1), 154–172. https://doi.org/10.7758/rsf.2020.6.1.07

Lamont, M. (2001). The dignity of working men: Morality and the boundaries of race, class, and immigration. *Symbolic Interaction*, 24(4), 505–508.

Lamont, M., Beljean, S., & Clair, M. (2014). What is missing? Cultural processes and causal pathways to inequality. *Socio-Economic Review*, 12(3), 573–608.

Lampe, N. M., Carter, S. K., & Sumerau, J. E. (2019). Continuity and change in gender frames: The case of transgender reproduction. *Gender & Society*, 33(6), 865–887. https://doi.org/10.1177/0891243219857979

Lane, S. D., Rubinstein, R. A., Bergen-Cico, D., Jennings-Bey, T., Fish, L. S., Larsen, D. A., Fullilove, M. T., Schimpff, T. R., Ducre, K. A., & Robinson, J. A. (2017). Neighborhood trauma due to violence: A multilevel analysis. *Journal of Health Care for the Poor and Underserved*, 28(1), 446–462. https://doi.org/10.1353/hpu.2017.0033

Lareau, A. (2011). *Unequal childhoods* (2nd ed.). University of California Press.

Lauffer, K. (2002). Access to US federal government information for people with disabilities. In M. Pendakur and R. Harris (Eds.), *Citizenship and participation in the information age*. Garamond Press.

Lauritsen, J. L., & Heimer, K. (2008). The gender gap in violent victimization, 1973–2004. *Journal of Quantitative Criminology*, 24(2), 125–147.

Lauritsen, J. L., Rezey, M. L., & Heimer, K. (2014). Violence and economic conditions in the United States, 1973–2011: Gender, race, and ethnicity patterns in the National Crime Victimization Survey. *Journal of Contemporary Criminal Justice*, 30(1), 7–28.

Lawson, M. (2017, July 19). Inequality is not inevitable, it's a policy choice. For proof, look at Namibia. *The Guardian*. https://www.theguardian.com/inequality/2017/jul/19/inequality-not-inevitable-policy-choice-namibia-commitment-reducing-inequality-index-oxfam

Lawson, M., & Martin, M. (2018). *The commitment to reducing inequality index 2018: A global ranking of governments based on what they are doing to tackle the gap between rich and poor*. Oxfam International.

Leavitt, P. A., Covarrubias, R., Perez, Y. A., & Fryberg, S. A. (2015). "Frozen in time": The impact of Native American media representations on identity and self-understanding. *Journal of Social Issues*, 71(1), 39–53.

Lebron, C. J. (2017). *The making of Black Lives Matter: A brief history of an idea*. Oxford University Press.

Lee, B. A., Tyler, K. A., & Wright, J. D. (2010). The new homelessness revisited. *Annual Review of Sociology*, 36, 501–521.

Lee, J., & Bean, F. D. (2004). America's changing color lines: Immigration, race/ethnicity, and multiracial identification. *Annual Review of Sociology*, 30, 221–242.

Lee, J., & Ramakrishnan, K. (2017, May 16). *How do we define "Asian American"?* NBC News. https://www.nbcnews.com/think

Lee, J. Y. (2014). The plateau in US women's labor force participation: A cohort analysis. *Industrial Relations: A Journal of Economy and Society*, 53(1), 46–71.

Lee, M., Pitesa, M., Pillutla, M. M., & Thau, S. (2018). Perceived entitlement causes discrimination against attractive job candidates in the domain of relatively less desirable jobs. *Journal of Personality and Social Psychology*, 114(3), 422–442. https://doi.org/10.1037/pspi0000114

Lee, M. R., & Slack, T. (2008). Labor market conditions and violent crime across the metro–nonmetro divide. *Social Science Research*, 37(3), 753–768.

Lehmann, J. M. (1995). The question of caste in modern society: Durkheim's contradictory theories of race, class, and sex. *American Sociological Review*, 60, 566–585.

Leicht, K., & Fitzgerald, S. T. (2006). *Postindustrial peasants: The illusion of middle-class prosperity*. Worth.

Lemi, D. C., & Brown, N. E. (2019). Melanin and curls: Evaluation of Black women candidates. *The Journal of Race, Ethnicity, and Politics*, 4(2), 259–296. https://doi.org/10.1017/rep.2019.18

Lengermann, P., & Niebrugge-Brantley, J. (1998). Marianne Weber (1870–1954): A woman-centered sociology. In P. Lengermann, & J. Niebrugge-Brantly (Eds.), *The women founders: Sociology and social theory, 1830–1930* (pp. 193–228). McGraw-Hill.

Lensmire, T., McManimon, S., Tierney, J. D., Lee-Nichols, M., Casey, Z., Lensmire, A., & Davis, B. (2013). McIntosh as synecdoche: How teacher education's focus on White privilege undermines antiracism. *Harvard Educational Review*, 83(3), 410–431.

Leonardo, Z. (2004). The color of supremacy: Beyond the discourse of White privilege. *Educational Philosophy and Theory*, 36(2), 137–152.

Leppel, K. (2016). The Labor force status of transgender men and women. *International Journal of Transgenderism*, 17(3–4), 155–164.

Leppel, K. (2019). Transgender men and women in 2015: Employed, unemployed, or not in the labor force. *Journal of Homosexuality*, 68(2), 203–229. https://doi.org/10.1080/00918369.2019.1648081

Leslie, S.-J., Cimpian, A., Meyer, M., & Freeland, E. (2015). Expectations of brilliance underlie gender distributions across academic disciplines. *Science*, 347(6219), 262–265.

Levine, S. B. (1980). The rise of American boarding schools and the development of a national upper class. *Social Problems*, 28, 63–94.

Levinson, M. (2017, March 23). Cash handouts for everyone. *Wall Street Journal*. http://search.proquest.com/docview/1880193989/citation/FDC9476B8DCE4DE1PQ/1

Lewis, C., Abrams, M. K., & Seervai, S. (2017). *Obstacles for low-income patients*. The Commonwealth Fund. https://www.commonwealthfund.org/blog/2017/listening-low-income-patients-obstacles-care-we-need-when-we-need-it

Lewis, G. B., & Edelson, J. L. (2000). DOMA and ENDA: Congress votes on gay rights. In C. A. Rimmerman, D. Wald, & C. Wilcox (Eds.), *The politics of gay rights* (pp. 193–216). University of Chicago Press.

Lewis, K. M., Byrd, D. A., & Ollendick, T. H. (2012). Anxiety symptoms in African-American and Caucasian youth: Relations to negative life events, social support, and coping. *Journal of Anxiety Disorders*, 26(1), 32–39.

Lewis, O. (1966). The culture of poverty. *Scientific American*, 215(4), 19–25.

Lieb, D. (2018, November 17). Midterm elections reveal effects of gerrymandered districts. *The Tifton Gazette*. https://www.tiftongazette.com/cnhi_network/midterm-elections-reveal-effects-of-gerrymandered-districts/article_b2266a8b-5d74-510f-b30e-4ab1595a4672.html

Liebler, C. A., Wise, J., & Todd, R. M. (2018). Occupational dissimilarity between the American Indian/Alaska Native and the White workforce in the contemporary United States. *American Indian Culture and Research Journal*, 42(1), 41–70. https://doi.org/10.17953/aicrj.42.1.liebler

Lindert, P. H., & Williamson, J. G. (2016). *Unequal gains*. Princeton University Press. https://press.princeton.edu/books/hardcover/9780691170497/unequal-gains

Lindsay, C. A., Lee, V., & Lloyd, T. (2018, June 21). *The prevalence of police officers in US schools*. Urban Institute. https://www.urban.org/urban-wire/prevalence-police-officers-us-schools

Liptak, A. (2010, January 21). Supreme Court blocks ban on corporate political spending. *The New York Times*. https://www.nytimes.com/2010/01/22/us/politics/22scotus.html

Lloyd, M. (2007). *Judith Butler: From norms to politics*. Polity.

LoBianco, T. (2016, March 23). Aide says Nixon's war on drugs targeted Blacks, hippies. *CNN*. https://www.cnn.com/2016/03/23/politics/john-ehrlichman-richard-nixon-drug-war-blacks-hippie/index.html

Loftus, J. (2001). America's liberalization in attitudes toward homosexuality, 1973 to 1998. *American Sociological Review*, 66, 762–782.

Logan, J. R., & Molotch, H. (2007). *Urban fortunes: The political economy of place*. University of California Press.

Logan, J. R., Zhang, W., & Alba, R. D. (2002). Immigrant enclaves and ethnic communities in New York and Los Angeles. *American Sociological Review*, 67(2), 299–322.

Logan, R. I., Melo, M. A., & Castañeda, H. (2021). Familial vulnerability: Legal status and mental health within mixed-status families. *Medical Anthropology*, 40(7), 639–652. https://doi.org/10.1080/01459740.2021.1879061

Lohr, S. (2022, January 11). Economists pin more blame on tech for rising inequality. *The New York Times*. https://www.nytimes.com/2022/01/11/technology/income-inequality-technology.html

Long, J., & Ferrie, J. (2013). Intergenerational occupational mobility in Great Britain and the United States since 1850. *American Economic Review*, 103(4), 1109–1137.

Longmore, P. K., & Goldberger, D. (2000). The League of the Physically Handicapped and the Great Depression: A case study in the new disability history. *The Journal of American History*, 87(3), 888–922.

Looney, A., & Turner, N. (2018). *Work and opportunity before and after incarceration* (Economic Studies). Brookings Institution. https://www.brookings.edu/wp-content/uploads/2018/03/es_20180314_looneyincarceration_final.pdf

Lorber, J. (2001). *Gender inequality*. Roxbury.

Loveless, T. A. (2020). *Supplemental Nutrition Assistance Program (SNAP) receipt for households: 2018* (ACSBR/20-01). US Bureau of the Census.

Loveman, M., & Muniz, J. O. (2007). How Puerto Rico became White: Boundary dynamics and intercensus racial reclassification. *American Sociological Review*, 72(6), 915–939.

Lowrey, A. (2018, January 2). The great, overlooked tax policy for getting people to work. *The Atlantic*. https://www.theatlantic.com/business/archive/2018/01/eitc-getting-people-to-work/549416/

Lowrey, A. (2021, March 3). Stockton's basic-income experiment pays off. *The Atlantic*. https://www.theatlantic.com/ideas/archive/2021/03/stocktons-basic-income-experiment-pays-off/618174/

Lucal, B. (1996). Oppression and privilege: Toward a relational conceptualization of race. *Teaching Sociology*, 24, 245–255.

Lucchesi, A., & Echo-Hawk, A. (2017). *Missing and murdered Indigenous women and girls*. Urban Indian Health Institute.

Ludwig, J., Sanbonmatsu, L., Gennetian, L., Adam, E., Duncan, G. J., Katz, L. F., Kessler, R. C., Kling, J. R., Lindau, S. T., & Whitaker, R. C. (2011). Neighborhoods, obesity, and diabetes: A randomized social experiment. *New England Journal of Medicine*, 365(16), 1509–1519.

Lurie, A. (1987). Fashion and status. In I. Robertson (Ed.), *The social world* (3rd ed., pp. 124–130). Worth.

Lurie, N. O. (1982). The American Indian: Historical background. In N. R. Yetman and C. H. Steele (Eds.), *Majority and minority: The dynamics of race and ethnicity in American life* (3rd ed.). Allyn and Bacon.

MacFarlane, S., Yarborough, R., & Barnes, S. (2021, June 9). US Capitol Insurrection Defendant Says He Has No Regrets, Sought to Confront Lawmakers. *NBC4 Washington*. https://www.nbcwashington.com/news/national-international/us-capitol-insurrection-defendant-says-he-has-no-regrets-was-seeking-to-confront-lawmakers/2692996/

MacInnis, C. C., & Hudson, G. (2012). Intergroup bias toward "Group X": Evidence of prejudice, dehumanization, avoidance, and discrimination against aesexuals. *Group Processes & Intergroup Relations*, 15(6), 725–743.

MacLeod, J. (2008). *Ain't no makin' it: Aspirations & attainment in a low-income neighborhood* (3rd ed.). Westview Press.

Maddow, R. (2015, December 22). Snyder administration allowed Flint to drink toxic water despite warnings. *The Rachel Maddow Show*. MSNBC. http://www.msnbc.com/rachel-maddow/watch/snyder-admin-knew-flint-water-toxicity-mails-590489667731

Madowitz, M., Price, A., & Weller, C. E. (2020, October 23). *Public work provides economic security for Black families and communities*. Center for American Progress. https://www.americanprogress.org/issues/economy/reports/2020/10/23/492209/public-work-provides-economic-security-black-families-communities/

Maldonado, M. M. (2009). It is their nature to do menial labour': The racialization of 'Latino/a workers' by agricultural employers. *Ethnic and Racial Studies*, 32(6), 1017–1036.

Mallory, C., Brown, T. N. T., & Conron, K. (2018). *Conversion therapy and LGBT youth*. Williams Institute. https://williamsinstitute.law.ucla.edu/demographics/conversion-therapy-and-lgbt-youth/

Mandel, H., & Semyonov, M. (2016). Going back in time? Gender differences in trends and sources of the racial pay gap, 1970 to 2010. *American Sociological Review*, 81(5), 1039–1068.

Manning, A. (2021). The elusive employment effect of the minimum wage. *Journal of Economic Perspectives*, 35(1), 3–26. https://doi.org/10.1257/jep.35.1.3

Marcus, E. (2020, August 1). The war on frats. *The New York Times*. https://www.nytimes.com/2020/08/01/style/abolish-greek-life-college-frat-racism.html

Marger, M. N. (1997). *Race and ethnic relations: American and global definitions*. Wadsworth.

Marinescu, I. (2017). *No strings attached: The behavioral effects of US unconditional cash transfer programs*. Roosevelt Institute. https://www.nber.org/papers/w24337

Marinescu, I., Skandalis, D., & Zhao, D. (2021). *The impact of the federal pandemic unemployment compensation on job search and vacancy creation* (Working Paper No. 28567; Working Paper Series). National Bureau of Economic Research. https://doi.org/10.3386/w28567

Markowitz, F. E. (2006). Psychiatric hospital capacity, homelessness, and crime and arrest rates. *Criminology*, 44(1), 45–72.

Martin, K. A. (2009). Normalizing heterosexuality: Mothers' assumptions, talk, and strategies with young children. *American Sociological Review*, 74(2), 190–207. https://doi.org/10.1177/000312240907400202

Marx, K. (1967). *Capital* (S. Moore and E. Aveling, Trans.; Vol. 1). International Publishers.

Marx, K., & Engels, F. (1969). *Selected works* (Vol. 1). Progress Publishers.

Marx, K., & Engels, F. (1970). *Selected works* (Vol. 2). Progress Publishers.

Masci, D. (2016). *How income varies among US religious groups*. Pew Research Center. https://www.pewresearch.org/fact-tank/2016/10/11/how-income-varies-among-u-s-religious-groups/

Massey, D. S. (2007). *Categorically Unequal: The American Stratification Series*. Russell Sage Foundation. http://www.jstor.org/stable/10.7758/9781610443807.6

Massey, D. S., & Denton, N. A. (1993). *American apartheid: Segregation and the making of the underclass*. Harvard University Press.

Massey, D. S., Durand, J., & Pren, K. A. (2015). Border enforcement and return migration by documented and undocumented Mexicans. *Journal of Ethnic and Migration Studies*, 41(7), 1015–1040.

Massey, D. S., & Pren, K. A. (2012). Unintended consequences of US immigration policy: Explaining the post-1965 surge from Latin America. *Population and Development Review*, 38(1), 1–29.

Massey, S. G., Mattson, R. E., Chen, M.-H., Hardesty, M., Merriwether, A., Young, S. R., & Parker, M. M. (2021). Trending queer: Emerging adults and the growing resistance to compulsory heterosexuality. In E. M. Morgan, & M. Van Dulmen (Eds.), *Sexuality in emerging adulthood* (pp. 181–198). Oxford University Press.

Mathema, S., Svajlenka, N. P., & Hermann, A. (2018, September 2). *Revival and opportunity.* Center for American Progress. https://www.americanprogress.org/issues/immigration/reports/2018/09/02/455269/revival-and-opportunity/

Matsick, J. L., & Rubin, J. D. (2018). Bisexual prejudice among lesbian and gay people: Examining the roles of gender and perceived sexual orientation. *Psychology of Sexual Orientation and Gender Diversity, 5*(2), 143–155.

Matsuzawa, S. (2019). *Activating China: Local actors, foreign influence, and state response.* Routledge.

Matthews, D. (2017, April 27). Child poverty in the US is a disgrace. Experts are embracing this simple plan to cut it. *Vox.* https://www.vox.com/policy-and-politics/2017/4/27/15388696/child-benefit-universal-cash-tax-credit-allowance

Maume, D. J. (2004). Wage discrimination over the life course: A comparison of explanations. *Social Problems, 51*(4), 505–527.

Maxwell, J., Bourgoin, A., & Lindenfeld, Z. (2020, February 10). *Battling the mental health crisis among the underserved through state Medicaid reforms.* Health Affairs Blog. https://www.healthaffairs.org/do/10.1377/hblog20200205.346125/full/

Mayerson, A. (1992). *The history of Americans with Disabilities Act.* Disability Rights Education & Defense Fund. https://dredf.org/about-us/publications/the-history-of-the-ada/

Mazumder, B. (2005). Fortunate sons: New estimates of intergenerational mobility in the United States using Social Security earnings data. *Review of Economics and Statistics, 87*(2), 235–255.

Mazza, E. (2017, January 27). GOP lawmaker in Mississippi proposes fines And psychological counseling for saggy pants. *Huffington Post.* http://www.huffingtonpost.com/entry/sagging-pants-bill-mississippi_us_588aed2ce4b0230ce61b2e9c

McAdam, D. (2003). Beyond structural analysis: Toward a more dynamic understanding of social movements. In M. Diani, & D. McAdam (Eds.), *Social movements and networks* (pp. 281–298). Oxford University Press.

McAdam, D. (2010). *Political process and the development of Black insurgency, 1930–1970.* University of Chicago Press.

McAdam, D. (2017). Social movement theory and the prospects for climate change activism in the United States. *Annual Review of Political Science, 20*(1), 189–208.

McBride, A., Hebson, G., & Holgate, J. (2015). Intersectionality: Are we taking enough notice in the field of work and employment relations? *Work, Employment & Society, 29*(2), 331–341.

McCaffrey, O., & Shifflett, S. (2021, June 27). During COVID-19, most Americans got ahead—Especially the rich. *Wall Street Journal.* https://www.wsj.com/articles/during-covid-19-most-americans-got-richerespecially-the-rich-11624791602

McCall, L. (2005). The complexity of intersectionality. *Signs: Journal of Women in Culture and Society, 30*(3), 1771–1800.

McCall, L (2014). The political meanings of social class inequality. *Social Currents, 1*(1), 25–34.

McClellan, F. M., White, A. A., Jimenez, R. L., & Fahmy, S. (2012). Do poor people sue doctors more frequently? Confronting unconscious bias and the role of cultural competency. *Clinical Orthopaedics and Related Research, 470*(5), 1393–1397. https://doi.org/10.1007/s11999-012-2254-2

McCluney, C. L., Durkee, M. I., Smith, R. E., Robotham, K. J., & Lee, S. S.-L. (2021). To be, or not to be … Black: The effects of racial codeswitching on perceived professionalism in the workplace. *Journal of Experimental Social Psychology, 97,* 104199. https://doi.org/10.1016/j.jesp.2021.104199

McCulloch, H. (2017). *Closing the women's wealth gap: What it is, why it matters, and what can be done about it.* Closing the Women's Wealth Gap Project.

McDade, A. (2022, January 4). 300 low-income residents to receive $500 a month from city of Atlanta in pilot program. *Newsweek.* https://www.newsweek.com/300-low-income-residents-receive-500-month-city-atlanta-pilot-program-1665545

McDonald, S. (2011). What's in the "old boys" network? Accessing social capital in gendered and racialized networks. *Social Networks, 33*(4), 317–330.

McDow, K. B., Nguyen, D. T., Herrick, K. A., & Akinbami, L. J. (2019). *Attempts to lose weight among adolescents aged 16–19 in the United States* (Data Brief No. 340). Centers for Disease Control. https://www.cdc.gov/nchs/products/databriefs/db340.htm

McFarland, A. S. (2007). Neopluralism. *Annual Review of Political Science, 10*(1), 45–66.

McGrail, S. (2013). *The Philadelphia Negro.* Encyclopedia of Greater Philadelphia. http://philadelphiaencyclopedia.org/archive/philadelphia-negro-the/#5032

McIntosh, P. (1988). *White privilege and male privilege: A personal account of coming to see correspondences through work in women's studies*

(Working Paper No. 189). Center for Research on Women.

McIntosh, P. (2004). White privilege: Unpacking the invisible knapsack. In P. S. Rothenberg (Ed.), *Race, class, and gender in the United States: An integrated study* (pp. 188–192). MacMillan.

McLanahan, S. (2009). Fragile families and the reproduction of poverty. *The Annals of the American Academy of Political and Social Science, 621*(1), 111–131.

McLeod, J. D., & Nonnemaker, J. M. (1999). Social stratification and inequality. In C. S. Aneshensel and J. C. Phelan (Eds.), *Handbook of the sociology of mental health*. Springer.

McRuer, R. (2006). *Crip theory: Cultural signs of queerness and disability*. New York University Press.

McVeigh, R. (2006). Structural influences on activism and crime: Identifying the social structure of discontent. *American Journal of Sociology, 112*(2), 510–566.

McVeigh, R. (2009). *The rise of the Ku Klux Klan: Right-wing movements and national politics*. University of Minnesota Press.

Meadows, S., Engel, C., Collins, R., Beckman, R., Cefalu, M., Hawes-Dawson, J., Doyle, M., Kress, A., Sontag-Padilla, L., Ramchand, R., & Williams, K. (2018). *2015 health related behaviors survey: Summary findings and policy implications* (RR-1695-OS). RAND Corporation. https://doi.org/10.7249/RB9955

Meltzer, H., Bebbington, P., Brugha, T., Jenkins, R., McManus, S., & Stansfeld, S. (2010). Job insecurity, socio-economic circumstances and depression. *Psychological Medicine, 40*(8), 1401–1407.

Mental Health America. (2016). *Access to mental health care and incarceration*. Mental Health America. http://www.mentalhealthamerica.net/issues/access-mental-health-care-and-incarceration

Merikangas, K. R., He, J., Burstein, M., Swanson, S. A., Avenevoli, S., Cui, L., Benjet, C., Georgiades, K., & Swendsen, J. (2010). Lifetime prevalence of mental disorders in US adolescents: Results from the National Comorbidity Survey Replication–Adolescent Supplement. *Journal of the American Academy of Child & Adolescent Psychiatry, 49*(10), 980–989.

Messerschmidt, J. W. (1993). *Masculinities and crime: Critique and reconceptualization of theory*. Rowman & Littlefield.

Metin-Orta, I., & Metin-Camgöz, S. (2020). Attachment style, openness to experience, and social contact as predictors of attitudes toward homosexuality. *Journal of Homosexuality, 67*(4), 528–553. https://doi.org/10.1080/00918369.2018.1547562

Meyer, B. D., & Corinth, K. (2021, October 14). Why extending the current child tax credit would do more harm than good. *Washington Post*. https://www.washingtonpost.com/opinions/2021/10/14/press-pause-rush-extend-child-tax-credit/

Meyer, I. H. (2019, June 27). *How do you measure the LGBT population in the US?* Gallup Polls. https://news.gallup.com/opinion/methodology/259457/measure-lgbt-population.aspx

Meyer, L., & Floyd, I. (2020, November 30). *Cash assistance should reach millions more families to lessen hardship*. Center on Budget and Policy Priorities. https://www.cbpp.org/research/family-income-support/cash-assistance-should-reach-millions-more-families-to-lessen

Michelmore, K., & Lopoo, L. M. (2021). The effect of EITC exposure in childhood on marriage and early childbearing. *Demography, 58*(6), 2365–2394. https://doi.org/10.1215/00703370-9506903

Migration Policy Institute. (2021). *Profile of the unauthorized population*. Data Hub: Unauthorized Immigrant Population. https://www.migrationpolicy.org/data/unauthorized-immigrant-population/state/US

Miles, T. (2019). Beyond a boundary: Black lives and the settler-native divide. *The William and Mary Quarterly, 76*(3), 417–426. https://doi.org/10.5309/willmaryquar.76.3.0417

Miliband, R. (1977). *Marxism and politics*. Oxford University Press.

Miller, C. C. (2021, May 18). The pandemic created a child-care crisis. Mothers bore the burden. *The New York Times*. https://www.nytimes.com/interactive/2021/05/17/upshot/women-workforce-employment-covid.html

Miller, N. (2006). *Out of the past: Gay & lesbian history from 1869 to the present* (Updated). Alyson Books.

Miller, S. M. (Ed.). (1963). *Max Weber: Selections from his work*. Thomas Y. Crowell.

Mills, C. W. (1956). *The power elite*. Oxford University Press.

Milner, M. (2016). *Freaks, geeks, and cool kids: Teenagers in an era of consumerism, standardized tests, and social media*. Routledge.

Minkoff, S. L., & Lyons, J. (2019). Living with inequality: Neighborhood income diversity and perceptions of the income gap. *American Politics Research, 47*(2), 329–361. https://doi.org/10.1177/1532673X17733799

Mirowsky, J., & Ross, C. E. (2003). *Social causes of psychological distress* (2nd ed.). Aldine.

Mishel, L., & Kandra, J. (2020a). *CEO compensation surged 14% in 2019 to $21.3 million: CEOs now earn 320 times as much as a typical worker*. Economic Policy Institute. https://www.epi.org/publication/ceo-compensation-surged-14-in-2019-to-21-3-million-ceos-now-earn-320-times-as-much-as-a-typical-worker/

Mishel, L., & Kandra, J. (2020b, December 1). *Wages for the top 1% skyrocketed 160% since 1979 while the share of wages for the bottom 90% shrunk:*

Time to remake wage pattern with economic policies that generate robust wage-growth for vast majority. *Economic Policy Institute*. https://www.epi.org/blog/wages-for-the-top-1-skyrocketed-160-since-1979-while-the-share-of-wages-for-the-bottom-90-shrunk-time-to-remake-wage-pattern-with-economic-policies-that-generate-robust-wage-growth-for-vast-majority/

Mishel, L., & Kandra, J. (2021). *CEO pay has skyrocketed 1,322% since 1978*. Economic Policy Institute.

Mishel, L. R., Bernstein, J., & Allegretto, S. (2007). *The state of working America 2006/2007*. Cornell University Press.

Mistry, R. S., Brown, C. S., White, E. S., Chow, K. A., & Gillen-O'Neel, N. (2015). Elementary school children's reasoning about social class: A mixed-methods study. *Child Development, 86*(5), 1653–1671.

Mitropolous, A. (2021, March 2). Thousands of students reported "missing" from school systems nationwide amid COVID-19 pandemic. *ABC News*. https://abcnews.go.com/US/thousands-students-reported-missing-school-systems-nationwide-amid/story?id=76063922

Mitzman, A. (1970). *The iron cage: An historical interpretation of Max Weber*. Transaction Publishers.

Mize, R. L. (2016). *The invisible workers of the US-Mexico Bracero Program: Obreros olvidados*. Lexington Books.

Mizruchi, M. (2017). The Power Elite in historical context: A reevaluation of Mills's thesis, then and now. *Theory & Society, 46*(2), 95–116. https://doi.org/10.1007/s11186-017-9284-4

Moffitt, R. A. (2015). The deserving poor, the family, and the US welfare system. *Demography, 52*(3), 729–749.

Mohamed, B. (2021). Muslims are a growing presence in US, but still face negative views from the public. *Pew Research Center*. https://www.pewresearch.org/fact-tank/2021/09/01/muslims-are-a-growing-presence-in-u-s-but-still-face-negative-views-from-the-public/

Mohanty, A. (2019). *Poverty dynamics: An overview of longitudinal poverty estimates produced by the United States Census Bureau* (No. 2019-38). US Census Bureau. https://www.census.gov/content/dam/Census/library/working-papers/2019/demo/SEHSD-WP2019-38.pdf

Moledina, A. A., McConnell, D. L., Sugars, S. A., & Connor, B. R. (2014). Amish economic transformations: New forms of income and wealth distribution in a traditionally "flat" community. *Journal of Amish and Plain Anabaptist Studies, 2*(1), 1–22.

Molina, N. (2014). *How race is made in America: Immigration, citizenship, and the historical power of racial scripts*. University of California Press.

Monk, E. P. Jr. (2014). Skin tone stratification among Black Americans, 2001–2003. *Social Forces, 92*(4), 1313–1337.

Moore, B. J., Stocks, C., & Owens, P. L. (2017). *Trends in emergency department visits, 2006–2014* (HCUP Statistical Brief No. 227). Agency for Healthcare Research and Quality. https://www.hcup-us.ahrq.gov/reports/statbriefs/sb227-Emergency-Department-Visit-Trends.jsp?utm_source=ahrq&utm_medium=en1&utm_term&utm_content=1&utm_campaign=ahrq_en10_17_2017

Mora, G. C. (2014). Cross-field effects and ethnic classification: The institutionalization of Hispanic panethnicity, 1965 to 1990. *American Sociological Review, 79*(2), 183–210.

Morgan, E., Salomon, N., Plotkin, M., & Cohen, R. (2014). *The school discipline consensus report*. The Council of State Governments Justice Center. http://csgjusticecenter.org/wp-content/uploads/2014/06/The_School_Discipline_Consensus_Report.pdf

Morgan, R. E., & Thompson, A. (2021). *Criminal victimization, 2020* (NCJ 301775). National Crime Victimization Survey, Bureau of Justice Statistics. Vol. 4

Morris, A. D. (1986). *Origins of the civil rights movements*. Simon and Schuster.

Morris, A. D. (1999). A retrospective on the civil right movement: Political and intellectual landmarks. *Annual Review of Sociology, 25*(1), 517–539. https://doi.org/10.1146/annurev.soc.25.1.517

Morris, A. D. (2015). *The scholar denied: W.E.B. Du Bois and the birth of modern sociology*. University of California Press.

Morris, T., & Howard, B. (2019). *Tribal technology assessment: The state of internet service on tribal lands*. American Indian Policy Institute. https://www.ssrn.com/abstract=3427547

Morrison, A., Stafford, K., & Swanson, E. (2021, March 12). AP-NORC poll: People of color bear COVID-19's economic brunt. *ABC News*. https://abcnews.go.com/Health/wireStory/ap-norc-poll-people-color-bear-covid-19s-76412750

Morrissey, T. W., & Vinopal, K. M. (2018). Neighborhood poverty and children's academic skills and behavior in early elementary school: Neighborhoods in early elementary school. *Journal of Marriage and Family, 80*(1), 182–197.

Morrow, A. (2021, May 10). Jeff Bezos' superyacht is so big it needs its own yacht. *CNN*. https://www.cnn.com/2021/05/10/business/jeff-bezos-yacht/index.html

Moss, K. (2021). Russia's queer science, or how anti-LGBT scholarship is made. *The Russian Review, 80*(1), 17–36. https://doi.org/10.1111/russ.12296

Mouw, T., & Kalleberg, A. L. (2010). Occupations and the structure of wage inequality in the United

States, 1980s to 2000s. *American Sociological Review, 75*(3), 402–431.

Movement Advancement Project. (2018). *Local non-discrimination ordinances.* http://www.lgbtmap.org/equality-maps/non_discrimination_ordinances

Movement Advancement Project. (2021a). *Foster and adoption laws.* Equality Maps. https://www.lgbtmap.org//equality-maps/foster_and_adoption_laws

Movement Advancement Project. (2021b). *State nondiscrimination laws.* Equality Maps. https://www.lgbtmap.org//equality-maps/non_discrimination_laws

Mowen, T., & Brent, J. (2016). School discipline as a turning point: The cumulative effect of suspension on arrest. *Journal of Research in Crime and Delinquency, 53*(5), 628–653.

Mower, L., & Taylor, L. (2020, October 7). Florida's felon voting law leaves thousands wondering whether it's safe to vote. *Tampa Bay Times.* https://www.tampabay.com/news/florida-politics/elections/2020/10/07/florida-ruled-felons-must-pay-to-vote-now-it-doesnt-know-how-many-can/

Murnane, R. J., Mbekeani, P. P., Reardon, S. F., & Lamb, A. (2018, July 17). Who goes to private school? *Education Next.* https://www.educationnext.org/who-goes-private-school-long-term-enrollment-trends-family-income/

Murray, S. O. (1996). *American gay.* University of Chicago Press.

Myers, L. A. Jr. (2014). Globalization, corporate social responsibility, and ethical considerations. *Journal of Management, 2*(2), 45–61.

Na, C., & Gottfredson, D. C. (2013). Police officers in schools: Effects on school crime and the processing of offending behaviors. *Justice Quarterly, 30*(4), 619–650. https://doi.org/10.1080/07418825.2011.615754

Nachescu, V. (2008). Radical feminism and the nation. *Journal for the Study of Radicalism, 3,* 29–54.

Nadal, K. L., Davidoff, K. C., Davis, L. S., Wong, Y., Marshall, D., & McKenzie, V. (2015). A qualitative approach to intersectional microaggressions: Understanding influences of race, ethnicity, gender, sexuality, and religion. *Qualitative Psychology, 2*(2), 147–163.

Nam, Y. (2004). Is America becoming more equal for children? Changes in the intergenerational transmission of low- and high-income status. *Social Science Research, 33*(2), 187–205.

Nandi, A., Jahagirdar, D., Labreque, J., Strumpf, E., Kaufman, J., Vincent, I., Atabay, E., Sam, H., Earle, A., & Heyman, J. (2018). The impact of parental and medical leave policies on socioeconomic and health outcomes in OECD countries. *Milbank Quarterly, 96*(e), 434–474.

Nasrin, S., & Fisher, D. R. (2021). Understanding collective identity in virtual spaces: A study of the youth climate movement. *American Behavioral Scientist,* 000276422110562. https://doi.org/10.1177/00027642211056257

Nathans, S. J. (2001). Twelve years after Price Waterhouse and still no success for Hopkins in drag: The lack of protection for the male victim of gender stereotyping under Title VII. *Villanova Law Review, 46,* 713–744.

National Alliance to End Homelessness. (2018). *State of homelessness.* https://endhomelessness.org/homelessness-in-america/homelessness-statistics/state-of-homelessness-report/

National Archives. (2016, August 15). *Brown v. Board of Education.* National Archives. https://www.archives.gov/education/lessons/brown-v-board

National Association of Black Journalists. (2020, June). *NABJ style guide.* https://www.nabj.org/page/styleguide

National Center for Education Statistics. (2020). *Digest of education statistics, 2019.* https://nces.ed.gov/programs/digest/d19/tables/dt19_322.20.asp

National Center for Health Statistics. (2010). *Health: United States 2009.* U.S. Department of Health and Human Services.

National Council of Urban Indian Health. (n.d.). *Relocation.* National Council of Urban Indian Health. https://www.google.com/url?sa=t&rct=j&q=&esrc=s&source=web&cd=6&ved=0ahUKEwiaqdeEmLHcAhWIiOAKHewbD7MQFghwMAU&url=https%3A%2F%2Fwww.ncuih.org%2Faction%2Fdocument%2Fdownload%3Fdocument_id%3D120&usg=AOvVaw1mkslucICyidJQDxnPBsDM

National Institute on Drug Abuse. (2021a, January 29). *Overdose death rates.* https://www.drugabuse.gov/drug-topics/trends-statistics/overdose-death-rates

National Institute on Drug Abuse. (2021b, March 11). *Opioid overdose crisis.* https://www.drugabuse.gov/drug-topics/opioids/opioid-overdose-crisis

National Institute of Health. (2021). *Table 16: Respondent-assessed fair or poor health status, by selected characteristics: United Sates selected years 1991–2018.* https://www.ncbi.nlm.nih.gov/books/NBK569311/table/ch3.tab16/

National Park Service. (2021, November 29). *American Indians and the Homestead Act—Homestead National Historical Park.* https://www.nps.gov/home/learn/historyculture/american-indians-and-the-homestead-act.htm

National Restaurant Association. (2021). *State of the restaurant industry: Mid-year update.* https://go.restaurant.org/rs/078-ZLA-461/images/2021-SOI_Mid-Year%20Update%20Final.pdf

NCSL. (2021, June 9). *Undocumented student tuition: Overview.* National Conference of State Legislatures. https://www.ncsl.org/research/education/undocumented-student-tuition-overview.aspx

Nelson, K. (2012). Counteracting material deprivation: The role of social assistance in Europe. *Journal of European Social Policy*, 22(2), 148–163. https://doi.org/10.1177/0958928711433658

Newkirk, V. R. (2017, October 28). We're a lot better at gerrymandering than we used to be. *The Atlantic.* https://www.theatlantic.com/politics/archive/2017/10/gerrymandering-technology-redmap-2020/543888/

Ng, M. K., Ng, K. K., Song, S., Emara, A. K., Ngo, J., Patel, A., Shah, N., Mossialos, E., Salas-Vega, S., Mont, M., & Piuzzi, N. (2020). US healthcare insurance market concentration from 2001 to 2016: Increased growth in direct written premiums and overall decreased market consolidation. *Cureus*, 12(3), e7491. https://doi.org/10.7759/cureus.7491

Nicholson, P. Y. (2004). *Labor's story in the United States.* Temple University Press.

Nielsen, A. L., Martinez, R., & Lee, M. T. (2005). Alcohol, ethnicity, and violence: The role of alcohol availability for Latino and Black aggravated assaults and robberies. *The Sociological Quarterly*, 46(3), 479–502.

Nielsen, F., Roos, J. M., & Combs, R. M. (2015). Clues of subjective social status among young adults. *Social Science Research*, 52, 370–388.

NIH. (2021). *Table 16, Respondent-assessed fair or poor health status, by selected characteristics: United States, selected years 1991–2018.* National Center for Health Statistics (US). https://www.ncbi.nlm.nih.gov/books/NBK569311/table/ch3.tab16/

NIMH. (2021). *Mental illness.* National Institutes of Mental Health. https://www.nimh.nih.gov/health/statistics/mental-illness

Noack, R. (2015, February 4). Why Danish students are paid to go to college. *Washington Post.* https://www.washingtonpost.com/news/worldviews/wp/2015/02/04/why-danish-students-are-paid-to-go-to-college/

Noe-Bustamante, L., Mora, L., & Lopez, M. H. (2020, August 11). Latinx used by just 3% of US Hispanics; about one-in-four have heard of it. *Pew Research Center's Hispanic Trends Project.* https://www.pewresearch.org/hispanic/2020/08/11/about-one-in-four-u-s-hispanics-have-heard-of-latinx-but-just-3-use-it/

Nowotny, K. M., Omori, M., McKenna, M., & Kleinman, J. (2020). Incarceration rates and incidence of sexually transmitted infections in US counties, 2011–2016. *American Journal of Public Health*, 110(S1), 130–136. https://doi.org/10.2105/AJPH.2019.305425

NPR. (2010, June 10). A *"queer"* argument against marriage. https://www.npr.org/templates/story/story.php?storyId=127740436

NPR, Robert Wood Johnson Foundation, and the Harvard T.H. Chan School of Public Health.

(2020). *Life experiences and income inequality in the United States.* https://apps.npr.org/documents/document.html?id=6603517-Income-Inequality-Report-January-2020

NSF. (2019, September 19). *Scientists project northward expansion of valley fever by end of 21st century.* National Science Foundation Research News. https://nsf.gov/discoveries/disc_summ.jsp?cntn_id=299221&org=NSF&from=news

Nurse, A. M. (2002). *Fatherhood arrested: Parenting from within the juvenile justice system.* Vanderbilt University Press.

Nurse, A. M. (2017). Knowledge and behavioral impact of adult participation in child sexual abuse prevention: Evaluation of the Protecting God's Children program. *Journal of Child Sexual Abuse*, 26(5), 608–624. https://openworks.wooster.edu/cgi/viewcontent.cgi?article=1230&context=facpub

Nurse, A. M. (2020). *Confronting child sexual abuse: Knowledge to action.* Lever Press. https://doi.org/10.3998/mpub.12085149

OECD. (2021a). *Employment: Time spent in paid and unpaid work, by sex.* https://stats.oecd.org/index.aspx?queryid=54757

OECD. (2021b). *Family database.* https://www.oecd.org/els/family/database.htm

OECD. (2021c). *Inequality: Poverty rate.* OECD Data. http://data.oecd.org/inequality/poverty-rate.htm

OECD. (2022). *Income inequality.* https://data.oecd.org/inequality/income-inequality.htm

Office of the Historian. (2016). *Chinese immigration and the Chinese Exclusion Acts.* US Department of State. https://history.state.gov/milestones/1866-1898/chinese-immigration

Oliver, M. L., & Shapiro, T. M. (2006). *Black wealth, White wealth: A new perspective on racial inequality.* Taylor & Francis.

Ollman, B. (1968). Marx's use of "class." *American Journal of Sociology*, 73, 573–580.

Olsen, E. O. (2007). *Promoting homeownership among low-income households.* The Urban Institute.

Omi, M., & Menendian, S. (2014). *Responding to rising inequality: Policy interventions to ensure opportunity for all.* Haas Institute for a Fair and Inclusive Society.

Omi, M., & Winant, H. (2005). The theoretical status of the concept of race. In C. McCarthy, W. Crichlow, G. Dimitriadis, and N. Dolby (Eds.), *Race, identity, and representation in education* (2nd ed.). Routledge.

Omi, M., & Winant, H. (2015). *Racial formation in the United States* (3rd ed.). Routledge/Taylor & Francis Group.

Onishi, N. (2015, December 20). US support of gay rights in Africa may have done more harm than good. *The New York Times.* http://www.nytimes.

com/2015/12/21/world/africa/us-support-of-gay-rights-in-africa-may-have-done-more-harm-than-good.html

Open Secrets. (2021). *2020 outside spending, by super PAC.* https://www.opensecrets.org/outsides-pending/summ.php?cycle=2020&chrt=V&disp=O&type=S

Ortega, F., Edwards, R. D., & Hsin, A. (2018). *The economic effects of providing legal status to DREAMers* (IZA DP 11281). Institute of Labor Economics.

OSCE/ODIHR. (2021). *Hate crime reporting.* Organization for Security and Co-operation in Europe: Office for Democratic Institutions and Human Rights. https://hatecrime.osce.org/

Osterman, M. J. K., & Martin, J. A. (2018). *Timing and adequacy of prenatal care in the United States, 2016.* National Center for Health Statistics.

Ostrander, S. (1983). *Women of the upper class.* Temple University Press.

Overberg, P. (2018, January 30). Census change to race, ethnicity questions shelved by Trump administration delay. *Wall Street Journal.* https://www.wsj.com/articles/census-change-to-race-ethnicity-questions-shelved-by-trump-administration-delay-1517262931

Oxfam International. (2021, February 19). *Mega-rich recoup COVID-losses in record-time yet billions will live in poverty for at least a decade.* https://www.oxfam.org/en/press-releases/mega-rich-recoup-covid-losses-record-time-yet-billions-will-live-poverty-least

Padavic, I., & Reskin, B. F. (2002). *Women and men at work.* Pine Forge Press.

Padilla, A. M. (1994). Ethnic minority scholars, research, and mentoring: Current and future issues. *Educational Researcher, 23*(4), 24–27.

Page, B. I., & Jacobs, L. R. 2009. *Class War? What Americans really think about economic inequality.* University of Chicago Press.

Pager, D. (2003). The mark of a criminal record. *American Journal of Sociology, 108*(5), 937–975.

Painter, N. (2020, July 22). Why 'White' should be capitalized, too. *Washington Post.* https://www.washingtonpost.com/opinions/2020/07/22/why-white-should-be-capitalized/

Palmer, B., & Simon, D. (2010). *Breaking the political glass ceiling: Women and Congressional elections.* Routledge.

Parasurama, P., Ghose, A., & Ipeirotis, P. G. (2020). *Determinants of occupational segregation across race and gender: Evidence from sourcing, screening, and hiring in IT firms* (Scholarly Paper No. 3672484). Social Science Research Network. https://doi.org/10.2139/ssrn.3672484

Parent, M. C., Hammer, J. H., Bradstreet, T. C., Schwartz, E. N., & Jobe, T. (2018). Men's mental health help-seeking behaviors: An intersectional analysis. *American Journal of Men's Health, 12*(1), 64–73.

Parenti, M. (1970). Power and pluralism: A view from the bottom. *The Journal of Politics, 32*(3), 501–530.

Parijs, P. V., & Vanderborght, Y. (2017). *Basic income: A radical proposal for a free society and a sane economy.* Harvard University Press.

Parisi, D., Lichter, D. T., & Taquino, M. C. (2011). Multi-scale residential segregation: Black exceptionalism and America's changing color line. *Social Forces, 89*(3), 829–852.

Parker, K., Doherty, C., & Rohal, M. (2016). *Most Americans say government doesn't do enough to help middle class.* Pew Research Center.

Parreñas, R. (2015). *Servants of globalization* (2nd ed.). Stanford University Press.

Passel, J., & Rohal, M. (2015). *Modern immigration wave brings 59 million to US, driving population growth and change through 2065.* Pew Research Center.

Pastor, L., & Veronesi, P. (2018). *Inequality aversion, populism, and the backlash against globalization* (Working Paper No. 24900). National Bureau of Economic Research. http://www.nber.org/papers/w24900

Paxton, P., Hughes, M. M., & Green, J. L. (2006). The international women's movement and women's political representation, 1893–2003. *American Sociological Review, 71*(6), 898–920.

Pedace, R., & Rohn Kumar, S. (2014). A warm embrace or the cold shoulder? Wage and employment outcomes in ethnic enclaves. *Contemporary Economic Policy, 32*(1), 93–110.

Pell, M. B., & Schneyer, J. (2016). Thousands of US areas afflicted with lead poisoning beyond Flint's. *Scientific American.* https://www.scientificamerican.com/article/thousands-of-u-s-areas-afflicted-with-lead-poisoning-beyond-flints

Penner, A. M., & Willer, R. (2019). Men's overpersistence and the gender gap in science and mathematics. *Socius: Sociological Research for a Dynamic World, 5,* 237802311882183. https://doi.org/10.1177/2378023118821836

Peoples, C. D., & Gortari, M. (2008). The Impact of campaign contributions of policymaking in the US and Canada: Theoretical and public policy implications. *Politics and Public Policy, 17,* 43–64.

Pérez Huber, L., Vélez, V. N., & Solórzano, D. (2018). More than "papelitos:" a quantcrit counterstory to critique Latina/o degree value and occupational prestige. *Race Ethnicity and Education, 21*(2), 208–230. https://doi.org/10.1080/13613324.2017.1377416

Peri, G. (2014). Does immigration hurt the poor? *Pathways, Summer,* 15–18.

Peri, G., Shih, K., & Sparber, C. (2015). *Foreign and native skilled workers: What can we learn from H-1B lotteries?* (Working Paper No. 21175). National Bureau of Economic Research. https://doi.org/10.3386/w21175

Perry, A. M., &Ray, R. (2020). *Why we need reparations for Black Americans.* Brookings Institution. https://www.brookings.edu/policy 2020/bigideas/why-we-need-reparations-for-black-americans/

Persmark, A., Wemrell, M., Evans, C. R., Subramanian, S. V., Leckie, G., & Merlo, J. (2020). Intersectional inequalities and the US opioid crisis: Challenging dominant narratives and revealing heterogeneities. *Critical Public Health, 30*(4), 398–414. https://doi.org/10.1080/09581596.2019.1626002

Petersen, T., & Saporta, I. (2004). The opportunity structure for discrimination. *American Journal of Sociology, 109*(4), 852–901.

Peterson, R. D., & Krivo, L. J. (2009). Segregated spatial locations, race-ethnic composition, and neighborhood violent crime. *The Annals of the American Academy of Political and Social Science, 623*(1), 93–107.

Peterson-Withorn, C. (2021, April 30). How much money America's billionaires have made during the Covid-19 pandemic. *Forbes.* https://www.forbes.com/sites/chasewithorn/2021/04/30/american-billionaires-have-gotten-12-trillion-richer-during-the-pandemic/

Petsko, C. D., & Bodenhausen, G. V. (2019). Racial stereotyping of gay men: Can a minority sexual orientation erase race? *Journal of Experimental Social Psychology, 83*, 37–54. https://doi.org/10.1016/j.jesp.2019.03.002

Pettigrew, T. F., & Tropp, L. R. (2006). A meta-analytic test of intergroup contact theory. *Journal of Personality and Social Psychology, 90*(5), 751–783. https://doi.org/10.1037/0022-3514.90.5.751

Pew Research Center. (2012). *For the public, it's not about class warfare, but fairness.* http://www.people-press.org/2012/03/02/for-the-public-its-not-about-class-warfare-but-fairness/

Pew Research Center. (2015a). *Multiracial in America.* http://www.pewsocialtrends.org/2015/06/11/multiracial-in-america/

Pew Research Center. (2015b). *Changing attitudes on gay marriage.* Pew Research Center. http://www.pewforum.org/2015/07/29/graphics-slideshow-changing-attitudes-on-gay-marriage/

Pew Research Center. (2016a). *Do limits on family assets affect participation in, costs of TANF?* Issue Brief. http://pew.org/29n0ICJ

Pew Research Center. (2016b). *Having a parent behind bars costs children, states.* http://pew.org/1U9FMzl

Pew Research Center. (2016c, October 26). The links between religious upbringing, current religious identity. *Pew Research Center's Religion & Public Life Project.* https://www.pewforum.org/2016/10/26/links-between-childhood-religious-upbringing-and-current-religious-identity/

Pew Research Center. (2017a, July 26). Demographic portrait of Muslim Americans. *Pew Research Center's Religion & Public Life Project.* https://www.pewforum.org/2017/07/26/demographic-portrait-of-muslim-americans/

Pew Research Center. (2017b). *US Muslims concerned about their place in society, but continue to believe in the American dream.*

Pew Research Center. (2018). *Shifting public views on legal immigration into the US.* https://www.pewresearch.org/politics/2018/06/28/shifting-public-views-on-legal-immigration-into-the-u-s/

Pew Research Center. (2019a, May 2). Most Blacks say someone has acted suspicious of them or as if they weren't smart. *Pew Research Center's Social & Demographic Trends Project.* https://www.pewresearch.org/social-trends/wp-content/uploads/sites/3/2019/05/PSDT_03.25.19_race_update-03.png

Pew Research Center. (2019b, July 23). How Americans feel toward religious groups. *Pew Research Center's Religion & Public Life Project.* https://www.pewforum.org/2019/07/23/feelings-toward-religious-groups/

Pew Research Center. (2020a). *Why are people rich or poor? Most Americans point to circumstances, not work ethic.* https://www.pewresearch.org/politics/2020/03/02/most-americans-point-to-circumstances-not-work-ethic-as-reasons-people-are-rich-or-poor/

Pew Research Center. (2020b). *Most Americans say immigrants mainly fill jobs US citizens don't want.* https://www.pewresearch.org/fact-tank/2020/06/10/a-majority-of-americans-say-immigrants-mostly-fill-jobs-u-s-citizens-do-not-want/

Pew Research Center. (2020c). *Important issues in the 2020 election.* https://www.pewresearch.org/politics/2020/08/13/important-issues-in-the-2020-election/

Philbrick, I. P. (2022, January 5). Why isn't Biden's expanded child tax credit more popular? *The New York Times.* https://www.nytimes.com/2022/01/05/upshot/biden-child-tax-credit.html

Phillips, J., & Land, K. C. (2012). The link between unemployment and crime rate fluctuations: An analysis at the county, state, and national levels. *Social Science Research, 41*(3), 681–694.

Phillips, S. (2018, January 31). Latinos are the key to taking back the Senate in 2018. *The Nation.* https://www.thenation.com/article/latinos-are-the-key-to-taking-back-the-senate-in-2018/

Picchi, A. (2021, December 3). Americans are quitting their jobs at record rates—here are the 10 states leading the trend. *CBS News.* https://www.cbsnews.com/news/great-resignation-workers-quit-jobs-states-trend/

Pichardo, N. A. (1997). New social movements: A critical review. *Annual Review of Sociology, 23*(1), 411–430.

Piff, P. K., Kraus, M. W., Côté, S., Cheng, B. H., & Keltner, D. (2010). Having less, giving more: The influence of social class on prosocial behavior. *Journal of Personality and Social Psychology, 99*(5), 771–784. https://doi.org/10.1037/a0020092.

Piketty, T. (2014). *Capital in the twenty-first century* (A. Goldhammer, Trans.). Belknap Press of Harvard University.

Pipes, D., & Durán, K. (2002). *Muslim immigrants in the United States.* Center for Immigration Studies. https://www.cis.org/sites/cis.org/files/articles/2002/back802.pdf

Piven, F. F., & Cloward, R. (2012). *Regulating the poor: The functions of public welfare.* Vintage Books.

Piven, F. F., & Cloward, R. A. (1979). *Poor people's movements: Why they succeed, how they fail.* Vintage Books.

Plumer, B. (2012, September 18). Who doesn't pay taxes, in eight charts. *The Washington Post.* http://www.washingtonpost.com/news/wonkblog/wp/2012/09/18/who-doesnt-pay-taxes-in-charts/

Pollard, K., & Jacobsen, L. A. (2021). *The Appalachian region: A data overview from the 2015–2019 American Community Survey.* Appalachian Regional Commission. https://www.arc.gov/income-and-poverty-in-appalachia/

Polletta, F., & Jasper, J. M. (2001). Collective identity and social movements. *Annual Review of Sociology, 27*(1), 283–305.

Popovich, N., & Choi-Schagrin, W. (2021, August 11). Hidden toll of the northwest heat wave: Hundreds of extra deaths. *The New York Times.* https://www.nytimes.com/interactive/2021/08/11/climate/deaths-pacific-northwest-heat-wave.html

Portes, A., & Rumbaut, R. G. (2005). Not everyone is chosen. In T. M. Shapiro (Ed.), *Great divides: Readings in social inequality in the United States* (3rd ed.). McGraw-Hill.

Prahalad, C. K. (2019, June 20). How many Americans live on $2 a day? *The Economist.* https://www.economist.com/democracy-in-america/2019/06/20/how-many-americans-live-on-2-a-day

Pressman, S. (2007). The decline of the middle class: An international perspective. *Journal of Economic Issues, 41,* 181–200.

Price Waterhouse v. Hopkins, Pub. L. No. 490 US 228, 231 (1989).

Principe, C. P., & Langlois, J. H. (2013). Children and adults use attractiveness as a social cue in real people and avatars. *Journal of Experimental Child Psychology, 115*(3), 590–597.

PRRI. (2020). *The 2020 census of American religion.* Public Religion Research Institute. https://www.prri.org/research/2020-census-of-american-religion/

Public Broadcasting Service. (2014). *Islam In America.* History Detectives. http://www.pbs.org/opb/historydetectives/feature/islam-in-america/

Puckett-Pope, L. (2020, August 26). *Here's how you can support the Equal Rights Amendment.* Harper's Bazaar. https://www.harpersbazaar.com/culture/politics/a32175363/what-is-the-equal-rights-amendment-today/

Rabito, F. A., Iqbal, S., Perry, S., Arroyave, W., & Rice, J. C. (2012). Environmental lead after Hurricane Katrina: Implications for future populations. *Environmental Health Perspectives, 120*(2), 180–184.

Rafa, A. (2019). *The status of school discipline in state policy.* Education Commission of the States.

Rafferty, A. (2012). Ethnic penalties in graduate level over-education, unemployment and wages: Evidence from Britain. *Work, Employment & Society, 26*(6), 987–1006.

Raifman, J., Moscoe, E., Austin, S. B., & McConnell, M. (2017). Difference-in-differences analysis of the association between state same-sex marriage policies and adolescent suicide attempts. *JAMA Pediatrics, 171*(4), 350–356.

Raissian, K. M., & Bullinger, L. R. (2017). Money matters: Does the minimum wage affect child maltreatment rates? *Children and Youth Services Review, 72,* 60–70. https://doi.org/10.1016/j.childyouth.2016.09.033

Ramakrishnan, K., Wong, J., Lee, J., & Lee, T. (2016). *2016 post-election national Asian American survey.* http://naasurvey.com/wp-content/uploads/2017/05/NAAS16-post-election-report.pdf

Rank, M. R. (2004). *One nation, underprivileged: Why American poverty affects us all.* Oxford University Press.

Rasmussen, A., Crager, M., Baser, R. E., Chu, T., & Gany, F. (2012). Onset of posttraumatic stress disorder and major depression among refugees and voluntary migrants to the United States: Onset of PTSD and depression in refugees. *Journal of Traumatic Stress, 25*(6), 705–712.

Ratha, D. (2018). What are remittances? *Finance and Development, 76*–77.

Ravallion, M. (2020). On measuring global poverty. *Annual Review of Economics, 12,* 167–188.

Ray, R. (2014). Stalled desegregation and the myth of racial equality in the US labor market. *Du Bois Review: Social Science Research on Race, 11*(2), 477–487.

Read, J. G., & Gorman, B. K. (2010). Gender and health inequality. *Annual Review of Sociology, 36,* 371–386.

Reardon, S. F., Bischoff, K., Owens, A., & Townsend, J. B. (2018). Has income segregation really increased? Bias and bias correction in sample-based segregation estimates. *Demography, 55*(6), 2129–2160.

Reddy, C. (2011). *Freedom with violence: Race, sexuality, and the US state.* Duke University Press.

Reeves, R. V., Bucher, E., & Smith, E. (2021). *The unreported gender gap in high school graduation rates.* Brookings Institution. https://www.brookings.edu/blog/up-front/2021/01/12/the-unreported-gender-gap-in-high-school-graduation-rates/

Reich, R. B. (2021). *The system: Who rigged it, how we fix it.* Knopf Doubleday Publishing Group.

Reiman, J. H., & Leighton, P. (2012). *The rich get richer and the poor get prison: Ideology, class, and criminal justice* (10th ed.). Routledge.

Reskin, B. F., & Roos, P. A. (2009). *Job queues, gender queues: Explaining women's inroads into male occupations.* Temple University Press.

Retelsdorf, J., Schwartz, K., & Asbrock, F. (2015). "Michael Can't Read!" Teachers' gender stereotypes and boys' reading self-concept. *Journal of Educational Psychology, 107*(1), 186–194.

Rhode, D. L. (2010). *The beauty bias: The injustice of appearance in life and law.* Oxford University Press.

Rich, A. (1979). Disloyal to civilization: Feminism, racism, gynephobia. In *On lies, secrets, and silence: Selected prose 1966–1978* (pp. 275–310). W.W. Norton & Company.

Richardson, S. S. (2013). *Sex itself: The search for male and female in the human genome.* The University of Chicago Press.

Ridgeway, C. L. (1997). Interaction and the conservation of gender inequality: Considering employment. *American Sociological Review, 62*(2), 218–235.

Ridgeway, C. L. (2009). Framed before we know it: How gender shapes social relations. *Gender & Society, 23*(2), 145–160. https://doi.org/10.1177/0891243208330313

Ridgeway, C. L. (2011). *Framed by gender how gender inequality persists in the modern world.* Oxford University Press.

Ridgeway, C. L. (2014). Why status matters for inequality. *American Sociological Review, 79*(1), 1–16. https://doi.org/10.1177/0003122413515997

Ridgeway, C. L., Backor, K., Li, Y. E., Tinkler, J. E., & Erickson, K. G. (2009). How easily does a social difference become a status distinction? Gender matters. *American Sociological Review, 74*(1), 44–62.

Ridgeway, C. L., & Correll, S. J. (2004). Unpacking the gender system: A theoretical perspective on gender beliefs and social relations. *Gender & Society, 18*(4), 510–531.

Ridgeway, C. L., & Kricheli-Katz, T. (2013). Intersecting cultural beliefs in social relations: Gender, race, and class binds and freedoms. *Gender & Society, 27*(3), 294–318.

Ridgeway, C. L., & Nakagawa, S. (2014). Status. In J. D. McLeod, E. J. Lawler, & M. Schwalbe (Eds.), *Handbook of the social psychology of inequality* (pp. 3–25). Springer.

Ridley, M., Rao, G., Schilbach, F., & Patel, V. (2020). Poverty, depression, and anxiety: Causal evidence and mechanisms. *Science, 370*(6522). https://doi.org/10.1126/science.aay0214

Riegle-Crumb, C., & Humphries, M. (2012). Exploring bias in math teachers' perceptions of students' ability by gender and race/ethnicity. *Gender & Society, 26*(2), 290–322.

Riley, L. (2016, June 22). A misunderstood area of ADA compliance: Existing facilities. *Burnham.* https://www.burnhamnationwide.com/final-review-blog/a-misunderstood-area-of-ada-compliance-existing-facilities

Risman, B. J. (2004). Gender as a social structure: Theory wrestling with activism. *Gender & Society, 18*(4), 429–450.

Risman, B. J. (2018). *Where the millennials will take us: A new generation wrestles with the gender structure.* Oxford University Press.

Risman, B. J., & Davis, G. (2013). From sex roles to gender structure. *Current Sociology, 61*(5–6), 733–755.

Rivera, D. P., Forquer, E. E., & Rangel, R. (2010). Microaggressions and the life experience of Latina/o Americans. In D. W. Sue (Ed.), *Microaggressions and marginality: Manifestation, dynamics, and impact* (pp. 59–83). Wiley.

Rivera, L. A. (2015). *Pedigree: How elite students get elite jobs.* Princeton University Press.

Rivers, D. (2010). "In the best interests of the child": Lesbian and gay parenting custody cases, 1967–1985. *Journal of Social History, 43*(4), 917–943.

Robbins, A. (2004). *Pledged: The secret life of sororities.* Hyperion.

Roberts, L. L. (2019). Changing worldwide attitudes toward homosexuality: The influence of global and region-specific cultures, 1981–2012. *Social Science Research, 80*, 114–131. https://doi.org/10.1016/j.ssresearch.2018.12.003

Roberts, N. (2019, January 28). Undocumented immigrants quietly pay billions into Social Security and receive no benefits. In *Marketplace.* https://www.marketplace.org/2019/01/28/undocumented-immigrants-quietly-pay-billions-social-security-and-receive-no/

Robertson, D. L. (2015). Invisibility in the color-blind era: Examining legitimized racism against Indigenous peoples. *American Indian Quarterly, 39*(2), 113–153.

Rocksborough-Smith, I. (2018). *Black public history in Chicago: Civil rights activism from World War II into the Cold War.* University of Illinois Press.

Rodriguez, S. F., Curry, T. R., & Lee, G. (2006). Gender differences in criminal sentencing: Do effects vary across violent, property, and drug offenses? *Social Science Quarterly, 87*(2), 318–339.

Rogers, S. A., & Rogers, B. A. (2021). Trans men's pathways to incarceration. *Sociological Spectrum,*

41(1), 115–134. https://doi.org/10.1080/027321
73.2020.1850376

Romo, V. (2021, March 11). Number of unaccompanied minors entering US soared in February. *NPR.* https://www.npr.org/2021/03/11/975916980/number-of-unaccompanied-minors-entering-u-s-soared-in-february

Ronan, W. (2021, April 19). *North Dakota Governor Doug Burgum signs anti-LGBTQ House Bill 1503 into law.* Human Rights Campaign. https://www.hrc.org/press-releases/north-dakota-gov-doug-burgum-signs-anti-lgbtq-house-bill-1503-into-laww

Rose, M., & Baumgartner, F. R. (2013). Framing the poor: Media coverage and US poverty policy, 1960-2008. *Policy Studies Journal, 41*(1), 22–53.

Rosen, R. (2006). *The world split open: How the modern women's movement changed America* (Revised). Penguin Books.

Rosenblum, M. (2017, September 23). *The US bisexual+ movement: A #BiWeek history lesson.* GLAAD. https://www.glaad.org/blog/us-bisexual-movement-biweek-history-lesson

Rosenfeld, J. (2010). Economic determinants of voting in an era of union decline. *Social Science Quarterly, 91*(2), 379–395.

Rothenberg, P. S. (2008). *White privilege.* Worth Publishing.

Rothstein, J., & Rouse, C. E. (2011). Constrained after college: Student loans and early-career occupational choices. *Journal of Public Economics, 95*(1–2), 149–163.

Rothwell, J. (2019, November 8). If people were paid by ability, inequality would plummet. *The New York Times.* https://www.nytimes.com/2019/11/08/upshot/inequality-paying-by-ability.html?searchResultPosition=1

Rothwell, J. T., & Massey, D. S. (2015). Geographic effects on intergenerational income mobility: Geographic effects on income mobility. *Economic Geography, 91*(1), 83–106.

Roy, S. (2015, September 8). *Our sampling of 252 homes demonstrates a high lead in water risk: Flint should be failing to meet the EPA lead and copper rule.* Flint Water Study Updates. http://flintwaterstudy.org/2015/09/our-sampling-of-252-homes-demonstrates-a-high-lead-in-water-risk-flint-should-be-failing-to-meet-the-epa-lead-and-copper-rule/

Roy, S. (2016). *The surreal Flint experience: 2014–2015 water crisis.* Flint Water Study Updates. http://flintwaterstudy.org/2015/12/the-surreal-flint-experience-2014-2015-water-crisis-video-of-resident-getting-arrested-for-questioning-safety-of-water/

Rubenstein, R. (2001). *Dress codes: Meanings and messages in American culture.* Westview Press.

Rufrancos, H., Power, M., Pickett, K. E., & Wilkinson, R. (2013). Income inequality and crime: A review and explanation of the time-series evidence. *Sociology and Criminology, 1*(1). https://doi.org/10.4172/2375-4435.1000103

Ruiz, R. R. (2017, December 22). US charges 412, including doctors, in $1.3 billion health fraud. *The New York Times.* https://www.nytimes.com/2017/07/13/us/politics/health-care-fraud.html

Rural Health Research Gateway. (2018). *Opioid use and treatment availability.* https://www.ruralhealthresearch.org/assets/925-3046/opioid-use-and-treatment-availability-recap.pdf

Rush, N. (2016). *Somali refugees in the US.* Center for Immigration Studies. https://cis.org/Rush/Somali-Refugees-US

Rushovich, T., Boulicault, M., Chen, J. T., Danielsen, A. C., Tarrant, A., Richardson, S. S., & Shattuck-Heidorn, H. (2021). Sex disparities in COVID-19 mortality vary across US racial groups. *Journal of General Internal Medicine, 36*(6), 1696–1701. https://doi.org/10.1007/s11606-021-06699-4

Russell-Brown, K. (2018). The academic swoon over implicit bias: Costs, benefits, and other considerations. *Du Bois Review: Social Science Research on Race, 15*(1), 185–193.

Ryabov, I. (2018). Childhood obesity and academic outcomes in young adulthood. *Children, 5*(11), Article 11. https://doi.org/10.3390/children5110150

Ryan, B. (2013). *Feminism and the women's movement: Dynamics of change in social movement ideology and activism.* Routledge.

Ryan, C., Toomey, R. B., Diaz, R. M., & Russell, S. T. (2020). Parent-initiated sexual orientation change efforts with LGBT adolescents: Implications for young adult mental health and adjustment. *Journal of Homosexuality, 67*(2), 159–173. https://doi.org/10.1080/00918369.2018.1538407

Ryan, M. T., Hutchison, R., & Gottdiener, M. (2015). *The new urban sociology.* Routledge.

Saad, L. (2012). *US acceptance of gay/lesbian relations is the new normal.* Gallup Polls. http://www.gallup.com/poll/154634/Acceptance-Gay-Lesbian-Relations-New-Normal.aspx

Sacks, M., Sainato, V. A., & Ackerman, A. R. (2015). Sentenced to pretrial detention: A study of bail decisions and outcomes. *American Journal of Criminal Justice, 40*(3), 661–681.

Saez, E., & Zucman, G. (2019, October 11). How to tax our way back to justice. *The New York Times.* https://www.nytimes.com/2019/10/11/opinion/sunday/wealth-income-tax-rate.html

Safawi, A., & Floyd, I. (2020, October 8). *TANF benefits still too low to help families, especially Black families, avoid increased hardship.* Center on Budget and Policy Priorities. https://www.cbpp.org/research/family-income-support/tanf-benefits-still-too-low-to-help-families-especially-black

Safawi, A., & Schott, L. (2021, January 12). *To lessen hardship, states should invest more TANF dollars in basic assistance for families*. Center on Budget and Policy Priorities. https://www.cbpp.org/research/family-income-support/to-lessen-hardship-states-should-invest-more-tanf-dollars-in-basic

Sahlins, M. D. (1968). *Tribesman*. Prentice Hall.

Sainato, M. (2021, December 21). "They are fed up": US labor on the march in 2021 after years of decline. *The Guardian*. https://www.theguardian.com/us-news/2021/dec/21/labor-organizing-pandemic-decline

Sakamoto, A., & Kim, C. (2010). Is rising earnings inequality associated with increased exploitation? Evidence for US manufacturing industries, 1971–1996. *Sociological Perspectives*, *53*(1), 19–43. https://doi.org/10.1525/sop.2010.53.1.19

Sampson, R. J. (2008). Moving inequality: Neighborhood effects and experiments meet structure. *American Journal of Sociology*, *114*(11), 189–231.

Sampson, R. J. (2012). *Great American city: Chicago and the enduring neighborhood effect*. University of Chicago Press.

Sampson, R. J., & Bean, L. (2006). Cultural mechanisms and killing fields: A revised theory of community-level racial inequality. In *The many colors of crime: Inequalities of race, ethnicity, and crime in America* (pp. 19–44). New York University Press.

Sampson, R. J., Morenoff, J. D., & Raudenbush, S. (2005). Social anatomy of racial and ethnic disparities in violence. *American Journal of Public Health*, *95*(2), 224–232.

Sampson, R. J., & Wilson, W. J. (1995). Toward a theory of race, crime, and urban inequality. In J. Hagan & R. D. Peterson (Eds.), *Race, crime, and justice: A reader* (pp. 177–190). Stanford University Press.

Samuels, E. (2014). *Fantasies of identification: Disability, gender, race*. NYU Press.

Sanches, C., & Nadworny, E. (2017, May 24). *Preschool, a state-by-state update*. NPR. https://www.npr.org/sections/ed/2017/05/24/529558627/preschool-a-state-by-state-update

Sanchez, T. (2018, March 19). Stuck in limbo, DACA recipients consumed by fear and anxiety. *The Mercury News*. https://www.mercurynews.com/2018/03/09/stuck-in-limbo-daca-recipients-are-consumed-with-fear-and-anxiety/

Sandbakk, Ø., Solli, G. S., & Holmberg, H.-C. (2018). Sex differences in world-record performance: The influence of sport discipline and competition duration. *International Journal of Sports Physiology & Performance*, *13*(1), 2–8.

Sandel, M. (2012). *What money can't buy: The skyboxification of American life*. Farrar, Straus and Giroux.

Santiago, A. M. (2015). Fifty years later: From a war on poverty to a war on the poor. *Social Problems*, *62*(1), 2–14.

Saperstein, A., & Penner, A. M. (2012). Racial fluidity and inequality in the United States. *American Journal of Sociology*, *118*(3), 676–727.

Sapinski, J., & Carroll, W. (2018). Interlocking directorates and corporate networks. In A. Nölke and C. May (Eds.), *Handbook of the international political economy of the corporation*. Edward Elgar Publishing.

Sassen, S. (2014). *Expulsions*. Harvard University Press.

Sawhill, I. V. (2014). *Generation unbound: Drifting into sex and parenthood without marriage*. Brookings Institution Press.

Sawhill, I. V., & Pulliam, C. (2018). *Money alone doesn't buy happiness, work does*. Brookings Institution. https://www.brookings.edu/blog/up-front/2018/11/05/money-alone-doesnt-buy-happiness-work-does/

Sawyer, W. (2018). *The gender divide: Tracking women's state prison growth*. Prison Policy Initiative. https://www.prisonpolicy.org/reports/women_overtime.html

Scarborough, W. J., & Risman, B. J. (2017). Changes in the gender structure: Inequality at the individual, interactional, and macro dimensions. *Sociology Compass*, *11*(10), e12515. https://doi.org/10.1111/soc4.12515

Schaefer, R. T. (2015). *Racial and ethnic groups* (14th ed.). Pearson.

Schaeffer, K. (2020). *Racial, ethnic diversity increases yet again with the 117th Congress*. Pew Research Center. https://www.pewresearch.org/fact-tank/2021/01/28/racial-ethnic-diversity-increases-yet-again-with-the-117th-congress/

Scheid, T. L. (2005). Stigma as a barrier to employment: Mental disability and the Americans with Disabilities Act. *International Journal of Law and Psychiatry*, *28*(6), 670–690.

Schervish, P. G., Coutsoukis, P. E., & Lewis, E. (1994). *Gospels of wealth: How the rich portray their lives*. Praeger Publishers.

Schieman, S., & Jung, J. H. (2012). "Practical divine influence": Socioeconomic status and belief in the prosperity gospel. *Journal for the Scientific Study of Religion*, *51*(4), 738–756.

Schilt, K., & Wiswall, M. (2008). Before and after: Gender transitions, human capital, and workplace experiences. *The BE Journal of Economic Analysis & Policy*, *8*(1 [39]). https://www.degruyter.com/view/j/bejeap.2008.8.1/bejeap.2008.8.1.1862/bejeap.2008.8.1.1862.xml

Schmitt, M. T., Branscombe, N. R., Postmes, T., & Garcia, A. (2014). The consequences of perceived discrimination for psychological well-being: A meta-analytic review. *Psychological Bulletin*, *140*(4), 921–948.

Schneebaum, A., & Badgett, M. V. L. (2019). Poverty in US lesbian and gay couple households. *Feminist Economics*, 25(1), 1–30. https://doi.org/10.1080/13545701.2018.1441533

Schroeder, R. (2015). *Republican aims to block export-import aid to companies with hefty CEO pay.* MarketWatch. https://www.marketwatch.com/story/republican-aims-to-block-export-import-aid-to-companies-with-hefty-ceo-pay-2015-11-03

Schwalbe, M. (2008). *Rigging the game: How inequality is reproduced in everyday life.* Oxford University Press.

Schwalbe, M., Godwin, S., Holden, D., Schrock, D., Thompson, S., & Wolkomir, M. (2000). Generic processes in the reproduction of inequality: An interactionist analysis. *Social Forces*, 79(2), 419–452.

Schwalbe, M., & Shay, H. (2014). Dramaturgy and dominance. In J. D. McLeod, E. J. Lawler, & M. Schwalbe (Eds.), *Handbook of the social psychology of inequality* (pp. 155–180). Springer.

Schwartz, N. D. (2016, January 3). Economists take aim at wealth inequality. *The New York Times.* http://www.nytimes.com/2016/01/04/business/economy/economists-take-aim-at-wealth-inequality.html

Scott, S., & Dawson, M. (2015). Rethinking asexuality: A symbolic interactionist account. *Sexualities*, 18(1–2), 3–19.

SEARAC/AAAJ (2020). *Southeast Asian American journeys.* Southeast Asia Resource Action Center and Asian Americans Advancing Justice.

Selden, T. M., & Berdahl, T. A. (2020). COVID-19 and racial/ethnic disparities in health risk, employment, and household composition. *Health Affairs*, 39(9), 1624–1632. https://doi.org/10.1377/hlthaff.2020.00897

Seltzer, R. (2017, October 25). Tuition and fees still rising faster than aid: College Board report shows. *Inside Higher Education.* https://www.insidehighered.com/news/2017/10/25/tuition-and-fees-still-rising-faster-aid-college-board-report-shows

Semple, K. (2013, June 8). New York City's newest immigrant enclaves. *The New York Times.* https://www.nytimes.com/interactive/2013/06/09/nyregion/new-york-citys-newest-immigrant-enclaves.html

Semuels, A. (2015). Imagining a post-coal Appalachia. *The Atlantic.* https://www.theatlantic.com/business/archive/2015/04/imagining-a-post-coal-appalachia/389817/

Sen, A., & Anand, S. (1997). Concepts of human development and poverty: A multidimensional perspective. In *Human development papers 1997: Poverty and human development:* (pp. 1–20). United Nations. http://clasarchive.berkeley.edu/Academics/courses/center/fall2007/sehnbruch/UNDP%20Anand%20and%20Sen%20Concepts%20of%20HD%201997.pdf

Sevak, P., & Schmidt, L. (2014). Immigrants and retirement resources. *Social Security Bulletin*, 74(1), 27–45.

Sewell, T. A. (2021, September 14). *Text—H.R.4—117th Congress (2021–2022): John R. Lewis Voting Rights Advancement Act of 2021* (2021/2022) [Legislation]. https://www.congress.gov/bill/117th-congress/house-bill/4/text

Shachar, C., Wise, T., Katznelson, G., & Campbell, A. L. (2020). Criminal justice or public health: A comparison of the representation of the crack cocaine and opioid epidemics in the media. *Journal of Health Politics, Policy and Law*, 45(2), 211–239. https://doi.org/10.1215/03616878-8004862

Shaked, D., Williams, M., Evans, M. K., & Zonderman, A. B. (2016). Indicators of subjective social status: Differential associations across race and sex. *SSM—Population Health*, 2, 700–707. https://doi.org/10.1016/j.ssmph.2016.09.009

Shallal, A. (2021, March). Yellen says COVID-19 having "extremely unfair" impact on women's income, jobs. *Reuters.* https://www.reuters.com/article/us-usa-treasury-yellen-women-idUSKBN2B01UP

Shams, T. (2015). The declining significance of race or the persistent racialization of Blacks? A conceptual, empirical, and methodological review of today's race debate in America. *Journal of Black Studies*, 46(3), 282–296.

Shapiro, A. (2020, June 10). "CAHOOTS": How social workers and police share responsibilities in Eugene, Oregon. In *All Things Considered*. NPR. https://www.npr.org/2020/06/10/874339977/cahoots-how-social-workers-and-police-share-responsibilities-in-eugene-oregon

Shapiro, D., Dundar, A., Huie, F., Wakhungu, P. K., Yuan, X., Nathan, A., & Hwang, Y. (2017). *A national view of student attainment rates by race and ethnicity—Fall 2010 cohort* (Signature Report #12b). National Student Clearinghouse Research Center.

Shapiro, J. (2020, December 21). Oregon hospitals didn't have shortages. So why were disabled people denied care? *NPR.* https://www.npr.org/2020/12/21/946292119/oregon-hospitals-didnt-have-shortages-so-why-were-disabled-people-denied-care

Shapiro, T. M. (2004). *The hidden cost of being African American: How wealth perpetuates inequality.* Oxford University Press.

Sharkey, P. (2013). *Stuck in place: Urban neighborhoods and the end of progress toward racial equality.* University of Chicago Press.

Sharrow, E. A. (2021). Sports, transgender rights and the bodily politics of cisgender supremacy. *Laws*, 10(63), Article 3. https://doi.org/10.3390/laws10030063

Sheasley, C. (2021, April 20). In a roiled Minneapolis, schools are testing new model for safety. *Christian Science Monitor*. https://www.csmonitor.com/USA/Education/2021/0420/In-a-roiled-Minneapolis-schools-are-testing-new-model-for-safety

Sherman, R. (2017). *Uneasy Street: The anxieties of affluence*. Princeton University Press.

Sherwood, J. H. (2013). *Wealth, whiteness, and the matrix of privilege: The view from the country club* (Reprint ed.). Lexington Books.

Shiffer-Sebba, D., & Behrman, J. (2021). Gender and wealth in demographic research: A research brief on a new method and application. *Population Research and Policy Review*, 40(4), 643–659. https://doi.org/10.1007/s11113-020-09603-w

Shihadeh, E. S., & Barranco, R. E. (2010). Latino employment and Black violence: The unintended consequence of US immigration policy. *Social Forces*, 88(3), 1393–1420.

Shor, F. (2015). "Black Lives Matter": Constructing a new civil rights and Black freedom movement. *New Politics*, 15(3), 28–32.

Shrider, E. A., Kollar, M., Chen, F., & Semega, J. (2021). *Income and poverty in the United States: 2020* (Current Population Reports No. P60-273). US Census Bureau.

Siegler, K. (2020, November 18). Biden's win shows rural-urban divide has grown since 2016. In *Morning edition*. NPR. https://www.npr.org/2020/11/18/934631994/bidens-win-shows-rural-urban-divide-has-grown-since-2016

Silberner, J. (2021). Covid-19: How Native Americans led the way in the US vaccination effort. *BMJ*, *374*, n2168. https://doi.org/10.1136/bmj.n2168

Silva Junior, C. H. L., Pessôa, A. C. M., Carvalho, N. S., Reis, J. B. C., Anderson, L. O., & Aragão, L. E. O. C. (2021). The Brazilian Amazon deforestation rate in 2020 is the greatest of the decade. *Nature Ecology & Evolution*, 5(2), 144–145. https://doi.org/10.1038/s41559-020-01368-x

Silverman, A. M., & Cohen, G. L. (2014). Stereotypes as stumbling-blocks how coping with stereotype threat affects life outcomes for people with physical disabilities. *Personality and Social Psychology Bulletin*, 40(10), 1330–1340.

Simon, L. H. (1994). *Selected writings: Karl Marx*. Hackett.

Siripurapu, A. (2020, July 15). *The US inequality debate*. Council on Foreign Relations. https://www.cfr.org/backgrounder/us-inequality-debate

Siripurapu, A., & Speier, M. (2021, April 13). *Is rising student debt harming the US economy?* Council on Foreign Relations. https://www.cfr.org/backgrounder/rising-student-debt-harming-us-economy

Sitkoff, H. (1981). *The Black struggle for equality, 1954–1980*. Hill and Wang.

Siwach, G. (2018). Unemployment shocks for individuals on the margin: Exploring recidivism effects. *Labour Economics*, *52*, 231–244. https://doi.org/10.1016/j.labeco.2018.02.001

Skocpol, T. (2007). Government activism and the reorganization of American civic democracy. In T. Skocpol, & P. Pierson (Eds.), *The transformation of American politics: Activist government and the rise of conservatism* (pp. 39–67). Princeton University Press.

Small, M. L., Harding, D. J., & Lamont, M. (2010). Reconsidering culture and poverty. *The ANNALS of the American Academy of Political and Social Science*, 629(1), 6–27. https://doi.org/10.1177/0002716210362077

Smeeding, T. (2005). Public policy, economic inequality, and poverty: The United States in comparative perspective. *Social Science Quarterly*, 86, 955–983.

Smeeding, T. (2016). Poverty measurement. In D. Brady, & L. M. Burton (Eds.), *The Oxford handbook of the social science of poverty* (pp. 21–46). Oxford University Press.

Smeeding, T. (2018). Poorer by comparison. In D. B. Grusky and S. Szelényi (Eds.), *The inequality reader* (2nd ed., pp. 153–158). Routledge. https://doi.org/10.4324/9780429494468-17

Smith, N. C. (2021). Black-White disparities in women's physical health: The role of socioeconomic status and racism-related stressors. *Social Science Research*, 99, 102593. https://doi.org/10.1016/j.ssresearch.2021.102593

Smith, S. J., Axelton, A. M., & Saucier, D. A. (2009). The effects of contact on sexual prejudice: A meta-analysis. *Sex Roles*, 61(3–4), 178–191.

Snipp, C. M. (2003). Racial measurement in the American census: Past practices and implications for the future. *Annual Review of Sociology*, 29, 563–588.

Snyder, R. C. (2008). What is third-wave feminism? A new directions essay. *Signs: Journal of Women in Culture and Society*, 34(1), 175–196.

Social Security Administration. (2021, June). *Monthly statistical snapshot, May 2021*. https://www.ssa.gov/policy/docs/quickfacts/stat_snapshot/

Solow, R. (2015, August 11). The future of work: Why wages aren't keeping up. *Pacific Standard*. https://psmag.com/economics/the-future-of-work-why-wages-arent-keeping-up

Solt, F. (2008). Economic inequality and democratic political engagement. *American Journal of Political Science*, 52(1), 48–60.

Solt, F., Habel, P., & Grant, J. T. (2011). Economic inequality, relative power, and religiosity. *Social Science Quarterly*, 92(2), 447–465. https://doi.org/10.1111/j.1540-6237.2011.00777.x

Sørensen, J. B. (2007). Organizational diversity, labor markets, and wage inequality. *American Behavioral Scientist*, 50(5), 659–676.

Southern Poverty Law Center. (2021). *Hate map*. Southern Poverty Law Center. https://www.splcenter.org/hate-map

Spain, D. (2014). Gender and urban space. *Annual Review of Sociology*, 40(1), 581–598.

Spector, M., & Kitsuse, J. I. (1977). *Constructing social problems*. Cummings Publishing.

Speer, I. (2016). Race, wealth, and class identification in 21st-century American society. *The Sociological Quarterly*, 57(2), 356–379.

Speri, A. (2021, June 10). The NYPD Is still stopping and frisking Black people at disproportionate rates. *The Intercept*. https://theintercept.com/2021/06/10/stop-and-frisk-new-york-police-racial-disparity/

Spinaris, C. (2019, September 8). *Mandatory overtime and partial chronic sleep deprivation—Part 1*. Corrections1. https://www.corrections1.com/officer-safety/articles/mandatory-overtime-and-partial-chronic-sleep-deprivationpart-1-apZHCJhDY3KHrWdQ/

Spring, J. (2020, March 4). Exclusive: Brazil exported thousands of shipments of unauthorized wood from Amazon port. *Reuters*. https://www.reuters.com/article/us-brazil-environment-lumber-exclusive-idUSKBN20R15X

Springer, K. (2002). Third wave black feminism? *Signs: Journal of Women in Culture and Society*, 27(4), 1059–1082.

Springer, K. W., Lee, C., & Carr, D. (2019). Spousal breadwinning across 30 years of marriage and husbands' health: A gendered life course stress approach. *Journal of Aging and Health*, 31(1), 37–66.

Staff, J., & Uggen, C. (2003). The fruits of good work: Early work experiences and adolescent deviance. *Journal of Research in Crime and Delinquency*, 40(3), 263–290.

Staggenborg, S. (2015). *Social movements*. Oxford University Press.

Stalnaker-Shofner, D. M. (2020). Colorism and racial identity development in Black/African American women: An autoethnographic perspective. *Journal of Black Sexuality and Relationships*, 7(2), 75–98. https://doi.org/10.1353/bsr.2020.0018

Starr, S. B. (2012). *Estimating gender disparities in federal criminal cases* (Scholarly Paper No. 2144002). Social Science Research Network. http://papers.ssrn.com/abstract=2144002

Statista Research Department. (2021, December 10). *Murders of transgender and gender-diverse people US 2021*. Statista. https://www.statista.com/statistics/944726/murders-transgender-gender-diverse-people-us/

Steen, S., Engen, R. L., & Gainey, R. R. (2005). Images of danger and culpability: Racial stereotyping, case processing, and criminal sentencing. *Criminology*, 43, 435–468.

Steffesnmeier, D., & Demote, S. (2000). Ethnicity and sentencing outcomes in US federal courts: Who is punished more harshly? *American Sociological Review*, 65, 705–729.

Steffensmeier, D., Painter-Davis, N., & Ulmer, J. (2017). Intersectionality of race, ethnicity, gender, and age on criminal punishment. *Sociological Perspectives*, 60(4), 810–833.

Stein, M., & Cacciola, S. (2018, July 1). LeBron James joining Lakers on 4-Year $154 million deal. *New York Times*. https://www.nytimes.com/2018/07/01/sports/lebron-james-lakers.html

Stellar, J. E., Manzo, V. M., Kraus, M. W., & Keltner, D. (2012). Class and compassion: Socioeconomic factors predict responses to suffering. *Emotion*, 12(3), 449–459. https://doi.org/10.1037/a0026508

Stern, M. J. (2015, January 12). Oklahoma Republican proposes bill banning hoodies in public. *Slate*. http://www.slate.com/blogs/the_slatest/2015/01/12/hoodie_ban_oklahoma_republican_proposes_bill_to_outlaw_wearing_hoods_in.html

Steuerle, C. E. (2021, August 3). *Biden's expanded EITC adds significant marriage penalties*. Tax Policy Center. https://www.taxpolicycenter.org/taxvox/bidens-expanded-eitc-adds-significant-marriage-penalties

Steverman, B. (2020, April 29). The pandemic will reduce inequality—Or make it worse. *Bloomberg*. https://www.bloomberg.com/news/features/2020-04-29/how-will-the-coronavirus-pandemic-affect-inequality

Streib, J. (2015). *The power of the past: Understanding cross-class marriages*. Oxford University Press.

Stringer, A. (2018). Crossing the border: Latino attitudes toward immigration policy. *Journal of International Migration and Integration*, 19(3), 701–715.

Stroshine, M. S., & Brandi, S. G. (2011). Race, gender, and tokenism in policing: An empirical elaboration. *Police Quarterly*, 14(4), 344–365.

Stuart, F. (2016). *Down, out, and under arrest: Policing and everyday life in skid row*. University of Chicago Press.

Stults, B. J., Hernandez, J. L., & Hay, C. (2021). Low self-control, peer delinquency, and crime: Considering gendered pathways. *Journal of Research in Crime and Delinquency*, 002242782110014. https://doi.org/10.1177/00224278211001416

Sullivan, K., & Adams, T. (2010). *Summary of Citizens United V. Federal Election Commission*. Connecticut General Assembly. https://www.cga.ct.gov/2010/rpt/2010-R-0124.htm

Sullivan, L., Meschede, T., Shapiro, T., Kroger, T., & Escobar, F. (2019). *Not only unequal paychecks: Occupational segregation, benefits, and the racial wealth gap*. Institute on Assets and Social Policy, Brandeis University.

https://heller.brandeis.edu/iere/pdfs/racial-wealth-equity/asset-integration/occupational_segregation_report_40219.pdf

Summers Sandoval, T. Jr. (2009, July 13). Mexicans after the US-Mexican War. *Latino Like Me.* https://latinolikeme.wordpress.com/2009/07/13/mexican-after-the-u-s-mexican-war/

Sutch, R. (2017). The one percent across two centuries: A replication of Thomas Piketty's data on the concentration of wealth in the United States. *Social Science History, 41*(4), 587–613. https://doi.org/10.1017/ssh.2017.27

Sutin, A. R., Stephan, Y., & Terracciano, A. (2015). Weight discrimination and risk of mortality. *Psychological Science, 26*(11), 1803–1811.

Swanson, G. E. (1964). *The birth of the gods: The origin of primitive beliefs.* University of Michigan Press.

Szymanski, A. (1978). *The capitalist state and the politics of class.* Winthrop Publishers.

Tapia, M. (2010). Untangling race and class effects on juvenile arrests. *Journal of Criminal Justice, 38*(3), 255–265.

Tarrow, S. G. (2011). *Power in movement: Social movements and contentious politics.* Cambridge University Press.

Tax Policy Center. (2020). *How do taxes affect income inequality?* Urban Institute and Brookings Institution. https://www.taxpolicycenter.org/briefing-book/how-do-taxes-affect-income-inequality

Teachman, J., & Tedrow, L. M. (2004). Wages, earnings, and occupational status: Did World War II veterans receive a premium? *Social Science Research, 33*(4), 581–605.

Temko, N. (2021, June 30). Why Europe's far-right parties are losing steam. *Christian Science Monitor.* https://www.csmonitor.com/World/2021/0630/Why-Europe-s-far-right-parties-are-losing-steam

Tharps, L. L. (2014, November 19). The case for Black with a capital B. *The New York Times.* https://www.nytimes.com/2014/11/19/opinion/the-case-for-black-with-a-capital-b.html

The CAP Immigration Team, and Nicholson, M. D. (2017, April 20). *The facts on immigration today: 2017 edition.* Center for American Progress. https://www.americanprogress.org/issues/immigration/reports/2017/04/20/430736/facts-immigration-today-2017-edition/

The College Board. (2018). *Undergraduate enrollment and percentage receiving Pell Grants over time.* Trends in Higher Education. https://trends.collegeboard.org/student-aid/figures-tables/undergraduate-enrollment-and-percentage-receiving-pell-grants-over-time

The Commonwealth Fund. (2020). *Percentage of GDP spent on health care.* https://www.commonwealthfund.org/international-health-policy-center/system-stats/percentage-gdp-spent-health-care

The Economist. (2015, July 30). *If India's monsoon fails: A billion-person question.* https://worldif.economist.com/article/12127/billion-person-question

The Education Trust (2015). *The Pell partnership: Ensuring a shared responsibility for low-income student success.* The Education Trust.

The LGBT+ Bar. (2021). *LGBTQ+ "panic" defense.* https://lgbtbar.org/programs/advocacy/gay-trans-panic-defense/

The Marshall Project. (2020, October 30). The state of bail reform. *The System, 4.* https://www.themarshallproject.org/2020/10/30/the-state-of-bail-reform

The Pluralism Project. (2018). *The first American Muslims.* Harvard University. http://pluralism.org/religions/islam/islam-in-america/the-first-american-muslims/

The Sentencing Project. (2017). *Immigration and public safety fact sheet.* https://www.sentencingproject.org/wp-content/uploads/2017/04/Immigration-and-Public-Safety-Fact-Sheet.pdf

The Sentencing Project. (2021). *Criminal justice facts.* https://www.sentencingproject.org/criminal-justice-facts/

The Trevor Project. (2020, July 29). *Pronouns usage among LGBTQ youth.* https://www.thetrevorproject.org/research-briefs/pronouns-usage-among-lgbtq-youth/

The Urban Institute. (2017, October 5). *Nine charts about wealth inequality in America (Updated).* http://urbn.is/wealthcharts

The World Bank. (2020, October 7). *COVID-19 to add as many as 150 million extreme poor by 2021.* https://www.worldbank.org/en/news/press-release/2020/10/07/covid-19-to-add-as-many-as-150-million-extreme-poor-by-2021

The World Bank. (2021). *Life expectancy at birth.* The World Bank: Data. https://data.worldbank.org/indicator/SP.DYN.LE00.IN

Thiede, B., Greiman, L., Weiler, S., Beda, S. C., & Conroy, T. (2017, March 16). Six charts that illustrate the divide between rural and urban America. *The Conversation.* http://theconversation.com/six-charts-that-illustrate-the-divide-between-rural-and-urban-america-72934

Thomas, C. L., Laguda, E., Olufemi-Ayoola, F., Netzley, S., Yu, J., & Spitzmueller, C. (2018). Linking job work hours to women's physical health: The role of perceived unfairness and household work hours. *Sex Roles, 79*(7–8), 476–488.

Thomas, K. C., Shartzer, A., Kurth, N. K., & Hall J. P. (2017). Impact of ACA health reforms for people with mental health conditions. *Psychiatric Services.* https://ps.psychiatryonline.org/doi/10.1176/appi.

ps.201700044

Thomas, L. (2014, June 14). Hospitals, doctors moving out of poor city neighborhoods to more affluent areas. *Milwaukee Journal Sentinel*. https://archive.jsonline.com/news/health/hospitals-doctors-moving-out-of-poor-city-neighborhoods-to-more-affluent-areas-b99284882z1-262899701.html/

Thompson, A. (2020, August 11). COVID outbreaks at Ohio meatpacking plants hit immigrants extra hard. *The Columbus Dispatch*. https://www.dispatch.com/story/lifestyle/health-fitness/2020/08/11/covid-outbreaks-at-ohio-meatpacking-plants-hit-immigrants-extra-hard/42201967/

Thompson, B. (2018, February 18). The racial wealth gap: Addressing America's most pressing epidemic. *Forbes*. https://www.forbes.com/sites/brianthompson1/2018/02/18/the-racial-wealth-gap-addressing-americas-most-pressing-epidemic/

Thompson, J., & Conley, D. (2016). Health shocks and social drift: Examining the relationship between acute illness and family wealth. *The Russell Sage Foundation Journal of the Social Sciences*, 2(6), 153–171. https://doi.org/10.7758/RSF.2016.2.6.08

Thompson, M. (2010). Race, gender, and the social construction of mental illness in the criminal justice system. *Sociological Perspectives*, 53(1), 99–126.

Thorpe, R. J., Bell, C. N., Kennedy-Hendricks, A., Harvey, J., Smolen, J. R., Bowie, J. V., & LaVeist, T. A. (2015). Disentangling race and social context in understanding disparities in chronic conditions among men. *Journal of Urban Health: Bulletin of the New York Academy of Medicine*, 92(1), 83–92.

Tilcsik, A., Anteby, M., & Knight, C. R. (2015). Concealable stigma and occupational segregation: Toward a theory of gay and lesbian occupations. *Administrative Science Quarterly*, 60(3), 446–481. https://doi.org/10.1177/0001839215576401

Tilly, C. (1998). *Durable inequalities*. University of California Press.

Tilly, C. (2003). Changing forms of inequality. *Sociological Theory*, 21(1), 31.

Tilly, C., & Wood, L. J. (2015). *Social movements 1768-2012*. Routledge.

Tillyer, R., Hartley, R. D., & Ward, J. T. (2015). Differential treatment of female defendants: Does criminal history moderate the effect of gender on sentence length in federal narcotics cases? *Criminal Justice and Behavior*, 42(7), 703–721.

Timberg, C., Dwoskin, E., & Albergotti, R. (2021, October 22). Inside Facebook, Jan. 6 violence fueled anger, regret over missed warning signs. *Washington Post*. https://www.washingtonpost.com/technology/2021/10/22/jan-6-capitol-riot-facebook/

Tirado, L. (2014). *Hand to mouth: Living in bootstrap America*. G.P. Putnam's Sons.

Tobias, S. (2018). *Faces of feminism: An activist's reflections on the women's movement*. Routledge.

Tofig, D. (2017, January 11). *Education and training opportunities in America's prisons*. National Center for Education Statistics. https://nces.ed.gov/blogs/nces/2017/01/11/default

Tomaskovic-Devey, D. (2014). The relational generation of workplace inequalities. *Social Currents*, 1(1), 51–73.

Toossi, M., & Morisi, T. L. (2017). *Women in the workforce before, during, and after the great recession*. US Bureau of Labor Statistics. https://www.bls.gov/spotlight/2017/women-in-the-workforce-before-during-and-after-the-great-recession/home.htm

Tredway, K. (2014). Judith Butler redux—the heterosexual matrix and the out lesbian athlete: Amélie Mauresmo, gender performance, and women's professional tennis. *Journal of the Philosophy of Sport*, 41(2), 163–176.

Truth, S. (1867, May 9). *Address to the first annual meeting of the American Equal Rights Association*. https://www.lehigh.edu/~dek7/SSAWW/writTruthAddress.htm

Tumin, M. M. (1953). Some principles of stratification: A critical analysis. *American Sociological Review*, 18, 387–394.

Turner, B. S. (1986). *Equality*. Methuen.

Turner, R. J., Brown, T. N., & Hale, W. B. (2017). Race, socioeconomic position, and physical health: A descriptive analysis. *Journal of Health and Social Behavior*, 58(1), 23–36. https://doi.org/10.1177/0022146516687008

Ueno, K., Vaghela, P., & Nix, A. N. (2018). Gender composition of the occupation, sexual orientation, and mental health in young adulthood. *Stress and Health*, 34(1), 3–14.

Uggen, C., Larson, R., & Pulido-Nava, A. (2020). *Locked out 2020: Estimates of people denied voting rights due to a felony conviction*. The Sentencing Project. https://www.sentencingproject.org/publications/locked-out-2020-estimates-of-people-denied-voting-rights-due-to-a-felony-conviction/

Uggen, C., Larson, R., & Shannon, S. (2016). *Six million lost voters: State-level estimates of felony disenfranchisement, 2016*. The Sentencing Project.

Ulmer, J. T., & Bradley, M. S. (2018). Punishment in Indian country: Ironies of federal punishment of Native Americans. *Justice Quarterly*, 35(5), 751–781. https://doi.org/10.1080/07418825.2017.1341540.

UN Women. (2021, January). *Facts and figures: Women's leadership and political participation*. UN Women. https://www.unwomen.org/en/what-we-do/leadership-and-political-participation/facts-and-figures

Undem, T., & Wang, A. (2018). *The state of gender equality for US adolescents*. Plan USA. https://www.planusa.org/docs/state-of-gender-equality-summary-2018.pdf

United Nationals Development Programme. (2020). *Charting pathways out of multidimensional poverty: Achieving the SDGs*. http://hdr.undp.org/en/2020-MPI

United Nations. (2020). *Policy brief: The impact of COVID-19 on women*. https://www.unwomen.org/sites/default/files/Headquarters/Attachments/Sections/Library/Publications/2020/Policy-brief-The-impact-of-COVID-19-on-women-en.pdf

United Nations Development Programme. (2021). *Human development data center*. Human Development Reports. http://hdr.undp.org/en/data

Unnever, J. D. (2016). The racial invariance thesis revisited: Testing an African American theory of offending. *Journal of Contemporary Criminal Justice, 32*(1), 7–26.

Unnever, J. D., & Owusu-Bempah, A. (2018). A Black criminology matters. In J. D. Unnever, S. L. Gabbidon, and C. Chouhy (Eds.), *Building a Black criminology: Race, theory and crime* (Vol. 24). Routledge.

Urban Institute. (2017). *Nine charts about wealth inequality in America (updated)*. Urban Institute. http://urbn.is/wealthcharts

Urbatsch, R. (2018). Things are looking up: Physical beauty, social mobility, and optimistic dispositions. *Social Science Research, 71*, 19–36.

US Bureau of Labor Statistics. (2021a). *Correctional officers and bailiffs*. Occupational Outlook Handbook. https://www.bls.gov/ooh/protective-service/correctional-officers.htm#tab-5

US Bureau of Labor Statistics. (2021b, January 22). *2020 annual averages—Employed persons by detailed occupation, sex, race, and Hispanic or Latino ethnicity*. https://www.bls.gov/cps/cpsaat11.htm

US Bureau of Labor Statistics. (2021c, January 22). *Union members summary*. https://www.bls.gov/news.release/union2.nr0.htm

US Bureau of Labor Statistics. (2021d, February 24). *Persons with a disability: Labor force characteristics summary*. Economic News Release. https://www.bls.gov/news.release/disabl.nr0.htm

US Bureau of Labor Statistics. (2021e, April 23). *Median weekly earnings were $900 for men, $1,089 for men, in first quarter 2021*. TED: The Economics Daily. https://www.bls.gov/opub/ted/2021/median-weekly-earnings-were-900-for-women-1089-for-men-in-first-quarter-2021.htm

US Bureau of Labor Statistics. (2021f). *A profile of the working poor, 2019* (No. 1093). https://www.bls.gov/opub/reports/working-poor/2019/home.htm

US Bureau of Labor Statistics. (2021g). *The employment situation: May 2021* (USDL-21-0980). https://www.bls.gov/news.release/archives/empsit_06042021.pdf

US Bureau of Labor Statistics. (2021h, September 9). *Consumer expenditures—2020*. https://www.bls.gov/news.release/cesan.nr0.htm

US Bureau of Labor Statistics. (2021i). *National census of fatal occupational injuries in 2020* [News Release]. The Department of Labor.

US Census Bureau. (1979). *The social and economic status of the Black population in the United States: An historical view, 1790–1978* (Series P-21, No. 80; Current Population Reports). US Government Printing Office.

US Census Bureau. (2014a). *ACS demographic and housing estimates—Flint, Michigan*. American FactFinder. http://factfinder.census.gov/faces/tableservices/jsf/pages/productview.xhtml?src=CF

US Census Bureau. (2014b). *Poverty status in the past 12 months—Flint, Michigan* [American Fact Finder]. American Fact Finder. http://factfinder.census.gov/faces/tableservices/jsf/pages/productview.xhtml?src=CF

US Census Bureau. (2020a). *Average number of people per household, by race and Hispanic origin, marital status, age, and education of householder: 2020* [Table AVG1]. https://www2.census.gov/programs-surveys/demo/tables/families/2017/cps-2017/tabavg1.xls

US Census Bureau. (2020b). *Characteristics of same-sex couple households: 2019*. https://www.census.gov/data/tables/time-series/demo/same-sex-couples/ssc-house-characteristics.html

US Census Bureau. (2020c). *Flint City, Michigan*. Quickfacts. https://www.census.gov/quickfacts/flintcitymichigan

US Census Bureau. (2020d). *The Supplemental Poverty Measure: 2019*. https://www.census.gov/library/publications/2020/demo/p60-272.html

US Census Bureau. (2020e, September 17). *2019 poverty rate in the United States*. https://www.census.gov/library/visualizations/interactive/2019-poverty-rate.html

US Census Bureau. (2021a). *New Household Pulse survey data reveal differences between LGBT and non-LGBT respondents during COVID-19 pandemic*. https://www.census.gov/library/stories/2021/11/census-bureau-survey-explores-sexual-orientation-and-gender-identity.html

US Census Bureau. (2021b). *POV-32. Mean number of persons per primary family, by family structure, age of householder, and poverty status*. https://www.census.gov/data/tables/time-series/demo/income-poverty/cps-pov/pov-32.html

US Census Bureau. (2021c). *QuickFacts: United States*. https://www.census.gov/quickfacts/fact/table/US/LFE046219

US Census Bureau. (2021d, April). *Voting and registration*. https://www.census.gov/topics/public-sector/voting.html

US Census Bureau. (2021e). *Historical poverty tables: People and families—1959 to 2020.* https://www.census.gov/data/tables/time-series/demo/income-poverty/historical-poverty-people.html

US Census Bureau. (2021f, May). *Research to improve data on race and ethnicity.* https://www.census.gov/about/our-research/race-ethnicity.html

US Census Bureau. (2021g, June 16). *Week 31 Household Pulse Survey.* Census.Gov. https://www.census.gov/data/tables/2021/demo/hhp/hhp31.html

US Census Bureau. (2021h, August 12). *Local population changes and nation's racial and ethnic diversity.* https://www.census.gov/newsroom/press-releases/2021/population-changes-nations-diversity.html

US Census Bureau. (2021i, September). *Income, poverty and health insurance coverage in the United States: 2020.* https://www.census.gov/newsroom/press-releases/2021/income-poverty-health-insurance-coverage.html

US Census Bureau. (2021j, September 14). *Income and poverty in the United States: 2020.* https://www.census.gov/library/publications/2021/demo/p60-273.html

US Census Bureau. (2021k, November 1). *Historical income tables: Households.* Census.Gov. https://www.census.gov/data/tables/time-series/demo/income-poverty/historical-income-households.html

US Census Bureau. (2021l, November 4). *Sexual orientation and gender identity in the Household Pulse Survey.* https://www.census.gov/library/visualizations/interactive/sexual-orientation-and-gender-identity.html

US Census Bureau. (2021m, November 9). *Historical income tables: People.* https://www.census.gov/data/tables/time-series/demo/income-poverty/historical-income-people.html

US Census Office. (1903). *Statistical atlas of the United States, 1900.* US Government Printing Office.

US Department of Commerce and Labor, Bureau of Statistics. (1911). *Statistical abstract of the United States.* US Government Printing Office.

US Department of Housing and Urban Development. (2021). *The 2020 annual homeless assessment report to Congress.*

US Department of Labor. (2020 May 14). *Labor force participation rate by sex, race and Hispanic ethnicity.* https://www.dol.gov/agencies/wb/data/lfp/lfp-sex-race-hispanic

US Department of the Interior. (2021, April 1). Secretary Haaland creates new missing & murdered unit to pursue justice for missing or murdered American Indians and Alaska Natives. *DOI News.* https://www.doi.gov/news/secretary-haaland-creates-new-missing-murdered-unit-pursue-justice-missing-or-murdered-american

USDA. (2021a, June). *SNAP data tables.* USDA Food and Nutrition Service. https://www.fns.usda.gov/pd/supplemental-nutrition-assistance-program-snap

USDA. (2021b, June 7). *SNAP and P-EBT accounted for more than one-ninth of total food-at-home spending from April to September 2020.* US Department of Agriculture, Economic Research Service. http://www.ers.usda.gov/data-products/chart-gallery/gallery/chart-detail/?chartId=101399

USDA. (2021c, June). *Reaching those in need: Estimates of state supplemental nutrition assistance Program Participation Rates in 2018.* USDA Food and Nutrition Service. https://hungersolutionsny.org/reaching-those-in-need-estimates-of-state-supplemental-nutrition-assistance-program-participation-rates-in-2018-may-2021-usda-fns/

Useem, M. (1984). *The inner circle large corporations and the rise of business political activity in the US and UK.* Oxford University Press.

Valadez, M., & Wang, X. (2017). Citizenship, legal status, and federal sentencing outcomes: Examining the moderating effects of age, gender, and race/ethnicity. *The Sociological Quarterly,* 58(4), 670–700. https://doi.org/10.1080/00380253.2017.1354736

Valdes, F. (1995). *Queers, sissies, dykes, and tomboys: Deconstructing the conflation of "sex," "gender," and "sexual orientation" in Euro-American law and society.* Stanford University.

Valentino, L. (2019). *What is a "good" job? Cultural logics of occupational prestige.* Duke University.

Vallas, R., & Valenti, J. (2014). Asset limits are a barrier to economic security and mobility. *Center for American Progress.* https://www.americanprogress.org/article/asset-limits-are-a-barrier-to-economic-security-and-mobility/

van Doorn, B. W. (2015). Pre-and post-welfare reform media portrayals of poverty in the United States: The continuing importance of race and ethnicity. *Politics & Policy,* 43(1), 142–162.

VanHeuvelen, T. (2020). The right to work, power resources, and economic inequality. *American Journal of Sociology,* 125(5), 1255–1302. https://doi.org/10.1086/708067

Veblen, T. (1953). *The theory of the leisure class.* New American Library.

Verba, S., Burns, N., & Schlozman, K. L. (2003). Unequal at the starting line: Creating participatory inequalities across generations and among groups. *The American Sociologist,* 34(1–2), 45–69.

VerBruggen, R., & Wang, W. (2019). *The real housewives of America: Dad's income and mom's work.* Institution for Family Studies. https://ifstudies.org/blog/the-real-housewives-of-america-dads-income-and-moms-work

Vincent, W., Peterson, J. L., & Parrott, D. J. (2009). Differences in African American and White women's attitudes toward lesbians and gay men. *Sex Roles*, 61(9–10), 599–606.

Viruell-Fuentes, E. A. (2007). Beyond acculturation: Immigration, discrimination, and health research among Mexicans in the United States. *Social Science & Medicine*, 65(7), 1524–1535. https://doi.org/10.1016/j.socscimed.2007.05.010

Viruell-Fuentes, E. A., Miranda, P. Y., & Abdulrahim, S. (2012). More than culture: Structural racism, intersectionality theory, and immigrant health. *Social Science & Medicine*, 75(12), 2099–2106. https://doi.org/10.1016/j.socscimed.2011.12.037

Wacquant, L. (2007). *Urban outcasts: A comparative sociology of advanced marginality*. Polity Press.

Wacquant, L. (2009). *Prisons of poverty*. University of Minnesota Press.

Waggoner, J. (2021, April 8). *9 states that don't have an income tax*. AARP. https://www.aarp.org/money/taxes/info-2020/states-without-an-income-tax.html

Wakamo, B. (2020, November 9). *14 Successful ballot initiatives to reduce inequality*. Inequality. Org. https://inequality.org/great-divide/ballot-initiatives-reduce-inequality/

Wakefield, S., & Uggen, C. (2010). Incarceration and stratification. *Annual Review of Sociology*, 36, 387–406.

Walasek, L., & Brown, G. D. A. (2015). Income inequality and status seeking: Searching for positional goods in unequal US states. *Psychological Science*, 26(4), 527–533.

Wallace, M. (1997). Revisiting Broom and Cushing's "Modest test of an immodest theory." *Research in Social Stratification Mobility*, 15, 239–253.

Wang, H. L. (2015, January 18). Broken promises on display at Native American treaties exhibit. In *Code Switch*. National Public Radio. https://www.npr.org/sections/codeswitch/2015/01/18/368559990/broken-promises-on-display-at-native-american-treaties-exhibit

Wang, D., Piazza, A., & Soule, S. A. (2018). Boundary-spanning in social movements: Antecedents and outcomes. *Annual Review of Sociology*, 44(1), 167–187.

Wang, W., Phillips, P. C. B., & Su, L. (2019). The heterogeneous effects of the minimum wage on employment across states. *Economics Letters*, 174, 179–185. https://doi.org/10.1016/j.econlet.2018.11.002

Ward, M. (2020, August 11). How decades of US welfare policies lifted up the White middle class and largely excluded Black Americans. *Business Insider*. https://www.businessinsider.com/welfare-policy-created-white-wealth-largely-leaving-black-americans-behind-2020-8

Warren, J. R. (2009). Socioeconomic status and health across the life course: A test of the social causation and health selection hypotheses. *Social Forces*, 87(4), 56–80.

Warren, P., Chiricos, T., & Bales, W. (2012). The imprisonment penalty for young Black and Hispanic males: A crime-specific analysis. *Journal of Research in Crime and Delinquency*, 49(1), 56–80.

Waters, M. C., Kasinitz, P., & Asad, A. L. (2014). Immigrants and African Americans. *Annual Review of Sociology*, 40(1), 369–390.

Watkins, N. L., LaBarrie, T. L., & Appio, L. M. (2010). Black undergraduates' experience with perceived racial microaggressions in predominantly White colleges and universities. In D. W. Sue (Ed.), *Microaggressions and marginality: Manifestation, dynamics, and impact* (pp. 25–58). Wiley.

Webb, J. B., Warren-Findlow, J., Chou, Y., & Adams, L. (2013). Do you see what I see?: An exploration of inter-ethnic ideal body size comparisons among college women. *Body Image*, 10(3), 369–379.

Weber, D. (2006). *The US-Mexican War: The aftermath of war*. PBS. http://www.pbs.org/kera/usmexicanwar/aftermath/many_truths.html

Weber, M. (1905). *The protestant ethic and the spirit of capitalism* (T. Parsons, Ed.). Dover Publications.

Weber, M. (1947). *The theory of social and economic organization* (T. Parsons, Ed.; A. M. Henderson, Trans.). Free Press.

Weber, M. (1963). *Max Weber: Selections from his work* (S. M. Miller, Ed.). Thomas Y. Crowell.

Weber, M. (1968). *Capitalism and the oppression of women: Marx revisited* (M. Roth and M. Wittich, Eds.). Bedminster Press.

Weeden, K. A. (2002). Why do some occupations pay more than others? Social closure and earnings inequality in the United States. *American Journal of Sociology*, 108(1), 55–101. https://doi.org/10.1086/344121

Weeden, K. A. (2019). Occupational segregation. *Pathways, Special Issue*, 33–36.

Weeden, K. A., Gelbgiser, D., & Morgan, S. L. (2020). Pipeline dreams: Occupational plans and gender differences in STEM major persistence and completion. *Sociology of Education*, 93(4), 297–314. https://doi.org/10.1177/0038040720928484

Weisman, J. (2021, October 22). Sinema's blockade on tax rates prods Democrats toward billionaires' tax. *The New York Times*. https://www.nytimes.com/2021/10/22/us/politics/sinema-wealth-taxes.html

Weller, C. E., & Helburn, A. (2009). *Public policy options to build wealth for America's middle class* (Working Paper No. 210). Political Economy Research Institute.

Werft, M. (2017). *7 laws that show why Iceland ranks first for gender equality*. Global Citizen. https://www.globalcitizen.org/es/content/7-iceland-feminist-law-women/

West, C., & Fenstermaker, S. (1995). Doing difference. *Gender & Society, 9*(1), 8–37.

West, C., & Zimmerman, D. H. (1987). Doing gender. *Gender & Society, 1*(2), 125–151.

Westbrook, L., & Schilt, K. (2014). Doing gender, determining gender: Transgender people, gender panics, and the maintenance of the sex/gender/sexuality system. *Gender & Society, 28*(1), 32–57.

Western, B., & Pettit, B. (2010). *Collateral costs*. The Pew Charitable Trusts. https://csgjusticecenter.org/wp-content/uploads/2010/09/2010-Pew.pdf

Western, B., & Rosenfeld, J. (2011). Unions, norms, and the rise in US wage inequality. *American Sociological Review, 76*(4), 513–537.

Western, M., & Wright, E. O. (1994). The permeability of class boundaries to intergenerational mobility among men in the United States, Canada, Norway and Sweden. *American Sociological Review, 59*, 606–629.

Weston, W. (2010). The power elite and the Philadelphia gentlemen. *Society, 47*(2), 138–146.

White, D. (2021). A multinational overview of the LGBTQ+ panic defense in remembrance to its victims. *Towson University Journal of International Affairs*. https://wp.towson.edu/iajournal/2021/05/03/a-multinational-overview-of-the-lgbtq-panic-defense-in-remembrance-to-its-victims/

Whitley, B. E., Childs, C. E., & Collins, J. B. (2011). Differences in Black and White American college students' attitudes toward lesbians and gay men. *Sex Roles, 64*(5–6), 299–310.

WHO. (2015). *Lead poisoning and health* [Fact Sheet #379]. World Health Organization. http://www.who.int/mediacentre/factsheets/fs379/en/

Widra, E. (2021). *Data update: As the delta variant ravages the country, correctional systems are dropping the ball (again)*. Prison Policy Initiative. https://www.prisonpolicy.org/blog/2021/10/21/october2021_population/

Wiersma, J. E., van Oppen, P., van Schaik, D. J. F., van der Does, A. J. W., Beekman, A. T. F., & Penninx, B. W. J. H. (2011). Psychological characteristics of chronic depression: A longitudinal cohort study. *Journal of Clinical Psychiatry, 72*(3), 288–294.

Wildeman, C. (2012). Mass incarceration. In *Oxford bibliographies*. Oxford University Press. http://www.oxfordbibliographies.com/view/document/obo-9780195396607/obo-9780195396607-0033.xml

Wilkerson, I. (2020). *Caste: The origins of our discontents*. Random House.

Wilks, S. (2013). *The political power of the business corporation*. Elgar Publishing.

Williams, C. (2021, November 2). *Detroit voters OK launching reparations commission*. https://www.detroitnews.com/story/news/politics/2021/11/02/reparations-proposal-leads-early-detroit-returns/8570995002/

Williams, C. L. (2013). The glass escalator, revisited: Gender inequality in neoliberal times. *Gender & Society, 27*(5), 609–629.

Williams, R. (2021, October 22). *State House committee hears pitch to give Georgia DACA students in-state tuition*. Georgia Public Broadcasting. https://www.gpb.org/news/2021/10/22/state-house-committee-hears-pitch-give-georgia-daca-students-in-state-tuition

Williams, R. Y. (2014). *Concrete demands: The search for Black Power in the 20th century*. Routledge. https://doi.org/10.4324/9780203122228

Williams, Y. (2015). *Rethinking the black freedom movement*. Routledge.

Williamson, L. L. (2021). COVID-19 incidence and mortality among American Indian/Alaska Native and White persons—Montana, March 13–November 30, 2020. *MMWR. Morbidity and Mortality Weekly Report, 70*. https://doi.org/10.15585/mmwr.mm7014a2

Willson, A. E. (2003). Race and women's income trajectories: Employment, marriage, and income security over the life course. *Social Problems, 50*(1), 87–110.

Wilson, D. (2012), April 3). The history of the hoodie. *Rolling Stone*. http://www.rollingstone.com/culture/news/the-history-of-the-hoodie-20120403

Wilson, V., & Mokhiber, Z. (2017). *2016 ACS shows stubbornly high Native American poverty and different degrees of economic well-being for Asian ethnic groups*. Economic Policy Institute. https://www.epi.org/blog/2016-acs-shows-stubbornly-high-native-american-poverty-and-different-degrees-of-economic-well-being-for-asian-ethnic-groups/

Wilson, W. J. (1982). The declining significance of race: Revisited but not revised. In N. R. Yetman, & C. H. Steele (Eds.), *Majority and minority: The dynamics of race and ethnicity in American life* (pp. 399–405). Allyn and Bacon.

Wilson, W. J. (2012). *The truly disadvantaged: The inner city, the underclass, and public policy*. University of Chicago Press.

Wiltz, T. (2020, June 25). *Black homeowners pay more than "fair share" in property taxes*. Pew Charitable Trust. https://pew.org/37V2N6i

Wise, J. (2021). Covid-19: Highest death rates seen in countries with most overweight populations. *BMJ, 372*(623). https://doi.org/10.1136/bmj.n623

Wiseman, P. (2021, April 20). What Trump's new North American trade deal actually does. *AP News*. https://apnews.com/article/mexico-donald-trump-us-news-ap-top-news-international-news-222da26d3fe441dc0afca4194addfc6f

Wiser, M. C. (2014). Lacrosse history, a history of one sport or two? A comparative analysis of men's lacrosse and women's lacrosse in the United States. *The International Journal of the History of Sport, 31*(13), 1656–1676. https://doi.org/10.1080/09523367.2014.930709

Witko, C. (2006). PACs, issue context, and congressional decision-making. *Political Research Quarterly, 59*(2), 283–295.

Wiwad, D., Mercier, B., Piff, P. K., Shariff, A., & Aknin, L. B. (2021). Recognizing the impact of COVID-19 on the poor alters attitudes towards poverty and inequality. *Journal of Experimental Social Psychology, 93*, 104083. https://doi.org/10.1016/j.jesp.2020.104083

Wolbring, T., & Riordan, P. (2016). How beauty works: Theoretical mechanisms and two empirical applications on students' evaluation of teaching. *Social Science Research, 57*, 253–272.

Wolf, N. (2002). *The beauty myth: How images of beauty are used against women* (Reprint ed.). Harper Perennial.

Wolfe, J., & Blair, H. (2019, September 11). Government programs kept tens of millions out of poverty in 2018. *Economic Policy Institute.* https://www.epi.org/blog/government-programs-keep-tens-of-millions-out-of-poverty/

Wolff, E. (2021). *Household wealth trends in the United States, 1962 to 2019: Median wealth rebounds… but not enough* (No. 28383). National Bureau of Economic Research. https://doi.org/10.3386/w28383

Wolff, E. N., & Gittleman, M. (2014). Inheritances and the distribution of wealth or whatever happened to the great inheritance boom? *The Journal of Economic Inequality, 12*(4), 439–468.

Woodly, D. R. (2021). *Reckoning: Black Lives Matter and the democratic necessity of social movements.* Oxford University Press.

Woolf, N. (2016, December 8). Portland city council passes tax on CEOs who earn 100 times more than staff. *The Guardian.* https://www.theguardian.com/us-news/2016/dec/08/portland-oregon-ceo-pay-tax-passes-income-inequality

World Economic Forum. (2021). *Global gender gap report.* https://www3.weforum.org/docs/WEF_GGGR_2021.pdf

World Inequality Database. (2021). *Data.* https://wid.world/data/

World Prison Brief. (2021). *Highest to lowest—Prison population rate.* https://www.prisonstudies.org/highest-to-lowest/prison_population_rate?field_region_taxonomy_tid=All

Worthen, M. G. F. (2018). "Gay equals White"? Racial, ethnic, and sexual identities and attitudes toward LGBT individuals among college students

at a Bible Belt university. *The Journal of Sex Research, 55*(8), 995–1011.

Wright, E. O. (2000). *Class counts: Comparative studies in class analysis* (Reprinted). Cambridge University Press.

Wright, E. O., & Cho, D. (1992). The relative permeability of class boundaries to cross-class friendships: A comparative study of the United States, Canada, Sweden, and Norway. *American Sociological Review, 57*, 85–102.

Wrye, H. K. (2009). The fourth wave of feminism: Psychoanalytic Perspectives introductory remarks. *Studies in Gender and Sexuality, 10*(4), 185–189.

Wysong, E., Perrucci, R., & Wright, D. (2014). *The new class society: Goodbye American dream?* (4th ed.). Rowman & Littlefield Publishers, Inc.

Xie, M., & Lauritsen, J. L. (2012). Racial context and crime reporting: A test of Black's stratification hypothesis. *Journal of Quantitative Criminology, 28*(2), 265–293.

Yanco, J. J. (2014). *Misremembering Dr. King: Revisiting the legacy of Martin Luther King Jr.* Indiana University Press.

Yang, J., McCuish, E. C., & Corrado, R. R. (2017). Foster care beyond placement: Offending outcomes in emerging adulthood. *Journal of Criminal Justice, 53*, 46–54. https://doi.org/10.1016/j.jcrimjus.2017.08.009

York, E. (2021, February 3). Summary of the latest federal income tax data. *Tax Foundation.* https://taxfoundation.org/publications/latest-federal-income-tax-data/

Yost, M. R., & Thomas, G. D. (2012). Gender and binegativity: Men's and women's attitudes toward male and female bisexuals. *Archives of Sexual Behavior, 41*(3), 691–702. https://doi.org/10.1007/s10508-011-9767-8

Yuen, D. N. W., Smith, D. S. L., Pieper, D. K., Choueiti, M., Yao, K., & Dinh, D. (2021). *The prevalence and portrayal of Asian and Pacific Islanders across 1,300 popular films.* Annenberg Inclusion Initiative.

Yun, J., Fukushima-Tedor, M., Mallett, C. A., Quinn, M. I., & Quinn, L. M. (2021). Examining trauma and crime by gender and sexual orientation among youth: Findings from the Add Health National Longitudinal Study. *Crime & Delinquency*, 0011128721999342. https://doi.org/10.1177/0011128721999342

Zamarripa, R. (2020, October 21). *Closing Latino labor market gap requires targeted policies to end discrimination.* Center for American Progress. https://www.americanprogress.org/issues/economy/reports/2020/10/21/491619/closing-latino-labor-market-gap-requires-targeted-policies-end-discrimination/

Zamberlan, A., Gioachin, F., & Gritti, D. (2021). Work less, help out more? The persistence of gender inequality in housework and childcare during UK COVID-19. *Research in Social Stratification and Mobility, 73*, 100583. https://doi.org/10.1016/j.rssm.2021.100583

Zauzmer, J. (2017, August 3). Christians are more than twice as likely to blame a person's poverty on lack of effort. *Washington Post*. https://www.washingtonpost.com/news/acts-of-faith/wp/2017/08/03/christians-are-more-than-twice-as-likely-to-blame-a-persons-poverty-on-lack-of-effort/

Zeitlin, I. M. (1968). *Ideology and the development of sociological theory*. Prentice-Hall.

Zhao, N., Zhao, M., Shi, Y., & Zhang, J. (2015). Face attractiveness in building trust: Evidence from measurement. *Social Behavior and Personality, 43*(5), 855–866.

Zieger, R. H. (1986). *American workers, American unions, 1920–1985*. Johns Hopkins University Press.

Zimmer, M. J., Sullivan, C. A., Calloway, D., & Richards, R. (2000). *Cases and materials on employment discrimination* (5th ed.). Aspen Law & Business.

Zivony, A., & Saguy, T. (2018). Stereotype deduction about bisexual women. *The Journal of Sex Research, 55*(4–5), 666–678. https://doi.org/10.1080/00224499.2018.1437116

Zuckerman, P. (2004). *The social theory of W.E.B. Du Bois*. Sage Publications.

Index

Note: *Italicized* page numbers indicate figures and **bold** page numbers indicate tables in the text.

middle class 2–3, 22, 41, 45, 59, 118, 172, 223, 296, 304; civil rights movement 309; neighborhoods 328; and poor 39; relative mobility of 60; upper 43, 114; women 255, 315
Middle Eastern and North African (MENA) 206
middle quintile 21
Milano, A. 317
Miliband, R. 110
military 53; ban of homosexual people from service 187; commander becoming CEO 86; desegregation 306; and discrimination 211; independent power 87; industrial complex 86, 96; occupational training 59; stigma 261
Miller, F. 314
million dollar blocks 291
Mills, C. W. 86–87, 96, 100
minimum wage 22, 37, 47, 55–56, 61, 75, 320, 323
minority stress 192–193, 194, 253
Mississippi Freedom Democratic Party (MFDP) 309
mixed status families 234; see also family
mobility: from 1850s to 1990s 58–59; absolute 58–60; class 57–61; downward 4, 60; economic 209, 223; gap 60; impairments 82; intergenerational vs. intragenerational 58; of minority workers 215; patterns in the US 59–61; and race 60; rags-to-riches 61; relative 58–60; social 59, 247, 327; structural vs. circulation 58; United States 59–61; upward 77, 118, 180, 326
model minority 218
mode of production 109–112
Molotch, H. 148
money 98–99; benefits 72; defined 19; impact on elections 99; income 18; lower quintiles 27; poor waste 74–75; soft 97
Moore, W. 136–138
Mormons 237, 239
mortality rates 256
mortgage: deduction 54–55, 211; interest-free program 75; interest tax deductions 327; loans and 211, 242, 246
motherhood penalty 171
Mott, L. 312
Moving to Opportunity (MTO) 327–328
Mulvaney, M. 323
Murray, C. 321
Musk, E. 18, 54, 321

National Academy of Sciences 32
National Association for the Advancement of Colored People (NAACP) 127, 303, 308
National Association of Black Journalists 10
National Association to Advance Fat Acceptance (NAAFA) 76
National Council on Public Polls 13
National Crime Victimization Survey (NCVS) 273

National Institute on Drug Abuse 264–265
National Labor Relations Board (NLRB) 301
National Organization for Women (NOW) 314, 316, 329
National Survey of Family Growth (NSFG) 185, 187
National Woman's Party (NWP) 313–314, 315
National Woman Suffrage Association 313
nativism 237, 240, 242, 251, 253, 274
neighborhood effects 30, 148
neoclassical models of inequality 138, 140
neopluralism 86; see also pluralism
net worth 18, 26, 28–29, 324
Never Again gun control movement 297
New Deal 47, 80, 301, 305
The New Jim Crow (Alexander) 129, 289
New Leaders Council 330
new social movements 296
Nixon, R. 287
Nixon administration 322
nonbinary 11, 161
non-governmental organizations (NGOs) 47, 86
North American Free Trade Agreement 57
nouveaux riches (new rich) 68

Obamacare see Affordable Care Act
Obergefell v. Hodges 190
obesity 79, 247, 252, 254, 262–263
occupational prestige 66–67, 119
occupational segregation 140–141, 178, 180, 191, 215, 262
occupational status 42–44, 67, 219, 225
occupational structure 22
Office of Management and Budget 206
old social movements 296
Omi, M. 144, 152, 205, 224
opioid epidemic 264–266
opportunity hoarding 144–145
opportunity structure 147, 180
oppressive othering 149
Organization for Economic Cooperation and Development (OECD) 39, 170–171
Organization for Security and Co-operation in Europe 280
othering 143, 149, 165, 170, 237

Painter, N. 10
panethnic group 206
pansexuality 184
parental leave policy 181
parents 2, 7, 32, 58–60; Catholic 239; gay and lesbian 188; gendered expectations of work and family 171; and grandparents 130; income 41, 290; of intersex babies 161; medical insurance